MACINTOSH OLE 2

Programmer's Reference

BARRY POTTER

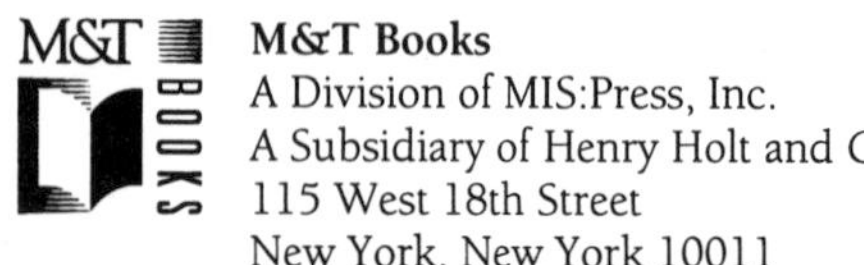

M&T Books
A Division of MIS:Press, Inc.
A Subsidiary of Henry Holt and Company, Inc.
115 West 18th Street
New York, New York 10011

Printed in the United States of America

ISBN 1-55851-420-1

This title is listed with the Library of Congress Cataloging-in-Publication Data.

97 96 95 94 4 3 2 1

Contents

About This Book .... **xxixi**
How This Book Is Organized xxix
Document Conventions xxxi

Chapter 1 Architectural Overview **1**
What is OLE? 1
Component Object Model 2
- Interfaces 4
- Interface Negotiation 6
- Reference Counting 6
- Memory Management 7
- Error and Status Reporting 9
- Inter-process Communication 10
- Dynamic Loading of Object Implementations 11

Data Transfer Model 11
Structured Storage Model 11
Compound Document Management 12
- Overview 12
- Linked Objects vs. Embedded Objects 13
- Architecture of Compound Documents 14
- Types of Object Handlers 17
- Link Objects 19
- Data Cache 20
- Container Applications 20
- Object Applications 22
- Object States 23
  - Entering the Loaded State 25
  - Entering the Running State 25
  - Entering the Passive State 26

Chapter 2 User Interface Guidelines **27**
Object Type 27
Class Registration 29

Objects and Other Object Applications 31
Activating an Object Having an Upgraded Version 32
Converting an Object from One Type to Another 32
Emulating Different Object Types 33
Creating Objects 39
Embedded versus Linked Objects 44
Automatic and Manual Updating 45
Verbs and Links 45
Types and Links 46
Maintaining Links 47
States and the Visual Appearance of Objects 49
The Inactive State 50
The Selected State 52
The Active State 53
The Open State 56
Outside-in Activation 59
Inside-out Activation 60
Undo for Active and Open Objects 60
Menus 63
Workspace Menu 63
Active Editor Menu 65
Selected Object (Sub)Menu 65
Menu Summary 66
Command Keys 67
Pop-Up Menus 67
Control Bars, Frame Adornments, and Floating Palettes 71
Object Transfer Model 77
Clipboard Method 77
Drag and Drop Method 81
Dialog Box Messages 84
Balloon-Help Messages 87

Chapter 3 Programming Considerations 89
Designing Component Objects 89
Component Objects: C Nested Structures 90
Component Objects: C++ Nested Classes 91
Component Objects: C++ Multiple Inheritance 97
Aggregation 98
Grouping Interfaces 101

Implementing OLE Applications 103
Starting OLE Applications 103
Registering to Receive OLE 2 Apple Events 103
Verifying Entries in the Registration Database 104
Initializing the Microsoft OLE Extension 104
Verifying Build Version Compatibility of OLE Libraries 104
Initializing the C-Based Interface VTBL Data Structures 105
Registering the IMessageFilter Interface Implementation 105
Determining the Start-Up Method 106
Registering Class Objects and Object Classes 106
Locking an Application in Memory 108
Opening Compound Documents 109
Initializing the Document Structure 110
Creating and Registering File Monikers 111
Opening Storage Objects 111
Loading Objects from Storage 112
Changing the User Interface 112
Registering a Document for Drag and Drop 113
Showing the Document and Setting the Dirty Flag 113
Using the Insert Object Dialog 114
Activating Objects 117
Activating an Embedded Object 118
Activating a Linked Object 119
Binding a File Moniker 121
Binding an Item Moniker 121
Binding a Generic Composite Moniker 122
Verifying Links 122
Registering an Object's Verbs 122
Managing Notifications 123
Managing Notification Registration 124
Notification Flow 126
Sending Notifications 129
Receiving Notifications 130
Saving OLE Compound Documents 131
File Save As Command 132
File Save Command 138
Saving to Temporary Files 138
Saving Objects in Low Memory 140

Full Save Operations 141
Incremental Save Operations 143
Saving Data to Compound Files Using Transacted Mode 143
Supporting Link Updating 145
Closing OLE Compound Documents 145
Checking Documents for Changes 145
Closing Pseudo Objects: Object Application Only 146
Closing Loaded Objects: Container Only 146
Hiding the Document Window 146
Sending Close Notifications: Object Applications Only 147
Releasing Reference Locks 148
Closing Scenarios 148
Closing an Application With the File Quit Command 148
Closing an Embedded Object from its Container 152
Closing Data Transfer Objects 154
Closing OLE Applications 155
Safeguarding the Application Object 155
Hiding the Application Window 156
Closing OLE Libraries 156

Chapter 4 Registering Object Applications 157
How to Register an Application 157
OLE 2 Registration Database File 158
Syntax of Entries in the Registration Database 158
Programmatic Identifiers 159
Converting CLSIDs and ProgIDs 159
The ProgID Key and Subkeys 160
The CLSID Key and Subkeys 161
The Version-Independent ProgID Key and Subkeys 163
The FileExtension Key 163
The FileType Key and Subkeys 163
The Interface Key and Subkeys 164
OLE 1 Compatibility Subkeys 164
OLE 1 Application Entries 164
Adding Information to the Registration Database 165
ProgID Key Entry 166
Human-Readable String Subkey Entry 166
Information for OLE 1 Applications Subkey Entries 166
Insertable Subkey Entry 166
Entry Point Subkey 167

- CLSID Key Entry 167
  - CLSID Subkey Entry 167
  - LocalServer Subkey Entry 167
  - InprocHandler Subkey Entry 168
  - Verb Subkey Entry 168
  - AuxUserType Subkey Entry 168
  - MiscStatus Subkey Entry 169
  - DataFormats Subkey Entry 169
  - Insertable Subkey Entry 170
  - ProgID Subkey Entry 170
  - Conversion Subkey Entry 170
  - DefaultIcon Subkey Entry 170
- Version-Independent ProgID Key Entry 171
- FileExtension Key Entry 171
- MacFInfo Key Entry 171
- Automation Key Entry 172

Registering OLE 2 Libraries 172

Accommodating OLE 1 Versions of the Object Application 173
- Overwriting the OLE 1 Application 173

Using the Registration Database for Localization 175

OLE 2 Registration Functions 176
- OleRegGetUserType 177
- OleRegGetMiscStatus 177
- OleRegEnumVerbs 178
- OleRegEnumFormatEtc 179
- RegCloseKey 180
- RegCreateKey 180
- RegDeleteKey 181
- RegDeleteValue 181
- RegEnumKey 182
- RegEnumProgID 183
- RegEnumValue 185
- RegFlush 187
- RegInitialize 187
- RegOpenKey 188
- RegQueryValue 188
- RegQueryValueEx 189
- RegSetValue 190
- RegSetValueEx 191

OLE 1 Registration Functions ... 192
Function Return Values ... 192
OleregOpenRegistration ... 193
OleregCloseRegistration ... 194
OleregGetValue ... 194
OleregSetValue ... 196
OleregRemoveKey ... 197

Chapter 5 Component Object Interfaces and Functions ... 199

IUnknown Interface ... 199
Reference Counting Rules ... 199
Avoiding Reference Counting Cycles ... 200
Optimizing Reference Counting ... 202
IUnknown::QueryInterface ... 204
IUnknown::AddRef ... 206
IUnknown::Release ... 206
IClassFactory Interface ... 207
Creating Instances of an Object Class ... 207
Creating New CLSIDs and IIDs ... 209
IClassFactory::CreateInstance ... 210
IClassFactory::LockServer ... 212
IMalloc Interface ... 213
IMalloc::Alloc ... 213
IMalloc::Free ... 214
IMalloc::Realloc ... 214
IMalloc::GetSize ... 215
IMalloc::DidAlloc ... 216
IMalloc::HeapMinimize ... 216
IExternalConnection Interface ... 216
IExternalConnection::AddConnection ... 217
IExternalConnection::ReleaseConnection ... 218
IEnumX Interface ... 219
Example Enumerator ... 220
IEnumX::Next ... 220
IEnumX::Skip ... 221
IEnumX::Reset ... 222
IEnumX::Clone ... 222

IMarshal Interface 223
Data Structures 224
MSHCTX Enumeration 224
MSHLFLAGS Enumeration 224
IMarshal::GetUnmarshalClass 226
IMarshal::GetMarshalSizeMax 227
IMarshal::MarshalInterface 229
IMarshal::UnmarshalInterface 230
IMarshal::ReleaseMarshalData 231
IMarshal::DisconnectObject 232
IStdMarshalInfo Interface 232
IStdMarshalInfo::GetClassForHandler 233
Custom Marshaling Functions 233
Overview to Custom Marshaling 234
Storing Marshaled Interface Pointers in Global Tables 235
CoGetStandardMarshal 236
CoMarshalHresult 238
CoUnmarshalHresult 238
CoMarshalInterface 239
CoUnmarshalInterface 241
CoReleaseMarshalData 242
Component Object Functions 243
CoCreateInstance 244
CoGetClassObject 245
CoRegisterClassObject 248
CoRevokeClassObject 251
CoLockObjectExternal 251
CoDisconnectObject 255
CoIsHandlerConnected 256
DLL Initialization Functions 256
CoLoadLibrary 256
CoFreeAllLibraries 257
CoFreeLibrary 257
CoFreeUnusedLibraries 258
File Time Conversion Functions 258
FILETIME Data Structure 258
CoFileTimeToMacDateTime 258
CoMacDateTimeToFileTime 259
CoFileTimeNow 259

DLL Object Class Functions ... 260
DllCanUnloadNow ... 260
DllGetClassObject ... 261
OLE Library Functions ... 261
CoBuildVersion ... 262
CoGetCurrentProcess ... 263
CoGetMalloc ... 263
CoCreateStandardMalloc ... 264
CoInitialize ... 265
CoUninitialize ... 266
Object Class Conversion and Emulation Functions ... 266
Tagging Objects for Automatic Conversion and Emulation ... 267
Converting Objects ... 268
Container Responsibilities ... 268
Object Application Responsibilities ... 269
Activating Objects of a Different Class ... 270
Container Responsibilities ... 270
Object Application Responsibilities ... 271
CoGetTreatAsClass ... 272
CoTreatAsClass ... 272
OleDoAutoConvert ... 273
OleGetAutoConvert ... 274
OleSetAutoConvert ... 275
SetConvertStg ... 276
GetConvertStg ... 277
Error Handling Functions and Macros ... 278
OLE Error Information ... 278
Handling Error Information ... 279
Structure of OLE Error Codes ... 281
Severity Field ... 281
Context Field ... 281
Facility Field ... 282
Code Field ... 282
Codes in FACILITY_ITF ... 283
PropagateResult ... 284
GetScode ... 284
ResultFromScode ... 285

Status Code Macros 285
SCODE_CODE 285
SCODE_FACILITY 285
SCODE_SEVERITY 285
SUCCEEDED 286
FAILED 286
MAKE_SCODE 286
String and CLSID Conversion Functions 286
IsEqualGUID 287
IsEqualIID 287
IsEqualCLSID 288
CLSIDFromProgID 288
ProgIDFromCLSID 289
CLSIDFromString 290
StringFromCLSID 290
IIDFromString 291
StringFromIID 292
StringFromGUID2 292

Chapter 6 Compound Document Interfaces and Functions 293
IAdviseSink Interface 293
IAdviseSink::OnDataChange 294
IAdviseSink::OnViewChange 295
IAdviseSink::OnRename 296
IAdviseSink::OnSave 296
IAdviseSink::OnClose 296
IAdviseSink2 Interface 297
IAdviseSink2::OnLinkSrcChange 298
IEnumOLEVERB Interface 298
IOleAdviseHolder Interface 299
IOleAdviseHolder::Advise 300
IOleAdviseHolder::Unadvise 300
IOleAdviseHolder::EnumAdvise 301
IOleAdviseHolder::SendOnRename 301
IOleAdviseHolder::SendOnSave 302
IOleAdviseHolder::SendOnClose 302
IOleClientSite Interface 303
IOleClientSite::SaveObject 303
IOleClientSite::GetMoniker 304

IOleClientSite::GetContainer 306
IOleClientSite::ShowObject 307
IOleClientSite::OnShowWindow 307
IOleClientSite::RequestNewObjectLayout 308
IOleContainer Interface 308
IOleContainer::EnumObjects 310
IOleContainer::LockContainer 311
IOleItemContainer Interface 312
IOleItemContainer::GetObject 312
IOleItemContainer::GetObjectStorage 315
IOleItemContainer::IsRunning 316
IOleObject Interface 316
IOleObject::SetClientSite 317
IOleObject::GetClientSite 317
IOleObject::SetHostNames 318
IOleObject::Close 318
IOleObject::SetMoniker 321
IOleObject::GetMoniker 322
IOleObject::InitFromData 322
IOleObject::GetClipboardData 324
IOleObject::DoVerb 325
IOleObject::EnumVerbs 328
IOleObject::Update 330
IOleObject::IsUpToDate 330
IOleObject::GetUserClassID 331
IOleObject::GetUserType 331
IOleObject::SetExtent 333
IOleObject::GetExtent 333
IOleObject::Advise 334
IOleObject::Unadvise 335
IOleObject::EnumAdvise 335
IOleObject::GetMiscStatus 336
IOleObject::SetColorScheme 339
IRunnableObject Interface 339
IRunnableObject::GetRunningClass 340
IRunnableObject::Run 341
IRunnableObject::IsRunning 341
IRunnableObject::LockRunning 342
IRunnableObject::SetContainedObject 343

Compound Document Functions........343
CreateOleAdviseHolder........344
OleIsRunning........344
OleRun........345
OleLockRunning........346
OleNoteObjectVisible........347
OleSetContainedObject........347
Object Creation Functions........348
Object Creation Parameters........349
OleCreate........351
OleCreateDefaultHandler........352
OleCreateEmbeddingHelper........353
OleCreateFromData........355
OleCreateFromFile........357
OleCreateFromFSp........358
OleCreateLink........359
OleCreateLinkFromData........360
OleCreateLinkToFile........361
OleCreateLinkToFSp........361
OleCreateStaticFromData........362
OleQueryCreateFromData........363
OleQueryCreateAll........364
OleQueryLinkFromData........365
OLE Initialization Functions........365
OleBuildVersion........365
OleInitialize........367
OleUninitialize........368
InitOleManager........368
UninitOleManager........370
IsOleManagerRunning........371
OleInitDBCSCountry........371
Apple Event Functions........371
OleProcessDdeAE........372
OleProcessLrpcAE........372
OleProcessClipboardAE........373

Chapter 7 Data Transfer/Caching Interfaces and Functions........375
Overview of Data and Presentation Transfer........375

Data Structures and Enumerations 375
FORMATETC Data Structure 376
STGMEDIUM Data Structure 379
DVTARGETDEVICE Data Structure 380
ADVF Enumeration 382
TDFLAGS Enumeration 383
OLE Clipboard Formats 384
Embed Source Format 384
Link Source Format 385
Custom Link Source Format 385
Embedded Object Format 386
Object Descriptor Format 387
Link Source Descriptor Format 389
Copying Data to the Clipboard 389
Pasting Data From the Clipboard 391
IDataObject Interface 392
IDataObject::GetData 393
IDataObject::GetDataHere 394
IDataObject::QueryGetData 395
IDataObject::GetCanonicalFormatEtc 396
IDataObject::SetData 397
IDataObject::EnumFormatEtc 398
IDataObject::DAdvise 400
IDataObject::DUnadvise 402
IDataObject::EnumDAdvise 402
CreateDataAdviseHolder 403
IDataAdviseHolder Interface 404
IDataAdviseHolder::Advise 405
IDataAdviseHolder::Unadvise 406
IDataAdviseHolder::EnumAdvise 406
IDataAdviseHolder::SendOnDataChange 407
IEnumFORMATETC Interface 408
IEnumSTATDATA Interface 409
IViewObject Interface 409
IViewObject::Draw 410
IViewObject::GetColorSet 413
IViewObject::Freeze 414
IViewObject::Unfreeze 415

- IViewObject::SetAdvise ... 415
- IViewObject::GetAdvise ... 416
IViewObject2 Interface ... 417
- IViewObject2::GetExtent ... 418
IOleCache Interface ... 419
- IOleCache::Cache ... 419
- IOleCache::Uncache ... 421
- IOleCache::EnumCache ... 422
- IOleCache::InitCache ... 422
- IOleCache::SetData ... 423
IOleCache2 Interface ... 424
- IOleCache2::UpdateCache ... 425
- IOleCache2::DiscardCache ... 426
IOleCacheControl Interface ... 427
- IOleCacheControl::OnRun ... 428
- IOleCacheControl::OnStop ... 429
Clipboard Functions ... 429
- OleSetClipboard ... 430
- OleSetClipboardEx ... 431
- OleGetClipboard ... 432
- OleFlushClipboard ... 433
- OleIsCurrentClipboard ... 433
Data Transfer, Caching, and Drawing Functions ... 434
- OleDraw ... 434
- OleDuplicateData ... 435
- CreateDataCache ... 436
- ReleaseStgMedium ... 437
Icon Extraction Functions ... 437
- OleIconSource Data Structure ... 438
- Macintosh Icon Picture Formats ... 439
- OleGetIconOfFile ... 440
- OleGetIconOfFSp ... 441
- OleGetIconOfClass ... 442
- OlePictFromIconAndLabel ... 442
- OleGetIconFromIconSuite ... 443

Chapter 8 Linking Interfaces and Functions **445**
What is a Moniker 445
Monikers and Linked Objects 446
IMoniker Interface 447
IMoniker::BindToObject 449
IMoniker::BindToStorage 451
IMoniker::Reduce 453
IMoniker::ComposeWith 455
IMoniker::Enum 456
IMoniker::IsEqual 457
IMoniker::Hash 458
IMoniker::IsRunning 458
IMoniker::GetTimeOfLastChange 461
IMoniker::Inverse 462
IMoniker::CommonPrefixWith 463
IMoniker::RelativePathTo 464
IMoniker::GetDisplayName 465
IMoniker::ParseDisplayName 466
IMoniker::IsSystemMoniker 468
IParseDisplayName Interface 468
IParseDisplayName::ParseDisplayName 469
IBindCtx Interface 470
IBindCtx::RegisterObjectBound 471
IBindCtx::RevokeObjectBound 472
IBindCtx::ReleaseBoundObjects 472
IBindCtx::SetBindOptions 473
IBindCtx::GetBindOptions 476
IBindCtx::GetRunningObjectTable 477
IBindCtx::RegisterObjectParam 477
IBindCtx::GetObjectParam 478
IBindCtx::EnumObjectParam 478
IBindCtx::RevokeObjectParam 479
IEnumMoniker Interface 479
IOleLink Interface 480
IOleLink::SetUpdateOptions 480
IOleLink::GetUpdateOptions 481
IOleLink::SetSourceMoniker 481
IOleLink::GetSourceMoniker 482

IOleLink::SetSourceDisplayName 483
IOleLink::GetSourceDisplayName 483
IOleLink::BindToSource 484
IOleLink::BindIfRunning 486
IOleLink::GetBoundSource 486
IOleLink::UnbindSource 487
IOleLink::Update 487
IRunningObjectTable Interface 488
IRunningObjectTable::Register 489
IRunningObjectTable::Revoke 491
IRunningObjectTable::IsRunning 492
IRunningObjectTable::GetObject 492
IRunningObjectTable::NoteChangeTime 493
IRunningObjectTable::GetTimeOfLastChange 494
IRunningObjectTable::EnumRunning 495
Linking Functions 495
BindMoniker 496
CreateAntiMoniker 496
CreateBindCtx 497
CreateFileMoniker 497
CreateFileMonikerFSp 498
CreateItemMoniker 499
CreatePointerMoniker 499
CreateGenericComposite 501
GetRunningObjectTable 502
MkParseDisplayName 502
MkParseDisplayNameMac 506
MonikerRelativePathTo 507
MonikerCommonPrefixWith 508
MkGetMacNetInfo 510

Chapter 9 Persistent Storage Interfaces and Functions 511
Summary of Storage Interfaces 511
OLE Storage Model 513
Overview to Structured Storage 513
Storage Objects on the Macintosh 520
Saving Objects to Storage 521
Storage Access Mode Flags 522
Overview 522

Storage Creation Flags 523
STGM_CREATE 524
STGM_CONVERT 524
STGM_FAILIFTHERE 524
Temporary Storage Creation Flag 524
Transaction Flags 524
STGM_DIRECT 525
STGM_TRANSACTED 525
STGM_PRIORITY 525
Access Permission Flags 526
STGM_READ 526
STGM_WRITE 527
File Sharing Privileges 527
STGM_READWRITE 527
STGM_SHARE_DENY_READ 527
STGM_SHARE_DENY_WRITE 528
STGM_SHARE_EXCLUSIVE 528
STGM_SHARE_DENY_NONE 528
Storage Naming Conventions 528
String Name Block (SNB) 530
STATSTG Structure 530
IEnumSTATSTG Interface 533
IStorage Interface 533
IStorage::CreateStream 535
IStorage::OpenStream 536
IStorage::CreateStorage 537
IStorage::OpenStorage 539
IStorage::CopyTo 541
IStorage::MoveElementTo 543
IStorage::Commit 544
IStorage::Revert 547
IStorage::EnumElements 547
IStorage::DestroyElement 548
IStorage::RenameElement 549
IStorage::SetElementTimes 550
IStorage::SetClass 551
IStorage::SetStateBits 552
IStorage::Stat 552

IStream Interface 553
IStream::Read 554
IStream::Write 555
IStream::Seek 557
IStream::SetSize 558
IStream::CopyTo 559
IStream::Commit 560
IStream::Revert 561
IStream::LockRegion 562
IStream::UnlockRegion 563
IStream::Stat 564
IStream::Clone 564
IRootStorage Interface 565
IRootStorage::SwitchToFile 565
ILockBytes Interface 566
ILockBytes::ReadAt 568
ILockBytes::WriteAt 569
ILockBytes::Flush 570
ILockBytes::SetSize 570
ILockBytes::LockRegion 571
ILockBytes::UnlockRegion 572
ILockBytes::Stat 573
IPersist Interface 574
IPersist::GetClassID 574
IPersistFile Interface 575
IPersistFile::IsDirty 576
IPersistFile::Load 576
IPersistFile::Save 577
IPersistFile::SaveCompleted 578
IPersistFile::GetCurFile 578
IPersistFile::LoadFSP 579
IPersistFile::SaveFSP 579
IPersistFile::SaveCompletedFSP 581
IPersistFile::GetCurFSP 581
IPersistStorage Interface 581
IPersistStorage::IsDirty 582
IPersistStorage::InitNew 583
IPersistStorage::Load 583

- IPersistStorage::Save ... 584
- IPersistStorage::SaveCompleted ... 585
- IPersistStorage::HandsOffStorage ... 587

IPersistStream Interface ... 587
- IPersistStream::IsDirty ... 588
- IPersistStream::Load ... 588
- IPersistStream::Save ... 589
- IPersistStream::GetSizeMax ... 590

Storage Creation Functions ... 590
- OleMakeFSSpec ... 591
- OleFullPathFromFSSpec ... 592
- CreateILockBytesOnHGlobal ... 592
- CreateStreamOnHGlobal ... 593
- StgCreateDocfile ... 594
- StgCreateDocfileFSp ... 597
- StgCreateDocfileMac ... 599
- StgCreateDocfileOnILockBytes ... 600

Storage Query Functions ... 602
- StgIsStorageFile ... 603
- StgIsStorageFileFSp ... 604
- StgIsStorageFileMac ... 604
- StgIsStorageILockBytes ... 605

Input/Output Storage Functions ... 606
- GetClassFile ... 607
- GetClassFSp ... 608
- GetHGlobalFromILockBytes ... 609
- GetHGlobalFromStream ... 609
- ReadClassStg ... 610
- ReadClassStm ... 610
- ReadFmtUserTypeStg ... 611
- ReadOle1FmtProgIDStgMac ... 612
- StgOpenStorage ... 613
- StgOpenStorageFSp ... 616
- StgOpenStorageMac ... 618
- StgOpenStorageOnILockBytes ... 619
- StgSetTimes ... 621
- StgSetTimesMac ... 622
- StgSetTimesFSp ... 623

WriteClassStg 624
WriteClassStm 625
WriteFmtUserTypeStg 625
WriteOle1FmtProgIDStgMac 626
StgGetFRefFromIStorage 627
StgGetFSpFromIStorage 628
Compound Document Storage Functions 629
OleLoad 629
OleLoadFromStream 630
OleSave 631
OleSaveToStream 632

Chapter 10 Drag and Drop Interfaces and Functions 633
DROPEFFECT Enumeration 634
IDropSource Interface 635
Drag Source Responsibilities 635
Drag Distance and Delay Values 637
Generating Drag Feedback 637
Ending the Drop Operation 638
IDropSource::QueryContinueDrag 638
IDropSource::GiveFeedback 639
IDropTarget Interface 640
Drop Target Responsibilities 640
Registering as a Drop Target 641
Determining Drop Effect Values 641
Drag Scrolling and Related Values 642
Ending the Drag Operation 643
IDropTarget::DragEnter 643
IDropTarget::DragOver 645
IDropTarget::DragLeave 646
IDropTarget::Drop 646
Drag and Drop Functions 647
RegisterDragDrop 648
RevokeDragDrop 648
DoDragDrop 649

Chapter 11 In-Place Activation Interfaces and Functions 653
In-Place Activation:Programing Considerations 653
Hierarchical Menu Ranges 653
Activating Objects while Background Utilities Are Running 653
Container not Receiving Low-Level Events 653
In-Place Object Documents not Clipped to Container's Window 654
Hide Others Application Menu Option 654
UI Deactivating a Session 654
Click in Scroll Bars Causes UI Deactivate 654
In-Place Object UI Deactivates After Taking the Foreground 655
Handling Floating Windows 655
In-Place Data Structures 655
BORDERWIDTHS 656
OLEINPLACEFRAMEINFO 656
OleMBarRec Data Structure 658
IOleWindow Interface 658
IOleWindow::GetWindow 659
IOleWindow::ContextSensitiveHelp 659
IOleInPlaceObject Interface 660
IOleInPlaceObject::InPlaceDeactivate 661
IOleInPlaceObject::UIDeactivate 662
IOleInPlaceObject::SetObjectRects 663
IOleInPlaceObject::ReactivateAndUndo 664
IOleInPlaceActiveObject Interface 665
IOleInPlaceActiveObject::TranslateAccelerator 666
IOleInPlaceActiveObject::OnFrameWindowActivate 667
IOleInPlaceActiveObject::OnDocWindowActivate 668
IOleInPlaceActiveObject::ResizeBorder 668
IOleInPlaceActiveObject::EnableModeless 669
IOleInPlaceUIWindow Interface 670
IOleInPlaceUIWindow::GetBorder 671
IOleInPlaceUIWindow::RequestBorderSpace 671
IOleInPlaceUIWindow::SetBorderSpace 672
IOleInPlaceUIWindow::SetActiveObject 673
IOleInPlaceFrame Interface 674
IOleInPlaceFrame::InsertMenus 675
IOleInPlaceFrame::AdjustMenus 675
IOleInPlaceFrame::RemoveMenus 676

IOleInPlaceFrame::SetStatusText ... 676
IOleInPlaceFrame::EnableModeless ... 677
IOleInPlaceFrame::TranslateAccelerator ... 678
IOleInPlaceSite Interface ... 679
IOleInPlaceSite::CanInPlaceActivate ... 680
IOleInPlaceSite::OnInPlaceActivate ... 680
IOleInPlaceSite::OnUIActivate ... 681
IOleInPlaceSite::OnUIVisible ... 682
IOleInPlaceSite::GetObjectRects ... 683
IOleInPlaceSite::GetWindowContext ... 684
IOleInPlaceSite::Scroll ... 685
IOleInPlaceSite::OnUIDeactivate ... 685
IOleInPlaceSite::OnInPlaceDeactivate ... 686
IOleInPlaceSite::DiscardUndoState ... 687
IOleInPlaceSite::DeactivateAndUndo ... 687
IOleInPlaceSite::OnPosRectChange ... 687
In-Place Activation Functions ... 688
OleSendLowLevelEvent ... 689
OleSendLLE ... 691
OleNewMBar ... 691
OleDisposeMBar ... 692
OleInsertMenus ... 692
OleHashMenuID ... 693
OleUnhashMenuID ... 693
OlePatchGetMHandle ... 694
OleUnpatchGetMHandle ... 695
OleAddMBarMenu ... 695
OleSetInFrontOf ... 696
OleSetInPlaceWindow ... 697
OleUnSetInPlaceWindow ... 697
OleClipWindows ... 698
OleClipWindow ... 699
OleUnclipWindow ... 699
OleMoveWindow ... 700
OleDragParentWindow ... 701
OleDragObjectWindow ... 701
OleSizeParentWindow ... 702
OleSizeObjectWindow ... 703

OleZoomParentWindow 704
OleGrowParentWindow 704
OleGrowObjectWindow 705
OleWhichGrowHandle 706
OleGetCursor 707
OleSetCursor 707
OleUpdateCursor 708
OleSetInPlaceRects 709
OleSetParentRgns 710
OleMaskMouse 711

Chapter 12 Compatibility with OLE 1 713
Overview 713
Working with OLE 1 Containers 714
Working with OLE 1 Object Applications 715
Upgrading Applications 717
OLE 1 Compatibility Functions 719
CoIsOle1Class 719
OleConvertIStorageToOLESTREAM 719
OleConvertIStorageToOLESTREAMEx 720
OleConvertOLESTREAMToIStorage 722
OleConvertOLESTREAMToIStorageEx 723

Chapter 13 Concurrency Management 725
Overview 725
IMessageFilter Interface 726
IMessageFilter::HandleIncomingCall 727
IMessageFilter::RetryRejectedCall 729
IMessageFilter::MessagePending 730
CoRegisterMessageFilter 733

Appendix A Object Handlers 735
Introduction 735
OLE Default Object Handler 736
Interfaces Implemented by the Default Handler 738
IOleObject Interface 738
IDataObject Interface 741
IPersistStorage Interface 742
Interfaces Implemented by the Cache 743
IPersistStorage Interface 743

IDataObject Interface 744
IViewObject2 Interface 745
IOleCache2 Interface 745
Strategies for Caching Data 746
Custom Object Handlers 748
Rendering Handlers 749
Rendering Objects from Native Data 750
Interfaces Implemented by Rendering Handlers 750
Writing a Custom Object Handler 751
Required Interface Implementations 751
Aggregating the OLE Default Object Handler 753
Registering Object Handlers 755
Loading Object Handlers 756
Unloading Object Handlers 756
DLL Object Applications 757
Overview 757
Required Interfaces for DLL Object Applications 758
IRunnableObject Interface and DLL Object Applications 759
IExternalConnection Interface and Silent Updates to Linked Objects 759

Appendix B Creating Distribution Disks 761
Disk Contents 761
Installing Your Application 761

Appendix C Data Structures and Enumerations 763
Data Structures 763
BIND_OPTS 763
BORDERWIDTHS 765
DVTARGETDEVICE 765
FILETIME 767
FORMATETC 767
INTERFACEINFO 769
OBJECTDESCRIPTOR 769
OleIconSource 771
OLEINPLACEFRAMEINFO 773
OleMBarRec 775
OLEVERB 775
STATDATA 776
STATSTG 776
STGMEDIUM 778

Enumerations 779
ADVF 779
BINDFLAGS 781
BINDSPEED 782
CALLTYPE 783
CLSCTX 784
DATADIR 784
DISCARDCACHE 785
DROPEFFECT 786
DVASPECT 787
EXTCONN 787
LOCKTYPE 788
MEMCTX 788
MKRREDUCE 789
MKSYS 789
MSHCTX 790
MSHLFLAGS 790
OLECLOSE 791
OLECONTF 792
OLEGETMONIKER 793
OLEGROWHANDLES 793
OLELINKBIND 794
OLEMANAGER 794
OLEMISC 795
OLEREG_KEYWORD 797
OLERENDER 797
OLEUPDATE 799
OLEWHICHMK 799
PENDINGTYPE 800
REGCLS 800
REGENUMPROGIDF 801
STATFLAG 802
STGC 802
STGMOVE 803
STGTY 803
STREAM_SEEK 804
TDFLAGS 804
TYMED 805
USERCLASSTYPE 806

Appendix D OLE 2 for the Macintosh: How It Differs from OLE 2 for Windows.....807

Differences in Architecture 807
- OLE Packaging 808
- In-Place Activation 808
- Interprocess Communication 808
- Structured Storage 808
- Using Structured Storage 809
- Concurrency 811

Differences in Implementation 811
- Object Design 811
- Enumerations and Data Structures 811
  - OBJECTDESCRIPTOR 812
  - OLEINPLACEFRAMEINFO 814
- Data Types and Parameter Usage 815
- Application Initialization and Shutdown 816
- Data Transfer Issues 816
- Format Conversion 817
- Monikers on the Macintosh 817
- Event Handling 817
- Miscellaneous Differences 818

Interface Differences 818
- IMessageFilter 818
- IViewObject 818
- IPersistFile 819
- IOleInPlaceObject 819
- IOleInPlaceFrame 820
- IOleInPlaceSite 820

API Function Differences 821
- API Functions Not Supported 821
  - CoCreateGuid 821
  - In-Place Activation 821
  - Validation Functions 822
- Static and DLL Versions of OLE Functions 822
  - Registration Database Functions Having Static and DLL Versions 823
  - Storage Functions Having Static and Runtime Versions 823
- Enhanced Functions for Use on the Macintosh 823

New API Functions 824
- Initialization 824
- In-Place Activation 824
- Object Creation 826
- FileTime Conversion 826
- Clipboard 826
- Apple Event Processing 827
- Icon Extraction 827
- Storage Related 827
- Registration Database 828
- Object Linking 828

Glossary 829

Index 837

About This Book

The *Object Linking and Embedding Programmer's Reference*, version 2.01, provides a complete reference to the extensible application protocol known as OLE (Object Linking and Embedding). Although OLE can run on other platforms, such as Microsoft Windows operating system, version 3.1 and Microsoft Windows NT, this book focuses on OLE applications that are being developed for the Macintosh operating system, version 7.0. (Minimal OLE support is available for version 6 of the Macintosh operating system; most noticeably is the support for static compound files.)

To get the most out of this book, you should be familiar with:

- The C/C++ programming language concepts.

  While not a prerequisite for programming OLE, the inherent properties of C++ can make a difference in programming OLE.

  To aid in moving from C to C++, Microsoft provides sample OLE applications written in C to mimic and teach the object-oriented principles behind C++ and OLE.
- The Macintosh programming environment, version 7.0. The OLE protocols are used in conjunction with other Macintosh programs.

Note For brevity, this book uses the shorthand notation of OLE 2 when referring to material specific to version 2.01 of OLE.

How This Book Is Organized

The following sections summarize the book's contents:

Chapter 1, "Architectural Overview," introduces the basic concepts of OLE and presents a high-level overview of the design principles behind OLE, including the component object model and an introduction to common interfaces. Illustrations are used to show the architecture of and the relationship between component objects.

Chapter 2, "User Interface Guidelines," describes the visual and interactive interfaces that support component objects. Where appropriate, illustrations are provided to show the details of dialog boxes and OLE concepts where they concern the end user of the OLE application.

Chapter 3, "Programming Considerations," describes guidelines on a variety of subjects that pertain to the implementation of OLE in a general sense. This chapter also discusses implementation issues specific to container applications that deal with compound documents.

Chapter 4, "Registering Object Applications," describes the registration database, which contains information about OLE object applications. Information is also provided regarding the entry and modification of database keys, OLE 1 compatibility issues, and the set of API functions used to create and modify the registration entries.

Chapter 5, "Component Object Interfaces and Functions," covers much of the functionality that forms the underlying foundation on which OLE 2 is built. The **IUnknown** interface, from which all other interfaces inherit, plus the object-class creation interface, **IClassFactory**, is described in this chapter. This chapter also describes issues such as reference counting (the mechanism used to keep track of valid objects), error handling, and the marshaling of pointers across process boundaries.

Chapter 6, "Compound Document Interfaces and Functions," describes the interfaces and functions that form the heart of compound document functionality. This chapter covers the **IOleObject** interface, the interface that exposes basic embedding functionality. Also covered is **IOleClientSite**, the interface that allows an embedded object to communicate with and request services from its embedding container.

Chapter 7, "Data Transfer/Caching Interfaces and Functions," describes the interfaces and functions that support displaying and rendering objects, caching presentation data for objects, and setting up advisory connections to keep applications informed of changes made to OLE objects.

Chapter 8, "Linking Interfaces and Functions," describes the interfaces that enable linked objects to be tracked and kept current to their source data, as well as API functions for creating application-specific instances of these OLE-provided interface implementations.

Chapter 9, "Persistent Storage Interfaces and Functions," describes the OLE object storage model and the interfaces and API functions that support storing and retrieving objects to and from disk and memory.

Chapter 10, "Drag and Drop Interfaces and Functions," describes the interfaces that will need to be implemented to enable users to selectively drag and drop objects from one application to another, or to iconic representations of target devices, such as a printer or fax.

Chapter 11, "In-Place Activation Interfaces and Functions," describes the interfaces and API functions that support activating objects within the context of their container application; activation could be editing, play, or any of the actions an object is capable of providing to the user.

Chapter 12, "Compatibility with OLE 1," describes the API functions that allow objects created by an OLE 1 object application to be embedded in and linked to by OLE 2 containers. OLE provides these capabilities by means of a built-in compatibility layer in the core code that include a set of API functions for conversion.

Chapter 13, "Concurrency Management," describes interfaces and functions that allow OLE applications to correctly deal with user input while processing one or more calls from OLE or the operating system. OLE calls, when made between processes, are categorized as synchronous calls, asynchronous notifications, and input-synchronized calls.

Appendix A, "Object Handlers," describes the basics of object handlers, a library of interfaces and functions that provide services on behalf of OLE object applications while an object is in its loaded state, eliminating the need to start the object application. The appendix discusses the default object handler, custom handlers, and DLL object applications.

Appendix B, "Creating Distribution Disks," describes issues related to the distribution of OLE applications. The appendix lists the files that must be included on an application's distribution disk(s) and discusses special considerations for distributing OLE applications.

Appendix C, "Data Structures and Enumerations," summarizes in one location, all of the data structures and enumeration used with OLE.

Appendix D, "OLE 2.01 for the Macintosh: How It Differs from OLE 2.01 for Windows," summarizes the major differences between OLE for the Windows operating system and OLE for the Macintosh operating system.

Glossary, contains an alphabetical listing of special terms and their definitions as used in this book.

Document Conventions

The following typographical conventions are used throughout this book:

Typographical Convention	Meaning
Bold	Indicates a word that is a function name, method name, structure name, data type, or other fixed part of the Microsoft Windows and OLE Application Programming Interface. For example, **OleSave** is an OLE-specific function. Words in bold must always be typed exactly as they are printed.
Italic	Indicates a word that is a place holder or a variable value. For example, *ClassName* would be a place holder for any OLE object class name. Function parameters in API reference material will be in italic to indicate that any variable name can be used. In addition, italic is used to highlight the first time use of OLE terms and to emphasize meaning.
MixedCase	Indicates filenames and paths as well as constants. For example, Macole:Current:Src:IncludesS:Ole2.h is a Macintosh path and filename. CF_METAFILEPICT is an OLE constant.

`monospace`	Indicates source code and syntax spacing. For example:
	`typedef struct _APPSTREAM`
	`{`
	`  OLESTREAM      olestream;`
	`  int            fh;`
	`} APPSTREAM;`

Note Much of the interface syntax in this book follows the variable-naming convention known in programming jargon as Hungarian notation where variables are prefixed with lower-case letters that indicate their data type. For example, *lpszNewDocname* would be a long pointer to a zero-terminated string named *NewDocname*. For more information about Hungarian notation, see *Programming Windows 3.1* by Charles Petzold.

CHAPTER 1

Architectural Overview

This chapter provides an architectural overview of OLE, version 2.01. The Component Object Model, the object-oriented programming model that is the basis for the OLE infrastructure, is first described, followed by a. brief description of the OLE infrastructure services. The remainder of the chapter discusses compound documents and related topics, including the differences between linked and embedded objects, the various roles an application can play in compound document creation and management, and the components that provide communication between applications.

What is OLE?

Microsoft Object Linking and Embedding (OLE) enables developers to create sophisticated and extensible applications that operate across multiple platforms. OLE is the first step in presenting applications as a collection of independently installed components.

With OLE, users interact with and manipulate information in an intuitive manner, using an environment that is more "document-centric" and less "application-centric." This enables users to focus directly on their data rather than on the applications responsible for the data. Users can create compound documents, which contain objects of different formats. The objects can be embedded within the document, or linked to it, so that only a reference to the objects data is stored in the document.

OLE facilitates application integration by defining a set of standard interfaces, groupings of semantically related methods through which one application accesses the services of another. The concept of exposing functionality through interfaces makes OLE an open, extensible system. It is open in the sense that anyone can provide an implementation of a defined interface and anyone can develop an application that uses it. It is extensible because new or extended interfaces can be defined and integrated into existing applications without requiring changes to existing code.

Applications that implement or access the new interfaces can exploit them while continuing to operate with other applications through the older interfaces. Interfaces can be implemented within a single process or across processes in application objects. As a developer, you can take advantage of the built-in functionality provided by OLE, or you can either add to it or fully replace it as best suits your needs.

The set of OLE services can be viewed as a two-tier hierarchy. The lower level contains the infrastructure services; basic services that provide the means by which features can be implemented and used. The infrastructure services include interface negotiation, memory management, error and status reporting, inter-process communication, structured storage, and data transfer. Application features are those services that benefit the end user; they comprise the upper level of the OLE service hierarchy. Some of the features that are currently available include compound document management, in-place activation, programmability, and drag and drop operations. Because OLE is open and extensible, others will be added by developers as needs are recognized.

Figure 1.1 illustrates the relationship between the infrastructure services and the features. Each service and feature represents one or more interfaces made up of semantically related functions.

FEATURES

Compound Document Management	In-Place Activation	Programmability	Drag and Drop	Future

Interface Negotiation	Memory Management	Error and Status Reporting	Interprocess Communication	Structured Storage	Data Transfer	Naming and Binding

INFRASTRUCTURE

Figure 1.1 OLE as a layered architecture

Component Object Model

The Component Object Model specifies how objects interact within a single application or between applications. A component object conforms to this model, implementing and using the interfaces that support object interaction. Implementing component objects is a matter of style: they can be implemented using C++ classes or C structures.

The Component Object Model is the key to OLE's extensible architecture, providing the foundation on which the rest of OLE is built. Each of the mechanisms described below is supported by one or more interfaces.

The Component Object Model defines the following:

- The concept of an interface by which a client of a service communicates with the provider of that service. The service provider, whether it is implemented in a DLL or an application, is referred to as the class of object.
- An architecture by which object classes can support multiple interfaces, providing a way for potential clients to query an object about support for a specific interface.
- A reference counting model for object management that permits simultaneous use of object classes by multiple clients. It also provides a way to determine when an object class is no longer in use and can be safely destroyed.
- A mechanism by which memory passed between clients and an object class can be allocated and freed.
- A model for reporting error and status information.
- A mechanism for allowing object classes to communicate transparently across process boundaries.
- A mechanism by which a specific object implementation (DLL or application) can be identified and dynamically loaded into the running system. The implementation may be local (within one application process) or remote (between two different application processes). The difference is handled transparently by OLE.

Figure 1.2 shows the OLE infrastructure divided into the services supported by the Component Object Model (interface negotiation, memory management, error and status reporting, and inter-process communication) and other basic services built on the model. The feature set is divided into two groups: those that are currently provided and features that might be available in the future.

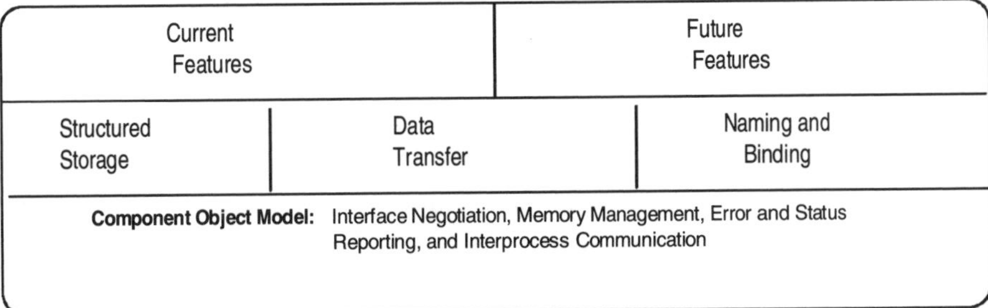

Figure 1.2 Component Object Model as OLE's foundation layer

Component objects can be independent, stand-alone entities or be composed of other objects. With a composition technique known as aggregation, a new object can be built using one or more existing objects that support some or all of the new object's required interfaces. This technique enables the new object to appear as a seamless whole rather than as a collection of independent parts. For more information on aggregation, see Chapter 3, "Programming Considerations."

Interfaces

Interfaces are the binary standard for component object interaction. Each interface contains a set of functions that defines a contract between the object implementing the interface and the client using it. The contract includes the name of the interface, the function names, and the parameter names and types. Under this contract, the object must implement all of the functions defined for that interface and the implementations must conform to the contract.

Clients use pointers to reference interface instances, obtaining them either when the object is instantiated or by querying the object. An interface pointer points to an array of function pointers known as a virtual table (VTBL). The functions that are pointed to by the members of the VTBL are called the methods, or member functions, of the interface.

Figure 1.3 shows the run-time representation of an interface instance. A variable supplied by the client of the component object points to the object's VTBL pointer that points to the VTBL instance. In addition to the VTBL pointer, the component object contains private data that cannot be used by the object's client. Each function pointer in the VTBL points to the actual method implementation.

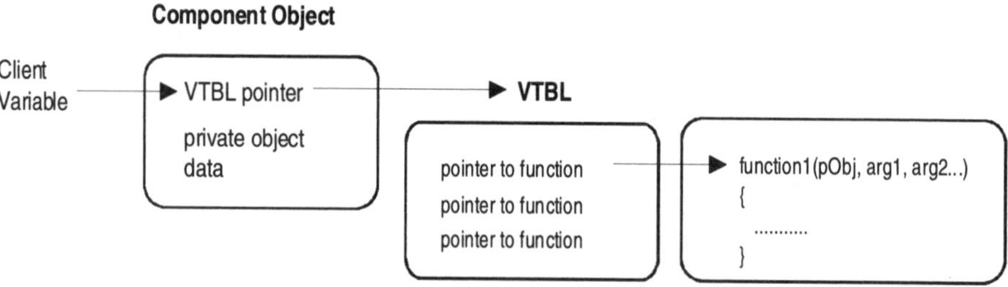

Figure 1.3 OLE interface model

Interfaces, using C++ terminology, are abstract base classes that specify behavior in a general manner with no implementation. Interfaces are defined by OLE to be pure virtual, which means without implementation specified here. OLE provides implementations for the interfaces that support the Component Object Model and other pieces of the infrastructure as well as for some of the interfaces that support application features. Applications typically implement some of the infrastructure interfaces, such as those that support data transfer, and some of the feature-specific interfaces. Also, if an OLE implementation of a particular interface is somehow unsuitable, an application can provide its own unique implementation, either adding onto what OLE has provided or completely replacing it.

Figure 1.4 shows by functional area all of the OLE interfaces available to applications. The Component Object Model interfaces are placed in the center of the diagram because they provide the foundation on which all other interfaces are built. The Component Object Model interfaces support the services described above in the Component Object Model section. For example, **IUnknown** provides the reference counting model and **IMalloc** supports memory management.

All interface names are prefixed with either "IOle" or "I." Interfaces that begin with "IOle" provide services relating to compound document management; those that begin with "I" provide services that are more general in nature. For example, **IOleObject** contains methods used by a client of an embedded or linked compound document object. **IOleObject** is implemented and used only by applications that participate in compound document management. **IDataObject**, however, contains methods that are used by all applications to transfer data of all types.

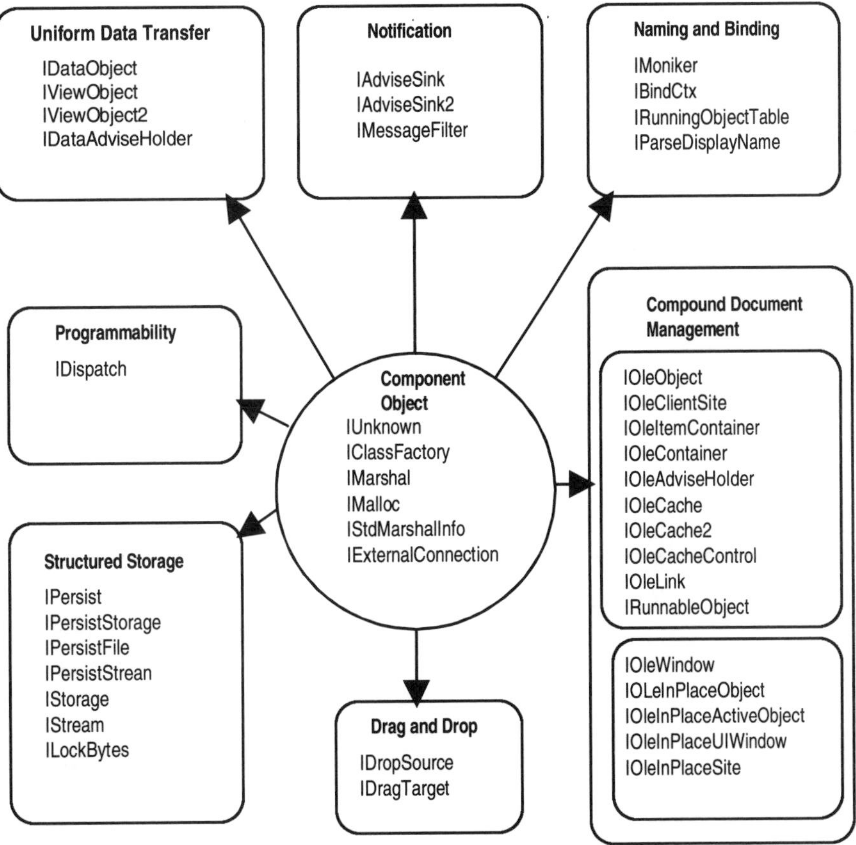

Figure 1.4 Functional view of OLE

Interface Negotiation

Objects use interfaces through a mechanism known as *interface negotiation*. Each interface has a globally unique interface identifier (IID) by which it is known at run time. The IID allows a client to dynamically determine (via a call to **IUnknown::QueryInterface**) the interfaces supported by other objects.

IUnknown::QueryInterface is the method that allows clients of objects to query for and obtain pointers to needed interfaces. **IUnknown** is implemented by all component objects because it is the base interface from which all other OLE 2 interfaces are derived. Given the interface pointer *pInterface1*, a caller can invoke *pInterface1*->**QueryInterface** to get pointers to other interface implementations that are supported by the object supporting the interface pointed to by *pInterface1*. The caller passes the IID of the desired interface to **IUnknown::QueryInterface**, which then returns either a NULL pointer, signifying that the interface is not supported, or a valid pointer to the interface.

Note Even though **IUnknown** is the OLE base interface, it is possible to implement or use an interface that does not derive directly from it. If an interface is implemented in an object containing an implementation of another interface that does derive from **IUnknown**, it is possible to request the new interface using **QueryInterface** by passing it a pointer to the derived interface.

There are two strategies for obtaining interface pointers in OLE applications. Some applications acquire all the interface pointers they will use over the lifetime of the application at initialization time. These applications typically store copies of the pointers with the objects that make calls to the interfaces' methods. Other applications postpone the acquisition of interface pointers until an interface is needed. These applications do not store pointer copies. The interface pointer is used and then released.

Reference Counting

Reference counting is keeping a count of each instance of a pointer to an interface that is derived from **IUnknown**. Reference counting ensures that an object is not destroyed before all references to it are released. Objects are kept alive if there are one or more references to one or more of their interfaces. Under no circumstances is an object to be deleted when its reference count is greater than zero. The reference counting mechanism enables independent components to obtain and release pointers to a single object with no coordination required.

The rules for accurate reference counting and suggestions for optimization are described in Chapter 5, "Component Object Interfaces and Functions."

Memory Management

Most of the OLE interface methods in are called by code written by one programming organization and implemented by code written by another. Many of the parameters and return values of these methods are of types that can be passed around by value; however, sometimes there is a need to pass data structures for which this is not the case and for which it is necessary that the caller and the callee agree on the allocation and deallocation policy.

Memory management of pointers to interfaces is always provided by member functions in the interface in question. For all of the interfaces defined by OLE, these are the **AddRef** and **Release** methods found in the **IUnknown** interface, from which all other OLE interfaces are derived. (The memory management discussed in this section relates only to non-by-value parameters, which are not pointers to interfaces, but are instead more mundane things like strings and pointers to structures.)

OLE uses two different kinds of memory: local application task memory, and shared (between process) memory, also called "global" memory. Each kind of memory has a different memory allocator implementation. All non-shared memory allocated by the OLE libraries or by object handlers is allocated using an application-supplied memory allocator passed as a parameter to **CoInitialize**. If the application doesn't want to provide its own allocator, then it can pass NULL to **CoInitialize**. This gives the application control of how memory is actually allocated, while still allowing for the improved efficiency that results from often not having to allocate copies of data merely to pass as parameters to OLE functions. It also results in improved robustness in case of application crashes, since the task memory is owned by an application and will be freed by the operating system when the application terminates.

Shared memory is used much less frequently in OLE than is task memory. The primary use of shared memory is to optimize data copying that might otherwise need to occur in an interface call: if the caller knows that the data it is allocating will be passed as a parameter to a function that results in a remote procedure call to another process, allocating it in shared memory will be more efficient. In OLE, "shared memory" specifically means memory that is allocated with the memory allocator returned by **CoGetMalloc**(MEMCTX_SHARED, *&pmalloc*).

Each parameter passed in and the value returned from a function can be classified into one of three groups: an In parameter, an Out parameter, or an In/Out parameter (the return value is treated as an out parameter). In each class of parameter, the responsibility for allocating and freeing non-by-value parameters is as follows:

Parameter Type	How It Is Allocated and Freed
In Parameter	In parameters are both allocated and freed by the caller.
Out Parameter	Out parameters are allocated by the callee, but freed by the caller.
In/Out Parameter	In/Out parameters are to be initially allocated by the caller, then freed and reallocated by the callee if necessary. As with out parameters, the caller is responsible for freeing the final returned value.

In the latter two cases, one piece of code does the allocation but another piece of code does the freeing. To be successful, these two pieces of code must have knowledge of which memory allocator is being used. So that the system as a whole can operate correctly, the following rules govern which memory allocators can be used and when:

Parameter Type	How Allocated
In Parameter	Allocated by either the task or the shared allocator.
Out Parameter	Only the task allocator may be used.
In/Out Parameter	Only the task allocator may be used.

The treatment of Out and In/Out parameters in failure conditions needs special consideration. If a function returns a status code which is a failure code, then the calling application has no way to clean up the Out or In/Out parameters returned to it. Therefore, the following rules should be followed in failure conditions:

Parameter Type	How Allocated
Out Parameter	In error returns, out parameters must be reliably set to a value which will be cleaned up without any action on the caller's part. All Out pointer parameters (usually passed in a pointer-to-pointer parameter, but which can also be passed as a member of a caller-allocate callee-fill structure) must explicitly be set to NULL. The most straightforward way to ensure this is to set these values to NULL on function entry. (On successful returns, the semantics of the function determine the legal return values.)
In/Out Parameter	In error returns, all In/Out parameters must either be left alone by the callee or be explicitly set as in the Out parameter error return case. If left alone by the callee, they remain set to the value to which they weres initialized by the caller; if the caller didn't initialize them, then they are an Out parameter, not an In/Out parameter.

Note Interface pointers passed as In parameters to a method cannot be modified in the implementation of the method. Modifying these interface pointer parameters can lead to reference counting errors. In parameters that are interface pointers must be treated as "**const char ***" regardless of whether they are declared as such in the header files. Methods that need to hold onto data longer than a call's duration need to make a copy of that data.

These memory management conventions apply only to public interfaces and APIs. Memory allocation internal to applications does not need to be managed this way.

Error and Status Reporting

Most OLE interface methods and API functions return result handles called HRESULTs that are comprised of a severity code, context information, a facility code, and a status code. The returned HRESULT can be interpreted at two levels. At the simplest level, zero indicates success and nonzero indicates failure or nonsuccess. At a more complex level, the nonzero value can be examined to determine a more detailed reason for the failure.

In the current release of OLE 2, an HRESULT does little more than wrap the status code. In future releases, however, the HRESULT will be transparently enhanced to convey more information about the error and where it occurred.

The return values described for a given interface method specify status code constants that incorporate information about the facility, severity, and status. For example, STG_E_MEDIUMFULL is returned when there is no space left on a storage device. The STG prefix indicates the storage facility, the E indicates that the status code represents an error, and the MEDIUMFULL provides specific information about the error.

Success codes are defined when the interface's designer ships that interface (that is, makes it public). Although success codes cannot be altered, error codes can be changed by the designer of the interface. At the present time, most interfaces have been designed by Microsoft, but in the future, other developers will design and ship interfaces.

For more information about OLE error handling, see Chapter 5, "Component Object Interfaces and Functions."

Inter-process Communication

OLE uses a lightweight remote procedure call (LRPC) communication mechanism based on posting messages or events to window handles to transfer data between processes. The communication mechanism is referred to as "lightweight" because, at present, it only handles communication between processes on one machine. In the future, communication will be across machines. LRPC is not a protocol because there is no need for a conversation between the communicating processes. Data is simply sent to a predefined space in memory.

The sending and receiving of interface parameters across process boundaries, referred to as marshaling and unmarshaling, is the job of proxy and stub component objects. Every interface has its own proxy object that can package method parameters for that interface. On the receiving side, there is an interface-specific stub object that unpackages the parameters and makes the required method call. A proxy manager exists to establish connections to the LRPC channel and to load and unload proxy objects as needed. In most cases, callers of interface methods are not affected when calls cross a process boundary.

Several component object interfaces manage the marshaling and unmarshaling process. For more information about this process and how it works, see Chapter 5, "Component Object Interfaces and Functions."

Dynamic Loading of Object Implementations

One of the key features of the Component Object Model is that a client of a component object can locate the code that is responsible for the object and dynamically load it into a running system. By associating each component object with a class identifier (CLSID), OLE can match the CLSID with the code containing the implementation of the associated object. Once it is loaded, OLE makes a call to the object implementation to retrieve an instance of the specific interface requested by the client.

Data Transfer Model

OLE's data transfer model allows users to transfer data uniformly with a drag and drop operation, a copy/paste operation, or programmatically. The data transfer model is supported by the **IDataObject**. By implementing **IDataObject**, an application can provide data to be pasted or dropped in a variety of formats across a range of mediums. Once it has obtained a pointer to the **IDataObject** implementation, an application can call **IDataObject** methods to query for appropriate formats and mediums, set up data advises, and send or receive the actual data.

OLE associates two types of data with a compound document object: presentation data and native data. The presentation data is needed to render the object on an output device, while the native data is needed for editing. There are data formats that are used to describe both types of data. Applications that copy to the clipboard or that can act as drag sources publish formats that best describes the source data. These can be standard formats (PICT), private formats, or OLE formats. OLE formats support the creation of compound document objects so one or more of these formats must be available to create a linked or embedded object.

Non-OLE applications that copy data to the clipboard do not offer OLE data formats; data transfers remain unchanged. In an analogous way, OLE 1 applications offer the OLE 1 set of clipboard formats that can be understood by OLE 2 applications. OLE 2 sources offer OLE 2 clipboard formats and the OLE system then synthesizes additional corresponding OLE 1 formats. Some source applications might not follow the rules of offering preferred formats first. A target application pasting from such a source might end up with a non-typical result.

Structured Storage Model

OLE's structured storage model specifies how data is saved and retrieved from storage. In this model, multiple streams are multiplexed onto one underlying file (or byte array) so this layer looks like a file system directory tree, a file system within a file. There are two types of objects in a file system: directories and files. The structured storage model has two equivalent types of objects: storages and streams.

A storage object is analogous to a directory in that each storage may contain nested storages and streams. Stream objects are analogous to files. The structured storage model enables objects to control their own storage, loading directly from and saving directly to disk.

Storage objects are binary compatible across all OLE-supported development platforms. OLE writes information to an object's storage so that the information can be read on other platforms. All supporting data that OLE stores about an object is converted as needed on each platform.

Figure 1.5 shows the hierarchical nature of the structured storage model. A container creates the root storage object needed to store the document. The document's outermost storage object is referred to as the root storage object. Root storage objects, like all storage objects, can be marshaled from one process to another. The root storage object contains a stream for OLE data and one or more streams for native data. The two embedded objects have storage objects with their own streams for OLE and native data.

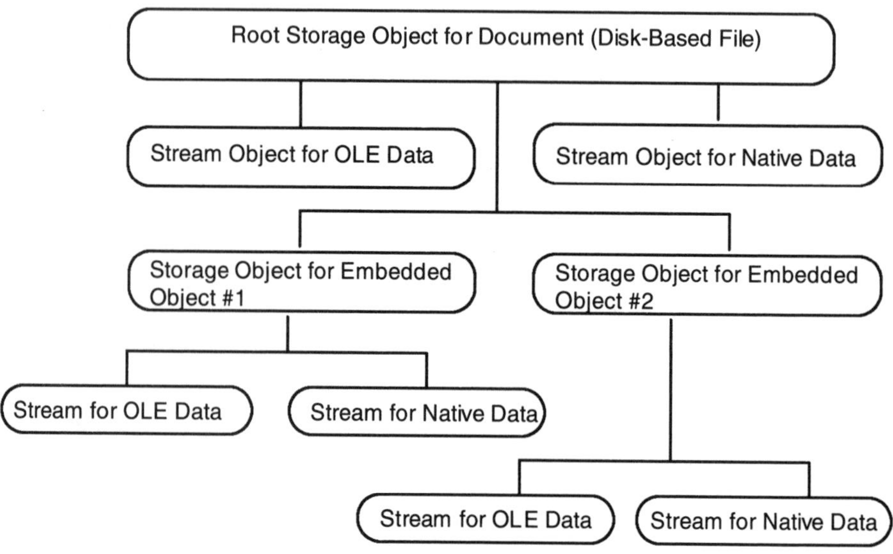

Figure 1.5 Hierarchy of the OLE structured storage model

Compound Document Management

Overview

A compound document is a document within a container application that seamlessly integrates data of different formats, such as sound clips, spreadsheets, text, and bitmaps. Each piece of integrated data, referred to as a compound document object, is created and maintained by the application that created it. End users feel as though they are using a single application, with all the functionality of each of the object's application. Therefore, rather than being concerned with managing multiple object applications, they focus solely on the compound document and the task being performed.

A compound document object is a specific type of component object. In addition to using the component object interfaces, container and object applications that deal with compound document objects implement and use a set of interfaces specifically for creating and managing compound documents. There are various types of container and object applications and the type relates to the features offered by the application. The type determines the specific set of interfaces to be implemented. For example, container applications either can be pure containers, providing sites for compound document objects, or linking containers that allow other containers to link to their embedded objects. Object applications can support linking to file-based objects only or linking to portions of their file-based objects, referred to as pseudo objects.

The following table describes the types of OLE applications:

Application Types	Description
Pure Container	Contains linked and embedded objects within its documents. Does not allow other applications to link to its data.
Link Container	Contains linked and embedded objects within its documents. Allows other applications to link to its embedded objects.
Simple Object Application	Creates object(s) that can be embedded or linked. Allows linking only to the whole object.
Pseudo Object Application	Creates object(s) that can be embedded or linked. Allows linking to whole object and to selections of data.
Link Object Application	Acts as a link source only. Cannot create object(s) to be embedded in a container (is not insertable).
Container/Object Application	Creates object(s) that can be embedded or linked and can embed or link objects within its documents.

Linked Objects vs. Embedded Objects

Users can create two types of compound document objects: linked or embedded. The difference between the two is how and where the actual source data comprising the object is stored. This, in turn, affects the object's portability, its method(s) of activation, and the size of the compound document.

When an object is linked, the source data, or link source, continues to physically reside wherever it was initially created, either at another point within the document or within a different document or application altogether. Only a reference, or link, to the object and appropriate presentation data is kept with the compound document. Linked objects cannot "travel" with documents to another machine; they must remain within the local file system or be copied explicitly.

Linking objects is efficient and keeps the size of the compound document small. Users may choose to link when the source object is owned or maintained by someone else because a single instance of the object's data can serve many documents. Changes made to the source object are automatically reflected in any compound documents that have a link to the object. From the user's point of view, a linked object appears to be wholly contained within the document. In addition to simple links, it is possible to get arbitrarily complex by nesting links and combining linked and embedded objects.

In the case of an embedded object, a copy of the original object is physically stored in the compound document as is all the information needed to manage the object. As a result, the object becomes a physical part of the document. A compound document containing embedded objects will be larger than one containing the same objects as links. However, embedding offers several advantages that might outweigh the disadvantages of the extra storage overhead. For example, compound documents with embedded objects can be transferred to another computer and edited there. The new user of the document need not know where the original data resides because a copy of the object's source (native) data travels with the compound document.

Embedded objects can be edited, or activated, in place. This means all maintenance of the object can be done without leaving the compound document. Because each user has a copy of the object's source data, changes made to an embedded object by one user will not affect other compound documents containing an embedding of the same original object. However, if there are links to this object, changes to it will be reflected in each document containing a link.

Architecture of Compound Documents

Several component objects participate to enable compound document interaction. The object handler is a piece of object-specific code loaded in the container's space so that communication is by function call rather than remote messaging. The object handler services container requests that do not require the services of the object application, such as requests for drawing. The object handler, therefore, is needed only if the object and container applications are not in the same process space. When implemented as a DLL, the object application can handle all container requests by function call.

OLE provides a default object handler that object applications can use. For object applications that require special behavior, a custom handler can be implemented that either replaces the default version or uses it to provide selected default behavior. For more general information about object handlers, see Appendix A, "Object Handlers."

When an object is embedded in a container application, data flows both from the container application to the object application and from the object application to the container application. Proxy and stub objects facilitate the transfer of the data across process boundaries as described earlier in the section, "Inter-process Communication." Data flowing from the container to the object application always goes through the object handler. When data flows from the object application, however, there are two possible routes using these remoting objects on either side of the process boundary. Data can flow directly either to the container application or to the object handler.

Figure 1.6 shows the flow between applications for an embedded object. The more general term, LRPC Remoting, is used in this diagram for the proxy and stub objects. The object handler is a composite, or aggregate, object made of three pieces: a remoting piece, a controlling piece, and a cache. Notice that the container and object applications, as well as the object handler, can access the structured storage for the compound document.

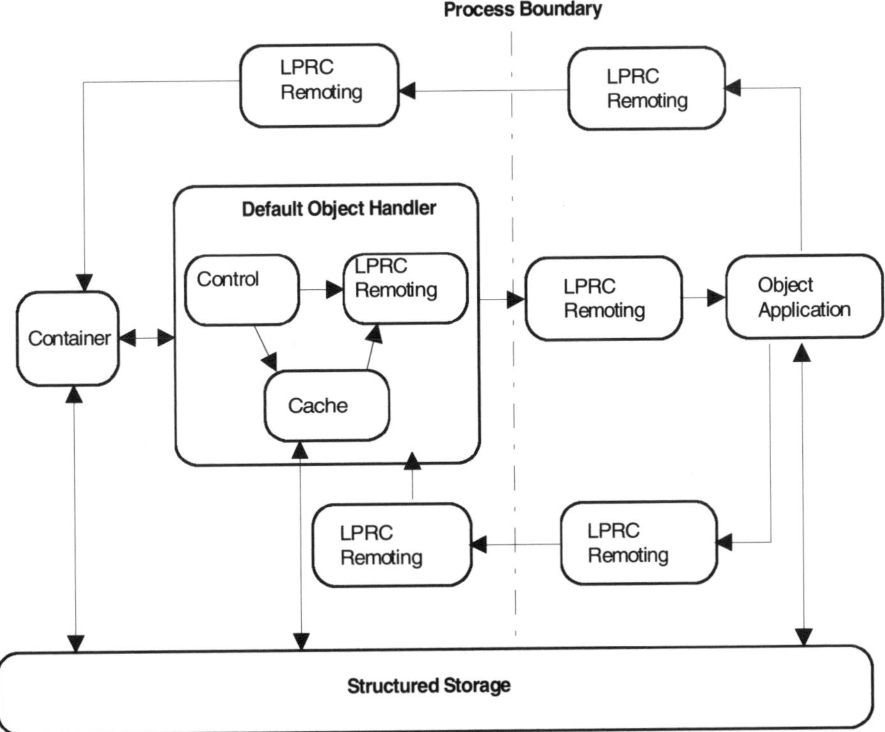

Figure 1.6 Data flow for an embedded object

Figure 1.7 illustrates the flow of a linked compound document object whose link source is in a separate process. For linked compound document objects, OLE instantiates a component object referred to as the link object. The link object and the object handler are instantiated in the container's process space. However, only the link object has access to the compound document's storage. Rather than holding a pointer to the object handler as is the case with embedded object, the container of a linked object holds a pointer to the link object. When the linked object in the container is activated, this link object initiates the binding process whereby the link source application is located and run.

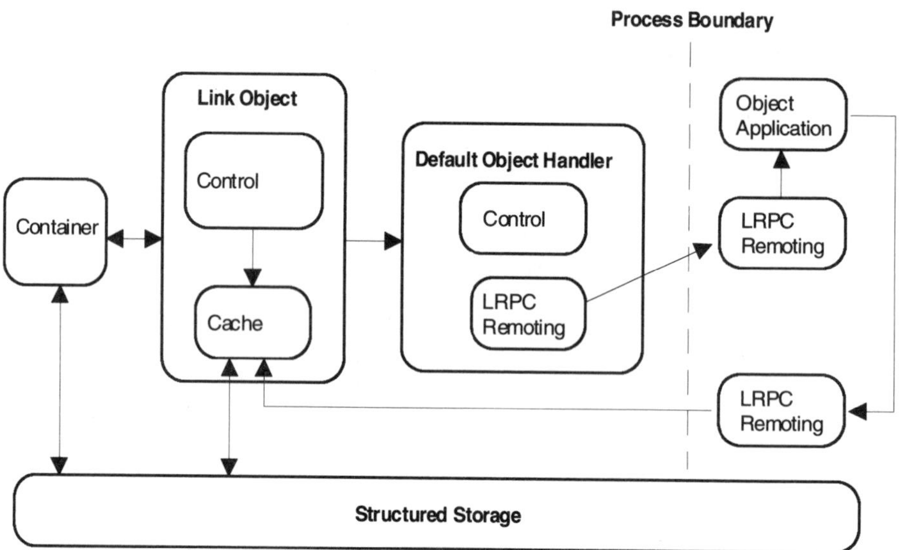

Figure 1.7 Data flow for a linked object

Both of the preceding illustrations describe the compound document architecture when a container application and object application reside in separate processes. Object applications can be written either as a separate task in a separate process space, providing services to containers remotely, or as a dynamic linked library in the container process space, providing services to containers through local function calls. Object applications that run in a separate process space are referred to as local servers. Object applications that run in the container's process space are referred to as in-process servers.

When an object application is implemented as an in-process server, it replaces the majority of functionality provided by the object handler. Implementing the object application in-process does not preclude it from using some or all of the services provided by the default object handler. The remoting object may or may not exist. However, if there is a remoting object, OLE is not affected by its existence.

Figure 1.8 shows the flow for in-process servers and container applications.

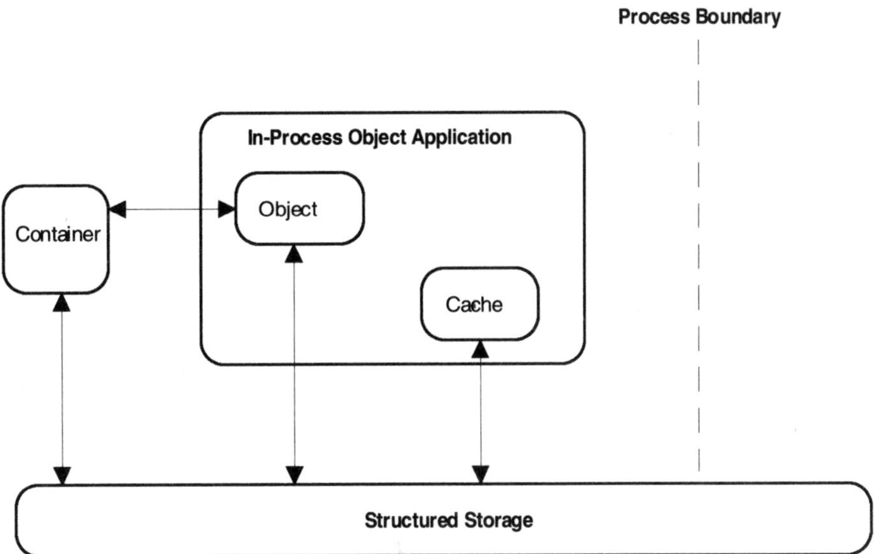

Figure 1.8 Data flow for an in-process object application

Types of Object Handlers

An object handler provides a partial implementation of a particular object class. The object handler is an aggregate object, a composite object made up of a remoting piece for marshaling and unmarshaling interface parameters across the process boundary, the cache, an optional link object, and a controlling object that coordinates between the pieces. There is a one-to-one relationship between an object class and its handler. An object handler is unique to an object class. Once instantiated, it is not possible to interchange or share a handler between object classes. When used for a compound document, the object handler implements the container-side data structures when objects of a particular class are accessed remotely.

Figure 1.9 shows the different ways in which the object handler can be structured.

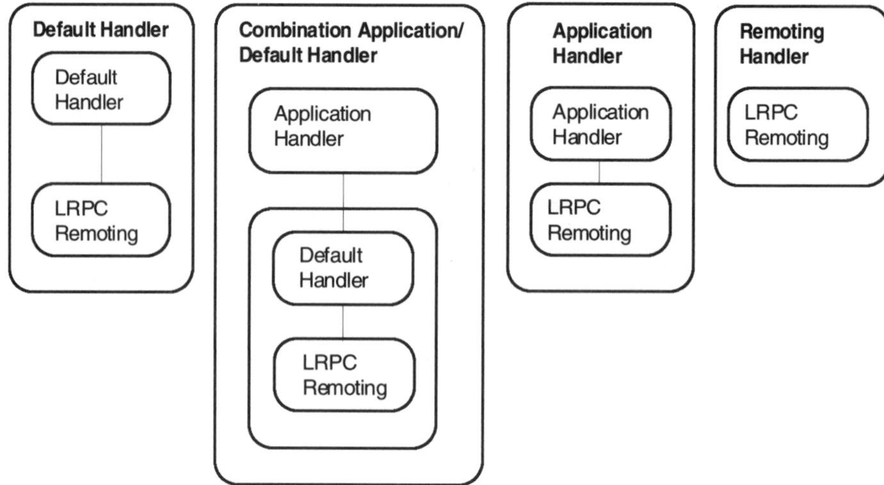

Figure 1.9 Structure of object handlers

The default handler, an implementation provided by OLE, is used by most applications as the handler. An application implements a custom handler when the default handler's capabilities are insufficient. A custom handler can either completely replace the default handler or use parts of the functionality it provides where appropriate. In the latter case, the application handler is implemented as an aggregate object composed of a new control object and the default handler. Combination application/default handlers are also known as in-process handlers. The remoting handler is used for objects not assigned a CLSID in the Registration Database file or that have no specified handler. All that is required from a handler for these types of objects is to pass information across the process boundary. For more information on the Registration Database file, see Chapter 4, "Registering Object Applications."

Figure 1.10 shows how objects communicate through interfaces across process boundaries using the default and remoting handlers. Object A's private functions make calls to Object B's interface methods. Similarly, Object B's private functions make calls to Object A's interface methods. The communication between the two objects is maintained through the handler. Object A uses a remote handler because it has no assigned CLSID, whereas Object B uses the default handler. The remoting part of the object handler packages parameters in each function call into a known format and sends them to the appropriate object.

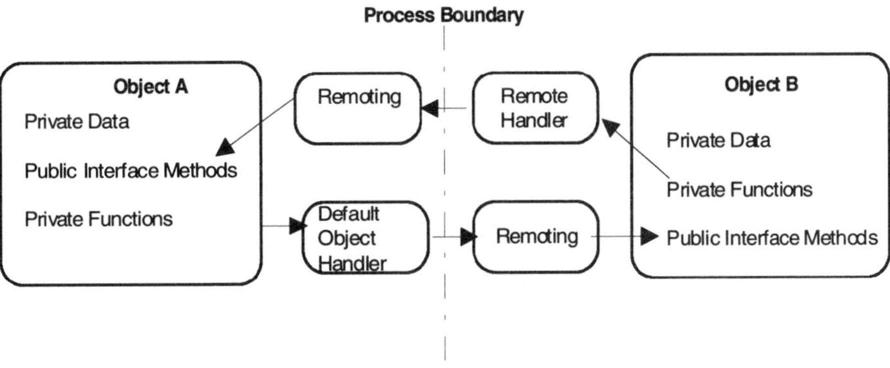

Figure 1.10 Component objects using interfaces

For more information on implementing custom object handlers, see Appendix A, "Object Handlers."

Link Objects

The link object is a component object that is instantiated Whenever a linked compound document object is created or loaded, OLE instantiates a special component object called a *link object*. The link object manages the naming of linked objects and the tracking of link sources. Object naming is accomplished through a mechanism known as a moniker. A moniker is a conceptual handle to the linked object at the source of the link that can be persistently stored with the container. Similar to a pointer in programming languages, the moniker can be bound, or dereferenced, to locate and load the object to which it refers.

The important properties of a moniker are:

- A moniker's representation is opaque to applications. Monikers are to name components what OLE is to data formats.
- Applications can compose (concatenate) and decompose a moniker without knowing its syntax. This allows an application to give a composite moniker that describes, for example, a range within a spreadsheet. The application is able to do this without recognizing the syntax name by which the spreadsheet is known.
- OLE defines a set of moniker (component) types that provide standard ways for applications to participate in naming support. The main type is the item moniker. An item moniker is an encapsulation of an item name that can be composed with other monikers, which encapsulate other names, such as path names. Item names are strings assigned by the object or container.

When a running application contains data to which another application can potentially create a link, the application names the data by creating a moniker. When a linked compound document object is created, the instantiated link object acts like an in-process server. For example, when the user of the container activates the linked object with a double-click, the link object locates and launches the appropriate object application so that editing (or other supported verbs) can be initiated.

Data Cache

The data cache is responsible for transferring an embedded object's data from storage to memory and back to storage, where it is persistently saved. OLE provides an implementation of the cache used by OLE's default object handler and the link object. The cache stores data in formats needed by the object handler to satisfy container draw requests. When an object's data changes, the object sends a notification to the cache so that an update can occur.

Container Applications

Container applications are the compound document object's consumer, providing storage, a place for object display, and access to this display site, referred to as the client site. Containers can be pure containers that simply hold embedded and linked objects, or more sophisticated containers that allow other containers to link to their embedded objects. Combination container/object applications can be used to embed and link to objects created by other applications as well as to create and service their own class(es) of objects.

The following table list the interfaces that are implemented by various kinds of container applications. Other interfaces can be optionally implemented to add functionality. This includes support for drag and drop operations and in-place activation. If an application does not support these features, the interfaces need not be implemented. Only two of the interfaces are required: **IOleClientSite** and **IAdviseSink**. **IOleClientSite** is the primary interface by which a container provides services to the compound document object. **IAdviseSink** supports the flow of notifications between an object and its container.

Pure Container	Link Container	Container/Object
IOleClientSite	IOleClientSite	IOleClientSite
IAdviseSink	IAdviseSink	IAdviseSink
IAdviseSink2	IAdviseSink2	IAdviseSink2
IMessageFilter	IMessageFilter	IMessageFilter
IOleInPlaceSite	IOleInPlaceSite	IOleInPlaceSite
IOleInPlaceFrame	IOleInPlaceFrame	IOleInPlaceFrame
IDataObject	IDataObject	IDataObject
IDropSource	IOleItemContainer	IOleItemContainer

Pure Container	Link Container	Container/Object
IDropTarget	IPersistFile	IPersistFile
	IClassFactory	IClassFactory
	IDropSource	IDropSource
	IDropTarget	IDropTarget
		IPersistStorage
		IOleObject

Container applications are typically structured so that particular interfaces are grouped together in an object. These groupings are shown in Figure 1.11. The **IOleInPlaceFrame**, **IClassFactory**, and **IMessageFilter** interfaces are each implemented in a separate object, instantiated once per application instance. At the document level, there is an object that exposes **IPersistFile** and **IOleItemContainer** to support linking to embeddings and **IDropTarget** to allow data to be dropped onto the document window. There is an additional data transfer object to support clipboard and drag and drop operations that exposes **IDropSource** and **IDataObject**. The container site object contains the required interfaces, **IOleClientSite** and **IAdviseSink**, and **IOleInPlaceSite**.

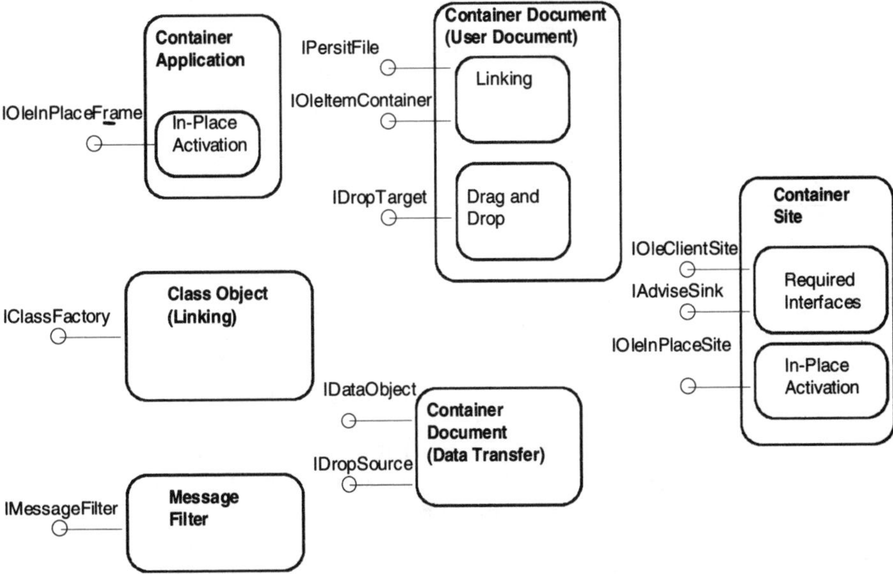

Figure 1.11 Interface groupings for a container

Object Applications

Object applications create embedded or linked objects at the request of the user working with a compound document in the container. Because some object applications act as containers also, this could be the same application. Object applications are responsible for creating one or more objects of a specific class.

Object applications must provide a persistent representation of each object and one or more presentations for the container's use. Object applications also supply user interface and editing capabilities.

Object applications can allow linking to file-based documents or to pieces of data within those documents. When linking to pieces of data is allowed, the object application is said to support pseudo objects. These pseudo objects implement the same interfaces as the registered objects that are supported.

The following table lists the interfaces that object applications of various types typically implement.

Simple Object Application	Pseudo Object Application	Link Object Application
IOleObject	IOleObject	IOleObject
IClassFactory	IClassFactory	IClassFactory
IDataObject	IDataObject	IDataObject
IMessageFilter	IMessageFilter	IMessageFilter
IPersistFile	IPersistFile	IPersistFile
IOleInPlaceObject	IOleInPlaceObject	IOleInPlaceObject
IOleInPlaceActiveObject	IOleInPlaceActiveObject	IOleInPlaceActiveObject
IDropSource	IDropSource	IDropSource
IDropTarget	IDropTarget	IDropTarget
IPersistStorage	IPersistStorage	IOleItemContainer
	IOleItemContainer	

Some object applications are referred to as mini servers. A mini server is one that cannot run as a stand-alone application; it always runs from another application. Mini servers, with their simplified user interface, can only support embedded objects and they cannot open or save files independently. Microsoft Graph is an example of a mini server that cannot run by itself; it is always run from Microsoft Excel. A mini server is useful to create when limited functionality is required or when there is a predefined partnership with specific containers.

Object applications, like container applications, structure their implemented interfaces so that grouped interfaces are implemented within the same object. Figure 1.12 shows the typical structure of an object application. As with container applications, there are two types of document objects: one for the user document and one for data transfer, which exposes **IDataObject** and **IDropSource**. However, in object applications, the user document object also implements **IDataObject** and a variety of other interfaces. The pseudo object is implemented only if the object application supports linking to selections of data.

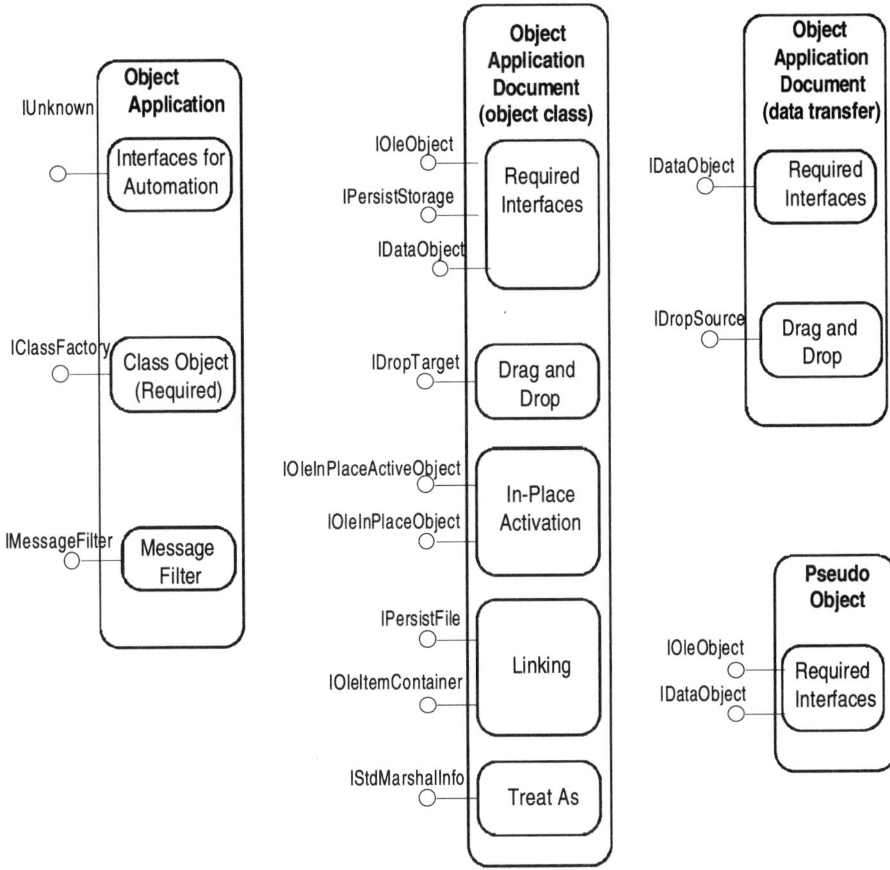

Figure 1.12 Interface groupings for an object application

Object States

A compound document object's state describes the relationship between the object in its container and the application responsible for its creation. Compound document objects have three states: passive, loaded, and running. The loaded and running states are referred to as active.

Note These object states do not correlate with the end user object states described in Chapter 2, "User Interface Guidelines."

The compound document object states are described as follows:

Object State	Description
Passive	The compound document object is not selected or active. It is in its stored state (on disk or in a database).
Loaded	The object's data structures created by the object handler are in the container's memory. The container has established communication with the object handler and there is cached presentation data available for rendering the object. Calls are processed by the object handler.
Running	The object application is running. It is possible to edit the object, access the object's interfaces, and receive notification of changes. The objects that control remoting have been created. The object handler delegates calls to the real object (in the object application).

Figure 1.13 shows the three states and the method calls that cause an object to transition from one state to another.

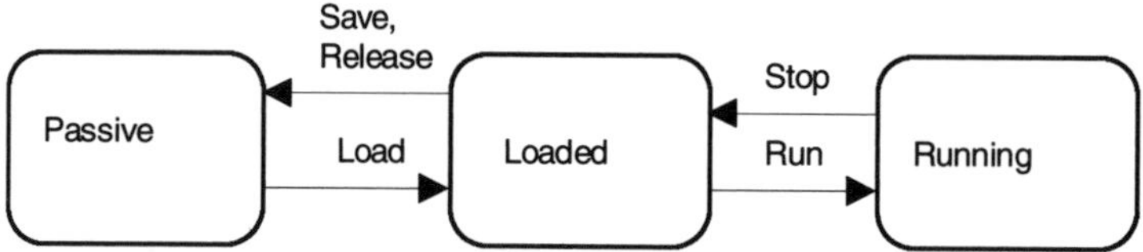

Figure 1.13 States of an object

Figure 1.14 shows the relationship between a container for an embedded object, its object handler, and its executable object application as the object transitions to each of the three states. In-process servers have no object handler in the container process; it is up to the server to keep track of its state (loaded vs. running).

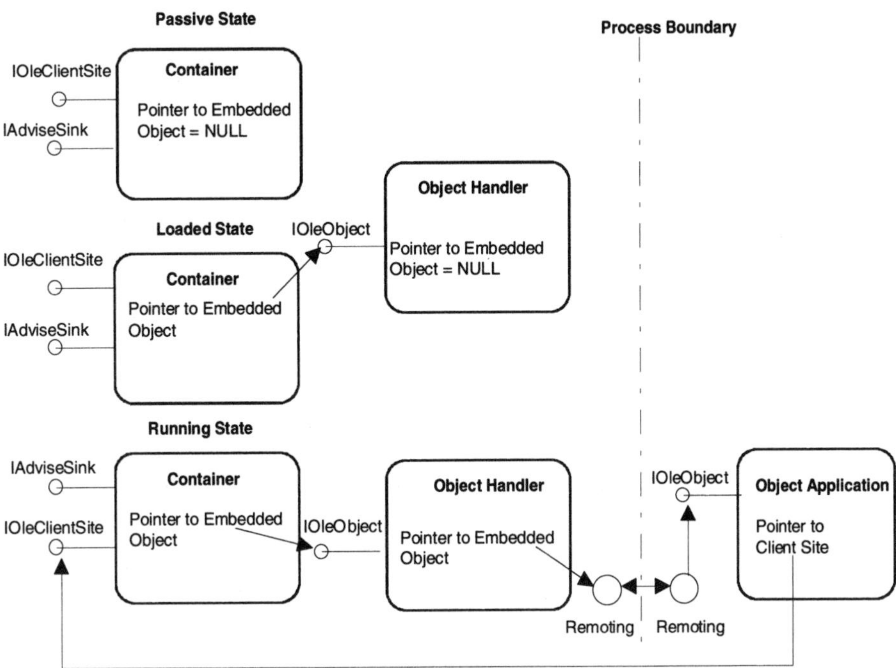

Figure 1.14 States of an embedded object

Entering the Loaded State

When an object enters the loaded state, the in-memory structures representing the object are created so that operations can be invoked on it. The object's handler or in-process server is loaded. This process, referred to as instantiation, occurs when an object is loaded from persistent storage (a transition from the passive to the loaded state) or when an object is being created for the first time.

Internally, instantiation is a two-phase process. An object of the appropriate class is created, after which a method on that object is called to perform initialization and give access to the object's data. The initialization method is defined in one of the object's supported interfaces. The particular initialization method called depends on the context in which the object is being instantiated and the location of the initialization data.

Entering the Running State

When an embedded object transitions to the running state, the object application must be located and run so that the object application's services can be utilized. Embedded objects are placed in the running state either explicitly through a request by the container, such as a need to draw a format not presently cached, or implicitly by OLE as a side effect of invoking an operation, such as when the user of the container double-clicks the object.

The process of transitioning a linked object into the running state is known as *binding*. Binding involves first locating the object data before the object application can be located and run.

At first glance, binding a linked object appears to be no more complicated than running an embedded object. However, the following points complicate the process:

- OLE allows a link to refer to objects (and possibly parts of objects) that are embedded in other containers. This implies a potential for nested embeddings. The link must include sufficient information to allow it to locate the object inside the other container(s). This information is maintained through the use of monikers, the naming mechanism described earlier. Typically, an object's moniker is part of a filename (path) concatenated with a series of item name parts. During binding, names are reduced before the steps in binding take place; this allows for important functionality such as link tracking and user aliases to be implemented transparently.
- Because linking permits multiple references to a given object, it is possible that the object may already be running, in which case OLE binds to the running object. At any point in the containment hierarchy, OLE might be able to bind to an already running object.
- Running an object requires accessing the storage area for the object. When an embedded object is run, OLE is given a pointer to the storage during the load process, which it passes on to the object application. However, for linked objects, there is no standard interface for accessing storage. The object application may use the file system interface or another mechanism.

OLE manages the binding process for applications. For more information, see Chapter 8, "Linking Interfaces and Functions."

Entering the Passive State

Object closure forces an embedded or linked object into the passive state. It is normally initiated from the object application's user interface, such as when the user selects the File Close command. In this case, the object application notifies the container, who releases its reference count on the object. When all references to the object have been released, the object can be freed. When all objects have been freed, the object application can safely terminate.

A container application can also initiate object closure. When the container wants to close an object, it releases its reference count after optionally completing a save. Containers will normally release objects in a lazy manner when they are deactivating after in-place activation. This will allow the user to click outside the object but not lose the active editing session until some other action causes the client to stop and/or release the object.

CHAPTER 2

User Interface Guidelines

This chapter describes guidelines to implementing the user interface for OLE applications. In general, the concepts in this chapter are a superset of the OLE 1 principles. These concepts unify the style of interaction with objects from both releases of OLE.

The goals of the OLE user interface include the following:

- To express a unified model of compound document composition and interaction that allows users to efficiently accomplish tasks.
- To fully exploit the integration power of OLE 2 using current user-interface frameworks and mechanisms.
- To establish a sound user model of compound documents that meets current application needs and that gracefully leads to more data-centric systems in the future.

Simply put, a user creates and manipulates various types of information (objects) that reside in a containing document. As a user focuses on a particular object, its corresponding commands and tools become available, allowing the user to interact with the object directly from within the document (in-place activation). Objects may be transferred within and across documents and still retain their full-featured editing and operating capabilities. In addition, information may be connected so that changes in one object are automatically reflected in another (*linking*).

Object Type

An object's type is the human-readable form of its class and conveys the object's behavior or capability to the user in dialog boxes and menu commands throughout the OLE 2 interface. The string "Claris Resolve 1.0 Spreadsheet" is a typical example. An object's type is not meant to imply its storage format. Two different object types may use the same storage format, but their types are distinct if they are handled by different object applications.

As shown in the following table, the four components of the object type name convey a wide range of useful information to the user:

Object Name Component	Description
brandname	Differentiates and identifies the application.
application	Indicates which application is responsible for activating the object.
data type	Suggests the basic nature or category of the object (such as drawing, spreadsheet, sound); should be a maximum of 15 characters.
version	When there are multiple versions of the same basic type, a version number is necessary to distinguish types for purposes of upgrading.

An object's type is expressed to the user in dialog boxes as a string (maximum of 40 characters) in one of the three recommended forms listed below:

- <brandname> <application> [<version>] <data type>

  For example, "Claris Resolve 1.0 Spreadsheet."

- *<brandname-application>* [*<version>*] *<data type>*, for cases when the brandname and application are the same.

  For example, "WordPerfect Text."

- *<brandname>* *<application>* [*<version>*], for cases where the application sufficiently describes the item.

  For example, "Microsoft Powerpoint 3.0."

Object type names provide users with a precise language for referring to objects. The full object type name should be used in dialog boxes and messages; this will help users become conscious of an object's type and its associated behavior.

Because of the restrictions on the length of type names, only their <data type> should be used in menus (both pull-down and pop-up), title bars, and in the list pane of the Links dialog box.

The data type is considered to be the shortform of the full object type name. If a short form name is not available for an object (because it is an OLE 1 object or the string was simply not registered), the full type name should be used instead. For example, a "Claris Resolve 1.0 Spreadsheet" is simply referred to as a "Spreadsheet" in menus and in the list pane of the Links dialog.

All dialogs that display the full type name must allocate enough space for 40 characters in width. Likewise dialog boxes must accommodate 15 characters when using the short form name.

Class Registration

Object applications must register the class of their service, including object types, in the OLE 2 Registration Database file, either during installation or when they are first started. For registration to occur during installation, the object application must supply a setup program that includes the registration. If there is no setup program, registration must occur when the application is first started, or each time it is started from the Finder.

The Registration Database file has two main purposes:

- It allows object applications to make information about the objects they create available to other OLE applications.
- It allows the OLE libraries to find the object application when the user clicks on one of the corresponding objects previously embedded or linked in a container document.

When referring to the registration database, an object type is called an object class.

As shown in Figure 2.1, when an object class is registered, such as during the installation of the object application that supports its class, the application should first determine if a previous version of the same class already exists in the registration database. If a previous version does exist, the user has the option of upgrading all of the older-version objects to the new version automatically the next time each is activated. (If a previous version is not detected, the new version is simply registered without prompting the user.)

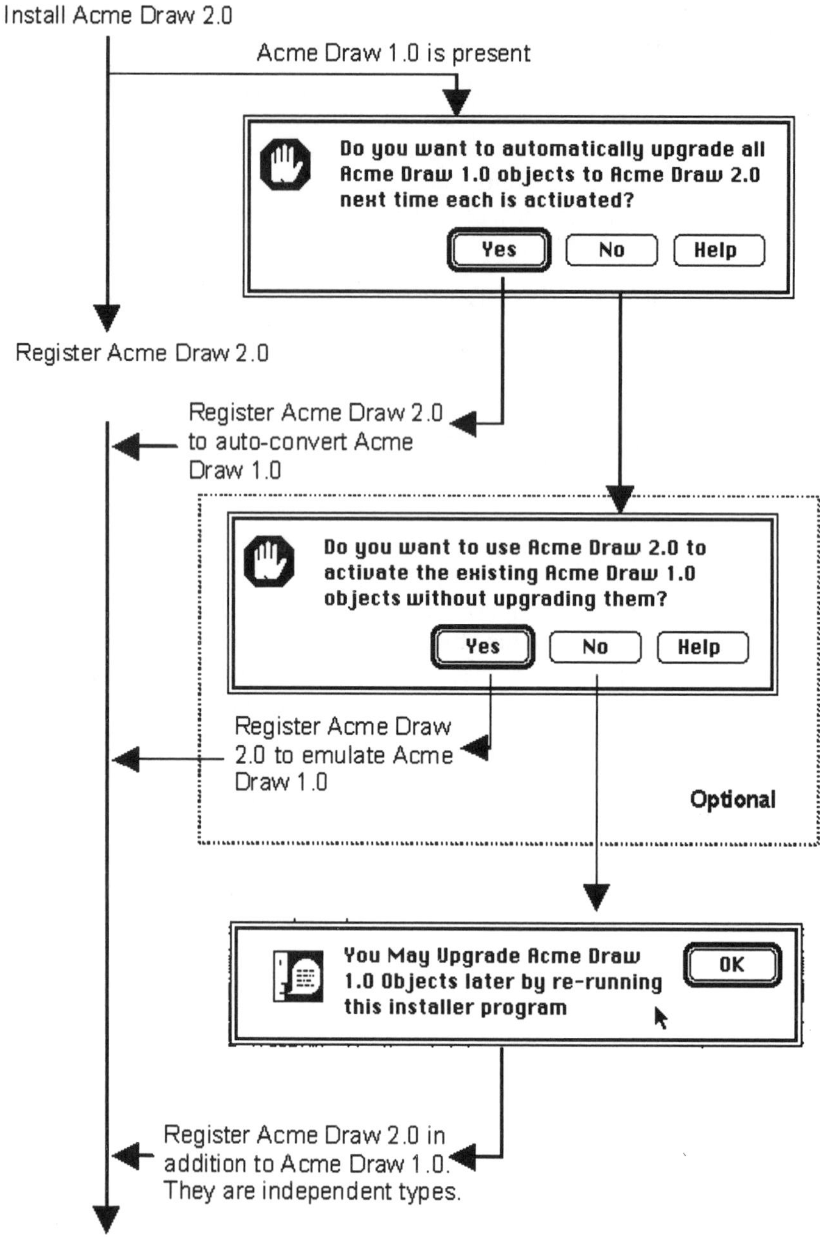

Figure 2.1 Installing a new version of an object application

When appropriate, a message dialog box should mention any important differences between object versions to help the user decide whether or not to upgrade. If the user elects to upgrade all of the older objects, the older version is replaced by the newer in the registration database. From that point, the older objects are activated with the new version of the application and are saved in its format.

Optionally, the new object application can offer to emulate the older version's objects without actually converting them to the new format. This allows a user to use the desirable features of the new object application while maintaining the object in its old format. However, if the user makes use of a particular feature of the new object application that cannot be accommodated by the old type's format, the user should be prompted with the option of abandoning such edits and staying within the old format or keeping the edits and accepting the necessary conversion to the new format. If the user specifies no upgrading or emulating, the new object application is registered in addition to the old one, and the two are considered completely independent types. The user may rerun the setup program for the object application any time later to respecify version-upgrading options.

As part of the class registration procedure, a setup program may register a list of data formats, such as PICT or TIFF, that the object application is capable of reading and activating, as well as a list of formats it is capable of writing. These formats are listed in the Registration Database file, described in Chapter 3, "Registering Object Applications."

Objects and Other Object Applications

To the user, an OLE object is a unit of information that resides in a document and whose behavior is constant no matter where it is located. The object's intrinsic behavior is defined by the object itself rather than by the document that holds it. The user may interact with an object as a whole (via OLE verbs and container commands), or edit/change its contents using the proper tools provided by its object application.

Objects can be nested arbitrarily within other objects; in addition, objects may be moved, copied, or linked from one location to another.

Although an object is normally activated by the object application corresponding to its class in the Registration Database file, this is not always the case. By comparing the lists of data formats registered in the database with other types of object applications, an application can determine which other object types a newly registered object application is capable of converting and emulating. For example, if a newly registered object application reads and write objects saved in the TIFF format and an existing object application also writes objects in the TIFF format, the new object application can convert objects saved by the existing object application. (The Convert dialog box shown in Figure 2.2 provides users with the means to convert and emulate object types.)

There are three specific situations in which an existing object is not activated by the object application corresponding to its class in the Registration Database file, each of which is discussed in the following sections.

Activating an Object Having an Upgraded Version

If the user activates an object whose object application version has been reassigned to a newer version, the object is activated and saved by the new object application.

Converting an Object from One Type to Another

Permanently converting an object from one type to another is frequently necessary. To do so, the user selects the object and, using the Edit/Object submenu, chooses the Convert . . . command. This opens the Convert dialog box, which allows the user to select the Convert to: option button. This button displays a list of other types (classes) to which the object may be converted. It is selected by default when Convert is chosen using the menus or if the selected object's type is registered in the database. This list of other object types is composed of all types that have registered themselves as capable of reading the selected object's format. (The list does not guarantee that a reverse conversion is possible).

As shown in Figure 2.2, the list of object types also contains the selected object's current type. This enables the user to change to Display As Icon without necessarily converting the selection's type. If a new type is chosen from list and the dialog box selection is committed, the selected object is immediately and silently converted to the new type. (If the object is open, the container closes it before performing conversion). If, however, the Convert dialog box results from an attempt by the user to edit an unregistered object, the new type application should immediately activate after the Convert dialog and the actual conversion should take place as part of loading the object.

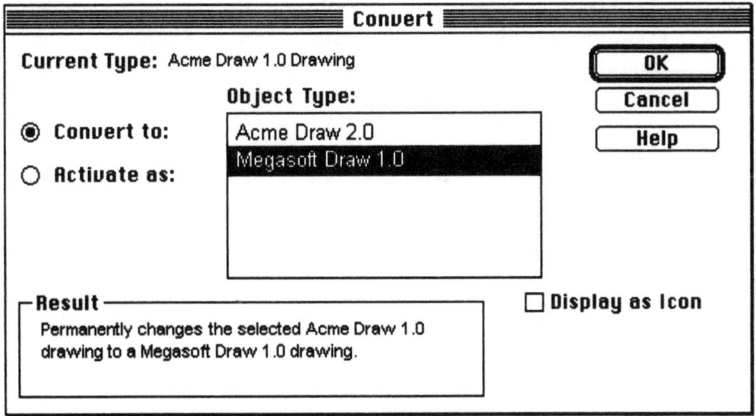

Figure 2.2 The Convert dialog box: converting an object

Emulating Different Object Types

Because users will be exchanging OLE documents between different machines, it will be common for them to receive an object for which they do not have the object application available to activate it. In addition, users may want to use other than default applications with their own objects to exploit unique editing features of a particular object application. The Convert dialog box shown in Figure 2.3 supports these situations.

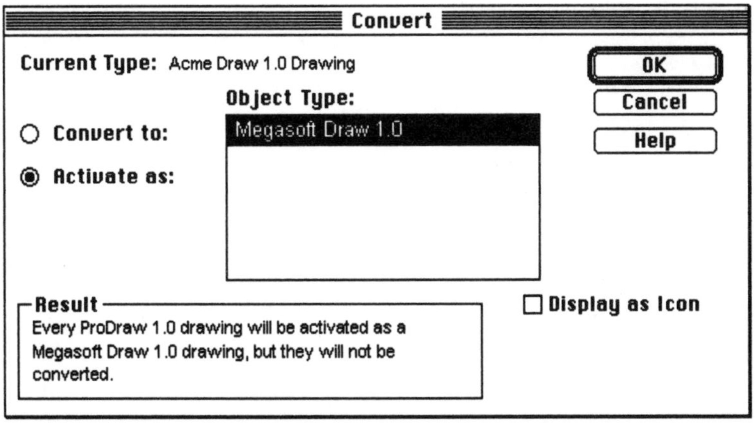

Figure 2.3 The Convert dialog box: activating an object

By choosing the Activate as: option button (chosen by default if the object's type is not registered) in the Convert dialog box, the subset of types capable of emulating (reading and writing) the selected object are displayed in the Object Type list box. The remaining types, which are only capable of conversion, do not appear.

When the user chooses an object type and responds Yes to the resulting message box, every object of the selected type is activated as an object of the emulating type. This provides an alternate type to be used thereafter. This means that these objects take on the alternate type's verbs in the Edit Object submenu and are activated by using the alternate object application. However, they still keep their original type name throughout the entire user interface because they continue to be stored in their original type's format.

Because the alternate application does not actually convert the objects, they can continue to be exchanged among users in their original type. (Behind the user interface, this dialog box registers the alternate application for the selected object's type in the database. As a result, the emulation applies only to a particular machine; each machine activates the type with the particular object application registered in its own database.)

An Error dialog box, which provides immediate access to the Convert dialog box, should appear when a user attempts to activate (double click) an unregistered object. Figure 2.4 shows the result of trying to activate an unregistered ProDraw 1.0 drawing, and the ensuing error and Convert dialog boxes. Note that in this example both Acme Draw 2.0 and Megasoft Draw 1.0 are possible conversions of the ProDraw 1.0 drawing, but only Megasoft Draw 1.0 is a legal emulating type.

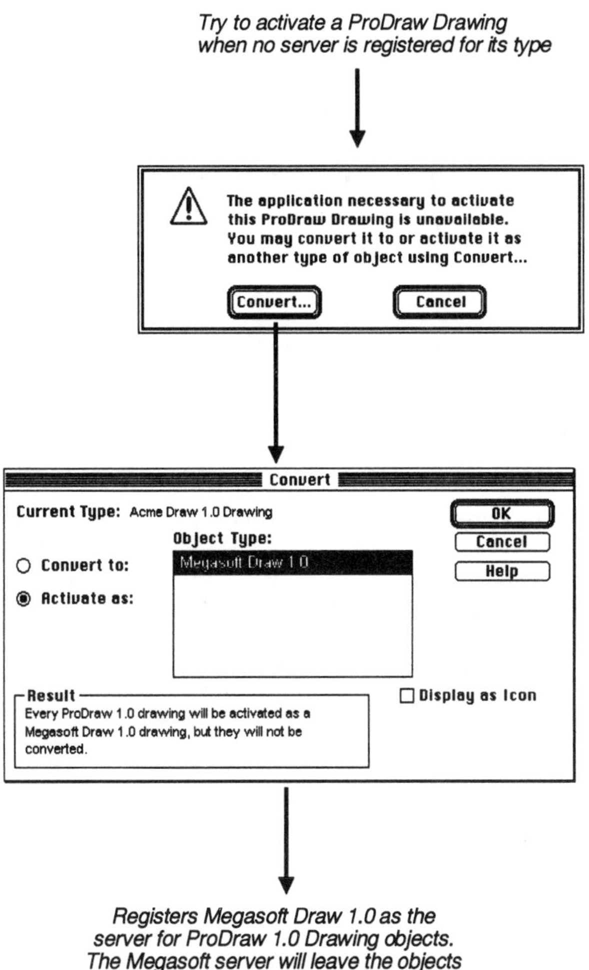

Figure 2.4 The Convert dialog box: emulating object types

Additionally, the user may voluntarily access the Convert dialog through the Edit / Object > Convert... command (the only command available for an unregistered object since its verbs are unknown). Because the Convert dialog box can be invoked at any time, the users may respecify an alternate type whenever necessary. Even if there are no conversions or alternate types available for the selected object's type, the Convert dialog box should still be available as a means of simply respecifying the icon of the object, as shown in Figure 2.5.

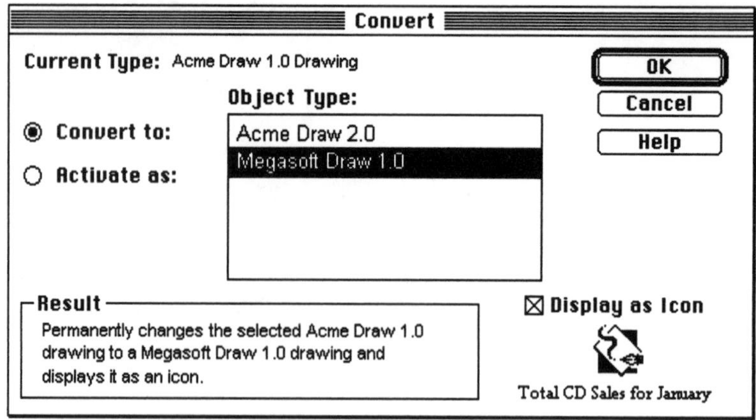

Figure 2.5 The Convert dialog box: displaying object as an icon

The following tables outline the result text that should be used for messages in the Convert dialog box.

When an embedded object is selected . . .

Task	Result Text
Convert to Original Type	The selected *<original type>* will not be converted.
Convert to Original Type + Display As Icon	The selected *<original type>* will not be converted. It will be displayed as an icon.
Convert to Different Type	Permanently changes the selected <original type> to a *<selected type>*.
Convert to Different Type + Display As Icon	Permanently changes the selected <original type> to a *<selected type>*. It will be displayed as an icon.

When a linked object is selected . . .

Task	Result Text
Convert to Original Type (only)	The selected *<original type>* will not be converted.
Convert to Original Type (only) + Display as Icon	The selected *<original type>* will not be converted. It will be displayed as an icon.

When either a linked or embedded object is selected—the Display As Icon check box is disabled . . .

Task	Result Text
Activate as Original Type	Every *<original type>* will be activated as a *<selected type>*.
Activate as Emulating Type	Every *<original type>* will be activated as a *<selected type>*, but it will not be converted.

Figure 2.6 shows how these cases are handled on a system that has three registered object applications, Acme Draw 1.0, Acme Draw 2.0, and Megasoft Draw 1.0. Notice how the "Result" help text elaborates on the outcome of the conversion and emulation options.

Beginning at the point "Select an Acme Draw 1.0 object," the user would normally follow the straight down path of activation and de-activation. However, if Acme Draw 1.0 was replaced by Acme Draw 2.0, or if the user wanted to convert or emulate Acme Draw 1.0, the appropriate alternate routes are taken.

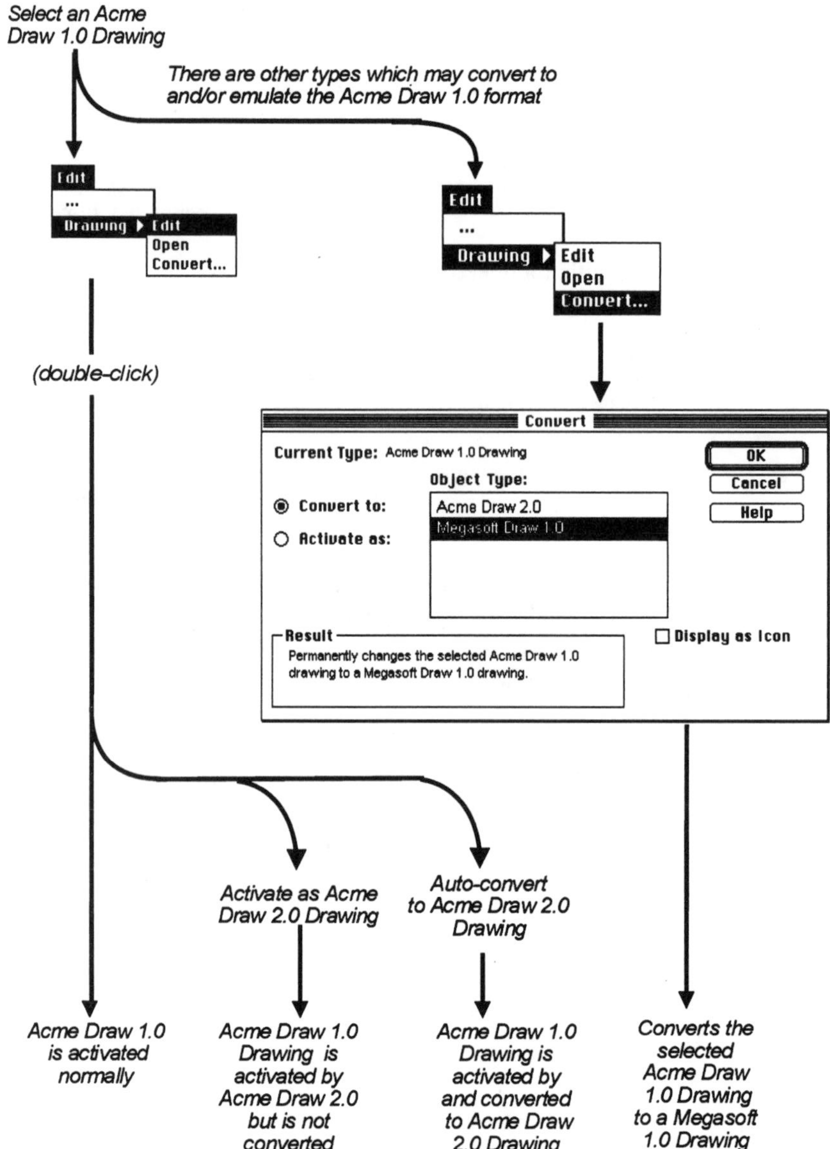

Figure 2.6 Upgrading and converting object types

A user who specified activation of all Acme Draw 1.0 objects as Acme Draw 2.0 objects could have specified this either 1) while running the program that installs Acme Draw 2.0 (if applicable) or 2) at any point afterwards using the Activate As option in the Convert dialog box. If the user uses any of features unique to Acme Draw 2.0 that cannot be accommodated in the Acme Draw 1.0 format, the warning message shown in Figure 2.7 should appear when the object is deactivated (when using an in-place object application) or closed (using an open object application).

Selecting Yes performs the conversion and saves the object with all of its changes intact. Selecting No discards certain changes to preserve the object in Acme Draw 1.0 format. This dialog box should not only be issued with different versions of the same type, but also with competitor type emulations that may incur a loss of data or compromise the integrity of the object's image if saved in the emulating type's format.

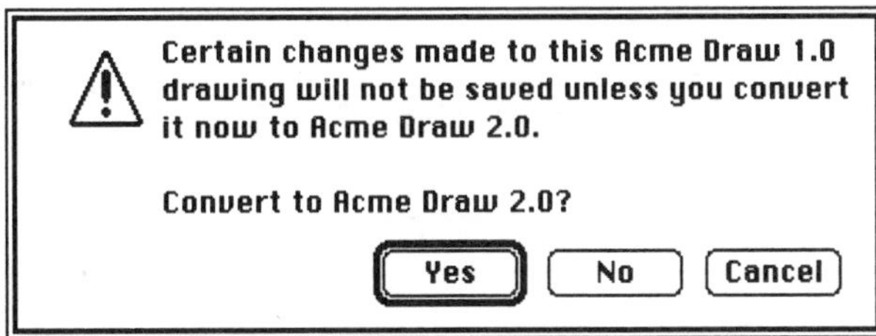

Figure 2.7 Possible warning message for emulation data loss

Creating Objects

Users can create objects either from existing objects or from "scratch." When creating objects from existing objects, users can modify a copy of an existing object of the same type (class) or convert an object from one type to another using the Convert dialog box (such as when converting spreadsheet cells to a word processor table).

The Insert Object dialog box allows the user to create new objects by:

- Embedding an object of a selected class (type), as shown in Figure 2.8.
- Inserting a file as an embedded object, as shown in Figure 2.9.
- Inserting a file as a linked object, as shown in Figure 2.10.

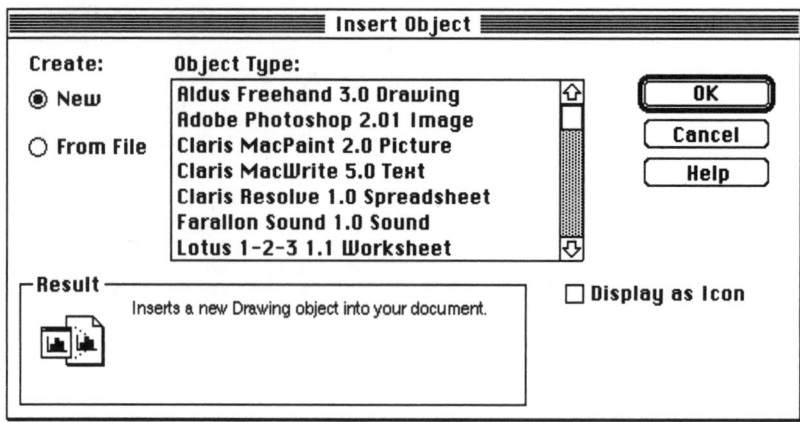

Figure 2.8 The Insert Object dialog box: embedding an object of a selected class

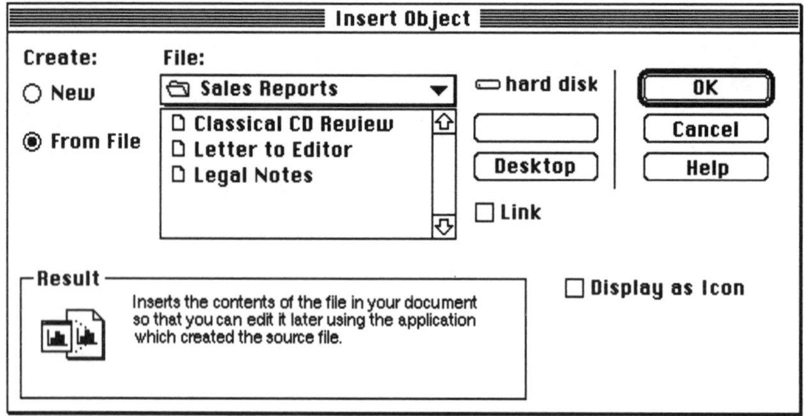

Figure 2.9 The Insert Object dialog box: inserting a file as an embedded object

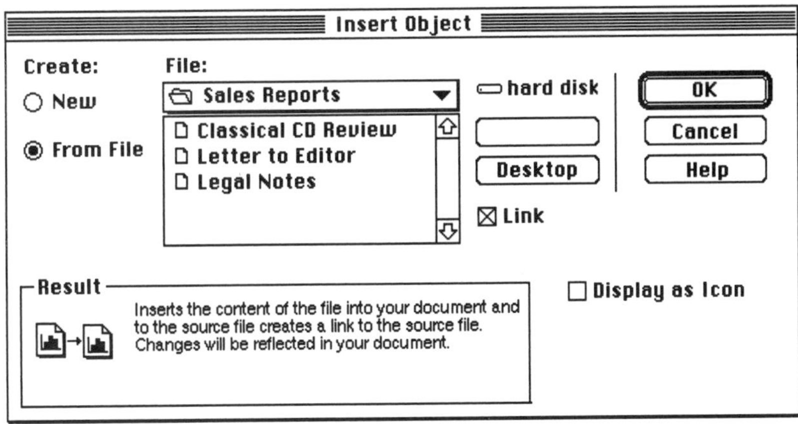

Figure 2.10 The Insert Object dialog box: inserting a file as a linked object

The Insert Object... command provides access to the Insert Object dialog box and should be placed within the menu responsible for instantiating or importing new objects into the document. If no such menu exists, use the Edit menu.

The user can embed a new object by choosing a type from the list box and selecting OK. Certain types of new objects may make use of the current selection in the container document and build themselves accordingly. For example, an object created by an object application whose function is to create charts may assume an appearance that reflects the values of data contained in a selected word processor table.

To ensure predictable behavior, the following guidelines should be followed when implementing the Insert Object dialog:

- If a newly inserted object is not based on the current selection, the selection should be replaced by the new object, effectively pasting over it.
- If the new object will remain linked to the selection, the new object should be inserted in addition to the selection and become the new selection.
- If the object is based on, but will not remain linked to, the selection, it is up to the new object's application whether or not to remove the given selection. Whether to replace or add depends on the specific use of an object type.

The user can either link an existing file as an object by checking the Link check box. Leaving it unchecked embeds the file as an object. When the user selects the Create from File option button, the Object Type list box is replaced with a File text box and a Browse command button because the Object Type list box is unrelated to the file options. The embedded or linked file specifies the class of the inserted or linked object. The Result box contains text that describes the final outcome of the insert operation to the user.

Insert Object Operation	Result Text
Create New	Inserts a new *<object type name>* into the document.
Create New as Icon	Inserts a new *<object type name>* into the document. It will be displayed as an icon.
Create From File	Inserts the contents of the file as an object into the document so that the user may activate it using the application which created it.
Create From File as Icon	Inserts the contents of the file as an object into the document so that the user may activate it using the application which created it. It will be displayed as an icon.
Create From File + Link	Inserts an iconof the file contents into the document. The icon will be linked to the file so that changes to the file will be reflected in the document.
Create From File as Icon + Link	The icon will be linked to the file so that changes to the file will be reflected in the document.

Whether the inserted object is new or previously exists, the user may specify to insert it as an icon in appearance by selecting the Display As Icon check box as shown in Figure 2.11. If the user has chosen a non-OLE file for insertion, it may only be inserted as an icon, effectively packaging the file.

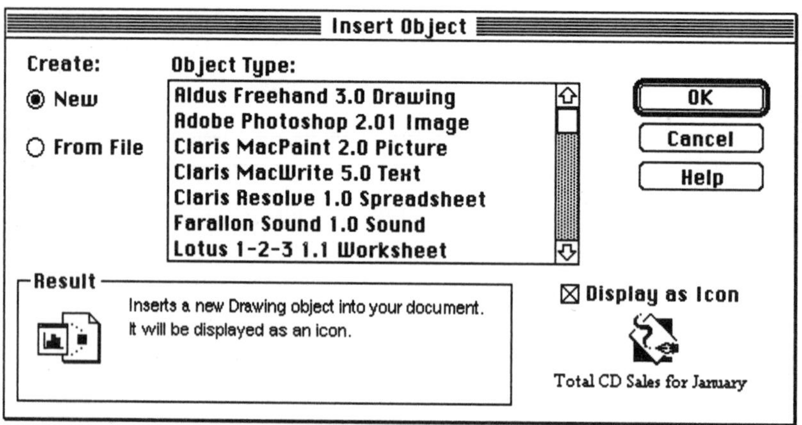

Figure 2.11 The Insert Object dialog box: displaying an object as an icon

Because a newly created object does not exist in another file, it may only be inserted as an embedded object. Only objects created from existing files may be inserted as linked objects. When the user selects the Link File option button, the icon appears beneath the Display as Icon check box. The Display as Icon check box in the Convert dialog box allows the user to respecify at any time whether to have the object appear as an icon.

Note The Convert dialog box may be used to change the icon of an object at any time. When the Convert dialog box is invoked for an object which already has an icon assigned, that icon is assumed to be a user-chosen icon. Consequently, the dialog box will not automatically change it to the default icon of the new type after the conversion. To adopt the default icon of the new conversion type, the user chooses the Default icon option button in the Change Icon dialog box. By doing so, the Convert dialog box will dynamically display the appropriate icon of the selected type in the Convert type list.

If an item is embedded as an icon (by means of Paste Special, Insert Object, or drag/drop from the File Manager), its default label should be one of the following:

- For an OLE object the label should be the short form of its object type name (such as Picture, Worksheet, ...).
- For an OLE object that has not registered a shortform, it should use its full object type name (such as Microsoft Excel Worksheet).
- For an item that is not associated with an OLE class the label is simply "Document."

If a file is linked into a container as an icon (via Insert Object Create from File + Link) its default label is the source file's filename in lower case. If a portion of a document is linked via the Paste Special dialog box as an icon, its default label should be formed from the display name of the link source.

In general, the display name of a link source can have a completely arbitrary syntax; consequently, the following algorithm for determining the default label is inherently heuristic. The default label should be formed as follows.

- From the end of the display name of the link source, scan for the last and second to last occurrence of the following characters:

  \ / ! :

  The label should be formed from the display name starting at the next-to-last scanned-for character through the end of the string.

- If this scan does not consume the whole display name, then the first line of the label should begin with ellipses (. . .). Following this, the portion of the display name between the next-to-last and the last scanned-for characters (inclusive) should be displayed.
- The second line of the label should contain the portion of the display name that follows the last scanned-for character.

If the entire label fits on one line, then there is no need to break it into pieces. Applications can display the full display name of the link source, although the above algorithm may produce results more pleasing to the user.

The label of an icon persists with the object as it is transferred between containers and can only be changed by the user via the Change Icon dialog box.

After an in-place object has been inserted, its application becomes active. If the inserted object appears in an open object application, then an open-style hatch rectangle appears in the container until an image from the object application is available for an update (similar to the open selected object shown later in Figure 2.21).

Note Applications can also display buttons in their control bar that insert objects directly. These buttons function in the same manner as the Insert Object dialog box.

Embedded versus Linked Objects

An embedded object contains data that retains the original editing and operating capability of the object application while it resides in a container document of another application. An embedded object is wholly and exclusively contained within the container document and is saved and moved with that document.

A linked object is an updating image of another piece of data that resides at another point in the same document or within a different document altogether. A linked object does not contain data that can be edited, but rather an image of the data referred to as presentation data, which is often a PICT file. This image of the source data provides the user with a visual representation of the linked object and gives the user access to the object's verbs.

Note Based on appearances, the user may interact with a linked object as if the source data of the object were contained in the document. In many instances, users pay little attention to the type of object (embedded or linked) they are working with.

Automatic and Manual Updating

When a link is created, it is an automatic link by default. Whenever the appearance of its source data changes, the linked object's appearance automatically changes without any request from the user. The user can specify a link to be manual by means of the Links... dialog box. A manual link means that the linked object can only be updated when requested by the user. The update request is issued by choosing the Update Now button within the Links... dialog box and optionally in conjunction with the container's usual "update fields" or "recalc" action.

Verbs and Links

An object responds to the same set of verbs defined for its class regardless of whether it is embedded or linked. Issuing verbs like "play" or "rewind" to a linked sound object will appear to activate the object in-place. However, issuing a verb that is intended to alter the object's content data (such as "open" or "edit"), exposes the linked source data by launching the associated object application.

While links can play in-place, they cannot edit in-place. Editing in-place implies that the actual data resides, even if only temporarily, in the document that contains the link. It is important to remember that the link source holds the object's data and that the data does not move to the container of the link for editing. In order for link sources to respond to editing verbs, the source object (and any containing objects and documents) must be opened to properly respond to the verb.

The most common case of a link responding to an edit verb is when the user double-clicks a link whose primary verb is edit. The source document will open to reveal the link source object for editing. This functionality may appear similar to opening an embedded object into a separate window, but this is not the case. Editing a linked object is functionally identical to launching an application on the link source's document, such as through the Finder. Unlike an opened embedded object application, which is bound to the container application window and causes the hatch pattern across the object, there is no special association between the link source and link destination application windows. The applications operate and close independently.

Note The link source can be on an unmounted network object application; this might require the user to first establish access to the source before OLE can open it. If the user tries to open an available source document, the container should post a message such as "Please connect to *foo:bar* and retry opening the *<object_type>* link."

When implementing the execution of an editing verb, it is the object application's responsibility to notify the object's immediate container that the source needs to be exposed. There are three different situations in which an object might notify its container:

- **Embedded.** If the verb is executed by an embedded object, the container document and parent objects are already exposed (there is no need to start the object's container).
- **Already Opened Link Source Document.** If the verb is issued to a link source whose document is already opened, then the currently active view of that document (in the case of a multi-view or multi-pane application) will scroll as necessary and unveil the source object ready for interaction.
- **Closed Linked Source Document.** The verb notifies its immediate container requesting it to expose the source to the user. All additional containers are opened resulting in the link source being fully exposed and ready for editing.

Types and Links

A link's type is a cached copy of its source's type taken when the last update was issued. Since it is possible to change the type of a link source object, all links derived from a converted object will bear the old type and verbs until either an update occurs or the link object application is launched. Because out-of-date links might display obsolete verbs to the user, the container should, upon issuing a verb from a link to its source, compare the cached link type with that of its sources. If the cached link type has changed, the container should do one of the following:

- If the verb issued from the old link is syntactically identical to one of verbs registered for the source's new type, execute the verb index of that new verb.
- If the issued verb is no longer supported by the link source's new type, issue an error message similar to that shown in Figure 2.12.

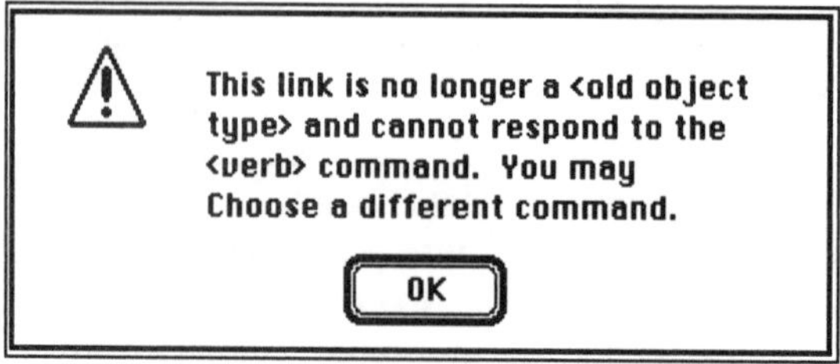

Figure 2.12 Error message for obsolete link verbOBSLTMSG.BMP

The link should adopt the source's new type and bear the new verbs in its menu.

Maintaining Links

A link has three properties: its type (or class as its known internally), the name of its source data, and its updating basis, either automatic (default) or manual, as shown in Figure 2.13. The container application supplies a Links... dialog box that allows the user to change the name of its source data and its updating basis. A link's type is determined by its source's type, and can be changed by converting it to another type.

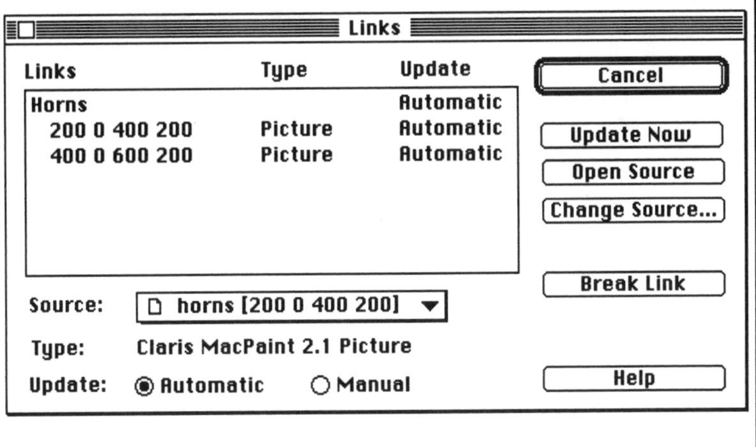

Figure 2.13 The Links dialog box

If a link's source can't be found, "Unavailable" should appear in the application'sstatus column. Multiple link sources from the same file are grouped and indented beneath the common filename. Only the filename appears in the list box; the full pathname is exposed in the lower portion of the dialog box.

By choosing the filename line (such as Horns in Figure 2.13), the user can edit the attributes of its listed source items as a group. Editing attributes as a group expedites the common actions of renaming a source file that contains many links and of switching between manual and automatic updating for the entire file. The indented list is only two levels: the filename and the source items. Sub-file nestings of link sources do not continue the indention scheme to deeper levels.

Applications should allow 15 characters for the Type field and enough space for "Automatic," "Manual," and "Unavailable" to appear completely. As each link in the list is selected, its type, name, and updating status appear in their entirety at the bottom of the dialog box.

Break Link effectively disconnects the selected link(s). Update Now forces the selected link(s) to connect to their sources and retrieve the latest information.

Open Source opens the source document(s) for the selected link(s). The Open Source button should be default when clicking within the links list, therefore double-clicking a list item opens the source of the particular link.

Choosing the Change Source button in the Links dialog box invokes the Change Source dialog box shown in Figure 2.14, which is similar to the standard File Open dialog box. The Change Source dialog box allows the user to respecify the link source.

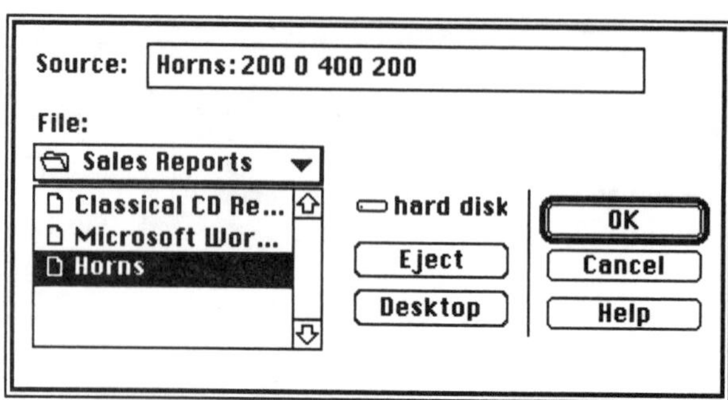

Figure 2.14 The Change source dialog box

The Change Source dialog box edits only the file portion of the link source; it is up to the user to manually enter the sub-document portion of the string if the source points to within the file. Although some containers may allow users to connect only to presently valid links, the user may want to key in a source name that does not designate an object that already exists. This would allow the user to create a new object to link to. Upon selecting OK, the Change Source dialog box will prompt "Invalid Source. Do you want to correct it? Yes, No." Answering Yes will return to the Change Source dialog box so the string may be corrected; answering No will cause the container to hold onto the unparsed display name of the link source until the user successfully causes the link to connect to a newly created object that satisfies the dangling reference.

If multiple links share any portion of their source's names and the user edits that common portion for one link, the user is given the option of making the same change for all other similar links. The dialog box shown in Figure 2.15 is the means by which users redirect links to new locations, such as when folder or file names have been changed.

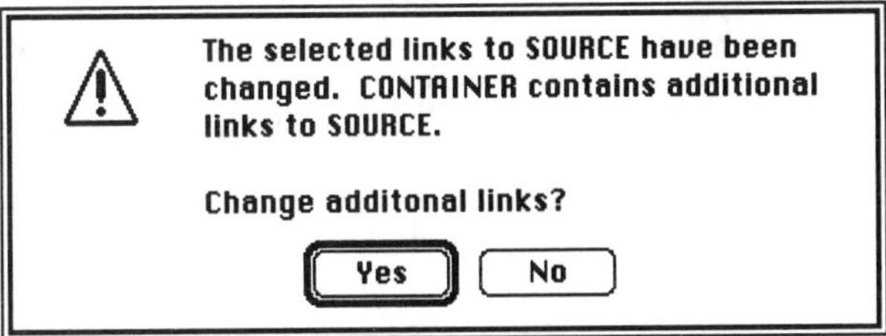

Figure 2.15 Changing additional links with same source message

States and the Visual Appearance of Objects

Visual editing enhances the conceptual structure of a compound document by exposing the entire hierarchy of containment in a single window.

Note OLE 1 handled two kinds of objects, the container (or client) and the embedded objects it contained. That the contained objects themselves might also contain embedded objects was of no consequence; because they were not accessible to the container, it was not necessary to consider embedded objects as containers.

In OLE 2, however, the open object becomes the root of a hierarchy of embedded objects, each of which may be a container of another object (or objects) and each of which may be edited. For example, a word processor document can contain a range of cells from a spreadsheet program, which in turn contains a chart representing the values contained in those cells. The chart is accessible from within the word processor document even though the chart's container is the range of spreadsheet cells. Figure 2.16 illustrates this concept.

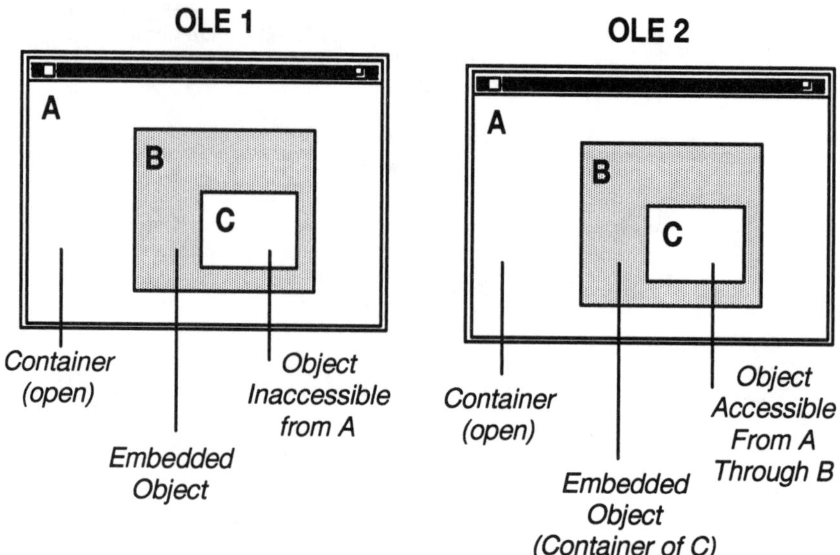

Figure 2.16 Hierarchy of OLE 1 and OLE 2 objects

As the user navigates through the object hierarchy within a document, OLE objects assume different states and appearances, as described in the following sections.

The Inactive State

An object is said to be inactive when it is neither active nor part of a selection. It is displayed in its presentation form, which is (usually) conveyed through its cached PICT description. A user may want to know whether an object is embedded or linked without having to interact with it. Therefore, container applications should provide a Show Objects command that places a single pixel wide black solid border around the extent of an embedded object and a dotted border around linked objects, as shown in Figure 2.17.

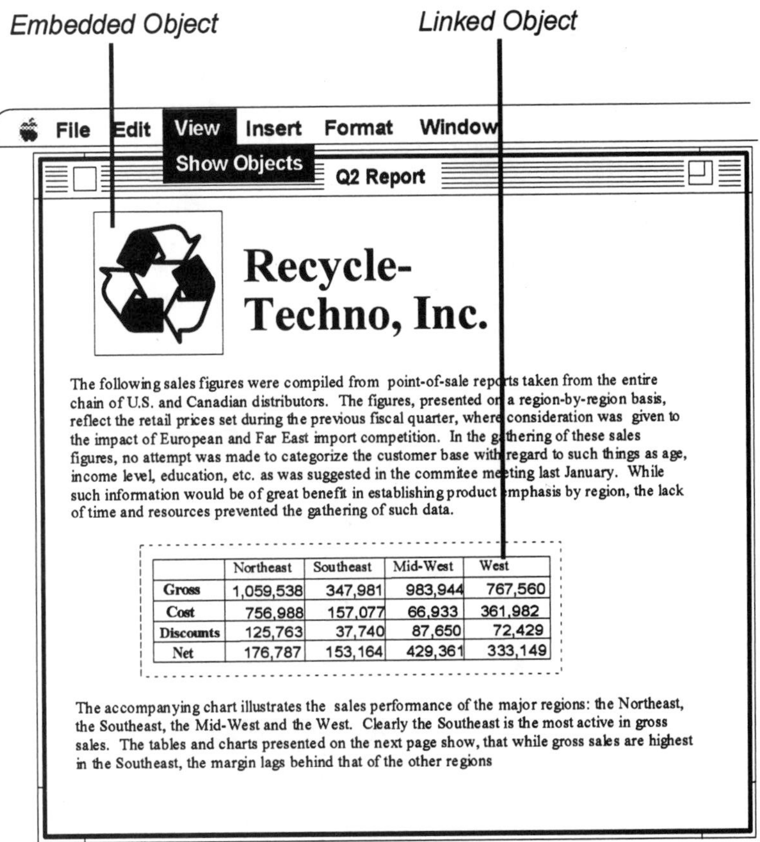
Embedded Object
Linked Object
File
Edit
View
Insert
Format
Window
Show Objects
Q2 Report
Recycle-
Techno, Inc.
The following sales figures were compiled from point-of-sale reports taken from the entire chain of U.S. and Canadian distributors. The figures, presented on a region-by-region basis, reflect the retail prices set during the previous fiscal quarter, where consideration was given to the impact of European and Far East import competition. In the gathering of these sales figures, no attempt was made to categorize the customer base with regard to such things as age, income level, education, etc. as was suggested in the commitee meeting last January. While such information would be of great benefit in establishing product emphasis by region, the lack of time and resources prevented the gathering of such data.

	Northeast	Southeast	Mid-West	West
Gross	1,059,538	347,981	983,944	767,560
Cost	756,988	157,077	66,933	361,982
Discounts	125,763	37,740	87,650	72,429
Net	176,787	153,164	429,361	333,149

The accompanying chart illustrates the sales performance of the major regions: the Northeast, the Southeast, the Mid-West and the West. Clearly the Southeast is the most active in gross sales. The tables and charts presented on the next page show, that while gross sales are highest in the Southeast, the margin lags behind that of the other regions

Figure 2.17 The Show Objects command allows user to know object's linked or embedded status

If the container cannot guarantee that a linked object is up to date with its source (because an automatic update was unsuccessful or the link is manual), the dotted border should appear in the disabled-text color, suggesting the link is out of date. Only the container document's first level objects should be bordered. For example, if the Show Objects command was chosen from an outer-level container, then only those objects that are directly embedded would be bordered; nested objects would not be bordered. These borders should be distinct from the visual appearance given to the other object states.

An inactive object may be selected by single clicking anywhere within its extent, or it may be double-clicked, which will perform its primary verb.

The Selected State

An object is selected when the user clicks it or when it is included in a selection of multiple objects. An object is selected (and deselected) and rendered according to the normal highlight rules of its container. When an object is selected, object-specific tasks can be done using the verbs associated with the object. The container application retrieves the verbs from the system registry. When the object is selected, as shown in Figure 2.18, the container can supply handles (for resizing) that affect the object as a unit with respect to the container. It is recommended that resizing an OLE object, while it is selected, should result also in a scaling operation.

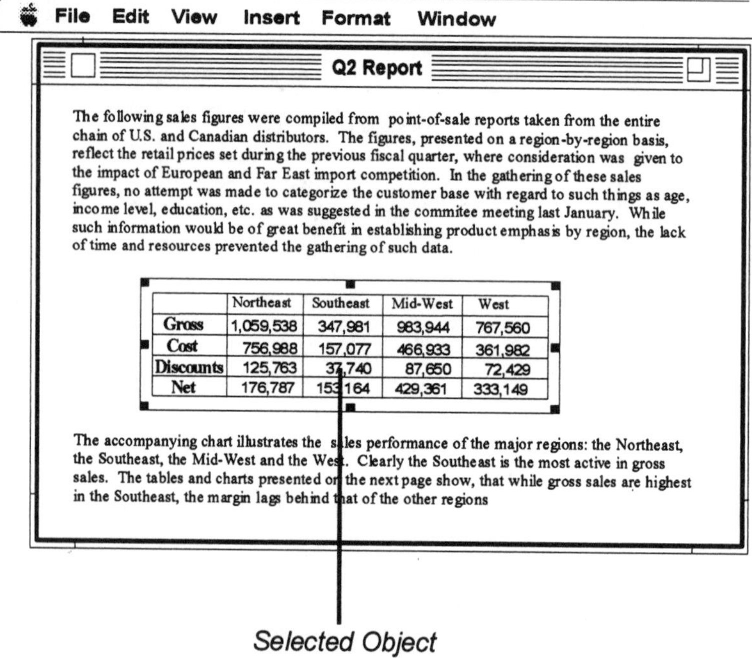
File Edit View Insert Format Window
Q2 Report
The following sales figures were compiled from point-of-sale reports taken from the entire chain of U.S. and Canadian distributors. The figures, presented on a region-by-region basis, reflect the retail prices set during the previous fiscal quarter, where consideration was given to the impact of European and Far East import competition. In the gathering of these sales figures, no attempt was made to categorize the customer base with regard to such things as age, income level, education, etc. as was suggested in the commitee meeting last January. While such information would be of great benefit in establishing product emphasis by region, the lack of time and resources prevented the gathering of such data.

	Northeast	Southeast	Mid-West	West
Gross	1,059,538	347,981	983,944	767,560
Cost	756,988	157,077	466,933	361,982
Discounts	125,763	37,740	87,650	72,429
Net	176,787	153,164	429,361	333,149

The accompanying chart illustrates the sales performance of the major regions: the Northeast, the Southeast, the Mid-West and the West. Clearly the Southeast is the most active in gross sales. The tables and charts presented on the next page show, that while gross sales are highest in the Southeast, the margin lags behind that of the other regions
Selected Object

Figure 2.18 A selected OLE object

When an object is selected, but not as part of a multiple selection, any of its registered verbs can be applied. For example, the verbs Edit and Open will activate and open the object respectively, but verbs such as Play might operate and leave the object in the selected state. Any number of single clicks will simply reselect the object, while clicking outside the object will deselect it.

Verbs that are meaningful only for certain states of the object should be enabled and disabled appropriately. For example, a media object that has Play and Rewind as verbs should disable Rewind when the object is already at the beginning. Similarly, if an object has two verbs Edit (for in-place editing) and Open (for opened editing), Edit should be disabled when the object is open because the object cannot directly achieve the in-place active state without first closing.

The Active State

When an OLE object is active, the user interacts with the object's contents in-place, using the container document's window to display the object application's menus and interface controls. The user can make an object active either by selecting its appropriate verb (Edit), double clicking the object (the primary verb will be Edit for many objects), or selecting the object and pressing RETURN. If the RETURN key is already used by the container application, then OPTION+RETURN should be used.

When an object becomes active, its object application's menus and interface controls are grafted onto the document window and applied over the extent of the active object. Frame adornments appear outside the extent of the object, and can temporarily cover neighboring material in the document.

The active object and its frame adornments are surrounded by a black diagonal hatch border as an indication of the active state and to suggest the area of focus. The hatch pattern border consists of four right-ascending diagonal lines with three transparent pixels between the lines. Since the border is translucent, underlying material will show between the diagonal lines. The hatch border is considered to be part of the object's layout; consequently, it is the object's pointer that appears when over the border.

In the active state, the object takes on the appearance that is best suited for its own editing. Frame adornments such as table gridlines, handles, scroll bars, as well as other editing aids may be shown with the object. Figure 2.19 shows row/column headers as adornments to the active worksheet object. Scroll bars could be included if the object was large and scrolling was needed to show the entire object in its viewport.

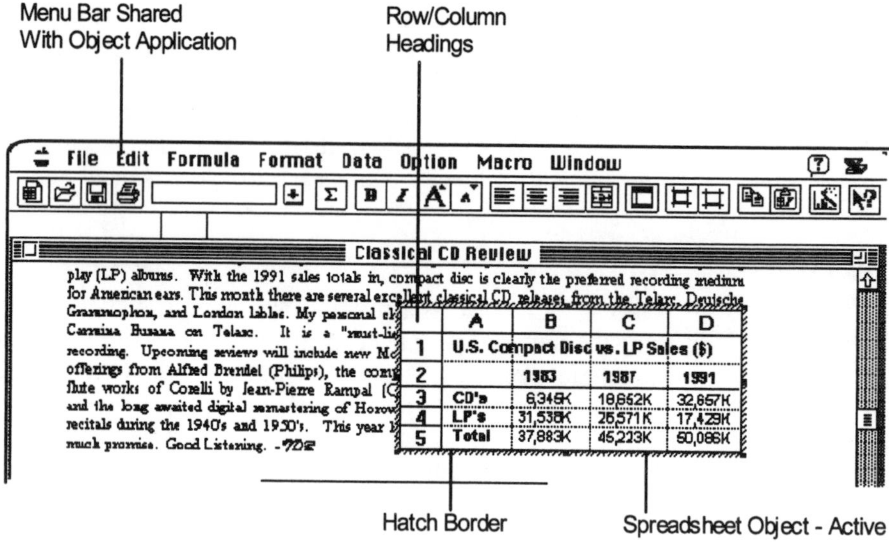

Figure 2.19 An in-place active object

Clicking the hatch pattern (not the resize handles) should be interpreted by the object as clicking just inside the edge of the object border. The hatch area is effectively a click slop zone that prevents inadvertent deactivations and makes it easier to select the contents of the object which lies right along its edge.

Those objects that support resizing while in-place active should include square resize handles within the active hatch pattern as shown in Figure 2.20. The solid black handles should be of the same width as the hatch pattern. To provide optimum clarity to the user, resize handle can have a single white pixel separation from the diagonal lines of the hatch pattern.

It is recommended that in-place resizing expose more or less of the object's content (for example, adding or removing rows/columns in the case of a spreadsheet). In-place resizing should be seen as adjusting the view rather than scaling the object's appearance. Certain objects may default to in-place scaling if cropping is not meaningful.

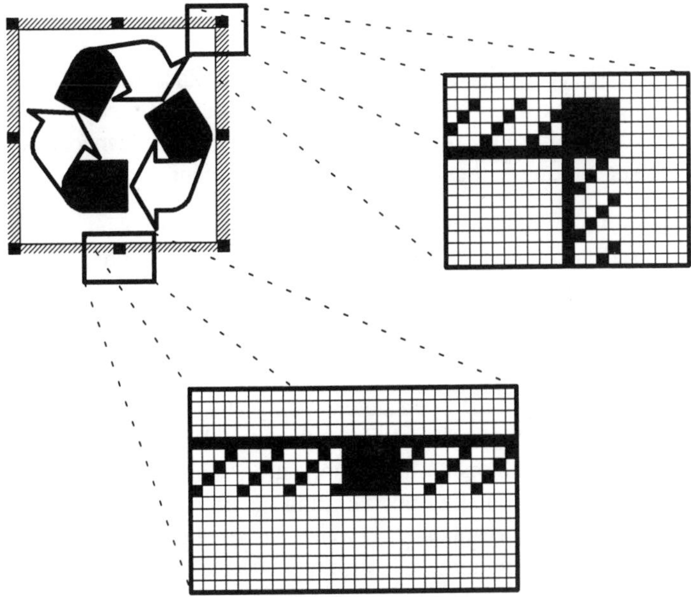

Figure 2.20 Hatch border and resize handles for an object active in place

If the object cannot match the container's zoom ratio while activating, the object should open into a separate window. If the object does not support being open in a separate window, then it should display an appropriate error message and not respond to the verb.

Only one object may be activated at any given time. Also, all objects that use the same object application cannot be activated as a set. For example, if all PowerPoint objects in a document were activated, commands such as Clear All or Delete would be ambiguous since the user may not know which objects would be affected by such document-scoped commands.

Edits made to an active object immediately and automatically become a part of the container document. Consequently, there is no "Update changes?" prompt when an in-place active object deactivates. Of course, changes to the entire document, embedded or otherwise, can be abandoned by declining to save the file to disk.

A single click in the container area, or a double click on a new OLE object (which may be nested in the currently active object) deactivates the current object and gives the focus to the new object. An active object can be deactivated by clicking outside its extent in the container document or by pressing the ESC key . If an in-place object already uses the ESC key for getting out of its own internal modes, ESC should return focus to the container, making the object the selection, when the object "escapes" from all its internal modes. If an object uses the ESC key at all times, it is recommended that SHIFT+ESC be used to deactivate the object.

The Open State

Open object applications unify open and in-place activation. In both cases, the user is interacting with objects at the document level directly without updating latencies. The only difference is where the interaction is performed, in place or in an alternate viewer looking at the same site in the document.

Any number of objects may be in the opened state. The object is deactivated (closed) by closing its object application window, which updates the embedded object in the container document. Since object application windows can be modal, the user is free to switch between object application and document windows and edit independently.

The semantics of the open state are similar to that of the open state introduced in OLE 1, with one important distinction. In OLE 1, the open object was seen by the user in a separate open object application. Changes made to the object were then updated in the container upon exiting the object application. In OLE 2, the open object application appears to the user as an alternate viewer on the same object, under the hatch pattern, still within the container document.

Figure 2.21 shows how a selected open object appears to the user. In this example, the container application is a word processor while the object application for the object is a drawing program.

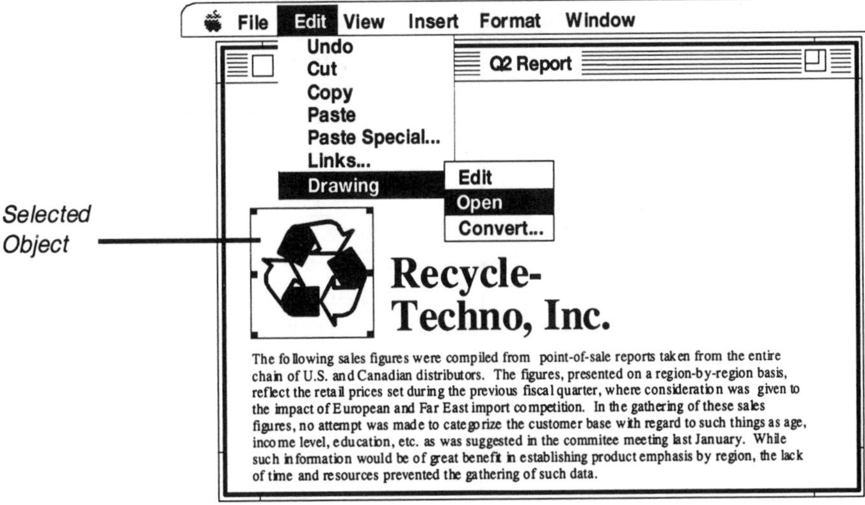
File Edit View Insert Format Window
Undo
Cut
Copy
Paste
Paste Special...
Links...
Drawing
Edit
Open
Convert...
Q2 Report
Selected Object
Recycle-
Techno, Inc.
The following sales figures were compiled from point-of-sale reports taken from the entire chain of U.S. and Canadian distributors. The figures, presented on a region-by-region basis, reflect the retail prices set during the previous fiscal quarter, where consideration was given to the impact of European and Far East import competition. In the gathering of these sales figures, no attempt was made to categorize the customer base with regard to such things as age, income level, education, etc. as was suggested in the commitee meeting last January. While such information would be of great benefit in establishing product emphasis by region, the lack of time and resources prevented the gathering of such data.

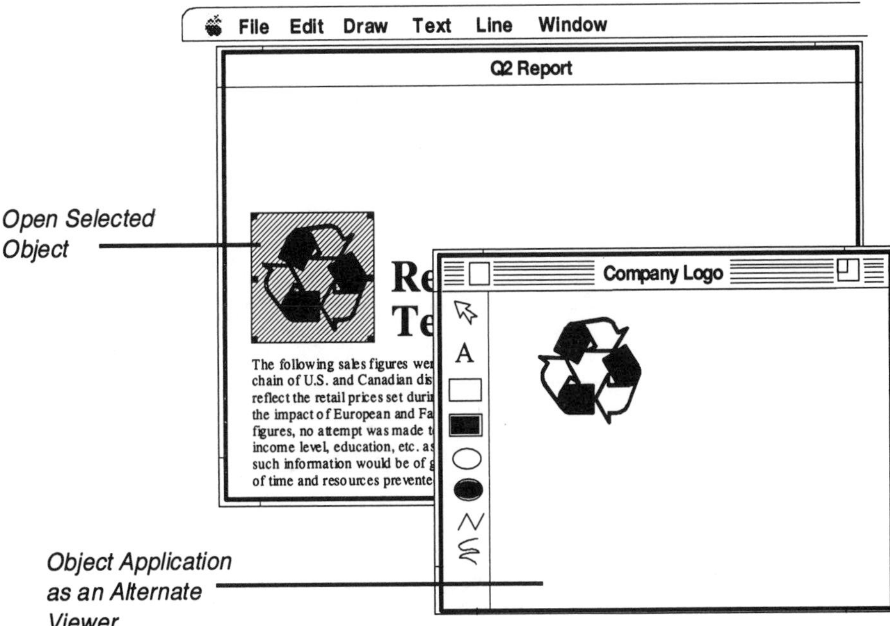
File Edit Draw Text Line Window
Q2 Report
Open Selected Object
Company Logo
A
Object Application as an Alternate Viewer

Figure 2.21 An open selected object

If the user clicks elsewhere in the container document, the object becomes unselected but remains in the open state as indicated in Figure 2.22.

When an object is opened, it becomes the selected object of the container document. Also, when the container document is printed, the presentation form of objects should be used. Neither the open nor active hatch patterns should appear in the printed document because these are meta-appearances (like selection indication) and not part of the content.

To the user, there is no sense of a local version kept within the object application; the opened object in the document and the object within the object application are the same. As a result, changes to the open object made within the object application window are immediately and automatically reflected in the object (beneath the hatch pattern) in the container. There is no longer the need for the Update command or the update confirmation upon quitting the object application.

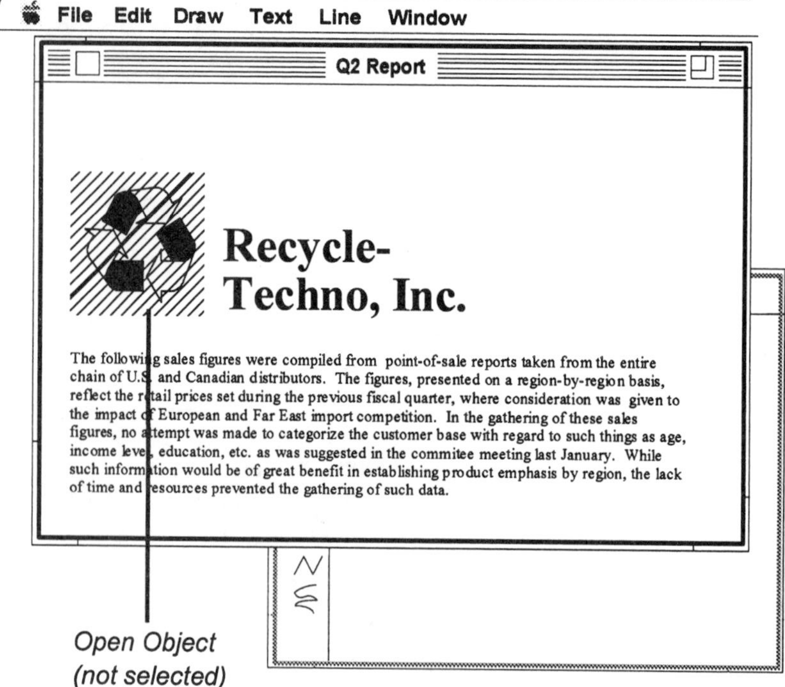
File Edit Draw Text Line Window
Q2 Report
Recycle-
Techno, Inc.
The followi g sales figures were compiled from point-of-sale reports taken from the entire
chain of U.S and Canadian distributors. The figures, presented on a region-by-region basis,
reflect the r tail prices set during the previous fiscal quarter, where consideration was given to
the impact f European and Far East import competition. In the gathering of these sales
figures, no ttempt was made to categorize the customer base with regard to such things as age,
income leve education, etc. as was suggested in the commitee meeting last January. While
such inform tion would be of great benefit in establishing product emphasis by region, the lack
of time and esources prevented the gathering of such data.
Open Object
(not selected)

Figure 2.22 An open object, not selected

Nevertheless, open object applications can still include an Update "<*source file*>" command so that user can make an update at any time. This is useful when the application's "real-time" image updates are not very frequent, often because they are computationally expensive. In any event, an update is always automatically performed at the time that the open window is closed.

The "Import File..." commands are still appropriate because they conceptually import a file into the document directly.

An OLE object that is capable of in-place activation should include the Open verb. The Open verb gives the user the opportunity of seeing more of the object or seeing the object in a different view state. Ideally, an in-place object should support in-place activation at arbitrary view scales because its container may be scaled unpredictably. If an object cannot accommodate in-place activation in the container's current view scale, or if the container does not support in-place editing, the object should be opened in a separate window.

Outside-in Activation

Objects are activated in OLE 2 using the outside-in rule of activation; that is, any number of single-clicks within or on the border of an object selects the object but does not activate or open it. An explicit activation (or open) verb, or double-clicking is necessary to tunnel into the object and interact with its contents.

From the user's perspective, outside-in objects must be selected and require explicit action to activate them. Container applications should display the "northwest" arrow pointer above an outside-in object when it is not activated, as an indication that it behaves as a single opaque item.

The following result from the outside-in rule:

- Requiring the user to perform a deliberate action to activate the object, insures that the activated objects are manageable.
- Because the user need only click somewhere within the object's extent, outside-in objects can be easily selected.

Figure 2.23 shows the state transition diagram for outside-in object applications. Not pictured in the diagram is the effect of double-clicking an opened object; this action brings the object application window to the front and activates it (similar to surfacing a window by double-clicking its open icon).

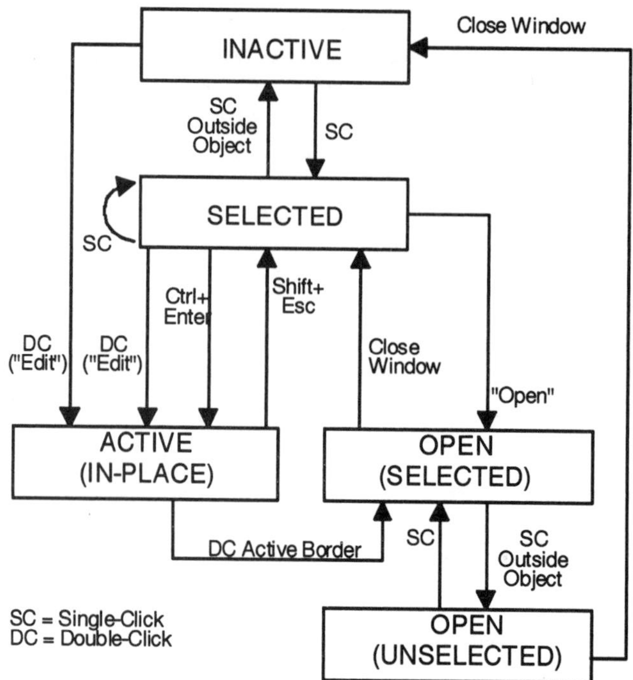

Figure 2.23 Object state transition diagram for outside-in object applications

Inside-out Activation

The contents of some objects should be accessible immediately, such as form controls, list panes, buttons, and so on. Such control-like objects should follow the inside-out rule of activation. With inside-out activation, the object's contents are effectively active at all times. The object may be selected as a whole by clicking its border (or some other appropriate "dead spot"). Since their behavior is indistinguishable from that of native data, inside-out objects are seamless with respect to the container's native document.

Undo for Active and Open Objects

Because different applications take control of a window during in-place activation, commands like "Undo" or "Redo" require special considerations. When defining the undo functionality, the main consideration is how the actions performed within an in-place object are reconciled with actions performed on the native data of the container with regards to undo is the main consideration for undo functionality.

The OLE undo model specifies a single undo stack per open window; that is, all actions that can be undone, whether generated by an in-place object application or the container application, conceptually accumulate on the same undo state sequence. This means that issuing Undo from either the container application's menus or from the in-place object application's menus will undo the last action (that is capable of being undone) performed in that open window, whether it ocurred within an in-place object or not.

If the container has the focus and the last action in the window occurred within an embedded object, then undo will activate the embedded object, revert the action, and leave the embedded object active in-place. In open object applications, each open window manages a single stack of states that can be undone. Actions performed in an open object application are local to that application's window and consequently must be undone from there. Actions in the open object application (even if they cause updates in the container) do not contribute to the undo state of the container.

Sending a verb to an object (or double-clicking) is not an action that can be undone, so it does not add to a container's undo stack. This includes opening an object into another window for editing: if the user unintentionally opens an object, the object application must be closed normally since the "open" action cannot be undone from the container.

Figure 2.24 shows two windows: container Window A has an in-place active object and Window B has an open object application. Between the two windows there are nine actions, all of which can be undone in the order and at the location indicated by the circled numbers. The resulting undo stacks are displayed beneath the windows. The in-place and native actions within Window A have been serialized into the same stack, while the actions in Window B have accumulated on Window B's own separate stack.

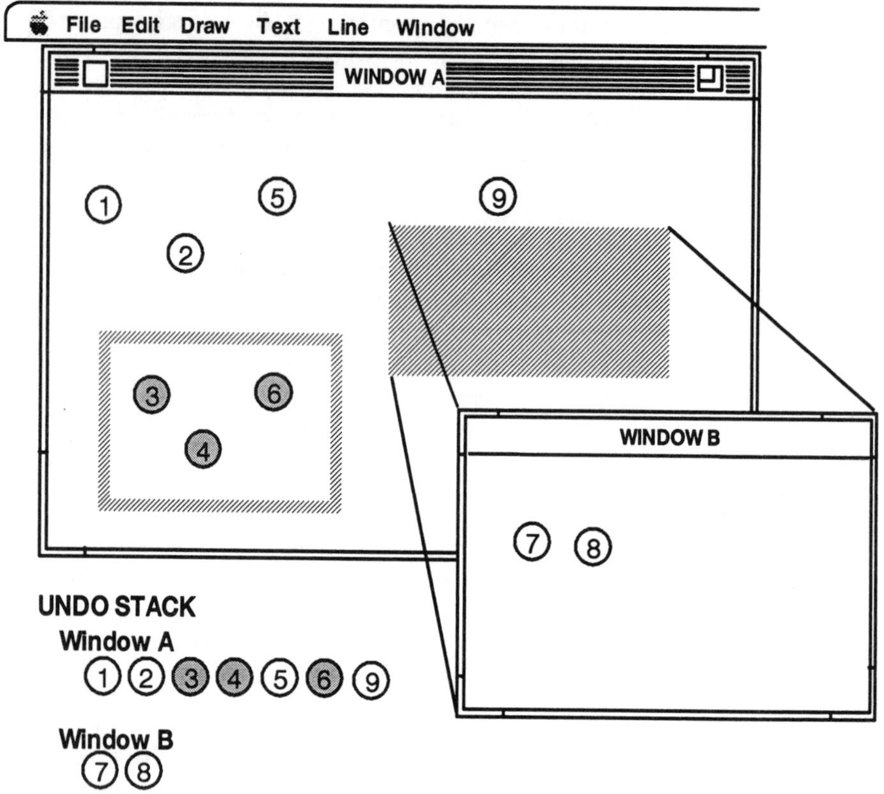

Figure 2.24 Undo stacks of in-place and open objects

Note The stack of undo states pictured in Figure 2.24 is not meant to imply a specific number of undo levels, but presents a timeline of actions that may be undone at different levels, depending on the degree of undo the container/object supports.

The undo actions discussed so far are bound to a single window. When a single action spans multiple windows, it can be undone from the last window involved. In most cases, the user will be focused on that window when the mistake is realized.

For example, if the user has dragged and dropped an item from Window A into Window B, the action would be appended to Window B's undo stack. The entire effect of the action will be undone even if multiple windows were affected. OLE 2 provides no technical support for this sort of multi-window undo coordination. As a result, multi-window actions at best create an independent undo state in each window that participates in the action.

Menus

The addition of in-place activation functionality presents potential problems, as several objects may need to expose their commands in the interface. If no restrictions are imposed on where these commands can appear, users may be faced with an interface that changes unpredictably. In addition, the user will be unable to reliably identify the object to which a given command applies. Developers are faced with the task of accommodating complex negotiations among objects to build the menus.

To avoid these problems, OLE defines a classification of menus that segregates the interface based on menu groupings. This classification is designed to enhance the usability of the interface by regularizing and limiting the changes that occur as different objects come and go from the interface. The following sections describe these menu categories.

Workspace Menu

The top-level container in an application controls the workspace of that application. Top-level containers are responsible for the organization of windows (in a multiple-document-instance, MDI, application), file-level operations, and how edits are ultimately saved. These top-level containers must supply a single File menu that contains file-level commands such as Open, Close, Save, and Print. If an object is opened in-place, the commands in the container's File menu are modified according to the guidelines shown in Figure 2.25. OLE updates are automatic between the open object application window and the container document, eliminating the need for the Update command or the update confirmation upon closing the open object application.

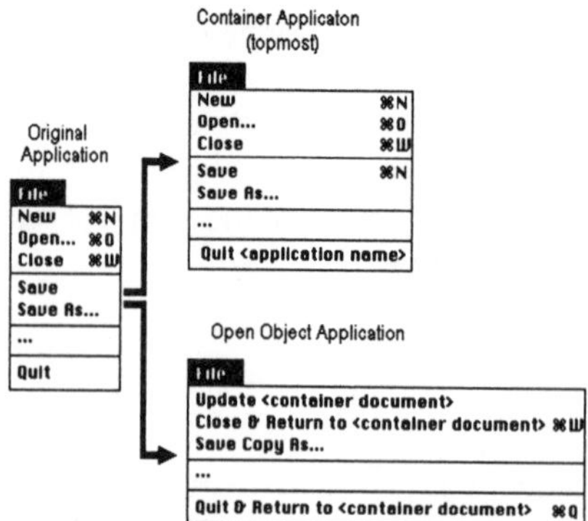

Figure 2.25 The object application and container file menus

As shown in Figure 2.26, MDI applications must supply a Window menu that controls the child windows of the application. Workspace menus remain in the menu bar at all times no matter which object is active. The View menu is not a workspace menu, so any document-level viewing/zooming commands that the container wants to have available must be moved to a workspace menu, preferably the Window menu, if present.

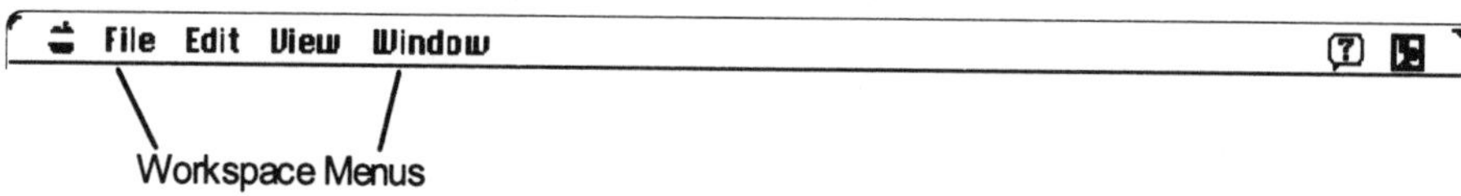

Figure 2.26 Workspace menus for MDI applications

Note Since first-time users may not expect the File menu to remain under the container application's control, they may assume that File/Quit only closes the in-place object application and returns to the main document. If the user makes this assumption and chooses File/Quit, the unwanted action of closing the entire document will happen. To minimize the chance of this happening, container applications should use Quit *<application name>* for the Quit command instead of just Quit, making the effect of the command more precise.

Active Editor Menu

Most OLE object applications must supply Active Editor menus that hold the bulk of their commands, similar to that shown in Figure 2.27. This includes those commands that actually operate on object content. Commands like moving, deleting, searching, replacing, creating new items, and applying tools, styles, and help should be located in these menus. Active Editor menus occupy the majority of the menu bar and can be slightly different depending on whether the object is activated in-place or opened. As the name suggests, they are executed by whichever object is currently active (which may be the top container application). None of these menus may be named File or Window because those titles are reserved for Workspace menus.

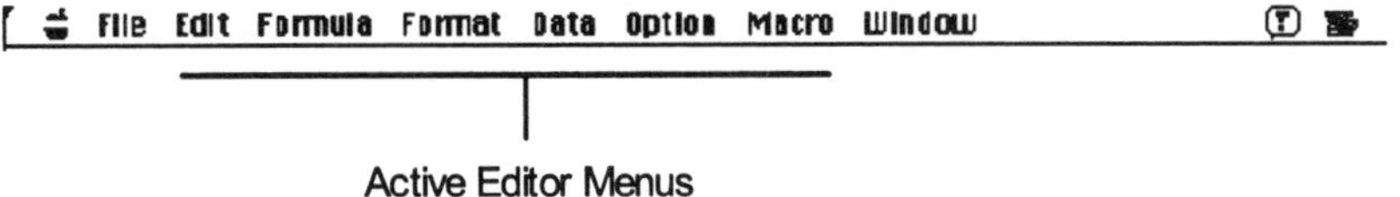

Figure 2.27 Active editor menus

The title bar always displays the name of the application that has its Active Editor menus present. This can either be the name of the container application or the name of the object application during in-place activation. In-place objects that do not require menus different from the container's menus will not have their application name displayed in the title bar; the container application name will remain in this case. If the title bar does display the in-place object application name, then it should add the string "<*shortform*> in" before the document name.

The View menu applies only to the active object; if it needs to contain a zoom command, this command name should indicate scaling of the object rather than suggest it zooms the entire document.

Objects that use direct-manipulation or OLE verbs as their sole user interface do not provide Active Editor menu or alter the menu bar when activated.

Selected Object (Sub)Menu

All container applications must include a menu that contains the verbs for any currently selected OLE object. This menu is preferably a submenu of an Active Editor menu, such as the Edit menu (although it could possibly be its own menu on the menu bar). The submenu uses the short form of the object type name. The submenu includes the word "Linked" preceding the object type name if the object is a link.

As illustrated in Figure 2.28, the syntax for the submenu of the Active Editor menu is:

[Linked] <*shortform*> Object -> <*verb0*>, ..., <*verbN*>, Convert....

The Convert... command is grayed if there are no other types (classes) registered that are capable of converting or emulating the selected object.

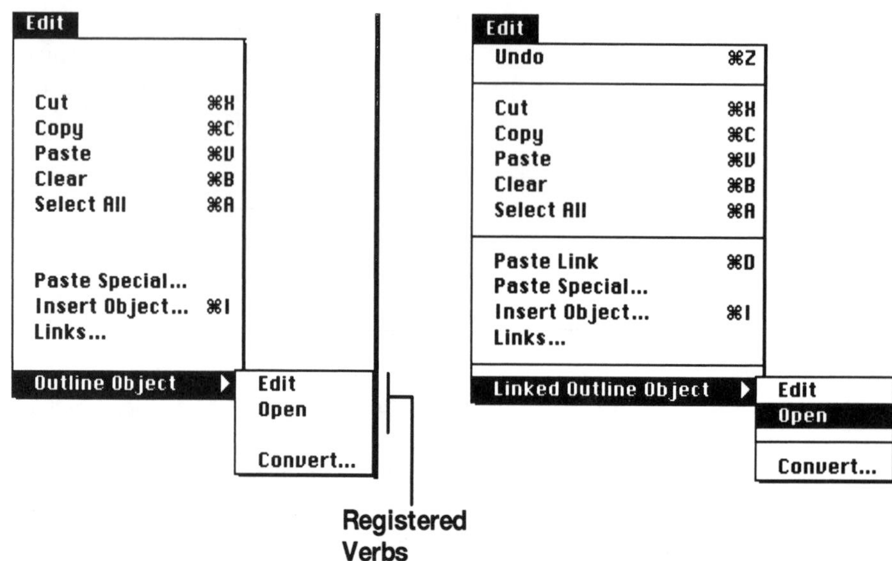

Figure 2.28 Selected object menu

Menu Summary

To summarize how the Workspace, Active Editor, and Selected Object menus mesh on the menu bar:

- Workspace menus are always present in each window, whether the menu is in the container application or an opened object application.
- The File menu commands in an open object application window are modified to point back to the container document and do not necessarily include the Update command or the update confirmation found in the OLE 1 user interface.
- The currently active object (possibly the container itself) supplies the Active Editor menu(s) as the bulk of the menu bar.
- If an object is selected, its commands are available through its selected object submenu within an Active Editor menu.

Command Keys

The object application always has the first opportunity to intercept a command key. If it is not one that it uses, the object application passes it on to the container application. It is important for the object application to avoid using command keys that are likely to be used by a container application. Active Editor commands should make use of the standard editing command keys and not the Workspace menu command keys.

In the event that the container and object application share a common command key, the Active Editor intercepts it. That is, if the object application is active it will get the command key and take appropriate action, with no negotiation or passing to the container application. Similarly, if the container application is the Active editor (even if an OLE object is selected), it will intercept and service the key command. In these collision cases, users will need to select the application that they want to respond to the command key.

Pop-Up Menus

Just as keyboard commands are shortcuts to the pull-down menu commands, pop-up menus (also called shortcut or context menus) provide quick access to frequently used and contextual commands, by means of the mouse. If an application implements pop-up menus, they should be used as described in this section.

Pop-up menus are an auxiliary command interface and therefore contain a subset of the pull-down menu commands. Pop-up menus are popped-up at the pointer's location, as shown in Figure 2.29, eliminating the need for the user to navigate to a menu or button bar. Pop-up menus take up no screen space because they are only displayed upon demand.

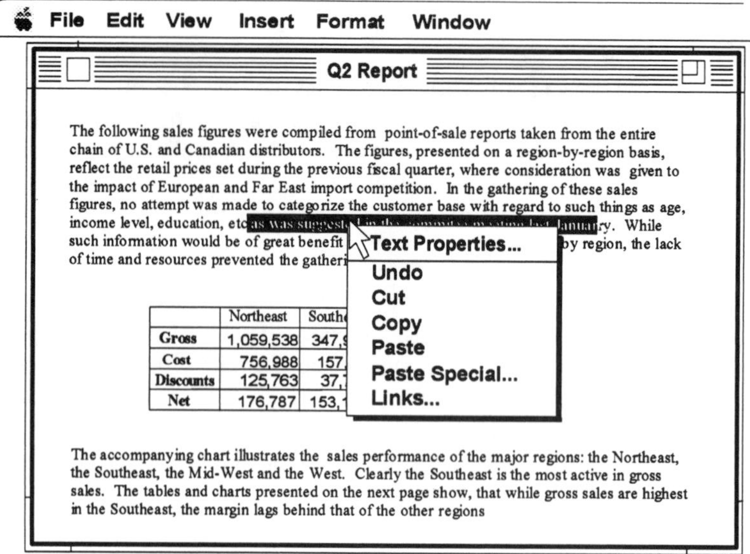

Figure 2.29 Text selection Pop-up menu displayed by a word processor

A pop-up menu looks similar to a standard drop-down menu in that it contains a frame, a shadow, and a list of commands with ellipses (where appropriate) and separator lines. By pressing COMMAND (⌘) OPTION and clicking the mouse button, a pop-up menu appears two pixels beneath and to the right of the current pointer position to display commands that relate to the object beneath the pointer.

Generally, a pop-up menu is displayed over an explicit selection; such as highlighted text in a word processor document. However, pressing COMMAND OPTION and the mouse button over certain objects will both determine the selection and bring up the pop-up menu. For example, pressing COMMAND OPTION and the mouse button over a discrete target such as a spreadsheet cell or an icon could automatically make it the current selection and display its pop-up menu.

To prevent the user from inadvertently selecting a command, the pointer is not initially positioned on any of the menu commands. Upon being displayed, no items on the pop-up menu should initially be highlighted; it is only after the pointer has entered into the menu that a command should be highlighted. The position of the menu allows the user to conveniently move the pointer down into the menu.

To display the popup menu, the user presses COMMAND OPTION and the mouse button while the pointer is over an object or selection of objects. If the pointer is moved into the menu and the button is released, the command beneath the pointer is executed. If the button is simply released at the button down point (specifically within four pixels of the button down point), then the menu remains displayed.

However, if the pointer is moved and the button is released outside the menu, then the menu is removed (cancelled). This behavior is identical to the that of drop-down menus when clicked in the menu bar.

Pointing to a command and clicking the mouse button within the pop-up menu performs that command and removes the menu. While the mouse button is held down, selection highlight feedback is provided on the selected command. The action is not executed until the button is released on the command, allowing the user to drag through the menu and highlight other commands or drag off and release to cancel the menu.

While a pop-up menu is displayed, clicking the mouse button outside the menu cancels the menu. This implies that there is at most one pop-up menu displayed at any time. Unlike drop-down menus, the top command of a pop-up menu should not be initially highlighted when the menu first appears; it is only after the mouse pointer is dragged down the menu that any command should be highlighted. As with drop-down menus, the ESC key cancels the menu.

The COMMAND OPTION keys and mouse button may be pressed over items contained outside a normal selection context, such as over interface controls or the screen background. For instance, a pop-up menu over a scroll bar may display useful navigation commands; a pop-up menu over a control bar button may display commands to re-program its function. Invoking pop-up menus on these objects has no effect on the selection within a window's content; they are completely separate domains.

If the pointer is positioned so that the menu would be appear off the bottom or right side of the screen, the menu position is adjusted so that it is fully visible. Generally, this means that the top-left corner of the menu is moved to the left to avoid the right screen edge or moved up to avoid the bottom screen edge. If the menu would appear both off the bottom and the right edge of the screen, the pop-up menu would be positioned to the left and above the pointer.

Because they are defined in terms of the drop-down menus, the pop-up menu interface provides no mnemonic keys or command keys. Pop-up menus are an efficient means of accessing commonly-used contextual commands and should contain only frequently-used commands and not simply repeat entire drop-down menus. Applications should arrange commands in pop-up menus from top to bottom in decreasing frequency of use.

Note It may defeat the purpose of the pop-up menu to include too many commands or multi-level cascade/hierarchical submenus. While cascade submenus are acceptable, they should be limited to a single level.

When an object is active, its pop-up menu provided by the object application is in effect. Figure 2.30 shows how a pop-up menu for an active bitmap object might appear.

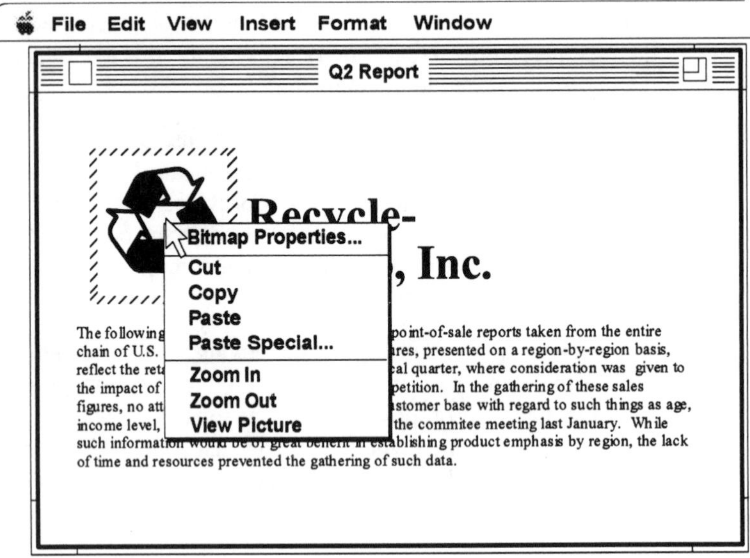

Figure 2.30 Pop-up menu for an active picture object

When an object is selected, the pop-up menu, provided by the container application, should list each of the objects verbs in-line rather than present them in a cascade menu. The syntax should be:

> *<verb>* [Linked] *<shortform>*

It is not necessary to append the word "Object" after the short form because mnemonics are not present in pop-up menus and including "Object" would make the menu unreasonably large.

Typical pop-up menu commands for verbs could be Edit Picture Link or Play Recording. The Convert... command follows the verb(s) (for example, Edit Picture) as shown in Figure 2.31.

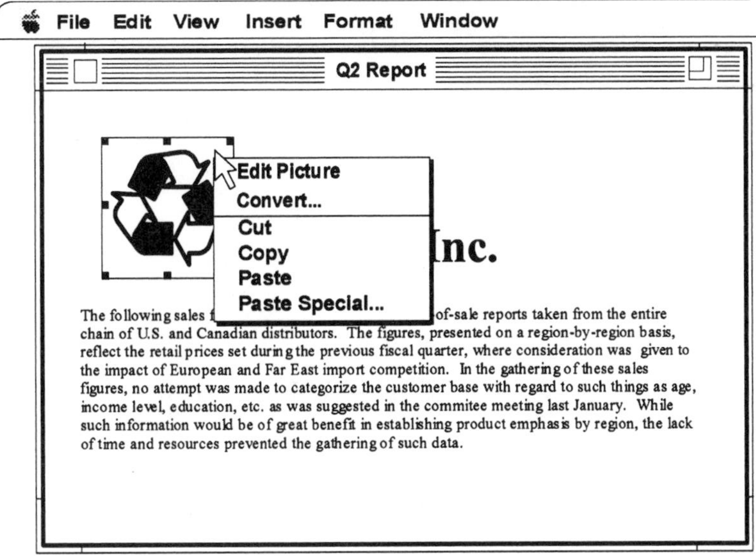
File Edit View Insert Format Window
Q2 Report
Edit Picture
Convert...
Cut
Copy
Paste
Paste Special...
Inc.
The following sales f of-sale reports taken from the entire chain of U.S. and Canadian distributors. The figures, presented on a region-by-region basis, reflect the retail prices set during the previous fiscal quarter, where consideration was given to the impact of European and Far East import competition. In the gathering of these sales figures, no attempt was made to categorize the customer base with regard to such things as age, income level, education, etc. as was suggested in the commitee meeting last January. While such information would be of great benefit in establishing product emphasis by region, the lack of time and resources prevented the gathering of such data.

Figure 2.31 Pop-up menu for an embedded picture object

Control Bars, Frame Adornments, and Floating Palettes

So that users have full access to an object application's functionality, the application's commands and interface controls should be presented in their entirety during in-place activation. OLE 2 employs a replacement strategy for arbitrating control bars, frame adornments, and floating palettes. Figure 2.32, Figure 2.33, and Figure 2.34 show some examples of these adornments.

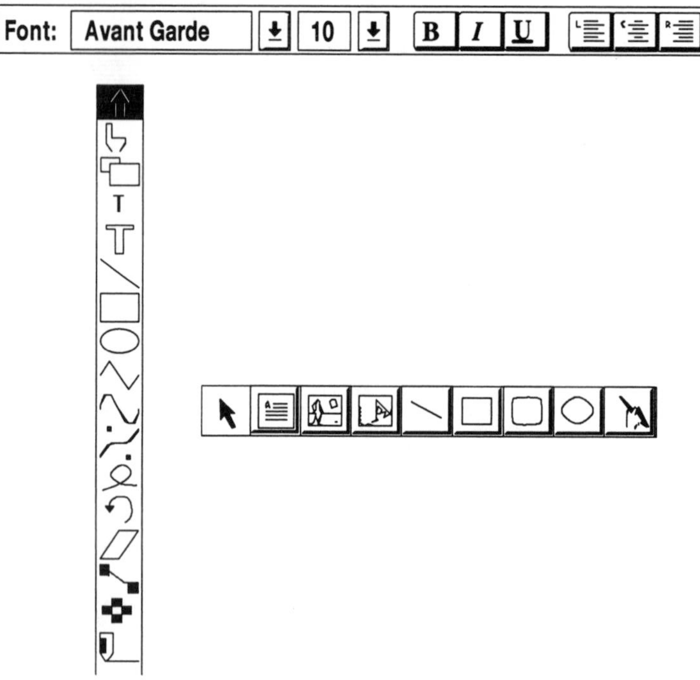

Figure 2.32 Control bar examples

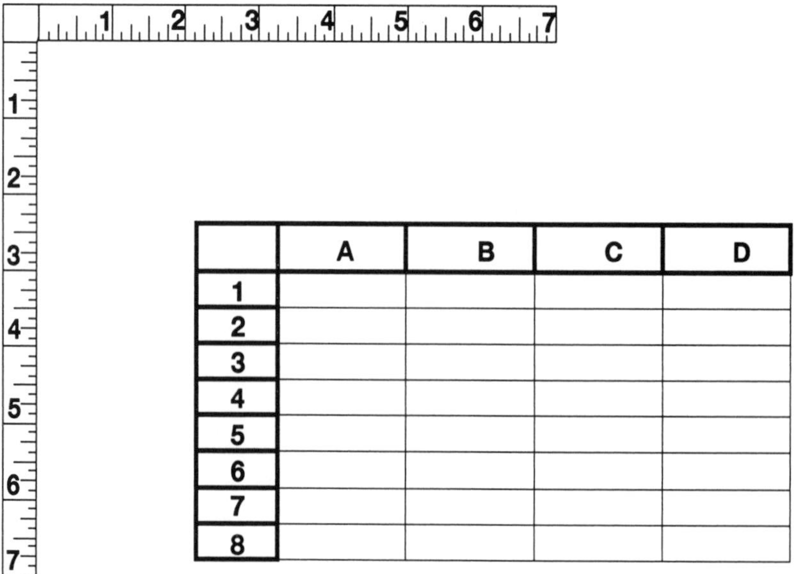

Figure 2.33 Frame adornment examples

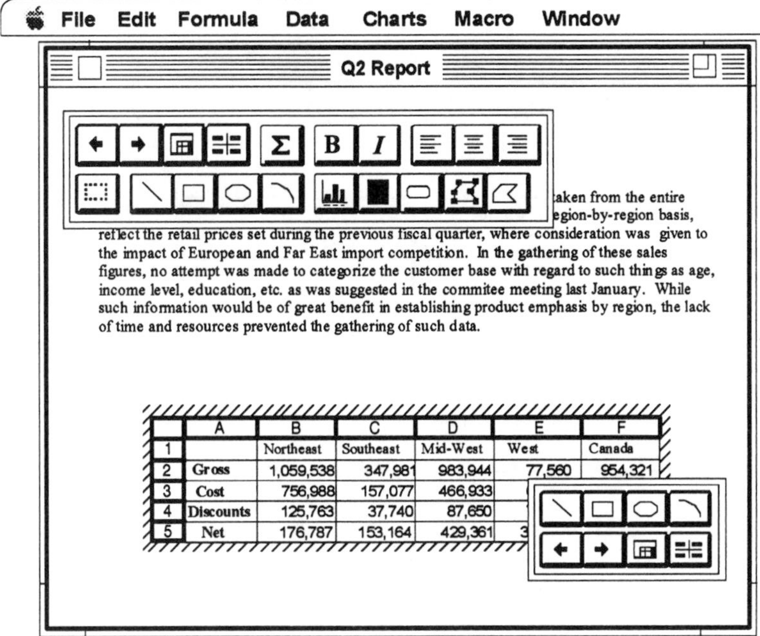
File Edit Formula Data Charts Macro Window
Q2 Report
taken from the entire
egion-by-region basis,
reflect the retail prices set during the previous fiscal quarter, where consideration was given to the impact of European and Far East import competition. In the gathering of these sales figures, no attempt was made to categorize the customer base with regard to such things as age, income level, education, etc. as was suggested in the commitee meeting last January. While such information would be of great benefit in establishing product emphasis by region, the lack of time and resources prevented the gathering of such data.
A B C D E F
1 Northeast Southeast Mid-West West Canada
2 Gross 1,059,538 347,981 983,944 77,560 954,321
3 Cost 756,988 157,077 466,933
4 Discounts 125,763 37,740 87,650
5 Net 176,787 153,164 429,361

Figure 2.34 Floating palette examples

Just as with menus on the menu bar, control bars, floating palettes, and frame adornments are displayed and removed in their entirety. The display of floating palettes, which are independent from the container window and are solely under the control of the active object, is relatively simple. The display of control bars and frame adornments is more complex, since it may require using the same space in the container application window. This may mean repainting, relocating, or resizing objects.

In keeping with document-centered interaction, swapping active objects' interfaces should not disturb the document's appearance and position. Since drop-down and pop-up menus are confined within a particular area, their integration into the container is fairly straightforward. However, tool bars and frame adornments are less predictably integrated.

From OLE's perspective control bars, frame adornments, and floating palettes are all basically the same devices differing primarily in their location and the degree of shared control between the container and object application. As shown in Figure 2.35, there are four locations in the user interface where these types of controls may reside; the location is principally determined by the scope over which the control applies.

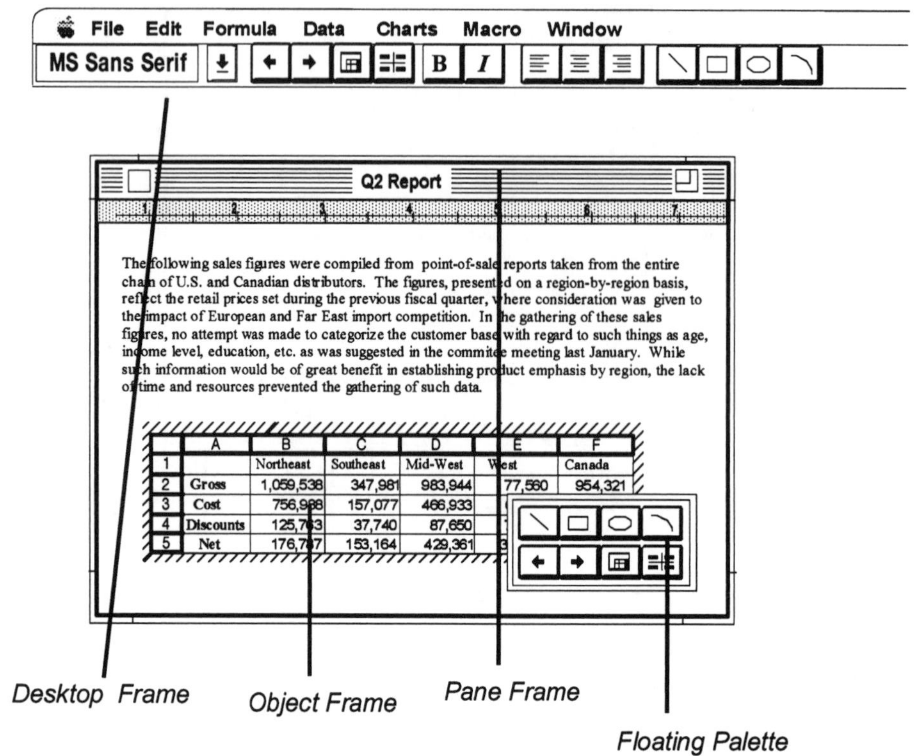

Figure 2.35 Possible locations for optional interface controls

These possible locations should be used as follows:

- **Object Frame.** Object specific controls like a table header or a local coordinate ruler can be placed directly adjacent to the object itself for tightly coupled interaction between the object and its interface. An object (such as a spreadsheet) may include scrollbars if its content extends beyond the boundaries of its frame.
- **Pane Frame.** Controls that are specific to a view or a single document should be located at the pane level. Rulers and viewing tools are common examples.

- **Desktop Frame.** Tools that apply to the entire document (or documents in the case of a MDI application) can be attached just inside any edge of the desktop frame. Such tools include ribbons, drawing tools, and status lines. MDI windows will typically shift up and down to accommodate different sized tool bars as they come and go with context switches. Because the vertical movement of the document windows can be disruptive to the user, it is recommended that tool bars either "float" or be placed elsewhere when MDI windows are returned to the restored state.
- **Floating Palette.** Objects may want to float their tools above the document allowing the user to arrange them as desired.

As an object becomes active it requests a specific area from its container to post its tools. In response, the container can take one of the following actions:

- Replace its tool(s) with the object's if the requested space is already occupied by a container tool.
- Add the object's tool(s) requested space if not already occupied by a container tool.
- Refuse to put up the tool(s)at all (least desirable).

Since container control bars may still be visible while an object is active (like the pane ruler in Figure 2.35), they are still available for use simply by interacting with them. If object application control bars contain "workspace" commands, such as save, print, or open icons, they must be disabled and should be visually distinguished as unavailable.

As windows are resized and the document is scrolled, these interface controls will be forced to clip with respect to their containers. An active object and its frame adornments will be clipped by its immediate window pane just like all document content; frame adornments can be thought of as handles that lie in the same plane as the object. When the object is clipped, the visible part of the object can be edited in-place and the visible frame adornments are operational.

Some containers may scroll at certain increments that will prevent portions of an embedded object from being activated in place. For example, a large picture embedded in a worksheet cell of a spreadsheet application could exhibit this behavior. The spreadsheet application scrolls vertically in one-row increments so that the top of the pane is always aligned with the top edge of a row. If the embedded picture is too large to fit within the pane at one time, then its bottom portion will always be clipped and consequently never viewed or edited in-place as indicated in Figure 2.36. In such cases, the user will likely open the picture into its own object application window for editing. Frame adornments of nested embedded objects are also clipped by the immediate window pane, but not by the extent of any parent object.

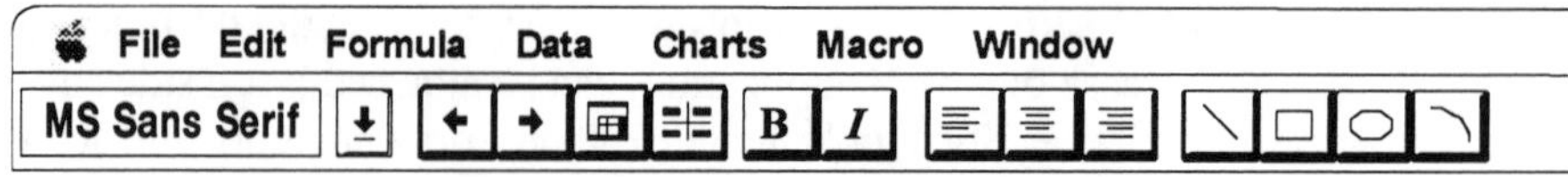
File Edit Formula Data Charts Macro Window
MS Sans Serif
B I

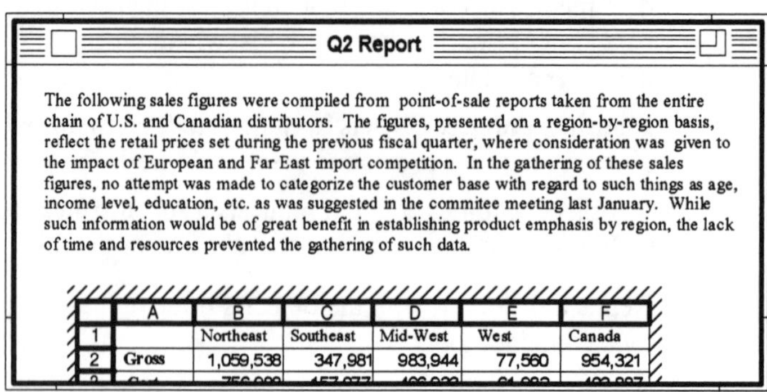
Q2 Report
The following sales figures were compiled from point-of-sale reports taken from the entire chain of U.S. and Canadian distributors. The figures, presented on a region-by-region basis, reflect the retail prices set during the previous fiscal quarter, where consideration was given to the impact of European and Far East import competition. In the gathering of these sales figures, no attempt was made to categorize the customer base with regard to such things as age, income level, education, etc. as was suggested in the commitee meeting last January. While such information would be of great benefit in establishing product emphasis by region, the lack of time and resources prevented the gathering of such data.
A B C D E F
1 Northeast Southeast Mid-West West Canada
2 Gross 1,059,538 347,981 983,944 77,560 954,321

Figure 2.36 Interface control clipping

Alternating between different size control bars in the pane frame should have no effect on the document's position within the pane. That is, there will be no automatic scrolling provision to guarantee that the active object remains in view, since in many cases that is not achievable. Consequently pane control bars are thought to lay atop the document's content, requiring the container to repaint parts of the pane as control bars are removed or replaced with smaller ones.

By preserving the document's position, the user's focus will not be disturbed by the active object bumping down to accommodate the new set of control bars, and bumping back up when it is deactivated. This rule should be followed even if the arriving control bars will clip the object of interest. There is one exception to the container scrolling the document as a result of a control bar change: if the document is at its very top or bottom, and removing a control bar would expose an undefined area (area beyond the document's extent), then the document may scroll to take up the space left by the control bar.

Object Transfer Model

This section explains how objects are moved, copied, and linked within and across documents. This is done using:

- The standard clipboard method invoked through commands from either drop-down or pop-up menus.
- The drag and drop method which enables users to directly drag objects from one location to another.

The clipboard method allows the user to move, copy, and link data, and optionally specify data formats. The drag and drop method allows the user to quickly perform moves, copies, and links when little navigation is needed. The two approaches cooperate to give the user both a global and expedient means of arranging information in documents.

Clipboard Method

Using the clipboard method, a user performs the following steps to transfer an object:

1. Select an object in the source document.
2. Using either Cut (⌘+x) or Copy (⌘+v) from the menu (either the Edit pull-down menu or a pop-up menu), transfer the object to the clipboard.
3. Choose an insertion point (or a selection if it is to be replaced) within the destination document.
4. Choose Paste [<*shortform*>] (⌘+v) or Paste Special... to insert the clipboard contents, as shown in Figure 2.37.

Figure 2.37 The Paste [*shortform*] and Paste Link [*shortform*] menu commands

A Cut and Paste operation removes the user's selection from the source document and relocates it at the insertion point in the destination document. A Copy and Paste operation inserts an independent duplicate of the selection, leaving the original unaffected.

Choosing Paste Special... displays the Paste Special dialog box shown in Figure 2.38, which gives the user explicit control over how to paste the clipboard's contents. The default Paste operation embeds the object if possible. If the destination document application can edit the clipboard data, the application pastes the data format which itself can edit. For example, pasting a bitmap object from one bitmap editor to the document of another causes the object to become part of the destination document's data instead of an embedded object.

If the default settings for the Paste operation results in embedding the object, the command should read Paste <*shortform*>; for example, Paste Worksheet and Paste Recording. Similarly, if the container application includes the Paste Link command, the command should read Paste Link Worksheet, Paste Link Recording, and so on.

The Paste command appearing on the menu with no item extension simply means the data is pasted as native information without OLE intervention. Note that the short form of the object type is used for <*shortform*>.

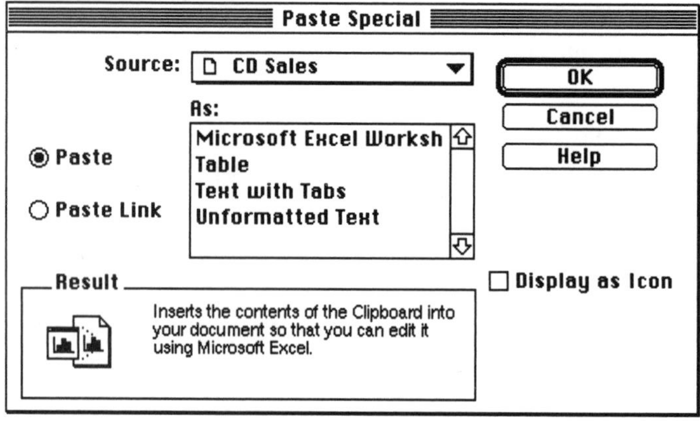

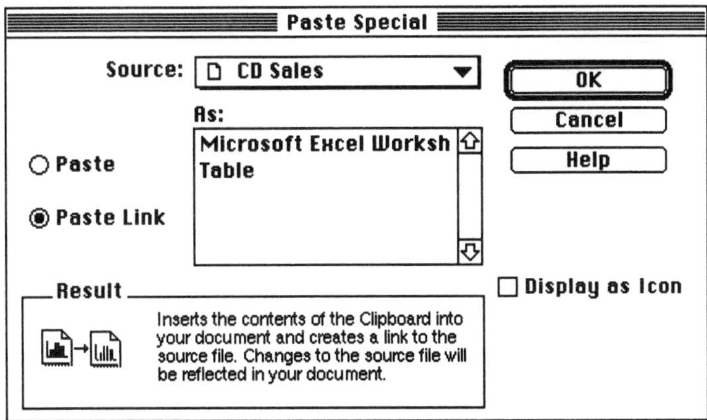

Figure 2.38 The Paste Special dialog box, showing different selections

The Paste Special dialog box shows the name of the source data (using moniker-type syntax), provides the Paste and Paste Link option buttons, and lists the possible data formats associated with each option button. A section of result text describes the result of the currently chosen function and format. Pictures are displayed with the help text to communicate the end result of the chosen operation. Also note the same Display as Icon option button found in the other dialog boxes.

When the Paste option button is selected, the listbox shows the full object type name (without the trailing "object") and other native data forms. When the clipboard contains an already linked object, its object type should be preceded by "Linked" in the format list. For example, if the user copied a linked Microsoft Excel 5.0 Worksheet to the clipboard, Paste Special would show "Linked Microsoft Excel 5.0 Worksheet" under the Paste format options (since a Paste would insert an exact duplicate of the original linked worksheet).

Native data formats should be expressed in the same terms that the destination application uses in its own menus. When Paste Link is chosen, both the object type (full form) and any native format that will support linking appears. The default formats for The Paste and Paste Link options use the same default formats that the default Paste [*<shortform>*] and Paste Link [*<shortform>*] use.

The following table shows the recommended Result text for the Paste Special dialog box:

Paste Special Operation	**Result Text**
Paste.[Linked] Object	Inserts the contents of the clipboard into user's document so that it can be activated using *<object app name>*.
Paste.[Linked] Object as Icon	Inserts the contents of the clipboard into user's document so that it can be activated using *<object app name>*. The object is displayed as an icon.
Paste. Data	Inserts the contents of the clipboard into user's document as *<native type name, and optionally an additional help sentence>*.
Paste Link. Object	Inserts a picture of the clipboard contents into user's document. Paste Link creates a link to the source file so that changes to the source file will be reflected in the document.
Paste Link. Object as Icon	Inserts an icon into user's document which represents the clipboard contents. Paste Link creates a link to the source file so that changes to the source file will be reflected in the document.
Paste Link. Data	Inserts the contents of the clipboard into user's document as *<native type name>*. Paste Link creates a link to the source file so that changes to the source file will be reflected in the document.

When implementing the Paste Special and Insert Object dialogs, the container application should use monikers to hold the pathnames to link sources. Monikers bind to the object and properly track names across networks.

Drag and Drop Method

Using the drag and drop method for object movement, a user can directly transfer objects from document to document as well as supply objects to system resources such as printers and mailboxes. The steps for performing a drag and drop are:

1. Press the mouse button when the pointer is over the object. The pointer should change to a "move" pointer. For objects such as text or table cells, it may be necessary to first select the desired range. Depending on their visual representation, objects may also be dragged by a move handle or its frame border.
2. Hold the mouse button and drag the object to the intended target location.
3. Release the button over the intended insertion point to drop the object.

If a drop target is invalid, the pointer should change to the shape shown in Figure 2.39:

Figure 2.39 Invalid drop target pointer

Note The "not allowed" pointer should be displayed when dragging over a linked object because OLE does not support dropping on linked targets.

When moving an object from one location in a document to another place in the same document, move (not copy) is the default drag function. The user may force a copy operation by holding down the OPTION key or force a link operation by holding down both the SHIFT and OPTION keys. When dragging an object from one document to another, the OPTION key forces a move operation.

The drag is qualified by the modifier keys only while they are held down; releasing the modifiers before the drop results in a default drop. The pointer's appearance indicates which type of transfer is to be performed and provides feedback to the user. Figure 2.40, shows how the pointer changes depending on the type of drag operation.

	No Modifier	OPTION Key	SHIFT + OPTION Keys
Drag Operation Within the Same Document	Move	Force Copy	Force Link
Drag Operation Between Two Documents	Copy	Force Move	Force Link

Figure 2.40 Drag pointers change to indicate the type of drag operation

Typically, the pointer's appearance generally suggests which type of transfer is to be performed.

For example, for a cell selected in a range of embedded worksheet cells, as shown in Figure 2.41, the user would start the drag by grabbing the selection's border with the mouse and pointer.

	A	B	C	D	E	F
1		Northeast	Southeast	Mid-West	West	Canada
2	Gross	1,059,538	347,981	983,944	767,560	954,321
3	Cost	756,988	157,077	466,933	361,982	403,887
4	Discounts	125[illegible]63	37,740	87,650	72,429	91,872
5	Net	176[illegible]7	153,164	429,361	333,149	458,562

Figure 2.41 Select and start drag

The "move" pointer appears by default and the user has a choice of six different categories of targets. These are enumerated in Figure 2.42.

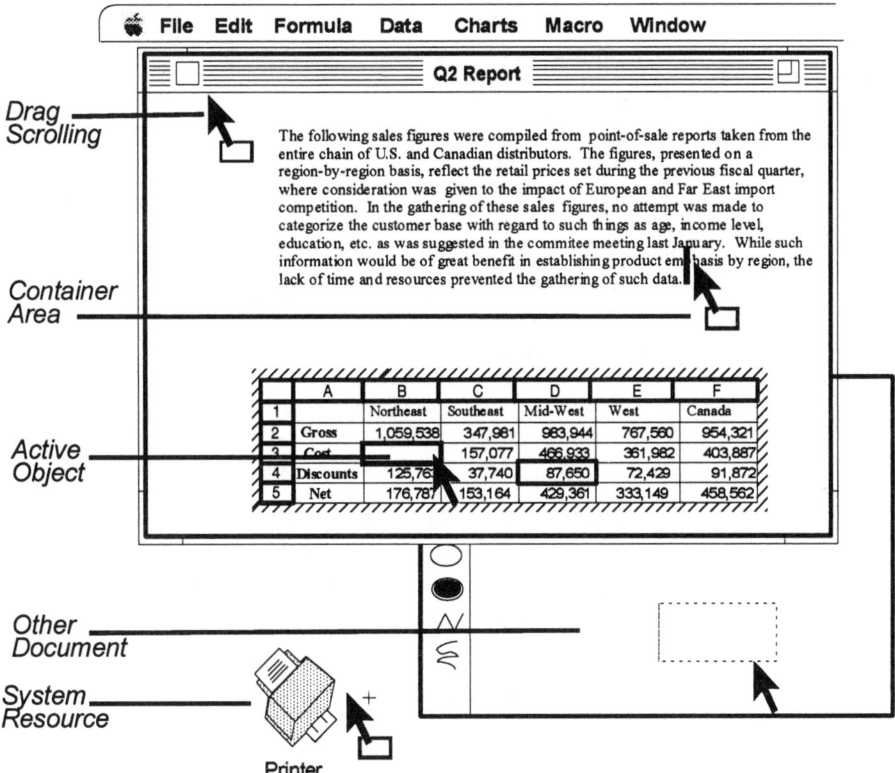
File Edit Formula Data Charts Macro Window
Q2 Report
Drag Scrolling
The following sales figures were compiled from point-of-sale reports taken from the entire chain of U.S. and Canadian distributors. The figures, presented on a region-by-region basis, reflect the retail prices set during the previous fiscal quarter, where consideration was given to the impact of European and Far East import competition. In the gathering of these sales figures, no attempt was made to categorize the customer base with regard to such things as age, income level, education, etc. as was suggested in the commitee meeting last January. While such information would be of great benefit in establishing product emphasis by region, the lack of time and resources prevented the gathering of such data.
Container Area
Active Object
Other Document
System Resource
Printer

	A	B	C	D	E	F
1		Northeast	Southeast	Mid-West	West	Canada
2	Gross	1,059,538	347,981	983,944	767,560	954,321
3	Cost		157,077	466,933	361,982	403,887
4	Discounts	125,76	37,740	87,650	72,429	91,872
5	Net	176,787	153,164	429,361	333,149	458,562

Figure 2.42 Possible drag and drop targets

The significance of each of the target categories in Figure 2.42 is as follows:

- **Drag Scrolling**. Dragging should follow the conventions implemented within System 7 with regard to dragging over pane borders and over out-of-view drop targets. After the document has scrolled to the proper point, the user can drop the object at the intended target.
- **Container Area**. An object can be dropped in the container of the currently active object.
- **Active Object**. This drag is completely internal to the application (as shown in the spreadsheet in Figure 2.42) and is handled in the same way as normal dragging in the application.
- **Illegal Target**. When the target cannot accept a drop (such as the screen background in Figure 2.42), the "not allowed" pointer should be displayed.
- **System Resource (Icon)**. The object is being dropped on a particular resource that highlights with the selection color. Copy is the default operation for the drag and drop operation to a system resource.

- **Other Document**. In this case, the drag has left the pane (and application window), and is being dropped into another application.
- **Inside-out Activated Object** (not shown in Figure 2.42). Because inside-out objects are effectively always active, they can serve as a drop target. They should provide accurate drop target feedback to indicate the result of the dropping item.

Drag scrolling, container area, and active object targets are possible in any window, not just the active application window. However, an inactive object cannot be a drop target because it cannot give precise feedback on where within itself an item would be dropped.

Because drag and drop operations produce the same end result as Cut/Paste, Copy/Paste, and Copy/Paste Link respectively, there is no implied bearing on the state of the clipboard since the two transfer methods are completely independent.

The "drop-point" indicator (checkered I-beam) shown in Figure 2.43 should be displayed with the pointer as target feedback when dragging over text areas. Because text areas are a common drop site, it is particularly necessary for the user to see this consistent feedback.

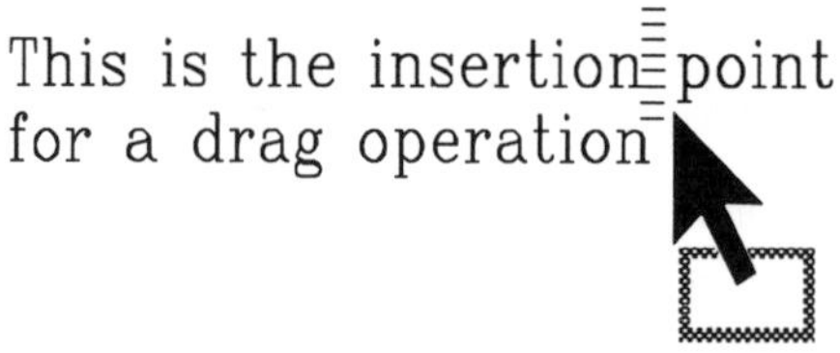

This is the insertion point
for a drag operation

Figure 2.43 Checkered "I-Beam" pointer used in drag operation

When dragging an icon from the Finder into a document, it should effectively perform an "insert object from file," exposing the contents of the object, if at all possible. If the application that created the file is not an OLE-aware file, then it is embedded and continues to be displayed as a document icon.

Dialog Box Messages

The following are a listing of standard dialog box messages.

If the user attempts to launch an object application that cannot be run as a stand-alone application, the error message of Figure 2.44 should be issued.

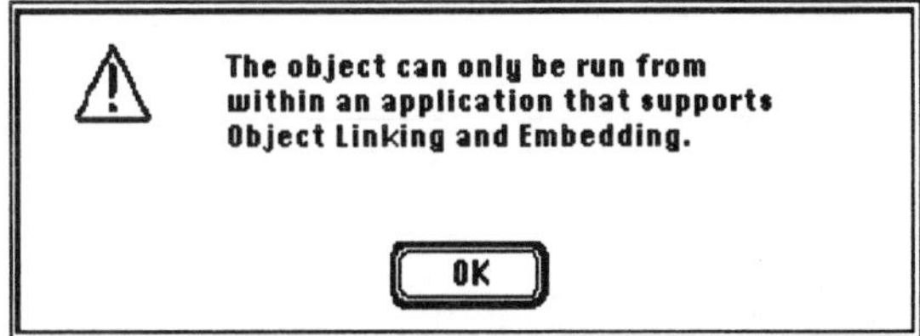

Figure 2.44 Warning message for an object application that cannot be run as a stand-alone application

If the container application fails to locate the requested object application (that is registered in the database) when the user selects an entry from the Insert Object dialog or when the user double clicks on an object, the error message shown in Figure 2.45 should be displayed. Browse... invokes the standard File Open dialog box. The user-supplied path should be entered in the registration as the new object application pathname.

Note To ensure that the Registration Database file is current, object applications should register themselves, or verify registration, each time they are started. For more information, see Chapter 4, "Registering Object Applications."

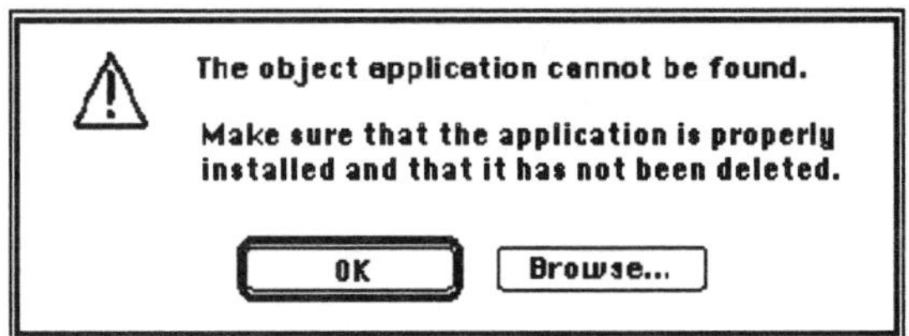

Figure 2.45 Warning message for when the object application cannot be found

An object application may be busy or unavailable for several reasons. For example, it may be busy printing, waiting for user input to a modeless error message, hung, or accidentally deleted. If the object application is not available, the warning message in Figure 2.46 should be displayed. The object should not display the message until both the time out expires and a user event (for example, mouse down) has been received through **IMessageFilter::MessagePending**; this eliminates unnecessarily displaying the warning.

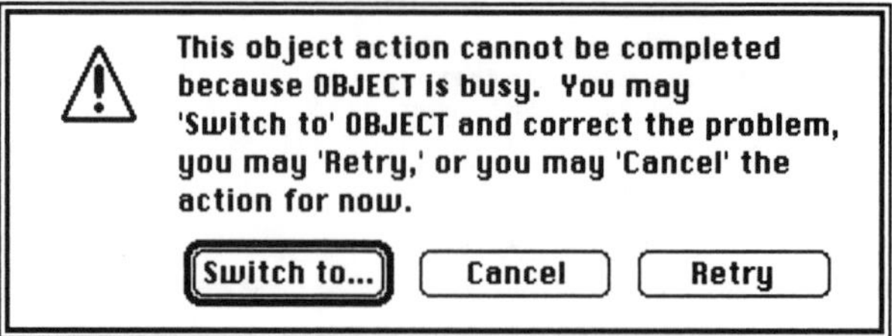

Figure 2.46 Object application busy warning message

The progress indicator shown in Figure 2.47 should be displayed while the links are being updated (when a document that contains automatic links is opened). The Cancel button interrupts the update process and returns the data to its state before the operation was initiated. If a return to the original state of the data is not possible, Stop should be used instead of Cancel. The Stop buttons halts the updating but does not reverse any changes that the operation has already caused.

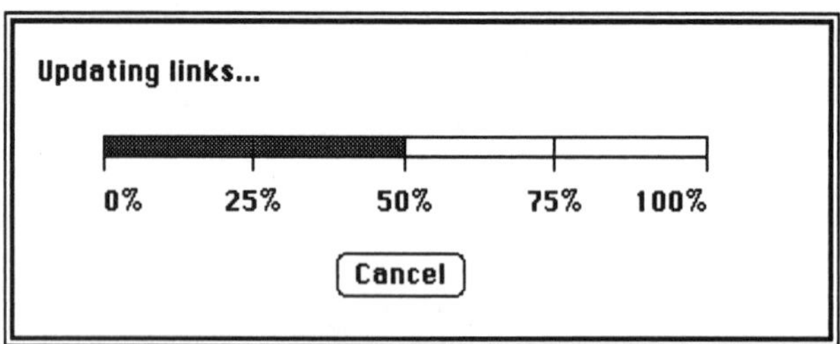

Figure 2.47 Progress Indicator for Link Updating

If some of the linked files are unavailable, the warning shown in Figure 2.48 is displayed. This dialog box contains OK and Links... buttons. The OK button closes the dialog box without updating the links. The Links... button displays the Links dialog box (see Figure 2.13) with all the links listed in a list box. Unavailable linked files are marked with the word "Unavailable" in the third column of the list box. The user can attempt to locate the unavailable files by using the Change Source dialog (see Figure 2.14), which is available from the Change Source... command button in the Links dialog box.

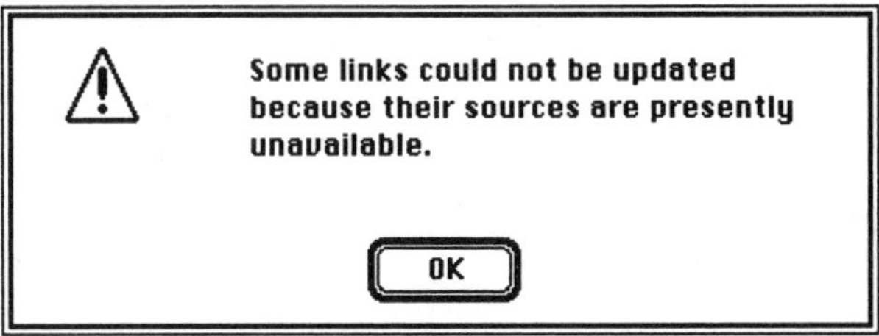

Figure 2.48 Warning message for unavailable links

If the user issues a command to a link whose source is unavailable, the warning message in Figure 2.49 should be issued. The unavailable link is marked as such in the Links dialog.

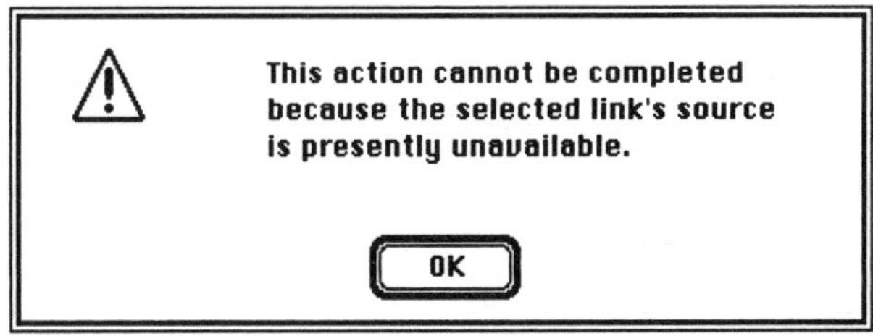

Figure 2.49 Warning message for issuing a command to an unavailable link

Balloon-Help Messages

The following tables describes the recommended balloon-help messages that should be displayed against the given user actions:

Menu Commands	Balloon-Help Message
File Menu	
Update *<container-document>*	Updates the appearance of this *<object type name>* in *<container document>*
Save Copy As...	Saves a copy of *<object type name>* in a separate file
Quit & Return to *<container-document>*	Quits *<object application>* and return to *<container-document>*

Menu Commands	Balloon-Help Message
Edit Menu	
Paste <*shortform*>	Inserts clipboard contents as <*object type name*> *
Paste Special...	Inserts clipboard contents as a linked object, embedded object, or other format
Paste Link <*shortform*>	Inserts a link to <*descriptive class name*> object from <*source-document*>
Insert Object...	Inserts a new embedded object
<*verb*> [Linked] <*shortform*>**	None
[Linked] <*shortform*> Object ->	Apply the following commands to <*descriptive class name*> object
[Linked] <*shortform*> Object -> <*verb*>	None
Links...	Allows links to be viewed, updated, opened, or cancelled
Options (Preferences) Menu	
Show Objects	Displays (toggles) the borders around objects
Mouse Interface	
When an object is selected	Double click to <*primary-verb*> <*object type name*> object

* The <*descriptive type name*> is identical to the initially highlighted value in the list box in the Paste Special dialog box. This status bar message indicates the data format used to paste clipboard contents.

** If no verb in the Registration Database file is specified, "Activate" should be used as a default verb.

CHAPTER 3

Programming Considerations

This chapter contains helpful guidelines for developing OLE applications. Many of the key subjects that pertain to the programming implementation of OLE are introduced.

Designing Component Objects

Component objects contain one or more interface implementations and data that is specific to the object. The data is private and inaccessible from outside the object, while the interface implementations are public and can be accessed through pointers.

Because interfaces are a binary standard, interface implementation is language independent. However, C++ is the preferred language because it supports many of the object-oriented concepts inherent in OLE.

Using a procedural language such as C involves extra work, as is summarized below:

- VTBLs must be initialized explicitly either at compile or run time. VTBLs should be unchangeable; once a VTBL is initialized with function pointers, those pointers should remain unchanged until the application shuts down. VTBLs in C++ are declared as constants to prevent them from being modified inadvertently. However, in C there is no way to ensure that a VTBL will remain unchanged.

  OLE provides a mechanism that allows C developers to choose how their VTBLs should be declared. If you want to declare constant VTBLs, place the following statement before the #include statement for the OLE2.H header file:

  ```
  #define CONST_VTABLE
  ```

- Each method requires a pointer to the object that owns the method. With C++, all members are implicitly dereferenced off the **this** pointer. With C, there must be an additional first parameter passed to each method that is a pointer to the interface in which the method is declared.
- Methods in C++ can have identical names because methods are actually known by a name that is the result of concatenating the method name to the class name. Methods in C must have a unique name to designate the object with which they are associated.

  For example, the following C++ code sample defines an implementation of **IUnknown::QueryInterface**. The method name is **QueryInterface** and there are two parameters: a REFIID and a pointer to where to return the requested interface instance.

  ```
  CUnknown::QueryInterface (REFIID riid, void * * ppvObj);
  ```

  A similar C implementation would require a more complex name and an additional first parameter to indicate the object owning the method:

  ```
  IUnknown_Doc_QueryInterface (LPUNKNOWN pUnk, REFIID riid,
      void * * ppvObj);
  ```

Component Objects: C Nested Structures

In the following code example, the demonstration object, called *CObj*, supports two interfaces that are derived from **IUnknown**, InterfaceA and InterfaceB. The object's private data includes a pointer to another component object in the application (*m_pCDoc*), a count of all the external references to the object (*m_ObjRefCount*), and pointers to two interfaces implemented by other component objects and used by *CObj (m_pOleObj* and *m_pStg)*. All object members use the *m_* prefix to make it easy to distinguish between member variables and other variables.

A C interface implementation is comprised of data structures nested within the object's data structure. Each interface structure contains a VTBL pointer as its first member (*pVtbl*), a pointer to the object (*pCObj*), and a count of the external references to the interface (*m_RefCount*). The order of the members in the interface structures is identical to facilitate code sharing.

```
typedef struct CObj {
    unsigned long        m_ObjRefCount;
    LPSTORAGE            m_pStg;
    LPOLEOBJECT          m_pOleObj;
    struct CDOC   *      m_pCDoc;

    struct InterfaceA  {
        LPVTBL           pVtbl;
        struct CObj *    pCObj;
        unsigned long    m_RefCount;
    } m_InterfaceA;

    struct InterfaceB {
        LPVTBL           pVtbl;
        struct Obj   *   pCObj;
        unsigned long    m_RefCount;
    } m_InterfaceB;

} COBJ;
```

Component Objects: C++ Nested Classes

The following code examples shows how to declare a nested C++ class using OLE 2 macros.

```
class CObj : public IUnknown
{
private:
    unsigned long m_ObjRefCount; LPSTORAGE       m_pStg;
    LPOLEOBJECT      m_pOleObj;
private:
    STDMETHOD(QueryInterface)(REFIID riid, void **ppvObj);
    STDMETHOD_(unsigned long,AddRef)(void) { return ++m_ObjRefCount;}
    STDMETHOD_(unsigned long,Release)(void)
    {
        if ( --m_ObjRefCount == 0)
        {
            delete this;
            return 0;
         }
         else
            return m_ObjRefCount;
    }
```

```
public:
    // Constructor
    CObj(): m_Unknown(this), m_InterfaceA(this), m_InterfaceB(this)
    {
        m_ObjRefCount = 0;
        m_pStg = NULL;
        m_pOleObj = NULL;
    }
    ~CObj();

    struct CUnknown : IUnknown
    {
    private:
        unsigned long m_RefCount;
        CObj *    m_pCObj;
    public:
        CUnknown(CObj *pCObj)
        {
            m_pCObj = pCObj;
            m_RefCount = 0;
        }

        STDMETHOD(QueryInterface) (REFIID riid, void **ppvObj)
        {
            return m_pCObj->QueryInterface(riid,ppvObj);
        }
        STDMETHOD_(unsigned long,AddRef)(void)
        {
            ++m_RefCount;
            return m_pCObj->AddRef();
        }
        STDMETHOD_(unsigned long,Release) (void)
        {
            --m_RefCount;
            return m_pCObj->Release();
        }
    };

    friend CUnknown;
    CUnknown m_Unknown;

    struct CInterfaceA : InterfaceA
    {
    private:
        unsigned long m_RefCount;
        CObj *    m_pCObj;

    public:
        CInterfaceA(CObj *pCObj)
            {  m_pCObj = pCObj; m_RefCount = 0; }
        STDMETHOD(QueryInterface) (REFIID riid, void **ppvObj)
```

```
        {
            return m_pCObj->QueryInterface(riid,ppvObj);
        }
        STDMETHOD_(unsigned long,AddRef)(void)
        {
            ++m_RefCount;
            return m_pCObj->AddRef();
        }
        STDMETHOD_(unsigned long,Release) (void)
        {
            --m_RefCount;
            return m_pCObj->Release();
        }
        STDMETHOD(MethodA1)(void **ppvObj);
        STDMETHOD(MethodA2)(unsigned long dwArg);
    };

    friend CInterfaceA;
    CInterfaceA m_InterfaceA;

    struct CInterfaceB : InterfaceB
    {
    private:
        unsigned long m_RefCount;
        CObj *    m_pCObj;
    public:
        CInterfaceB(CObj *pCObj)
            {
                m_pCObj = pCObj;
                m_RefCount = 0;
            }
        STDMETHOD(QueryInterface) (REFIID riid, void **ppvObj)
        {
            return m_pCObj->QueryInterface(riid,ppvObj);
        }
        STDMETHOD_(unsigned long,AddRef)(void)
        {
            ++m_RefCount;
            return ++m_pCObj->m_ObjRefCount;
        }
        STDMETHOD_(unsigned long,Release) (void)
        {
            --m_RefCount;
            return m_pCObj->Release();
        }
        STDMETHOD(MethodB1)(void);
        STDMETHOD(MethodB2)(unsigned long dwArg1,unsigned long dwArg2);
    };
    friend CInterfaceB;
    CInterfaceB m_InterfaceB;
};
```

```
// QueryInterface for this would look like the following:

OLEMETHODIMP CObj::QueryInterface(REFIID riid, void **ppvObj)
{
    if (riid == IID_IUnknown)
        *ppvObj = &(this->m_Unknown);
    else if (riid == IDD_InterfaceA)
        *ppvObj = &(this->m_InterfaceA);
    else if (riid == IDD_InterfaceB)
        *ppvObj = &(this->m_InterfaceA);
    else
    {
        *ppvObj = NULL;
        return ResultFromScode(E_NOINTERFACE);
    }
         ((IUnknown * ) *ppvObj)->AddRef();
    return NOERROR;
};
```

The following code example shows how to declare a nested C++ class Macintosh base types:

```
class CObj : public IUnknown
{
private:
    unsigned long m_ObjRefCount;
    LPSTORAGE        m_pStg;
    LPOLEOBJECT      m_pOleObj;
private:
    HRESULT QueryInterface(REFIID riid, LPVOID *ppvObj);
    unsigned long AddRef(void)
    {
        return ++m_ObjRefCount;
    }
    unsigned long Release(void)
    {
        if ( --m_ObjRefCount == 0)
        {
            delete this;
            return 0;
        }
    else
        return m_ObjRefCount;
    }
    public:
    // Constructor
    CObj(): m_Unknown(this), m_InterfaceA(this), m_InterfaceB(this)
    {
        m_ObjRefCount = 0;
        m_pStg = NULL;
```

```
    m_pOleObj = NULL;
}
~CObj();

struct CUnknown : IUnknown
{
private:
    unsigned long m_RefCount;
    CObj *    m_pCObj;
public:
    CUnknown(CObj *pCObj)
        {
            m_pCObj = pCObj;
            m_RefCount = 0;
        }
    HRESULT QueryInterface(REFIID riid, void **ppvObj)
    {
        return m_pCObj->QueryInterface(riid,ppvObj);
    }
    unsigned long AddRef(void)
    {
        ++m_RefCount;
        return m_pCObj->AddRef();
    }
    unsigned long Release(void)
    {
        --m_RefCount;
        return m_pCObj->Release();
    }
};
friend CUnknown;
CUnknown m_Unknown;

struct CInterfaceA : InterfaceA
{
private:
    unsigned long m_RefCount;
    CObj *    m_pCObj;

public:
    CInterfaceA(CObj *pCObj)
        {
            m_pCObj = pCObj;
            m_RefCount = 0;
        }
    HRESULT QueryInterface(REFIID riid, void **ppvObj)
    {
        return m_pCObj->QueryInterface(riid,ppvObj);
    }
    unsigned long AddRef(void)
    {
```

```
            ++m_RefCount;
            return m_pCObj->AddRef();
        }
        unsigned long Release(void)
        {
            --m_RefCount;
            return m_pCObj->Release();
        }
        HRESULT MethodA1(void **ppvObj);
        HRESULT MethodA2(unsigned long dwArg);
    };
    friend CInterfaceA;
    CInterfaceA m_InterfaceA;

    struct CInterfaceB : InterfaceB
    {
    private:
        unsigned long m_RefCount;
        CObj *    m_pCObj;

    public:
        CInterfaceB(CObj *pCObj)
            {
                m_pCObj = pCObj;
                m_RefCount = 0;
             }
        HRESULT QueryInterface(REFIID riid, void **ppvObj)
        {
            return m_pCObj->QueryInterface(riid,ppvObj);
        }
        unsigned long AddRef(void)
        {
            ++m_RefCount;
            return ++m_pCObj->m_ObjRefCount;
        }
        unsigned long Release(void)
        {
            --m_RefCount;
            return m_pCObj->Release();
        }
        HRESULT MethodB1(void);
        HRESULT MethodB2(unsigned long dwArg1,unsigned long dwArg2);
    };
    friend CInterfaceB;
    CInterfaceB m_InterfaceB;
};

// The QueryInterface for this would look like the following:

HRESULT CObj::QueryInterface(REFIID riid, void **ppvObj)
```

```
{
    if (riid == IID_IUnknown)
        *ppvObj = &(this->m_Unknown);
    else if (riid == IDD_InterfaceA)
        *ppvObj = &(this->m_InterfaceA);
    else if (riid == IDD_InterfaceB)
        *ppvObj = &(this->m_InterfaceA);
    else
    {
        *ppvObj = NULL;
        return ResultFromScode(E_NOINTERFACE);
    }
         ((IUnknown * ) *ppvObj)->AddRef();
    return NOERROR;
};
```

Component Objects: C++ Multiple Inheritance

The following example illustrates the use of C++ multiple inheritance. The main advantage to using multiple inheritance lies in its simplicity. Only the prototypes for each of the interface methods are listed; no interface data structures or class definitions are necessary.

Because both InterfaceA and InterfaceB inherit from **IUnknown**, **IUnknown** does not need to be explicitly listed in the class statement and a single implementation of the **IUnknown** methods (**QueryInterface**, **AddRef**, and **Release**) is sufficient.

```
class FAR CObj : public InterfaceA, public InterfaceB
{
private:
    unsigned long    m_ObjRefCount;
    LPSTORAGE        m_pStg;
    LPOLEOBJECT      m_pOleObj;
    CDOC *           m_pCDoc;

public:
    CObj();
    ~CObj();

    HRESULT QueryInterface(REFIID riid, void * * ppvObj)
    unsigned long AddRef(void) { return ++m_ObjRefCount; }
    unsigned long Release(void);

    HRESULT MethodA1(void * * ppvObj);
    HRESULT MethodA2(unsigned long dwArg);

    HRESULT MethodB1(void);
    HRESULT MethodB2(unsigned long dwArg1, unsigned long dwArg2);
};
```

There are two disadvantages to using multiple inheritance with OLE. First, it is not possible to have an interface-level reference count. (For more information about reference counting, see the section "Reference Counting Rules" in Chapter 5, "Component Object Interfaces and Functions.")

Second, there is the potential for confusion over the interpretation of the class statement. A standard C++ multiple inheritance declaration implies there is a relationship when an object inherits implementations. In OLE, however, interfaces are attributes of the object and implementations are not inherited.

Aggregation

An aggregate object is like any other object in that it implements one or more interfaces. Internal to the aggregate, the implementation of certain interfaces is actually provided by one or more contained objects. Users of the object are unaware of this internal structure. They cannot tell and do not care that the object is an aggregate: aggregation is purely an implementation technique.

Figure 3.1 shows an aggregate object consisting of a control object that implements Interface A and Interface B, and a noncontrol object, which implements Interface C. All these interface implementations are exposed publicly, as indicated by the line and circle extending to the outside of the aggregate.

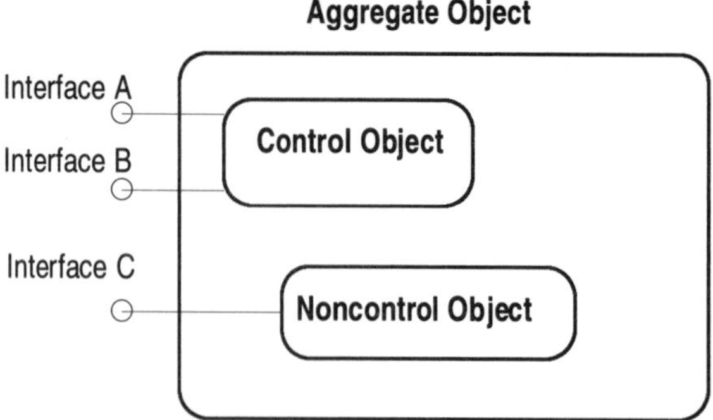

Figure 3.1 Aggregate containing two internal objects

In the aggregation model, the control object forms the aggregate's personality and determines how it operates, making decisions about which interfaces are exposed outside of the object and which interfaces remain private. The control object has a special instance of the **IUnknown** interface known as the controlling unknown. The controlling unknown is always implemented as part of the new code written when the aggregate is put together from other objects.

The other objects can be implemented at any time. These noncontrol objects can be instantiated separately or as part of the aggregate. However, if these objects are to be aggregatable, they must be written to cooperate with the control object by forwarding their **QueryInterface**, **AddRef**, and **Release** calls to the controlling unknown. A reference count for the aggregate as a whole is maintained so that it is kept alive if there are one or more references to any of the interfaces supported by either the control or noncontrol objects.

It is possible for an object to call a method that may cause the object to be released. A technique known as artificial reference counting can be used to guard against this untimely release. The object calls **IUnknown::AddRef** before the potentially destructive method call and **IUnknown::Release** after it. If the object in question is aggregatable, it must call the controlling unknown's implementations of **AddRef** and **Release** (*pUnkOuter*->**AddRef** and *pUnkOuter*->**Release**) to artificially increment the reference count rather than its own implementations. For more information about reference counting, see "Reference Counting Rules" in Chapter 5, "Component Object Interfaces and Functions."

When shutting down, aggregatable objects should either not attempt to use their *pUnkOuter* pointer or should set *pUnkOuter* to their own **IUnknown** implementation.

Figure 3.2 shows how the coordination between the control and noncontrol object works. The control object exposes the controlling unknown, Interface A and Interface B. The noncontrol object supports Interface C. All three interfaces derive from **IUnknown**.

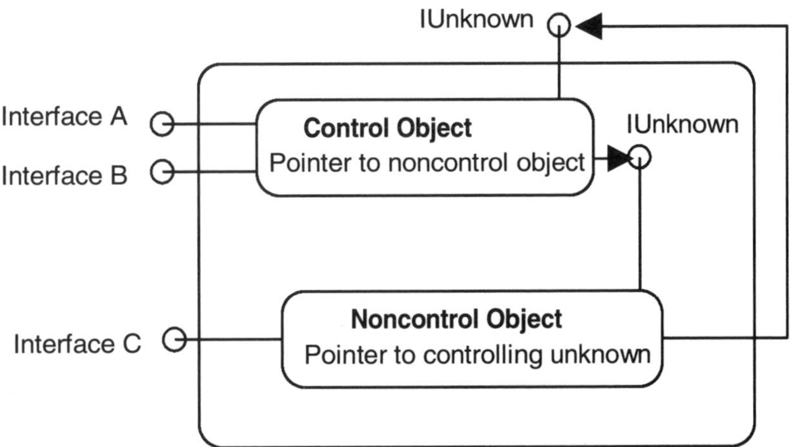

Figure 3.2 Internal structure of an aggregate

The control object holds a pointer to the noncontrol object's **IUnknown** implementation so it can call the noncontrol methods when appropriate. The noncontrol object holds a pointer to the controlling unknown for the same reason. The pointer to the controlling unknown is supplied when the noncontrol object is instantiated. Whereas the controlling unknown is available to the outside, as is indicated by the line and circle identifying it extending past the bounds of the aggregate, the noncontrol object's **IUnknown** implementation works locally and is not obtainable from outside the aggregate. It is called solely by the controlling unknown to obtain instances of the noncontrol interfaces, such as Interface C, to expose to the outside.

Aggregation is entirely optional and designing for it is an optional decision to be made for each object. However, providing support for aggregation costs little in time and complexity. The reward is larger than the cost; it enables the effective reuse of interface implementations. The key in implementing an aggregate object is making the correct delegation decision in both the aggregated and non-aggregated situations.

The following code example is an aggregate object implemented using C++ nested classes. The constructor takes as an argument the pointer to the control object's **IUnknown** implementation, or controlling unknown. If this pointer is NULL, indicating that the new object is not being aggregated, the *m_pUnkOuter* member is set to the address of *m_Unknown*, the local implementation of **IUnknown**. If **pUnkOuter** is not NULL, indicating that the new object is being aggregated, *m_pUnkOuter* is set to *pUnkOuter*. The **InterfaceA** implementations of the **IUnknown** methods forward their calls to the controlling unknown implementations. The controlling unknown **IUnknown** implementations manage queries for interfaces for the aggregate and maintain a master reference count.

```
class cAggregateObj
{
public:
    CAggregateObj(LPUNKNOWN pUnkOuter);
    ~CAggregateObj();

    HRESULT CreateObj(REFCLSID rclsid, REFIID riid, void * * ppvObj);
private:
    struct CUnknown : IUnknown
    {
        CUnknown(CAggregateObj * pAgg)
        { m_pAgg = pAgg; }

        HRESULT QueryInterface(REFIID riid, void * * ppvObj)
        unsigned long AddRef(void) { return ++m_ObjRefCount; }
        unsigned long Release(void);
      private:
        CAggregateObj * m_pAgg;
    }
    friend CUnknown;
    CUnknown m_Unknown;

    struct CInterfaceA : InterfaceA
    {
        CInterfaceA(CAggregateObj * pAgg)
        { m_pAgg = pAgg; }
```

```
        HRESULT QueryInterface(REFIID riid, void * * ppvObj)
        { return m_pAgg->m_pUnkOuter->QueryInterface
            (riid, ppvObj); }
        unsigned long AddRef(void) {return m_pAgg->m_pUnkOuter-
>AddRef();}
        unsigned long Release(void)
        {return m_pAgg->m_pUnkOuter->Release();}

        HRESULT MethodA1(void * * ppvObj);
        HRESULT MethodA2(unsigned long dwArg);

      private:
        CAggregateObj FAR * m_pAgg;
    }
    friend CInterfaceA;
    CInterfaceA m_InterfaceA;

private:
    unsigned long    m_ObjRefCount;
    LPUNKNOWN        m_pUnkOuter;
    LPSTORAGE        m_pStg;
    LPOLEOBJECT      m_pOleObj;
};
```

Grouping Interfaces

Interface relationships are based on the ability to successfully obtain interface pointers by using **IUnknown::QueryInterface**. Although interface implementors are advised to design objects in such a way that many interfaces are accessible from many other interfaces, there is generally no guarantee to an interface user, that a specific interface is accessible from another interface. This means that given one interface, it usually cannot be assumed that **QueryInterface** returns a pointer to a second interface because implementations of **QueryInterface** are application-specific.

There are three ways in which two interfaces can be related. For example, consider Interfaces A and B in the following list:

1. Given a pointer to Interface A, it should be possible to obtain a pointer to Interface B. Interface A and Interface B are managed by a single reference count. OLE defines the following interfaces that fall in this category:
   - **IOleObject**, **IDataObject**, **IViewObject**, **IOleCache**, **IOleInPlaceObject,** and **IPersistStorage**. If the object is a link, **IOleLink** should also be available.
   - **IPersistFile** and **IOleItemContainer**.
   - **IOleClientSite** and **IOleInPlaceSite**.
2. Given a pointer to Interface A, it must not be possible to obtain a pointer to Interface B. Interface A and Interface B can be managed by either a single reference count or separate reference counts. **IOleInPlaceActiveObject** and **IOleInPlaceObject** fall in this category. **IStorage** and **IStream**, typically implemented by OLE, also fall in this category.
3. Given a pointer to Interface A, it might be possible to obtain a pointer to Interface B, depending on the implementing application. Interface A and Interface B can be managed by a single reference count. Clients of the interfaces **cannot** assume it is always possible to obtain the same set of interfaces in this category from all implementing applications. The decision to group these interfaces is up to the implementor, and there is no guarantee they will be implemented in the same manner by all applications.

All OLE interfaces not mentioned as belonging to the first or second groups belong to the third type. These interfaces can be grouped in a manner that works best for the application. It is wise to implement interfaces together whenever possible, because it leads to greater flexibility and interconnectivity. Implementing interfaces together implies they are within a single object supported by one piece of memory. The interfaces share one **IUnknown::QueryInterface** implementation that recognizes all related interfaces. Pointers to the interfaces are managed by a single reference count.

An object that has multiple groups of interfaces, each managed by its own reference count, is kept alive if there is at least one reference to any interface in one of the groups.

For interfaces that cannot be implemented together, there are two possible approaches. They can be implemented either in separate objects, or in a single object that manages the interfaces independently. In the single object approach, there can be one **IUnknown::QueryInterface** implementation or several, depending on the number of interface groups in the object. In the single **QueryInterface** implementation, explicit steps must be taken to return pointers only to related interfaces.

Implementing OLE Applications

This section describes key implementation tasks that pertain to OLE container and object applications. Where implementation differs depending on the type of application, these differences are described.

Starting OLE Applications

The following list of tasks are performed by OLE applications before they display their main window and begin processing events. These tasks are described in greater detail in the following sections.

- Register to receive OLE 2 apple events by registering the class of event interested in receiving with the **AEInstallEventHandler** function.
- Verify that the correct registry information is in the OLE 2 Registration Database file, located in the Extensions folder. (Containers that do not support linking to embedded objects do not need to do this.)
- Call **InitOleManager** to start Microsoft OLE Extension, which exposes the OLE libraries.
- Check the application's compatibility with the OLE libraries.
- Initialize the OLE libraries.
- **C-based applications only:** Initialize the OLE interface VTBL data structures.
- Register the **IMessageFilter** interface implementation to manage concurrency.
- Determine how the application was started.
- Register the application's class object(s), if required.
- Initialize any flags and variables used to maintain the state of OLE objects and/or interfaces.

Registering to Receive OLE 2 Apple Events

In order to receive OLE 2 apple events, an application must register to receive the class of event using **AEInstallEventHandler**, passing in the Class and Event ID, as shown in the following example:

```
myErr = AEInstallEventHandler ('OLE2', 'EVNT', (EventHandlerProcPtr)
RemoteLowLevelEvt, 0, false);
```

The following table describes the classes of OLE events an application might register to receive.

Class of event	Event ID	Meaning
OLE2	EVNT	This event allows an in-place container to receive mouse down events.
OLE2	AUTO	This event indicates that an application was started by an OLE container application. An application will always receive this event when launched by OLE.
DDE	EMBD	This event indicates that an application was started for programmatic access. An application that supports OLE automation will receive this event when launched by OLE if its registration entry contains the /Automation switch.

Verifying Entries in the Registration Database

On startup, an object application should verify the existence of itself and OLE default object handler are present in the Registration Database file. If the information is incorrect or missing, the object application should automatically update it, otherwise the application will not be found should a user try to activate an object belonging to the object application. In addition, an application should also check for the existence of its own object handlers and in-process object applications. Mini object applications should do these same steps before they exit.

For more information on registering applications, see Chapter 4, "Registering Object Applications."

Initializing the Microsoft OLE Extension

Before an application can use the OLE libraries, it must initialize the extension, "Microsoft OLE Extension," which runs in the background and exposes the OLE libraries for use by an application. To start Microsoft OLE Extension, applications call **InitOleManager**.

Verifying Build Version Compatibility of OLE Libraries

Applications can be compiled to run against only one released major build version of the OLE library and the Component Object library while they are using any of the incremental minor build versions. For example, an application that was compiled against build version 23.0 of the libraries would safely run against 23.0 and any of the minor build version releases, provided the minor build versions are greater than or equal to the minor version that the application was compiled against.

With any given release of the OLE library there is a file called OLE*x*VER.H, which contains the major and minor build versions, defined as "rmm" and "rup." To get the build versions, applications call **OleBuildVersion** or **CoBuildVersion**. These functions return the major and minor build version numbers from this file. It is unlikely that the major build version would change between releases, but applications should still ensure compatibility by calling the functions before intializing the libraries. If the library was updated to another major build version and the application had not been compiled against that build version, then the application should not call OleInitialize (or CoInitialize) to initialize the OLE library or the Component Object library, respectively.

Initializing the C-Based Interface VTBL Data Structures

A C-based OLE application typically implements its interfaces as nested data structures. Interface data structure initialization involves allocating memory and setting each member to an initial value. These structures can be allocated and initialized in any order but, it is required that the **IUnknown** and **IClassFactory** interface structures be initialized before registering a class of object(s).

Applications written in C must explicitly initialize each interface VTBL. Typically the VTBLs are initialized as part of creating the application object's window, before the window is shown to the user. Initializing the VTBLs involves setting each of the VTBL pointers to the appropriate method implementation.

The following code sample illustrates how a C program might initialize the VTBL for the **IUnknown** interface. The **IUnknown** interface is implemented in a data structure nested in *MyObject*. The members in the VTBL are set to the application's unique implementations of the **IUnknown** methods, IUnknown_MyObj_QueryInterface, IUnknown_MyObj_AddRef, and IUnknown_MyObj_Release.

```
myUnknownVtbl.QueryInterface = IUnknown_MyObj_QueryInterface;
myUnknownVtbl.AddRef         = IUnknown_MyObj_AddRef;
myUnknownVtbl.Release        = IUnknown_MyObj_Release;
pMyObject->m_Unknown->pVtbl  = &myUnknownVtbl;
```

Registering the IMessageFilter Interface Implementation

The **IMessageFilter** interface *must* be implemented by OLE applications in order to manage concurrency-related issues. On startup, a Macintosh OLE application must register its **IMessageFilter** interface implementation so that it can correctly handle concurrency issues while it is involved in remoted calls (such as the processing of events while awaiting the reply to a remoted call).

To register an **IMessageFilter** interface implementation, an application calls **CoRegisterMessageFilter**. For more information on the **IMessageFilter** interface and concurrency issues, see Chapter 13, "Concurrency Management."

Determining the Start-Up Method

Because an application's set of initialization tasks is affected by its method of start-up, an OLE application must determine whether it was started by a user or as part of activating a linked or embedded object. Applications started by OLE on behalf of a container of an embedded or linked object will receive a DDE class EMBD type Apple event. The absence of the Apple event indicates that the user is in control.

How an application initializes itself depends on its method of start-up:

- An application started by OLE registers its class object(s), providing a pointer to the **IClassFactory** interface. The application window is kept hidden until either **IOleObject::DoVerb** (with an *iVerb* parameter value of OLEIVERB_SHOW) is called for an object application or **IOleClientSite::ShowObject** is called for a container.
- An application started by the user creates either an untitled document or, if a OpenDocument ApplkeEvent is received, a document initialized to the contents of the specified file. The application window is made visible immediately. An application registers its class object(s), indicating that multiple objects can be handled or created. Because a single-document interface (SDI) application can only work with one user document at a time, it does not register its class object(s).

For more information on creating and opening documents, see "Opening Compound Documents," later in this chapter.

Registering Class Objects and Object Classes

A class object is an object that exposes the **IClassFactory** interface, which is used to create instances of a particular object class. Applications must implement a separate instance of **IClassFactory** for each supported object class. For example, a spreadsheet application that supports a spreadsheet, a graph, and a chart would register three separate object classes.

Each class of object is assigned a unique class identifier (CLSID) that is registered in the Registration Database file. Applications call the **CoRegisterClassObject** function to register the class object, passing it a pointer to its **IClassFactory** interface and the CLSID of the object, which OLE then registers in the internal Class Factory Table.

When registering the CLSID in the table, OLE creates a stub manager that is used to keep track of the number of external references and explicit locks on the object. (An explicit lock is one that results from **CoLockObjectExternal** being called on the object.) Later, OLE will locate this class factory instance registered in the Class Factory Table and use it to create an instance of the object.

Note Every application must have a unique CLSID for each class of object that it supports. By contacting Microsoft directly, you can obtain a unique block of CLSID values. Please specifiy the number of values needed; unless specified, a block of 256 values will be assigned per request.

As shown in Figure 3.3, the class object's *cRef* counter has a value of two, which reflects the reference from the stub manager and the pointer reference from the application.

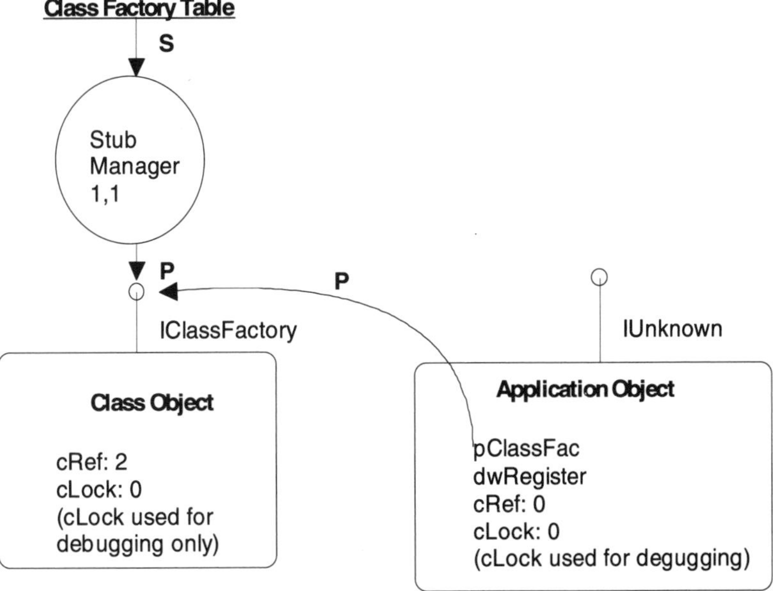

S Strong reference lock (CoLockObjectExternal called on object)
P Interface pointer reference
n,n The sum of external references on an object (leftmost n) and the number that are strong (rightmost n)

Figure 3.3 Effect of registering an object with CoRegisterClassObject

In addition to the CLSID, three other parameters are passed to **CoRegisterClassObject**: a pointer to an instance of the **IClassFactory** interface, the context in which the object code is to be run, and a value that indicates how connections are to be made to the class of object. The context in which the code runs can be one or more of the following values:

Context Value	Meaning
CLSCTX_INPROC_SERVER	Object application is written completely as a DLL.
CLSCTX_INPROC_HANDLER	The code is written as an object handler that is designed to run with an application.
CLSCTX_INPROC_LOCAL	The code is written as a stand-alone application that can run independent of any other code or object handler.

Applications specify how connections are made to the class object with the *grfFlags* parameter to **CoRegisterClassObject**. The following table describes the use of the *grfFlags* parameter:

grfFlags **Value**	**Meaning**
REGCLS_SINGLEUSE	Allows a single connection to the object. Typically specified for object applications that support only one instance of a document.
REGCLS_MULTIPLEUSE	Enables multiple connections to the object. Typically used with object applications that allow more than one document to be opened at a time.

On shutdown, the OLE application must revoke the register the register class object(s) by calling **CoRevokeClassObject**.

Locking an Application in Memory

OLE uses the concept of strong and weak locks. Whereas a strong lock on an object will keep it in memory, a weak lock will not. Strong locks are required, for example, when there are links to embedded objects that need to be updated. The embedded object's container must remain in memory until the update process is complete. There must also be a strong lock on an application's class object to ensure the application stays alive until it has finished providing object services to its containers. All external references to an object result in a strong reference lock being placed on the object.

After an application calls **CoRegisterClassObject**, it should call **CoLockObjectExternal** to ask OLE to maintain a strong lock on its class object. **CoLockObjectExternal** locks any object so that its reference count cannot decrement to zero. It can also be used to release such a lock.

Note A user has explicit control over the lifetime of an application, even if there are external locks on the application. Thus, if a user decides to close the application (File Quit), the application must shut down. In the presence of external locks on an object, the application can call **CoDisconnectObject** to force these connections closed prior to shut down.

Opening Compound Documents

Note The information presented in this section assumes an application is saving its native data using the OLE structured storage model. While there is no prerequisite for using structured storage, using it can simplify solutions to storage needs. For an overview of the OLE storage model, see Chapter 9, "Persistent Storage Interfaces and Functions."

A user typically initiates the opening of a compound document by choosing the File New command for new documents or the File Open command for existing documents. The tasks an application has to perform to open existing documents and new ones are the same, except for the added steps of loading an existing document into memory.

Before making an open compound document visible, container applications must complete the following tasks:

1. Allocate memory for the document object, using a class or a structure, and initialize its members.
2. Lock the application object in memory.
3. Create and register a file moniker, if linking to the file is supported.
4. Open a storage object.
5. Load the data (for existing documents only).
6. Change the user interface as appropriate.
7. Register as a drop target (if applicable).
8. Show the document to the user and set the document's dirty flag, as appropriate.
9. If the document was opened by the user, lock the document in memory.

Initializing the Document Structure

Before allocating memory for a new document object, SDI applications check to see whether there is a document already open that needs to be saved. If there is and the document has changes, the application should prompt the user to save the document. An application can open a new document while others are open. For more information on closing a document, see "Closing OLE Compound Documents," later in this chapter.

The type of document being opened determines the user interface changes needing to be made, if any. For example, when the user opens a new untitled document in an object application started by OLE, the application needs to change its user interface menus. When saving a document, applications check the document type in order to call the correct save routine. For information on saving OLE documents, see "Saving OLE Compound Documents," later in this chapter.

To help keep track of the document type and how it is being initialized, applications can define and use constants like the following:

Document Type	Description
DOCTYPE_UNKNOWN	A newly allocated document object exists but has not been initialized with application data yet.
DOCTYPE_NEW	A new document was created by the user by means of the File New command. The document is initialized as an untitled document. The usual user interface for user documents is displayed.
DOCTYPE_FROMFILE	The document was initialized from an existing file using the File Open command (or by using **IPersistFile::Load** being called when binding a link source).The normal user interface for user documents is displayed.
DOCTYPE_EMBEDDED	The document was initialized as an embedded compound document object using the **IStorage** opened by its container. The usual user interface is replaced with the modified user interface for an embedded object.
DOCTYPE_FROMSTG	The document is initialized using data from the **IStorage** provided by using **IPersistStorage::Load**. The usual user interface for user documents is displayed.

The document type is initially set to DOCTYPE_UNKNOWN because the actual document type is not known until the document object is initialized with data.

Applications should keep track of references to its document object in a data member of the object. To guard this object from accidental destruction while it is being initialized, the reference counter should be intentionally incremented at the beginning of the initialization process. When initialization is complete, the counter can be decremented. This technique is known as artificial reference counting and is explained more fully in the section "Reference Counting Rules" in Chapter 5, "Component Object Interfaces and Functions."

A document-level reference counter can work in conjunction with a corresponding counter in the application object. To guarantee the application is not accidentally closed while the document is open, both counters should be incremented.

Creating and Registering File Monikers

Applications that allow containers to link to their file-based documents must create a file moniker to represent the open document and register the moniker in the running object table. The file moniker is created by passing in the document's complete path in a call to **CreateFileMoniker**. To register the moniker, make the following two calls: **GetRunningObjectTable** to retrieve a pointer to the running object table and **IRunningObjectTable::Register** to complete the registration. For more information about monikers and the running object table, see Chapter 8, "Linking Interfaces and Functions."

Opening Storage Objects

Storage objects are handled differently, depending on whether the application is an object application or a container and whether the File New or File Open command was selected.

When opening a new untitled document, a container creates a temporary root storage object in which to create child objects for saving compound document objects. This outermost root object forms the base from which all object storage elements are created in the container.

To create a temporary root storage object, containers call **StgCreateDocfile**, specifying NULL for the document filename (*pwcsName*) and STGM_DELETEONRELEASE as one of the values to the *grfMode* parameter. Additional values for the *grfMode* parameter determine the access mode (transacted or direct) in which to open the object.

In transacted mode, the changes to an object are buffered in temporary files until the application commits (saves) or reverts (destroys) the changes. In direct mode, the changes are immediately saved to the open storage object with no chance of undoing the changes. By default, if no mode value is specified, the storage object is opened in direct mode.

Containers must provide scribble-enabled storage to the objects they contain. However, sometimes there is a need to instantiate an object in read-only mode. If the object's storage is read-only, it must also be opened in transacted mode, since transacted mode is the only scribble-enabled read-only mode. An object can call **IStorage::Stat** to determine its storage mode.

A root storage object opened in direct mode and that can be written to must always specify STGM_SHARE_EXCLUSIVE for its access mode.

When opening a file-based document, an application needs to be able to open the document as an **IStorage** object and read the document's data. Object applications typically read in the data and then close the storage object until it is time to save the document. Containers, on the other hand, must keep their root storage object open at all times to ensure compound document objects have access to their storage.

To open an existing storage object, an application calls **StgOpenStorage**, passing it the filename and the access mode to use.

Loading Objects from Storage

An application that saves its application data to compound files will, after opening an existing storage object, proceed to initialize the document object with the contents of the contained stream object(s).

To read the contents of a storage object, an application calls **IStorage::OpenStream**, which opens an existing named **IStream** instance using the access mode specified by the *grfMode* parameter. To read the contents of an open data stream into memory, an application calls **IStream::Read**.

A storage object can have nested child storage objects, which are accessed through **IStorage::OpenStorage**.

As part of opening and reading storage objects, applications should test the compatibility of the document with the current version of the application. If the document is incompatible, the application should display an error message and open an untitled document instead. Testing for compatibility can be done easily by storing the version number of the application as part of its native data.

Changing the User Interface

An application sets the title of the document window either to the name of the file from which the document was initialized or to an untitled document name.

If an SDI object application started by OLE opens a document, the File New and File Open commands are disabled and the File Save and File Quit commands are replaced with the File Save Copy As and File Quit and Return to <*container document*> commands. The File Save Copy As command enables a user to save an embedded object in a document other than its containing document.

An object application started by OLE makes the same user interface changes as does an SDI object application, except these changes are made when the document window changes from a user-opened document to one needed to service an embedded object. Also, an object application does not disable the File Open and File New menu commands.

Registering a Document for Drag and Drop

Application windows that can accept dropped data must register as valid drop targets by calling **RegisterDragDrop**, passing a pointer to their **IDropTarget** implementation. The object exposing the **IDropTarget** interface must have at least one external reference lock on it. Without an external lock, the object is in an unstable state and might be destroyed prematurely. Calling **CoLockObjectExternal** just before the document is made visible to the user and before **RegisterDragDrop** is called safeguards the object.

Showing the Document and Setting the Dirty Flag

The application needs to make the document visible to the user and set a flag to indicate whether data has changed since it was last saved to storage. For a document opened by OLE, the document dirty flag should be set to TRUE to ensure the container always gets the most up-to-date representation of the object. Documents created or opened by the user should set their dirty flag to FALSE. To explicitly lock the document in memory on behalf of the user, the application calls **CoLockObjectExternal** (*pUnk*, TRUE, NULL).

Figure 3.4 shows the state of a document object opened by OLE. This document object is the data source for a linked object in a container. OLE opened the document via a moniker bind operation. (Had the document been opened by the user in an SDI application, the class object would not have been registered.) The reference counts for the objects are stored in the data member *cRef*. As shown, the document and application objects have a reference count of one, reflecting the external reference held by the stub managers. The stub managers keep track of the total number of external references (leftmost number) to the objects and how many of those references are strong (rightmost number).

The class object has a reference count of two: the one that OLE holds on the object on behalf of the class factory table registration, and the pointer reference to the object's **IClassFactory** interface.

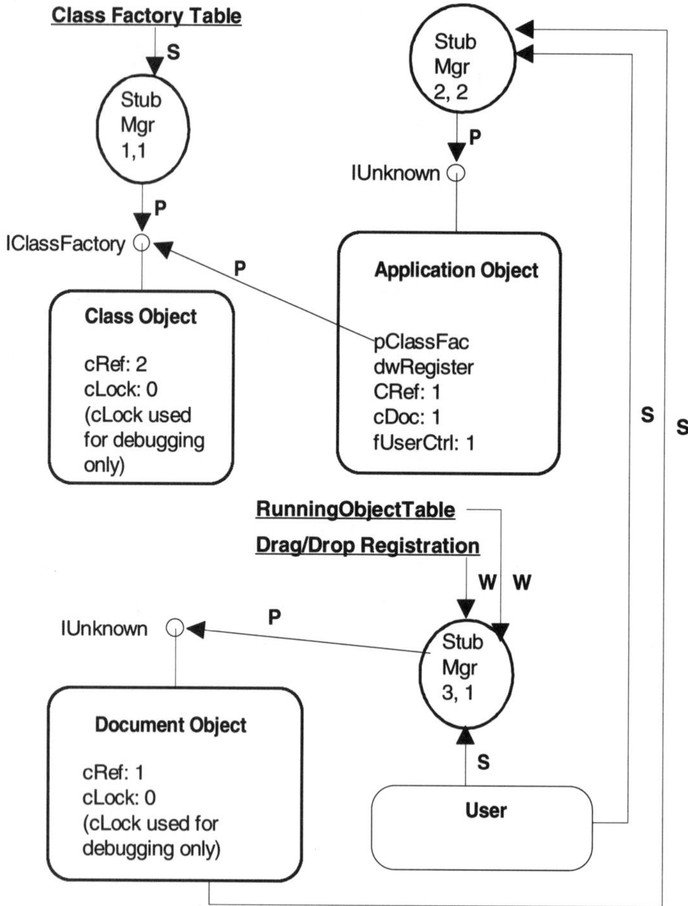

Figure 3.4 Reference locks on a document during a file moniker bind

Using the Insert Object Dialog

The Insert Object dialog box, which is accessed from the Edit menu, allows a user to create a new or embedded object from either a default object application object or a file.

The Insert Object dialog, provides three options for creating objects: Create New, Create From File, and Display as Icon. The Create New option creates an embedded object from a list of registered object application object types. When the

Create New option is selected, a list of currently registered objects is displayed from which the user can choose. The helper function **OleUIInsertObject** from the sample user interface library can be called to display the dialog box, accept the user's selection, and optionally go on to create the necessary object.

The Create From File option allows users to create either a new embedded object from a file or a link to a file if the Link check box is chosen. The Display as Icon check box allows users to insert an object as an icon.

The Insert Object dialog in Figure 3.5 shows the Create From File option.

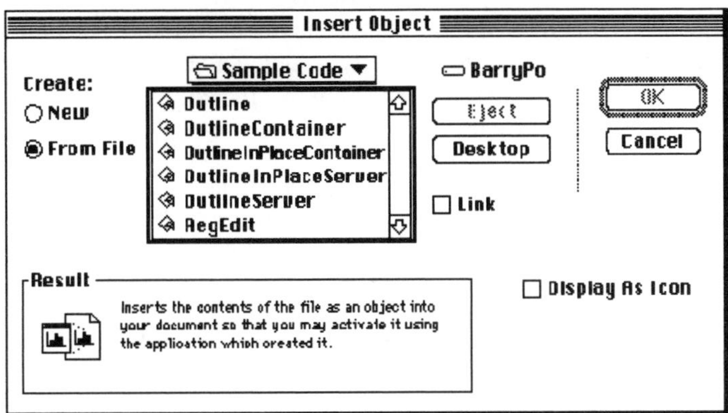

Figure 3.5 Insert Object dialog for creating an object from a file

The implementation of the three options is identical from the container's point of view, with one exception. A different OLE creation API function is called for each option. The container does the following steps:

1. Displays the Insert Object dialog box, whichallows the user to make a selection.
2. Allocates a storage object and allocates and initializes the container site.
3. Depending on the user's selection, calls the appropriate OLE creation API.
4. Sets up advisory connections between the object application and the newly initialized container site.
5. Integrates the object into the container document.
6. Makes the object visible.
7. Marks the document as changed.

Calling OLE to Create the Object

OLE provides several helper functions for creating embedded and linked objects. As noted above, depending on the option selected by the user, a different OLE creation function is called.

The following table lists the OLE creation functions used with the Insert Object dialog and provides a brief description:

OLE Object Creation Function	Type of Object Created
OleCreate	New embedded object.
OleCreateFromFile	Embedded object from a file.
OleCreateLinkToFile	Linked object to a file.

The OLE creation functions take several parameters, among them the CLSID of the object being created, the name of the file (if appropriate), the interface ID to be returned, the render option for cache initialization, and a pointer to the container's **IOleClientSite** interface. The typical container sets the render option to OLERENDER_DRAW, indicating that the compound document object should determine the formats to cache.

Containers, if they choose, can implement the functionality provided in the creation helper functions. However, most developers will want to use these functions to minimize errors and speed implementation.

If preferred, containers can implement this functionality in a different way. The function calls made in **OleCreate** and the purpose of each call is listed in the following table in the order in which they are made:

Object Creation Function Called	Purpose of Call
CoCreateInstance	Creates a class object for the object to be created and returns a pointer to that class object (**IClassFactory** interface).
IClassFactory::CreateInstance	Allocates and initializes the new object.
IOleObject::SetClientSite	Passes a pointer to the container's **IOleClientSite** interface to the object.
IPersistStorage::InitNew	Passes a pointer to the storage object.
OleRun	Runs the object and initializes the cache if a cache has been requested.

Setting Up Advisory Connections

When the OLE creation function returns, the container registers to receive either OLE notifications and data or view notifications. Typical compound document containers that rely on OLE to draw their embedded and linked objects register for OLE and view notifications. Containers handling the caching of their own presentation data can register for data notifications rather than view notifications. These containers pass OLERENDER_NONE in the render option in the call to the OLE creation function and then call **IUnknown::QueryInterface** asking for the **IOleCache** interface, creating the cache(s) needed with the **IOleCache** methods.

The following table indicates the interface methods that should be called to set up notification registration and the type of notifications handled by each method:

Interface Method Called	Type of Notification Registered For
IViewObject::SetAdvise	Registers for view notifications.
IOleObject::Advise	Registers for OLE notifications.
IDataObject::DAdvise	Registers for data change notifications.

When containers are finished registering, they call **IOleObject::SetHostNames** to inform the object of its name in the container. The object is made visible with a call to **IOleObject::DoVerb**.

Activating Objects

Activation refers to invoking a particular operation, or verb, available for a compound document object when it is selected in its container. The operations can be invoked on both embedded and linked objects. Activation requires that the compound document object be in the running state so the object application is available to supply the requested operation.

The process of getting the object into the running state is known as binding. Because binding is handled by OLE, it is transparent to containers and object applications.

An embedded object is activated when the user selects a verb from the Edit or popup menus or double-clicks the object. The container makes a call to **IOleObject::DoVerb**, and the object application either activates the object in place or in a separate window in the object application process space, as is appropriate. Binding an embedded object involves locating and running the object application with the object data passed from the container.

From the container's perspective, activating a linked object is the same as activating an embedded object. However, the internal process required to activate the link source is much different from the process for activating an embedded object. When a linked object is bound, each of the pieces that make up the link source's moniker, typically a generic composite moniker, is evaluated. When the binding process is complete, the link source's application, if not already running, is forced into the running state.

Linked objects must be edited in their original source application. This usually means that the linked object must be edited in a separate window rather than in place. The use of the separate window indicates that an edit process is occurring, which is important because changes made to a linked object might potentially impact other objects. However, if the link is to an embedded object whose object application supports in-place editing, the embedded object can be edited in place. Other types of activation, such as play or rewind, can also be done in place.

Activating an Embedded Object

Binding an embedded object involves locating and running the object's object application using the unique CLSID stored with the object. The object application is sent a DDE class EMBD type Apple event, indicating it is being launched to support an OLE operation. For information on initializing an object application for OLE operations, see "Starting OLE Applications," earlier in this chapter.

Figure 3.6 shows what happens after a container makes a call to **IOleObject::DoVerb** to activate an embedded object. The site for the embedded object in the container has a pointer to one of the object's interfaces in the object handler, typically **IOleObject**. The object handler is responsible for locating and starting the object application. A pointer to the object in the object application is stored in the object handler.

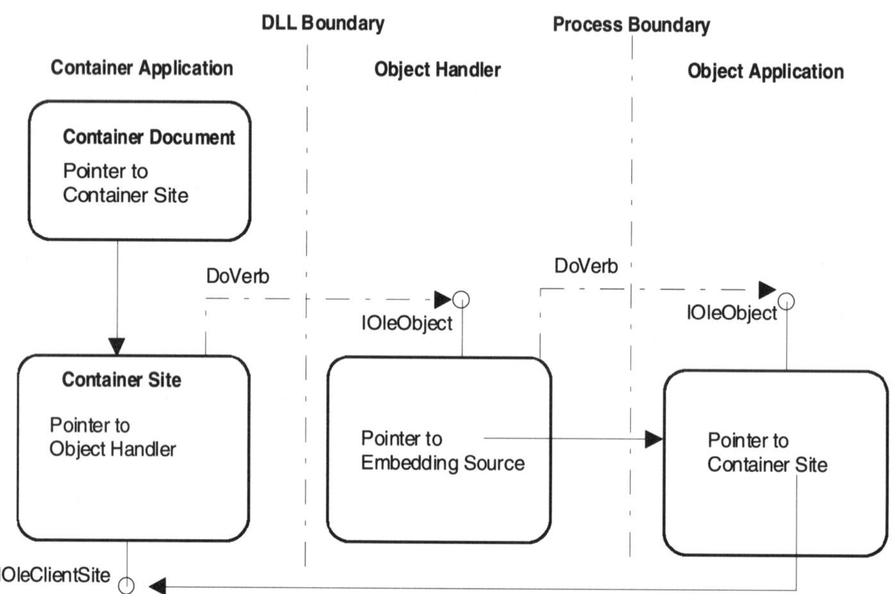

Figure 3.6 Relationship between an embedded object, the object handler, and the object application

An object application's implementation of **IOleObject::DoVerb** for activating in open mode is quite simple: **IOleObject::DoVerb** determines which of the supported verbs have been requested and then initiates the action required. The object returns OLEOBJ_S_INVALIDVERB if the verb is invalid.

Activating a Linked Object

The link source for a linked object can be a file-based document, a selection of data within a document, an embedded object, or a selection of data within an embedded object. Each of these link sources is represented by a moniker that is itself made up of one or more monikers of the following types:

- **Item moniker**: a null terminated string for naming an item or object.
- **File moniker**: a wrapper for the path name in the native file system (always the leftmost piece in a generic composite moniker).
- **Generic composite moniker**: a concatenation of two or more monikers. A generic composite moniker is made up of one file moniker and one or more item monikers.

The following table briefly describes the types of monikers typically assigned to link source data:

Link Source Type	Type of Moniker
Document stored in a disk file.	File moniker.
Range of data within a document that might or might not be explicitly named by the user (pseudo object).	Generic composite moniker comprised of a file moniker and an item moniker to represent the pseudo object.
Part or all of an embedded object (either within the same container or in a different container)	Generic composite moniker comprised of a file moniker and two item monikers, one for the object in the container and one for the data in the object application

A pseudo object is created when a link is made to a selection of data within a document. Pseudo objects are not associated with an identifiable storage location. The pseudo object is assigned a generic composite moniker consisting of the file moniker for its document and an item moniker for the data range. Figure 3.7 shows the typical components of a generic composite moniker.

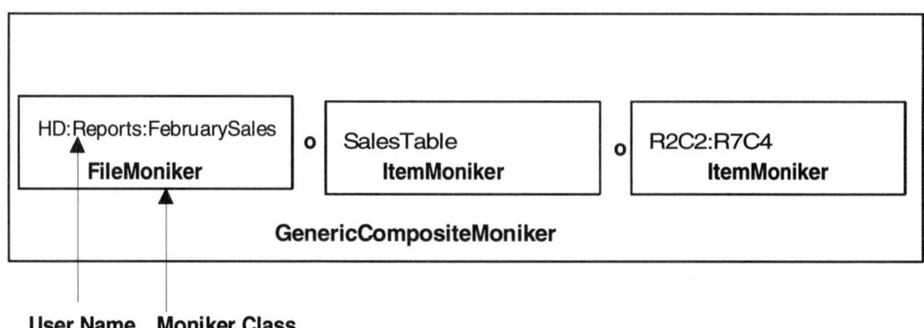

Figure 3.7 Components of a generic composite moniker

Figure 3.8 shows what happens after a container makes a call to **IOleObject::DoVerb** to activate a linked object. Except for the insertion of the OLE link object between the container site and the object handler, the flow of control for linked objects is identical to the flow of control for embedded objects. The OLE link object's implementation of **IOleObject::DoVerb** initiates the moniker binding process.

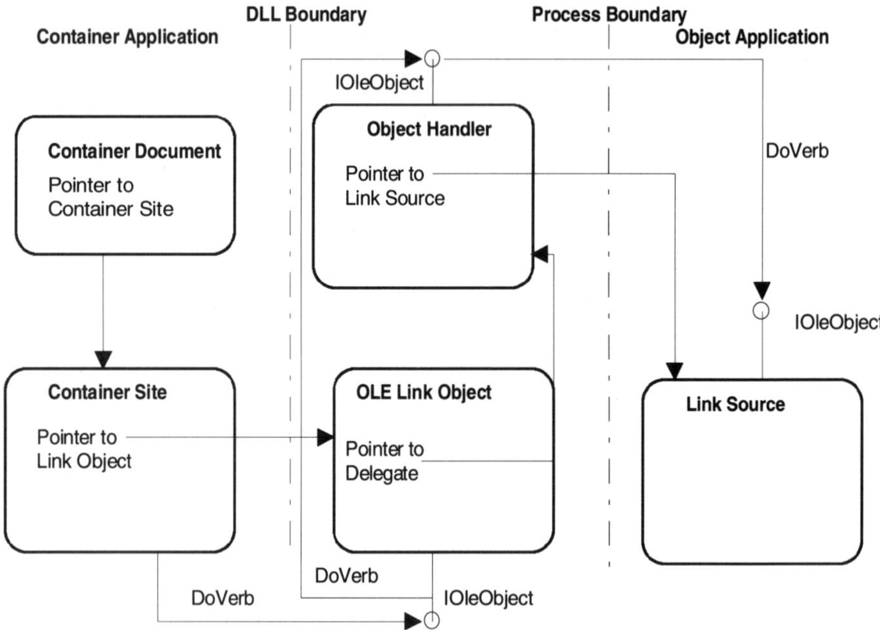

Figure 3.8 Relationship between a linked object, the OLE link, the class handler, and the object application

Figure 3.9 illustrates how editing a link to an embedded object that is typically edited in place might appear to the user. Two containers are involved, one to hold the linked object and the other to hold the embedded object. When the user double-clicks the linked object, the moniker for its link source is bound. This starts the object application for the embedded object. Because the object application's **IOleObject::DoVerb** implementation supports in-place editing, the link source is edited in place within its embedding container.

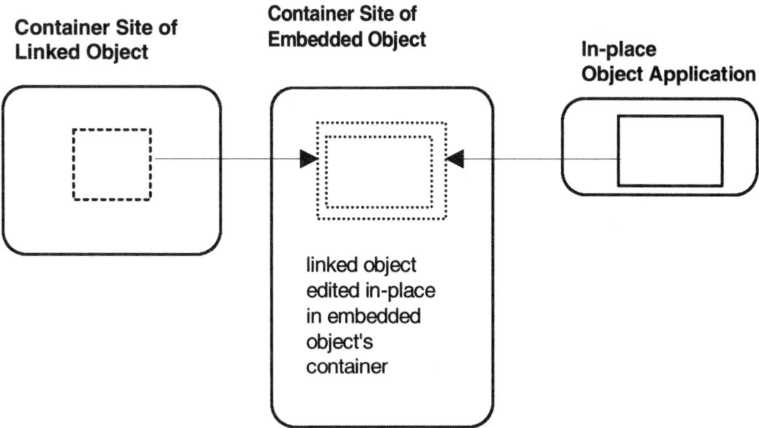

Figure 3.9 Editing a link to an in-place embedded object

Binding a File Moniker

When a file moniker is bound, the running object table is checked first to see whether the object is already running. If it is, the file moniker then binds to the running object. If the object is not currently running, applications call the OLE function **GetClassFile** to determine the object class associated with the file. **GetClassFile** runs the appropriate object application, if it is not already running, and then calls **IPersistFile::Load** to open the file and **IClassFactory::CreateInstance** to instantiate the object. For more information on the strategies that GetClassFile uses to determine the object's class, see the description of **GetClassFile** in Chapter 9, "Persistent Storage Interfaces and Functions."

Binding an Item Moniker

An item moniker requires the **IOleItemContainer** interface of the object to its left to bind. **IOleItemContainer** is implemented by all object applications that allow linking to pseudo objects and all containers that allow linking to embedded objects. When the item moniker gains access to the interface, **IOleItemContainer::GetObject** is called to locate and run the object represented by the item name and to return a pointer to one of the object's interfaces. The caller passes the item name, a value that indicates the amount of time the caller is willing to wait for the object, an interface identifier, and a place to return the object. The object application's implementation of **IOleItemContainer::GetObject** returns the pointer to an active pseudo object. The container's implementation of **GetObject** returns a pointer to an interface belonging to the running object. **GetObject** cannot be recursive; it must get the object and then return.

Binding a Generic Composite Moniker

Binding a generic composite moniker involves binding all its pieces. The process starts with the rightmost piece, typically an item moniker. OLE locates and loads the object represented by the item moniker by calling **IOleItemContainer::GetObject**, and then initiates binding on the piece to the left. This process is repeated until the binding of the leftmost moniker, a file moniker, causes the object application to be run (if it is not already running). The file containing the link source is opened and loaded, and the link source is placed in the running state.

Verifying Links

IOleItemContainer::IsRunning provides an application with a way to determine whether an object identified by a specific name is running. Determining the state of a link source is important for maintaining active link connections.

Containers call **IOleObject::IsUpToDate** to find out whether they have the most up-to-date data. Linked objects can be outdated if the document containing the link source has changed. If **IOleObject::IsUpToDate** returns FALSE, containers of manual links that are connected can get updated data by calling **IOleLink::GetBoundSource** to get a pointer to the link source. The container can then call **QueryInterface** on the returned pointer asking for a pointer to **IDataObject**. **IDataObject:GetData** can then be called to get the most up-to-date data.

Registering an Object's Verbs

Verbs are the set of operations supported by a particular object. The set of object-specific verbs can differ for each object type because different verbs make sense for different objects. For example, a sound object's verbs displayed to the user might include play, rewind, and edit, while a text object might only support edit. An object application registers a set of object-specific verbs in the Registration Database file for each type of object supported. These user-selectable verbs are assigned sequentially positive values, beginning with 0 for the primary verb (in order to maintain compatibility with OLE 1 containers).

Compound document objects must also register and support a set of special OLE verbs. (These verbs are not to be confused with those that appear on the Edit and popup menus for the user to select.) The OLE verbs have a predefined meaning and value for each supported object. The OLE verbs include OLEIVERB_PRIMARY, OLEIVERB_SHOW, OLEIVERB_OPEN, OLEIVERB_HIDE, and a few other verbs that apply only to in-place activation. For detailed information about verbs, see **IOleObject::DoVerb**.

OLE verbs are typically invoked programmatically and are registered in the Registration Database file. OLEIVERB_PRIMARY has a value of 0; the other OLE verbs have negative values in sequential order beginning with -1. Refer also to Chapter 4, "Registering Object Applications."

Managing Notifications

Notifications are callbacks generated by an object when it detects a change. Containers and other clients of an object register to receive notifications of interest by setting up an advisory connection to the object. Through this connection, the object undergoing the change notifies the advisory sink. Some of the changes that cause a notification to be sent include when the object is renamed, saved to persistent storage, closed, or its view changes. Notifications ensure that a container has the most up-to-date information about its embedded and linked objects.

There are three types of notifications: OLE (or compound document), data, and view. The OLE notifications include OnRename, OnSave, OnLinkSrcChange, and OnClose. Containers and other objects interested in receiving OLE notifications call the object's **IOleObject::Advise** method, passing it a pointer to its **IAdviseSink** interface implementation. (Advise connections are not saved with objects.) The **IAdviseSink** interface is implemented by all objects interested in receiving notifications of any type. An extension of **IAdviseSink**, **IAdviseSink2**, is implemented by objects that are interested in receiving OnLinkSrcChange notifications. Each type of notification maps to one of the methods in **IAdviseSink** or **IAdviseSink2**. For example, when an object application is saving an embedded object, it generates an OnClose notification that causes the container's **IAdviseSink::OnClose** method to be called.

Notification registration is handled by methods in three different interfaces. To register for OLE notifications, an object calls **IOleObject::Advise.** To register for data change notifications, an object calls **IDataObject::DAdvise**. To register for view notifications, an object calls **IViewObject::SetAdvise**. **IDataObject** and **IOleObject** are implemented by the object application and object handler; **IViewObject** is implemented by the cache.

The five types of notifications are described below:

Notification	Description
OnRename	Sent when the object application's full moniker is initially set or changed. (OLEWHICKMK_OBJFULL is passed as a parameter to **IOleObject::SetMoniker**). Tells the OLE link object to update its moniker. Containers can ignore this notification.
OnSave	Sent when the object application saves the object. If the ADVF flag ADVFCACHE_ONSAVE was specified, tells the OLE link object or object handler to update its cache.

Notification	Description
OnClose	Sent when the object application is closing the object. Tells an OLE link object to release its pointer to the bound link source. Containers can revert the storage to ensure that uncommitted changes are flushed.
OnViewChange	Sent when the object's view (presentation) has changed. Containers need to redraw. Can be sent when the object is in either the running or loaded state.
OnDataChange	Sent when the object's data has changed. Cache might need updating. Linked objects with manual links do not update the cache with OnDataChange.
OnLinkSrcChange	Sent by the OLE link object when it receives the **OnRename** notification from the link source (object) application. The link object updates its moniker and calls **IAdviseSink2::OnLinkSrcChange**

There are a few other methods related to notification registration. **IDataObject::DUnadvise** and **IOleObject::Unadvise** remove a registration; **IDataObject::EnumDAdvise**, **IOleObject::EnumAdvise**, and **IViewObject::GetAdvise** list the registrations currently in effect for the object.

Managing Notification Registration

An object application must manage registration requests, keeping track of who is interested in which notifications and sending those notifications when appropriate. OLE provides two component objects to simplify this task: the OleAdviseHolder for OLE notifications and the DataAdviseHolder for data notifications.

The OleAdviseHolder, created with a call to the OLE API function **CreateOleAdviseHolder**, is an object provided by OLE that implements the **IOleAdviseHolder** interface. **IOleAdviseHolder** contains methods for managing registration requests and sending notifications to **IAdviseSink** sites.

The DataAdviseHolder is an object provided by OLE that implements the **IDataAdviseHolder** interface and is used to manage data notifications. Applications can call the OLE API function **CreateDataAdviseHolder** to instantiate a DataAdviseHolder.

When an object application uses one of the advise holder objects, a call to one of the registration methods in **IOleObject** or **IDataObject** results in the corresponding function being called in the advise holder object. For example, the following implementation of **IDataObject::DAdvise** illustrates the use of the DataAdviseHolder to handle data change notification registration:

```
HRESULT IDataObject_DAdvise(
    LPDATAOBJECT     pThis,
    FORMATETC *      pFormatetc,
    unsigned long    advf,
    LPADVISESINK     pAdvise,
    unsigned long *  pdwConnection )
{
    HRESULT hrErr;
    struct MYDOC * pDoc =
        ((struct CDocDataObjectImpl *)pThis)->pDoc;
    *pdwConnection = NULL;

    if (pDoc->m_pDataAdviseHldr == NULL && CreateDataAdviseHolder
         (&pDoc->m_pDataAdviseHldr) != NOERROR)
            return ResultFromScode(E_OUTOFMEMORY);
    else  {
        hrErr = pDoc->m_pDataAdviseHldr->pVtbl->DAdvise(
            pDoc->m_pDataAdviseHldr,
            (LPDATAOBJECT)&pDoc->m_pDataObject,
            pFormatetc,
            advf,
            pAdvise,
            pdwConnection    );
        return hrErr;
    }
```

Among the parameters passed to **IDataObject::DAdvise** is a group of flags, the *advf* parameter in the above example, that controls the advisory connection. These flags are also used with the **IOleCache** methods. The value for the parameter is taken from the enumeration **ADVF**; one or more of these values (or-ed together) can be used.

When a caller specifies ADVF_PRIMEFIRST as the *advf* parameter, **DAdvise** immediately sends an OnDataChange notification, thus enabling the caller to get the data immediately.

A possible scenario for setting these flags involves a user selecting the Display as Icon check box in the Paste Special dialog. The object is requested with the DVASPECT_ICON aspect value that causes an icon to be placed in the cache. When a data change notification is set up, the caller could specify ADVF_NODATA | ADVF_ONLYONCE | ADVF_PRIMEFIRST in its call to **IDataObject::DAdvise**. The result would be that the only one data change notification would ever be sent and no data would be sent with it. The ADVF_NODATA value can be used whenever the caller does not want OLE to update the cache.

Notification Flow

Notifications originate in the object application and flow to the container by using the object handler. If the object is a linked object, the OLE link object intercepts the notifications from the object handler and notifies the container directly.

All containers, the object handler, and the OLE link object register for OLE notifications. The typical container also registers for view notifications. Data notifications are usually sent to the OLE link object and object handler. A special purpose container, such as a container that renders the data itself (instead of calling the OLE helper function **OleDraw**), might want data notifications instead of view notifications. For example, an embedded chart container with a link to a table can register for data notifications. Because a change to the table affects the chart, the receipt of a data notification would direct the container to call **IDataObject::GetData** to get the new tabular data.

Figure 3.10 shows the notification flow from an object application to an embedded object container that has registered for OLE and view notifications. The solid lines represent memory pointers; the dotted lines represent notifications. Note that the notifications go directly to the **IAdviseSink** interface. Data notifications sent to the object handler are forwarded to the appropriate cache element in the object handler's cache object. If a container has registered for view notifications rather than data notifications, the cache generates an OnViewChange notification that it sends to the container site.

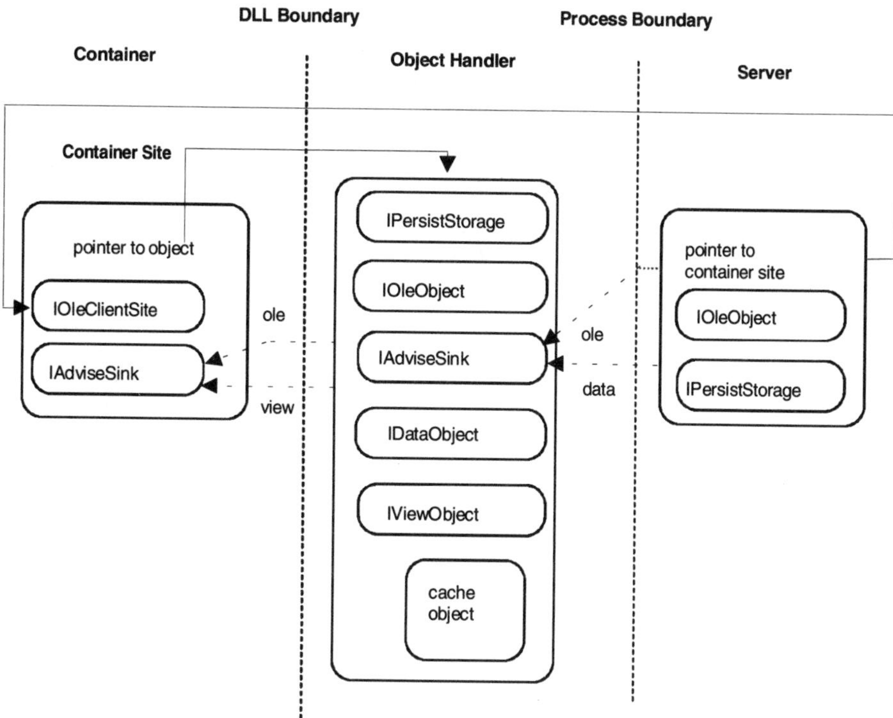

Figure 3.10 Notification flow for an embedded object

For a linked object, the flow is slightly different. Instead of holding a pointer to the object handler, the container points to the OLE link object. The OLE link object points to its delegate, the object handler. There is no pointer from the object application back to the container site. The object application, or link source, sends data and OLE notifications to the object handler which in turn sends them on to the OLE link object. The OLE link object generates a view notification it sends to the container, if it has registered for view notifications, and a link source change notification, if appropriate. Figure 3.11 shows the flow for a linked object.

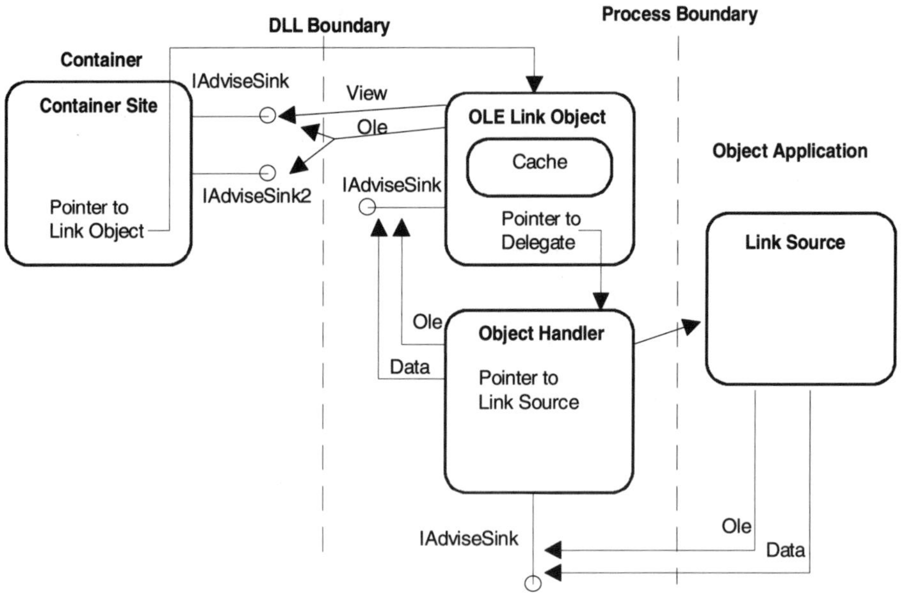

Figure 3.11 Notification flow for a linked object

Figure 3.12 shows how notifications are sent to container sites in separate container applications. The container sites contain linked objects that are linked to the same link source. Note that each container has its own OLE link object and object handler within its process space. The advise holders are objects provided by OLE to keep track of the objects that have registered for advises. The OleAdviseHolder manages OLE notifications; the DataAdviseHolder manages data notifications.

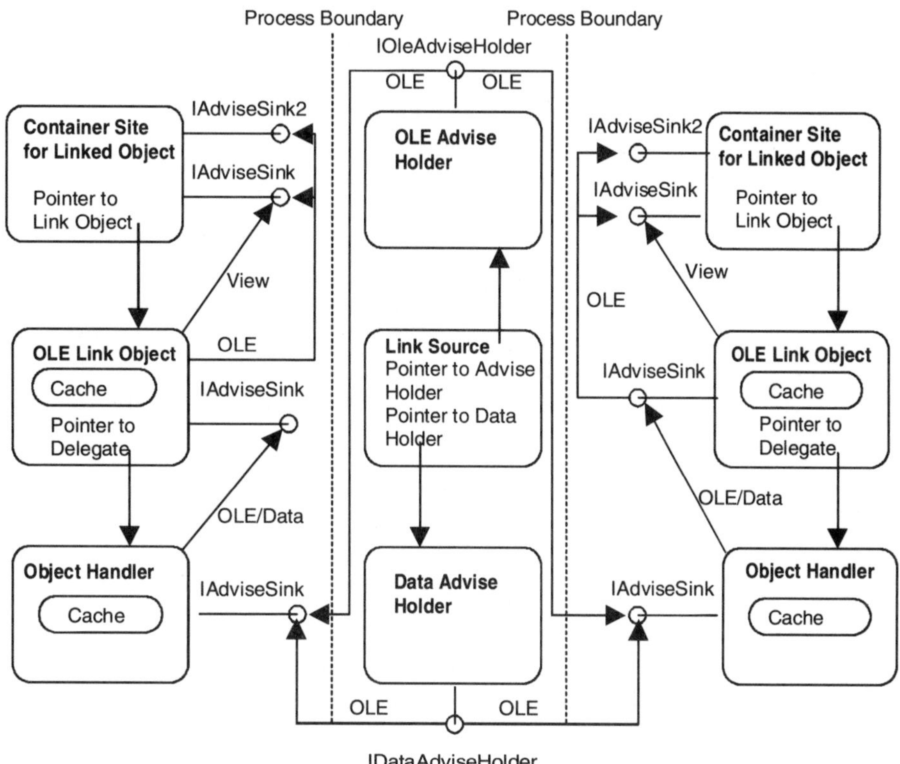

Figure 3.12 Notification flow to separate container processes

Notifications can be synchronous or asynchronous. With synchronous notifications, the remoting object responsible for marshaling the data across the process boundary waits for a response from the remoting object on the other side of the boundary before returning control back to the object that sent the notification. With asynchronous notifications, the remoting object does not wait for a response before returning. For more information about the types of method calls in OLE, see Chapter 13, "Concurrency Management."

Sending Notifications

Object applications determine the conditions that prompt the sending of each specific notification and the frequency with which each notification should be sent. When it is appropriate for multiple notifications to be sent, it does not matter which notification is sent first; they can be sent in any order.

Each notification maps to one or more conditions. The following table lists the common conditions that generate each notification. The view and link source change notifications are not included because object applications do not send them.

Condition in Object application	Notification Generated
User selects Close	OnClose
User selects Save or Save As	OnSave
Document or Pseudo Object name first assigned or changed	OnRename
Object's data changed	OnDataChange

The timing of notifications affects the performance, and coordination between, an object application and its containers. Whereas notifications sent too frequently slow processing, notifications sent too infrequently result in an out-of-sync container. Notification frequency can be compared with the rate at which an application repaints. Therefore, using similar logic for the timing of notifications (as is used for repainting) is wise.

Object applications that support linking to ranges need to consider how pseudo objects are to be informed of the need to send notifications. For example, when a document is saved, the OnSave notification must be sent to both the container sites of the standard objects and the container sites of the pseudo objects. Two approaches can be considered:

- Any change in the document causes a notification to be sent to all container sites for all pseudo objects in the document.
- A mechanism can be implemented for determining the specific pseudo object affected by a change. Notification is sent only to the container sites of those affected.

Some object applications disable the sending of notifications for an extended period of time so certain operations are not interrupted. Notification requests are placed in a queue, and when the operation completes, these pending notifications are sent. For example, a graphic object application can ensure that the repainting of its image is not interrupted; notifications are not sent until the repaint operation has completed.

There are a few considerations for object applications that implement pseudo objects to support linking to ranges. If such an object application supports the queueing of notifications, a mechanism to queue pseudo object notifications must be implemented. Notifications must be sent to all pseudo object container sites when the OnRename and OnSave conditions arise.

Receiving Notifications

A container is responsible for registering for notifications and responding if necessary after a notification is received. Containers register to receive notifications when a new embedded or linked object is created and when an object is loaded.

The **IAdviseSink** interface implementation dictates the necessary response for each notification. **IAdviseSink** is implemented by containers, the OLE link object, and the object handler; and each implementation is different. For example, the OLE link object's implementation of the **IAdviseSink::OnRename** method updates the moniker for a linked object, but the object handler and container versions of **OnRename** do nothing.

A container that does not use OLE's caching support should get data change notifications through **IAdviseSink::OnDataChange**. It is not valid to call **IDataObject::GetData** within **IAdviseSink::OnDataChange** (calling **GetData** results in a synchronous call nested inside of an asynchronous call).

IAdviseSink::OnViewChange handles view and extent changes.

Containers can postpone receiving view notifications so an operation, such as printing, can continue uninterrupted. A call to **IViewObject::Freeze** causes view notifications to be queued until **IViewObject::Unfreeze** is called.

Saving OLE Compound Documents

Users typically initiate a document save by selecting the File Save or File Save As commands. An SDI object application opened by OLE also offers the File Save Copy As command, which is used to save the embedded object in a file that is separate from its containing document's file. Saving an object with the File Save Copy As command does not break the connection to the object's container application.

Note Unlike OLE 1 object applications, OLE 2 object applications do not need a File Update command to update changes made to an open OLE 2 embedded object. The changes are automatically reflected in the object's container document. However, if the object application is going to support OLE 1 objects, they also need to support the File Update command. For more information on OLE user interface recommendations, see Chapter 2, "User Interface Guidelines."

When saving untitled documents, OLE applications need to create a new file moniker for the document and register it in the running object table. If the untitled document had a temporary file moniker registered in the running object table, this temporary moniker must be revoked by calling **IRunningObjectTable::Revoke**.

File Save As Command

Opening an IStorage Object

Handling Monikers

Resetting the Document's Dirty Flag

Note An OLE object application started by OLE does not have a File Save As command; instead, the File Save As command is replaced with the File Save Copy As command. In a File Save Copy As operation, the application does not reinitialize the document object to the file in which the document is being saved, because this would break the connection with the object's container application. This model is different from OLE 1.

To save a document using the File Save As command, an OLE application performs the following tasks:

1. Prompt the user for the filename in which to save the document. If the user cancels the save operation, leave the document object initialized in the state it was in before the user chose the save operation.
2. Set the document's title to the filename specified by the user.
3. If linking is supported, create and register a new file moniker for the document in the running object table. Destroy and revoke the registration of the document's temporary file moniker (if it exists).
   - **Object application only:** Notify all linking containers and/or pseudo objects that the document has been renamed by calling **IAdviseSink::OnRename** either directly or via **IOleAdviseHolder::SendOnRename**. Direct all pseudo objects to notify their registered linking clients. Each pseudo object sends a notification in a similar fashion by calling **IAdviseSink::OnRename** for each of its registered sinks or **IOleAdviseHolder::SendOnRename**.
   - **Container only:** Notify all compound document objects that have monikers assigned that the document's moniker has changed by calling **IOleObject::SetMoniker**. If the container is a top-level container, this is done when the container's filename changes.
4. Open the specified file in which to save the document as an OLE compound file by calling **StgOpenStorage**.
5. Open a stream in the open **IStorage** object and save the object's CLSID by calling **WriteClassStg**. Save the object's user type name and clipboard data format by calling **WriteFmtUserTypeStg**. (When saving an embedded object, the object application does not call **WriteClassStg**; it is called automatically when the container calls **OleSave** to save the object.)
6. Open as many streams as needed to write the document's native data.

7. **Container only:** If the document contains objects, save them as child **IStorage** objects of the opened **IStorage** instance.
8. **Object application only:** If the object application loads all of its native data into memory, it can release the pointer to its open **IStorage** object. However, a container, even if it loads all of its native data into memory, cannot release its **IStorage** pointer because it must keep the storage object open at all times so its loaded embedded objects have access to their storage.
9. Set the document's title to the filename specified by the user.
10. Reset the document's dirty flag.

Opening an IStorage Object

IStorage objects can be opened in one of two access modes: direct or transacted. In direct mode, the changes to the **IStorage** are committed immediately with no chance of undoing the changes. In transacted mode, the **IStorage** is opened in a buffered state, whereby changes are saved to temporary files until they are committed with a call to **IStorage::Commit**.

The access mode can be combined with the ability to read and write to the **IStorage**, and to deny others the right to do the same.

StgCreateDocfile uses its *grfMode* parameter (a set of flags) to control how the **IStorage** object is created and subsequently accessed. Valid values for *grfMode* are taken from the following constants defined in STORAGE.H:

```
#define STGM_DIRECT          0x00000000L
#define STGM_TRANSACTED      0x00010000L

#define STGM_READ            0x00000000L
#define STGM_WRITE           0x00000001L
#define STGM_READWRITE       0x00000002L

#define STGM_SHARE_DENY_NONE     0x00000040L
#define STGM_SHARE_DENY_READ     0x00000030L
#define STGM_SHARE_DENY_WRITE    0x00000020L
#define STGM_SHARE_EXCLUSIVE     0x00000010L

#define STGM_PRIORITY        0x00040000L
#define STGM_DELETEONRELEASE 0x04000000L

#define STGM_CREATE      0x00001000L
#define STGM_CONVERT     0x00020000L
#define STGM_FAILIFTHERE 0x00000000L
```

The *grfMode* parameter values are meant to be used together. Only one value from each of the five groups of flags can be specified at one time. As an example, the following combination of flag values opens the storage object in transacted mode, with read and write access granted to the caller and write access denied to all other objects:

```
STGM_TRANSACTED | STGM_READWRITE | STGM_SHARE_DENY_WRITE
```

Except for the root storage object, each storage object and its contained stream object(s) are always opened in the context of some other open storage object. Child storage objects inherit the access mode of the parent; thus, the child storage object can only be opened in a more restrictive mode.

Writing OLE Data to IStorage

OLE uses one or more stream objects for saving information about the document in the root storage object. This information includes the object's CLSID, which is written to the root storage object using **WriteClassStg**. Note that an object application launched to service an embedded object does not save the object's CLSID. The object's container saves this in a stream of the object's storage. OLE also saves the moniker of a linked object, the clipboard data format of the document's native data, and the user type name by calling the **WriteFmtUserTypeStg** function.

Writing Native Data to IStorage

Before it can write its native data to an **IStream** instance in the root storage object, an application must create a stream; this is done by calling the **IStorage::CreateStream** method. After creating the stream object, the application calls the **IStream::Write** method to write its data to the **IStream** instance.

Saving Compound Document Objects to IStorage

Consider the compound document illustrated in Figure 3.13. The root storage object, *pStg1*, contains nested embedded objects, which also contain nested embeddings. For simplicity, the streams are represented by the small circles.

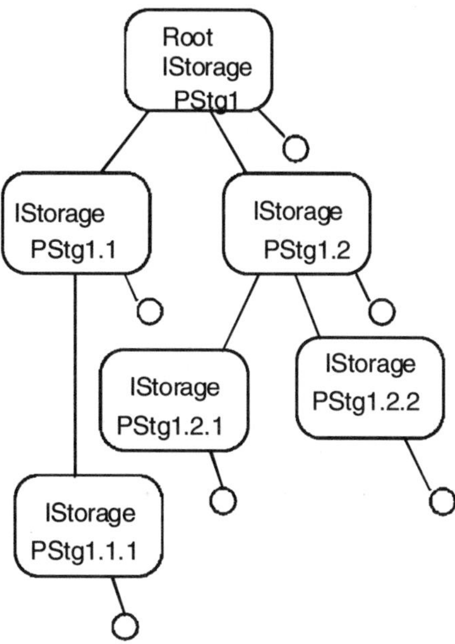

Figure 3.13 Saving a compound document object

To save its contained embeddings, the top-level container must do the following tasks:

1. Call **OleSave** on the storage object of each immediate embedded object, passing the storage object a pointer to where the object is to be saved. The object then recursively calls **OleSave** on any of its nested embeddings.

   OleSave first calls **WriteClassStg** to save the object's CLSID before calling the object handler's **IPersistStorage::Save** method. (Usually, the object handler is the OLE-provided default handler.) The default handler's implementation of **IPersistStorage::Save** first saves the object's presentation cache and then calls **IPersistStorage::Save** on the running object to save the native data.

   Finally, **OleSave** calls **IStorage::Commit** on the storage object to commit the changes back one level to the transaction state of the root storage object.

2. After the return from **OleSave**, the top-level container must call **IPersistStorage::SaveCompleted** on the immediate embedded objects to return them and any of their nested embeddings to the normal storage mode. Unless this is done, the object is left in the no scribble mode it was put in when **OleSave** called **IPersistStorage::Save**. Because of this, **SaveCompleted** should be called immediately on the object after the return from **OleSave** to put the object and any of its nested embeddings back in the normal storage mode with full read and write access.

Note **IPersistStorage::SaveCompleted** is always called on the **IStorage** object that contains the object; it is a call that recurses to all currently loaded or running embedded objects. Should **SaveCompleted** fail, the object(s) does not return to normal storage mode. In this case the container should back out any changes that have been committed and instead try to save the object following the recommendations for saving an object in low-memory situations. See "Saving Objects in Low Memory," later in this chapter.

Saving a linked object is no different from saving an embedded object. To save a linked object that is not loaded or running, **IStorage::CopyTo** can be used. When an object is in the loaded or running state, **OleSave** should be called because it saves all changes.

OleSave and **IPersistStorage::Save** use the *fSameAsLoad* flag to determine whether the storage object that the object is being saved to is the same one from which the object was loaded. The value of *fSameAsLoad* can be combined with the value of the *pStg* passed to these functions to determine the save routine being used to save the compound document, as shown in the following table:

Value of *fSameAsLoad*	Value of *pStg* passed to IPersistStorage:: SaveCompleted	Save Routine to call
TRUE	NULL	File Save
FALSE	*pStg*	File Save As
FALSE	NULL	File Save Copy As

A container should save both the document's native data stream and any information on behalf of the compound document object, including the following data:

Data Saved on Behalf of a Compound Document Object	Description
m_szStgName	Stores the name of object's persistent **IStorage** element.
m_fMoniker-Assigned	Keeps track of whether or not a moniker was assigned to the compound document object.
m_dwAspect	Determines how to display the object when it is later loaded into memory: as an embedded object, a thumbnail representation (appropriate for browsing tools), an iconic representation, or as a sequence of pages (as if the object had been printed).

Handling Monikers

Saving an untitled document requires that the application revoke the temporary file moniker created and registered for the untitled document, if any.

If a linking container established links to an object application's untitled document and then shuts down before the object application saves the untitled document, the links to the untitled document are broken. To repair the links, the user needs to use the Edit Links dialog. For this reason, some applications might not allow linking to untitled documents.

Notifying Linking Clients of File Moniker Changes: Object Application Only

When the file moniker to a document changes, OLE object applications need to notify all registered linking clients. A linking client must have previously registered to receive change notifications by calling the **IOleObject::Advise** and/or **IDataObject::DAdvise** methods, as appropriate. To notify the linking clients, the object application calls the OLE-provided **IOleAdviseHolder::SendOnRename** method.

Notifying Pseudo Objects of Moniker Change: Object Application Only

Just as they notify linking clients of a change in the document's file moniker, OLE object applications that support linking to pseudo objects must notify the registered linking clients that the pseudo object's file moniker has changed. Again, the application can use the OLE-provided implementation of the **IOleAdviseHolder** and **IDataAdviseHolder** interface to notify the linking clients of the file moniker change.

Notifying Compound Document Objects of File Moniker Change: Containers Only

A container that supports linking to its embedded objects must notify each of its linking containers that the file moniker used to represent its document has changed when either the document is saved for the first time or when it is saved to a new file. Otherwise, all links to the container's embedded objects are broken.

To notify an embedded object of its document's moniker change, containers call the **IOleObject::SetMoniker** method, passing in the new moniker and a flag that specifies that the name of the object's container has changed (OLEWHICHMK_CONTAINER). Calling **IOleObject::SetMoniker** on a running object forces the object to revoke its currently registered moniker from the running object table and register the new moniker.

Resetting the Document's Dirty Flag

After saving the document, applications reset their dirty flag on the document to FALSE. However, if the document is being saved as the result of a File Save Copy As operation, the flag is not reset.

File Save Command

Saving a document with the File Save command follows the same logic as File Save As, except when saving documents with File Save, the application does not need to prompt the user for the name of the file or call the routines that create and register new monikers.

To save a document using the File Save command, OLE applications perform the following tasks. For a discussion of these tasks, see the preceding section, "File Save As Command."

1. Open the specified file in which to save the document as a compound file.
2. Open as many **IStream** instances as needed to save the OLE information to the document's root storage object, including the CLSID, user type name, and clipboard data format.
3. Save the document's native data to the root storage object.
4. If the document contains objects, save them as child **IStorage** instances to the open root storage object. After saving all objects, call **IPersistStorage::SaveCompleted** on each storage object to return it and any of its nested embeddings to the normal storage mode.
5. Reset the document's dirty flag.

Saving to Temporary Files

A document saved to a compound file can choose to implement its save functionality by doing a complete save to a temporary file residing in the same directory as the original. After the temporary file has been created, the original file is deleted, and the temporary one is renamed to have the name of the original. As far as the object is concerned, the process of saving documents this way works in three steps:

1. The object's container calls **IPersistStorage::Save**. This call temporarily removes the object's right to scribble into its storage; putting the object into the no scribble storage mode. While in this mode, the object cannot write to its storage object, although it can read from it. Thus, the duration of the no scribble storage mode should be kept to the absolute minimum.
2. The container does whatever it needs to do to safely retain the changes the object saved. Usually containers call **IStorage::Commit**.
3. The container returns the object to normal storage mode by calling **IPersistStorage::SaveCompleted**.

Notice that in either normal or no scribble storage mode an object can hold on to its open **IStorage** instance. With OLE compound files, the object application also has the actual disk file open. Because of this, a file cannot be deleted or renamed while it is open, which prevents the application from doing a full save operation. To solve this problem, an object can be put into the hands-off storage mode, which is similar to but somewhat more severe than the no scribble storage mode. In this mode, the object must release the **IStorage** instance it owns. If the object is also an OLE container, it recursively causes any of its loaded or running objects to enter the hands-off storage mode. When the object returns to the normal storage mode, its container gives the object back its storage pointer.

To put an object into the hands-off storage mode, the container calls the **IPersistStorage::HandsOffStorage** method. To return the object to its normal storage mode, the **IPersistStorage::SaveCompleted** method is called with a *pStg* to the object's **IStorage** instance. The contents of the just-passed *pStg* is guaranteed to be identical to the contents of the *pStg* that the object had but which was revoked in the call to **IPersistStorage::HandsOffStorage**. Thus, the object does not have to do a full reload; it only needs to reopen any substreams in the normal storage mode.

Note Calling **IPersistStorage::Save** always causes the object to enter the no scribble state. This is done to guarantee that low-memory saves work while ensuring efficiency in the high-memory cases. Thus, every call to **IPersistStorage::Save** must be followed by a call to **IPersistStorage::SaveCompleted** to return the object and any of its child objects to the normal storage state. In addition, the container can make an intervening call to **IPersistStorage::HandsOffStorage**, which is useful for implementing the application's File Save As routine.

From the perspective of a client of an object, the hands-off storage mode is very similar to the no scribble storage mode. In neither mode can the client expect anything at all to work on the object. From the object's perspective, in no scribble state the object can read but not write to its storage; in the hands-off state, it clearly can no longer read from the storage object.

Saving Objects in Low Memory

Often an object is asked to save itself in low-memory situations. Conceptually, this can be thought of as doing a File Save As operation. For example, suppose there is a root document in a file and all the changes to its embedded objects have been saved, but not yet committed at the document level, as shown in Figure 3.14:

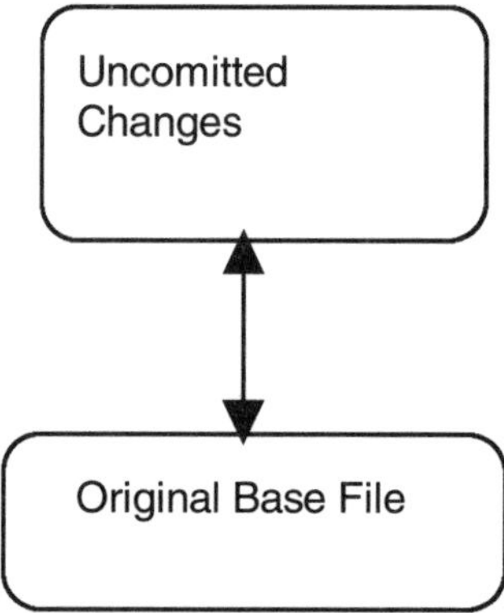

Figure 3.14 State of an unsaved object in a low-memory situation

Here, the uncommitted changes are those written to the compound file that have yet to be committed. In low-memory situations, an application needs to be guaranteed a way to save its compound document to a new base file without consuming any new memory, as shown in Figure 3.15.

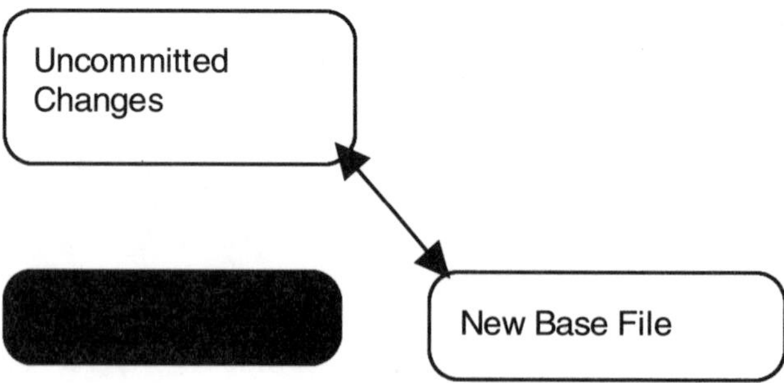

Figure 3.15 Saving objects to a new base file in low-memory situations

The new base file is a copy of the original file. The uncommitted compound file changes are now associated with the new file; the old file is inaccessible. If an **IStorage::Commit** is now made, the changes go to the new file. In this situation, **IStorage::Commit** is guaranteed to work without consuming additional memory.

When saving compound documents in this manner, it is recommended that any loaded or running embedded objects be in the hands-off storage mode, which simplifies the implementation of this low-memory save operation in compound files.

When saving an object in low-memory situations, the following interface methods are guaranteed to work:

IStream::Read	**IStream::Write**
IStream::SetSize	**IStream::Seek**
IStream::Commit	**IStream::Revert**
IStream::AddRef	**IStream::Release**
IStorage::QueryInterface	**IStorage::SetClass**
IStorage::SetStateBits	**IStorage::Commit**
IStorage::Revert	**IStorage::AddRef**
IStorage::Release	**IRootStorage::QueryInterface**
IRootStorage::AddRef	**IRootStorage::Release**
IRootStorage::SwitchToFile	

Full Save Operations

To do a full save of a document, an application completes the following steps:

1. The object creates and opens a temporary destination file in direct mode.
2. The container then creates the appropriate **IStorage** instances for each object, also using direct mode for these storage objects.
3. The container then asks each loaded or running embedding to save to the new storage by calling **IPersistStorage::Save** (*pStg*, FALSE).
4. If the object's **IStorage** instance was opened in transacted mode, the container then writes the root level document's data to the compound file and flushes the root storage object by calling **IStorage::Commit**.

   If any of these steps fail for low memory reasons, the container should back each object out by calling **IPersistStorage::SaveCompleted** (NULL) and try to save the document using the sequence of steps for saving in low-memory situations.

5. Once the data is in the new file, the container calls **IPersistStorage::HandsOffStorage** on each object and releases the **IStorage** instance that the root document is holding on to. This then allows the container to delete the original file and to rename the new one to be the old name.
6. The container reloads each object by calling **IPersistStorage::SaveCompleted** (*pStgNew*).

If any errors occur after the data is saved in the new file but before completion, error handlers need to note that some objects are either in the no scribble or hands-off storage mode and need to be returned to the normal storage mode eventually.

Doing a Full Save in Low Memory

To do a full save in low memory, a container does the following steps:

1. Ask each object to save to its current **IStorage** by calling **IPersistStorage::Save**(*pStg*, TRUE). Objects are responsible for ensuring that this operation works without consuming additional memory.
2. Commit the storage of each of the objects by calling **IStorage::Commit** to percolate the changes out to the next transaction level.
3. Write any changes made to the root-level document to the appropriate streams immediately contained within the root **IStorage** instance.
4. Put each object in the hands-off storage mode by calling **IPersistStorage::HandsOffStorage** on the object.
5. Close any streams the root-level document might be holding on to.
6. Call **IRootStorage::SwitchToFile**(*lpszNewFile*) to switch the files.
7. Call **IStorage::Commit** on the root **IStorage** instance to commit the new file. This **Commit** can safely be done using STGC_OVERWRITE, which reduces the size of the final file.
8. After the data is in the new file, close and delete the original file before renaming the new one to the old name. Then reattach the objects by calling **IPersistStorage::SaveCompleted**(*pStgNew*).
9. Reopen any root-level streams.

The error handling cautions for doing a full save in high memory apply to the low-memory case as well.

The Save As case is the same, except the container need not bother with deleting the original file and renaming the new one.

Backing Out of a Save As

In the File Save As sequence, a container recursively calls **IPersistStorage::Save** followed by a call to **IPersistStorage::SaveCompleted** on its contained embedded objects. However, suppose the Save As operation cannot be completed. In this case, some of the objects will be holding on to a storage object in the new location, while some are holding on to the old location. There are two steps a container can follow to get the objects that have been saved to back out:

1. The container can ask these objects to "Save As" back to their original location. This is slow, but might be an acceptable solution for the container, especially if this scenario happens infrequently.
2. The container can close and reload the object from the original location. If the object is loaded, this has no visible effect on the user; however, if the object is running, this closes the object on the user's screen.

Incremental Save Operations

Incremental saves are somewhat less complicated, because the presence of transactioning and the lack of a need of a new temporary file makes things easier. Incremental saving assumes that the root storage object is open in transacted mode.

To do an incremental save, the container does the following tasks:

1. Ask each object to save to its current **IStorage** by calling **IPersistStorage::Save** (*pStg*, TRUE). This is guaranteed by contract with the object not to fail for lack of memory.
2. Commit the storage of each of the objects by calling **IStorage::Commit** to percolate the changes out to the next transaction level; compound files are guaranteed that this works in low memory.
3. Write any changes made to the root-level document to the root **IStorage** instance. As with objects, the root document is responsible for ensuring this works in low memory.
4. Call **IStorage::Commit** on the root **IStorage** instance to commit the compound file.
5. Return the objects to their normal storage mode by calling **IPersistStorage::SaveCompleted** (NULL).

Saving Data to Compound Files Using Transacted Mode

When repeatedly saving (writing then committing) data to compound files in transacted mode, the size of the resulting file may not reflect the actual amount of data written to the file. This is because the new data does not immediately overwrite the old data in the file in order to allow changes to be discarded and reverted back to the original, intact file.

This concept is best illustrated by a simple example. Consider a document being saved to a compound file; after the save operation, the file size is approximately 50K, as shown below:

The black and white blocks represent the internal structures of the compound file which help support transacted mode. These blocks form a chain that refers to the most recently committed data in the file.

If the document is now rewritten into the same file, the new data will be written at the end of the file along with a white reference block (below); a final commit operation will automatically update the references in the black, master reference block to point to the new data as well as to the now unused area where the previously saved data lay. This file is now about 100K, of which only 50K is used for the document's data.

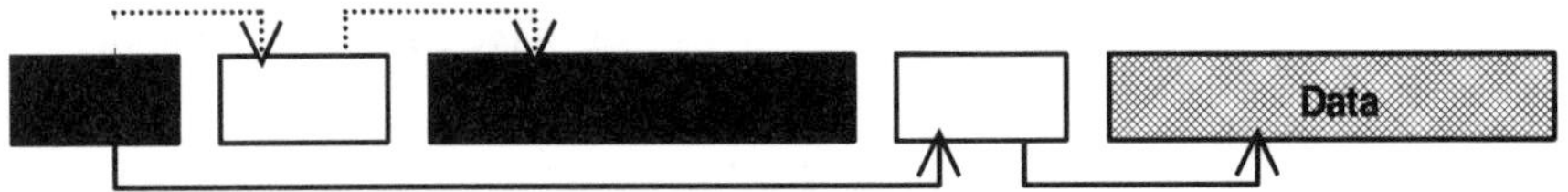

Now, consider a third save operation on the same file where the data is again completely rewritten. This time, the write operation will reclaim the unused area of the compound file (below, A), and shrink the size of the file by discarding the unused portions at the end of the file (below, B). At the end of this save, the size of the file is again 50K; just as it was when it was originally saved.

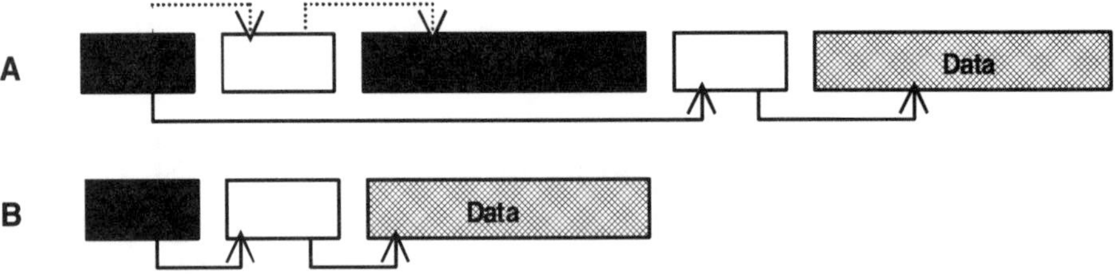

To avoid problems like this, file formats should be designed so that the application only has to write the data that has changed; the transactioning will take care of the robustness issues and will also prevent the file from growing in size. If an application needs to rewrite the entire contents of the file, it should just save to another file and not use transactioning (saving to a new file guarantees the smallest file possible).

Supporting Link Updating

Applications that act as file-level link sources can better handle all cases of manual links and nearly all cases of automatic links by setting the change time in the running object table to the time of the file's last save.

Closing OLE Compound Documents

On shutdown, an application might have many documents to close (an SDI application will have only one open document to close). To close a document, OLE applications do the following tasks:

1. Check the open document(s) for changes. If a file-based document has changed, prompt the user to save the document; otherwise, do nothing. If an embedded object has changed, tell the object's container to save it.
2. Safeguard both the application and document objects from premature closing by intentionally incrementing the objects' reference counters.
3. Revoke the registration of the document's moniker from the running object table.
4. If the document is the source for the data on the clipboard, flush the clipboard.
5. Hide the document window and unlock the document on behalf of the user. If the application supports drag and drop operations, revoke the document as a drop target.
   - **Object application only:** Force all pseudo objects to close.
   - **Object application only:** Send a final OnDataChange to all clients that have registered to receive data notifications when the object stops running (ADVF_DATAONSTOP). After sending the notification, release the DataAdviseHolder.
   - **Object application only:** Send an OnClose advisory notification to all registered containers; after sending it, release the OleAdviseHolder.
   - **Container only:** Force all loaded embedded and linked objects to close.
6. To guarantee the document object has been freed of all external and pointer references, call **CoDisconnectObject**.
7. Release the intentional reference count on the document and application objects. When the document object's reference count goes to zero, destroy the object.

Checking Documents for Changes

When closing documents, an application should ensure that its application and document objects are prevented from accidentally closing. To guard the objects, an application intentionally increments the reference counts on these objects. The reference counts remain until all other external memory pointers have been released.

Application shutdown begins by first checking all open documents to see whether there are changes that need to be saved. If the application was started by the user, it should prompt the user to save any changes made to the document. This model is different from OLE 1, where the application prompted the user to save the object in its container.

If the document is dirty, the object application should check to see whether or not OLE opened the document. If the document was opened by OLE, the object application should call the container's **IOleClientSite::SaveObject** method to save the object. Otherwise, the object application should prompt the user to save the changes made to the document.

Closing Pseudo Objects: Object Application Only

Object applications that support linking to pseudo objects need to close the pseudo objects as part of closing the open document(s). The object application also needs to send an OnClose notification to all registered linking containers of the pseudo object, telling them the pseudo object is being closed. Upon receipt of the OnClose notification, the linking container is automatically disconnected from the pseudo object. This disconnection is done by the OLE link object, which is part of the container's object handler. To forcefully close any connections to its pseudo object, the object application can call the **CoDisconnectObject** function.

Closing Loaded Objects: Container Only

To forcefully close all loaded objects, including links and embeddings, containers can call **CoDisconnectObject**. The container passes to **CoDisconnectObject** a pointer to one of the interfaces being maintained on behalf of the object. Usually, this is a pointer to the **IUnknown** interface.

Note Care should be taken when calling **CoDisconnectObject** because it forcefully closes all objects. An application should not call **CoDisconnectObject** to routinely disconnect and release an interface pointer to an object; instead, it should call the object's **IUnknown::Release** method. **CoDisconnectObject** should only be called by the process that manages the object and only when that process wants to exit.

Hiding the Document Window

As the last part of closing a document, the application hides the document's window from the user. At the time of hiding the window, the application needs to revoke the document's registered file moniker from the running object table and take control of the document away from the user. (If the application supports drag and drop operations, it also unregisters itself as a drop target.)

As discussed earlier in the section, "Opening Compound Documents," applications that support linking to pseudo objects create and register a file moniker for every document they open. Registering the file moniker results in a weak reference lock being placed on the document object on behalf of the registered moniker. Before the document can be closed, this moniker should be revoked from the running object table by calling the **IRunningObjectTable::Revoke** method, passing it the *dwRegister* token returned by the **IRunningObjectTable::Register** method when the moniker was registered.

Note Registering a moniker in the running object table results in a weak reference lock being placed on the document which is not strong enough to keep the document object alive should all the other external connections be released. Still, the application should release the moniker from the table before closing the document.

If the object application activated the object in a window in the object application process space, it must call **IOleClientSite::OnShowWindow** (FALSE) to tell the container to remove the hatching around the open object.

When there are no more documents visible to the user and the application is not under user control, the application should hide its application window. This leaves the application in a hidden, running state. Only when the application object's last external reference is freed, does the application actually shut down.

Taking Control Away from the User

If the document was visible to the user when closing on shutdown, the application takes control of the document away from the user. To free this external user reference, the application calls **CoLockObjectExternal** (*pDoc*, FALSE, TRUE).

Sending Close Notifications: Object Applications Only

When closing a document, an object application sends a final OnDataChange notification to all clients registered with the ADVF_DATAONSTOP flag, telling them the object has stopped running. After sending the notification, the object application releases its **IDataAdviseHolder** pointer.

The object application also sends an OnClose advisory notification to all registered containers telling them it is shutting down. The object application then releases its **IOleAdviseHolder** pointer.

For more information on sending notifications, see "Managing Notifications," earlier in this chapter.

Releasing Reference Locks

Just as **CoLockObjectExternal** (*pDoc*, FALSE, TRUE) was called to release the external reference on behalf of the user, the application needs to call **CoLockObjectExternal** (*pApp*, FALSE, TRUE) to release the lock on the application made when the document was first created.

Closing Scenarios

How an OLE container or object application was started and subsequently used affects the closing of the application. There are three scenarios for closing applications:

- The user started the container or object application and initiated application shutdown by choosing the File Quit command or the system Close command.
- The object application was started by OLE to service a linked or embedded object. Application shutdown was initiated by the container calling the object's **IOleObject::Close** method.
- The object application was started to service a linked or embedded object. Application shutdown was initiated by the user choosing the File Quit command or the system Close command.

The procedure for closing an application started by the user is the same for both object and container applications; the sequence of shutdown tasks begin with the application object. However, for an object application started by OLE, shutdown is initiated by the object's container application and begins with the document object.

The following sections describe each of these scenarios in greater detail.

Closing an Application With the File Quit Command

Figure 3.16 shows the state of an object application at the time the user initiated program shutdown by choosing the File Quit command (the application was started explicitly by the user).

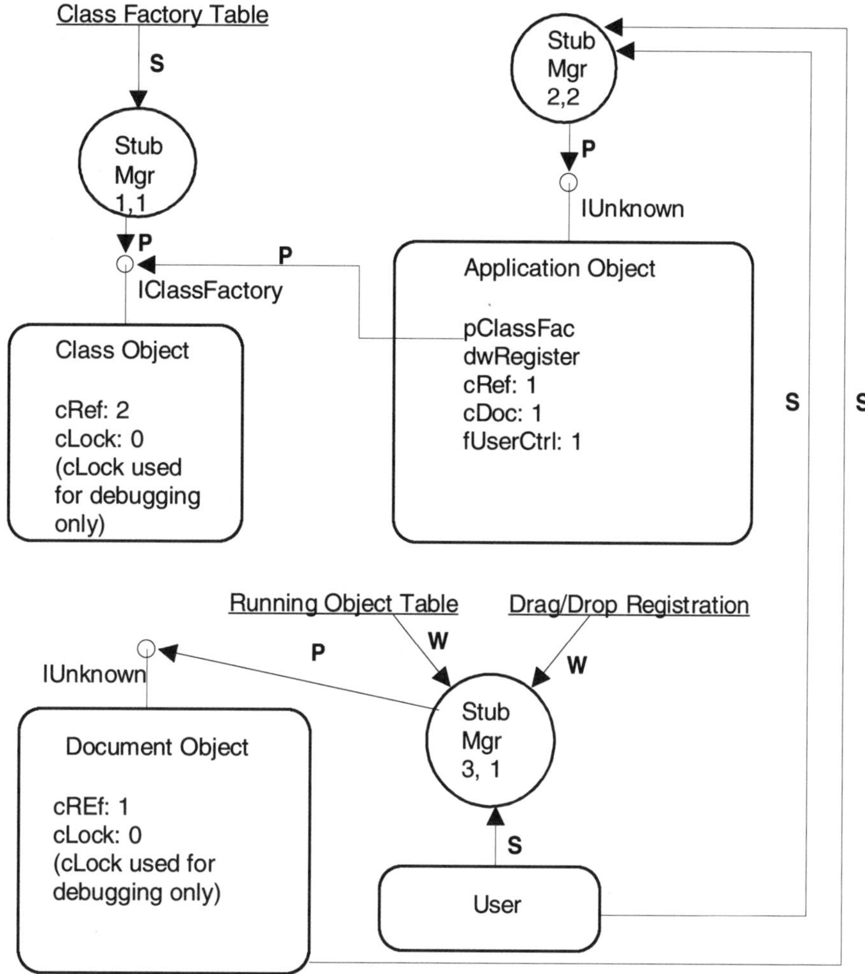

S Strong reference lock (CoLockObjectExternal called on object)
W Weak reference lock
P Interface pointer reference
n,n The sum of references on an object (leftmost n) and the number that are strong (rightmost n)

Figure 3.16 Object application shutdown initiated by user choosing File Quit command

As shown, the application object's reference count is one, which reflects the reference on behalf of the stub manager. The document object also has a reference count of one on behalf of the user opening the document. (If a data transfer object had been created during a Copy/Paste operation, the clipboard object would also maintain similar reference counts).

Closing an application with the File Quit command starts a sequence of shutdown events beginning with the application object. Upon receiving the Quit command, the application object begins shutdown by first closing the open document. After the document has been saved, the document's moniker is revoked from the running object table, the document window is hidden, the document is unregistered as a drag and drop target, and control of the document is taken away from the user. These acts cause the document object's reference counter to be decremented to zero. Only when the reference count goes to zero, can the document be safely destroyed.

After destroying the document object, the application object's reference count maintained on behalf of the document object is released, leaving the object application in the state shown in Figure 3.17.

Note The scenario described around Figure 3.17 reflects an object application with one open document; it is possible there could have been multiple document objects to close. Each open document in an application would have been reflected in the application object's application and document reference counts.

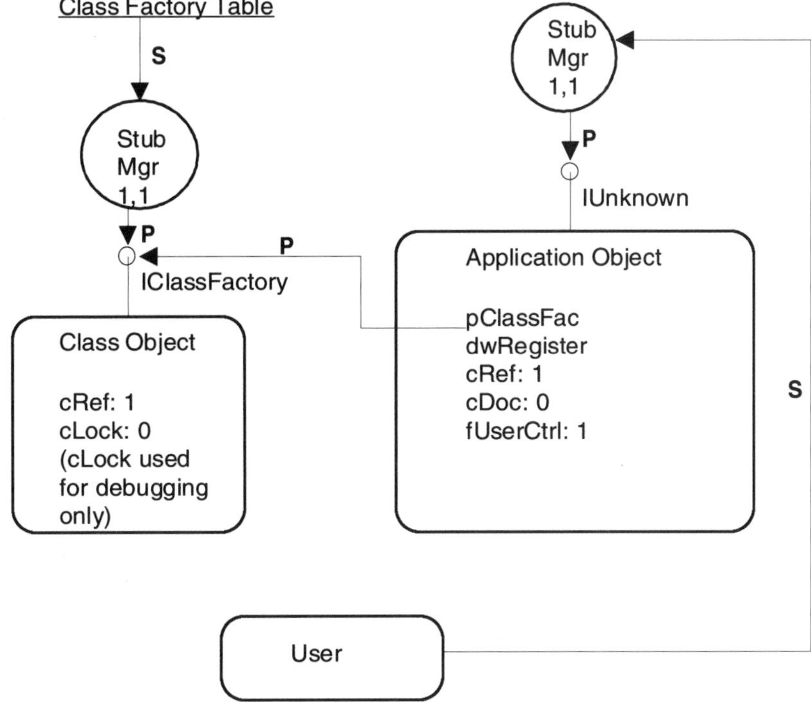

S Strong reference lock (CoLockObjectExternal called on object)
W Weak reference lock
P Interface pointer reference
n,n The sum of references on an object (leftmost n) and the number that are strong (rightmost n)

Figure 3.17 Object application after closing open document

After all documents have been closed, the application object removes control of the application from the user and hides the application frame window. Figure 3.18 shows the state of the application immediately after control of the application is removed from the user.

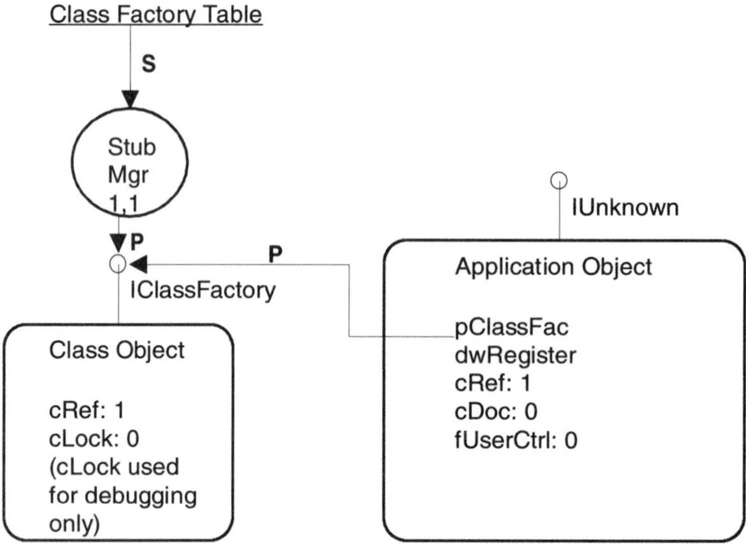

S Strong reference lock (CoLockObjectExternal called on object)
W Weak reference lock
P Interface pointer reference
n,n The sum of references on an object (leftmost n) and the number that are strong (rightmost n)

Figure 3.18 Object application after removing user control

After calling **CoLockObjectExternal** (*pApp*, FALSE, TRUE) to remove control from the user, the application object's reference count is generally zero. When this count reaches zero, the application calls its destructor routine. Because **CoLockObjectExternal** was called with *fLastUnlockReleases* set to TRUE, the application object is freed when control is removed from the user and there are no outstanding external references. As part of its destructor routine, the application should call **CoRevokeClassObject** to release the class object from the class factory table and then release the **IClassFactory** interface pointer. This destroys the **IClassFactory** object.

Closing an Embedded Object from its Container

Figure 3.19 shows the state of an SDI object application started to service an embedded object. Because the object is visible, the user controls the lifetime of the running embedded object but not the application itself. The embedded object, in turn, holds the application alive.

Application shutdown is forced by the object's container calling **IOleObject::Close** on the loaded object. (If the embedding container were to simply release the object, the application would not necessarily shutdown.)

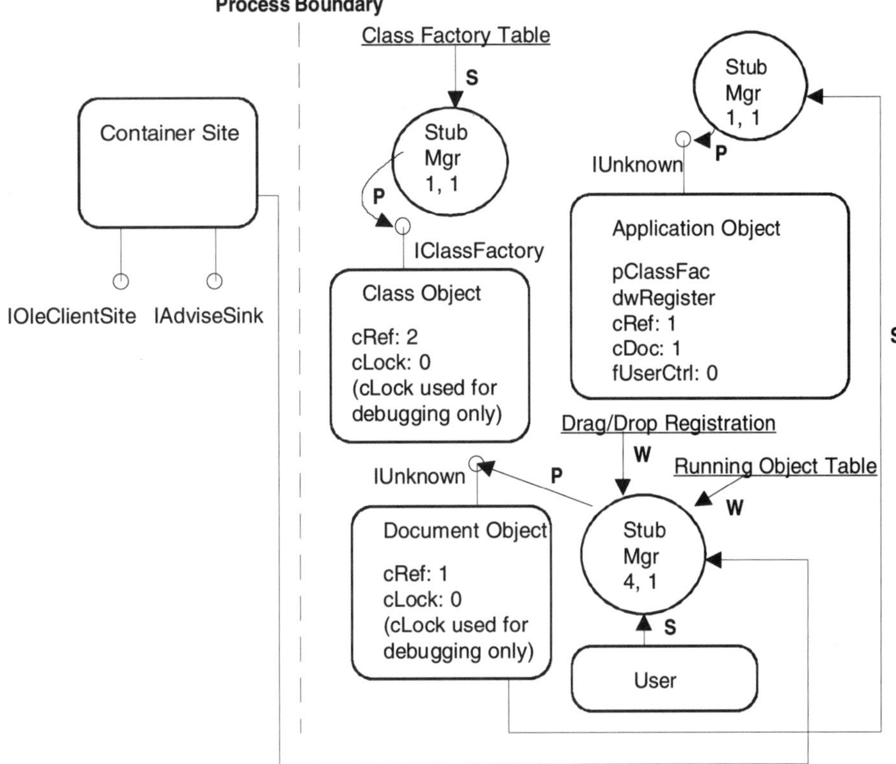

S Strong reference lock (CoLockObjectExternal called on object
W Weak reference lock
P Interface pointer reference
n,n The sum of references on an object (leftmost n) and the number that are strong (rightmost n)

Figure 3.19 SDI object application at the time the object's container called IOleObject::Close

As shown, the document object has a *cRef* of one on behalf of the document being visible to the user. The application object has a *cRef* of one on behalf of the open document. Because the user is not in control of the application or document, the *fUserCtrl* flag is FALSE on the application object.

The embedding container initiates shutdown by calling the **IOleObject::Close** method on the running OLE object. Closing begins with the open document object instead of with the application object as is done when the user explicitly initiates shutdown by using the File Quit command.

As part of closing, the document object closes all open pseudo and embedded objects before revoking the document's registered moniker from the running object table. Only when all external connections are disconnected does the document object receive its final release. To release the reference, the document object sends an OnClose notification to the container, telling it the document is being closed. The OnClose notification is first received by the object handler in the container's process. Upon receipt of the notification, the handler disconnects its LRPC connection to the running object application document, and then forwards the notification on to advisory sink in the container. On receiving the OnClose advisory, the container should revert the OLE object's **IStorage** to flush any uncommitted changes.

In conjunction with sending the OnClose notification, the document object calls **CoDisconnectObject** to forcefully disconnect any existing external connections to the document. Once the document object's reference count goes to zero, the document object's destructor routine is called and the document is destroyed.

Note Because any changes made to the open document would have already been saved by the time of sending the OnClose notification, an object application can safely call the **CoDisconnectObject** function to release all references to the object.

After the document object has been destroyed, the application object's *cDoc* reference count maintained on behalf of the document object is released. If this was the only open document and the user was not in control of the application, the application would be in a state similar to that shown previously in Figure 3.19, with one *cRef* reference count remaining on behalf of the registered class object. To release its class object, the object application calls the **CoRevokeClassObject** function as part of calling its destructor routine.

Object Application Considerations

If the user creates a new untitled document or opens a file-based document in an application started to service a linked or embedded object, the application object sets its *fUserCtrl* flag to TRUE. On a shutdown initiated by the container application calling **IOleObject::Close**, the loaded OLE object would first be closed. After the document object's destructor routine is called, control of the shutdown process is passed to the application object. This leaves the application in a state similar to that of an application started by the user (see Figure 3.19). Because the user is in control, the application would not shut down until the user chose the File Quit or system Close commands.

Closing Data Transfer Objects

How the data transfer object is destroyed depends on how application shutdown was initiated: by the user choosing the File Quit command or by the container calling **IOleObject::Close** on its loaded object. If the object is being closed by the user, the object is responsible for closing the clipboard data object and flushing it of any data pertaining to the application.

When a container calls **IOleObject::Close** to initiate shutdown on an object application document that is the source for a data transfer object, the object application's document object flushes the clipboard of data pertaining to the document.

To empty the clipboard, an application calls **OleFlushClipboard** if it is desirable to have all hGlobal-based formats and OLE 1 compatibility formats remain on the clipboard. Otherwise, **OleSetClipboard**(NULL) can be called.

Closing OLE Applications

As part of application shutdown, OLE containers and object applications do the following tasks. These tasks are described in the following sections.

1. Safeguard the application against premature shutdown by intentionally incrementing the reference count on the application object.
2. Close all open documents. For more information on closing open compound document objects, see "Closing OLE Compound Documents," earlier in this chapter.
3. Flush the clipboard of any data object pertaining to the application. (Object applications usually flush the clipboard when closing the document that is the source of the clipboard data.)
4. If the user had control, release the external reference lock on behalf of the user and hide the application frame window.
5. To ensure that all references to the application have been freed, call **CoDisconnectObject** on the application object.
6. When the reference count on the application object transitions to zero, destroy the application object, freeing all application-specific structures from memory.
7. Close the OLE libraries.

Safeguarding the Application Object

On initiating application shutdown, applications should take precautions to ensure they are not exited until all shutdown procedures have been performed. To safeguard itself, the application can increment *cRef*, which controls the lifetime of the application. This reference count remains until all other counted references to the application object have been released. Only after all other references have been released, does the application release the reference count.

Hiding the Application Window

If the user has control of the application after the document and clipboard data transfer objects have been closed, release user control of the application by calling **CoLockObjectExternal** (*pApp*, FALSE, TRUE) on behalf of the user. After releasing this last external reference on behalf of the user, hide any open windows from the user for the remainder of the shutdown process.

Upon return from **CoLockObjectExternal**, the application's destructor routine is called. As part of its destructor's routine, the application should revoke the registered class factory object from the class factory table. This is done by calling **CoRevokeClassObject**, passing in the *dwRegister* token returned by **CoRegisterClassObject**.

Closing OLE Libraries

As part of its shutdown process, an application needs to close any OLE libraries initialized at program startup. To close the libraries, an application calls the **OleUninitialize** function. This function must be the last call made to the libraries on behalf of the application.

To guard against **OleUninitialize** being called if **OleInitialize** was never called, applications can set a flag as part of initializing the libraries. Before calling **OleUninitialize**, the application checks the flag to ensure that the libraries were properly initialized.

After closing the OLE libraries, the application should call the Macintosh **CleanupLibraryManager** function to resolve any ASLM issues.

CHAPTER 4

Registering Object Applications

This chapter describes how to register OLE 2 object applications on the Macintosh. Information is provided regarding the entry and modification of database keys, OLE 1 compatibility issues, and the API functions used to create and modify the database entries.

How to Register an Application

In order for an object application to support OLE activities, it must be properly registered. Registration is typically done during installation, or when the application is started for the first time. Object applications must register their objects with their full names (for example, Microsoft Excel Graph); failure to do so may result in improper displays when using the Insert Object dialog.

Note Unless the Registration Database properly reflects the services offered by OLE and object applications, neither OLE nor the applications can be used. That is, if the database gets corrupted, it will need to be recreated with all of the OLE information and that of the application(s) previously registered.

The OLE registration database on the Macintosh is comprised of two files: one contains information about OLE 2 applications and the other contains similiar information about OLE 1 applications. The OLE 2 file is called "Registration Database" and the OLE 1 file is called "Embedding Preferences." Both of these files are stored in the Preferences Folder.

To register applications, OLE has two sets of API functions: one set is used to register OLE 2 applications while the other set is used for compatibility with OLE 1 applications. The OLE 2 information is stored in the Registration Database file in the Extensions folder and the OLE 1 information is stored in the Embedding Preferences file in the Systems Preferences folder.

So that their object class(es)can be used by both OLE 1 and OLE 2 containers, OLE 2 object applications must register information in both places.

OLE 2 Registration Database File

The OLE 2 registration database, called "Registration Database," is located in the Preferences folder. This file stores information in the form of a hierarchically structured tree with each node in the tree comprised of a case insensitive key name and a case sensitive value. Each key name is unique with respect to the key immediately above it in the hierarchy.

OLE 2 registration information is comprised of a variety of subkeys. The type and amount of information stored for an object class depends on an object's characteristics. Most of the available keys and subkeys are the same for all platforms.

Applications register their data using the API functions described in the section, "OLE 2 Registration Functions."

Note To be OLE 1 compatible, an OLE 2 application must register in both the OLE 1 and OLE 2 database files.

Syntax of Entries in the Registration Database

Keys in the Registration Database file are case insensitive, while values in it are case sensitive. The names of the keys are not localized or altered for non-English versions of the application being installed, although user-type names (all forms) and verb names are localized for language considerations.

Commas, which are used to separate values into individual items, are not localized. All digits in the CLSID are in uppercase hexadecimal notation with no spaces; this format is the same as the OSF DCE standard.

Note In the registration database, the numerical value of the CLSID is always placed between "curly" braces, such as in {12345678-9ABC-DEF0-C000-000000000046}. The braces are not shown in the CLSID examples in this chapter, but are implied. Similarly, IID is a shorthand notation for an interface identifier. As with the CLSID, the required surrounding braces are not shown in the examples.

Numbers that appear as keys (usually on the left side of an = sign) are always decimal. Numbers on the right side (values) can be either decimal or hexadecimal but hexadecimal values must be preceded by 0x. Negative numbers are always in decimal (for example, -1).

A clipboard format is represented as a **long**.

Programmatic Identifiers

Every OLE 2 object class that is to appear in an Insert Object dialog box (hereafter referred to as an "insertable class") must have a programmatic identifier (ProgID). This string uniquely identifies a given class. Additionally, the ProgID is the "class name" used for an OLE 2 class when placed in an OLE 1 container.

The ProgID string must:

- Have no more than 39 characters.
- Contain no punctuation (including underscore). The only exception is that it may contain one or more periods.
- Not start with a digit.
- Be different from the class name of any OLE 1 application, including the OLE 1 version of the same application, if there is one.

Relative to the conversion process, it is important to note that there are two kinds of ProgIDs. One depends on the version of the object application (version dependent) and the other is version independent. The version-dependent ProgID is the string used when OLE 1 is trying to contact OLE 2 by using DDE. Version-dependent ProgID-to-CLSID conversions must be specific, well defined, and one to one.

An example of using a version-independent ProgID is when a container creates a chart or table with a toolbar button. In this situation, the application could use the version-independent ProgID to determine the latest version of the needed object application.

The version-independent ProgID is stored and maintained solely by application code. When given the version-independent ProgID, **CLSIDFromProgID** returns the CLSID of the current version. **CLSIDFromProgID** works on the version-independent ProgID because the subkey, CLSID, is the same as for the version-dependent one.

A ProgID must never be shown to the user; if you need to display a short human-readable string for an object, call **IOleObject::GetUserType**(USERCLASSTYPE_SHORT, *lpszShortName*).

Converting CLSIDs and ProgIDs

To convert a CLSID into a string of printable characters, use **StringFromCLSID**, which always converts different CLSIDs to different strings. **StringFromIID** can be used to produce an IID string.

The **CLSIDFromProgID** and **ProgIdFromCLSID** functions can be called to convert back and forth between the two representations of the CLSID. These functions use the entries in the registration database to perform the conversion.

Converting a ProgID to a CLSID is done using the ROOT\<ProgID>\CLSID key. The reverse translation is done using the ROOT\CLSID\<clsid>\ProgID subkey. (This means that the ProgID subkey under ROOT\CLSID\<clsid> is version dependent.)

The ProgID Key and Subkeys

Note In the registration database examples that follow, **boldface** indicates a literal standard key or subkey, <*italics*> indicates an application-supplied string or value, and <***boldface-italics***> indicates an application-supplied key or subkey. In the first example, "OLE1ClassName," "OLE1UserTypeName," and "CLSID" are all supplied by the application.

Before an OLE 2 class can be displayed in the Insert Object dialog box, it must have a ProgID. The value registered under the **ProgID** key is the human-readable name that is displayed in the dialog box; it should be the same as the "MainUserTypeName" of the class. If this class is insertable in an OLE 2 container, the **ProgID** key must have an immediate subkey named **Insertable** and it must have no value assigned to it.

Because OLE 2 provides a built-in OLE 1/OLE 2 compatibility layer, it will be rare that an OLE 2 class that is insertable in an OLE 2 container will not be insertable in an OLE 1 container.

If a particular class is insertable in an OLE 1 container, the **ProgID** root key will contain a **Protocol\StdFileEditing** subkey with appropriate subkeys **Verb**, **Server**, and so on, as in OLE 1. The application registered under the **Server** subkey is the full pathname to the executable file of the OLE 2 object application. An OLE 1 container uses the path and executable file names to launch the OLE 2 object application. The initialization of this application, in turn, causes the OLE 2 compatibility layer to be loaded. This layer handles subsequent interactions with the OLE 1 client (container), turning them into OLE 2-like requests to the OLE 2 application. An OLE 2 object application need take no special action beyond setting up these registration database entries for its objects to be insertable into an OLE 1 container.

The **ProgID** key and subkeys appear in the registration database as shown in the following example, where <Progid> is the key, and **Insertable**, **Protocol**, **StdFileEditing**, **Verb**, and so on are subkeys.

```
<ProgId> = <MainUserTypeName>
Insertable                    // class is insertable in OLE 2 containers
Protocol
    StdFileEditing            // OLE 1 compatibility information; present
if, and only if, objects of this
                              // class are insertable in OLE 1 containers.
        Server = <creator signature of object application>
```

```
            Verb
                0 = <verb 0>// Verb entries for the OLE 2 application must
start with zero as the
                1 = <verb 1>// primary verb and run consecutively.
CLSID = <CLSID>             // The corresponding CLSID. Needed by
GetClassFile.
```

To summarize, any root key that has either an **Insertable** or a **Protocol\StdFileEditing** subkey is the ProgID (or OLE 1 class name) of a class that should appear in the Insert Object dialog box. The value of that root key is the human-readable name displayed in the Insert Object dialog box.

The CLSID Key and Subkeys

Most of the OLE 2 object application information is stored in subkeys under the **CLSID** root key (unlike OLE 1 in which all information is kept immediately under the root). As a result, only classes explicitly intended to be user-visible appear when the registration database viewer, Reg Viewer, is run.

The immediate subkey of the **CLSID** root key is a string version of the CLSID. This subkey indicates where the code that services this class can be found.

Most of the information found under the CLSID root key is used by the OLE default object handler to return various information about an object's class when the object is in the loaded state. Examples of this include the **Verb**, the **AuxUserType**, and the **MiscStatus** entries. The **Insertable** subkey appears under both this key and the **ProgID** key.

```
CLSID
<CLSID> = <Main User Type Name>
// local (same machine) server; see "Server =" under ProgID key.
    LocalServer = <creator signature of app>
    InprocServer = <name of dll> // Reserved for use with in process server; relatively
rare for
                                    // insertable classes.
    InprocHandler = <name of dll>   // in process handler. "OLE2:Def$DefFSet" for the
                                    // default OLE 2 handler
    Verb                            // info returned in IOleObject::EnumVerbs().
        verb number = <name, menu flags, verb flags>
                                    // several examples follow:
            0 = Edit, 0, 2          // primary verb; often Edit; on menu; possibly dirties
object,
                                    // MF_STRING | MF_UNCHECKED | MF_ENABLED == 0.
           1 = Play, 0, 3           // other verb; appears on menu; leaves object clean
          -3 = Hide, 0, 1           // pseudo verb for hiding window; not on menu, opt.
          -2 = Open, 0, 1           // pseudo verb for opening in sep. window; not on
menu, opt.
          -1 = Show, 0, 1           // pseudo verb for showing in preferred state; not on
menu, opt.
```

```
    AuxUserType                   // auxiliary user types (main user type above)
        <form of type> = <string>   // See IOleObject::GetUserType(); for example:
        2 = <ShortName>           // key 1 should not be used
        3 = <Application name>      // Contains the human-readable name of the
application. Used
                                    // when the actual name of the app is needed (for
example in
                                    // the Paste Special dialog's result field) Example:
Acme Draw
    MiscStatus = <default>          // def status used for all aspects; see
IOleObject::GetMiscStatus
        <aspect> = <integer>      // exceptions to above;  for example:4 = 1
                                    // DVASPECT_ICON = OLEMISC_RECOMPOSEONRESIZE
    DataFormats
        DefaultFile = <format>      // default main file/object format of objects of this
class.
        GetSet                      // list of formats for default impl. of EnumFormatEtc;
very similar
                                    // to Request/SetDataFormats in OLE 1 entries
        <n> = <format ,aspect, medium, flag>
                                            // in the preceding  line,
                                    // n  is a zero-based integer index;
                                    // format is clipboard format;
                                    // aspect is one or more of DVASPECT_*, -1 for "all";
                                    // medium is one or more of TYMED_*;
                                    // flag is one or more of DATADIR_*.
                                    // three examples follow:
                                    // 0 = PICT, -1, 32, 1
                                    // PICT, all aspects, TYMED_MFPICT,
                                    // DATADIR_GET
                                    // 1 = BIF3, 1, 15, 3 shows
                                    // Microsoft Excel's Biff format version 3,
                                    // DVASPECT_CONTENT,
                                    // TYMED_HGLOBAL | TYMED_FILE |
                                    // TYMED_ISTREAM | TYMED_ISTORAGE,
                                    // (DATADIR_SET | DATADIR_GET)
                                    // 2 = RTF, 1,1,3
    Insertable                      // when present, the class appears in the Insert
Object dialog.
                                    // (not present for internal classes like the moniker
classes)
    ProgID = <ProgID>               // the programmatic identifier for this class.
    TreatAs = <CLSID>               // see CoGetTreatAs()
    AutoConvertTo = <CLSID>       // see OleGetAutoConvert()
    Conversion                      // support for Change Type dialog box
        Readable
            Main = <format,format,format,format, ...>
        Readwritable
            Main = <format,format,format,format, ...>
    DefaultIcon = <index>           // parameters passed to ExtractIcon
```

```
    Interfaces = <IID, IID, ...>      // optional. If this key is present, then its values
are the
                                      // total interfaces supported by this class:if the IID
is not in this list,
                                      // then the interface is never supported by an
instance of this class.
    VersionIndependentProgID = <VersionIndependentProgID>
```

The Version-Independent ProgID Key and Subkeys

An OLE object application must register a version-independent ProgID in the **Version-Independent ProgID** root key. This key provides a constant name, called the "MainUserTypeName," which refers to the currently installed version of the application's class. The MainUserTypeName must correspond to the name of the latest version of the object application.

```
<VersionIndependentProgID> = <MainUserTypeName>
    CLSID = <CLSID>                 // the class id of the newest installed
version of that class
    CurVer = <ProgID>                   // the ProgID of the newest
installed version of that class
```

In additon to the above entry, you should add the following entry to the **CLSID** root key:

```
CLSID
<CLSID> = <Main User Type Name>
        VersionIndependentProgID = <VersionIndependentProgID>
```

The FileExtension Key

OLE applications may optionally register a file extension in the registration database, which may be used at various times to associate files of this type with a specific application (this key is maintained for compatibility with the Windows version of OLE). To register the file extension, an application must first create the **FileExtension** root key as shown in the following example:

```
<.ext>  = <ProgID>  //used by GetClassFile and File Monikers
```

The FileType Key and Subkeys

Note The FileType key and subkeys are not supported in version 2.01 of OLE.

The Interface Key and Subkeys

If your application implements a new interface, the Interface key must be completed in order for OLE 2 to register the new interface. There needs to be one IID subkey for each new interface, as shown in the following example:

```
Interface
    <IID> = <textual name of interface> // for example: "IOleObject"
        ProxyStubClsID = <CLSID >    // Used internally by OLE 2 for interprocess
                                             // communication.
        NumMethods = <integer>       // Number of methods in the interface.
        BaseInterface = <IID>            // Interface from which this was derived. Absence
                                             // of key means IUnknown. Key present but
empty
                                             // value means derived from nothing.
```

OLE 1 Compatibility Subkeys

To handle two-way compatibility, the OLE 2 compatibility layer creates OLE 2-style entries for OLE 1 classes it discovers and places them under the **CLSID** key. When registering an OLE 2 object application on a system that contains an OLE 1 version of the same application, it might be necessary to add "AutoConvertTo" or "TreatAs" subkeys to the original OLE 1 application portion of the registration database. For more information, see "Overwriting the OLE 1 Application."

```
CLSID
    <CLSID> = <OLE1UserTypeName>     // This is an entry auto-generated by OLE 2 for an OLE
1 class.
        OLE1Class = <OLE 1 class name>   // This entry is created the first time an object
of that class
                                             // is inserted in an OLE 2 container.
        ProgId = <OLE 1 class name>      // Allows OLE 2 to convert CLSID back to an OLE 1
class name
        LocalServer = <creator signature of app>
```

OLE 1 Application Entries

When an OLE 1 class is inserted into an OLE 2 container for the first time, a new **CLSID** subkey is added to the original OLE 1 registration information by the OLE 2 compatibility layer. The value given to this key is a CLSID assigned by OLE 2 to this OLE 1 class, as shown in the following example:

```
<OLE1ClassName> = <OLE1UserTypeName>
    Protocol
        StdFileEditing
        Verb
    CLSID = <CLSID>
```

Adding Information to the Registration Database

Figure 4.1 shows a portion of the OLE 2 Registration Database file that contains the CLSID key and subkey entries created by the OLE 2 sample object application, OutLineInPlaceServer.

```
CLSID
 {00000402-0000-0000-0000-000000000046} = Ole 2.0 InPlace Server Sample Outline
   Local Server = OTIS
   InprocHandler = OLE2:Def$DefFSet
   ProgID = OLE2ISvrOutl
   Insertable
   AuxUserType
       2 = Outline
       3 = Ole 2.0 In-Place Outline Server
   Conversion
       Readwritable
           Main = OUTL
       Readable
           Main = OUTL
   DataFormats
       GetSet
           0 = OUTL, 1, 1, 3
           1 = EMBS, 1, 8, 1
           2 = TEXT, 1, 1, 3
           3 = PICT, 1, 32, 1
     MiscStatus = 512
           1 = 896
     Verb
           0 = Edit, 0, 2
           1 = Open, 0, 2
```

Figure 4.1 CLSID key and subkey entries

Figure 4.2 show a portion of the OLE 2 Registration Database file that contains the ProgID key and subkey entries.

```
OLE2ISvrOutl
    CLSID = {00000402-0000-0000-0000-000000000046}
    Insertable
    protocol
        StdFileEditing
            verb
                0 = Edit
                1 = Open
            server = OTIS
```

Figure 4.2 ProgID key and subkey entries

The following sections describe the HKEY_CLASSES_ROOT statements that make up the entries in the registration database.

The Registration Database file is a binary file containing a single-line entry for each key/value to be stored. The key and the value must be separated by an equal sign surrounded by spaces.

At the left side of the equal signs in the following examples, the "OLE2ISvrOtl" string should be replaced by the ProgID string associated with your own application. Also, the CLSID used in the examples {00000402-0000-0000-C000-000000000046} should be replaced by the CLSID assigned to your application.

ProgID Key Entry

The following sections describe examples of registering values in the registration database. The values of each key in the examples are those used to register the "Ole 2 In-Place Server Outline" sample application. You will need to set these values as required and used by your application.

Human-Readable String Subkey Entry

The entry to register the human-readable string (long form), such as that used in The Insert New dialog box, is as follows. The recommended maximum length for the string is 40 characters. For example:

```
HKEY_CLASSES_ROOT\OLE2ISvrOtl = Ole 2 In-Place Server Outline
```

Information for OLE 1 Applications Subkey Entries

To maintain OLE 1 compatibility, include the following OLE 1 information. The **Server** key entry should contain the full path to the object application. The entries for verbs must start with 0 as the primary verb and be consecutively numbered.

```
HKEY_CLASSES_ROOT\OLE2ISvrOtl\protocol\StdFileEditing\server = OTIC
HKEY_CLASSES_ROOT\OLE2ISvrOtl\protocol\StdFileEditing\verb\0 = Edit
HKEY_CLASSES_ROOT\OLE2ISvrOtl\protocol\StdFileEditing\verb\1 = Open
```

Insertable Subkey Entry

The **Insertable** subkey entry indicates that the object application should appear in the Insert New dialog box's list box when used by OLE 2 container applications.

```
HKEY_CLASSES_ROOT\OLE2ISvrOtl\Insertable
```

Entry Point Subkey

This entry points to the start of the application's OLE 2 information in the registration database.

```
HKEY_CLASSES_ROOT\OLE2ISvrOtl\CLSID = {00000402-0000-0000-C000-000000000046}
```

CLSID Key Entry

The subkey entries described in the following sections are subkeys to your **CLSID** root key. Not all possible subkeys are described.

CLSID Subkey Entry

Use the following statement to create a CLSID subkey under the **CLSID** key in the registration database.

```
HKEY_CLASSES_ROOT\CLSID\{00000402-0000-0000-C000-000000000046} =
Ole 2.01 In-Place Server Outline
```

LocalServer Subkey Entry

The **LocalServer** subkey designates where the application is located. The LocalServer subkey has the same value as the "OLE2ISvrOtl\Protocol\StdFileEditing\Server" key and should contain a full path name.

```
HKEY_CLASSES_ROOT\CLSID\{00000402-0000-0000-C000-000000000046}
\LocalServer = OTIC
```

Applications can optionally register an alias that points to the application file in the "Alias" value field of the \HKEY_CLASSES_ROOT\CLSID\{<*clsid-string*>}\LocalServer key. The alias must be registered as a REG_BINARY value.

When launching a LocalServer, OLE will first try to launch the application pointed to by the registered alias. If this fails, OLE will then try to launch according to the creator signature registered under the LocalServer key.

If an application registers a LocalServer alias it should still register a creator signature, especially if it is registering the "/Automation" switch.

The following example shows how to register a LocalServer alias (this example shows no error checking):

```
AliasHandle hAlias = <Alias pointing to LocalServer application file>;
HKEY hkeyLocalSrvr;

RegOpenKey(HKEY_CLASSES_ROOT, "CLSID\\{<clsid-string>}\\LocalServer",
        &hkeyLocalSrvr);
```

```
RegSetValueEx(hkeyLocalSrvr, "Alias", NULL, REG_BINARY,
              (char *)*hAlias, GetHandleSize((Handle)hAlias));
RegCloseKey(hkeyLocalSrvr);
```

InprocHandler Subkey Entry

The **InprocHandler** subkey designates whether the application uses a custom object handler. If no custom handler is used, the entry should be set to the default handler as shown in the following example.

```
HKEY_CLASSES_ROOT\CLSID\{00000402-0000-0000-C000-000000000046}
\InprocHandler = OLE2:Def$DefFSet
```

Verb Subkey Entry

The verbs for the application must be numbered consecutively in the registration database.

The second value after a verb indicates whether the verb will dirty the object. It also indicates whether the verb should appear in the menu (as defined by OLEVERBATTRIB_). For more information, see **IOleObject::EnumVerbs** in Chapter 6, "Compound Document Interfaces and Functions."

The entry for Verb 0: "Edit"

appears as follows:

```
HKEY_CLASSES_ROOT\CLSID\{00000402-0000-0000-C000-000000000046}\Verb\0 = Edit,0,0
```

The entry for Verb 1: "Open"

appears as:

```
HKEY_CLASSES_ROOT\CLSID\{00000402-0000-0000-C000-000000000046}\Verb\1 = Open,0,0
```

AuxUserType Subkey Entry

The **AuxUserType** key describes the short and actual human-readable names of the application. The short name is used in the menus, including pop ups, and the recommended maximum length for the string is 15 characters. A short name example follows.

```
HKEY_CLASSES_ROOT\CLSID\{00000402-0000-0000-C000-000000000046}\AuxUserType\2 = In-Place
Outline
```

For more information on displaying a short readable name, see **IOleObject::GetUserType** in Chapter 6, "Compound Document Interfaces and Functions."

The long human-readable name of the application is used in the Results field of the Paste Special dialog box. This string should contain the actual name of the application (such as "Acme Draw 2.0").

```
HKEY_CLASSES_ROOT\CLSID\{00000402-0000-0000-C000-000000000046}\AuxUserType\3 = Ole 2 In-
Place Server
```

MiscStatus Subkey Entry

Use the following statement to set the **MiscStatus** subkey. For information on the different settings, see **IOleObject::GetMiscStatus** in Chapter 6, "Compound Document Interfaces and Functions."

```
HKEY_CLASSES_ROOT\CLSID\{00000402-0000-0000-C000-000000000046}\MiscStatus = 0
```

DataFormats Subkey Entry

The **DataFormats** subkey lists the default and main data formats supported by the application. This entry is used by the **IDataObject::GetData**, **IDataObject::SetData** and **IDataObject::EnumFormatEtc** methods.

The values defined in the following example entry are 'TEXT', DVASPECT_CONTENT, TYMED_HGLOBAL, and DATADIR_GET | DATADIR_SET. For other examples, see the section, "OLE 2 Registration Database File" earlier in this chapter.

```
HKEY_CLASSES_ROOT\CLSID\{00000402-0000-0000-C000-000000000046}\DataFormats\GetSet\0 =
TEXT,1,1,3
```

The values defined in the following entry are: 'PICT', DVASPECT_CONTENT, TYMED_MFPICT, DATADIR_GET.

```
HKEY_CLASSES_ROOT\CLSID\{00000402-0000-0000-C000-000000000046}\DataFormats\GetSet\1 =
PICT,1,32,1
```

The values defined in the following entry are: 2 = 'EMBS', DVASPECT_CONTENT, TYMED_ISTORAGE, and DATADIR_GET.

```
HKEY_CLASSES_ROOT\CLSID\{00000402-0000-0000-C000-000000000046}\DataFormats\GetSet\2 =
EMBS,1,8,1
```

The values defined in the following entry are: 3 = 'OUTL' (cfOutline), DVASPECT_CONTENT, TYMED_HGLOBAL, and DATADIR_GET | DATADIR_SET

```
HKEY_CLASSES_ROOT\CLSID\{00000402-0000-0000-C000-000000000046}\DataFormats\GetSet\3 =
OUTL,1,1,3
```

The following example entry declares the default File Format supported by this application to be CF_OUTLINE:

```
HKEY_CLASSES_ROOT\CLSID\{00000402-0000-0000-C000-000000000046}\DataFormats\DefaultFile =
OUTL
```

Insertable Subkey Entry

The **Insertable** subkey entry indicates that this application should appear in the Insert New... dialog box's list box when used by OLE 2 container applications. This entry is required for future use.

```
HKEY_CLASSES_ROOT\CLSID\{00000402-0000-0000-C000-000000000046}\Insertable
```

ProgID Subkey Entry

Every insertable object class must have an associated ProgID that is registered under the **ProgID** subkey entry. For information on the creation and syntax of ProgIDs, see "Programmatic Identifiers" earlier in this chapter.

```
HKEY_CLASSES_ROOT\CLSID\{00000402-0000-0000-C000-000000000046}\ProgID = OLE2ISvrOtl
```

Conversion Subkey Entry

Information under the **Conversion** subkey is used in the Convert dialog box to determine which formats the application can read and write. The following entry registers a file format that the application can read (convert from):

```
HKEY_CLASSES_ROOT\CLSID\{00000402-0000-0000-C000-000000000046}\Conversion\Readable\Main =
OUTL
```

The following entry registers a file format that the application can read and write (activate as):

```
HKEY_CLASSES_ROOT\CLSID\{00000402-0000-0000-C000-000000000046}\Conversion\Readwritable\Main
= OUTL
```

DefaultIcon Subkey Entry

The **DefaultIcon** subkey provides default icon information for iconic presentations of objects. This entry contains the index of the icon within the executable.

```
HKEY_CLASSES_ROOT\CLSID\{00000402-0000-0000-C000-000000000046}\DefaultIcon = 128
```

Version-Independent ProgID Key Entry

The **ProgID** key describes the version-independent programmatic ID used for this class (for more information, see "Programmatic Identifiers" earlier in this chapter).

The following example statements show that "Ole 2 In-Place Server Outline" is the version-independent ProgID for the CLSID {0000402-0000-0000-C000-000000000046}.

```
HKEY_CLASSES_ROOT\ISvrOtl.Outline = Ole 2 In-Place Server Outline
HKEY_CLASSES_ROOT\ISvrOtl.Outline\CLSID = {0000402-0000-0000-C000-000000000046}
HKEY_CLASSES_ROOT\ISvrOtl.Outline\CurVer = OLE2ISvrOtl
```

FileExtension Key Entry

The **FileExtension** key can be used to optionally register a file extension for use by by your application (although not often used, this key remains primarily for compatibility with Windows). The value of the key is the application's ProgID, which in the following example is "OLE2ISvrOtl."

```
HKEY_CLASSES_ROOT\.oln = OLE2ISvrOtl
```

MacFInfo Key Entry

So that other applications can obtain the CLSID of an OLE object (using **GetClassFile**), object applications must register their *CreatorSigs*, *FileTypes*, and corresponding CLSIDs under the MacFInfo key in the registration database, using the following form:

```
MacFInfo
    Creator(<Hex representation of CreatorSig1>) = CreatorSig1
        CLSID = {Default CLSID for this CreatorSig1}
        Type(<Hex representation of FileTypeA>) = FileTypeA
            CLSID = {CLSID for (CreatorSig1,FileTypeA)}
        Type(<Hex representation of FileTypeB>) = FileTypeB
            CLSID = {CLSID for (CreatorSig1,FileTypeB)}
```

An application does not have to register a default CLSID for its *CreatorSig* if it does not want to.

As an example, consider the following fictional entries for Microsoft Word and Microsoft Excel:

```
MacFInfo
    Creator(4D535744) = MSWD
        Type(5744424e) = WDBN
        CLSID = {000...00046}         // Word
```

```
Creator(5843454C) = XCEL
    Type(584c4333) = XLS3
    CLSID = {000........00046}        // ExcelWorksheet
```

Given the file's *CreatorSig* "CREA" and *FileType* "TYPP," **GetClassFile** looks for the CLSID under

```
MacFInfo\Creator(<Hex-CREA>)\Type(<Hex-TYPP>)\CLSID
```

If not found, **GetClassFile** looks for the default CLSID under

```
MacFInfo\Creator(<Hex-CREA>)\CLSID
```

If **GetClassFile** is called on an OLE 1 file and the OLE 1 object application is not registered for OLE 2, *CreatorSig* and *FileType* are used to search for the OLE 1 class name (ProgID) in the OLE 1 Embedding Preferences file. If found, then the OLE 1 class is registered in the OLE 2 Registration Database file via **CLSIDFromProgID**, and the resulting CLSID is returned from **GetClassFile**.

When **CLSIDFromProgID** registers an OLE 1 class in the OLE2 Registration Database file, then the MacFInfo data is registered according to the *CreatorSig* and *FileTypes* that were registered in the OLE 1 Embedding Preferences file for that OLE 1 class. A default CLSID for the *CreatorSig* will be registered if there were no particular *FileTypes* registered for that class in the OLE 1 database. **CLSIDFromProgID** will not overwrite MacFInfo data that is already registered for a particular creator signature.

When registering MacFInfo keys for a particular creator signature, an application should overwrite or remove any MacFInfo data previously registered for that creator signature. An easy way to do this is to remove the MacFInfo\Creator('Hex-CREA') key before registering the new MacFInfo information.

Automation Key Entry

An application that supports OLE automation must register the /Automation switch in order to receive OLE 2 /Auto apple events when being launched by OLE. This is done using the following form:

```
Local Server = CreatorSig /Automation
```

Registering OLE 2 Libraries

The OLE 2 libraries require that many internal interfaces be registered. Therefore, if your application installs the OLE 2 libraries on a machine that does not have them already, it should register OLE 2 specific information in the Registration Database file.

Also, if your program has overwritten older versions of the application on the user's hard disk, it will need to register information in the registration database.

If your program does not install OLE 2 libraries because it found more recent libraries on the hard disk, it should not register the OLE 2 interface information.

Note When checking the version numbers in the Vers Resource on existing OLE 2 libraries to determine whether or not to replace them on the user's hard disk, do so on a file-by-file basis.

Accommodating OLE 1 Versions of the Object Application

There are two basic situations that can arise when the OLE 1 version of an object application is superseded by an OLE 2 version on the user's system, such as when upgrading:

- An OLE 1 version of the application is present on the user's system and the OLE 2 version overwrites the OLE 1 version.
- An OLE 1 version of the application is present on the user's system, but the OLE 2 version does not overwrite it.

Note Even if an OLE 1 object application is not present on the user's system, it is recommended that the OLE 2 object application register itself as being able to service OLE 1 objects. To do this, follow the guidelines in the section "Overwriting the OLE 1 Application," plus, add the following entry to the root of the registration database:

<OLE 1 class name>/CLSID = *<CLSID of OLE 1 application>*

Overwriting the OLE 1 Application

When replacing an OLE 1 object application with an OLE 2 version, the OLE 2 object application must do the following steps to add the OLE 2 information to the registration database.

1. Register the Ole 2 application in the registration database file as previously described.
2. Modify the *original* registration database entries of the OLE 1 object application by changing the executable path to point to the OLE 2 object

application. For example, the **Server** subkey for the OLE 1 executable, named **svrapp1** in this example, changes from

OLE1ISvrOtl\Protocol\StdFileEditing\Server = svrapp

to

OLE1ISvrOtl\Protocol\StdFileEditing\Server = svrapp2

where **svrapp2** is the name of the OLE 2 object application.

3. If the OLE 2 application will automatically convert OLE 1 objects to the OLE 2 object format (during a save operation), create or modify the following registration database entries:

    a. Modify the original registration database entry of the OLE 1 application by changing the "Value of the ProgID = Main User Type Name" key of the registration database to the name of the OLE 2 application. For example, the ProgID of the OLE 1 application

    OLE1App = Ole 1 Object Application

    becomes

    OLE1App = Ole 2 Object Application

    b. Set the "AutoConvertTo = CLSID" subkey entry for the OLE 1 application under the **CLSID** key (not under the original OLE 1 entries at the root of the registration database) to the CLSID of the OLE 2 application. (See also "OLE 1 Compatibility Subkeys," earlier in this chapter.)

CLSID\{*CLSID of OLE 1 app.***}\AutoConvertTo = {***CLSID of OLE 2 app***}**

Note You can obtain the CLSID of the OLE 1 object application for inclusion in registration database by calling **CLSIDFromProgID**.

---

    c. Modify the original registration database entry of the OLE 1 application by setting the verbs to those of the OLE 2 application. For example, change

    OLE1App\Protocol\StdFileEditing\Verb\0 = Edit

    to

    OLE1App\Protocol\StdFileEditing\Verb\0 = Edit
    OLE1App\Protocol\StdFileEditing\Verb\1 = Open

4. If the user is allowed to open OLE 1 objects and save them back to disk in the OLE 1 format:

    a. Set the "TreatAs = CLSID" entry to the CLSID of the OLE 2 application using the following form:

    CLSID\{CLSID of OLE 1 app**}\TreatAs = {**CLSID of OLE 2 app**}**

    b. Set the OLE 1 object application verbs to those of the OLE 2 object application as described earlier (see step 3).

When the OLE 1 object application is not replaced by the OLE 2 version, but the user is allowed to open OLE 1 objects with the OLE 2 application and save them back to disk in the OLE 1 format, set the "TreatAs = CLSID" entry to the CLSID of the OLE 2 application (see step 4).

If the OLE 1 version of the application is not overwritten, or if the user does not want to set the "Treat As" option, register the OLE 2 version as a separate and new application.

Using the Registration Database for Localization

It is possible to address a pair of product-localization issues by inserting a special key in the registration database. This key allows functions to return a specified string instead of a default value or the string "Unknown."

With OLE 1, an object application can be registered in the registration database without specifing any verbs. In this case, the application has a single implied verb that is understood to be "Edit" by OLE 1 containers.

When an OLE 2 application calls **IOleObject::EnumVerbs** or **OleRegEnumVerbs** on an object of this class, one verb is enumerated. By default, the name of the verb is "Edit." To avoid having the string "Edit" as the enumerated verb, the following key can be included in the registration database:

\Software\Microsoft\OLE1\UnregisteredVerb = *<verbname>*

The *verbname* is the value that will be returned from the enumeration and allows for localization of the default verb to a specified string to accommodate a specific language.

Note Do not attempt to register a verb (under ProgID\Protocol\StdFileEditing) for an application that did not register the verb itself.

The OLE 2 default handler's implementation of **IOleObject::GetUserType** first examines the registration database by calling **OleRegGetUserType**. If the object's class is not found in the database, the User Type from the object's **IStorage** is returned. If the class is not found, the string "Unknown" is returned.

By inserting the following key in the registration database, **IOleObject::GetUserType** returns the value of the string specified by *<usertype>*. This string can be localized for a different language user-type name, instead of using the "Unknown" string, for the User Type.

\Software\Microsoft\OLE2\UnknownUserType = *<usertype>*

OLE 2 Registration Functions

The following functions are used to manipulate the OLE 2 Registration Database file, which is stored in the Extensions folder. These functions are defined in macapi.h:

```
HRESULT OleRegGetUserType (REFCLSID clsid, unsigned long dwFormOfType, char * * pszUserType);
HRESULT OleRegGetMiscStatus (REFCLSID clsid, unsigned long dwAspect, unsigned long * pdwStatus);
HRESULT OleRegEnumFormatEtc (REFCLSID clsid, unsigned long dwDirection,
        LPENUMFORMATETC * ppenumFormatetc);
HRESULT OleRegEnumVerbs (REFCLSID clsid, LPENUMOLEVERB * ppenumOleVerb);
long RegCloseKey (OLEREG_HKEY, hKey);
long RegCreateKey (HKEY hKey, const char * lpszSubKey, HKEY lphkResult);
long RegDeleteKey (HKEY hKey, const char * lpszSubKey);
long RegEnumKey (HKEY hKey, unsigned long iSubkey, char * lpszBuffer, unsigned long cbBuffer);
long RegEnumProgID (HKEY hKey, unsigned long isubKey, char * lpszSubKey, unsigned long cbSubKeyBuf,
        char * lpszMainUserType, unsigned long cbMainUserTypeBuf, unsigned long * lpgrfFlags);
long RegFlush (void);
long RegInitialize (void);
long RegOpenKey (HKEY hKey, const char * lpszSubKey, HKEY * lphkresult);
long RegDeleteValue(HKEY hKey, const char * lpszValue);
long RegEnumValue(HKEY hKey, unsigned long dwIdx, char * lpszValue, unsigned long * lpcbValue,
        unsigned long * lpdwReserved, unsigned long * lpdwType, unsigned char * lpbData,
        unsigned long * lpcbData);
long RegQueryValue (HKEY hKey, const char * lpszSubKey, char * lpszValue, long * lpcb);
long RegQueryValueEx(HKEY hKey, const char * lpszSubKey, char * lpszValue, unsigned long * dwType,
        long * lpcb);
long RegSetValue (HKEY hKey, const char * lpszSubKey, unsigned long fdwType, char * lpszValue,
        unsigned long cb);
long RegSetValueEx(HKEY hKey, const char * lpszValueName, unsigned long dwReserved, unsigned long dwType,
        const char * lpszValue, unsigned long dwValSize);
```

Note There are three API versions for the preceding list of OLE 2 registration functions, as illustrated below for **RegCloseKey**:

```
RegCloseKey (OLEREG_HKEY, hKey);
_RegCloseKey (HKEY hKey);
StaticRegCloseKey (HKEY hKey);
```

Applications should call the **Reg*** version when they are using the DLL version of the OLE libraries. Applications using the static version of the OLE libraries should call the **StaticReg*** functions.

To determine at runtime which of these functions to call, use the **_Reg*** version. The **_Reg*** version calls the appropriate function depending on the value of the externally defined constant **_bregstatic**: TRUE results in the **StaticReg*** version being called while FALSE results in the **Reg*** version being called.

OleRegGetUserType

HRESULT OleRegGetUserType (*clsid, dwFormOfType, pszUserType*)
REFCLSID *clsid*
unsigned long *dwFormOfType*
char * * *pszUserType*

OleRegGetUserType returns the user type of the indicated class from the registration database.

Parameters

clsid
Specifies the CLSID of the object class whose user type is requested.

dwFormOfType
Specifies the form of the user-presentable string; valid values are taken from the enumeration **USERCLASSTYPE**; for more information, see **IOleObject::GetUserType**.

pszUserType
Points to where to return the user type.

Return Values

Value	Meaning
S_OK	The user type was returned successfully.
E_OUTOFMEMORY	There is insufficient memory to complete the operation.
REGDB_E_CLASS-NOTREG	There is no CLSID registed for the class object.
REGDB_E_READ-REGDB	There was an error reading the registration database.
OLE_E_REGDB_KEY	The *ProgID = MainUserTypeName* and *CLSID = MainUserTypeName* keys are missing from the registration database.

See Also

IOleObject::GetUserType

OleRegGetMiscStatus

HRESULT OleRegGetMiscStatus (*clsid, dwAspect, pdwStatus*)
REFCLSID *clsid*
unsigned long *dwAspect*
unsigned long * *pdwStatus*

OleRegGetMiscStatus returns the miscellaneous status information for the given class from the registration database.

Parameters

clsid
Specifies the class whose status information is requested.

dwAspect
Specifies the aspect of the class whose information is requested.

pdwStatus
Points to where to return the status.

Return Values

Value	Meaning
S_OK	The status information was returned successfully.
REGDB_E_CLASS-NOTREG	No CLSID is registed for the class object.
REGDB_E_READ-REGDB	An error occured reading the registration database.
OLE_E_REGDB_KEY	The GetMiscStatus key is missing from the registration database.

See Also **IOleObject::GetMiscStatus**

OleRegEnumVerbs

HRESULT OleRegEnumVerbs (*clsid, ppenumOleVerb*)
REFCLSID *clsid*
LPENUMOLEVERB * *ppenumOleVerb*

OleRegEnumVerbs returns an enumerator that enumerates the entries in a **OLEVERB** data structure.

Parameters

clsid
Specifies the object class whose verbs are requested.

ppenumOleVerb
Points to where to return the enumerator.

Return Values

Value	Meaning
S_OK	The eunumerator was returned successfully.
E_OUTOFMEMORY	An out of memory condition occurred.
OLEOBJ_E_NOVERBS	There are no verbs registered for the class.
REGDB_E_CLASSNOTREG	No CLSID is registered for the class object.
REGDB_E _READREGDB	There was an error reading the registration database.
OLE_E_REGDB_KEY	The DataFormats/GetSet key is missing from the registration database.

Comments

For more information on the **OLEVERB** data structure, see **IOleObject::EnumVerbs**.

See Also **IOleObject::EnumVerbs**

OleRegEnumFormatEtc

HRESULT OleRegEnumFormatEtc (*clsid, dwDirection, ppenumFormatetc*)
REFCLSID *clsid*
unsigned long *dwDirection*
LPENUMFORMATETC * *ppenumFormatetc*

OleRegEnumFormatEtc returns an enumerator that enumerates the entries in a **FORMATETC** data structure containing the supported format information for the indicated class.

Parameters

clsid
Specifies the class whose verbs are requested.

dwDirection
Specifies the set of formats to be enumerated; valid values for *dwDirection* are taken from the enumeration **DATADIR**; for more information see the following comments.

ppenumFormatetc
Points to where to return the enumerator.

Return Values

Value	Meaning
S_OK	The eunumerator was returned successfully.
E_OUTOFMEMORY	An out of memory condition occurred.
REGDB_E_CLASSNOTREG	There is no CLSID registed for the class object.
REGDB_E_READREGDB	There was an error reading the registration database.
OLE_E_REGDB_KEY	The DataFormats/GetSet key is missing from the registration database.

Comments

The **DATADIR** enumeration is defined in DVOBJ.H as follows:

```
typedef enum tagDATADIR
{
    DATADIR_GET       = 1,
    DATADIR_SET       = 2,
```

DATADIR_GET enumerates those formats that can be passed to **IDataObject::GetData**; DATADIR_SET enumerates those formats that can be passed to **IDataObject::SetData**.

See Also **IDataObject::EnumFormatEtc**

RegCloseKey

long RegCloseKey(*hkey***)**
HKEY *hkey*

RegCloseKey closes a key, which releases the key's handle. When the database is closed, all changes are committed to disk.

Parameters

hkey
Specifies the handle of the key to close.

Return Values

Value	Meaning
ERROR_SUCCESS	The function completed successfully. Otherwise, it is an error.

Comments

RegCloseKey should be called only if a key has been opened by either **RegOpenKey** or **RegCreateKey**.

The handle for a given key should not be used after it has been closed, because it may no longer be valid. Key handles should not be left open any longer than necessary.

See Also

RegCreateKey, **RegDeleteKey**, **RegOpenKey**, **RegSetValue**

RegCreateKey

long RegCreateKey(*hkey, lpszSubKey, lphkResult***)**
HKEY *hkey*
const char * *lpszSubKey*
HKEY FAR * *lphkResult*

RegCreateKey creates the key identified by *lpszSubKey*. If the key already exists in the registration database, **RegCreateKey** opens it.

Parameters

hkey
Identifies an open key. The key opened or created by **RegCreateKey** (*lpszSubKey*) is a subkey of *hkey*. This value should not be NULL.

lpszSubKey
Points to a null-terminated string specifying the subkey to open or create.

lphkResult
Points to the handle of the key that is opened or created.

Return Values

Value	Meaning
ERROR_SUCCESS	The function completed successfully. Otherwise, it is an error.

Comments An application can create keys that are subordinate to the top-level root key of the database by specifying HKEY_CLASSES_ROOT for *hKey*. **RegCreateKey** can be used to create several keys at once.

See Also **RegCloseKey**, **RegOpenKey**, **RegSetValue**

RegDeleteKey

long RegDeleteKey(*hkey*, *lpszSubKey*)
HKEY *hkey*
const char * *lpszSubKey*

RegDeleteKey deleted the specified key. When a key is deleted, its value and all of its subkeys are deleted.

Parameters

hkey
Identifies an open key (which can be HKEY_CLASSES_ROOT). The key deleted by **RegDeleteKey** is a subkey of this key.

lpszSubKey
Points to a null-terminated string specifying the subkey to delete. This value should not be NULL.

Return Values

Value	Meaning
ERROR_SUCCESS	The function completed successfully.
ERROR_ACCESS_DENIED	Either the application does not have privileges for the specified key or another application has opened the specified key.

See Also **RegCloseKey**

RegDeleteValue

long RegDeleteValue(*hkey*, *lpszValue*)
HKEY *hkey*
const char * *lpszValue*

RegDeleteValue removes a named value from the given registry key.

Parameters

hkey
Identifies a currently open key or any of the following predefined reserved handle values:

HKEY_CLASSES_ROOT

lpszValue
Points to a null-terminated string that names the value to remove. If this parameter is NULL or points to an empty string, the value set by the **RegSetValue** function is removed.

Return Values

Value	Meaning
ERROR_SUCCESS	The function completed successfully.
ERROR_ACCESS_DENIED	Either the application does not have privileges for the specified key or another application has opened the key.

See Also **RegSetValueEx**

RegEnumKey

long RegEnumKey(*hkey, iSubKey, lpszBuffer, cbBuffer*)
HKEY *hkey*
unsigned long *iSubKey*
char * *lpszBuffer*
unsigned long *cbBuffer*

RegEnumKey enumerates the subkeys of a specified key.

Parameters

hkey
Specifies the handle of the key to query. Identifies an open key (which can be HKEY_CLASSES_ROOT) for which subkey information is retrieved.

iSubkey
Identifies an open key (which can be HKEY_CLASSES_ROOT) for which subkey information is retrieved.

lpszBuffer
Points to a buffer that contains the name of the subkey when the function returns. This function copies only the name of the subkey, not the full key hierarchy, to the buffer.

cbBuffer
Specifies the size, in bytes, of the buffer pointed to by *lpszBuffer*.

Return Values

Value	Meaning
ERROR_SUCCESS	The function completed successfully.

Comments

The first parameter of **RegEnumKey** must specify an open key.

Applications typically precede the call to **RegEnumKey** with a call to **RegOpenKey** and follow it with a call to **RegCloseKey**. Calling **RegOpenKey** and **RegCloseKey** is not necessary when the first parameter is HKEY_CLASSES_ROOT, because this key is always open and available; however, calling these functions is an optimization.

While an application is using **RegEnumKey**, it should not make calls to any registration functions that might change the key being queried.

See Also **RegQueryValue**

RegEnumProgID

long RegEnumProgID(*hKey*, *isubKey*, *lpszBuffer*, *cbBuffer*, *lpszMainUserType*, *cbMainUserTypeBuf*, *lpgrfFlags*)

HKEY *hKey*
unsigned long *isubKey*
char * *lpszSubKey*
unsigned long *cbSubKeyBuf*
char * *lpszMainUserType*
unsigned long *cbMainUserTypeBuf*
unsigned long * *lpgrfFlags*

RegEnumProgID enumerates the subkeys of a specified key, indicating which enumerated subkeys are ProgIDs. This function can be used to enuerate ProgIDs from both the registration database and the Embedding Preferences files.

Parameters

hKey
Specifies the handle of the key to query. Identifies an open key (which can be HKEY_CLASSES_ROOT) for which subkey information is retrieved.

iSubkey
Specifies the index of the subkey to retrieve. this value should be zero for the first call to **RegEnumProgID**.

lpszSubKey
Points to a buffer that contains the name of the subkey when the function returns. This function copies only the name of the subkey, not the full key hierarchy, to the buffer.

cbSubKeybuf
Specifies the size, in bytes, of the buffer pointed to by *lpszBuffer*.

lpszMainUserType
If non-NULL, returns the MainUserType (or human-readable) string of the returned subkey if the subkey is a ProgID. If the returned subkey is not a ProgID, or if an error occurred when obtaining the MainUserType string, then an empty string (" ")is returned in *lpszMainUserType*.

cbMainUserTypeBuf
Specifies the size, in bytes, of the buffer pointed to by *lpszMainUserType*.

lpgrfFlags
Points to the status information returned for the given subkey.Valid values are from the enumeration **REGENUMPROGIDF**; for more information, see the following comments.

Return Values

Value	Meaning
ERROR_SUCCESS	The function completed successfully. Any other return value indicates that there are no more entries in the Registration Database or Embedding Preferences files, and the application's enumeration of the ProgID loop can end.

Comments

RegEnumProgID is used the same way as **RegEnumKey**, with the following differences:

- When **RegEnumProgID** is used in a loop to find all of the registered ProgIDs, **RegEnumProgID** first enumerates all subkeys of *hkey* in Registration Database file, and then, if *hkey* == HKEY_CLASSES_ROOT, it enumerates all ProgIDs in the Embedding Preferences file.
- If **RegEnumProgID** returns a subkey and if *lpgrfFlags* is non-NULL, the function returns status in **lpgrfFlags*, indicating certain properties of the returned subkey. If the returned subkey is a ProgID from the Embedding Preferences file, but the subkey is also a ProgID found in Registration Database file, then **lpgrfFlags* returns REGENUMPROGIDF_EMBPREF, but no other flags are set. (This is used to avoid duplication when enumerating ProgIDs when a ProgID exists in both the Registration Database file and the Embedding Preferences file.)

The values for *lpgrfFlags* are taken from the enumeration **REGENUMPROGIDF**, which is defined in MACDEF.H:

```
typedef enum tagREGENUMPROGIDF
{
    REGENUMPROGIDF_ISPROGID    = 1;  //the returned subkey is a ProgID
    REGENUMPROGIDF_EMBPREF     = 2;  //the returned subkey came from the
                                      //Embedding Preferences folder
    REGENUMPROGIDF_INSERTABLE = 4;   //the returned subkey is an
                                      //insertable ProgID
} REGENUMPROGIDF;
```

REGENUMPROGIDF values have the following meaning:

Value	Meaning
REGENUMPROGIDF-_ISPROGID	A subkey SUB is a ProgID if HKEY_CLASSES_ROOT\SUB has a CLSID subkey or a Protocol\StdFileEditing subkey, or SUB came from the Embedding Prefernces file.
REGENUMPROGIDF-_EMBPREF	This flag is set if the returned subkey is a ProgID from Embedding Preferences file. If this is returned, then the ProgID did not come from the registration database, so an application should not look for subkeys/values of the ProgID in the registration file. To enter the ProgID into the registration database (along with its appropriate OLE1 information from the Embedding Preferences file), the application calls **CLSIDFromProgID**(*szProgID*, *&clsid*).
REGENUMPROGIDF-_INSERTABLE	A subkey SUB is insertable if HKEY_CLASSES_ROOT\SUB has a Insertable subkey or a Protocol\StdFileEditing, or SUB came from the Embedding Prefernces file.

RegEnumValue

long RegEnumValue(*hkey*, *dwIdx*, *lpszValue*, *lpcbValue*, *lpdwReserved*, *lpdwType*, *lpbData*, *lpcbData***)**

HKEY *hkey*
unsigned long *dwIdx*
char * *lpszValue*
unsigned long * *lpcchValue*
unsigned long * *lpdwReserved*
unsigned long * *lpdwType*
unsigned char * *lpbData*
unsigned long * *lpcbData*

The **RegEnumValue** function enumerates the values for the given open registry key. The function copies one indexed value name and data block for the key each time it is called.

Parameters

hkey
Identifies a currently open key or any of the following predefined reserved handle values:

HKEY_CLASSES_ROOT

The enumerated values are associated with the key identified by *hkey*.

dwIdx
Specifies the index of the value to retrieve. This parameter should be zero for the first call to the **RegEnumValue** function and then be incremented for subsequent calls.

Because values are not ordered, any new value will have an arbitrary index. This means that the function may return values in any order.

lpszValue
Points to a buffer that receives the name of the value, including the terminating null character.

lpcbValue
Points to a variable that specifies the size, in characters, of the buffer pointed to the *lpszValue* parameter. This size should include the terminating null character. When the function returns, the variable pointed to by *lpcbValue* contains the number of characters stored in the buffer. The count returned does not include the terminating null character.

lpdwReserved
Reserved; must be NULL.

lpdwType
Points to a variable that receives the type code for the value entry. The type code can be one of the following values:

Value	Meaning
REG_BINARY	Binary data in any form.
REG_SZ	A null-terminated string. It will be a UNICODE or ANSI string depending on whether you use the UNICODE or ANSI functions.

The *lpdwType* parameter can be NULL if the type code is not required.

lpbData
Points to a buffer that receives the data for the value entry. This parameter can be NULL if the data is not required.

lpcbData
Points to a variable that specifies the size, in bytes, of the buffer pointed to by the *lpbData* parameter. When the function returns, the variable pointed to by the *lpcbData* parameter contains the number of bytes stored in the buffer. This parameter can be NULL, only if *lpbData* is NULL.

Return Values

Value	Meaning
ERROR_SUCCESS	The function completed successfully.

Comments

To enumerate values, an application should initially call the **RegEnumValue** function with the *dwIdx* parameter set to zero. The application should then increment *dwIdx* and call **RegEnumValue** until there are no more values (until the function returns ERROR_NO_MORE_ITEMS).

The application can also set *dwIdx* to the index of the last value on the first call to the function and decrement the index until the value with index 0 is enumerated. To retrieve the index of the last value, use the **RegQueryValueEx** function.

While using **RegEnumValue**, an application should not call any registration functions that might change the key being queried.

To determine the maximum size of the name and data buffers, use the **RegQueryValueEx** function.

See Also

RegQueryValueEx

RegFlush

long RegFlush(*void*)

RegFlush forces a write of the Registration Database file to disk.

Return Values

Value	Meaning
long	0 indicates the function completed successfully; any other value indicates an error occurred.

Comments

Applications normally do not call **RegFlush**; OLE makes this call on behalf of the application.

RegInitialize

long RegInitialize(*void*)

RegInitialize initializes the Registration Database file for use by OLE.

Return Values

Value	Meaning
long	0 indicates the function completed successfully; any other value indicates an error occurred.

Comments

Applications normally do not call **RegInitialize**; this is call that OLE makes on behalf of the application when the application calls **OleInitialize**.

RegOpenKey

long RegOpenKey(*hKey, lpszSubKey, lphkResult*)
HKEY *hKey*
const char * *lpszSubKey*
HKEY FAR * *lphkResult*

RegOpenKey opens the specified key in the OLE registration database.

Parameters

hKey
Identifies an open key (which can be HKEY_CLASSES_ROOT). The key opened by **RegOpenKey** is a subkey of this key. The value of *hKey* should not be NULL.

lpszSubKey
Points to a null-terminated string specifying the subkey to open.

lphkResult
Points to the handle of the key that is opened.

Return Values

Value	Meaning
ERROR_SUCCESS	The function completed successfully.
ERROR_BADKEY	Key is invalid.

Comments

Unlike **RegCreateKey**, **RegOpenKey** does not create the specified key if the key does not exist in the registration database.

See Also

RegCreateKey

RegQueryValue

long RegQueryValue(*hkey, lpszSubKey, lpszValue, pcb*)
HKEY *hkey*
const char * *lpszSubKey*
const char * *lpszValue*
long FAR * *lpcb*

RegQueryValue retrieves the text string associated with a specified key.

Parameters

hkey
Specifies the handle of the key to query. Identifies an open key (which can be HKEY_CLASSES_ROOT). This value should not be NULL.

lpszSubKey
Points to a null-terminated string specifying the name of the subkey of *hkey* for which a text string is retrieved. If *lpszSubKey* is NULL or points to an empty string, **RegQueryValue** retrieves the value of *hkey*.

lpszValue
Points to a buffer that contains the text string when the **RegQueryValue** returns.

lpcb
Points to a null-terminated string specifying the size, in bytes, of the string pointed to be *lpszValue*. This value should not be NULL.

Return Values

Value	Meaning
ERROR_SUCCESS	Function completed successfully.
ERROR_BADKEY	Cannot find specified key.

See Also **RegEnumKey**

RegQueryValueEx

long RegQueryValueEx(*hKey*, *lpszValueName*, *dwReserved*, *lpdwType*, *lpszData*, *lpcb*)
HKEY *hKey*
const char * *lpszValueName*
unsigned long * *dwReserved*
unsigned long * *lpdwType*
char * *lpbData*
long * *lpcbData*

RegQueryValueEx RegQueryValue retrieves any data type associated with a specified key.

Parameters

hKey
Specifies the handle of the key to query. Identifies an open key (which can be HKEY_CLASSES_ROOT). This value should not be NULL.

lpszValueName
Points to a null-terminated string specifying the name of the subkey of *hkey* for which a text string is retrieved. If *lpszValueName* is NULL or points to an empty string, **RegQueryValueEx** retrieves the value of *hkey*.

dwReserved
Reserved for future use; must be NULL.

lpdwType
Points to an unsigned long that contains the type of data returned; the value is either REG_SZ or REG_BINARY.

lpbData
Points to a buffer that contains the text string when the **RegQueryValueEx** returns.

lpcbData
Points to a null-terminated string specifying the size, in bytes, of the string pointed to be *lpbData*. This value should not be NULL.

Return Values

Value	Meaning
ERROR_SUCCESS	Function completed successfully.
ERROR_BADKEY	Cannot find specified key.

See Also **RegQueryValue**

RegSetValue

long RegSetValue(*hkey, lpszSubKey, type, lpValue, cb*)
HKEY *hkey*
const char * *lpszSubKey*
unsigned long *fdwtype*
const char * *lpszValue*
unsigned long *cb*

RegSetValue associates a text string with a specified key.

Parameters

hkey
Specifies the handle of the open key (which can be HKEY_CLASSES_ROOT). This value should not be NULL.

lpszSubKey
Points to a null-terminated string specifying the subkey of *hkey* with which a text string is associated. If *lpszSubKey* is NULL or points to an empty string, **RegSetValue** sets the value of *hkey*.

fdwType
Specifies the string type; must be REG_SZ.

lpszValue
Points to a null-terminated string specifying the text string to set for the given key.

cb
Specifies the size, in bytes, of the string pointed to be *lpszValue*. Optional; if *cb* is zero, **RegSetValue** will calculate the size.

Return Values

Value	Meaning
ERROR_SUCCESS	Key set successfully.
ERROR_BADKEY	Cannot find specified key.

Comments If the key specified by *lpszSubKey* does not exist, **RegSetValue** creates it.

See Also **RegSetValueEx**, **RegCreateKey**, **RegQueryValue**

RegSetValueEx

long RegSetValueEx(*hkey*, *lpszValueName*, *dwReserved*, *dwType*, *lpszValue*, *dwValSize*)
HKEY *hkey*
const char * *lpszValueName*
unsigned long *dwReserved*
unsigned long *dwType*
const char * *lpszValue*
unsigned long *dwValSize*

RegSetValueEx associates any number of named values of any data type with a specified key.

Parameters

hkey
Identifies a currently open key or any of the following predefined reserved handle values:

HKEY_CLASSES_ROOT

lpszValueName
Points to a null-terminated string containing the name of the subkey with which a value is associated. This parameter can be Null or a pointer to an empty string. In this case, the value will be added to the key identified by the *hKey* parameter.

dwReserved
Reserved for future use; must be zero.

dwType
Specifies the data type.

lpszValue
Points to a null-terminated string containing the value to set for the given key.

dwValSize
Specifies the length, in characters, of the string pointed to by the *lpszValue* parameter, not including the terminating null character.

Return Values

Value	Meaning
ERROR_SUCCESS	Key set successfully.
ERROR_BADKEY	Cannot find specified key.

Comments

If the key specified by the *lpszValueName* parameter does not exist, the **RegSetValueEx** function creates it.

Value lengths are limited by available memory. Long values (more than 2048 bytes) should be stored as files with the filenames stored in the configuration registry. This will help the registry perform efficiently.

See Also

RegQueryValueEx, **RegSetValue**

OLE 1 Registration Functions

The OLE 1 registration database, located in a file called "Embedding Preferences" in the System 7 Preferences folder, has two main purposes:

- The database allows OLE 1 applications to provide information about the objects they support to other OLE 1 applications.
- The database enables OLE to locate the code needed to process an object.

The OLE 1 file stores information by database key, a combination of the object class name with a protocol, the convention used for manipulating the data. Protocol, however, is optional and, if it is omitted, the StdFileEditing protocol is assumed. Each object class can have several attributes below it in the hierarchy. Typical attribute entries include the name of the application that can edit the object class, the lists of verbs that the object class can invoke, and the name of the handler for the object class.

The following functions support OLE 1 objects and are defined in macapi.h:

OLEREG_HKEY OleregOpenRegistration (void);
OLEREGSTATUS OleregCloseRegistration (HKEY hKey);
OLEREGSTATUS OleregGetValue (const char * lpKey, OLELONG KeyWord, OLELONG Index, OLEREG_VALUE lpValue,OLELONG * dwSize);
OLEREGSTATUS OlerefSetValue (const char * lpKey, OLELONG KeyWord, OLEREG_ORDER wInsertOrder, OLEREG_VALUE lpvalue, OLELONG dwSize);
OLEREGSTATUS OleregRemoveKey (const char * lpKey, OLELONG KeyWord, OLELONG Index);

Function Return Values

OLE 1 registration functions typically return a value from the enumeration **OLEREGSTATUS**:

```
typedef enum {

    OLEREG_OK,                              // success
    OLEREG_INVALID_KEY,                     // invalid key to close
    OLEREG_INVALID_KEYWORD,                 // invalid keyword to query/set
    OLEREG_ITEM_NOT_FOUND,
    OLEREG_INDEX_NOT_FOUND,                 // no such index in item list
    OLEREG_ENUM_DONE = OLEREG_INDEX_NOT_FOUND,
    OLEREG_REG_NOT_OPEN,
    OLEREG_DB_NOT_FOUND,                    // emb pref file not found
    OLEREG_DB_LOCKED,                       // emb pref file locked
    OLEREG_DB_ERROR,                        // error reading/writing
    OLEREG_ERR_MEMORY,                      // not enough or bad memory
    OLEREG_DB_BADFORM,                      // invalid entries in reg db
```

```
        OLEREG_FILE_NOT_FOUND,            // specified file not found
        OLEREG_ERR_GENERIC,               // some general error
        OLEREG_ERR_BUFFER_SIZE            // buffer bad size

} OLEREGSTATUS;
```

OleregOpenRegistration

OLEREG_HKEY OleregOpenRegistration(void)

OleregOpenRegistration opens the registration database and keeps it open until **OleregCloseRegistration** is called.

Return Values

Value	Meaning
OLEREGSTATUS	The return values is one of the enumerated types from OLEREGSTATUS.

Comments

Successive calls to **OleregOpenRegistration** while the database is open will increment a lock count. Each call to **OleregOpenRegistration** must be balanced by a subsequent call to **OleregCloseRegistration**.

OleregOpenRegistration is for speed optimization only since keeping the database open for successive modifications or queries speeds up operation. However, keeping the database open also prevents access by other applications. Therefore, do not keep it open unnecessarily.

The registration database is contained in a resource fork. Consequently, if an application uses any of the "1" resource functions (for example, Get1Resource), you must close the registration database, since keeping it open will report it as the topmost resource file.

Once the registration database is open, the object application should check on the validity of its registration. The object application will need to reregister the information if the registration has been inadvertently destroyed.

See Also

OleregCloseRegistration

OleregCloseRegistration

OLEREGSTATUS OleregCloseRegistration (*hkey*)
OLEREG_HKEY *hkey*

OleregCloseRegistration decrements the lock count on the registration database and closes the database when the lock count reaches zero.

Parameters

hkey
Specifies the handle of the key to the registration database that is returned from **OleregOpenRegistration**.

Return Values

Value	Meaning
OLEREGSTATUS	The return values is one of the enumerated types from OLEREGSTATUS.

Comments

Each call to **OleregCloseRegistration** must be balanced by a previous call to **OleregOpenRegistration**.

See Also

OleregOpenRegistration

OleregGetValue

OLEREGSTATUS OleregGetValue (*lpKey, KeyWord, Index, lpValue, dwSize*)
char * *lpKey*;
OLEREG_KEYWORD *KeyWord*;
OLELONG *Index*;
OLEREGVALUE *lpValue*;
OLELONG * *dwSize*;

OleregGetValue queries the registration database for the information identified by the combination of *lpKey* and *KeyWord*. This function can be used as an enumerator by calling it repeatedly and incrementing the *Index* parameter by one on each successive call.

Parameter

lpKey
Points to the object class name followed by the protocol in the format <*class* >\<*protocol* >. The protocol is optional and, if omitted, StdFileEditing is assumed.

KeyWord
Identifies the type of service. Each object class may have multiple *KeyWords* registered for it, and within some of the *KeyWords*, multiple values. Valid values are from the enumeration **OLEREG_KEYWORD**; see the following comments.

Index
Specifies the position within a group of keyword values. To sequentially retrieve all values, *Index* should start at 0 and increase by 1 in subsequent calls.

lpValue
Points to where to return *KeyWord* values; may be NULL.

dwSize
Specifies the length of buffer *lpValue* and length of return data.

Return Values

Value	Meaning
OLEREGSTATUS	The return values is one of the enumerated types from OLEREGSTATUS.

Comments

Each object class is registered using its class name, which uniquely identifies the object. Since objects must be uniquely identified, there can be only one application on a workstation registered as an object application for a given class name.

For class names that support multiple protocols, concatenating the protocol with the class name in *lpKey* is required for queries where each protocol within the class may have a different attribute. For example, class signatures can be different for each protocol, but human readable names cannot. If the protocol is not supplied where needed, StdFileEditing is assumed.

Values for *KeyWords* are taken from the enumeration **OLEREG_KEYWORD**, which is defined in MacDef.H as follows:

```
typedef enum tagOLEREG_KEYWORD {
    OLEREG_ROOT,
    OLEREG_GENERIC,
    OLEREGSVR_CLASS,
    OLEREGSVR_HUMAN_READABLE,
    OLEREGSVR_EXTENSION,
    OLEREGSVR_FILE_TYPE =    OLEREGSVR_EXTENSION,
    OLEREGSVR_PROTOCOL,
    OLEREGSVR_SERVER,
    OLEREGSVR_SIGNATURE = OLEREGSVR_SERVER,
    OLEREGSVR_HANDLER,
    OLEREGSVR_VERB,
    OLEREGSVR_NET_DRIVE,

    //Following keywords can only be used with OleregGetValue
    OLEREG_QUERY_ONLY = 2000,
    OLEREGSVR_CLASS_FROM_HUMAN_READABLE,
    OLEREGSVR_CLASS_FROM_EXTENSION,
    OLEREGSVR_CLASS_FROM_SIG =
    OLEREGSVR_CLASS_FROM_EXTENSION
} OLEREG_KEYWORD;
```

OleregSetValue

OLEREGSTATUS OleregSetValue (*lpKey*, *KeyWord*, *wInsertOrder*, *lpValue*, *dwSize*)
char * *lpKey*;
OLEREG_KEYWORD *KeyWord*;
OLEREG_ORDER *wInsertOrder*;
OLEREGVALUE *lpValue*;
OLELONG *dwSize*;

OleregSetValue stores a data value for a combination of *lpKey* and *KeyWord*. To store all necessary class name information, **OleregSetValue** must be called repeatedly.

Parameter

lpKey
Points to the object class name followed by the protocol in the format <*class* >\<*protocol* >. The protocol is optional and if omitted, StdFileEditing is assumed.

KeyWord
Identifies the type of service. Each object class may have multiple *KeyWords* registered for it, and within each *KeyWord*, multiple values. Valid values are defined in the enumeration **OLEREG_KEYWORD**; for more information, see **OleregGetValue**.

wInsertOrder
Identifies the position within a list of multiple *KeyWord* values. *wInsertOrder* is only meaningful for those *KeyWords* that can have multiple values. For more information on the values for *wInsertOrder*, see the following comments.

lpValue
Points to the value that is to be stored for the specified *KeyWord*.

dwSize
Specifies the length of *lpValue*.

Return Values

Value	Meaning
OLEREGSTATUS	The return values is one of the enumerated types from OLEREGSTATUS.

Comments

For class names that support multiple protocols, concatenating the protocol with the class name in *lpKey* is required for storing information where each protocol within the class may have a different *KeyWord* value. For example, class signatures can be different for each protocol, but human readable names cannot.

If the protocol is not supplied where needed, StdFileEditing is assumed.

The value for *wInsertOrder* can be any of the following:

```
REG_APPEND,                  //append lpValue to end of list
REG_IGNORE = REG_APPEND,     //used as a place holder to maintain syntax
                             // when none of the parameters are appropriate
REG_INSERT,                  //place lpValue at the beginning of the list
                             //of entries specified by lpKey and KeyWord
REG_REPLACE,                 //
REG_DELETE = REG_REPLACE     //delete existing entries before adding
                             //new one(s)
```

REG_IGNORE should be used where there is only one *KeyWord* value possible for the *lpKey*.

Since *OleregSetValue* sets one value at a time, repeated calls are necessary to set multiple values for a *KeyWord* and multiple *KeyWords* for a *lpKey*.

Note **OleregSetValue** ("<*class*>," OLEREGSVR_SIGNATURE, ...) will automatically perform **OleregSetValue** ("<*class*>\\OLE2,"OLEREGSVR_SIGNATURE, ...), indicating that <*class*> is not an OLE 1 ProgID, but rather is an OLE 2 (or higher) ProgID. This allows OLE or an appplication to determine whether the <*class*> is an OLE 1 ProgID or not (in the rare situation in which <*class*> appears in the OLE 1 Embedding Preferences file but not in the OLE 2 Registration Database file).

In the rare case where an application is calling **OleregSetValue** in order to register an OLE 1 ProgID, it should call **OleregRemoveKey** ("<*class*>\\OLE2," OLEREGSVR_SIGNATURE, 0) after **OleregSetValue** ("<*class*>," OLEREGSVR_SIGNATURE, ...) so that "<*class*>\\OLE2" will not appear in the OLE 1 Embedding Preferences file.

OleregRemoveKey

OLEREGSTATUS OleregRemoveKey (*lpKey, KeyWord, Index*)
char * *lpKey*;
OLEREG_KEYWORD *KeyWord*;
OLELONG *Index*;

OleregRemoveKey removes the data identified by the combination of *lpKey* and *KeyWord*. **OleregRemoveKey** may be used to remove verbs from an object class, or to unregister the object application.

Parameters

lpKey
Points to the object class name from which to remove data.

KeyWord
Identifies the type of service. Valid values are from the enumeration **OLEREG_KEYWORD**; for more information, see **OleregGetValue**.

Index

Specifies a position within a group of keyword values. To sequentially retrieve all values, *Index* should start at zero and increase by one in subsequent calls.

Return Values

Value	Meaning
OLEREGSTATUS	The return values is one of the enumerated types from OLEREGSTATUS.

Comments

If *lpKey* is the class name for a protocol other than StdFileEditing, the *lpKey* format should be <*class* >\<*protoco l*>. This concatenation handles queries about a class where each protocol within the class may have a different attribute. For example, class signatures can be different for each protocol, but human-readable names cannot.

Calling **OleregRemoveKey**("<*class*>," OLEREGSVR_SIGNATURE, ...) will automatically unregister the "<*class*>\\OLE2" key (see **OleregSetValue**).

If the protocol is not supplied where needed, StdFileEditing is assumed.

Note Removing the signature for a protocol automatically unregisters the entire protocol without cleaning up the registration database. Similarly, removing the human-readable string for a class unregisters the entire class.

CHAPTER 5

Component Object Interfaces and Functions

This chapter describes the interfaces and API functions that comprise the Component Object Model of OLE.

IUnknown Interface

The **IUnknown** interface methods enable an application to obtain pointers to other interfaces supported by its objects and to manage the interface pointer(s) obtained on an object. **IUnknown** is used by OLE and all OLE-aware applications.

Because **IUnknown** is the interface from which all other OLE interfaces are derived, it must be implemented by all applications. **IUnknown** contains the following methods:

```
DECLARE_INTERFACE(IUnknown)
{
 HRESULT QueryInterface (REFIID riid, void * * ppvObj) ;
 unsigned long AddRef () ;
 unsigned long Release () ;
};
```

For more information, see the compobj.h header file.

Reference Counting Rules

The **IUnknown::AddRef** and **IUnknown::Release** methods keep track of the reference count for an object. When an application obtains access to interface pointer *pInterface*, the application calls *pInterface->AddRef* to increment the reference count. When the application is finished with the pointer, it calls *pInterface->Release*, in much the same way that one might call **DisposeHandle** to free a global memory block. If the reference count for a particular interface goes to zero, the interface implementation can be freed. Only when there are no more interface pointers on an object as a whole can the object be safely freed.

The general rules that apply to callers and callees of interface methods are described in the following paragraphs.

- If a local copy of an interface pointer is made from an existing global interface pointer, the local copy must be independently reference counted. This separate reference count is necessary because the global copy can be destroyed while the local copy is in use.
- If a pointer passed as a parameter is copied into one or more global variables, or as a variable that is not returned to the caller, each copy must be independently reference counted.
- Every instance of an interface pointer returned to a caller must be reference counted. For example, **IUnknown::QueryInterface**, **IOleItemContainer::GetObject**, **IOleContainer::EnumObjects**, and **IClassFactory::CreateInstance** all return interface pointers and must include a call to **AddRef** to increment the reference count on the returned pointer. Every function receiving an interface pointer must call **Release** on that interface.
- Interface pointers that are passed from a caller are temporarily owned. This implies that the methods of that interface can be called and that the object implementing that interface will remain alive during the call(s). If a pointer is returned from one of these interface method calls, the pointer is considered fully owned and its reference count must be incremented. For example, if the temporary pointer is used to call **QueryInterface,** and **QueryInterface** returns a pointer to an interface, the reference count on the returned pointer must be incremented. If this pointer is not returned to the caller, **Release** must be called to decrement its reference count.
- If pointers to two different interfaces are both obtained by calling **QueryInterface** on the same **IUnknown**, **Release** should be called once on each pointer; rather than on **IUnknown** or on one of the pointers twice. This constraint allows future implementations to store reference counts on parts of aggregates rather than on a whole aggregate.

Note When objects are created, their reference count may be initially zero. If a newly created object with a zero reference is passed as a function parameter, it is necessary to ensure the object's stability by incrementing the reference count prior to the function call. This technique is referred to as *artificial reference counting.* After the function returns, the reference count can be decremented. Safeguarding an object through artificial reference counting may also be necessary prior to the object's destruction, which is an unstable time for the object.

Avoiding Reference Counting Cycles

It is possible to create cycles whereby a reference count would never reach zero. This can occur when two objects hold pointers to each other and a third object holds a pointer to one of the other two objects. Two strategies can be implemented to avoid a potential cycle. Depending on the object and its use, it may be possible to avoid reference counting one of the interface pointers. An alternate strategy is to manage separate reference counts, whereby the object is not destroyed until all of the reference counts are zero.

Figure 5.1 illustrates a potential cycle scenario and the two strategies for avoiding that cycle. ObjectX and ObjectY both hold pointers to interfaces in ObjectAB; ObjectAB holds a pointer to InterfaceA in ObjectY. In the first case, ObjectAB avoids a cycle by not counting its reference to ObjectY, as is indicated by the dotted line.

In the second case, ObjectAB avoids a cycle by maintaining separate reference counts, as is indicated by the dotted line.

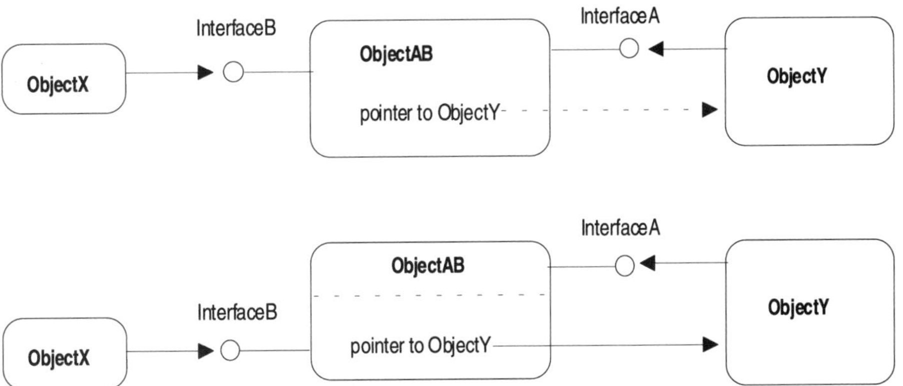

Figure 5.1 Avoiding a reference counting cycle

Figure 5.2 shows how a reference cycle can occur in an aggregate object. The controlling unknown points to the **IUnknown** implementation in the noncontrol object who in turn points to the controlling unknown. To avoid a cycle, the noncontrol object's pointer to the controlling unknown is not reference counted, as is indicated by the dotted line.

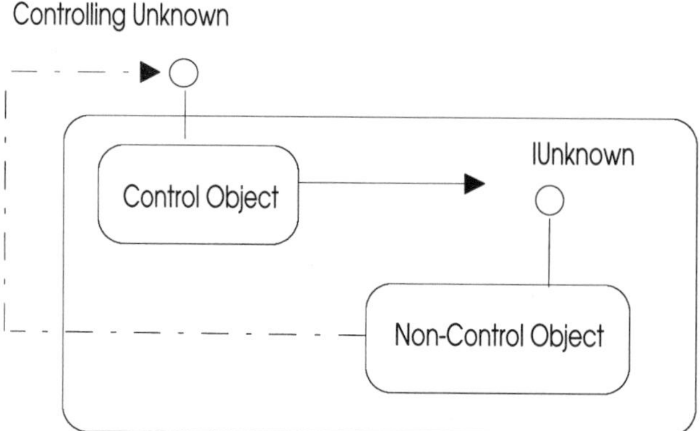

Figure 5.2 Reference counting cycle in an aggregate object

Optimizing Reference Counting

Reference counting manages the lifetimes of an object so that it is kept alive only if necessary. If it is possible to know the relationships between the lifetimes of two or more copies of an interface pointer, the reference counting process can be streamlined. Most relationships fall into two categories: 1) nested lifetimes and 2) overlapping lifetimes.

Figure 5.3 presents an illustration of the two types of relationships. In a nested lifetime relationship, the first copy of the interface pointer is created followed by the creation of the second copy. The second copy is destroyed before the end of the first copy's lifetime. The calls to **AddRef** (A2) and **Release** (R2) can be omitted. The overlapping lifetime relationship begins like the nested lifetime relationship's with the second interface pointer created after the first. However, with overlapping lifetimes, the first pointer copy is destroyed before the second pointer copy. The **AddRef** (A2) and **Release** (R1) calls can be omitted.

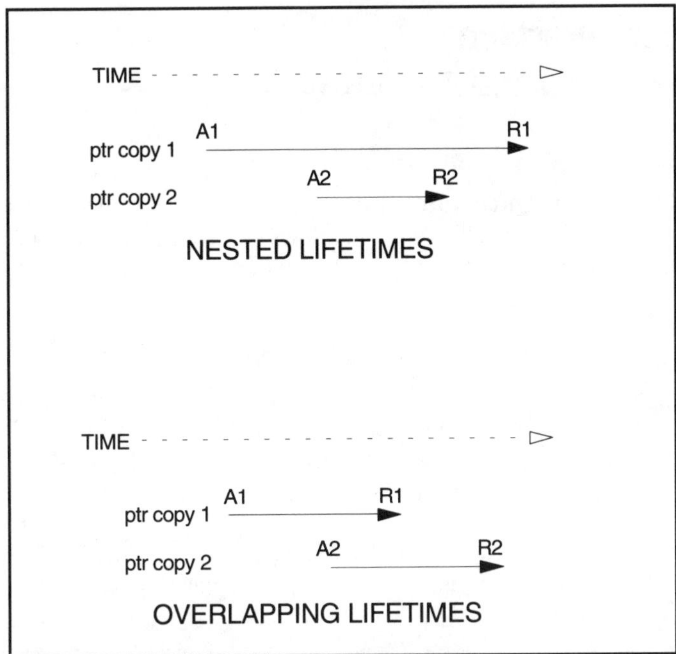

Figure 5.3 Nested versus overlapping lifetimes of an interface pointer

The following general rules are helpful in reference counting optimization:

- **In parameters to functions**. An interface pointer passed as a function parameter has a lifetime that is nested in the pointer used to initialize the parameter. Therefore, the function parameter need not be reference counted separately.
- **Out parameters from functions**. Parameters returned from function calls (including return values), must have a stable copy of the interface pointer. On exit, the caller must release the pointer. The returned parameter need not be reference counted separately.
- **Local variables**. A function clearly knows the lifetimes of each local pointer variable allocated on the stack frame. It can use this information to omit redundant **AddRef** and **Release** calls.
- **Back pointers**. Data structures often contain two components, A and B, each containing a pointer to the other. If A is known to contain the lifetime of B, then the pointer from B to A need not be referencecounted.

IUnknown::QueryInterface

HRESULT IUnknown::QueryInterface(*riid, ppvObj*)
REFIID *riid*
void ** *ppvObj*

IUnknown::QueryInterface returns a pointer to a specified interface on a particular object. This function allows a client to query an object to determine what interfaces it supports.

Parameters

riid
Specifies the IID of the interface being queried for.

ppvObj
Points to the object (on exit) whose interface is being queried. If the interface specified in *riid* is not supported by the object, E_NOINTERFACE is returned. All errors set **ppvObj* to NULL.

Return Values

Value	Meaning
S_OK	Interface is supported and **ppvObj* is set.
E_NOINTERFACE	Interface is not supported by the object; **ppvObj* is set to NULL.
CO_E_OBJNOTCONNECTED	Handler created but object application is not running. The object application must be running to determine whether it supports interface (much like OLE_E_NOTRUNNING but more general).
REGDB_E_IIDNOTREG	Object application is running, but *riid* cannot be remoted because no information exists in the Registration Database file to indicate how it is to be done.
E_OUTOFMEMORY	Out of memory.
E_INVALIDARG	One or more arguments are invalid.
E_UNEXPECTED	An unexpected error occurred.

Comments

If an object supports multiple interfaces that are each derived from **IUnknown**, calling **IUnknown::QueryInterface**(IID_IUnknown) on any one of the interfaces must return the same pointer, regardless of which interface is called. To determine whether two pointers point to the same object, call **IUnknown::QueryInterface**(IID_IUnknown,...) on both and compare the results.

In contrast, queries for interfaces other than **IUnknown** are not required to return the same pointer value each time **QueryInterface** is called to return a pointer to them.

The set of interfaces accessible on an object by using **IUnknown::QueryInterface** must be static, not dynamic. For example, consider the following pointer:

```
ISomeInterface *pSome = (some function returning an ISomeInterface *);
```

where **ISomeInterface** derives from **IUnknown**. Now suppose the following operation is attempted:

```
IOtherInterface * pOther;
HRESULT herr = pSome->QueryInterface(IID_IOtherInterface, &pOther); //line 3
```

Then, based on the assignment made in line 3, the following must be true:

- If *herr*==NOERROR, calling **IUnknown::QueryInterface** a second time from the same *pSome* pointer returns NOERROR again. This action is independent of whether *pOther* was released in the interim.
- If *herr*==E_NOINTERFACE, calling **IUnknown::QueryInterface** a second time from the same *pSome* pointer returns E_NOINTERFACE again.

IUnknown::QueryInterface must be symmetric, reflexive, and transitive with respect to the set of accessible interfaces as follows:

Symmetric:

```
pOther->QueryInterface(IID_ISomeInterface, ...)
```

must succeed.

Reflexive: If, in line 3, *pOther* were successfully obtained, then

```
pSome->QueryInterface(IID_ISomeInterface, ...)
```

must succeed.

Transitive: If in line 3, *pOther* were successfully obtained, and the following assignment were then made:

```
IYetAnother * pyet;
HRESULT herr = pother->QueryInterface(IID_IYetAnother, &pyet); // line 6
```

and `pyet` were successfully obtained in line 6, then

```
pyet->QueryInterface(IID_ISomeInterface, ...)
```

must succeed.

Notice that success does not mean that two **QueryInterface** calls on the same pointer asking for the same interface must succeed and return exactly the same pointer; all that is required is that **QueryInterface** not indicate that the interface is unavailable.

Calling **IUnknown::QueryInterface** on a non-running object will not force the object into the running state.

See Also **IUnknown::AddRef**, **IUnknown::Release**

IUnknown::AddRef

unsigned long IUnknown::AddRef()

IUnknown::AddRef is used to increment a reference count for every new instance of a pointer to a specified interface on a particular object.

Return Values

Value	Meaning
0 to *n*	The value of the reference count. When fully released, it is zero. This information is used for diagnostics and testing only. It cannot be used by shipping code because, in certain situations, it is unstable.

Comments

IUnknown::AddRef is used by container objects to stabilize a copy of an interface pointer. **IUnknown::AddRef** is also used in those instances where the life of the cloned pointer must extend beyond the lifetime of the original pointer. The cloned pointer must be released by calling **IUnknown::Release**.

The internal reference counter that **AddRef** maintains must be a 32-bit unsigned integer.

See Also **IUnknown::Release**

IUnknown::Release

unsigned long IUnknown::Release()

IUnknown::Release decrements the reference count on a specified interface of a particular object. If the object reference count goes to zero as a result of the **Release**, the object is freed from memory.

Return Values

Value	Meaning
0 to *n*	The value of the reference count on the whole object. When fully released, it is zero. This information can be used for diagnostics and testing only. It cannot be used by shipping code because, in certain situations, it is unstable. If a client needs to know that resources have been freed, it must use an interface with higher level semantics before calling **Release**.

Comments

If **IUnknown::AddRef** has been called on this object's interface *n* times and this is the *n+1th* call to **IUnknown::Release**, the interface pointer will free itself. An object frees itself if the released pointer is the only pointer and if the object supports multiple interfaces through **IUnknown::QueryInterface**.

Note Because of restrictions in the implementation of OLE 2, **IUnknown::Release** must return zero if the identity of the object has been destroyed. Therefore, clients cannot rely on zero having any special significance other than for debugging purposes. This restriction may be removed in future implementations.

The aggregation of an object restricts the ability to recover interface pointers.

See Also **IUnknown::AddRef**, **IUnknown::QueryInterface**

IClassFactory Interface

The **IClassFactory** interface is implemented by object applications and is used by OLE to create instances of an object class in memory. The interface is optionally implemented by container applications that allow linking to embedded objects.

IClassFactory contains the following methods:

```
DECLARE_INTERFACE_(IClassFactory, IUnknown)
{
  // *** IUnknown methods ***
 HRESULT QueryInterface (REFIID riid, void * * ppvObj) ;
 unsigned long  AddRef ();
 unsigned long  Release ();

  // *** IClassFactory methods ***
 HRESULT CreateInstance (LPUNKNOWN pUnkOuter, REFIID riid,  void * * ppvObj) ;
 HRESULT LockServer (unsigned long fLock) ;
};
```

For further information, see the compobj.h header file.

Creating Instances of an Object Class

Object applications and handler implementors implement one object class (that is, one instance of the **IClassFactory** interface) for each object they support.

Object applications register the public availability of their class of objects with **CoRegisterClassObject** so that container applications may connect to them. Object handlers implement and export the **DllGetClassObject** function in order to make available their object class(es).

Creating an instance of an object class is done using the appropriate variation of the following steps:

1. Determine the class of the object to instantiate.

   This step identifies the CLSID of which an instance is needed (see the following section, "Creating New CLSIDs and IIDs"). Depending on the task at hand, this differs from situation to situation. Following are some examples:

   - In the Insert Object Dialog, each object type in the list has a unique associated CLSID. If a user wants to insert a given type, an instance of this CLSID is required.
   - When an object is loaded into memory from persistent storage, the class of object that is to manipulate the object data is identified with a unique CLSID that is kept in persistent storage along with the object's data.

2. Obtain the class factory for the specified CLSID.

   This is done by calling **CoGetClassObject**, as shown in the following example (for brevity, this code and the other examples in this section omit error checking):

   ```
   LPCLASSFACTORY lpcf;
   CoGetClassObject(clsid, CLSCTX_INPROC, 0, IID_IClassFactory,
       (void**)&lpcf);
   ```

   The class context (second parameter) is used to specify the type of object application that is to be used. For more information on the class context, see **CoGetClassObject**, later in this chapter.

3. Create an uninitialized instance of the class.

   An uninitialized instance is created using **IClassFactory::CreateInstance**. The interface requested from the object should be the one by which the object is initialized. For OLE embeddings, this interface is **IPersistStorage**, but the particular interface to be used depends on the situation. If the object is being created as part of an aggregate, the controlling unknown is passed.

   ```
   LPPERSISTSTORAGE lpPersistStorage;
   lpcf->CreateInstance(NULL, IID_IPersistStorage,
               (void * *)&lpPersistStorage);   // non-aggregate case
   lpcf->Release();
   ```

4. Initialize the newly created instance.

   This involves invoking one or more methods in the requested initialization interface. For OLE embeddings, a reloaded object is initialized with **IPersistStorage::Load**, while a new blank object is initialized with **IPersistStorage::InitNew**.

Until an object is initialized, only the following operations are guaranteed to succeed:

- **QueryInterface** calls to either **IUnknown** or to an initialization interface on the object. Non-initialization interfaces are specifically excluded as the set of these may not be known until the object is initialized. For embedded objects, **IPersistStorage** is the initialization interface.
- **AddRef** and **Release** calls on any obtained interface derived from **IUnknown**.
- Calling initialization methods appropriate for the object. For embedded objects, **IPersistStorage::InitNew** and **IPersistStorage::Load** are the legal methods.

5. Query for some working interface on the instance and clean up.

   Often, when the interface needed on an object has been initialized, it is different than the interface by which initialization is done. In this final step, call **QueryInterface** for the working interface needed and then clean up by releasing the previously obtained pointers:

```
LPOLEOBJECT lpOleObject;
lpPersistStorage->QueryInterface(IID_IOleObject,
    (void **)&lpOleObject);
lpPersistStorage->Release();
```

Creating New CLSIDs and IIDs

Each class of object must have a unique CLSID registered in the Registration Database file so that the particular object can be identified in the presence of any other object(s). If an object application does not register the CLSID of an object class in the Registration Database file with the "Insertable" key and if the application does not support the **IPersistStorage** interface, then other applications will not be able to create an embedded object using that object class.

Note CLSIDs are obtained by contacting Microsoft directly (the easiest way is to post a message to Microsoft from Compuserve). To obtain a range of CLSID values:

1. Logon to Compuserve.
2. Type **GO WINOBJ**
3. Post a message (public or private), requesting the number of CLSIDs needed. To validate the request, Microsoft requires your company's name, address, and telephone number.

Unless specified, a block of 250 values will be assigned per request.

The string representation of a CLSID, as determined by **StringFromCLSID**, is the string surrounded by two braces. To create a CLSID from a string, call **CLSIDFromString**, as follows:

```
CLSID clsid;
CLSIDFromString("{80C11F40-7503-1068-8576-00DD01113F11}", &clsid);
```

Interface IDs (IIDs) are allocated in a similar way, except that **IIDFromString** is used in place of **CLSIDFromString**.

OLE also provides the **DEFINE_GUID** macro for declaring and initializing a GUID in hexadecimal. As an example, given the following GUID string, the **DEFINE_GUID** macro can be used to make the number available as an interface ID in a program (*name* is some user defined interface):

```
DEFINE_GUID(name, 0x00000301, 0x0000, 0x0000, 0xc0, 0x00, 0x00, 0x00, 0x00, 0x00, 0x00, 0x46)
```

The **DEFINE_GUID** macro also initializes the GUID if #define INITGUID was used before #include <COMPOBJ.H> or INITGUID.H was included after COMPOBJ.H.

IClassFactory::CreateInstance

HRESULT IClassFactory::CreateInstance(*pUnkOuter, riid, ppvObj***)**
LPUNKNOWN *pUnkOuter*
REFIID *riid*
void * * *ppvObj*

IClassFactory::CreateInstance creates an uninitialized instance of an object class. Initialization is subsequently performed using another interface-specific method, such as **IPersistStorage::InitNew**, **IPersistStorage::Load**, **IPersistStream::Load**, or **IPersistFile::Load**.

Parameters

pUnkOuter
Points to the controlling **IUnknown** interface if the object is being created as part of an aggregate. It is NULL if the object is not part of an aggregate.

riid
Identifies the interface by which the caller will communicate with the resulting object and through which it initializes the object.

ppvObj
Points to where the pointer to the object will be returned.

Return Values

Value	Meaning
S_OK	The specified class of the object was created.
CLASS_E _NOAGGREGATION	*pUnkOuter* was non-NULL and the object does not support aggregation.

Value	Meaning
E_NOINTERFACE	The object pointed to by *ppvObj* does not support the interface identified by *riid*.
E_UNEXPECTED	An unexpected error occurred.
E_OUTOFMEMORY	Out of memory.
E_INVALIDARG	One or more arguments are invalid.

Comments

The *pUnkOuter* parameter indicates whether the object is being created as part of an aggregation. Because object classes must be consciously designed to be aggregate objects, not all classes can participate in aggregation. If *pUnkOuter* is not NULL, indicating that the object is aggregatable, *riid* must represent a private interface. Private interfaces are never made available outside of the aggregate.

The container passes to **IClassFactory::CreateInstance** the interface to be used to communicate with the resulting object instance. The newly created object is usually initialized by using this interface. For OLE compound document objects (embedded and linked), this process is encapsulated by the **OleLoad** helper function.

In general, if an application supports one object class and the class object is registered for single use, only one instance of the object class can be created. The application must refuse to create other instances of the class, returning an error from **IClassFactory::CreateInstance**. The same is true for applications that support multiple object classes, each having a class object registered for single use: a **CreateInstance** for one class followed by a **CreateInstance** for any of the classes should return an error.

To avoid returning an error, applications that support multiple classes with single-use class objects can revoke the registered class object of the first class by calling **CoRevokeClassObject** when a request for instantiating a second class is received. For example, consider the two classes, A and B. When **IClassFactory::CreateInstance** is called for class A, revoke the **IClassFactory** for B. When B is created, revoke A. This solution complicates shutdown because one of the **IClassFactory** objects might have already been revoked (and cannot be revoked twice).

See Also

CoGetClassObject, **CoRegisterClassObject**, **CoRevokeClassObject**

IClassFactory::LockServer

HRESULT IClassFactory::LockServer(*fLock*)
unsigned long *fLock*

IClassFactory::LockServer keeps an open object application in memory. Keeping the object application alive in memory allows instances of this class to be created more quickly.

Parameters

fLock
Specifies the lock count. If TRUE, it increments the lock count; if FALSE, it decrements the lock count.

Return Values

Value	Meaning
S_OK	The specified object was either locked (*fLock* = TRUE) or unlocked from memory (*fLock* = FALSE).
E_FAIL	Indicates an unspecified error.
E_OUTOFMEMORY	Out of memory.
E_UNEXPECTED	An unexpected error occurred.

Comments

A container application can call this method to obtain better performance in situations where there is a need to create and release instances frequently.

All calls to **IClassFactory::LockServer** must be counted, not just the last one. Calls must be balanced; that is, for every **LockServer**(TRUE) call, there must be a **LockServer**(FALSE) call. If the lock count and the class object reference count are both zero, the class object can be freed.

Most clients do not need to call **IClassFactory::LockServer**. It is used primarily by sophisticated clients with special performance needs from certain object classes.

The process that locked the object application is responsible for unlocking it. Once the **IClassFactory** is released, there is no mechanism by which the caller can be guaranteed to later connect to the same class (for example, consider single-use classes). It is an error to call **IClassFactory::LockServer**(TRUE) and then release the **IClassFactory** without first releasing the lock with **IClassFactory::LockServer**(FALSE).

Most implementations of **IClassFactory::LockServer** do nothing more than call **CoLockObjectExternal**. For more information on locking objects in memory, see **CoLockObjectExternal**, later in this chapter.

IMalloc Interface

The **IMalloc** interface is implemented by OLE and is used by OLE and object handlers to manage memory. To use OLE's implementation of **IMalloc**, an application sets *pMalloc* to NULL in its call to **OleInitialize** and **CoInitialize**. **IMalloc** may also be implemented by applications that manage memory differently than OLE.

IMalloc contains the following methods, the first three of which are similar to the C library functions **malloc**, **realloc**, and **free**:

```
DECLARE_INTERFACE_(IMalloc, IUnknown)
{
 // *** IUnknown methods ***
 HRESULT QueryInterface (REFIID riid, void * * ppvObj) ;
 unsigned long  AddRef ()  ;
 unsigned long  Release () ;

 // *** IMalloc methods ***
 void * Alloc (unsigned long cb) ;
 void Free (void * pv) ;
 void *  Realloc (void * pv, unsigned long cb) ;
 unsigned long GetSize (void * pv) ;
 int DidAlloc (void * pv) ;
 void HeapMinimize () ;
};
```

For further information, see compobj.h

IMalloc::Alloc

void * IMalloc::Alloc(*cb***)**
unsigned long *cb*

IMalloc::Alloc allocates a block of memory.

Parameters

cb
Specifies the size (in bytes) of the memory block to allocate.

Return Values

Value	Meaning
Allocated memory block	Memory block allocated successfully.
NULL	Insufficient memory available.

Comments

The initial contents of the returned memory block are undefined; there is no guarantee that the block has been initialized. The allocated block may be larger than *cb* bytes because of the space required for alignment and for maintenance information.

If *cb* is 0, **IMalloc::Alloc** allocates a zero-length item and returns a valid pointer to that item. If there is insufficient memory available, **IMalloc::Alloc** returns NULL.

Applications should always check the return value from this method, even when requesting small amounts of memory, because there is no guarantee the memory will be allocated.

See Also **IMalloc::Free**, **IMalloc::Realloc**

IMalloc::Free

void IMalloc::Free(*pv***)**
void * *pv*

IMalloc::Free frees a block of memory previously allocated through a call to **IMalloc::Alloc** or **IMalloc::Realloc**.

Parameters

pv
Points to the memory block to be freed.

Comments

The number of bytes freed equals the number of bytes that were originally allocated or reallocated. After the call, the memory block pointed to by *pv* is invalid and can no longer be used.

The *pv* parameter can be NULL, in which case calling **IMalloc::Free** is a no-op.

See Also **IMalloc::Alloc**, **IMalloc::Realloc**

IMalloc::Realloc

void * IMalloc::Realloc(*pv*, *cb***)**
void * *pv*
unsigned long *cb*

IMalloc::Realloc changes the size of a previously allocated memory block.

Parameters

pv
Points to the memory block to be reallocated. It can be a NULL pointer, as discussed in the following comments.

cb
Specifies the size of the memory block (in bytes) to be reallocated. It can be zero, as discussed in the following comments.

Return Values

Value	Meaning
Reallocated memory block	Memory block successfully reallocated.
NULL	Insufficient memory or *cb* is zero and *pv* is not NULL.

Comments

The *pv* argument points to the beginning of the memory block. If *pv* is NULL, **IMalloc::Realloc** allocates a new memory block in the same way as **IMalloc::Alloc**. If *pv* is not NULL, it should be a pointer returned by a prior call to **IMalloc::Alloc**.

The *cb* argument specifies the size (in bytes) of the new block. The contents of the block are unchanged up to the shorter of the new and old sizes, although the new block can be in a different location. Because the new block can be in a different memory location, the pointer returned by **IMalloc::Realloc** is not guaranteed to be the pointer passed through the *pv* argument. If *pv* is not NULL and *cb* is zero, then the memory pointed to by *pv* is freed.

IMalloc::Realloc returns a void pointer to the reallocated (and possibly moved) memory block. The return value is NULL if the size is zero and the buffer argument is not NULL, or if there is not enough memory available to expand the block to the given size. In the first case, the original block is freed; in the second, the original block is unchanged.

The storage space pointed to by the return value is guaranteed to be suitably aligned for storage of any type of object. To get a pointer to a type other than **void**, use a type cast on the return value.

See Also

IMalloc::Alloc, **IMalloc::Free**

IMalloc::GetSize

unsigned long IMalloc::GetSize(*pv***)**
void * *pv*

IMalloc::GetSize returns the size (in bytes) of a memory block previously allocated with **IMalloc::Alloc** or **IMalloc::Realloc**.

Parameters

pv
: Points to the memory block whose size is requested. If it is a NULL pointer, -1 is returned.

Return Values

Size of allocated memory block in bytes.

See Also

IMalloc::Alloc, **IMalloc::Realloc**

IMalloc::DidAlloc

int IMalloc::DidAlloc(*pv*)
void * *pv*

IMalloc::DidAlloc determines if this **IMalloc** instance was used to allocate the specified block of memory.

Parameters

pv
Specifies the pointer to the memory block; can be a NULL pointer, in which case, -1 is returned.

Return Values

Value	Meaning
1	The memory block was allocated by this **IMalloc** instance.
0	The memory block was not allocated by this **IMalloc** instance.
-1	**DidAlloc** is unable to determine whether or not it allocated the memory block.

Comments

Pointers returned from the shared allocator cannot be directly manipulated using the host global memory allocator. Except when a NULL pointer is passed, the shared memory allocator does not return -1 to **IMalloc::DidAlloc**, the allocator always indicates that it either did or did not allocate the passed pointer.

It is permissible that the memory allocator passed to **CoInitialize** always respond with -1 in this function.

See Also

IMalloc::Alloc, **IMalloc::HeapMinimize**, **IMalloc::Realloc**

IMalloc::HeapMinimize

void IMalloc::HeapMinimize()

IMalloc::HeapMinimize minimizes the heap as much as possible by releasing unused memory to the operating system.

Comments

Calling **IMalloc::HeapMinimize** is useful when several memory blocks have been freed using **IMalloc::Free** and the application needs to make the freed memory available for other purposes.

See Also

IMalloc::Alloc, **IMalloc::Free**, **IMalloc::Realloc**

IExternalConnection Interface

The **IExternalConnection** interface is optionally implemented by DLL object applications to support the correct shutdown of links to embedded objects. Object handlers never implement this interface.

The stub manager calls **IExternalConnection** methods when external linking connections to an object are made and broken or when **CoLockObjectExternal** is called. Embedded objects should maintain a count of these connections and, when the count goes to zero, call **IOleObject::Close**.

The **IExternalConnection** interface contains the following methods:

```
DECLARE_INTERFACE_(IExternalConnection, IUnknown)
{
   // *** IUnknown methods ***
   HRESULT QueryInterface (REFIID riid, void * * ppvObj) ;
   unsigned long  AddRef () ;
   unsigned long  Release () ;

// *** IExternalConnection methods ***
  STDMETHOD_(unsigned long, AddConnection (unsigned long extconn, unsigned long reserved) ;
  STDMETHOD_(unsigned long, ReleaseConnection (unsigned long extconn, unsigned long reserved,
            unsigned long fLastReleaseCloses) ;
};
```

For further information, see the compobj.h header file.

IExternalConnection::AddConnection

unsigned long IExternalConnection::AddConnection(*extconn*, *reserved*)
unsigned long *extconn*
unsigned long *dwReserved*

IExternalConnection::AddConnection indicates that another strong external connection has been created on a running object.

Parameters

extconn
Specifies the type of external connection that exists on the object. The value is from the **EXTCONN** enumeration; for more information, see the following comments. EXTCONN_STRONG is currently the only value allowed.

reserved
Used by OLE to pass information about the connection; it can be zero, but not necessarily. Therefore, implementations of **IExternalConnection::AddConnection** should not include a check for zero.

Return Values

Value	Meaning
unsigned long	An unsigned long value containing the remaining number of reference counts on the object; used for debugging purposes only.

Comments

An external connection represents strong bindings (by means of a moniker bind) or external locks (by means of **CoLockObjectExternal**). As with all connections (weak or strong), the user can always override them and shutdown the application.

The *extconn* parameter specifies the type of external connection; its value is taken from the enumeration **EXTCONN**, which is defined in compobj.h as follows:

```
typedef enum tagEXTCONN
{
    EXTCONN_STRONG =    0x0001,     //strong connection
}EXTCONN
```

The following is a typical implementation for the **AddConnection** method:

```
unsigned long XX::AddConnection(unsigned long extconn,
                                unsigned long reserved)
{
    return extconn&EXTCONN_STRONG ? ++m_cStrong : 0;
}
```

See Also

CoLockObjectExternal, **IExternalConnection::ReleaseConnection**

IExternalConnection::ReleaseConnection

unsigned long IExternalConnection::ReleaseConnection(*extconn*, *reserved*, *fLastReleaseCloses*)
unsigned long *extconn*
unsigned long *reserved*
unsigned long *fLastReleaseCloses*

IExternalConnection::ReleaseConnection indicates the release of an external connection to a running object.

Parameters

extconn
Specifies the type of external connection that exists on the object; the value is obtained from the enumeration **EXTCONN**; for more information, see **IExternalConnection::AddConnection**.

reserved
Used by OLE to pass information about the connection; it can be zero, but not necessarily.

fLastReleaseCloses
TRUE specifies that if this is the last external reference to the object, the object should close. FALSE leaves the object in a state in which its closing is controlled by some other means.

Return Values

Value	Meaning
unsigned long	The remaining number of reference counts on the object; used for debugging purposes only.

Comments

Closing the last strong connection (along with *fLastReleaseCloses* == TRUE) causes the object to close. If an object has no closing semantics, then it is not required to count the strong connections. An enumerator object, for example, has no closing semantics.

The following is a typical implementation for **IExternalConnection::ReleaseConnection**:

```
unsigned long XX::ReleaseConnection(unsigned long extconn,
                                    unsigned long reserved,
                                    unsigned long fLastReleaseCloses)
{
    if (extconn & EXTCONN_STRONG)
    {
        if (--m_cStrong == 0 && fLastReleaseCloses)
            save if dirty
            close ...

        return m_cStrong;
    }
    else
        return 0;
}
```

See Also

IExternalConnection:AddConnection

IEnum*X* Interface

A frequent OLE 2 programming task is to iterate through a sequence of items. OLE 2 supports such enumerations through the use of enumerator objects.

Enumerators are just a concept; there is no OLE interface called IEnumerator or IEnum, because the method signatures in an enumerator interface must be specific to the type of items being enumerated. As a consequence, separate interfaces, such as **IEnumString** and **IEnumUnknown,** are instantiated for each type of item to be enumerated. The only difference between these interfaces is the type of item being enumerated; all enumerators are basically used in the same way.

An enumerator contains the following methods:

```
template <class ELT_T> interface IEnum : IUnknown {
virtual SCODE Next(unsigned long celt, char * * rgelt, unsigned long * pceltFetched) = 0;
virtual SCODE Skip(unsigned long celt) = 0;
virtual SCODE Reset() = 0;
virtual SCODE Clone(IEnum<ELT_T>* * ppenum) = 0;
};
```

Example Enumerator

The following code example illustrates a typical use of an enumerator. **StringContainer** contains an instance of the **IEnumString** interface that can enumerate a sequence of strings. **SomeFunc** takes a pointer to a **StringContainer** which provides access to the string enumerator. **SomeFunc** loops through each of the strings by calling the enumerator's **Next** method and then releases the enumerator by calling its **Release** method.

```
/* The following is a typical use of an enumerator.*/
interface StringContainer {
    virtual IEnumString ** EnumStrings() = 0;
    };

void SomeFunc(StringContainer * pstringcont) {
    char * lpsz;
    IEnumString ** penum;
    penum = pstringcont->EnumStrings();
    while (penum->Next(1, &lpsz, NULL) == S_OK)
        {
        // do something with the string in lpsz
        // free the string in lpsz with the allocator returned by
        // CoGetMalloc(MEMCTX_TASK, ...);
        }
    penum->Release();
    // penum is not valid here
    }
```

Note In general, the enumerators used in OLE are defined and documented with the functions that instantiate the enumerations.

For all enumerators, an application can determine results by keeping track of the total number of elements remaining in the enumeration before the current position.

IEnum*X*::Next

HRESULT IEnum*X*::Next(*celt, rgelt, pceltFetched***)**
unsigned long *celt*
<ELT_T> * *rgelt*
unsigned long * *pceltFetched*

IEnum*X*::Next retrieves the specified number of items in the enumeration sequence.

Parameters

celt
Specifies the number of elements to return. If the number of elements requested is more than remains in the sequence, only the remaining elements are returned. The number of elements returned is passed through the *pceltFetched* parameter (unless it is NULL).

rgelt
Points to the array in which to return the elements.

pceltFetched
Points to the number of elements actually returned in *rgelt*. The *pceltFetched* parameter cannot be NULL if *celt* is greater than one. If *pceltFetched* is NULL, *celt* must be one.

Return Values

Value	Meaning
S_OK	Returned requested number of elements—**pceltFetched* set if non-NULL. All requested entries are valid.
S_FALSE	Returned fewer elements than requested by *celt*. In this case, unused slots in the enumeration are not set to NULL and **pceltFetched* holds the number of valid entries, even if zero is returned.
E_OUTOFMEMORY	Out of memory.
E_INVALIDARG	Value of *celt* is invalid.
E_UNEXPECTED	An unexpected error occurred.

If an error value is returned, no entries in the *rgelt* array are valid on exit; they are all in an indeterminate state.

Comments

It is illegal to call

```
...Next(celt>1, ...,NULL);
```

Only one element can be specified without passing a valid value for *pceltFetched*.

IEnum*X*::Skip

HRESULT IEnum*X*::Skip(*celt***)**
unsigned long *celt*

IEnum*X*::Skip skips over a specified number of elements in the enumeration sequence.

Parameters

celt
Specifies the number of elements to be skipped.

Return Values

Value	Meaning
S_OK	The number of elements skipped is equal to *celt*.
S_FALSE	The number of elements skipped is fewer than *celt*.
E_OUTOFMEMORY	Out of memory.
E_INVALIDARG	Value of *celt* is invalid.
E_UNEXPECTED	An unexpected error occurred.

IEnum*X*::Reset

HRESULT IEnum*X*::Reset()

IEnum*X*::Reset resets the enumeration sequence back to the beginning.

Return Values

Value	Meaning
S_OK	The enumeration sequence was reset to the beginning.
S_FALSE	The enumeration sequence was not reset to the beginning.

Comments

There is no guarantee that the same set of objects will be enumerated the second time as was enumerated the first: it depends on the collection being enumerated. It is too expensive for some collections, such as files in a directory, to maintain this condition.

IEnum*X*::Clone

HRESULT IEnum*X*::Clone(*ppenum***)**
IEnum*X* * * *ppenum*

IEnum*X*::Clone returns another enumerator containing the same enumeration state as the current one.

Parameters

ppenum
Pointer to the place to return the cloned enumerator. The type of *ppenum* is the same as the enumerator name. For example, if the enumerator name is **IEnumFORMATETC**, *ppenum* is of **IEnumFORMATETC** type.

Return Values

Value	Meaning
E_OUTOFMEMORY	Out of memory.
E_INVALIDARG	Value of *ppenum* is invalid.
E_UNEXPECTED	An unexpected error occurred.

Comments

Using **IEnum*X*::Clone**, it is possible to record a particular point in the enumeration sequence, then return to that point at a later time. The enumerator returned is of the same interface type as the one being cloned.

IMarshal Interface

The **IMarshal** interface is implemented and used by OLE to package and send interface method arguments from one application process to another. In a given call, method arguments are marshaled and unmarshaled in one direction and return values are marshaled and unmarshaled in the other direction. Marshaling allows pointers to interfaces to be passed through remote procedure calls and enables clients in other processes to access and manipulate objects across process boundaries.

Object and container applications can optionally implement **IMarshal** to provide custom interface marshaling. For more information on custom marshaling, see the section "Overview to Custom Marshaling," later in this chapter.

The **IMarshal** interface contains the following methods:

```
DECLARE_INTERFACE_(IMarshal, IUnknown)
{
  // *** IUnknown methods ***
  HRESULT QueryInterface (REFIID riid, void * * ppvObj) ;
  unsigned long  AddRef ();
  unsigned long  Release () ;

  // *** IMarshal methods ***
  HRESULT GetUnmarshalClass (REFIID riid, void * pv, unsigned long dwDestContext,
            void * pvDestContext, unsigned long mshlflags, LPCLSID pclsid) ;
  HRESULT GetMarshalSizeMax (REFIID riid, void * pv, unsigned long dwDestContext,
            void * pvDestContext, unsigned long mshlflags, unsigned long * pSize) ;
  HRESULT MarshalInterface (LPSTREAM pStm, REFIID riid, void * pv,
            unsigned long dwDestContext, LPVOID pvDestContext,
            unsigned long mshlflags) ;
  HRESULT UnmarshalInterface (LPSTREAM pStm, REFIID riid, void * * ppvObj) ;
  HRESULT ReleaseMarshalData (LPSTREAM pStm) ;
  HRESULT DisconnectObject (unsigned long dwReserved) ;
};
```

For further information, see the compobj.h header file.

Data Structures

This section describes the data structures and enumerations that are used in the **IMarshal** interface methods and related marshaling functions.

MSHCTX Enumeration

The **MSHCTX** enumeration determines the destination context of the marshaling operation and is defined in compobj.h as follows:

```
typedef enum tagMSHCTX
{
    MSHCTX_LOCAL           = 0,
    MSHCTX_NOSHAREDMEM     = 1,
} MSHCTX;
```

Currently, only MSHCTX_LOCAL is a valid value.

MSHCTX values have the following meanings:

Value	Description
MSHCTX _LOCAL	Unmarshaling context is local; it has shared memory access.
MSHCTX _NOSHAREDMEM	Unmarshaling context does not have shared memory access with the marshaling context.

MSHLFLAGS Enumeration

The **MSHLFLAGS** enumeration contains a group of flags that determine how the marshaling is to be done; **MSHFLAGS** is defined in compobj.h as follows:

```
typedef enum tagMSHLFLAGS
{
    MSHLFLAGS_NORMAL = 0,
    MSHLFLAGS_TABLESTRONG = 1,
    MSHLFLAGS_TABLEWEAK = 2,
} MSHLFLAGS;
```

The **MSHLFLAGS** flags have the following meanings:

Value	Description
MSHLFLAGS _NORMAL	Marshaling is done by passing an interface from one process to another. The marshaled-data-packet that results from the call will be transported to the other process, where it will be unmarshaled (see **CoUnmarshalInterface**). By means of this flag, the marshaled data packet is unmarshaled either one or zero times. If it is unmarshaled successfully, **CoReleaseMarshalData** is not called on the data packet; and any necessary processing is done in the unmarshal itself. If unmarshaling fails, or it is not attempted, only then is **IMarshal::ReleaseMarshalData** called on the data packet.
MSHLFLAGS _TABLESTRONG	Marshaling is happening because the data packet is to be stored in a globally accessible table from which it is to be unmarshaled zero, one, or more times. Further, the presence of the data packet in the table is to count as a reference on the marshaled interface. When removed from the table, it is the responsibility of the table implementor to call **CoReleaseMarshalData** on the data-packet.
MSHLFLAGS _TABLEWEAK	Marshaling is happening because the data packet is to be stored in a globally accessible table from which it is to be unmarshaled zero, one, or more times. However, the presence of the data packet in the table does not count as a reference on the marshaled interface. Destruction of the data packet is done by calling **CoReleasemarshalData**.

IMarshal::GetUnmarshalClass

HRESULT IMarshal::GetUnmarshalClass(*riid, pv, dwDestContext, pvDestContext, mshlflags, pclsid*)

REFIID *riid*
void * *pv*
unsigned long *dwDestContext*
void * *pvDestContext*
unsigned long *mshlflags*
LPCLSID *pclsid*

IMarshal::GetUnmarshalClass determines the object class that should be used to create an uninitialized proxy in the unmarshaling process.

Parameters

riid
Specifies the IID of the object to be marshaled.

pv
Points to the interface pointer to be marshaled; can be NULL.

dwDestContext
Specifies the destination context relative to the current context in which the unmarshaling is to be done. Valid values are taken from the enumeration **MSHCTX. For** more information, see the section "Data Structures," at the beginning of the **IMarshal** interface description.

pvDestContext
Reserved for use with future **MSHCTX** values.

mshflags
Specifies why marshaling is taking place. Valid values are taken from the enumeration **MSHLFLAGS. For** more information, see the section "Data Structures," at the beginning of the **IMarshal** interface description.

pclsid
Points to the class to be used in the unmarshaling process.

Return Values

Value	Meaning
S_OK	Object class was successfully obtained.
E_INVALIDARG	An invalid argument was passed as a parameter.
E_UNEXPECTED	An unexpected error occurred.
E_OUTOFMEMORY	Out of memory.
E_FAIL	Object class could not be obtained.

Comments

The *dwDestContext* parameter identifies the destination context, which is relative to the current context in which the unmarshaling is to be done. For example, marshalling might be done differently depending on whether the unmarshaling will happen on the local workstation or on a network workstation. An object could do custom marshaling in one case but not the other.

An implementation of **IMarshal::GetUnmarshalClass** can delegate some destination contexts to the standard marshaling implementation, available by calling **CoGetStandardMarshal**. Delegating destination contexts should always be done if the *dwDestContext* parameter contains any flags that the **IMarshal::GetUnmarshalClass** does not understand.

The *mshlflags* parameter indicates the purpose for which the marshal is taking place.

If the caller already has the *riid* of the interface being marshaled, it should pass the interface pointer through *pv*. If the caller does not have the r*iid*, then it should pass NULL.

The *pv* pointer is sometimes used to determine the appropriate object class. If the **IMarshal** interface needs the class, it can call **QueryInterface** on itself to get the interface pointer. The pointer is passed here only to improve efficiency.

See Also **GetMarshalSizeMax**, **MarshalInterface**, **UnmarshalInterface**

IMarshal::GetMarshalSizeMax

HRESULT IMarshal::GetMarshalSizeMax(*riid, pv, dwDestContext, pvDestContext, mshlflags, lpdwSize***)**

REFIID *riid*
void * *pv*
unsigned long *dwDestContext*
void * *pvDestContext,*
unsigned long *mshlflags*
unsigned long * *lpdwSize*

IMarshal::GetMarshalSizeMax returns the upper memory bound needed to write the specified data into an **IMarshal::MarshalInterface** stream.

Parameters

riid
Identifies the interface of the object to be marshalled.

pv
The interface pointer that is to be marshalled; it can be NULL.

dwDestContext
Specifies the destination context relative to the current context in which the unmarshalling is to be done. Valid values are taken from the enumeration **MSHCTX.** For more information, see the section “Data Structures,” at the beginning of the **IMarshal** interface description.

pvDestContext
Reserved for use with future **MSHCTX** values.

mshlflags
Specifies why marshaling is taking place. Valid values are taken from the enumeration **MSHLFLAGS.** For more information, see the section "Data Structures," at the beginning of the **IMarshal** interface description.

lpdwSize
Points to where the maximum marshal size should be returned.

Return Values

Value	Meaning
S_OK	Maximum size needed for marshaling successfully returned.
E_INVALIDARG	An invalid argument was passed as a parameter.
E_UNEXPECTED	An unexpected error occurred.
E_OUTOFMEMORY	Out of memory.
E_FAIL	Object class could not be obtained.

Comments

Calling applications can optionally use the data size returned to preallocate stream buffers for use in the marshaling process.

The *dwDestContext* parameter identifies the destination context, which is relative to the current context in which the unmarshalling is to be done. For example, different marshaling might be done depending on whether the unmarshaling is to happen on the local workstation or on a network workstation. An object might do custom marshalling in one case but not the other.

When **IMarshal::MarshalInterface** is called, the **IMarshal** implementation cannot rely on the caller having already called **IMarshal::GetMarshalSizeMax**; it must still be aware of STG_E_MEDIUMFULL errors returned by the stream.

The return value is guaranteed to be valid only as long as the internal state of the object being marshalled does not change. Marshaling should be done immediately after **IMarshal::GetMarshalSizeMax** returns; otherwise, the caller runs the risk that the object might require more memory than was originally indicated for the marshal.

See Also

IMarshal::GetUnmarshalClass, **IMarshal::MarshalInterface**, **IMarshal::UnmarshalInterface**

IMarshal::MarshalInterface

HRESULT IMarshal::MarshalInterface(*pStm, riid, pv, dwDestContext, pvDestContext, mshlflags***)**
LPSTREAM *pStm*
REFIID *riid*
void * *pv*
unsigned long *dwDestContext*
void * *pvDestContext*
unsigned long *mshlflags*

IMarshal::MarshalInterface marshals a reference of the object's IID into the specified stream.

Parameters

pStm
Points to the stream in which the object is to be marshaled.

riid
Specifies the IID of the object to be marshaled.

pv
Points to the interface to be marshaled; it can be NULL.

dwDestContext
Specifies the destination context relative to the current context in which the unmarshaling will be done. Values are taken from the **MSHCTX** enumeration. For more information, see the section "Data Structures," at the beginning of the **IMarshal** interface description.

pvDestContext
Reserved for use with future **MSHCTX** values.

mshlflags
Specifies why unmarshaling is to be done. Valid values are taken from the enumeration **MSHLFLAGS.** For more information, see the section "Data Structures," at the beginning of the **IMarshal** interface description.

Return Values

Value	Meaning
S_OK	The interface ID reference was marshaled successfully.
E_FAIL	Indicates an unspecified error.
STG_E_MEDIUMFULL	The medium is full.
E_OUTOFMEMORY	Out of memory.
E_INVALIDARG	One or more arguments are invalid.
E_UNEXPECTED	An unexpected error occurred.

For information on possible stream access errors, see the **IStream** methods.

Comments

Once the contents of the stream are sent to the destination, the interface reference can be restored by using the CLSID used to create the handler and then calling

IMarshal::UnmarshalInterface. An implementation of **IMarshal::MarshalInterface** writes to the stream any data required for initialization of this proxy.

The *dwDestContext* parameter identifies the destination context, which is relative to the current context in which the unmarshaling is to be done. For example, different marshaling might be done depending on whether the unmarshaling will happen on the local workstation or on a network workstation; an object could do custom marshalling in one case but not the other.

An implementation of **IMarshal::MarshalInterface** can delegate some destination contexts to the standard marshaling implementation, which is available by calling the **CoGetStandardMarshal** function. Delegating destination contexts should always be done if the *dwDestContext* parameter contains any flags that the **MarshalInterface** function does not understand.

The data marshaled in a particular **IMarshal::MarshalInterface** call can be unmarshaled zero or more times; marshalers must be able to handle the unmarshaling. If a proxy implementation relies on state information in the object application (such as a stub interface whose functions unmarshal the arguments and then forward the call onto the real receiver), by implication this state must deal with zero or more proxies being created from the same initialization data.

If the caller already has the *riid* of the interface being marshaled, it should pass the interface pointer through *pv*. If the caller does not have the *riid*, it should pass NULL; **IMarshal::MarshalInterface** will call **QueryInterface** on itself to get the interface pointer. On exit from this method, the seek pointer in the data stream must be positioned after the last byte of data written.

See Also

IMarshal::GetUnmarshalClass, **IMarshal::GetMarshalSizeMax**, **IMarshal::UnmarshalInterface**

IMarshal::UnmarshalInterface

HRESULT IMarshal::UnmarshalInterface(*pStm, riid, ppvObj***)**
LPSTREAM *pStm*
REFIID *riid*
void * * *ppvObj*

IMarshal::UnmarshalInterface initializes a newly created proxy as part of the unmarshaling process.

Parameters

pStm
Points to the stream in which the interface is to be unmarshaled.

riid
Identifies the IID that the caller wants from the object.

ppvObj
Points to where the interface is to be returned.

Return Values

Value	Meaning
S_OK	The proxy was initialized successfully.
E_FAIL	Indicates an unspecified error.
E_OUTOFMEMORY	Out of memory.
E_INVALIDARG	One or more arguments are invalid.
E_UNEXPECTED	An unexpected error occurred.

For information on possible stream access errors, see the **IStream** interface.

Comments

To get the information required to complete the call, **IMarshal::UnmarshalInterface** often calls **QueryInterface**(*riid*, *ppvObj*) on itself immediately before returning. On exit from this method, the seek pointer in the data stream must be positioned after the last byte of data read.

See Also

IMarshal::GetUnmarshalClass, **IMarshal::GetMarshalSizeMax**, **IMarshal::MarshalInterface**

IMarshal::ReleaseMarshalData

HRESULT IMarshal::ReleaseMarshalData(*pStm*)
LPSTREAM *pStm*

IMarshal::ReleaseMarshalData is called by the unmarshaler (usually **CoReleaseMarshalData** or **CoUnMarshalInterface**) to destroy a marshaled data packet.

Parameters

pStm
Points to a stream that contains the data packet which is to be destroyed.

Return Values

Value	Meaning
S_OK	The data packet was released successfully.
E_FAIL	Indicates an unspecified error.
E_OUTOFMEMORY	Out of memory.
E_INVALIDARG	One or more arguments are invalid.
E_UNEXPECTED	An unexpected error occurred.

For information on possible stream access errors, see the **IStream** interface methods.

See Also

CoUnMarshalInterface, **CoReleaseMarshalData**

IMarshal::DisconnectObject

HRESULT IMarshal::DisconnectObject(*dwReserved***)**
unsigned long *dwReserved*

IMarshal::DisconnectObject is called by **CoDisconnectObject** when the object that is being disconnected supports custom marshaling. This is analogous to how **CoMarshalInterface** defers to **IMarshal::MarshalInterface** if the object supports **IMarshal**.

Parameters

dwReserved
Reserved for future use; must be set to zero by the caller. To ensure compatibility with future use, the callee must not check for zero.

Return Values

Value	Meaning
S_OK	The object was disconnected successfully.
E_FAIL	Indicates an unspecified error.
E_OUTOFMEMORY	Out of memory.
E_INVALIDARG	One or more arguments are invalid.
E_UNEXPECTED	An unexpected error occurred.

IStdMarshalInfo Interface

The **IStdMarshalInfo** interface returns the CLSID of the object handler that is to marshal data to and from the object. The interface is is implemented in an object handler. In order to activate objects as a different type (emulate), object applications use **IStdMarshalInfo** to to get the CLSID of the new object from the handler.

IStdMarshalInfo contains the following methods:

```
DECLARE_INTERFACE_(IStdMarshalInfo, IUnknown)
{
// *** IUnknown methods ***
  HRESULT QueryInterface (REFIID riid, void * * ppvObj) ;
  unsigned long  AddRef ()  ;
  unsigned long  Release () ;

// *** IStdMarshalInfo method ***
  HRESULT GetClassForHandler (unsigned long dwDestContext, void * pvDestContext, LPCLSID pclsid) ;
};
```

For more information, see the compobj.h header file.

IStdMarshalInfo::GetClassForHandler

HRESULT IStdMarshalInfo::GetClassForHandler(*dwDestContext, pvDestContext, pclsid***)**
unsigned long *dwDestContext*
void * *pvDestContext*
LPCLSID* *pclsid*

IStdMarshalInfo::GetClassForHandler retrieves the CLSID of the object handler that is used for standard marshaling in the destination process.

Parameters

dwDestContext
Specifies the type of destination context to which this object is being passed. Valid values are taken from the enumeration **MSHCTX**. For more information, see the section "Data Structures," at the beginning of the **IMarshal** interface description.

pvDestContext
Points to the destination context.

pclsid
Points to where to return the handler's CLSID.

Return Values

Value	Meaning
S_OK	The CLSID was retrieved successfully.
E_OUTOFMEMORY	Out of memory.
E_INVALIDARG	One or more arguments are invalid.
E_UNEXPECTED	An unexpected error occurred.

Comments

Object applications that support class conversion, for example, Activate As in the Convert dialog box, must implement the **IStdMarshalInfo** interface so that the correct object handler can be determined in all cases.

For more information on converting and emulating objects, see "Object Class Conversion and Emulation Functions," later in this chapter.

See Also

CoTreatAsClass, **CoGetTreatAsClass**

Custom Marshaling Functions

The following functions are used to marshal and unmarshal interface method parameters. These functions are defined as follows:

```
CoGetStandardMarshal(REFIID riid, LPUNKNOWN pUnk, unsigned long dwDestContext,
        void * pvDestContext,unsigned long mshlflags, LPMARSHAL * ppMarshal);
CoMarshalHresult(LPSTREAM pStm, HRESULT hresult);
CoMarshalInterface(LPSTREAM pStm, REFIID riid, LPUNKNOWN pUnk,
        unsigned long dwDestContext, void * pvDestContext, unsigned long mshlflags);
```

```
CoReleaseMarshalData(LPSTREAM pStm);
CoUmarshalHresult(LPSTREAM pStm, HRESULT * phresult);
CoUnmarshalInterface(LPSTREAM pStm, REFIID riid, void * * ppvObj);
```

For more information, see the compobj.h header file.

Overview to Custom Marshaling

OLE relies on shared memory access between the calling application and the called process. Therefore, only communication between processes on one machine is supported. An application is not informed whether a called interface method is local or remote, nor is the method told whether the application that called it is local or remote. OLE achieves this transparency between processes by using what are referred to as proxy and stub functions.

A proxy function is a stand-in for a remote method used in the context of a particular container application. The proxy function packages the in parameters to a interface method in a process known as marshaling and sends them across the process boundary to the receiving object application's process space. Here, the parameters are unmarshaled by a corresponding stub function. The stub function then calls a method in the object application to do the work. The out parameters and return value are marshaled by the stub function and passed back to the proxy function in the calling application's process space, where they are unmarshaled and returned to the calling application.

The process of marshaling and unmarshaling a method parameter depends on the type of the parameter. The differences usually center around how pointers are followed and when memory allocations are done in order to make a copy of the parameter to pass to the other process.

There are tables in the marshaling and unmarshaling code that describe, conceptually, how to marshal and unmarshal different types of data, including **int**, **long**, **double**, **char** * strings, and various kinds of structures.

If the object being remoted does not support custom marshaling (as indicated by the lack of support for the **IMarshal** interface), then OLE's standard marshaling is used. By using standard marshaling, the actual marshaling and unmarshaling of interface method parameters is handled by OLE.

The object being marshaled can make use of a custom object handler to do some processing locally; however, the majority of requests are sent to the object using the OLE-supplied standard marshaling mechanism. Custom object handlers must use standard marshaling, which means that custom handlers must aggregate the OLE 2 default handler, as is described in **OleCreateDefaultHandler**.

Once OLE determines that standard marshaling is to be used, it checks for a custom handler by querying the object for the **IStdMarshalInfo** and the **IPersist** interface.

If either of these interfaces is supported, the returned CLSID is used to identify the custom handler to be loaded in the container's process space (see **CoGetClassObject**). The CLSID is obtained by calling the method contained in each of the interfaces.

If a custom handler is not supported, the OLE default remoting handler is used. This is the common situation for components that are not embedded objects. It corresponds to the classic RPC scenario in which the remote proxy is little more than a forwarder of requests.

Objects can implement their own marshaling and unmarshaling functionality or let OLE do it for them. It may be useful to have the OLE object do custom marshaling for three reasons:

- Objects that are already proxies (or handlers) use custom marshaling to avoid creating proxies to proxies. Instead, new proxies are short circuited back to the original stub. This is an important consideration for both efficiency and robustness.
- An object, whose entire state is kept in shared memory, can often be remoted by creating an object in the container application that communicates directly with the shared memory rather than with the original object. This can improve performance significantly, because access to the remoted object does not result in context switches. The compound file implementations of **IStorage** and **IStream** are examples of this custom marshaling.
- From the time they are created, the internal state of some objects does not change. Monikers are an example of such objects. By using custom marshaling, these kinds of objects can be efficiently remoted by making independent copies of them in their client processes.

Note Because of the way in which an OLE object handler communicates with an object application when an object enters the running state, it is not possible for embedded objects to use custom marshaling unless they are completely implemented in the object handler.

Storing Marshaled Interface Pointers in Global Tables

Usually, marshaled interface pointers are sent across a process boundary from one process to another (container or object) where they are unmarshaled. In this usage, the data packet that results from the marshaling process is unmarshaled just once. However, there are occasions where marshaled interface pointers need to be stored in a globally accessible table. Once in the table, the data packet can be retrieved and unmarshaled zero, one, or more times.

The running object table and the internal table maintained by **CoRegisterClassObject** are examples of this concept. The marshaled data packet sitting in the table acts much like another pointer to the object. Depending on the semantics of the table in question, the data packet pointer may be either a reference-counted or nonreference-counted pointer to the interface. Thus, depending on the table in which the object is placed, the presence of the object in the table can or might not keep the object alive.

Because of this behavior, the marshaling code must execute at the time these data packets are removed from these tables and destroyed. The packets cannot be simply discarded, because the presence or absence of the internal state they maintain might be important to the object they indicate.

When an interface pointer is marshaled it is told why it is being marshaled. There are three possible reasons for marshaling:

- This is a typical case of marshal then unmarshal once (this is the responsibility of the unmarshaler).
- This is a marshal for storing into a global-table case, and the presence of the entry in the table is to count as an additional reference to the interface.
- This is a marshal for storing into a global-table case; the entry in the table should not count as an additional reference to the interface.

Whenever a marshaled data packet (from case two or three) is removed from the table, it is the responsibility of the table implementor to call **CoReleaseMarshalData**.

CoGetStandardMarshal

HRESULT CoGetStandardMarshal(*riid, pUnk, dwDestContext, pvDestContext, mshlflags, ppMarshal*)
REFIID *riid*
LPUNKNOWN *pUnk*
unsigned long *dwDestContext*
void * *pvDestContext*
unsigned long *mshlflags*
LPMARSHAL **ppMarshal*

CoGetStandardMarshal returns an **IMarshal** instance that performs standard default marshaling and unmarshaling of interface parameters across remote process boundaries.

Parameters

riid
Specifies the interface to be marshaled.

pUnk
Points to the object to be marshaled. This interface does not have to be of type *riid*; it can be any interface on the object which conforms to **IUnknown**. The standard marshaler will internally call **QueryInterface**.

dwDestContext
Specifies the destination context relative to the current context in which the unmarshaling is to be done.

pvDestContext
Points to the associated destination context.

mshlflags
Specifies the destination context relative to the current context in which the unmarshaling is to be done; valid values are from the enumeration **MSHCTX**. Currently there is only one valid destination context: MSHCTX_LOCAL. For more information, see the section "Data Structures," at the beginning of the **IMarshal** interface description.

ppMarshal
Points to where to return the standard marshaler.

Return Values

Value	Meaning
S_OK	The **IMarshal** instance was returned successfully.
E_OUTOFMEMORY	Out of memory.
E_INVALIDARG	One or more arguments are invalid.
E_UNEXPECTED	An unexpected error occurred.
E_FAIL	Indicates an unspecified error.

Comments

Custom marshaling implementations should delegate any destination contexts they do not understand and those they want the standard marshaler to handle. The standard marshaler is also used when the object being marshaled does not support the **IMarshal** interface.

Note **CoGetStandardMarshal** is not implemented in OLE 2, though a non-functional stub is present. Programmers of custom marshalers should write their code as indicated and call this stub for any destination contexts the application does not understand. For more information, see "Overview to Custom Marshaling," earlier in this chapter).

With OLE 2, this is guaranteed not to happen because OLE only supports one kind of destination context. By writing their code this way, programmers of custom marshalers pre-enable themselves for supporting different contexts as they become available (such as when networking support is added).

See Also

IMarshal Interface

CoMarshalHresult

HRESULT CoMarshalHresult(*pStm*, *hresult*)
LPSTREAM *pStm*
HRESULT *hresult*

CoMarshalHresult marshals an HRESULT to the specified stream so it can be unmarshaled using **CoUnmarshalHresult**.

Parameters

pStm
Points to the stream used for marshaling.

hresult
Specifies the HRESULT in the originating process.

Return Values

Value	Meaning
S_OK	The HRESULT was marshaled successfully.
STG_E_INVALID-POINTER	Bad pointer passed in for *pStm*.
STG_E_MEDIUM-FULL	The medium is full.
E_OUTOFMEMORY	Out of memory.
E_INVALIDARG	One or more arguments are invalid.
E_UNEXPECTED	An unexpected error occurred.

Comments

HRESULTs are process-specific; an HRESULT valid in one process might not be valid in another. **CoMarshalHresult** is used only by developers who are writing custom marshaling code to marshal HRESULTs, either as parameters or as return codes.

The HRESULT returned by **CoMarshalHresult** indicates the success or failure of the marshaling process and is unrelated to the HRESULT parameter.

See Also

CoUnmarshalHresult

CoUnmarshalHresult

HRESULT CoUnmarshalHresult(*pStm*, *phresult*)
LPSTREAM *pStm*
HRESULT * *phresult*

CoUnmarshalHresult unmarshals an HRESULT from the specified stream.

Parameters

pStm
Points to the stream from which the HRESULT is marshaled.

phresult
Points to the memory location into which the HRESULT is to be put.

Return Values

Value	Meaning
S_OK	The HRESULT was unmarshaled successfully.
STG_E_INVALID-POINTER	Bad pointer passed in for *pStm*.
E_OUTOFMEMORY	Out of memory.
E_INVALIDARG	One or more arguments are invalid.
E_UNEXPECTED	An unexpected error occurred.

Comments

CoUnmarshalHresult is needed only by applications that implement custom marshaling. Custom marshallers must use **CoUnmarshalHresult** to unmarshal all HRESULTs.

See Also

CoMarshalHresult

CoMarshalInterface

HRESULT CoMarshalInterface(*pStm, riid, pUnk, dwDestContext, pvDestContext, mshlflags***)**
LPSTREAM *pStm*
REFIID *riid*
LPUNKNOWN *pUnk*
void * *dwDestContext*
unsigned long *pvDestContext*
unsigned long *mshlflags*

CoMarshalInterface marshals the OLE 2 object instance into the specified stream so that it can be unmarshaled in the destination with **CoUnMarshalInterface**. **CoMarshalInterface** only marshals interfaces derived from **IUnknown**.

Parameters

pStm
Specifies the stream into which the object is to be marshaled.

riid
Specifies the interface to which the *pUnk* complies. This interface must be derived from **IUnknown**.

pUnk
Points to the IID of the object that is to be marshaled. Only objects derived from **IUnknown** can be marshaled.

dwDestContext
Specifies the destination context relative to the current context in which the unmarshaling is to be done; values are from the enumeration **MSHCTX**.For more information, see the section "Data Structures," at the beginning of the **IMarshal** interface description.

pvDestContext
Reserved for future use; must be set to zero by the caller. However, to ensure compatibility with future use, the callee must not check for zero.

mshlflags
Specifies the destination context relative to the current context in which the unmarshaling is to be done; valid values are from the enumeration **MSHLFLAGS**. For more information, see the section "Data Structures," at the beginning of the **IMarshal** interface description.

Return Values

Value	Meaning
S_OK	The object was marshaled successfully.
STG_E_MEDIUM-FULL	The medium is full.
STG_E_INVALID-POINTER	An **IStream** error dealing with the *pStm* parameter.
CO_E_OBJNOT-CONNECTED	Similar to OLE_E_NOTRUNNING. The object is loaded but no server is running.
E_OUTOFMEMORY	Out of memory.
E_INVALIDARG	One or more arguments are invalid.
E_UNEXPECTED	An unexpected error occurred.
E_FAIL	Indicates an unspecified error.

Comments

The *dwDestContext* parameter identifies the destination context, which is relative to the current context in which the unmarshaling is to be done.

Calling **CoMarshalInterface** on an OLE 1 object will always fail with CO_E_OBJNOTCONNECTED, even if the OLE 1 object is running . (To allow the function to succeed would introduce multiple DDE conversations between different processes, which is something OLE 1 was not designed to support).

CoMarshalInterface first tries to obtain an **IMarshal** interface from *pUnk* by calling **QueryInterface**. If that fails, the standard marshaler (accessible by **CoGetStandardMarshal**) is used. Having obtained an **IMarshal** interface, **CoMarshalInterface** uses the **GetMarshalClass** and **CoMarshalInterface** functions to marshal the interface. **IMarshal::GetMarshalSizeMax** is not used; the stream passed to the **CoMarshalInterface** function must be able to grow dynamically.

CoMarshalInterface is usually only called by code in interface proxies or stubs that marshal an interface pointer parameter, although it is sometimes used by objects that support custom marshaling.

To custom marshal an object, the sending application performs the following steps:

1. Get the CLSID to be used to create an uninitialized proxy in the unmarshaling context by calling **IMarshal::GetUnmarshalClass**.

2. [optional] Get an upper bound on the amount of memory needed to do the marshaling by calling **IMarshal::GetMarshalSizeMax**.
3. Do the marshaling by calling **IMarshal::MarshalInterface**. The CLSID and the data marshaled into the stream are then sent to the destination, where they are unmarshaled.

See Also **CoUnmarshalInterface**

CoUnmarshalInterface

HRESULT CoUnmarshalInterface(*pStm, riid, ppvObj***)**
LPSTREAM *pStm*
REFIID *riid*
void * * *ppvObj*

CoUnmarshalInterface unmarshals a previously marshaled object from the specified stream. This function is provided for convenience in unmarshaling previously marshaled objects.

Parameters

pStm
Points to the stream from which the object is to be unmarshaled.

riid
Specifies the interface that is to communicate with the unmarshaled object.

ppvObj
Points to the location where the interface pointer is to be returned.

Return Values

Value	Meaning
S_OK	The interface was unmarshaled successfully.
STG_E_INVALIDPOINTER	An **IStream** error dealing with the *pStm* parameter.
CO_E_OBJNOTCONNECTED	The object application has been disconnected from the remoting system (for example, as a result of **CoDisconnectObject**).
REGDB_E_CLASSNOTREG	An error occurred reading the Registration Database file.
E_OUTOFMEMORY	Out of memory.
E_INVALIDARG	One or more arguments are invalid.
E_UNEXPECTED	An unexpected error occurred.
E_NOINTERFACE	The final **QueryInterface** of this function for the requested interface returned E_NOINTERFACE.

Value	Meaning
E_FAIL	Indicates an unspecified error.
CoCreateInstance errors	An error occurred when creating the handler (standard or custom marshaling).

Comments

Unmarshaling an object requires the receiving application to perform the following steps:

1. Load the class object corresponding to the CLSID that the object application passed to **IMarshal::GetUnmarshalClass**:

```
LPCLASSFACTORY lpcf;
GetClassObject(cid, CLSCTX_INPROCHANDLER, IID_IClassFactory, &lpcf);
```

2. Instantiate the class, requesting the **IMarshal** interface:

```
LPMARSHAL lpProxy;
lpcf->CreateInstance(NULL, IID_IMarshal, &lpProxy);
```

Note If the proxy is being created as part of an aggregate, the **IUnknown** interface would be requested and the **IMarshal** interface would be queried.

3. Initialize the proxy by calling **IMarshal::UnmarshalInterface**. Use a copy of the data originally produced by **IMarshal::MarshalInterface** and request the interface that was originally marshaled:

```
IOriginal * pobj;
lpProxy->UnmarshalInterface(lpstm, IID_Original, &pobj);
lpProxy->Release();
lpcf->Release();
if (MSHLFLAGS_NORMAL){
    reset Stm;
    Release m_data;
}
```

See Also

CoMarshalInterface

CoReleaseMarshalData

HRESULT CoReleaseMarshalData(*pStm***)**
LPSTREAM *pStm*

CoReleaseMarshalData destroys a previously marshaled data packet.

Parameters

pStm
Points to a stream containing the data packet to be destroyed.

Return Values

Value	Meaning
S_OK	The data packet was successfully destroyed.
STG_E_INVALID-POINTER	An **IStream** error dealing with the *pStm* parameter.
E_OUTOFMEMORY	Out of memory.
E_INVALIDARG	*pStm* is invalid.
E_UNEXPECTED	An unexpected error occurred.
E_FAIL	Indicates an unspecified error.

Comments

CoReleaseMarshalData must be called to destroy data packets. The following situations are examples of when **CoReleaseMarshalData** should be called:

- An attempt was made to unmarshal the data packet, but failed.
- A marshaled data packet was removed from a global table.

See Also

IMarshal::ReleaseMarshalData

Component Object Functions

The following functions are used to create a class of object, to locate and connect to a class of object, to register a class of object, and to revoke the registration of an object class. These functions are defined as follows:

```
CoCreateInstance(REFCLSID rclsid, LPUnknown pUnkOuter, unsigned long dwClsContext, REFIID riid,
                 void * * ppvObj);
CoGetClassObject(REFCLSID rclsid, unsigned long dwClsContext, void * pvReserved,
                 REFIID riid, void * * ppvObj);
CoRegisterClassObject(REFCLSID rclsid, LPUNKNOWN pUnk, unsigned long dwClsContext,
                 unsigned long flags, unsigned long * lpdwRegister);
CoRevokeClassObject(unsigned long dwRegister);
CoLockObjectExternal(LPUNKNOWN pUnk, unsigned long fLock, unsigned long fLastUnlockReleases);
CoDisconnectObject(LPUNKNOWN pUnk, unsigned long dwReserved);
CoIsHandlerConnected(LPUNKNOWN pUnk);
```

For more information, see the compobj.h header file.

CoCreateInstance

HRESULT CoCreateInstance(*rclsid, pUnkOuter, dwClsContext, riid, ppvObj*)
REFCLSID *rclsid*
LPUnknown *pUnkOuter*
unsigned long *dwClsContext*
REFIID *riid*
void * * *ppvObj*

CoCreateInstance creates an instance of the specified object class.

Parameters

rclsid
Specifies the CLSID of the object class to create.

pUnkOuter
Specifies the controlling unknown of the aggregate.

dwClsContext
Specifies the context in which the executable is to be run. The values are taken from the enumeration **CLSCTX**. For more information, see **CoGetClassObject**.

riid
Specifies the IID to be used to communicate with the object.

ppvObj
Points to where to return the pointer to the requested interface.

Return Values

Value	Meaning
S_OK	An instance of the specified object class was successfully created.
REGDB_E_CLASS-NOTREG	Specified class not registered in Registration Database file.
E_OUTOFMEMORY	Out of memory.
E_INVALIDARG	One or more arguments are invalid.
E_UNEXPECTED	An unexpected error occurred.
CLASS_E_NO-AGGREGATION	This class cannot be created as part of an aggregate.

Comments

CoCreateInstance is a helper function that encapsulates the following functionality:

```
CoGetClassObject(rclsid, dwClsContext, NULL, IID_IClassFactory,
     &pCF);
hresult = pCF->CreateInstance(pUnkOuter, riid, ppvObj)
pCF->Release();
```

CoCreateInstance will not force the object into the running state.

See Also

CoGetClassObject, **IClassFactory::CreateInstance**

CoGetClassObject

HRESULT CoGetClassObject(*rclsid*, *grfContext*, *pvReserved*, *riid*, *ppvObj*)
REFCLSID *rclsid*
unsigned long *dwClsContext*
void * *pvReserved*
REFIID *riid*
void * * *ppvObj*

CoGetClassObject locates and connects to a specified class object.

Parameters

rclsid
Specifies the object class that is to be loaded.

dwClsContext
Specifies the context in which the executable code is to be run. The value is a group of flags taken from the enumeration **CLSCTX.** For more information, see the following comments.

pvReserved
Reserved for future use; must be NULL.

riid
Specifies the interface to be used to communicate with the class object.

ppvObj
Points to where the interface is to be stored.

Return Values

Value	Meaning
S_OK	The specified object was located and connected to successfully.
REGDB_E_CLASSNOTREG	CLSID is not properly registered.
E_NOINTERFACE	The object pointed to by *ppvObj* does not support the interface identified by *riid*.
REGDB_E_READREGDB	Error reading the Registration Database file.
CO_E_DLLNOTFOUND	DLL object application or handler not found (depends on context).
CO_E_APPNOTFOUND	Application not found (CLSCTX_LOCAL_SERVER only).
E_ACCESSDENIED	General access failure.
CO_E_WRONGOSFORAPP	Application or DLL is written for a different operating system than is currently running.
CO_E_ERRORINAPP	Application has an error in image.

Value	Meaning
CO_E_APPSINGLEUSE	Application can only be launched once.
CO_E_ERRORINDLL	Application has error in image.
CO_E_APPDIDNTREG	Application was launched, but it didn't register class object (may or may not have shutdown).
E_OUTOFMEMORY	Out of memory.
E_INVALIDARG	One or more arguments are invalid.
E_UNEXPECTED	An unexpected error occurred.
E_NOINTERFACE	The **QueryInterface** on the class object returned E_NOINTERFACE.

Comments

Given a CLSID, a container can opaquely locate and dynamically load the executable code that manipulates an object by calling **CoGetClassObject**. The container passes to **CoGetClassObject** the CLSID and the interface it wants to use to communicate with the object. Most often, this is the **IClassFactory** interface, through which the container can then make an instance of the object by calling **IClassFactory::CreateInstance**.

If necessary, the object's executable code can be dynamically loaded in order to locate and connect to the class object. The *riid* parameter specifies the interface used by the caller to communicate with the class object; this is usually **IID_IClassFactory**.

Different pieces of code can be associated with one *rclsid* for use in different execution contexts. The context in which the caller is interested is indicated by the parameter *dwClsContext*, which contains a group of flags taken from the enumeration **CLSCTX**.

CLSCTX is defined in compobj.h as follows:

```
typedef enum tagCLSCTX
{
    CLSCTX_INPROC_SERVER     = 1
    CLSCTX_INPROC_HANDLER    = 2,
    CLSCTX_LOCAL_SERVER      = 4,
} CLSCTX;
```

The contexts are tried in the order in which they are listed. Multiple values can be or-ed together, indicating that multiple contexts are acceptable to the caller; for example:

```
#define CLSCTX_INPROC (CLSCTX_INPROC_SERVER|CLSCTX_INPROC_HANDLER)
#define CLSCTX_SERVER (CLSCTX_INPROC_SERVER|CLSCTX_LOCAL_SERVER)
```

These contexts are used as follows:

Object Class Context Values	Description
CLSCTX_INPROC _SERVER	The code that creates and manages objects of this class is loaded in the container's process space (runs in same process as caller).
CLSCTX_INPROC _HANDLER	The DLL code that implements container-side structures of this class (when instances of it are accessed remotely) is loaded in the container's process space (runs in same process as caller).
CLSCTX_LOCAL _SERVER	The EXE code that creates and manages objects of this class is loaded in a separate process space (runs on same machine but in a different process).

CoGetClassObject operates by consulting (as appropriate for the context indicated) both the Registration Database file and the existing class objects registered using **CoRegisterClassObject**.

Example uses of particular flag combinations are as follows:

Function Called	Context Flag Used
OleLoad	CLSCTX_INPROC_HANDLER | CLSCTX_INPROC_SERVER Putting an OLE object into the loaded state requires in-process access; however, it doesn't matter if all of the object's functionality is presently available.
IRunnable-Object::Run	CLSCTX_INPROC_SERVER | CLSCTX_LOCAL_SERVER Running an OLE object requires connecting to the full code of the object wherever it is located.
CoUnMarshal-Interface	CLSCTX_INPROC_HANDLER Unmarshaling needs the form of the class designed for remote access.

See Also **CoRegisterClassObject**, **CoRevokeClassObject**

CoRegisterClassObject

HRESULT CoRegisterClassObject(*rclsid, pUnk, dwClsContext, flags, lpdwRegister*)
REFCLSID *rclsid*
LPUNKNOWN *pUnk*
unsigned long *dwClsContext*
unsigned long *flags*
unsigned long * *lpdwRegister*

CoRegisterClassObject registers a class object with OLE so that other applications can connect to it.

Parameters

rclsid
Specifies the object class being registered.

pUnk
Points to the class object whose availability is being published.

dwClsContext
Specifies the context in which the executable code is to be run: CLSCTX_INPROC_SERVER, CLSCTX_INPROC_HANDLER, or CLSCTX_LOCAL_SERVER. For more information on these context values, see **CoGetClassObject**.

flags
Determines how connections are made to the class object. Valid values are taken from the enumeration **REGCLS**. For more information, see the following comments.

lpdwRegister
Points to the value returned by **CoRegisterClassObject** that identifies the class object; later used by **CoRevokeClassObject** to revoke the class registration. **CoRegisterClassObject** will never return a value of zero.

Return Values

Value	Meaning
S_OK	The object was registered successfully.
CO_E_OBJISREG	Object class already registered in the class object table.
E_OUTOFMEMORY	Out of memory.
E_INVALIDARG	One or more arguments are invalid.
E_UNEXPECTED	An unexpected error occurred.

Comments

When an object application starts, it creates an **IClassFactory** instance and calls **CoRegisterClassObject** to register that class factory instance. Object applications that support several different object classes must allocate a different **IClassFactory** instance for each object class.

Multiple registrations of the same class object is not an error; each registration is independent. Each subsequent registration will yield a unique key in *lpdwRegister*.

CoRegisterClassObject is called by executable object applications only; it should not be called by object handlers or DLL object applications. These applications must instead implement and export **DllGetClassObject**.

SDI (single-document interface) applications that are being started with the **/Embedding** switch should not register their class of object; MDI (multiple-document interface) applications beings started with **/Embedding** (or **-Embedding**) must register their class of object.

When the subsequent reference count on the class object reaches zero, the class object can be destroyed, allowing the application to exit.

A sophisticated container can keep an object application running by obtaining its class object and calling **IClassFactory::LockServer**(TRUE) on it. However, because some class objects are single use, the container must hold on to the actual class object from which objects are instantiated. This prohibits the container application from using helper functions like **OleLoad**. Instead, the container has to code variants of such functions itself.

The *flags* parameter controls how connections are made to the class object; the values are taken from the enumeration **REGCLS**, which is defined in compobj.h as follows:

```
typedef enum tagREGCLS {
    REGCLS_SINGLEUSE         = 0,
    REGCLS_MULTIPLEUSE       = 1,
    REGCLS_MULTI_SEPARATE    = 2,
    } REGCLS;
```

REGCLS values have the following meaning:

Value	Description
REGCLS_SINGLE-USE	Once a container has connected to the class object with **CoGetClassObject**, the class object should be removed from public view so that no other container applications can similarly connect to it. This flag is commonly given for single document interface (SDI) applications. Specifying this flag does not affect the responsibility of the object application to call **CoRevokeClassObject**; it must always call **CoRevokeClassObject** when it is done by using an object class.
REGCLS_MULTIPLE-USE	Enables multiple **CoGetClassObject** calls to connect to the same class object.

Value	Description
REGCLS_MULTI _SEPARATE	Similar to REGCLS_MULTIPLEUSE, except that REGCLS_MULTI_SEPARATE does not automatically register the class object as CLSCTX_INPROC_SERVER for a local server; instead it provides separate control over each context.

Notice that registering as

```
CLSCTX_LOCAL_SERVER, REGCLS_MULTIPLEUSE
```

is the same as

```
(CLSCTX_INPROC_SERVER|CLSCTX_LOCAL_SERVER), REGCLS_MULTI_SEPARATE
```

but is different than registering as

```
CLSCTX_LOCAL_SERVER, REGCLS_MULTI_SEPARATE.
```

The following table summarizes the allowable flag combinations and the type of object registrations that are affected by the combinations:

	REGCLS_ SINGLEUSE	REGCLS_ MULTIPLE-USE	REGCLS_ MULTI_SEPARATE
CLSCTX_I NPROC_ SERVER	Error	Inproc	Inproc
CLSCTX_ LOCAL_ SERVER	Local	Inproc/local	Local
Both of the above	Error	Inproc/local	Inproc/local
Other	Error	Error	Error

The key difference is in the second and third columns and the middle rows. In the REGCLS_MULTIPLEUSE column, they are the same (registers multiple use for both inproc and local). In the REGCLS_MULTI_SEPARATE column, CLSCTX_LOCAL_SERVER is local only.

See Also **CoGetClassObject**, **CoRevokeClassObject**, **DllGetClassObject**

CoRevokeClassObject

HRESULT CoRevokeClassObject(*dwRegister***)**
unsigned long *dwRegister*

CoRevokeClassObject informs OLE that a class object previously registered with **CoRegisterClassObject** is no longer available for use.

Parameters

dwRegister
Specifies the token previously returned from **CoRegisterClassObject**.

Return Values

Value	Meaning
S_OK	The class object was successfully revoked.
E_OUTOFMEMORY	Out of memory.
E_INVALIDARG	The *dwRegister* parameter does not map to a registered class object.
E_UNEXPECTED	An unexpected error occurred.

Comments

The object application must call **CoRevokeClassObject** on all registered class objects prior to quitting program execution. **CoRevokeClassObject** should be called by class object implementors as part of their release sequence.

Specifying the value REGCLS_SINGLEUSE in a call to **CoRegisterClassObject** does not affect the responsibility of the object application to revoke registered class objects. This task must always be done prior to quitting.

See Also

CoGetClassObject, **CoRegisterClassObject**

CoLockObjectExternal

HRESULT CoLockObjectExternal(*pUnk, fLock, fLastUnlockReleases***)**
LPUNKNOWN *pUnk*
unsigned long *fLock*
unsigned long *fLastUnlockReleases*

CoLockObjectExternal locks an object so its reference count cannot decrement to zero; it is also used to release a lock on an object.

Parameters

pUnk
Points to the object to be locked or unlocked.

fLock
Specifies whether the object is to be locked. TRUE holds a reference to the object, locking it independently of external or internal **AddRef/Release** operations, registrations, or revokes. If TRUE, *fLastLockReleases* is ignored. FALSE releases such locks.

fLastLockReleases
Specifies whether a given lock is the last reference to an object that is supposed to keep it alive. TRUE means release all pointers to the object if this lock is the last reference to the object that is supposed to keep it alive. (There may be other references that are not supposed to keep it alive.)

Return Values

Value	Meaning
S_OK	The object reference count was locked successfully.
E_OUTOFMEMORY	Out of memory.
E_INVALIDARG	One or more arguments are invalid.
E_UNEXPECTED	An unexpected error occurred.

Comments

CoLockObjectExternal must be called in the process in which the object is loaded. From the object's point of view, the lock is implemented by having the system call **IUnknown::AddRef** on the object and then not calling **IUnknown::Release** on the object until **CoLockObjectExternal(**...,FALSE,...**)** is later called.

Because it acts external to the object, much like the user does, **CoLockObjectExternal** can be used to maintain a reference count on the object on behalf of the user.

CoLockObjectExternal adds a strong lock on the stubmanager associated with the object. The object's reference count will not go to zero until either this lock is freed by another call to **CoLockObjectExternal**(FALSE, ...) or **CoDisconnectObject** is called to forcibly break all external connections (including direct calls to **CoLockObjectExternal** by the object itself).

CoLockObjectExternal does not change the typical registration/revoking process for objects. **CoLockObjectExternal** can be used in **IOleContainer::LockContainer**, although the container must still keep a lock count so that it exits when the lock count reaches zero and the container is invisible.

CoLockObjectExternal is typically used in three places:

- Object applications call **CoLockObjectExternal**(*pUnk*, TRUE, TRUE) when they become visible. This call creates a strong lock on behalf of the user. When the application is closing, the lock must be freed with a call to **CoLockObjectExternal** (*pUnk,* FALSE, TRUE).

  The API function, **OleNoteObjectVisible**, can be called instead of **CoLockObjectExternal** in this context. **OleNoteObjectVisible** is simply a wrapper function for **CoLockObjectExternal**.

- A call to **CoLockObjectExternal** can be included in the implementation of **IClassFactory::LockServer**. Containers call **IClassFactory::LockServer** to keep an object application that handles a particular class of object(s) in memory, thereby eliminating startup time and allowing faster throughput during activation.
- A call to **CoLockObjectExternal** can also be in the implementation of **IOleContainer::LockContainer**. **IOleContainer::LockContainer** is called to keep an embedded object's container alive.

Conversely, a container must call **OleSetContainedObject** to weaken its connection to the object so other connections can determine what will happen to the object while it is visible. **OleSetContainedObject** is similar to calling **CoLockObjectExternal**(*pUnk*, FALSE, FALSE).

If an application manages all aspects of its application and document shutdown completely with calls to **CoLockObjectExternal**, it is not necessary to maintain a private count of calls to **IOleContainer::LockContainer**. Maintaining all aspects of shutdown means that **CoLockObjectExternal** is called whenever one of the following conditions occur:

- A document is created and destroyed or made visible or invisible.
- The application is started and shutdown by the user.
- A pseudo-object is created and destroyed.

For debugging purposes, it may be useful to keep a count of the number of external locks and unlocks made on the application.

Figure 5.4 shows the state of an application after **CoLockObjectExternal** is called. OLE creates a transparent stub manager that keeps track of the type and number of external references counts. As shown, the class object's reference count is two, which reflects the strong lock held by the stub manager and the weak lock held by the application object.

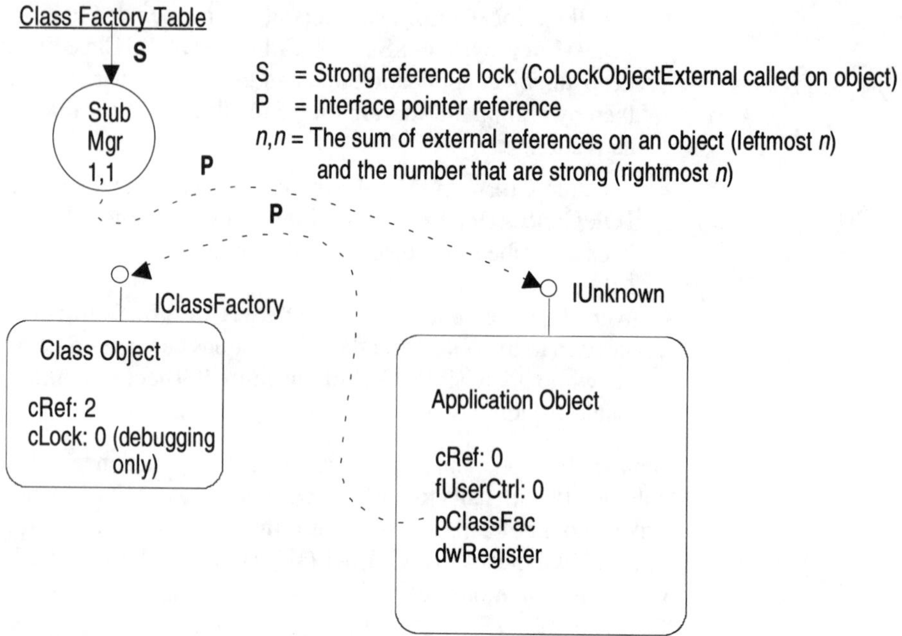

Figure 5.4 Creating a strong reference lock on an object

Weak locks are created when an object is registered in the running object table or typically when a drop target is registered. When there is a weak lock, the last external release releases the object. The object is still responsible for revoking its drag/drop registration and Running object table registration. This enables a moniker bind and release to shut down the object when it is invisible.

Note During drag and drop operations, the object that exposes the **IDropTarget** interface must have an external lock on it to ensure that a remote connection does not release the object after the drag and drop operation. To lock the drop object, call **CoLockObjectExternal** before calling **RegisterDragDrop**. The object should be freed after **RevokeDragDrop** has been called.

See Also **IOleContainer::LockContainer**, **OleSetContainedObject**

CoDisconnectObject

HRESULT CoDisconnectObject(*pUnk, dwReserved***)**
LPUNKNOWN *pUnk*
unsigned long *dwReserved*

CoDisconnectObject disconnects all remote process connections being maintained on behalf of all the interface pointers on a specified object.

Parameters

pUnk
Points to the object that is to be disconnected. Can be any interface on the object which is polymorphic with **IUnknown**, not necessarily the exact interface returned by **QueryInterface(IID_IUnknown**...).

dwReserved
Reserved for future use; must be set to zero by the caller; however, to ensure compatibility with future use, the callee must not check for zero.

Return Values

Value	Meaning
S_OK	All remote process connections were deleted successfully.
E_OUTOFMEMORY	Out of memory.
E_INVALIDARG	One or more arguments are invalid.
E_UNEXPECTED	An unexpected error occurred.
E_FAIL	Indicates an unspecified error.

Comments

CoDisconnectObject is not used in the typical course of processing (clients of interfaces should use **IUnknown::Release**). The primary purpose of **CoDisconnectObject** is to give an application process control over remote connections to other processes that might have been made from objects managed by the process. For example, suppose an OLE container loads an embedded object and then links are established between the embedded object and outside containers. If the container application process wanted to exit, it is not useful for these remote connections to keep the object active beyond the lifetime of its container. When the object's container closes, such links should go into a disconnected state. To forcefully close any existing connection(s), the object's container can call **CoDisconnectObject**.

CoDisconnectObject is a privileged operation, to be invoked only by the process in which the object actually is managed. **CoDisconnectObject** effectively causes a controlled crash of the remoting connections to the object.

Before calling **CoDisconnectObject**, the container process should first call **IOleObject::Close** for all OLE objects. The objects will send OnClose notifications to alert all clients of the impending closure.

CoIsHandlerConnected

BOOL CoIsHandlerConnected(*pUnk*)
LPUNKNOWN *pUnk*

CoIsHandlerConnected determines if the specifed handler is connected to its corresponding object.

Parameters

pUnk
Specifies the object in question.

Return Values

Value	Meaning
TRUE	Handler is connected to its object.
FALSE	Handler is not connected to its object.

Comments

If a pointer to the real object is passed instead of a pointer to the handler, then **CoIsHandlerConnected** returns TRUE.

DLL Initialization Functions

The following functions can be used to load and unload DLL libraries. They keep track of reference counts on the loaded library, removing them when the libraries are unloaded. The functions are defined as follows:

```
CoLoadLibrary(char * lpszLibName, unsigned long bAutoFree);
CoFreeAllLibraries(void);
CoFreeLibrary(long hInst);
CoFreeUnusedLibraries(void);
```

For more information, see also the compobj.h header file.

CoLoadLibrary

long CoLoadLibrary(*lpszLibName, bAutoFree*)
char * *lpszLibName*
unsigned long *bAutoFree*

CoLoadLibrary loads the DLL of the given name into the caller's process. Usually, this is not called directly by containers, but is called internally by **CoGetClassObject**.

Parameters

lpszLibName
Points to the name of the library to be loaded.

bAutoFree
Indicates, if TRUE, that this library is freed when it is no longer needed, either through **CoFreeUnusedLibraries** or at uninitialization time through **CoUninitialize**. If it is FALSE, the library should be explicitly freed with **CoFreeLibrary**.

Return Values

Value	Meaning
Module handle	Handle of the now-loaded library.
NULL	Library could not be loaded.

Comments
Internally, the loaded DLL is reference counted, by using **CoLoadLibrary** to increment the count and **CoFreeLibrary** to decrement it.

See Also
CoFreeAllLibraries, **CoFreeLibrary**, **CoFreeUnusedLibraries**

CoFreeAllLibraries

void CoFreeAllLibraries()

CoFreeAllLibraries frees all the DLLs that have been loaded with **CoLoadLibrary**, whether or not they are currently in use.

Comments
The component object model library maintains a list of loaded DLLs for each process that is used by **CoFreeAllLibraries** to unload the libraries. **CoFreeAllLibraries** is called internally by **CoUninitialize**; thus containers usually have no need to call this function directly.

See Also
CoLoadLibrary, **CoFreeLibrary**, **CoFreeUnusedLibraries**

CoFreeLibrary

void CoFreeLibrary(*hInst***)**
long *hInst*

CoFreeLibrary frees a library that was previously loaded with **CoLoadLibrary**.

Parameters
hInst
Specifies the handle to the library module that is to be freed, as was returned by **CoLoadLibrary**.

Comments
It is illegal to explicitly free a library whose corresponding **CoLoadLibrary** call specified auto-free (**CoLoadLibrary**(...,TRUE)).

See Also
CoFreeAllLibraries, **CoFreeUnusedLibraries**, **CoLoadLibrary**

CoFreeUnusedLibraries

void CoFreeUnusedLibraries()

CoFreeUnusedLibraries unloads any DLLs that have been loaded by **CoLoadLibrary** but are no longer in use.

Comments Applications should call this function periodically to free resources, either at the top of their message loop or in some idle-time task.

See Also **CoFreeLibrary**, **CoFreeUnusedLibraries**, **CoLoadLibrary**

File Time Conversion Functions

This section describes the functions used to convert 32-bit Macintosh representations of the time and date to 64-bit representations. The functions are defined as follows:

```
unsigned long CoFileTimeToMacDateTime(FILETIME * lpFileTime, unsigned long * psecs);
unsigned long CoMacDateTimeToFileTime(unsigned long secs, FILETIME * lpFileTime);
unsigned long CoFileTimeNow(FILETIME * lpFileTime);
```

For more information, see the compobj.h header file.

FILETIME Data Structure

The **FILETIME** data structure is a 64-bit value representing the number of 100-nanosecond intervals since January 1, 1601.

FILETIME is defined in compobj.h, as follows:

```
typedef struct FARSTRUCT tagFILETIME
{
    unsigned long dwLowDateTime;
    unsigned long dwHighDateTime;
} FILETIME;
```

CoFileTimeToMacDateTime

unsigned long CoFileTimeToMacDateTime (*lpFileTime*, *psecs*)
FILETIME * *lpFileTime*
unsigned long * *psecs*

CoFileTimeToMacDateTime converts a **FILETIME** data structure into Macintosh date and time values.

Parameters

lpFileTime
Points to the **FILETIME** structure that is to be converted.

psecs
Points to where to return the converted **FILETIME** date and time values. The value of *psecs* is the number of seconds since Midnight, January 1, 1904.

Return Values

Value	Meaning
TRUE	The FILETIME structure was converted successfully to Macintosh date and time values.
FALSE	The date and time values will not fit in the range of valid Macintosh values.

See Also **CoMacDateTimeToFileTime**

CoMacDateTimeToFileTime

unsigned long CoMacDateTimeToFileTime (*secs*, *lpFileTime*)
unsigned long *secs*
FILETIME * *lpFileTime*

CoMacDateTimeToFileTime converts the Macintosh representation of the time to a **FILETIME** structure, which is a 64-bit value representing the number of 100-nanosecond intervals since January 1, 1601.

Parameters

secs
Specifies the time value to convert.

lpFileTime
Points to where to return the **FILETIME** structure.

Return Values

Value	Meaning
TRUE	TRUE returned in all cases.

See Also **CoFileTimeToMacDateTime**

CoFileTimeNow

unsigned long CoFileTimeNow(*lpFileTime*)
FILETIME * *lpFileTime*

CoFileTimeNow returns the current time as a **FILETIME** structure.

Parameters

lpFileTime
Points to where to return the **FILETIME** structure.

Return Values

Value	Meaning
TRUE	TRUE returned in all cases.

See Also **CoMacDateTimeToFileTime**, **CoFileTimeToMacDateTime**

DLL Object Class Functions

The following functions can be implemented in DLL object handlers to enable containers to access a class of object implemented within an object handler or to indicate whether it is OK to unload a DLL handler from memory. The functions are defined as follows:

```
HRESULT DllCanUnloadNow(void);
HRESULT DllGetClassObject(REFCLSID rclsid, REFIID riid, void * * ppvObj);
```

For more information, see the compobj.h header file.

DllCanUnloadNow

HRESULT DllCanUnloadNow(void)

DllCanUnloadNow indicates whether the DLL is no longer in use and should be unloaded.

Return Values

Value	Meaning
S_OK	DLL can be unloaded now.
S_FALSE	DLL cannot be unloaded now.

Comments

DllCanUnloadNow is not provided with OLE; it is implemented and exported from DLLs supporting the Component Object Model.

DllCanUnloadNow should be exported from DLLs designed to be dynamically loaded in **CoGetClassObject** or **CoLoadLibrary** calls. A DLL is no longer in use when there are no existing instances of classes it manages; at this point, the DLL can be safely freed by calling **CoFreeUnusedLibraries**.

If the DLL loaded by **CoGetClassObject** fails to export **DllCanUnloadNow**, the DLL will be forcibly unloaded when **CoUninitialize** is called to release the OLE libraries.

If the DLL links to another DLL, returning S_OK from **DllCanUnloadNow** will also cause the second, dependent DLL to be unloaded. To prevent an inadvertent crash, the DLL should call **CoLoadLibrary**(*path to second DLL*, TRUE) which forces the component object model library to reload the second DLL and set it up for **CoFreeUnusedLibraries** to free it when appropriate.

S_FALSE should be returned if there are any references to any objects or if there has been an **IClassFactory::LockServer**(TRUE) call.

See Also

DllGetClassObject

DllGetClassObject

HRESULT DllGetClassObject(*rclsid, riid, ppvObj*)
REFCLSID *rclsid*
REFIID *riid*
void * * *ppvObj*

DllGetClassObject retrieves the class object from a DLL object handler or object application.

Parameters

rclsid
Identifies the CLSID of the object class that is to be loaded.

riid
Specifies the IID that the caller is to use to communicate with the class object. Most often, this is **IID_IClassFactory**.

ppvObj
Points to the location for the resulting interface.

Return Values

Value	Meaning
S_OK	The object was retrieved successfully.
CLASS_E_CLASS-NOTAVAILABLE	DLL does not support class.
E_OUTOFMEMORY	Out of memory.
E_INVALIDARG	One or more arguments are invalid.
E_UNEXPECTED	An unexpected error occurred.

Comments

If a call to **CoGetClassObject** results in the class object being loaded from a DLL, **CoGetClassObject** uses the DLL's exported **DllGetClassObject** function to retrieve the class.

DllGetClassObject is not provided with OLE; it is implemented and exported from DLLs supporting the Component Object Model.

See Also

CoGetClassObject, **DllCanUnloadNow**

OLE Library Functions

The following functions can be used to manage the OLE Component Object Model library. The functions are defined as follows:

```
CoBuildVersion(void);
CoCreateStandardMalloc(unsigned long dwDestContext, IMALLOC * * ppMalloc);
CoGetCurrentProcess(void);
```

```
CoGetMalloc(unsigned long dwDestContext, LPMALLOC * * ppMalloc);
CoInitialize(LPMALLOC pMalloc);
CoUnitialize(void);
```

For more information, see the compobj.h header file.

CoBuildVersion

unsigned long CoBuildVersion()

CoBuildVersion returns the major and the minor version number of Component Object Model library.

Return Values

Value	Meaning
unsigned long	The 16 high-order bits are the major build number; the 16 low-order bits are the minor build number.
E_OUTOFMEMORY	Out of memory.
E_UNEXPECTED	An unexpected error occurred.

Comments

Applications should call **CoBuildVersion** before using any other Component Object Model library API function or interface method. **CoBuildVersion** returns the major and minor build numbers in a DWORD where the high-order word is the major version number and the low-order word is the minor version number. Applications can run only one major version and any minor version. Therefore, the application must check that the returned major version is equal to the expected major version (the version that the application compiled against). If there are differences, **CoInitialize** must not be called.

For any given release of the Component Object Model library, there is a file called OLExVER.H, which defines the symbol "rmm" as the major version and "rup" as the minor version. It is unlikely that the major build version would change between releases, but applications should still ensure compatibility by calling **CoBuildVersion**.

CoBuildVersion is always the first function an application calls in the Component Object Model library.

See Also

CoInitialize, OleBuildVersion

CoGetCurrentProcess

unsigned long CoGetCurrentProcess()

CoGetCurrentProcess returns a value that is unique to the current process.

Return Values

Value	Meaning
unsigned long	Unique value for the current process.

Comments

CoGetCurrentProcess is useful in helping maintain tables that are keyed by processes.

CoGetMalloc

HRESULT CoGetMalloc(*dwDestContext, ppMalloc***)**
unsigned long *dwDestContext*
LPMALLOC * *ppMalloc*

CoGetMalloc retrieves either the task memory allocator originally passed to **CoInitialize** or the OLE-provided shared memory allocator. Object handlers should use the task allocator returned by **CoGetMalloc** for their local memory management needs.

Parameters

dwDestContext
Specifies a value that indicates whether the memory block is private to a task or shared between processes. Valid values are taken from the enumeration **MEMCTX**. For more information, see the following comments.

ppMalloc
Points to where the memory allocator is to be returned.

Return Values

Value	Meaning
S_OK	The allocator was retrieved successfully.
E_FAIL	Indicates an unspecified error.
E_INVALIDARG	One or more arguments are invalid.
CO_E_NOT-INITIALIZED	Must call **CoInitialize** first.
E_OUTOFMEMORY	Out of memory.

Comments

Legal values for the *dwDestContext* parameter are taken from the enumeration **MEMCTX**, which is defined in compobj.h as follows:

```
typedef enum tagMEMCTX
{
    MEMCTX_TASK      = 1,          //task (private) memory
    MEMCTX_SHARED    = 2,          //shared memory (between processes)
} MEMCTX;
```

MEMCTX_TASK returns the task allocator passed to **CoInitialize**. If **CoInitialize** has not yet been called, NULL will be returned through *ppMalloc* and CO_E_NOTINITIALIZED is returned. Specifying MEMCTX_SHARED returns the shared allocator.

The shared allocator returned by **CoGetMalloc** is the OLE-provided implementation of the **IMalloc** interface, which allocates memory so it can be accessed by other applications. Memory allocated by this shared allocator in one application can be freed by the shared allocator in another.

In versions of OLE 2 on platforms other than the Macintosh (or the 16-bit version of Windows), the shared memory allocator might not be available. In these cases, **CoGetMalloc**(MEMCTX_SHARED,...) will return E_INVALIDARG.

The possible unavailability of the shared memory allocator will not affect custom marshalers; for information on custom marshaling, see the IMarshal Interface, earlier in this chapter.

CoCreateStandardMalloc

HRESULT CoCreateStandardMalloc(*dwDestContext, ppMalloc***)**
unsigned long *dwDestContext*
IMALLOC * * *ppMalloc*

CoCreateStandardMalloc creates and returns an OLE-provided memory allocator for the given memory context.

Parameter

dwDestContext
Specifies how the memory block is to be allocated. Values are taken from the enumeration **MEMCTX**. For more information on the **MEMCTX** values, see **CoGetMalloc**. A value of 1 specifies that the memory block is private to a task (MEMCTX_TASK); 2 specifies that the block is shared between processes (MEMCTX_SHARED).

ppMalloc
Points to where to return the **IMalloc** memory allocator.

Return Values

Value	Meaning
S_OK	The memory allocator was created successfully.
E_OUTOFMEMORY	Out of memory.
E_INVALIDARG	One or more arguments are invalid.
E_UNEXPECTED	An unexpected error occurred.

Comments

The new allocator creates and maintains its own new heap. All memory allocated in the heap is freed when the last reference to the returned *ppMalloc* is released.

The allocator returned by **CoCreateStandardMalloc** is not the same allocator as that returned by **CoGetMalloc**. This means that the allocator returned here is not the one used for values passed across interface boundaries. Rather, **CoCreateStandardMalloc** provides a handy memory allocator that can be used internally by an object.

See Also **CoGetMalloc**

CoInitialize

HRESULT CoInitialize(*pMalloc*)
LPMALLOC *pMalloc*

CoInitialize initializes the Component Object Model library so that it can be used. With the exception of **CoBuildVersion**, this function must be called by applications before any other function in the Component Object Model library.

Parameters

pMalloc
Points to the memory allocator that is to be used for task memory by the library and by object handlers. To access the standard allocator, pass NULL.

Return Values

Value	Meaning
S_OK	The library was initialized successfully.
S_FALSE	Already initialized; didn't use *pMalloc*, if given.
E_OUTOFMEMORY	Out of memory.
E_INVALIDARG	*pMalloc* is invalid.
E_UNEXPECTED	An unexpected error occurred.

Comments

The design of the Component Object Model library allows the application that owns a given process space the opportunity to be in complete control of how memory is allocated and used by components in that space. To be in control, the application should implement the **IMalloc** interface and pass an instance of it (*pMalloc*) to **CoInitialize**; otherwise, it should pass NULL to use the OLE implementation of **IMalloc**.

Calls to **CoInitialize** must be balanced by corresponding calls to **CoUninitialize**. Usually, **CoInitialize** is called only once by the process that is to use the Component Object Library. In some instances (for example, two independent pieces of code written as DLLs), there may be competing calls to **CoInitialize**; in these cases, only the first successful call to **CoInitialize** initializes the library and only its corresponding balanced call to **CoUninitialize** will uninitialize it. **CoInitialize** returns S_FALSE if the library has already been initialized.

CoInitialize follows the usual reference counting rules described earlier in description of the **IUnknown** interface. Because **CoInitialize** retains the **IMalloc** pointer beyond the duration of the call, it calls *pMalloc*->**AddRef**.

CoInitialize is called internally by **OleInitialize** so most applications do not need to call **CoInitialize**.

See Also **CoUninitialize**, **OleInitialize**

CoUninitialize

void CoUninitialize()

CoUninitialize closes the Component Object Model library, freeing any resources that it maintains and forcing all connections closed.

Comments **CoInitialize** and **CoUninitialize** calls must be balanced; only the **CoUninitialize** call corresponding to the **CoInitialize** call that actually initialized the library can uninitialize it.

CoUninitialize should be called on application shutdown, as the last call made to the Component Object Model library and after the application hides its main windows and falls through its main message loop. If there are open conversations remaining, **CoUninitialize** starts a modal message loop and dispatches any pending messages from the containers or server for this OLE application. By dispatching the messages, **CoUninitialize** ensures that the application does not quit before receiving all its pending messages. Non-OLE messages are discarded.

Most applications do not need to call **CoUnInitialize** because it is called internally by **OleUnInitialize**.

See Also **CoInitialize**, **OleUnInitialize**

Object Class Conversion and Emulation Functions

The following functions are used to convert or emulate an object class of one type as a different class. The first two functions are defined in compobj.h while the rest of the functions are defined in ole2.h:

```
HRESULT CoGetTreatAsClass(REFCLSID clsidOld, LPCLSID pclsidNew);
HRESULT CoTreatAsClass(REFCLSID clsidOld, LPCLSID pclsidNew);
HRESULT OleDoAutoConvert(LPSTORAGE pStg, LPCLSID pclsidNew);
HRESULT OleGetAutoConvert(REFCLSID clsidOld, LPCLSID pclsidNew);
HRESULT OleSetAutoConvert(REFCLSID clsidOld, REFCLSID clsidNew);
HRESULT GetConvertStg(LPSTORAGE pStg);
HRESULT SetConvertStg(LPSTORAGE pStg, unsigned long fConvert);
```

Tagging Objects for Automatic Conversion and Emulation

An object's class determines the verbs and the application the user uses to interact with the object. Usually, an object is activated by the object application corresponding to its CLSID, as registered in the Registration Database file. However, implementing the Convert dialog box in a container application lets users change an object's current type to that of a different object type ("Convert to:"button) or to activate (emulate) objects of one type as if they were objects of another type (Activate as: option button).

In order to be the destination class of a Convert operation, the object application must register the formats it can read from other objects. These formats are registered under the CLSID\{*clsid*}\Conversion\Readable subkeys in the Registration Database file. An OLE 2 application registers itself using a four-letter OStype and an OLE 1 application registers itself using its ProgID as a string enclosed in quotes. For example:

```
CLSID
    {CLSID} = Main User Type Name
    .
    .
    .
    Conversion
        Readable
            Main = WDBN, "Word Document", "WordPerfect 3.0"
```

To activate an object of a different class as one of its own, the object application registers the formats it can both read and write under the "CLSID\{*clsid*}\Conversion\Readwritable" subkeys.

Note that converting an object to another type can destroy its original data format, while activating an object as a different type preserves the existing object's data format. Selecting an object to be activated as another class of object remains in effect until the user changes the class to a different one using the "Activate As" button.

Whenever a new version of an object application is being installed and an older version of the application is already present, the setup program should give the user the option of automatically converting the older version of the object class to the newer version the next time an object of that class is activated in the object's container.

If the user wants to tag the object class for automatic conversion, the setup program should call the **OleSetAutoConvert** function, passing the object's old and new CLSIDs to **OleSetAutoConvert**. This enables **OleSetAutoConvert** to register the new CLSID in the Registration Database file under the CLSID\{*clsid*}\AutoConvertTo = {*CLSID*} subkey entry. This means the object application of the destination class has to be able to manually convert an object to a different class on a case by case basis, as objects of the tagged class are loaded into memory.

When a container application loads an object that has been tagged for conversion, the container should check whether an automatic conversion is necessary by calling **OleDoAutoConvert**. (If the container loads the object with **OleLoad**, **OleDoAutoConvert** need not be called explicitly.)

Similarly, for automatically converting objects, an object application's setup program can offer to tag an object class for activation as a different class. If the user decides to tag an object class for activation under a different CLSID, the setup program should call **CoTreatAsClass**(*clsidOld*, *clsidNew*) to register the CLSID for the object under the "CLSID\{*clsidOld*}\TreatAs = {*CLSID*}" subkey entry in the Registration Database file. (The AutoTreatAs key is used in conjunction with the TreatAs key. If *clsidOld* has an AutoTreatAs key, then instead of treating *clsidOld* as itself, it is treated as the class indicated by AutoTreatAs.)

For more information on user interface considerations for installing OLE applications, see Chapter 2, "User Interface Guidelines." For information on the Registration Database file and its subkey entries, see Chapter 4, "Registering Object Applications."

Converting Objects

Container Responsibilities

To convert an object to a different object class as a result of the user selecting the Convert To: option button in the Convert dialog box, OLE containers do the following tasks:

1. Get the existing user type name and main data format from the object's **IStorage** by calling **ReadFmtUserTypeStg**. (The user type name is used to fill in the "Current Type:" and other strings in the Convert dialog box.)
2. Generate the appropriate list of object destination class types by examining the Registration Database file, looking for all object classes registered as being able to read the object's current main data format. These formats are registered under the "CLSID\{*clsid*}\Conversion\Readable" subkeys. For information on the Registration Database file and the "Conversion/ReadWritable" subkeys in particular, see Chapter 4, "Registering Object Applications."
3. If the object is currently loaded into memory, unload the object. Any objects that are not unloaded will not be used since the conversion takes place at load time, not when the object is put in its running state.
4. Write the object's new CLSID to its **IStorage** by calling **WriteClassStg**.

5. Write the object's new user type name and the existing main clipboard data format to the open **IStorage** object by calling **WriteFmtUserTypeStg**.
4. Set the conversion bit in the object's **IStorage** by calling **SetConvertStg** (TRUE). Now when the object is loaded into memory, it is loaded as an object with a new class type and is associated with a new object application.
5. Load the object into memory and call **IOleObject::Update** to achieve the actual conversion of the bits. For more information on loading objects, see the section "Loading Objects from Storage" in Chapter 9, "Persistent Storage Interfaces and Functions."

The **ConvertDlg** helper function, which is shipped with the OLE SDK, can be used to do steps one and two.

Object Application Responsibilities

To convert objects from one type to another, an OLE object application must register in the Registration Database file the data formats it can read from objects created by other applications. To activate an object as one of its supported types, the object application registers the data formats it can both read and write (when emulating an object, the object application needs to write the data changes to the object's **IStorage** in the container).

Each object application must be able to determine whether to convert an object to a class that it supports. If you do not want your object application to support this concept, do not implement any of the following tasks.

When the container initializes an object from its open storage, the object application must do the following tasks to convert the object:

1. Read the conversion bit from the object's storage by calling **GetConvertStg**.
2. If the conversion bit is set in the object's open storage, then:
   - Read the data from the object's storage according to its tagged format.
   - When the object is subsequently asked to save itself, write its native format by calling **IPersistStorage::Save**, then save the object's new data format and user type by calling **WriteFmtUserTypeStg**.
3. After saving the object, clear the conversion bit by calling **SetConvertStg**(FALSE).

The **ConvertDlg** helper function, which is shipped with the OLE SDK, can be used to do steps one and two.

Activating Objects of a Different Class

The Convert dialog box supports activating an object of one type as a different type. To activate an object as an object of a different class, both container and server applications need to do certain tasks, as described in the following sections.

Container Responsibilities

To support activating an object as a different class type, containers perform the following tasks:

1. Get the object's existing user type name and its main data format tag by calling **ReadFmtUserTypeStg**. (The object's type name is used to fill in the blanks in the "Activate as %s:" and other strings in the Convert dialog box.)
2. Generate the list of eligible classes that the object can be activated as by searching the Registration Database file looking for those classes that can both read and write the object's main data format. These entries are listed under the "Conversion\ReadWritable" subkeys for a particular CLSID. For more information on the Registration Database file and the "Conversion/ReadWritable" subkeys in particular, see Chapter 4, "Registering Object Applications."
3. If the object is currently loaded into memory, unload it. Any objects that are not unloaded will not be used since the conversion takes place at load time, not when the object is put in its running state.
4. Ensure that a Registration Database file entry for the existing class of the object is present. If an entry does not currently exist, create one. If the Registration Database file entry for the existing class of the object lacks a main user type entry, then set the main user type string in the database with the object's existing user type obtained from its **IStorage** by calling **ReadFmtUserTypeStg**.
5. Notify OLE that this object is to be treated as a new class of object by calling **CoTreatAsClass**. Note that calling this function causes all objects of the old class (other than those that were left in the loaded state) to subsequently be activated as object of the new class.
6. Before loading the object into memory, call **OleDoAutoConvert** to handle any needed object conversion. If the container calls **OleLoad** to load the object, the call to **OleDoAutoConvert** is done internally by **OleLoad**, and need not be called explicitly.
7. Load the object in the typical manner at a later time as needed. For more information on loading objects, see the section "Loading Objects from Storage" in Chapter 9, "Persistent Storage Interfaces and Functions."

Object Application Responsibilities

Just as it does when converting an object from one class to another, the object application must be able to determine whether to activate an object of a different class as one that it supports. Unless you want your object application to specifically support this, there is no code to implement in the object application.

When activating an object from a different object class as one of its supported class types, an object application only reads the source object's main data format. The conversion bit in the object's storage must be off.

Although the object is being activated as a different type, its behavior (in response to **IOleObject::EnumVerbs** being called on it) is unchanged from its usual behavior. Any changes made to the object are saved in the object's open **IStorage** object in the container.

Using the main data format that OLE saved with the object, an object application does the following tasks to activate a different object class as one of its own:

1. Get the object's current CLSID and user type from its storage by calling **IStorage::Stat** and **ReadFmtUserTypeStg**, respectively. The current CLSID can be the current class of the object but it might not be. Therefore, treating both cases the same is correct because it allows the former case (class is the same) to be simply a degenerate case of the latter (class not the same).
2. When asked for its CLSID and user type (in calls to **IPersist::GetClassID**,**IOleObject::GetUserClassID**, and **IOleObject::GetUserType**, the object must emulate the object found in the storage. Note that this will make the old class appear to have the verbs of the new class; however, the object's behavior in response to **IOleObject::EnumVerbs** will remain unchanged from its usual behavior.The class returned in **IStdMarshalInfo::GetClassForHandler** is always the CLSID of the object that is actually running. This is different than **IPersist::GetClassID** only in the Treat As case.
3. Read the data from the object's storage, which is in the format returned by **ReadFmtUserTypeStg**.

   When the object is subsequently asked to save itself, write the data in the format from which it was originally read.

CoGetTreatAsClass

HRESULT CoGetTreatAsClass(*clsidOld, pclsidNew*)
REFCLSID *clsidOld*
LPCLSID *pclsidNew*

CoGetTreatAsClass returns the existing emulation information for a given object class.

Parameter

clsidOld
Specifies the object class for which the emulation information is to be retrieved.

pclsidNew
Points to where to return the CLSID, if any, that emulates the *clsidOld* parameter. CLSID_NULL is returned if there is no such CLSID. The *pclsidNew* parameter cannot be NULL.

Return Values

Value	Meaning
S_OK	Indicates that a value was successfully returned through *pclsidNew*. This means **pclsidNew* is set to a new CLSID.
S_FALSE	Indicates that **pclsidNew* is set to *clsidOld*.
REGDB_E_READ-REGDB	Error reading the Registration Database file.

See **CLSIDFromString** for other possible errors.

See Also

CoTreatAsClass

CoTreatAsClass

HRESULT CoTreateAsClass(*clsidOld*, *clsidNew*)
REFCLSID *clsidOld*
REFCLSID *clsidNew*

CoTreatAsClass establishes or removes an emulation from one object class to another.

Parameter

clsidOld
Specifies the CLSID of the object class that is to be emulated.

clsidNew
Specifies the CLSID of the object class that should emulate *clsidOld*. This replaces any existing emulation for *clsidOld*. Can be CLSID_NULL, in which case any existing emulation for *clsidOld* is removed.

Return Values

Value	Meaning
S_OK	Emulation connection successfully established or removed.
REGDB_E_CLASS-NOTREG	*clsidOld* is not properly registered in the Registration Database file.
REGDB_E_READ-REGDB	Error reading from Registration Database file.
REGDB_E_WRITE-REGDB	Error writing to Registration Database file.

Comments

When *clsidNew* is emulating *clsidOld*, attempts by both **CoGetClassObject** and by object handlers (in particular, the OLE default handler) to consult the Registration Database file for *clsidOld* should be transparently forwarded to the entry for *clsidNew*. For example, launching the object application for *clsidOld* launches the object application for *clsidNew*. The default handler's **IOleObject::EnumVerbs** implementation will enumerate the verbs from *clsidNew* and so forth.

CoTreatAsClass does not check whether an appropriate Registration Database file entry for *clsidNew* currently exists.

During installation, setup programs should use **CoTreatAsClass**(*clsidOld*, NULL) to remove any existing emulation for the classes they install.

See Also

CoGetTreatAsClass

OleDoAutoConvert

HRESULT OleDoAutoConvert(*pStg*, *pclsidNew*)
LPSTORAGE *pStg*
LPCLSID *pclsidNew*

OleDoAutoConvert automatically converts an object to a new class. The object must have been previously tagged for automatic conversion, typically at setup time for the object application.

Parameter

pStg
Points to the persistent representation of the object to be converted.

pclsidNew
Points to the CLSID to which the object was converted; this might be the same as the original class if no auto-conversion was done.

Return Values

Value	Meaning
S_OK	No conversion is needed or a conversion was successfully completed.
REGDB_E_KEY-MISSING	Cannot read a key from the Registration Database file.
E_OUTOFMEMORY	Out of memory.
E_INVALIDARG	One or more arguments are invalid.
E_UNEXPECTED	An unexpected error occurred.

OleGetAutoConvert errors.

See **IStorage::OpenStorage** and **IStorage::OpenStream** for possible errors when accessing storage and stream objects.

IStream errors. Cannot determine existing CLSID or cannot update **IStorage** with new information.

Comments

The object to be converted is found in *pStg*.

OleDoAutoConvert first determines whether any conversion is required by calling **OleGetAutoConvert**. If not, it returns NOERROR. The object's storage is modified to convert the object. If the object being auto-converted is an OLE 1 object, the ItemName string is stored in a stream called "\1Ole10ItemName." If this stream does not exist, the object's item name is NULL.

A container application that supports object conversion should call **OleDoAutoConvert** each time it loads an object. Because it is called internally by **OleLoad**, **OleDoAutoConvert** need not be called explicitly by containers loading objects with **OleLoad**. The object must be in the unloaded state when **OleDoAutoConvert** is called.

See Also

OleSetAutoConvert

OleGetAutoConvert

HRESULT OleGetAutoConvert(*clsidOld*, *pclsidNew***)**
REFCLSID *clsidOld*
LPCLSID *pclsidNew*

OleGetAutoConvert returns the existing auto-conversion information for a given object class.

Parameter

clsidOld
Specifies the CLSID of the object class for which the auto-conversion information is to be retrieved.

pclsidNew
Points to where to return the class, if any, which auto-converts from *clsidOld*. If there is no such class, CLSID_NULL is returned. *pclsidNew* cannot be NULL.

Return Values

Value	Meaning
S_OK	Indicates that a value was successfully returned through *pclsidNew*.
REGDB_E_CLASSNOTREG	CLSID is not properly registered in the Registration Database file.
REGDB_E_READREGDB	Error reading the Registration Database file.
REGDB_E_KEYMISSING	Auto convert is not active or indicates that there was no registration entry for *clsidOld*.
E_OUTOFMEMORY	Out of memory.
E_INVALIDARG	One or more arguments are invalid.
E_UNEXPECTED	An unexpected error occurred.

Comments

During installation of an object application, the setup program can optionally tag a class of object for automatic conversion to a different class of object. This is done by calling **OleSetAutoConvert**, passing it the CLSIDs of the source and destination object classes. **OleSetAutoConvert** then creates the required "CLSID\{*clsid*}\AutoConvertTo = {CLSID}" entry in the Registration Database file.

On loading an object tagged for conversion, the container calls the **OleGetAutoConvert** function to retrieves the new CLSID from the Registration Database file. To perform the conversion, the container calls **OleDoAutoConvert**.

See Also

OleSetAutoConvert, **OleDoAutoConvert**

OleSetAutoConvert

HRESULT OleSetAutoConvert(*clsidOld*, *clsidNew***)**
REFCLSID *clsidOld*
REFCLSID *clsidNew*

OleSetAutoConvert tags an object for automatic conversion to a different class on being loaded.

Parameter

clsidOld
Specifies the CLSID of the object class to be converted.

clsidNew
Specifies the CLSID of the object class that should replace *clsidOld*. This replaces any existing conversion for *clsidOld*. May be CLSID_NULL. If so, any existing conversion for *clsidOld* is removed.

Return Values

Value	Meaning
S_OK	The object was tagged successfully.
REGDB_E_CLASS-NOTREG	The CLSID is not properly registered in the Registration Database file.
REGDB_E_READ-REGDB	Error reading from the Registration Database file.
REGDB_E_WRITE-REGDB	Error writing to the Registration Database file.
REGDB_E_KEY-MISSING	Cannot read a key from the Registration Database file.
E_OUTOFMEMORY	Out of memory.
E_INVALIDARG	One or more arguments are invalid.
E_UNEXPECTED	An unexpected error occurred.

Comments

OleSetAutoConvert does no validation of whether an appropriate Registration Database file entry for *clsidNew* currently exists. On being called, **OleSetAutoConvert** records the new CLSID for the object under the "CLSID\{*clsidOld*}\AutoConvertTo = CLSID" subkeys in the Registration Database file. For more information on tagging an object class for conversion at the time of setup, see Chapter 2, "User Interface Guidelines," and "Converting Objects," earlier in this chapter.

When installing a new CLSID, setup programs may call **OleSetAutoConvert** for various *clsidOld* values for older versions of their applications. They should also call **OleSetAutoConvert(***clsidNew*, NULL**)** to remove any existing conversion for the new class.

See Also

OleDoAutoConvert

SetConvertStg

HRESULT SetConvertStg(*pStg*, *fConvert***)**
LPSTORAGE *pStg*
unsigned long *fConvert*

SetConvertStg sets the conversion bit in an object's storage so that the setting is retrievable with **GetConvertStg**.

Parameter

pStg
Points to the **IStorage** instance in which the conversion bit is to be set.

fConvert
TRUE tags an object for conversion to another class of object; FALSE clears the conversion bit.

Return Values

Value	Meaning
S_OK	The object's IStorage conversion bit was set successfully.
STG_E_ACCESSDENIED	Access to the storage is not available.
E_OUTOFMEMORY	Out of memory.
E_INVALIDARG	One or more arguments are invalid.
E_UNEXPECTED	An unexpected error occurred.

See **IStorage::CreateStream**, **IStorage::OpenStream**, **IStream::Read**, and **IStream::Write** for possible storage and stream access errors.

Comments

As part of converting an object from one class to another, container applications call **SetConvertStg** to set the conversion bit in the object's storage. The bit is set to TRUE, indicating that the object has been tagged for conversion to a new class the next time it is loaded.

The value of the conversion bit is subsequently retrieved by calling **GetConvertStg**. To reset an object's conversion bit, call **SetConvertStg**(FALSE).

See Also

GetConvertStg

GetConvertStg

HRESULT GetConvertStorage(*pStg***)**
LPSTORAGE *pStg*

GetConvertStorage returns the current value of the conversion bit in an object's storage, which was previously set with **SetConvertStg**.

Parameter

pStg
Points to the **IStorage** instance from which to retrieve the conversion bit.

Return Values

Value	Meaning
S_OK	Indicates that the conversion bit is set (TRUE).
S_FALSE	Indicates the conversion bit has been turned off (FALSE) or never been set in this object's storage.
STG_E_ACCESSDENIED	Cannot access the **IStorage.**

See also **IStorage::OpenStream**, **IStorage::OpenStorage**, and **IStream::Read** for storage and stream access errors.

Comments

As part of converting an object from one class to another, object applications call **GetConvertStg** to retrieve the value of the conversion bit in an object's storage; this bit is usually set by the container application calling **SetConvertStg**(TRUE) as part of the user selecting the "Convert To:" option button in the Convert dialog box. After retrieving the bit value, the application should call **SetConvertStg**(FALSE) to clear the bit setting.

See Also **SetConvertStg**

Error Handling Functions and Macros

The following functions and macros can be used to handle error and status informatic ı returned from OLE interface methods and functions (see also scode.h):

```
PropagateResult(HRESULT hrPrev, SCODE scNew);

#define SCODE_CODE(scode)              ((scode) & 0xFFFF)
#define SCODE_FACILITY(scode)          (((scode)>> 16) & 0x000f)
#define SCODE_SEVERITY(scode)          (((scode) >> 31) & 0x1)
#define SEVERITY_SUCCESS               0
#define SEVERITY_ERROR                 1
#define SUCCEEDED(scode)               ((LONG)(scode) >= 0)
#define FAILED(scode)                  ((LONG)(scode)<0)
#define MAKE_SCODE(sev,fac,code)       ((SCODE) (((ULONG)(sev)<<31) |
                                       ((ULONG)(fac)<<16) | ((ULONG)(code))))
#define GetScode(hr)                   ((SCODE)(hr) & 0x800FFFFF)
#define ResultFromScode(sc)            ((HRESULT)((SCODE)(sc) & 0x800FFFFF))
```

Note Throughout the reference portion of this book, specific error codes are described for the individual methods and functions. However, there are three error codes that are common to all methods, even though they may not be specifically noted in all method descriptions.

These common error codes include: E_INVALIDARG, one or more arguments are invalid (only for methods that accept parameters); E_UNEXPECTED, an unexpected error occurred; and E_OUTOFMEMORY, an out of memory condition occurred.

OLE Error Information

OLE interface methods and API functions use a certain stylistic convention in order to pass back to the caller useful return values and/or status or error information. The return value is an opaque "result handle" of type HRESULT, and is otherwise passed as the return value in the absence of the need for status information. The return value is passed through a pointer as the last argument.

HRESULT values are defined to be zero for success, and non-zero if error or informational status is being returned. If the result value is non-zero, the application calls the **GetScode** macro to map the HRESULT into a known code. **GetScode** is defined to return S_OK for a zero HRESULT.

On the implementor's side, an interface method that wants to indicate a result other than simple success must call **ResultFromScode** to generate the corresponding HRESULT, and return that to its caller. For convenience, **ResultFromScode** is defined to return zero for a status code of S_OK. The constant NOERROR is defined as an HRESULT that corresponds to S_OK.

Sometimes functions will either return a Boolean result or, if the result is not currently available,return an error status. For functions of this type, two special status codes, S_OK and S_FALSE, are used to indicate the return value. This eliminates the need for a separate **unsigned long*** parameter for these functions.

HRESULTs do not need to be explicitly freed.

The status codes for the OLE interfaces and APIs are defined in FACILITY_ITF (see the header file SCODE.H for details). By design, none of the OLE-defined status codes have the same value, even if they are returned by different interfaces (although it would have been legal). The following basic interoperability rules and limitations apply to which errors can be returned by which methods or functions:

- Any OLE-defined status code can be returned by any OLE-defined interface method or API function.
- Any error in FACILITY_RPC or FACILITY_DISPATCH, even those not presently defined, can be returned.

The reference portion of this manual lists and describes the most common error codes that are appropriate for each interface method and API function. These are considered to be the legal error codes that can be returned.

Error codes are defined within the context of an inteface implementation. Once defined, success codes cannot be changed or new success codes added. However, new failure codes can be written since they generally only provide hints at what might have gone wrong. Microsoft reserves the right to define new failure codes (but not success codes) for the OLE interfaces in FACILITY_ITF or new facilities.

Handling Error Information

It is only legal to return a status code from the implementation of an interface method sanctioned as being legally returnable. Failure to observe this rule invites the possibility of conflict between returned error code values and those sanctioned by the application. In particular, pay attention to this potential problem when propagating error codes from internally called functions.

Applications that call interfaces should guard themselves from imprecise interface implementations by treating any unknown returned error code (in contrast with success code) as synonymous with E_UNEXPECTED. This practice of handling unknown error codes is required by clients of the OLE-defined interfaces and APIs. Because typical programming practice is to handle a few special error codes as special, but to treat the rest generically, this requirement of handling unexpected or unknown error codes is easily met.

The following code sample shows the recommended way of handling unknown errors:

```
HRESULT hrErr;
hrErr = xxMethod();

switch (GetScode(hrErr))  {
    case NOERROR:
        //success
        break;

    case x1:
        .
        .
        break;

    case x2:
        .
        .
        break;

    case E_UNEXPECTED:
    default:
        //general failure
        break;
}
```

The following error check is often used with those routines that don't return anything special (other than S_OK or some unexpected error):

```
if (xxMethod() == NOERROR)
    //success
else
    //general failure;
```

Structure of OLE Error Codes

As shown in Figure 5.5, OLE interface methods and API functions return a 32-bit result handle, which is comprised of a severity code, context information, a facility code, and a status code.

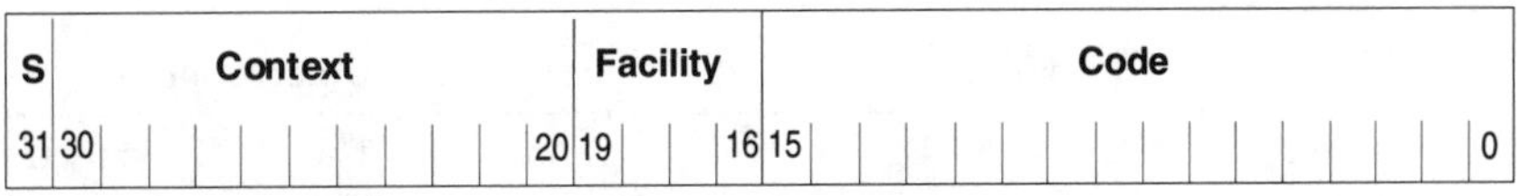

S	Context		Facility		Code	
31	30	20	19	16	15	0

S - severity code; 0= success and 1= error
Context - reserved for future use, may or may not be 0
Facility - facility code
Code - facility's status code

Figure 5.5 Order and size of error fields

Severity Field

Bit 31 of a status code is used to indicate success or failure of the given interface or API call. The following values indicate success or failure:

Severity Field Value	Meaning
00	The function completed successfully.
01	The function incurred an error and failed.

Context Field

Bits 20 - 30 of a status code are reserved for future use; applications that generate SCODEs must set this field to zero. In general, applications should not examine this field because it might be set to nonzero values in the implementation of **PropagateResult** in future system releases. None of the OLE-defined status codes set these bits.

Facility Field

Bits 16 - 19 of a status code are used to indicate which group of status codes this error belongs to. New facilities are allocated by Microsoft, because they must be unique. However, in nearly all cases FACILITY_ITF will be adequate, as described below:

Facility Field	Description
FACILITY_NULL	This facility is used for common status codes that are applicable to a broad range of functions. S_OK belongs to this facility, for example. This facility code has a value of zero.
FACILITY_RPC	Used for errors that result from an underlying remote procedure call (RPC) implementation. In general, RPC errors are not documented in this manual. This facility has a value of one.
FACILITY_DISPATCH	Used for late binding **IDispatch** interface errors. This facility has a value of two.
FACILITY_STORAGE	Used for persistent-storage-related errors. A Status code whose code value is in the range of Macintosh error codes has the same meaning as the corresponding Macintosh error. This facility has a value of three.
FACILITY_ITF	This facility is used for most status codes returned from an interface method. Use of this facility indicates that the meaning of the error code is defined solely by the definition of the particular interface in question. An SCODE with exactly the same 32-bit value returned from another interface might have a different meaning. This facility has a value of four.

Code Field

Bits 0 - 15 of a status code are used to describe the error that occurred. The meaning of the code value is related to the facility.

By convention, SCODEs generally have names in the following form:

```
<Facility >_<Severity >_<Reason >
```

where <*Facility* > is either the facility name or some other distinguishing identifier, <*Severity* > is a single letter, S or E, that indicates the severity of the error, and <*Reason* > is an identifier that describes the meaning of the code. For example, the status code STG_E_FILENOTFOUND indicates a storage-related error has occurred; specifically, a requested file does not exist. Status codes from FACILITY_NULL omit the <*Facility* >_ prefix.

Codes in FACILITY_ITF

Status codes with facilities such as FACILITY_NULL and FACILITY_RPC have universal meaning because they are defined at a single source, Microsoft. However, status codes in FACILITY_ITF are determined by the interface method (or API function) from which they are returned. That is, the same 32-bit value in FACILITY_ITF returned from two different interface methods might have different meanings.

The reason an SCODE in FACILITY_ITF can have a different meaning in different interfaces is that the SCODE is kept to an efficient data type size of 32 bits. Unfortunately 32 bits is not large enough for the development of an allocation system for error codes that avoid conflict between codes allocated by different non-communicating programmers at different times in different places (unlike the handling of interface IDs and CLSIDs). As a result, the 32-bit SCODE is structured in a way that allows Microsoft to define some universally defined error codes, while allowing other programmers to define new error codes without fear of conflict. The status code convention is as follows:

1. Status codes in facilities other than FACILITY_ITF can only be defined by Microsoft.
2. Status codes in facility FACILITY_ITF are defined solely by the developer of the interface or API that returns the status code. To avoid conflicting error codes, whoever defines the interface is responsible for coordinating and publishing the FACILITY_ITF status codes associated with that interface.

All the OLE-defined FACILITY_ITF codes have a code value in the range of 0x0000–0x01FF. While it is legal to use any codes in FACILITY_ITF, it is recommended that only code values in the range of 0x0200–0xFFFF be used. This recommendation is made as a means of reducing confusion with any OLE-defined errors.

It is also recommended that developers define new functions and interfaces to return error codes as defined by OLE and in facilities other than FACILITY_ITF. In particular, interfaces that have any chance of being remoted using RPC in the future should define the FACILITY_RPC codes as legal. E_UNEXPECTED is a specific error code that most developers will want to make universally legal.

PropagateResult

HRESULT PropagateResult(*hrPrev*, *scNew*)
HRESULT *hrPrev*
SCODE *scNew*

PropagateResult generates an HRESULT to return to a function's caller when the error being returned was caused by an internally called function, which was also returning an HRESULT error.

Parameters

hrPrev
Specifies the HRESULT returned from the internally called routine.

scNew
Specifies the new SCODE to return to the caller, wrapped in an HRESULT.

Return Values

Value	Meaning
HRESULT	The (new) HRESULT that should be returned to the caller.

See Also

GetScode, **ResultFromScode**

GetScode

SCODE GetScode(*hRes*)
HRESULT *hRes*

GetScode returns the status code contained in an HRESULT.

Parameters

hRes
Specifies the HRESULT returned from the internally called routine.

Return Values

Value	Meaning
SCODE	The status code extracted from the specified HRESULT.

Comments

GetScode should be used to return the HRESULT if an error is being returned as a result of some internal state error. By contrast, it should not be used if the error is being returned as a result of some internally called routine, itself returning an HRESULT error. Instead, the calling routine should use **PropagateResult** to return its error.

ResultFromScode

ResultFromScode(*sc***)**
SCODE *sc*

ResultFromScode creates a new HRESULT that contains the given SCODE.

Parameters

sc
Specifies the status code from which the HRESULT is to be returned.

Return Values

Value	Meaning
HRESULT	The HRESULT created from the specified status code.

Status Code Macros

The following macros can be used to manipulate status code values:

SCODE_CODE(*sc*)
SCODE_FACILITY(*sc*)
SCODE_SEVERITY(*sc*)
SUCCEEDED(*sc*)
FAILED(*sc*)
MAKE_SCODE(*sev,fac,sc*)

SCODE_CODE

SCODE_CODE(*sc***)**
SCODE *sc*

SCODE_CODE returns the error code part from a specified status code.

SCODE_FACILITY

SCODE_FACILITY(*sc***)**
SCODE *sc*

SCODE_FACILITY extracts the facility from a specified status code.

SCODE_SEVERITY

SCODE_SEVERITY(*sc***)**
SCODE *sc*

SCODE_SEVERITY extracts the severity field from the specified status code.

SUCCEEDED

SUCCEEDED(*sc*)
SCODE *sc*

SUCCEEDED returns TRUE if the severity of the SCODE is either success or information; otherwise, FALSE is returned. SUCCEEDED works on both status code and HRESULT values.

FAILED

FAILED(*sc*)
SCODE *sc*

FAILED returns TRUE if the severity of the status code is either a warning or error; otherwise, FALSE is returned. FAILED works on both status code and HRESULT values.

MAKE_SCODE

MAKE_SCODE(*sev,fac,sc*)
SEVERITY *sev*
FACILITY *fac*
SCODE *sc*

MAKE_SCODE makes a new status code given a severity, a facility, and a status code.

String and CLSID Conversion Functions

The following functions convert strings, GUIDs, CLSIDs, and ProgIDs from one form to another, using entries listed in the Registration Database file. The functions are defined as follows (see also compobj.h):

```
CoCreateGUID(GUID FAR* pguid);
IsEqualGUID(REFGUID rguid1, REFGUID rguid2);
IsEqualIID(REFGUID rguid1, REFGUID rguid2);
IsEqualCLSID(REFCLSID clsid1, REFCLSID clsid2);
CLSIDFromProgID(const char * lpszProgID, LPCLSID pclsid);
ProgIDFromCLSID(REFCLSID clsid, char * * lplpszProgID);
CLSIDFromString(char * lpsz, LPCLSID pclsid);
StringFromCLSID(REFCLSID rclsid, char * * lplpsz);
IIDFromString(char * lpsz, LPIID lpiid);
StringFromIID(REFIID rclsid, char * * lplpsz);
StringFromGUID2(REFGUID rguid, char * lpsz, int cbMax);
```

IsEqualGUID

unsigned long IsEqualGUID(*rguid1***,** *rguid2***)**
REFGUID *rguid1*
REFGUID *rguid2*

IsEqualGUID compares two GUIDs to see whether they are equal.

Parameters

rguid1
Specifies the GUID to compare with *rguid2*.

rguid2
Specifies the GUID that is to be compared with *rguid1*.

Return Values

Value	Meaning
TRUE	The GUIDs are equal.
FALSE	The GUIDs are not equal.

Comments

IsEqualGUID is used by **IsEqualCLSID** and **IsEqualIID**.

See Also

IsEqualCLSID, **IsEqualIID**

IsEqualIID

unsigned long IsEqualIID(*riid1***,** *riid2***)**
REFGUID *riid1*
REFGUID *riid2*

IsEqualIID compares two interface IDs to see whether they are equal.

Parameters

rclsid1
Specifies the IID to compare with *riid2*.

rclsid2
Specifies the IID to be compared with *riid1*.

Return Values

Value	Meaning
TRUE	The IIDs are equal.
FALSE	The IIDs are not equal.

See Also

IsEqualGUID, **IsEqualCLSID**

IsEqualCLSID

unsigned long IsEqualCLSID(*rclsid1*, *rclsid2*)
REFCLSID *rclsid1*
REFCLSID *rclsid2*

IsEqualCLSID compares two CLSIDs to see whether they are equal.

Parameters

rclsid1
Specifies the CLSID to compare with *rclsid2*.

rclsid2
Specifies the CLSID to be compared with *rclsid1*.

Return Values

Value	Meaning
TRUE	The CLSIDs are equal.
FALSE	The CLSIDs are not equal.

See Also

IsEqualGUID, **IsEqualIID**

CLSIDFromProgID

HRESULT CLSIDFromProgID(*lpszProgID*, *pclsid*)
const char * *lpszProgID*
LPCLSID *pclsid*

CLSIDFromProgID creates a CLSID from a ProgID.

Parameters

lpszProgID
Points to the ProgID whose CLSID is requested.

pclsid
Points to where to return the CLSID.

Return Values

Value	Meaning
S_OK	The CLSID was created successfully.
CO_E_CLASSSTRING	The registered CLSID for the ProgID is invalid.
REGDB_E_WRITEREGDB	Error writing to the Registration Database file.
E_OUTOFMEMORY	Out of memory.
E_INVALIDARG	One or more arguments are invalid.
E_UNEXPECTED	An unexpected error occurred.

Comments

A ProgID is a string that uniquely identifies a given object class. If the ProgID is the CLSID of an OLE 1 object class, **CLSIDFromProgID** automatically creates a

CLSID for it. Because of the restrictions placed on OLE 1 CLSID values, **CLSIDFromProgID** and **CLSIDFromString** are the only two functions that can be used to generate a CLSID for an OLE 1 object.

See Also **ProgIDFromCLSID**

ProgIDFromCLSID

HRESULT ProgIDFromCLSID(*clsid*, *lplpszProgID*)
REFCLSID *clsid*
char * * *lplpszProgID*

ProgIDFromCLSID retrieves the ProgID for a given CLSID.

Parameters

clsid
Specifies the CLSID for which the ProgID is requested.

lplpszProgID
Points to where to return the ProgID.

Return Values

Value	Meaning
S_OK	The ProgID was returned successfully.
REGDB_E_CLASSNOTREG	Class not registered in the Registration Database file.
REGDB_E_READREGDB	Error reading Registration Database file.

Comments

Every OLE 2 object class listed in the Insert Object dialog box must have a programmatic identifier (ProgID), a string that uniquely identifies a given object class. In addition to determining the eligibility for the Insert Object dialog box, the ProgID can be used as an identifier in a macro programming language to identify a class. Finally, the ProgID is also the class name used for an OLE 2 class when placed in an OLE 1 container.

ProgIDFromCLSID uses the entries in the Registration Database file to do the conversion. OLE 2 application authors are responsible for correctly configuring the Registration Database file at application installation time. For more information on the Registration Database file, see Chapter 4, "Registering Object Applications."

The ProgID string must be different from the class name of any OLE 1 application, including the OLE 1 version of the same application, if there is one. In addition, a ProgID string must not contain more than 39 characters or start with a digit. Except for a single period, it cannot contain any punctuation.

The ProgID is not shown to the user in the user interface. If you need a short human-readable string for an object, call **IOleObject::GetUserType**.

CLSIDFromProgID can be called to create a CLSID from a given ProgID. CLSIDs can be freed with the task allocator (see **CoGetMalloc**).

See Also **CLSIDFromProgID**

CLSIDFromString

HRESULT CLSIDFromString(*lpsz, pclsid***)**
char * *lpsz*
LPCLSID *pclsid*

CLSIDFromString converts a string generated by **StringFromCLSID** back into the original CLSID.

Parameters

lpsz
Points to the string representation of the CLSID.

pclsid
Points to where to return the CLSID.

Return Values

Value	Meaning
S_OK	CLSID returned successfully.
E_OUTOFMEMORY	Out of memory.
E_INVALIDARG	One or more arguments are invalid.
E_UNEXPECTED	An unexpected error occurred.

Comments Because of the restrictions placed on OLE 1 CLSID values, **CLSIDFromProgID** and **CLSIDFromString** are the only two functions that can be used to generate a CLSID for an OLE 1 object.

See Also **CLSIDFromProgID**, **StringFromCLSID**

StringFromCLSID

HRESULT StringFromCLSID(*rclsid, lplpsz***)**
REFCLSID *rclsid*
char * * *lplpsz*

StringFromCLSID converts the CLSID into a string of printable characters so that different CLSIDs always convert to different strings.

Parameters

rclsid
Specifies the class identifier of which we want a string representation.

lplpsz
Points to where to return the resulting string.

Return Values

Value	Meaning
S_OK	The character string was successfully converted and returned.
E_OUTOFMEMORY	Out of memory.

Comments

StringFromCLSID is used by OLE to look up CLSIDs as keys in the Registration Database file.

The returned string is freed in the standard way, using the task allocator (see **CoGetMalloc**).

See Also

CLSIDFromString

IIDFromString

HRESULT IIDFromString(*lpsz*, *lpiid***)**
char * *lpsz*
LPIID *lpiid*

IIDFromString converts a string generated by **StringFromIID** back into the original IID.

Parameters

lpsz
Points to the string representation of the IID.

lpiid
Points to where to return the IID.

Return Values

Value	Meaning
S_OK	The string was successfully converted.
E_OUTOFMEMORY	Out of memory.
E_INVALIDARG	One or more arguments are invalid.

Comments

The IID is converted in a way that guarantees different IIDs will always convert to different strings. One way this might work, for example, is to print the IID in hexadecimal.

See Also

StringFromIID

StringFromIID

HRESULT StringFromIID(*rclsid*, *lplpsz*)
REFIID *rclsid*
char * * *lplpsz*

StringFromIID converts an IID into a string of printable characters.

Parameters

rclsid
Specifies the IID to convert to a string representation.

lplpsz
Points to where to return the resulting string.

Return Values

Value	Meaning
S_OK	The character string was successfully returned.
E_OUTOFMEMORY	Out of memory.

The returned string is freed in the standard way, using the task allocator (see **CoGetMalloc**).

See Also

IIDFromString

StringFromGUID2

int StringFromGUID2(*rguid*, *lpsz*, *cbMax*)
REFGUID *rguid*
char * *lpsz*
unsigned short *cbMax*

StringFromGUID2 converts a globally unique IID (GUID) into a string of printable characters.

Parameters

rguid
Specifies the GUID to convert to a string representation.

lpsz
Points to where to return the resulting string.

cbMax
Specifies the maximum expected size of the returned string.

Return Values

Value	Meaning
0 (zero)	Buffer is too small for returned string.
Non-zero value	The number of characters in the returned string, including the null terminator.

CHAPTER 6

Compound Document Interfaces and Functions

Compound document interfaces are implemented and used to create and manage compound documents. The use of these interfaces depends on an application's role as a container application, object application, or combination container/object application.

Most of the compound document interfaces are implemented by at least one type of OLE application, as illustrated in the OLINE series of sample OLE applications shipped with the OLE SDK.

IAdviseSink Interface

The **IAdviseSink** interface, implemented by containers and OLE, is used to receive asynchronous notifications. There are three types of asynchronous notifications: compound document (also referred to as OLE notifications), data change, and view change.

Compound document notifications are generated when an object closes, is renamed, is saved, or its link source changes.

IAdviseSink implementors register for one or more types of notification and each **IAdviseSink** method is a callback for a specific notification. When an event occurs that applies to a registered notification type, the object application calls the appropriate **IAdviseSink** method. For example, when an embedded object closes, **IAdviseSink::OnClose** is called to notify the object's container of the change.

IAdviseSink contains the following methods:

```
DECLARE_INTERFACE_(IAdviseSink, IUnknown)
{
 // *** IUnknown methods ***
 HRESULT QueryInterface (REFIID riid, void * * ppvObj);
 unsigned long AddRef () ;
 unsigned long Release ();

 // *** IAdviseSink methods ***
 void OnDataChange (FORMATETC * pFormatetc, STGMEDIUM * pmedium);
```

```
    void OnViewChange (unsigned long dwAspect, long lindex);
    void OnRename (LPMONIKER pmk);
    void OnSave ();
    void OnClose ();
};
```

For more information, see the dvobj.h header file.

IAdviseSink::OnDataChange

void IAdviseSink::OnDataChange(*pFormatetc, pmedium*)
FORMATETC * *pFormatetc*
STGMEDIUM * *pmedium*

IAdviseSink::OnDataChange sends a notification that data in the calling object has changed.

Parameters

pFormatetc
Points to the **FORMATETC** data structure from which the data advise was originally set up. For more information about **FORMATETC**,see Chapter 7, "Data Transfers/Caching Interfaces and Functions."

pmedium
Points to the storage medium in which the data is passed.

Comments

In order to be notified when the object's data changes, the container must first call **IDataObject::DAdvise** to set up an advisory connection.

Not all containers register for data change notifications. Those that do not register have an empty implementation of **IAdviseSink::OnDataChange**. An example of a container that would register for data change notifications is one that does not use OLE's caching support.

The implementation of **IAdviseSink::OnDataChange** can invalidate the rectangle for the changed data by calling **InvalRect** and waiting for a Update Event.

Making synchronous calls within asynchronous methods is not valid. For example, **IAdviseSink::OnDataChange** cannot contain a call to **IDataObject::GetData**.

When **IAdviseSink::OnDataChange** is called on the cache, the cache is updated. Calling **OnDataChange** on a link object whose link type is automatic, automatically updates the link.

Data is passed in the storage medium pointed to by *pmedium*. Since the medium is owned by the caller, the sink should not free it. Also, if *pmedium* points to an **IStorage** or **IStream**, the sink must not increment the reference count.

The data is valid only for the duration of the call.

See Also

IDataObject::DAdvise

IAdviseSink::OnViewChange

void IAdviseSink::OnViewChange(*dwAspect, lindex***)**
unsigned long *dwAspect*
long *lindex*

IAdviseSink::OnViewChange notifies that an object's view or presentation has changed. These actions typically include redrawing the object.

Parameters

dwAspect
Specifies the aspect, or view, of the object. The value is taken from the enumeration **DVASPECT**. For more information, see the discussion of **DVASPECT** in Chapter 7, "Data Transfer/Caching Interfaces and Functions."

lindex
Identifies which piece of the view has changed, currently only -1 is valid.

Comments

Containers register to be notified when an object's view changes by calling **IViewObject::SetAdvise**. Once registered, the object will call the sink's **IAdviseSink::OnViewChange** method when appropriate.

dwAspect can represent only one value from **DVASPECT**; it cannot contain values from **DVASPECT** that have been or'ed together.

The *lindex* parameter represents the part of the aspect that is of interest. The value of *lindex* depends on the value of *dwAspect*. If *dwAspect* is either DVASPECT_THUMBNAIL or DVASPECT_ICON, *lindex* is ignored. If *dwAspect* is DVASPECT_CONTENT, *lindex* must be -1, which indicates that the entire view is of interest and is the only value that is currently valid.

To handle changes that affect the extent of the object, containers can set *fDoGetExtent* to TRUE in **IAdviseSink::OnViewChange** and then call **InvalRect** to force repainting. For example:

```
if (fDoGetExtent)  {
    fDoGetExtent = FALSE;
    IViewObject2::GetExtent(&newExtents);
    if (newExtents are different)
        relayout the contents.
}
draw the object
```

IAdviseSink::OnViewChange can be called when the object is in either the loaded or running state.

See Also

IViewObject::SetAdvise

IAdviseSink::OnRename

void IAdviseSink::OnRename(*pmk***)**
LPMONIKER *pmk*

IAdviseSink::OnRename notifies containers that an object has been renamed.

Parameters

pmk
Points to the new (full) name of the object.

Comments

The OnRename notification belongs to a group of notifications that containers register to receive by calling **IOleObject::Advise**.

IAdviseSink::OnRename is called when the object's name in the container changes or when the container's name changes. Although the container and the OLE link object typically receive this notification, the container can ignore it. On receiving the notification, OleLink objects must update their moniker to the link source in order to track the link source.

Most containers will not need to register for OLE advise notifications.

Linking containers can register to receive notifications of changes to the link source by calling **IAdviseSink2::OnLinkSrcChange**.

See Also

IAdviseSink2::OnLinkSrcChange

IAdviseSink::OnSave

void IAdviseSink::OnSave()

IAdviseSink::OnSave notifies registered advisory sinks that the object has been saved.

Comments

Objects call **IAdviseSink::OnSave** to send OnSave notifications when the object has been saved, either to the object's original storage or to a new one.

OnSave notifications are usually of interest only to object handlers; containers typically ignore them. When an object handler receives the OnSave notification, it updates its cache if the advise flag passed during registration specified ADVFCACHE_ONSAVE.

To register for OnSave notifications, containers call **IOleObject::Advise**.

IAdviseSink::OnClose

void IAdviseSink::OnClose()

IAdviseSink::OnClose notifies the container that an object has transitioned from the running into the loaded state and the object application has shut down.

Comments

Containers register to receive OnClose notifications by calling **IOleObject::Advise**. Object implementations call **IAdviseSink::Close** to inform its interested sinks that they are shutting down.

If the object is implemented in an object application, this method indicates that the object in the application is shutting down. If the object application is not servicing any other objects or if it has no other reason to remain in the running state (such as the presence of **IClassFactory::LockServer** locks or if the application is under user control), then this notification also indicates that the application itself is shutting down.

Upon receipt of this notification, the object handler and object link implementations should immediately release pointers to the object because the object in the application is shutting down. In the case of linked objects, the **OnClose** notification should always be interpreted to mean that the source link has closed and not that the linked object itself is no longer connected to the link source.

In the case of an object application supporting multiple instances of the object, **IAdviseSink::OnClose** is a notification that the object itself is being released. It does not indicate that the object application has shut down.

In the OLE link objects' implementation of **IAdviseSink::OnClose**, the link object releases its pointer to the bound link source. In the OLE default handler's implementation of this method, the handler releases its pointer to the object in the object application. A typical container application can ignore this notification. It need not release its pointers to the loaded object nor revert the object's storage.

IAdviseSink2 Interface

The **IAdviseSink2** interface is an extension of **IAdviseSink** and is optionally implemented by linking container applications.

When a linking container stores a representation of the link source outside of the link, it may be desirable to be notified when the link source changes; **IAdviseSink2::OnLinkSrcChange** can be used for this purpose.

IAdviseSink2 contains the following method:

```
DECLARE_INTERFACE_(IAdviseSink2, IAdviseSink)
{
  // *** IUnknown methods ***
  HRESULT QueryInterface (REFIID riid, void * * ppvObj);
  unsigned long AddRef () ;
  unsigned long Release ();

  // *** IAdviseSink methods ***
  void OnDataChange (FORMATETC * pFormatetc, STGMEDIUM * pmedium);
  void OnViewChange (unsigned long dwAspect, long lindex);
  void OnRename (LPMONIKER pmk);
```

```
    void OnSave ();
    void OnClose ();

    // *** IAdviseSink2 methods ***
    void OnLinkSrcChange (LPMONIKER pmk);
};
```

For more information, see the dvobj.h header file.

IAdviseSink2::OnLinkSrcChange

void IAdviseSink2::OnLinkSrcChange(*pmk*)
LPMONIKER *pmk*

IAdviseSink2::OnLinkSrcChange notifies containers that a link source has changed.

Parameters

pmk
Points to the new link source contained within the link object.

Comments

A container of linked objects implements this method so as to be notified of a change in the link source's moniker. A typical container uses the name of the link source as part of its application.

IAdviseSink2::OnLinkSrcChange is called by the OLE link object when it receives the OnRename notification from the link source (object) application. The link object updates its moniker and sends the change notification to containers that have implemented **IAdviseSink2**.

See Also

IAdviseSink::OnRename

IEnumOLEVERB Interface

The **IEnumOLEVERB** interface is implemented by OLE and by object applications that have a dynamically changing set of verbs. It is used by container applications to enumerate the verbs available for an object.

IEnumOLEVERB enumerates entries in the **OLEVERB** structure. For more information about **OLEVERB**, see **IOleObject::EnumVerbs** later in this chapter.

The **IEnumOLEVERB** interface contains the following methods, as do all enumerators (see also ole2.h):

```
DECLARE_INTERFACE_(IEnumOLEVERB, IUnknown)
{
 // *** IUnknown methods ***
 HRESULT QueryInterface (REFIID riid, void * * ppvObj);
 unsigned long AddRef () ;
 unsigned long Release ();
```

```
    // *** IEnumOLEVERB methods ***

    HRESULT Next (unsigned long celt, LPOLEVERB rgelt, unsigned long * pceltFetched);
    HRESULT Skip (unsigned long celt);
    HRESULT Reset ();
    HRESULT Clone (IEnumOLEVERB * * ppenumOleVerb);
};
```

For more information about emumerator interfaces in general, see the **IEnum*X*** interface in Chapter 5, "Component Object Interfaces and Functions."

IOleAdviseHolder Interface

The **IOleAdviseHolder** interface, implemented by OLE, is used by object applications to manage OLE notification registration and deregistration. It also sends notifications to registered sinks when appropriate.

Object applications can optionally provide their own notification management. **IOleAdviseHolder** is provided solely for the convenience of object application implementors.

IOleAdviseHolder contains the following methods

```
DECLARE_INTERFACE_(IOleAdviseHolder, IUnknown)
{
    // *** IUnknown methods ***
    HRESULT QueryInterface (REFIID riid, void * * ppvObj);
    unsigned long AddRef () ;
    unsigned long Release ();

    // *** IOleAdviseHolder methods ***
    HRESULT Advise (LPADVISESINK pAdvise, unsigned long * pdwConnection);
    HRESULT Unadvise (unsigned long dwConnection);
    HRESULT EnumAdvise (LPENUMSTATDATA * ppenumAdvise);
    HRESULT SendOnRename (LPMONIKER pmk);
    HRESULT SendOnSave ();
    HRESULT SendOnClose ();
};
```

For more information, see the ole2.h header file.

IOleAdviseHolder::Advise

HRESULT IOleAdviseHolder::Advise(*pAdvise, pdwConnection***)**
LPADVISESINK *pAdvise*
unsigned long * *pdwConnection*

IOleAdviseHolder::Advise sets up an advisory connection between the object and an advisory sink through which the sink can be informed of events that occur in the object.

Parameters

pAdvise
Points to the advisory sink that should be informed of changes.

pdwConnection
Points to a token that can later be used to delete the advisory connection.

Return Values

Value	Meaning
S_OK	Advisory connections set up successfully.
E_INVALIDARG	*pAdvise* is NULL.

Comments

Compound document notifications include OnSave, OnRename, OnLinkSrcChange, and OnClose. Advisory sinks register to receive compound document (OLE) notifications for an object by calling **IOleObject::Advise**.

An implementation of **IOleObject::Advise** generally will call **CreateOleAdviseHolder** to instantiate an **IOleAdviseHolder** interface instance and then delegate calls to **IOleAdviseHolder::Advise**.

If an advisory connection is successfully set up, the callee returns a nonzero value through *pdwConnection*. If a connection fails to be established, zero is returned.

To delete the connection, applications call **IOleAdviseHolder::Unadvise**.

See Also

IOleAdviseHolder::UnAdvise, **IOleAdviseHolder::EnumAdvise**, **IOleObject::Advise**

IOleAdviseHolder::Unadvise

HRESULT IOleAdviseHolder::Unadvise(*dwConnection***)**
unsigned long *dwConnection*

IOleAdviseHolder::Unadvise deletes an advisory connection previously established with **IOleAdviseHolder::Advise**.

Parameters

dwConnection
Contains a nonzero value previously returned from **IOleAdviseHolder::Advise** in *pdwConnection*.

Return Values

Value	Meaning
S_OK	Advisory connection deleted successfully.
OLE_E_NOCONNECTION	*dwConnection* does not represent a valid advisory connection.

See Also **IOleAdviseHolder::Advise**, **IOleAdviseHolder::EnumAdvise**, **IOleObject::Unadvise**

IOleAdviseHolder::EnumAdvise

HRESULT IOleAdviseHolder::EnumAdvise(*ppenumAdvise***)**
LPENUMSTATDATA * *ppenumAdvise*

IOleAdviseHolder::EnumAdvise enumerates the advisory connections currently established on the object.

Parameters

ppenumAdvise
Points to where the new enumerator should be returned. NULL indicates that there are no advisory connections on the object.

Return Values

Value	Meaning
S_OK	Enumerator returned successfully.
E_FAIL	Enumerator could not be returned.

Comments

While an enumeration is in progress, the effect of registering or revoking advisory connections on what is to be enumerated is undefined.

The returned enumerator is of type **IEnumSTATDATA**, which enumerates items of type **STATDATA**. For more information on **STATDATA**, see **IDataObject::EnumDAdvise**.

See Also **IEnumSTATDATA interface**, **IDataObject::EnumDAdvise**, **IOleAdviseHolder::Advise**, **IOleAdviseHolder::UnAdvise**, **IOleObject::EnumAdvise**

IOleAdviseHolder::SendOnRename

HRESULT IOleAdviseHolder::SendOnRename(*pmk***)**
LPMONIKER *pmk*

IOleAdviseHolder::SendOnRename notifies all advise sinks currently registered in the advise holder that the object has been renamed.

Parameters

pmk
Points to the new full moniker of the object.

Return Values

Value	Meaning
S_OK	Appropriate sinks were sent OnRename notifications.

IOleAdviseHolder::SendOnRename calls **IAdviseSink::OnRename** on all of the advisory sinks currently registered in the advise holder.

See Also **IAdviseSink::OnRename**

IOleAdviseHolder::SendOnSave

HRESULT IOleAdviseHolder::SendOnSave()

IOleAdviseHolder::SendOnSave notifies all advise sinks currently registered in the advise holder that the object has been saved.

Return Values

Value	Meaning
S_OK	Appropriate sinks were sent OnSave notifications.

IOleAdviseHolder::SendOnSave calls **IAdviseSink::OnSave** on all of the sinks currently registered in the advise holder.

See Also **IAdviseSink::OnSave**

IOleAdviseHolder::SendOnClose

HRESULT IOleAdviseHolder::SendOnClose()

IOleAdviseHolder::SendOnClose notifies all advise sinks currently registered in the advise holder that the object has been closed.

Return Values

Value	Meaning
S_OK	Appropriate sinks were sent OnClose notifications.

IOleAdviseHolder::SendOnClose calls **IAdviseSink::OnClose** on all of the sinks currently registered in the advise holder.

See Also **IAdviseSink::OnClose**

IOleClientSite Interface

The **IOleClientSite** interface, implemented by containers, is the object's view of its context: where it is anchored in the document, where it gets its storage, user interface, and other resources.

IOleClientSite is used by object applications to request services from the container. A container must provide one instance of **IOleClientSite** for every compound document object it contains.

IOleClientSite contains the following methods

```
DECLARE_INTERFACE_(IOleClientSite, IUnknown)
{
 // *** IUnknown methods ***
 HRESULT QueryInterface (REFIID riid, void * * ppvObj);
 unsigned long AddRef () ;
 unsigned long Release ();
 // *** IOleClientSite methods ***
 HRESULT SaveObject ();
 HRESULT GetMoniker (unsigned long dwAssign, unsigned long dwWhichMoniker,
      LPMONIKER * ppmk);
 HRESULT GetContainer (LPOLECONTAINER * ppContainer);
 HRESULT ShowObject ();
 HRESULT OnShowWindow (UNSIGNED long fShow);
 HRESULT RequestNewObjectLayout ();
};
```

For more information, see the ole2.h header file.

IOleClientSite::SaveObject

HRESULT IOleClientSite::SaveObject()

IOleClientSite::SaveObject requests that the object attached to this client site be saved.

Return Values

Value	Meaning
S_OK	Object was saved successfully.
E_FAIL	Object was not loaded.
Values returned from **IPersistStorage::Save**, **IPersistStorage::SaveCompleted**, or **IOleObject::Update**	For more information, see the method descriptions.

Comments

IOleClientSite::SaveObject is called by objects when the user chooses the File Update or File Quit commands. The method is synchronous; by the time it returns, the save will be completed.

See Also

IOleClientSite::GetMoniker, **IOleClientSite::GetContainer**, **IOleClientSite::RequestNewObjectLayout**

IOleClientSite::GetMoniker

HRESULT IOleClientSite::GetMoniker(*dwAssign, dwWhichMoniker, ppmk***)**
unsigned long *dwAssign*
unsigned long *dwWhichMoniker*
LPMONIKER **ppmk*

IOleClientSite::GetMoniker returns the container's moniker, the object's moniker relative to the container, or the object's full moniker.

Parameters

dwAssign
Specifies the type of moniker to be returned in *ppmk*. Values are taken from the enumeration **OLEGETMONIKER**; for more information, see the following comments.

dwWhichMoniker
Specifies which moniker to return in *ppmk*. Values are taken from the enumeration **OLEWHICHMK**; for more information, see the following comments.

ppmk
Points to where to return the moniker.

Return Values

Value	Meaning
S_OK	Requested moniker returned successfully.
E_FAIL	An unspecified error occurred.
E_UNEXPECTED	A relatively catastrophic failure has occurred.
E_NOTIMPL	This container cannot assign monikers to objects.

Comments

Every container that may contain links should support **IOleClientSite::GetMoniker** to give out OLEWHICHMK_CONTAINER. This enables link tracking when the link client and link source files move, but maintains the same relative position.

An object must not persistently store its full moniker or its container's moniker, because these can change while the object is not loaded.

When a link is made to an entire embedded object or to pieces of it, the embedded object needs a moniker to use in constructing a composite moniker indicating the source of the link. If the embedded object does not already have a moniker, it can call **IOleClientSite::GetMoniker** to request one.

Valid values for *dwAssign* are contained in the enumeration **OLEGETMONIKER**, which is defined in ole2.h as follows:

```
typedef enum tagOLEGETMONIKER
{
    OLEGETMONIKER_ONLYIFTHERE   = 1,
    OLEGETMONIKER_FORCEASSIGN   = 2,
    OLEGETMONIKER_UNASSIGN      = 3,
    OLEGETMONIKER_TEMPFORUSER   = 4,
} OLEGETMONIKER;
```

OLEGETMONIKER values have the following meaning:

Value	Meaning
OLEGETMONIKER _ONLYIFTHERE	Returns a moniker only if one has previously been assigned.
OLEGETMONIKER _FORCEASSIGN	Returns an assigned moniker. Forced moniker assignment should be postponed until such time that a Paste Link actually occurs.
OLEGETMONIKER _UNASSIGN	Removes moniker assignment and returns NULL.
OLEGETMONIKER _TEMPFORUSER	Returns a temporary, unassigned moniker. This flag is used when a moniker is needed, for example, to represent data being copied to the clipboard at the time of the copy.

Sometimes an object may not need the moniker previously assigned to it (such as high-frequency links used for object connections in a programming language). In this case, the object can call **IOleClientSite::GetMoniker** with OLEGETMONIKER_UNASSIGN to tell its container that it no longer needs the moniker. As part of its implementation, the container can unassign the moniker as an optimization.

The value for *dwWhichMoniker* is taken from the enumeration **OLEWHICHMK**, defined in ole2.h as follows:

```
typedef enum tagOLEWHICHMK {
    OLEWHICHMK_CONTAINER = 1,
    OLEWHICHMK_OBJREL    = 2,
    OLEWHICHMK_OBJFULL   = 3,
    }OLEWHICHMK;
```

OLEWHICHMK values have the following meaning:

Values	Meaning
OLEWHICHMK _CONTAINER	Returns the moniker belonging to the object's container, typically a file moniker.
OLEWHICHMK _OBJREL	Returns the object's moniker relative to the client site, typically an item moniker.
OLEWHICHMK _OBJFULL	Returns the object's full moniker, typically a composite moniker.

See Also

IOleClientSite::SaveObject, **IOleClientSite::GetContainer**, **IOleClientSite::RequestNewObjectLayout**

IOleClientSite::GetContainer

HRESULT IOleClientSite::GetContainer(*ppContainer*)
LPOLECONTAINER * *ppContainer*

IOleClientSite::GetContainer returns a pointer to the container's **IOleContainer** interface.

Parameters

ppContainer
Points to where the object's **IOleContainer** interface pointer is to be returned.

Return Values

Value	Meaning
S_OK	**IOleContainer** interface pointer successfully returned.
OLE_E_NOT _SUPPORTED	Client site is in OLE 1 container.
E_NOTIMPL	**IOleContainer** is not implemented by container.

Comments

IOleClientSite::GetContainer can be used to traverse up a hierarchy of compound document objects.

A successful call to **IOleClientSite::GetContainer** can be followed by **IOleContainer::QueryInterface**, asking for **IOleObject** and **IOleObject::GetClientSite** to get the client site for the next object. This sequence of calls can be repeated for each object.

Simple containers that do not support linking to embedded objects do not need to implement **IOleClientSite::GetContainer**. Instead, these containers should return E_NOINTERFACE and set * *ppContainer* to NULL.

See Also

IOleClientSite::SaveObject, **IOleClientSite::GetMoniker**, **IOleClientSite::RequestNewObjectLayout**

IOleClientSite::ShowObject

HRESULT IOleClientSite::ShowObject()

IOleClientSite::ShowObject tells the container to position the object so it is visible to the user. This method ensures that the container itself is visible and not minimized.

Return Values

Value	Meaning
S_OK	Container has tried to make the object visible.
OLE_E_NOT _SUPPORTED	Client site is in OLE 1 container.

Comments

IOleClientSite::ShowObject is typically part of an object's implementation of **IOleObject::DoVerb**. If the container itself is an embedded object, it will recursively invoke **IOleClientSite::ShowObject** on its container.

It is possible that the container is not able to position the object so it is either partially or completely visible at the present time. Therefore, when **IOleClientSite::ShowObject** returns, the object cannot rely on its degree of visibility. The intent of **IOleClientSite::ShowObject** is to respond to the request for visibility whenever possible.

After an object being edited in place scrolls into view, it is necessary to ask it to update its rectangle for the new clip **Rect** coordinates.

IOleClientSite::OnShowWindow

HRESULT IOleClientSite::OnShowWindow(*fShow*)
unsigned long *fShow*

IOleClientSite::OnShowWindow notifies a container when an object's windows become visible or invisible. This method is called when an object is open in its own window as opposed to being active in place.

Parameters

fShow
Indicates whether or not an object window is becoming visible.

Return Values

Value	Meaning
S_OK	Shading/hatching has been successfully removed or added.

Comments

The object calls **IOleClientSite::OnShowWindow** if an **IOleObject::DoVerb** call causes it to show its window.

IOleClientSite::OnShowWindow adds or removes object shading. If *fShow* is TRUE, the object is open in a window elsewhere and shading/hatching should be added. If *fShow* is FALSE, the window is not open elsewhere and shading/hatching should be removed and the application should be brought to the foreground.

IOleClientSite::RequestNewObjectLayout

HRESULT IOleClientSite::RequestNewObjectLayout()

IOleClientsite::RequestNewObjectLayout is called when a compound document object needs more or less room.

Return Values

Value	Meaning
S_OK	Request for new layout succeeded.
E_NOTIMPL	Client site does not support requests for new layout.

Comments

Currently, there is no standard mechanism by which a container would engage in a negotiation process to determine how much room the object would like. When such a mechanism is defined, responding to it will be optional on the container's part.

See Also

IOleClientSite::SaveObject, **IOleClientSite::GetMoniker**, **IOleClientSite::GetContainer**

IOleContainer Interface

The **IOleContainer** interface, implemented by containers and object applications, is used to enumerate objects in a container. **IOleContainer** is typically implemented by applications that support standard linking and linking to embeddings, however, it is useful for other applications as well.

IOleContainer is generic to many kinds of containers. It provides name parsing and enumeration of objects to provide an outside-in view of the composite set of objects managed by a container. To expose the contents of a container, OLE 2 applications will normally use **IOleItemContainer** (an extension of **IOleContainer**).

Simple, non-linking containers need not implement **IOleContainer**. The default object handler provides default behavior when a pointer to **IOleContainer** is not available.

The **IOleContainer** interface inherits from **IParseDisplayName**.

IOleContainer contains the following methods:

```
DECLARE_INTERFACE_(IOleContainer, IParseDisplayName)
{
 // *** IUnknown methods ***
 HRESULT QueryInterface (REFIID riid, void * * ppvObj);
 unsigned long AddRef () ;
 unsigned long Release ();

 // *** IParseDisplayName method ***
 HRESULT ParseDisplayName (LPBC pbc, char * lpszDisplayName, unsigned long * pchEaten,
      LPMONIKER * ppmkOut);

 // *** IOleContainer methods ***
 HRESULT EnumObjects (unsigned long grfFlags, LPENUMUNKNOWN * ppenumUnknown);
 HRESULT LockContainer (unsigned long fLock);
};
```

For further information, see the ole2.h header file.

IOleContainer::EnumObjects

HRESULT IOleContainer::EnumObjects(*grfFlags, ppenumUnknown***)**
unsigned long *grfFlags*
LPENUMUNKNOWN * *ppenumUnknown*

IOleContainer::EnumObjects enumerates the objects in the current container.

Parameters

grfFlags
Specifies a flag used to control the enumeration. Valid values are taken from the **OLECONTF** enumeration. For more information, see the following comments.

ppenumUnknown
Points to where the enumerator, of type **IEnumUnknown**, should be returned.

Return Values

Value	Meaning
S_OK	Enumerator successfully returned.
E_FAIL	An unspecified error occurred.
E_NOTIMPL	Object enumeration not supported.

Comments

IOleContainer::EnumObjects should be implemented to allow programmatic clients the ability to find out what elements the container holds. It is not called in standard linking scenarios.

Valid values for *grfFlags* are taken from the enumeration **OLECONTF**, which is defined in ole2.h as follows:

```
typedef enum tagOLECONTF
{
    OLECONTF_EMBEDDINGS     =  1,
    OLECONTF_LINKS          =  2,
    OLECONTF_OTHERS         =  4,
    OLECONTF_ONLYUSER       =  8,
    OLECONTF_ONLYIFRUNNING  = 16,
} OLECONTF;
```

OLECONTF values have following meanings:

Values	Meaning
OLECONTF_EMBEDDINGS	Enumerates the embedded objects in the container.
OLECONTF_LINKS	Enumerates the linked objects in the container.
OLECONTF_OTHER	Enumerates all objects in the container other than OLE compound document objects. If this flag is not given, pseudo objects in the container will be omitted.

Values	Meaning
OLECONTF_ONLYUSER	Enumerates only those objects the user is aware of. For example, hidden named-ranges in Microsoft Excel would not be enumerated using this value.
OLECONTF_ONLYIFRUNNING	Enumerates only the objects that are currently running inside this container.

For more information on enumerator interfaces in general, see the **IEnum*X*** interface in Chapter 5, "Component Object Interfaces and Functions."

See Also **IOleItemContainer** Interface

IOleContainer::LockContainer

HRESULT IOleContainer::LockContainer(*fLock*)
unsigned long *fLock*

IOleContainer::LockContainer is used by an embedded object to manually control the running of its container.

Parameters

fLock
Specifies whether to lock (TRUE) or unlock (FALSE) a container.

Return Values

Value	Meaning
S_OK	Container was locked successfully.
E_FAIL	An unspecified error occurred.
E_OUTOFMEMORY	Container could not be locked due to lack of memory.

Comments

An embedded object calls **IOleContainer::LockContainer** to ensure that its container remains in memory when other containers are linked to it and require an update. **IOleContainer::LockContainer** calls **CoLockObjectExternal** which keeps the running embedding container alive after all external references are released.

IOleContainer::LockContainer (TRUE) is called when an embedded object transitions to the running state. When the embedded object shuts down (transitions from running to loaded), it calls **IOleContainer::LockContainer** (FALSE).

The container must keep track of whether and how many **IOleContainer::LockContainer** (TRUE) calls have been made. Each call to **LockContainer** (TRUE) must be balanced by a call to **IOleContainer::LockContainer** (FALSE). If the user selects File Close from the menu, all outstanding locks are ignored and the document will shut down.

Object applications typically need not call **IOleContainer::LockContainer**; the default handler makes these calls automatically for object applications as the object transitions to and from the running state. Object applications not using the default handler, such as DLL object applications, must make the calls directly.

IOleItemContainer Interface

The **IOleItemContainer** interface, an extension to **IOleContainer**, is used to bind item monikers. Containers that use item monikers to identify contained objects must implement **IOleItemContainer**.

IOleItemContainer contains the following methods:

```
DECLARE_INTERFACE_(IOleItemContainer, IOleContainer)
{
 // *** IUnknown methods ***
 HRESULT QueryInterface (REFIID riid, void * * ppvObj);
 unsigned long AddRef () ;
 unsigned long Release ();

 // *** IParseDisplayName method ***
 HRESULT ParseDisplayName (LPBC pbc, char * lpszDisplayName, unsigned long * pchEaten,
      LPMONIKER * ppmkOut);

 // *** IOleContainer methods ***
 HRESULT EnumObjects (unsigned long grfFlags, LPENUMUNKNOWN *ppenumUnknown);
 HRESULT LockContainer (unsigned long fLock);

 // *** IOleItemContainer methods ***
 HRESULT GetObject (char * lpszItem, unsigned long dwSpeedNeeded, LPBINDCTX pbc,
      REFIID riid, void * * ppvObj);
 HRESULT GetObjectStorage (char * lpszItem, LPBINDCTX pbc, REFIID riid,
      void * * ppvStorage);
 HRESULT IsRunning (char * lpszItem);
};
```

For more information, see the ole2.h header file.

IOleItemContainer::GetObject

HRESULT IOleItemContainer::GetObject(*lpszItem, dwSpeedNeeded, pbc, riid, ppvObj***)**
char * *lpszItem*
unsigned long *dwSpeedNeeded*
LPBINDCTX *pbc*
REFIID *riid*
void * * *ppvObj*

IOleItemContainer::GetObject is called as part of binding an item moniker. It returns the object represented by *lpszItem*.

Parameters

lpszItem
Points to the item in this container to which the item moniker should be bound.

dwSpeedNeeded
Indicates how long the caller is willing to wait to get to the object. Valid values are taken from the enumeration **BINDSPEED**; for more information, see the following comments.

pbc
Points to an instance of the **IBindCtx** interface, which contains the actual bind context.

riid
Specifies the interface with which a connection to that object should be made.

ppvObj
Points to where the bound-to object is returned. If an object cannot be returned, NULL is returned.

Return Values

Value	Meaning
S_OK	Object returned successfully.
MK_E_EXCEEEDED-DEADLINE	Deadline was exceeded.
MK_E_SYNTAX	Error in parsing a display name or creating a file moniker.
MK_E_NOOBJECT	Intermediate object could not be found.
MK_E_INTERMEDIATE-INTERFACENOTSUPPORTED	Intermediate object needed did not support a required interface.
E_NOINTERFACE	The object cannot be returned because it does not support the interface identified by *riid*.
E_OUTOFMEMORY	Object cannot be returned due to lack of memory.

Comments

If MK_E_EXCEEEDEDDEADLINE was returned, the caller can retrieve the moniker of the object for which the deadline was exceeded by calling **IBindCtx::GetObjectParam** with the keys ExceededDeadline, ExceededDeadline1, ExceededDeadline2, and so on.

IOleItemContainer::GetObject first checks to see if the given item designates an embedded object. If the item is an embedded object, **IOleItemContainer::GetObject** loads and runs the object, and then returns it. If the item is not an embedded object, **IOleItemContainer::GetObject** checks to see if it designates a local object within the container. (This latter case is similar to **OLESERVERDOC::GetObject** in OLE 1.)

The parameter *dwSpeedNeeded* contains shorthand information found in the bind context. The value contained in *dwSpeedNeeded* is derived from the *dwTickCountDeadline* member in the **BIND_OPTS** structure that **IOleItemContainer::GetObject** receives in *pbc*. Instead of using *dwSpeedNeeded*, containers can call **IBindCtx::GetBindOptions** to get specific information about the time limit.

Values for *dwSpeedNeeded* are from the enumeration **BINDSPEED**, which is defined in ole2.h as follows:

```
typedef enum tagBINDSPEED
{
    BINDSPEED_INDEFINITE = 1,
    BINDSPEED_MODERATE   = 2,
    BINDSPEED_IMMEDIATE  = 3,
} BINDSPEED;
```

BINDSPEED values have the following semantics:

Value	Meaning
BINDSPEED_INDEFINITE	Caller will wait indefinitely. BINDSPEED_INDEFINITE is specified if the speed needed in the bind context is zero.
BINDSPEED_MODERATE	Caller will wait a moderate amount of time. BINDSPEED_MODERATE is specified if the speed needed in the bind context is greater than 2500 milleseconds. BINDSPEED_MODERATE includes those objects indicated by BINDSPEED_IMMEDIATE, plus those objects that are always running when loaded. In this case, the designated object should be loaded, checked to see whether it is running and if so, it should be returned. Otherwise, MK_E_EXCEEDEDDEADLINE should be returned.

Value	Meaning
BINDSPEED_IMMEDIATE	Caller will wait only a short time. If BINDSPEED_IMMEDIATE is specified, the object should be returned only if it is already running or if it is a pseudo-object. This is an object internal to the item container, such as a cell range in a spreadsheet or a character range in a word processor. Otherwise, MK_E_EXCEEDEDDEADLINE should be returned.

See Also **IBindCtx::GetBindOptions**

IOleItemContainer::GetObjectStorage

HRESULT IOleItemContainer::GetObjectStorage(*lpszItem, pbc, riid, ppvStorage*)
char * *lpszItem*
LPBINDCTX *pbc*
REFIID *riid*
void * * *ppvStorage*

IOleItemContainer::GetObjectStorage returns access to the object's storage using the indicated interface.

Parameters

lpszItem
Points to the item name for the object to whose storage access is being requested.

pbc
Points to the bind context. Can be ignored for most containers.

riid
Specifies the IID by which the caller wishes to access that storage. Often either **IID_IStorage** or **IID_IStream** is used.

ppvStorage
Place at which to return the requested interface.

Return Values

Value	Meaning
S_OK	Object's storage returned successfully.
E_FAIL	Cannot return object's storage.
MK_E_NOOBJECT	Object could not be found.
MK_E_NOSTORAGE	An attempt was made to access or bind to the storage of an object which does not have one.

In order for **IOleItemContainer::GetObjectStorage** to succeed, the object represented by *lpszItem* must have an independently identifiable piece of storage, as is the case of an embedded object. If no such storage exists, NULL is returned in *ppvStorage* and MK_E_NOSTORAGE is the return value.

IOleItemContainer::IsRunning

HRESULT IOleItemContainer::IsRunning(*lpszItem***)**
char * *lpszItem*

IOleItemContainer::IsRunning indicates whether the specified item in this item container is running.

Parameters

lpszItem
Points to the item name for the object whose status is being queried.

Return Values

Value	Meaning
S_OK	Object is running.
S_FALSE	Object does not allow linking inside.
MK_E_NOOBJECT	Object is not running.
E_OUTOFMEMORY	Ran out of memory while running the object.

IOleObject Interface

IOleObject, implemented by object applications and by OLE, contains methods for compound document object management. It is the primary interface by which a linked or embedded object provides functionality to its container.

IOleObject contains the following methods:

```
DECLARE_INTERFACE_(IOleObject, IUnknown)
{
 // *** IUnknown methods ***
 HRESULT QueryInterface (REFIID riid, void * * ppvObj);
 unsigned long AddRef () ;
 unsigned long Release ();

 // *** IOleObject methods ***
 HRESULT SetClientSite (LPOLECLIENTSITE pClientSite);
 HRESULT GetClientSite (LPOLECLIENTSITE * ppClientSite);
 HRESULT SetHostNames (const char * szContainerApp, const char * szContainerObj);
 HRESULT Close (unsigned long dwSaveOption);
 HRESULT SetMoniker (unsigned long dwWhichMoniker, LPMONIKER pmk);
 HRESULT GetMoniker (unsigned long dwAssign, unsigned long dwWhichMoniker,  LPMONIKER * ppmk);
 HRESULT InitFromData (LPDATAOBJECT pDataObject, unsigned long fCreation,
     unsigned long dwReserved);
```

```
HRESULT GetClipboardData (unsigned long dwReserved, LPDATAOBJECT * ppDataObject);
HRESULT DoVerb (long iVerb, Event Record * pEvt, LPOLECLIENTSITE pClientSite,
    long lindex, WindowPtr pWwndParent LPCRECT lprcPosRect);
HRESULT EnumVerbs (LPENUMOLEVERB * ppenumOleVerb);
HRESULT Update ();
HRESULT IsUpToDate ();
HRESULT GetUserClassID (CLSID * pclsid);
HRESULT GetUserType (unsigned long dwFormOfType, char * * lpszUserType);
HRESULT SetExtent (unsigned long dwAspect, LPSIZEL lpsizel);
HRESULT GetExtent (unsigned long dwAspect, LPSIZEL lpsizel);
HRESULT Advise (LPADVISESINK pAdvise, unsigned long * lpdwConnection);
HRESULT Unadvise (unsigned long dwConnection);
HRESULT EnumAdvise (LPENUMSTATDATA * ppenumStatData);
HRESULT GetMiscStatus (unsigned long dwAspect, unsigned long * pdwStatus);
HRESULT SetColorScheme (LPLOGPALETTE lpLogpal);
};
```

For more information, see the ole2.h header file.

IOleObject::SetClientSite

HRESULT IOleObject::SetClientSite(*pClientSite***)**
LPOLECLIENTSITE *pClientSite*

IOleObject::SetClientSite informs a newly created or loaded embedded object of its client site within the container.

Parameters

pClientSite
Points to the object's **IOleClientSite** interface.

Return Values

Value	Meaning
S_OK	Client site successfully set.
E_UNEXPECTED	Object is not embedded in a container.

Comments

Each embedded object has an associated client site through which the object communicates with its container. **IOleObject::SetClientSite** must be called whenever an embedded object is created or loaded.

IOleObject::GetClientSite

HRESULT IOleObject::GetClientSite(*ppClientSite***)**
LPOLECLIENTSITE * *ppClientSite*

IOleObject::GetClientSite queries an object for the pointer to its current client site within its container.

Parameters

ppClientSite
Points to the location at which to return the client site.

Return Values

Value	Meaning
S_OK	Client site pointer returned successfully.

Comments

The returned client site pointer will be NULL if the embedded object's client site has not yet been initialized.

IOleObject::SetHostNames

HRESULT IOleObject::SetHostNames(*lpszContainerApp, lpszContainerObj***)**
const char * *lpszContainerApp*
const char * *lpszContainerObj*

IOleObject::SetHostNames specifies window title information to be used when an object is open for editing.

Parameters

lpszContainerApp
Points to the user-presentable name of the container application.

lpszContainerObj
Points to the name of the container document that contains this object. Can be NULL.

Return Values

Value	Meaning
S_OK	Window title information set successfully.

Comments

Since these identifying strings are not stored as part of the persistent state of the object, **IOleObject::SetHostNames** must be called each time the object is loaded or run.

See Also

IOleObject::GetUserType

IOleObject::Close

HRESULT IOleObject::Close(*dwSaveOption***)**
unsigned long *dwSaveOption*

IOleObject::Close transitions a linked or embedded object from the running to the to the loaded state.

Parameters

dwSaveOption
Specifies whether the object is saved as part of the transition to the loaded state. Valid values are taken from the enumeration **OLECLOSE**; for more information, see the following comments.

Return Values

Value	Meaning
S_OK	Object closed successfully.
OLE_E_PROMPT-SAVECANCELLED	The user was prompted to save but chose the Cancel button from the prompt message box.

Comments

If the object is implemented by using an object application, this method causes the object in the application to shut down. If the object application is not servicing any other objects or if it has no other reason to remain in the running state (such as the presence of **IClassFactory::LockServer** locks or if the application is under user control), then it also causes the application itself to shut down.

IOleObject::Close is called by the object's linking or embedding container. This is one way that an object may be closed; the release of the object's last remaining interface pointer is another way. Calling **IOleObject::Close** when the object is not running has no effect.

When a link object is not connected to its link source, it is in the loaded state. As soon as it is connected, the link is in the running state. When using **OleLoad** on an automatic link, it tries to make a connection if the link source is running.

When **IOleObject::Close** is called on the link object, it disconnects from the link source. If the link source was visible to the user, the link source will not shut down, nor will it send an OnClose notification. Thus, even though the link object transitions from connected to disconnected (as well as from the running to the loaded state), an OnClose notification is not sent to the link container.

If **IOleObject::Close** is called on an open embedded object and there are no other visible documents, the application window should be hidden. If there are no other document/objects running, the application should also shut down. However, if there are other invisible documents/objects being used programmatically, such as in the silent update scenario, the application must only hide, postponing a shut down until the other documents are released by their clients.

Valid values for *dwSaveOption* are taken from the enumeration **OLECLOSE**, which is defined in ole2.h as follows:

```
typedef enum tagOLECLOSE
{
    OLECLOSE_SAVEIFDIRTY = 0,
    OLECLOSE_NOSAVE      = 1,
    OLECLOSE_PROMPTSAVE  = 2,
} OLECLOSE;
```

OLECLOSE values have the following meaning:

Value	Meaning
OLECLOSE_SAVEIFDIRTY	Indicates that the object is always to be saved if it is dirty.
OLECLOSE_NOSAVE	Indicates that a save is not to occur whether the object is dirty or not.
OLECLOSE_PROMPTSAVE	Indicates that the user should determine whether the save should occur by being prompted with a message.

NOTE: The OLE 2 user model dictates that embedded objects always be saved when closed without any prompting to the user. This is the recommendation regardless of whether the object is activated in place or in its own window.

This is a change from the OLE 1 user model in which object applications always prompted the user to save changes.

The following pseudo code shows the recommended way of handling *dwSaveOption*:

```
switch (dwSaveOption)  {
    case OLECLOSE_SAVEIFDIRTY:
        If dirty, save. Then close.

    case OLECLOSE_NOSAVE:
        Close

    case OLECLOSE_PROMPTSAVE:
        If object visible, but not in-place active:
            If not dirty, close.
            Otherwise, switch(prompt)   {
                case IDYES:
                    Save and close
                case IDNO:
                    Close
                case IDCANCEL:
                    return OLE_E_PROMPTSAVECANCELLED

        If object invisible (includes UI deactivated object)
            If dirty, save and close
            NOTE: No prompt - not appropriate to prompt if object
                  is not visible.

        If object is in-place active:
            If dirty, save and close
            NOTE: No prompt - not appropriate to prompt if object
                  is active in-place.
```

IOleObject::SetMoniker

HRESULT IOleObject::SetMoniker(*dwWhichMoniker, pmk)*
unsigned long *dwWhichMoniker*
LPMONIKER *pmk*

IOleObject::SetMoniker notifies the object of either its own moniker or its container's moniker.

Parameters

dwWhichMoniker
Specifies which moniker is passed in *pmk*; valid values are taken from the enumeration **OLEWHICHMK**. For more information about **OLEWHICHMK**, see **IOleClientSite::GetMoniker** earlier in this chapter.

pmk
Points to where to return the moniker.

Return Values

Value	Meaning
S_OK	Moniker successfully set.
E_FAIL	No client site for object.

Comments

IOleObject::SetMoniker is usually called only by the object's container, since the container is responsible for maintaining the object's identity.

If *dwWhichMoniker* is set to OLEWHICHMK_OBJREL, the moniker passed in *pmk* is the moniker of the object in the container's document. If this moniker is composed onto the moniker of the object's container and the resulting moniker is bound, then the object itself will be connected to it rather than the continer.

If *dwWhichMoniker* is OLEWHICHMK_CONTAINER, then the object is being notified that the name of its container has changed. If the object has registered itself as running and either of these monikers changes, then the object will need to change the name under which it is registered. For more information, see **IRunningObjectTable::Register**. Any nested embedded objects within the object presently loaded may need to be informed that the name of their container has changed.

The moniker of an object relative to its container is stored by the object handler as part of the object's persistent state. The moniker of the object's container must not be persistently stored inside the object, because the container can be renamed at any time.

See Also

IAdviseSink::OnRename, **IRunningObjectTable::Register**

IOleObject::GetMoniker

HRESULT IOleObject::GetMoniker(*dwAssign, dwWhichMoniker, ppmk***)**
unsigned long *dwAssign*
unsigned long *dwWhichMoniker*
LPMONIKER **ppmk*

IOleObject::GetMoniker returns a moniker that can be used to connect to the object.

Parameters

dwAssign
Specifies how the moniker is assigned to the object. Depending on the value of *dwAssign*, **IOleObject::GetMoniker** returns either an assigned or unassigned moniker. Values are taken from the enumeration, **OLEGETMONIKER**. For more information, see **IOleClientSite::GetMoniker,** earlier in this chapter.

dwWhichMoniker
Specifies the form of the moniker being requested. Values are taken from the enumeration **OLEWHICHMK**; for more information, see **IOleClientSite::GetMoniker** earlier in this chapter.

ppmk
Points to where to return the object's moniker.

Return Values

Value	Meaning
S_OK	Requested moniker returned successfully.
E_FAIL	Object cannot return a moniker.
MK_E_SYNTAX	Syntax error in **CreateFileMoniker**.
E_OUTOFMEMORY	**CreateFileMoniker** failed due to lack of memory.

Comments

It is not legal to pass OLEGETMONIKER_UNASSIGN to **IOleObject::GetMoniker**. For information on when to use OLEGETMONIKER_UNASSIGN, see **IOleClientSite::GetMoniker**.

See Also

IOleClientSite::GetMoniker

IOleObject::InitFromData

HRESULT IOleObject::InitFromData(*pDataObject, fCreation, dwReserved***)**
LPDATAOBJECT *pDataObject*
unsigned long *fCreation*
unsigned long *dwReserved*

IOleObject::InitFromData initializes the contents of an object with data available from *pDataObject*.

Parameters

pDataObject
Points to the data transfer object from which the initialization data is obtained; can be NULL, indicating that the caller wants to know if it is worthwhile trying to send data.

fCreation
TRUE indicates the initial creation of the object; FALSE indicates a more general programmatic data transfer.

dwReserved
Reserved for future use; must be zero.

Return Values

Value	Meaning
S_OK	Object successfully attempted to initialize if *pDataObject* is not NULL; object can attempt a successful initialization if *pDataObject* is NULL.
S_FALSE	Object made no attempt to initialize if *pDataObject* is not NULL; object can not attempt to initialize if *pDataObject* is NULL.
E_NOTIMPL	Object does not support **InitFromData**.
OLE_E _NOTRUNNING	Object must be running to perform the operation.

Comments

The container decides if it is OK to have a new object based on the current selection. The object returns S_OK if an attempt at initialization is made. The container should call **IOleObject::GetMiscStatus** to check the value of the OLEMISC_INSERTNOTREPLACE bit. If the bit is on, the new object is inserted after the selected data. If the bit is off, the new object replaces the selected data.

The object returns S_FALSE if it can never initialize itself from caller-provided data or cannot initialize itself with the data provided in this case. No return value is specified to indicate whether or not the call to **IOleObject::InitFromData** really did anything; subsequent *pDataObject* method calls to actually transfer the data will serve this purpose.

If *fCreation* is TRUE, the object is being initialized with data from its container as part of the creation sequence. The *pDataObject* provided by the container has the same contents as it would have for a copy operation. That is, if the container was to call **OleSetClipboard** rather than **IOleObject::InitFromData**, the contents of *pDataObject* would be identical.

If *fCreation* is FALSE, the caller is attempting to do a more general programmatic paste operation. The object should replace its current contents with the data pointed to by *pDataObject*, just as it would for a Paste operation. The normal constraints that an object applies when pasting should be applied here. For example, if the shape of the data provided is unacceptable, the object should fail to initialize and return S_FALSE.

See Also **IOleObject::GetMiscStatus**, **IDataObject::SetData**

IOleObject::GetClipboardData

HRESULT IOleObject::GetClipboardData(*dwReserved, ppDataObject***)**
unsigned long *dwReserved*
LPDATAOBJECT **ppDataObject*

IOleObject::GetClipboardData returns a data transfer object that contains exactly what would have been passed to **OleSetClipboard** in a copy operation.

Parameters

dwReserved
Reserved for future use; must be zero.

ppDataObject
Points to the location where the data transfer object is to be returned.

Return Values

Value	Meaning
S_OK	Data transfer object successfully returned.
E_NOTIMPL	**GetClipboardData** not supported.
OLE_E_NOTRUNNING	Object is not running.

Comments

The difference between the *pDataObject* returned from **IOleObject::GetClipboardData** and **IOleObject::QueryInterface** (IID_IDataObject,...) is that the former data transfer object is a snapshot copy that does not change as the object changes. The data object retrieved through the **QueryInterface** call may change as the object changes.

The **QueryInterface** method enables an object's client to perform a copy operation on the entire object without disturbing the contents of the real clipboard. This method could be used in a situation where it is necessary to convert a linked object to an embedded object, in which case the container application would call **IOleObject::GetClipboardData** to get the data and then pass that data to **OleCreateFromData**.

See Also **IOleObject::InitFromData**

IOleObject::DoVerb

HRESULT IOleObject::DoVerb(*iVerb, pEvt, pClientSite, lindex , pWndParent, lprcPosRect*
long *iVerb*
Event Record * *pEvt*
LPOLECLIENTSITE *pClientSite*
long *lindex*
WindowPtr *pWndParent*
LPCRECT *lprcPosRect*

IOleObject::DoVerb requests an object to perform one of its verbs.

Parameters

iVerb
Specifies the verb number associated with the action to take.

pEvt
Points to the event that caused the verb to be invoked.

pClientSite
Points to the client site of the embedding or linking container in which the verb was invoked.

lindex
Reserved for future use; must always be -1.

pWndParent
Specifies the WindowPtr of the document window containing the object.

lprcPosRect
Points to the rectangle containing the coordinates of the bounding rectangle in which the destination document displays the object. This position is in container window pixel coordinates with respect to *hwndParent*.

Return Values

Value	Meaning
S_OK	Object successfully invoked specified verb.
OLE_E_NOT_INPLACEACTIVE	*iVerb* set to OLEIVERB_UIACTIVATE or OLEIVERB_INPLACEACTIVATE and object is not currently open.
OLE_E _CANTBINDTOSOURCE	The object handler or link object cannot connect to the link source.
DV_E_LINDEX	Invalid *lindex*.
OLEOBJ_S_CANNOT _DOVERB_NOW	The verb is valid, but object cannot do it now.
OLEOBJ_S _INVALIDHWND	DOVERB was successful but *hwnd* is invalid.
OLEOBJ_E_NOVERBS	The object does not support any verbs.

Value	Meaning
OLEOBJ_S _INVALIDVERB	Object does not recognize a positive verb number. Verb is treated as OLEIVERB_PRIMARY.
MK_CONNECTMANUALLY	Link source is across a network that is not connected to a drive on this machine.
OLE_E_CLASSDIFF	Class for source of link has undergone a conversion.
E_NOTIMPL	Object does not support in-place activation or object does not recognize a negative verb number.

Comments

Verbs are available on an object while it is selected in its container. **IOleObject::DoVerb** can be invoked from either an object's container or one of its currently-connected link clients. In the first case, the client site pointer passed to **DoVerb** is the same as the embedding site, the pointer passed with **IOleObject::SetClientSite**. In the second case, the passed client site is not the same as the embedding site.

A container can determine the set of verbs available to an object by calling **IOleObject::EnumVerbs**, which returns an **OLEVERB** structure. The value of *iVerb* is matched against the *iVerb* member of **OLEVERB** to determine which verb to perform.

Except for a set of verbs predefined by OLE, the meaning of a particular verb is determined by the object's application. The following table describes the predefined verbs:

Verbs Defined by OLE	Purpose
OLEIVERB_PRIMARY (0L)	Verb that is invoked when the user double-clicks the object in its container. Object defines the semantics of the verb. If the object supports in-place activation, the primary verb usually activates the object in-place.
OLEIVERB_SHOW (-1L)	Indicates that the object is to be shown to the user for editing or viewing. Used to show a newly-inserted object to the user for initial editing.
OLEIVERB_OPEN (-2L)	Causes the object to be open-edited in a separate window. If the object does not support open editing, this verb has the same semantics as OLEIVERB_SHOW.
OLEIVERB_HIDE (-3L)	Causes the object to remove its user interface from the user's view.

Verbs Defined by OLE	Purpose
OLEIVERB_UI-ACTIVATE (-4L)	Used to activate the object in-place and show any user interface tools that it needs, such as menus or toolbars. If the object does not support in-place activation, it should return E_NOTIMPL.
OLEIVERB_INPLACE-ACTIVATE	Used to run the object and install its window, but not attempt to install user interface tools. In this state an inside-out style of object can take focus and then negotiate for menus and other tools. An outside-in style object returns E_NOTIMPL.
OLEIVERB_DISCARD-UNDOSTATE	Used to tell objects to discard any undo state that they may be maintaining without deactivating the object.

Any positive verb number that is not understood by the object should be treated as synonymous with the primary verb and OLE_S_INVALIDVERB returned. Negative verbs that are not understood should be ignored and E_NOTIMPL returned.

If the verb was invoked by some means other than a menu selection, the caller passes the Apple Event that caused the verb to be invoked through *pEvt*. On a double-click, an Event Record structure containing WM_LBUTTONDBLCLK, WM_MBUTTONDBLCLK, or WM_RBUTTONDBLCLK should be passed. If there is no event, *pEvt* should be NULL. The object should not examine the *pWnd* member of the passed Event Record structure. All of the other Event Record members, however, can be used.

Like the **OleActivate** function in OLE 1, **IOleObject::DoVerb** automatically runs the object application. If an error occurs during verb execution, the object application is shut down.

When **IOleObject::DoVerb** is invoked on an OLE link, it may return OLE_E_CLASSDIFF or MK_CONNECTMANUALLY. The former error is returned when a link has been made to an object that has been subjected to some sort of conversion while the link was passive. The latter error is returned when the link source is located on a network drive that is not currently connected to the caller's machine. The only way to connect a link under these conditions is to first call **QueryInterface**, asking for **IOleLink**, allocate a bind context, and run the link source by calling **IOleLink::BindToSource**.

Container applications that do not support in-place activation can still play multimedia players in-place using the *pWndParent* and *lprcPosRect* parameters. Containers must pass valid *pWndParent* and *lprcPosRect* parameters to **IOleObject::DoVerb**.

See Also **IOleObject::EnumVerbs**, **OleRun**, **IOleLink::BindToSource**

IOleObject::EnumVerbs

HRESULT IOleObject::EnumVerbs(*ppenumOleVerb***)**
LPENUMOLEVERB ** ppenumOleVerb*

IOleObject::EnumVerbs enumerates the verbs available for an object in increasing order by verb number.

Parameters

ppenumOleVerb
Points to where the new enumerator should be returned.

Return Values

Value	Meaning
S_OK	Verb(s) enumerated successfully.
OLE_S _USEREG	Delegate to the default handler to use the entries in the Registration Database file to provide the enumeration.
OLEOBJ_E _NOVERBS	Object does not support any verbs.

Comments

The default handler's implementation of **IOleObject::EnumVerbs** uses the Registration Database file to enumerate an object's verbs. If an object application wants to use the default handler's implementation, it should return OLE_S_USEREG.

The enumeration returned is of type **IEnumOLEVERB**:

```
typedef Enum < OLEVERB > IEnumOLEVERB;
```

where **OLEVERB** is defined in ole2.h as follows:

```
typedef struct tagOLEVERB
{
    long            iVerb;
    char *          lpszVerbName;
    unsigned long   fuFlags;
    unsigned long   grfAttribs;
} OLEVERB;
```

The following table describes the **OLEVERB** members:

OLEVERB Member	Description
iVerb	Verb number being enumerated. If the object supports OLEIVERB_OPEN, OLEIVERB_SHOW and/or OLEIVERB_HIDE (or other predefined verb), these will be the first verbs enumerated, since they have the lowest verb numbers.
lpszVerbName	Name of the verb. On the Macintosh, the following metacharacters may be included: • ! which marks the menu item with the subsequent character • < which sets the character style of the item • (which disables the item The meta-characters / and ^ are not permitted.
fuFlags	On Windows, a group of flags taken from the flag constants beginning with MF_ defined in **AppendMenu**. Container should use these flags in building the object's verb menu. All flags defined in **AppendMenu** are supported except for: • MF_BITMAP • MF_OWNERDRAW • MF_POPUP
grfAttribs	Group of flag bits taken from the enumeration OLEVERBATTRIB. OLEVERBATTRIB_NEVERDIRTIES indicates that the execution of this verb can never cause the object to become dirty and require saving to persistent storage. OLEVERBATTRIB_ONCONTAINERMENU indicates that this verb should be placed on the container's menu of object verbs when the object is selected. OLEIVERB_HIDE, OLEIVERB_SHOW, and OLEIVERB_OPEN never have this value set.

See Also **IOleObject::DoVerb**

IOleObject::Update

HRESULT IOleObject::Update()

IOleObject::Update ensures that any data or view caches maintained within the object are up-to-date.

Return Values

Value	Meaning
S_OK	All caches are up-to-date.
E_FAIL	An unspecified error occurred.
OLE_E_CANT_BINDTOSOURCE	Cannot run object to get updated data.
CACHE_E_NOCACHE_UPDATED	No caches were updated.
CACHE_S_SOMECACHES_NOTUPDATED	Some caches were not updated.

Comments

When applied to an OLE link object, **IOleObject::Update** first finds the link source and gets a new presentation from it. This process may involve running one or more object applications, which could be time consuming.

With an embedded object, **IOleObject::Update** works recursively, calling **IOleObject::Update** on each of its linked and embedded objects and running the object if needed. To see if an object is up-to-date, containers call **IOleObject::IsUpToDate**.

See Also

IOleObject::IsUpToDate

IOleObject::IsUpToDate

HRESULT IOleObject::IsUpToDate()

IOleObject::IsUpToDate recursively checks whether or not an object is up-to-date.

Return Values

Value	Meaning
S_OK	Object is up-to-date.
S_FALSE	Object is not up-to-date.
OLE_E_UNAVAILABLE	Status of object cannot be determined in a timely manner.

Comments

A linked object can become out-of-date if the link source has been updated. An embedded object that contains links to other objects can also become out-of-date. In general, determining whether an object is out-of-date can be as expensive as actually updating the object. In these cases, **IOleObject::IsUpToDate** should return OLE_E_UNAVAILABLE rather than do a lengthy query. In those cases where the answer may be learned efficiently, the function can return either S_OK or S_FALSE.

See Also **IOleObject::UpDate**

IOleObject::GetUserClassID

HRESULT IOleObject::GetUserClassID(*pclsid***)**
LPCLSID *pclsid*

IOleObject::GetUserClassID returns the CLSID of the object that corresponds to the type returned in **IOleObject::GetUserType**.

Parameters

pclsid
Points to the CLSID to be returned.

Return Values

Value	Meaning
S_OK	CLSID returned successfully.
E_FAIL	An unspecified error occurred.

Comments

IOleObject::GetUserClassID returns the CLSID as the user knows it. For embedded objects this is always the CLSID that is persistently stored with the object and is returned by **IPersist::GetClassID**. For linked objects, this is the CLSID of the last bound link source.

If a Treat As operation is taking place, the CLSID returned is that of the application being emulated (also the CLSID that will be written into storage).

See Also **IOleObject::GetUserType**, **IPersist::GetClassID**, **CoTreatAsClass**

IOleObject::GetUserType

HRESULT IOleObject::GetUserType(*dwFormOfType, lpszUserType***)**
unsigned long *dwFormOfType*
char * * *lpszUserType*

IOleObject::GetUserType returns the human-readable string for an object's type, such as "Word Document."

Parameters

dwFormOfType
Specifies a value that describes the form of the user-presentable string. Values are taken from the **USERCLASSTYPE** enumeration. For more information, see the following comments.

lpszUserType
Points to the place where the address of type string will be placed. The caller must free *lpszUserType* using the current **IMalloc** instance.

Return Values

Value	Meaning
S_OK	User type successfully returned.
OLE_S_USEREG	Delegate to the default handler's implementation using the Registration Database file to provide the requested information.

Comments

The printable information returned is the same as for **IOleObject::GetUserClassID**, which returns the information in binary form.

The default handler's implementation of **IOleObject::GetUserType** uses the object's CLSID (*pclsid* returned by **IOleObject::GetUserClassID**) and *dwFormOfType* as a key into the Registration Database file. If an entry is found that matches the whole key, then the entry is returned. If only the CLSID part of the key is found, the lowest-numbered entry available (usually USERCLASSTYPE_FULL) is used. If the CLSID is not found or there are no user types registered for the class, the user type currently found in the object's storage is used.

An object application can delegate to the default handler by returning OLE_S_USEREG. If the user type name is an empty string, "Unknown Object" is returned.

The parameter *dwFormOfType* takes its value from the **USERCLASSTYPE** enumeration, which is defined in ole2.h as follows:

```
typedef enum tagUSERCLASSTYPE {
    USERCLASSTYPE_FULL       = 1,
    USERCLASSTYPE_SHORT      = 2,
    USERCLASSTYPE_APPNAME     = 3,
} USERCLASSTYPE;
```

USERCLASSTYPE values have the following meaning:

Value	Meaning
USERCLASSTYPE_FULL	Full type name of the class.
USERCLASSTYPE_SHORT	A short name (maximum of 15 characters) that is used for popup menus and the Links dialog box.
USERCLASSTYPE_APPNAME	The name of the application servicing the class and is used in the Result text in dialogs.

See Also

IOleObject::SetHostNames, **IOleObject::GetUserClassID**, **ReadFmtUserTypeStg**

IOleObject::SetExtent

HRESULT IOleObject::SetExtent(*dwAspect, lpsizel)*
unsigned long *dwAspect*
LPSIZEL *lpsizel*

IOleObject::SetExtent sets the rectangular limits (logical size) that an object has available in the container.

Parameters

dwAspect
Describes the aspect of the object whose limit is to be set; the value is obtained from the enumeration **DVASPECT**. Different aspects of the object may have different extents. The most common value is DVASPECT_CONTENT.

lpsizel
Specifies the size limit for the object.

Return Values

Value	Meaning
S_OK	Object has resized successfully.
E_FAIL	Object's size is fixed.
OLE_E_NOTRUNNING	Object is not running.

Comments

Containers call **IOleObject::SetExtent** to inform objects how much space is available to them. If possible, the object should compose itself accordingly. The units are in pixels.

IOleObject::SetExtent may only be called when the object is running. Therefore, if a container resizes while the object is not running, the container must remember to inform the object by calling **IOleObject::SetExtent** at a later time when the object is running. If the OLEMISC_RECOMPOSEONRESIZE bit is set, the container should force the object to run before calling **IOleObject::SetExtent**.

If the object's size is fixed (that is, cannot be set by its container), **IOleObject::SetExtent** should return E_FAIL.

See Also

IOleObject::GetExtent, **IViewObject2::GetExtent**

IOleObject::GetExtent

HRESULT IOleObject::GetExtent(*dwAspect, lpsizel*)
unsigned long *dwAspect*
LPSIZEL *lpsizel*

IOleObject::GetExtent gets an object's current extent, that is, the extent that the object will actually use.

Parameters

dwAspect
Describes the aspect of the object whose limit is to be retrieved; the value is obtained from the enumeration **DVASPECT**. For more information, see the discussion of **DVASPECT** in Chapter 7, "Data Transfer/Caching Interfaces and Functions."

lpsizel
Points to where the object's extent is to be returned.

Return Values

Value	Meaning
S_OK	Extent information successfully returned.
E_INVALIDARG	Invalid value for *dwAspect*.

The extent returned from **IOleObject::GetExtent** may differ from the one last set by **IOleObject::SetExtent**. To the running object, **IOleObject::SetExtent** offers advice on what rectangle to use.

To get the extent from the cache, call **IViewObject2::GetExtent**.

See Also

IOleObject::SetExtent, **IViewObject2::GetExtent**

IOleObject::Advise

HRESULT IOleObject::Advise(*pAdvise, pdwConnection***)**
LPADVISESINK *pAdvise*
unsigned long * *pdwConnection*

IOleObject::Advise sets up an advisory connection between the object and an advisory sink through which the sink can be informed of events that happen in the object.

Parameters

pAdvise
Points to the advisory sink that should be informed of changes.

pdwConnection
Points to a token that can be passed to **IOleObject::Unadvise** to delete the advisory connection.

Return Values

Value	Meaning
S_OK	Advisory connection set up successfully.
E_OUTOFMEMORY	Cannot set up the connection due to lack of memory.

Comments

When an advisory sink registers for notifications using this call, the advisory sink will receive compound document (OLE) notifications via a call to the appropriate method in the sink's implementation of the **IAdviseSink** and/or **IAdviseSink2** interfaces.

Objects can take advantage of the functionality provided by **IOleAdviseHolder** interface, implemented by OLE, in their implementation of **IOleObject::Advise**, **IOleObject::Unadvise**, and **IOleobject::EnumAdvise**.

If an advisory connection is successfully set up, the callee returns a non-zero value through *pdwConnection* (if a connection fails to be established, zero is returned). The connection can be deleted by passing this non-zero token back to the object in a call to **IOleObject::Unadvise**.

See Also **IOleObject::UnAdvise**, **IOleObject::EnumAdvise**, **IOleAdviseHolder::Advise**

IOleObject::Unadvise

HRESULT IOleObject::Unadvise(*dwConnection*)
unsigned long *dwConnection*

IOleObject::Unadvise deletes an advisory connection previously established with **IOleObject::Advise**.

Parameters

dwConnection
Contains a non-zero value previously returned from **IOleObject::Advise** through its *pdwConnection* parameter.

Return Values

Value	Meaning
S_OK	Connection removed successfully.
E_FAIL	**IOleAdviseHolder** instance no longer available.
OLE_E _NOCONNECTION	*dwConnection* is not a valid connection ID.

See Also **IOleObject::Advise**, **IOleObject::EnumAdvise**

IOleObject::EnumAdvise

HRESULT IOleObject::EnumAdvise(*ppenumStatData*)
LPENUMSTATDATA * *ppenumStatData*

IOleObject::EnumAdvise enumerates the advisory connections registered for an object.

Parameters

ppenumStatData
Points to where the new enumerator should be returned. NULL is a legal return value; it indicates that the object does not have any advisory connections.

Return Values

Value	Meaning
S_OK	Enumerator returned successfully.
E_FAIL	**IOleAdviseHolder** instance no longer available.

Comments

IOleObject::EnumAdvise enumerates items of type **STATDATA**, which is defined in dvobj.h as follows:

```
typedef struct STRUCT tagSTATDATA
{
    FORMATETC        formatEtc;
    unsigned long    advf;
    LPADVISESINK     pAdvise;
    unsigned long    dwConnection;
} STATDATA;
```

While an enumeration is in progress, the effect of registering or revoking advisory connections on what is to be enumerated is undefined.

See Also

IOleObject::Advise, **IOleObject::UnAdvise**

IOleObject::GetMiscStatus

HRESULT IOleObject::GetMiscStatus(*dwAspect, pdwStatus***)**
unsigned long *dwAspect*
unsigned long * *pdwStatus*

IOleObject::GetMiscStatus returns status information about an object.

Parameters

dwAspect
Specifies the aspect of the object against which status information is being requested. The value is from the enumeration **DVASPECT**. For more information, see the discussion of **DVASPECT** in Chapter 7, "Data Transfer/Caching Interfaces and Functions."

pdwStatus
Points to where the status information is returned. May not be NULL.

Return Values

Value	Meaning
S_OK	Information returned successfully.
OLE_S_USEREG	Delegate to the default handler implementation to retrieve the MiscStatus information from the Registration Database file.
CO_E_CLASSNOTREG	There is no CLSID registered for the object.
CO_E_READREGDB	Error accessing the Registration Database file.

Comments

Objects store status information in the Registration Database file which the default handler's implementation of **IOleObject::GetMiscStatus** retrieves if the object is not running. If the object is running, the default handler calls **IOleObject::GetMiscStatus** on the running object.

The information stored varies depending on the object; the status values that can be returned are taken from the enumeration **OLEMISC**, which is defined in ole2.h:

```
typedef enum tagOLEMISC
{
    OLEMISC_RECOMPOSEONRESIZE              = 1,
    OLEMISC_ONLYICONIC                     = 2,
    OLEMISC_INSERTNOTREPLACE               = 4,
    OLEMISC_STATIC                         = 8,
    OLEMISC_CANTLINKINSIDE                 = 16,
    OLEMISC_CANLINKBYOLE1                  = 32,
    OLEMISC_ISLINKOBJECT                    = 64,
    OLEMISC_INSIDEOUT                      = 128,
    OLEMISC_ACTIVATEWHENVISABLE            = 256,
    OLEMISC_RENDERINGISDEVICEINDEPENDENT   = 512,
    } OLEMISC;
```

OLEMISC values have the following meanings:

Value	Description
OLEMISC_RECOMPOSE-ONRESIZE	If true, signifies that when the size that the container allocates to the object changes, the object would like the opportunity to recompose its picture. When resize occurs, the object is likely to do something other than scale its picture. The container should force the object to run so it can call **IOleObject::GetExtent.**
OLEMISC_ONLYICONIC	This object has no useful content view other than its icon. From the user's perspective, the Display As Icon checkbox (in the Paste Special dialog box) for this object should always be checked. Note that such an object should still have a drawable content aspect; it will look the same as its icon view.
OLEMISC_INSERTNOT-REPLACE	Indicates that this is the kind of object that when inserted into a document should be inserted beside the selection instead of replacing it. An object which linked itself to the selection with which it was initialized would set this bit. Containers should examine this bit after they have initialized the object with the selection. See **IOleObject::InitFromData**.

Value	Description
OLEMISC_STATIC	Indicates that this object is a static object. See **OleCreateStaticFromData**.
OLEMISC_CANTLINKINSIDE	Indicates that this is the kind of object that should not be the link source that when bound to runs the object. That is, if when the object is selected, its container wishes to offer the Link Source format in a data transfer, then the link, when bound, must connect to the outside of the object. The user would see the object selected in its container, not open for editing. Some objects that do not want to implement being the source of a link when they are embedded may want to set this bit.
OLEMISC_CANLINKBYOLE1	Indicates that this object can be linked to by OLE 1 containers. This bit is used in the *dwStatus* field of the OBJECTDESCRIPTOR structure transferred with the Object and Link Source Descriptor formats. An object can be linked by OLE 1 if it is not an embedded object or pseudo object contained within an embedded object.
OLEMISC_ISLINKOBJECT	This object is a link object. This bit is significant to OLE and is set by the OLE 2 link object; object applications have no need to set this bit.
OLEMISC_INSIDEOUT	This object is capable of activating in-place and running, without requiring installation of menus and toolbars. Several such objects can be active concurrently. Some containers, such as forms, may choose to activate such objects automatically.
OLEMISC_ACTIVATE-WHENVISIBLE	This bit is set only when OLEMISC_INSIDEOUT is set, and indicates that this object prefers to be activated whenever it is visible. Some containers may always ignore this hint.
OLEMISC_RENDERINGIS-DEVICEINDEPENDENT	This object does not pay any attention to target devices. Its presention data will be the same in all cases.

See Also **IViewObject::Draw**

IOleObject::SetColorScheme

HRESULT IOleObject::SetColorScheme(*lpLogPal***)**
LOGPALETTE * *lpLogPal*

IOleObject::SetColorScheme specifies the color palette that the object application should use when it edits the specified object.

Parameters

lpLogPal
Points to a container-defined **LOGPALETTE** structure that specifies the recommended color palette.

Return Values

Value	Meaning
S_OK	Color palette received successfully.
E_NOTIMPL	Object does not support setting palettes.
OLE_E _PALETTE	Invalid LOGPALETTE structure pointed to by *lpLogPal*.
OLE_E _NOTRUNNING	Object must be running to perform this operation.

Comments

IOleObject::SetColorScheme sends the object application the color palette recommended by the container; the object application does not have to use the recommended palette.The object application should:

1. Allocate and fill in its own **LOGPALETTE** structure that contains the colors passed via *lpLogPal*.
2. Create a palette from the **LOGPALETTE** structure. This palette can be used to render objects and color menus as the user edits objects in the document.

The first palette entry in the **LOGPALETTE** structure specifies the foreground color recommended by the container. The second palette entry specifies the background color. The first half of the remaining palette entries is fill colors and the second half is colors for the lines and text.

Container applications typically specify an even number of palette entries. When there is an uneven number of entries, the server should round up to the fill colors; that is, if there are five entries, the first three should be interpreted as fill colors and the last two as line and text colors.

IRunnableObject Interface

The **IRunnableObject** interface is implemented by object handlers and DLL object applications. The **IRunnableObject** interface supports the handling of silent updates and is also used by handlers and DLL object applications to find out when to transition into the running state and when to become a contained object.

In the running state, the DLL object application must keep a lock on the container (by calling **IOleContainer::LockContainer**), just as the default object handler does. This is necessary to make linking to embedded objects work correctly.

The **IRunnableObject** interface contains the following methods:

```
DECLARE_INTERFACE_(IRunnableObject, IUnknown)
{
 // *** IUnknown methods ***
 HRESULT QueryInterface (REFIID riid, void * * ppvObj);
 unsigned long AddRef () ;
 unsigned long Release ();

 // *** IRunnableObject methods ***
 HRESULT GetRunningClass (LPCLSID pclsid);
 HRESULT Run (LPBINDCTX lpbc);
 unsigned long IsRunning ();
 HRESULT LockRunning (unsigned long flock, unsigned long fLastUnlockCloses);
 HRESULT SetContainedObject (unsigned long fContained);
}
```

For more information, see the ole2.h header file.

IRunnableObject::GetRunningClass

HRESULT IRunnableObject::GetRunningClass(*pclsid***)**
LPCLSID *pclsid*;

IRunnableObject::GetRunningClass returns the CLSID of the embedded object.

Parameters

pclsid
Points to where to return the CLSID of the object.

Return Values

Value	Meaning
S_OK	CLSID was returned successfully.
E_INVALIDARG	One or more arguments are invalid.
E_UNEXPECTED	An unexpected error occurred.

Comments

In cases where the object is being emulated as a different object class (through a call to **CoTreatAsClass**), the CLSID returned is that of the object that is actually running. For example, suppose that ABC is emulating an XYZ object; calling **IRunnableObject::GetRunningClass** on XYZ would return the CLSID of ABC.

See Also

CoTreatAsClass

IRunnableObject::Run

HRESULT IRunnableObject::Run(*lpbc*)
LPBINDCTX *lpbc*

IRunnableObject::Run puts an object in its running state.

Parameters

lpbc
Points to the bind context for the run operation; may be NULL.

Return Values

Value	Meaning
S_OK	The object was successfully put into its running state.
E_OUTOFMEMORY	Out of memory.
E_UNEXPECTED	An unexpected error occurred.

Comments

If the object is not already running, calling **IRunnableObject::Run** can be an expensive operation, on the order of many seconds. If the object is already running, then this method has no effect on the object.

The object should register in the running object table if it has a moniker assigned. The object should not hold any strong locks on itself; instead, it should remain in the unstable, unlocked state and should be locked when the first external connection is made to the object. As part of their **IRunnableObject::Run** implementation, handlers and DLL object applications should call **IOleContainer::LockContainer**(TRUE) to lock the object.

When called on a linked object, **IRunnableObject::Run** may return OLE_E_CLASSDIFF in cases when the link has been made to an object that has been converted to a new class of object since the link was last activated. In this case, if the client wants to continue, it should call **IOleLink::BindToSource** before proceeding.

OleRun is a helper function that wraps the functionality offered by this method. It calls **QueryInterface**, asking for **IRunnableObject**, followed by a call to **IRunnableObject::Run**.

See Also

OleRun

IRunnableObject::IsRunning

unsigned long IRunnableObject::IsRunning()

IRunnableObject::IsRunning determines whether or not an object is currently in the running state.

Return Values

Value	Meaning
TRUE	The object is in its running state.
FALSE	The object is not in its running state.

Comments

OleIsRunning is a helper function that wraps the functionality offered by this method. It calls **QueryInterface**, asking for **IRunnableObject**, followed by a call to **IRunnableObject::IsRunning**.

See Also

OleIsRunning

IRunnableObject::LockRunning

HRESULT IRunnableObject::LockRunning(*fLock*, *fLastUnlockCloses***)**
unsigned long *fLock*
unsigned long *fLastUnlockCloses*

IRunnableObject::LockRunning locks an already-running object into its running state or unlocks it from its running state.

Parameters

fLock
TRUE locks the object into its running state, FALSE unlocks the object from its running state.

fLastUnlockCloses
Specifies how the object should be closed. TRUE closes the object if this is the last unlock on the object; FALSE leaves the object in its locked state.

Return Values

Value	Meaning
S_OK	The object was either locked or unlocked, depending on the value of *fLock*.
E_FAIL	The object was not running.
E_OUTOFMEMORY	Out of memory.
E_INVALIDARG	One or more arguments are invalid.
E_UNEXPECTED	An unexpected error occurred.

Comments

Most implementations of **IRunnableObject::LockRunning** will call **CoLockObjectExternal**.

See Also

CoLockObjectExternal

IRunnableObject::SetContainedObject

HRESULT IRunnableObject::SetContainedObject(*fContained***)**
unsigned long *fContained*

IRunnableObject::SetContainedObject indicates that the object is contained as an embedding in an OLE container.

Parameters

fContained
TRUE specifes that the object is contained in an OLE container; FALSE that it is not.

Return Values

Value	Meaning
S_OK	Object has been marked as a contained embedding.
E_OUTOFMEMORY	Out of memory.
E_INVALIDARG	One or more arguments are invalid.
E_UNEXPECTED	An unexpected error occurred.

Comments

IRunnableObject::SetContainedObject is called with *fContained* set to TRUE by embedding containers after calling **OleLoad**, or **OleCreate**. Normally, embedding containers call **IRunnableObject::SetContainedObject** with *fContained* set to TRUE once and never call it again, even before they close. Consequently, the use of this method with *fContained* set to FALSE is rare.

By default, all external connections to an object are strong reference locks in that the external connection controls the lifetime of the object. Calling **IRunnableObject::SetContainedObject** on a strong external connection transitions the strong lock to a weak lock, allowing other connections to determine the fate of the object while it is invisible. When an object is visible, it is controlled by **OleNoteObjectVisible(***pUnk*, TRUE) or **CoLockObjectExternal**.

OleSetContainedObject is a helper function that wraps the functionality offered by this method.

See Also

OleSetContainedObject, **OleNoteObjectVisible**, **CoLockObjectExternal**

Compound Document Functions

The functions described in this section are used by container and object applications to manage and send OLE notifications and to control the state of a compound document object. These functions are defines as follows:

```
HRESULT CreateOleAdviseHolder(LPOLEADVISEHOLDER * ppOAHolder);
unsigned long OleIsRunning(LPOLEOBJECT pOleObject);
HRESULT OleRun(LPUNKNOWN pUnk);
```

```
HRESULT OleLockRunning(LPUNKNOWN pUnk, unsigned long fLock, unsigned long fLastUnlockCloses);
HRESULT OleNoteObjectVisible(LPUNKNOWN pUnk, unsigned long fVisible);
HRESULT OleSetContainedObject(LPUNKNOWN pUnk, unsigned long fContained);
```

For more information, see the ole2.h header file.

CreateOleAdviseHolder

HRESULT CreateOleAdviseHolder(*ppOAHolder***)**
LPOLEADVISEHOLDER * *ppOAHolder*

CreateOleAdviseHolder returns an instance of the **IOleAdviseHolder** interface.

Parameters

ppOAHolder
Points to where to return the new **IOleAdviseHolder** instance.

Return Values

Value	Meaning
S_OK	**IOleAdviseHolder** instance returned successfully.
E_OUTOFMEMORY	Cannot return the **IOleAdviseHolder** instance because there is not enough memory.

OleIsRunning

unsigned long OleIsRunning(*pOleObject***)**
LPOLEOBJECT *pOleObject*

OleIsRunning determines whether an object is running.

Parameters

pOleObject
Points to the object in question.

Return Values

Value	Meaning
TRUE	Object is running.
FALSE	Object is not running.

Comments

OleIsRunning is a helper function that wraps the functionality offered by **IRunnableObject::IsRunning** and can be called in place of that method.

See Also

IRunnableObject::IsRunning

OleRun

HRESULT OleRun(*pUnk***)**
LPUNKNOWN *pUnk*

OleRun puts an object in the running state if it is not already running.

Parameters

pUnk
Points to the object that should be made running.

Return Values

Value	Meaning
S_OK	The object was successfully placed in the running state.
OLE_E_CLASSDIFF	Source of an OLE link has been converted.

Comments

If the object is not already in the running state, calling **OleRun** can be expensive since the object application must be launched. Calling **OleRun** has no effect if the object is already running.

When invoked on an OLE link object, **OleRun** may return OLE_E_CLASSDIFF, which indicates that the link source has been converted while the link has been passive. The caller can call **IOleLink::BindToSource** to proceed in this case.

OleRun is a helper function that wraps the functionality offered by **IRunnableObject::Run**.

See Also

IRunnableObject::Run

OleLockRunning

HRESULT OleLockRunning(*pUnk, fLock, fLastUnlockCloses***)**
LPUNKNOWN *pUnk*
unsigned long *fLock*
unsigned long *fLastUnlockCloses*

OleLockRunning locks an object into its running state or unlocks it from its running state.

Parameters

pUnk
Points to the object that is to be locked or unlocked.

fLock
TRUE locks the object into its running state, FALSE unlocks the object from its running state.

fLastUnlockCloses
Specifies how the object should be closed. TRUE closes the object if this is the last unlock on the object; FALSE leaves the object in its locked state.

Return Values

Value	Meaning
S_OK	The object was either locked or unlocked, depending on the value of *fLock*.
E_OUTOFMEMORY	Out of memory.
E_INVALIDARG	One or more arguments are invalid.
E_UNEXPECTED	An unexpected error occurred.

Comments

OleLockRunning is a helper function that wraps the functionality offered by **IRunnableObject::LockRunning**.

See Also

IRunnableObject::LockRunning

OleNoteObjectVisible

HRESULT OleNoteObjectVisible(*pUnk, fVisible***)**
LPUNKNOWN *pUnk*
unsigned long *fVisible*

OleNoteObjectVisible locks a visible object such that its reference count cannot decrement to zero; the function is also called to release such a lock.

Parameters

pUnk
Points to the object that is to be locked or unlocked.

fVisible
Indicates whether the object is visible. If TRUE, OLE holds the object visible and alive regardless of external or internal **AddRef** and **Release** operations, registrations, or revokes. If FALSE, OLE releases its hold and the object can lose visibility.

Return Values

Value	Meaning/Occurance
S_OK	Object locked or unlocked successfully.
E_OUTOFMEMORY	Lock/unlock operation could not be completed due to lack of memory.
E_INVALIDARG	One or more arguments are invalid.
E_UNEXPECTED	Lock/unlock operation could not be completed for reasons other than lack of memory or invalid arguments.

Comments

OleNoteObjectVisible is a wrapper for a call to **CoLockObjectExternal** (*pUnk*, *fVisible*, *TRUE*). It is provided as a separate API to reinforce the need to lock an object when it becomes visible to the user and to release the object when it becomes invisible.

Sophisticated objects may want to call **CoLockObjectExternal** directly.

See Also

CoLockObjectExternal

OleSetContainedObject

HRESULT OleSetContainedObject(*pUnk, fContained***)**
LPUNKNOWN *pUnk*
unsigned long *fContained*

OleSetContainedObject indicates that the object is contained as an embedding and facilitates linking to embedded objects.

Parameters

pUnk
Points to the object that is a contained embedding.

fContained
TRUE if the object is an embedded object; FALSE otherwise.

Return Values

Value	Meaning
S_OK	Object has been marked as a contained embedding.
E_OUTOFMEMORY	Object could not be marked as a contained embedding due to lack of memory.
E_INVALIDARG	One or more arguments are invalid.
E_UNEXPECTED	An unexpected error happened.

Comments

Normally containers call **OleSetContainedObject** with *fContained* set to TRUE one time, either after creating the object initially or after loading it, and never call it again, even before they close. Consequently, the use of **OleSetContainedObject** with *fContained* set to FALSE is rare.

Calling **OleSetContainedObject** is optional only when you know that the embedded object will not be reference by any client other than the container.

Although it is preferable that a container application that does not support linking to embedded objects call **OleSetContainedObject**, it is not necessary. However, a container application that does support linking to embedded objects must call this function.

If the container application does not call **OleSetContainedObject** on the object, the container will not shut down properly when another linking client does a silent update, such as when the user chooses Update Now in the Links dialog box. The reference from the container to the embedded object provided by **OleSetContainedObject** will keep the object alive and not let it shut down during a silent update.

Any external connection(s) to the embedded object start out strong (locked). Becoming a contained object weakens (unlocks) the connection(s) so that other connections can determine the fate of the object while it is visible.

OleSetContainedObject is a helper function that wraps the functionality offered by **IRunnableObject::SetContainedObject**.

See Also

IRunnableObject::SetContainedObject

Object Creation Functions

OLE provides several functions that create or aid in the creation of compound document object of different types. These functions are defined as follows:

```
HRESULT OleCreate(REFCLSID rclsid, REFIID riid, unsigned long renderopt, LPFORMATETC pFormatetc,
        LPOLECLIENTSITE pClientSite, LPSTORAGE pStg, void * * ppvObj);
```

```
HRESULT OleCreateDefaultHandler(REFCLSID rclsid, LPUNKNOWN pUnkOuter, REFIID riid, void * * ppvObj);
HRESULT OleCreateEmbeddingHelper(REFCLSID rclsid, LPUNKNOWN pUnkOuter, unsigned long flags,
    LPCLASSFACTORY pCF, REFIID riid, void * * ppvObj);
HRESULT OleCreateFromData(LPDATAOBJECT pDataObject, REFIID riid, unsigned long renderopt,
    LPFORMATETC pFormatetc, LPOLECLIENTSITE pClientSite, LPSTORAGE pStg, void * * ppvObj);
HRESULT OleCreateFromFile(REFCLSID rclsid, const char * lpszFileName, REFIID riid, unsigned long renderopt,
    LPFORMATETC lpFormatetc, LPOLECLIENTSITE pClientSite, LPSTORAGE pStg, void * * ppvObj);
HRESULT OleCreateFromFSp(REFCLSID rclsid, const FSSpec * pSpec, REFIID riid, unsigned long renderopt,
    LPFORMATETC lpFormatetc, LPOLECLIENTSITE pClientSite, LPSTORAGE pStg, void * * ppvObj);
HRESULT OleCreateLink(LPMONIKER pmk, REFIID riid, unsigned long renderopt, LPFORMATETC lpFormatetc,
    LPOLECLIENTSITE pClientSite, LPSTORAGE pStg, void * * ppvObj);
HRESULT OleCreateLinkFromData(LPDATAOBJECT pDataObject, REFIID riid, unsigned long renderopt,
    LPFORMATETC pFormatetc, LPOLECLIENTSITE pClientSite, LPSTORAGE pStg, void * * ppvObj);
HRESULT OleCreateLinkToFile(const char * lpszFileName, REFIID riid, unsigned long renderopt,
    LPFORMATETC lpFormatetc, LPOLECLIENTSITE pClientSite, LPSTORAGE pStg, void * * ppvObj);
HRESULT OleCreateLinkToFSp(const FSSpec * pFSSpec, REFIID riid, unsigned long renderopt,
    LPFORMATETC lpFormatetc, LPOLECLIENTSITE pClientSite, LPSTORAGE pStg, void * * ppvObj);
HRESULT OleCreateStaticFromData(LPDATAOBJECT pDataObject, REFIID iid, unsigned long renderopt,
    LPFORMATETC pFormatetc, LPOLECLIENTSITE pClientSite, LPSTORAGE pStg, void * * ppvObj);
HRESULT OleQueryLinkFromData(LPDATAOBJECT pDataObject);
HRESULT OleQueryCreateFromData(LPDATAOBJECT pDataObject);
unsigned long OleQueryCreateAll(LPDATAOBJECT lpSrcDataObj, unsigned long * pdwResult);
```

For more information, see the ole2.h header file.

Object Creation Parameters

Many of the object creation functions have parameters in common. The following table defines these parameters as they are used in the majority of the functions. For each function where the usage is different, additional comments are included with the description of the function.

Parameter	Description
renderopt	Indicates the caching that the container wants in the newly created object. Valid values are taken from the enumeration **OLERENDER**.
pDataObject	Points to the data transfer object from which a compound document object is to be created.
pFormatetc	Points to the data formats and medium information that control the caching to be done in the newly created object.
riid	Contains the interface to be used to communicate with the new object. The most common value is IID_IOleObject.

Parameter	Description
pClientSite	Points to the client site. May be NULL. If NULL, the caller must call **IOleObject::SetClientSite** before attempting any operations. If non-NULL, **OleCreate** calls **IOleObject::SetClientSite** before returning.
ppvObj	Points to the place at which the newly created instance of *riid* should be returned.
pStg	Points to the storage that will be used for the object. May not be NULL.
pStg	

The enumeration **OLERENDER** is defined in ole2.h as follows:

```
typedef enum tagOLERENDER
{
        OLERENDER_NONE          = 0,
        OLERENDER_DRAW          = 1,
        OLERENDER_FORMAT        = 2,
        OLERENDER_ASIS          = 3
} OLERENDER;
```

For most of the creation functions, **OLERENDER** values have the following meaning:

Value	Meaning
OLERENDER_NONE	The container is not requesting any locally cache drawing or data retrieval capabilities in the object. *pFormatetc* is ignored for this option.
OLERENDER_DRAW	The container will draw the contents of the object on the screen (a NULL target device) using **IViewObject::Draw**. The object determines the data formats that need to be cached. Only the *ptd* and *dwAspect* members of *pFormatetc* are significant, since the object may cache things differently depending on the parameter values. However, *pFormatetc* can legally be NULL here, in which case the object is to assume the display target device and the DVASPECT_CONTENT aspect.

Value	Meaning
OLERENDER_FORMAT	The container will pull one format from the object using **IDataObject::GetData**. The format of the data to be cached is passed in *pFormatetc*, which may not in this case be NULL.
OLERENDER_ASIS	The container is not requesting any locally cache drawing or data retrieval capabilities in the object. *pFormatetc* is ignored for this option. The difference between this and OLERENDER_NONE is important in other helper functions such as **OleCreateFromData** and **OleCreateLinkFromData**.

Some of the API functions have different or additional semantics for these values. Appropriate comments are included with each function description.

OleCreate

HRESULT OleCreate(*rclsid, riid, renderopt, pFormatetc, pClientSite, lpStg, ppvObj*)
REFCLSID *rclsid*
REFIID *riid*
unsigned long *renderopt*
LPFORMATETC *pFormatetc*
LPOLECLIENTSITE *pClientSite*
LPSTORAGE *lpStg*
void * * *ppvObj*

OleCreate creates an embedded object of a specified class. This method is typically used in implementing the Insert New Object scenario.

Parameters

rclsid
Specifies the CLSID of the embedded object that is to be created.

For a description of the *riid*, *renderopt*, *pFormatetc*, *pClientSite*,*lpStg*, and *ppvObj* parameters, see the section "Object Creation Parameters."

Return Values

Value	Meaning
S_OK	Embedded object created successfully.
E_OUTOFMEMORY	Embedded object cannot be created due to lack of memory.

Comments

When **OleCreate** returns, the object is blank and in the loaded state. Containers typically then call **OleRun** or **IOleObject::DoVerb** to show the object for initial editing.

The cache is not necessarily filled by the time that **OleCreate** returns. Instead, the cache is filled as appropriate for the passed *renderopt* and *pFormatetc* the first time the object enters the running state.

Between the return of **OleCreate** and a subsequent running of the object, the caller may add additional caching control by calling **IOleCache::Cache**.

See Also **IOleCache::Cache**

OleCreateDefaultHandler

HRESULT OleCreateDefaultHandler(*rclsid, pUnkOuter, riid, ppvObj*)
REFCLSID *rclsid*
LPUNKNOWN *pUnkOuter*
REFIID *riid*
**void * ** *ppvObj*

OleCreateDefaultHandler creates a new instance of the default handler to service the specified object class.

Parameters

rclsid
Specifies the CLSID of the object class to be loaded.

pUnkOuter
Points to the controlling IUnknown if the handler is to be aggregated; NULL if it is not to be aggregated.

For a description of the *riid* and *ppvObj* parameters, see the section "Object Creation Parameters."

Return Values

Value	Meaning
S_OK	Default handler created successfully.
E_OUTOFMEMORY	Default handler cannot be created due to lack of memory.

Comments

OleCreateDefaultHandler initializes the new default handler instance in such a way that when the running state needs to be entered, a local server of class *rclsid* will be created.

Calling **OleCreateDefaultHandler** is the same as calling **CoCreateInstance**(*rclsid, pUnkOuter, CLSCTX_INPROC_HANDLER, riid, ppvObj*) if the given class does not have a special object class handler.

OleCreateDefaultHandler is used internally when the *rclsid* is not registered and by handler writers that want to use the services of the default handler.

OleCreateEmbeddingHelper

HRESULT OleCreateEmbeddingHelper(*rclsid, pUnkOuter, flags, pCF, riid, ppvObj*)
REFCLSID *rclsid*
LPUNKNOWN *pUnkOuter*
unsigned long *flags*
LPCLASSFACTORY *pCF*
REFIID *riid*
void * * *ppvObj*

OleCreateEmbeddingHelper creates an embedding helper object using code supplied by the application which is then aggregated with pieces of the OLE default object handler. The resulting helper object can be used in a specific context and role, as determined by the caller.

Parameters

rclsid
Specifies the CLSID of the object class that is to be helped.

pUnkOuter
Points to the controlling **IUnknown** if the handler is to be aggregated; NULL if it is not to be aggregated.

flags
Specifies the role and creation context for the embedding helper; see the following comments for legal values.

pCF
Points to the application's **IClassFactory** instance; can be NULL.

riid
Specifies the interface ID of the desired by the caller.

ppvObj
Points to where to return the newly created embedding helper.

Return Values

Value	Meaning
S_OK	Embedding helper was created successfully.
E_NOINTERFACE	Interface not supported by the object.
E_OUTOFMEMORY	Out of memory.
E_INVALIDARG	One or more arguments are invalid.
E_UNEXPECTED	An unexpected error occurred.

Comments

OleCreateEmbeddingHelper is used to create a new instance of the OLE default handler that can be used to support objects in various roles. The caller passes to **OleCreateEmbeddingHelper** a pointer to its **IClassFactory** implementation; this object and the default handler are then aggregated to create the new embedding helper object.

OleCreateEmbeddingHelper is usually used to support one of the following implementations:

- An object application is being used as both a container and an object application. In this case, the application registers its CLSID for different contexts by calling **CoRegisterClassObject** (*Clsid*, *lpUnk*, CLSCTX_LOCAL_SERVER | CLSCTX_INPROC_SERVER, REGCLS_MULTI_SEPARATE, *lpdwRegister*). The local class is used to create the object and the in-process class creates the embedding helper, passing in the pointer to the first object's class factory in *pCF*.
- An in-process object handler. In this case, the DLL creates the embedding helper by passing in a private class factory in *pCF*.

The *flags* parameter indicates how the embedding helper is to be used and how and when the embedding helper is initialized. The values for *flags* are obtained by OR'ing together values from the following table:

Values for *flags* Parameter	Purpose
EMBDHLP_INPROC_HANDLER	EMBDHLP_INPROC_HANDLER creates an embedding helper that is used with an EXE object application; specifiying this flag is the same as calling **OleCreateDefaultHandler**.
EMBDHLP_INPROC_SERVER	EMBDHLP_INPROC_SERVER creates an embedding helper that can be used with DLL object applications; specifically the helper exposes the caching features of the default object handler.
EMBDHLP_CREATENOW	EMBDHLP_CREATENOW creates the application-supplied piece immediately.
EMBDHLP_DELAYCREATE	EMBDHLP_DELAYCREATE delays creating the application-supplied piece until the object is put into its running state.

Calling

```
OleCreateEmbeddingHelper
    (rclsid, pUnkOuter, EMBDHLP_INPROC_HANDLER | EMBDHLP_CREATENOW,
    NULL, riid, ppvObj)
```

is the same as calling

```
OleCreateDefaultHandler(rclsid, pUnkOuter, riid, ppvObj)
```

See Also

OleCreateDefaultHandler

OleCreateFromData

HRESULT OleCreateFromData(*pDataObject, riid, renderopt, pFormatetc, pClientSite, pStg, ppvObj***)**
LPDATAOBJECT *pDataObject*
REFIID *riid*
unsigned long *renderopt*
LPFORMATETC *pFormatetc*
LPOLECLIENTSITE *pClientSite*
LPSTORAGE *pStg*
void * * *ppvObj*

OleCreateFromData creates an embedded object from a data transfer object retrieved either from the clipboard or as part of a drag and drop operation.

Parameters

pDataObject
Points to the data transfer object that holds the data from which the object will be created.

riid
Identifies the interface that the caller uses to communicate with the new object.

renderopt
Indicates the type of caching desired for the newly created object. The use of *renderopt* is as defined in the section "Object Creation Parameters," with the following additional comments that relate to how the new object's cache is initialized:

Value	Meaning
OLERENDER_DRAW and OLERENDER _FORMAT	If the format to be cached is currently present in the appropriate cache initialization pool (the old object for the Embedded Object format, the other formats in *pDataObject* for Embed Source), then it is used. If the format is not present, then the cache is initially empty, but will be filled the first time the object is run. No other formats are cached in the newly created object.
OLERENDER_NONE	The newly created object has nothing cached. In the Embedded Object case, any copied existing cached data is removed.
OLERENDER_ASIS	In the Embedded Object case, the new object has exactly those things cached within itself that the original old source object had cached within itself. In the Embed Source case, the newly created object has nothing cached. The idea is that this option is to be used by more sophisticated containers. After this call, such containers will call **IOleCache::Cache** and **IOleCache::Uncache** calls to set up exactly what they want cached. In the Embed Source case, they will then also call **IOleCache::InitCache**.

For information on the *riid*, *pClientSite*, *pStg*, *pFormatetc*, and *ppvObj* parameters, see the section "Object Creation Parameters."

Return Values

Value	Meaning
S_OK	Embedded object created successfully.
OLE_E_STATIC	OLE can only create a static object.
DV_E_FORMATETC	No acceptable formats are available for object creation.

Comments

The *renderopt* and *pFormatetc* parameters can be used by the caller to control the caching that is done in the newly created object. The interaction between *renderopt* and *pFormatetc* in determining what is to be cached is described in the **OleCreate** function.

OleCreateFromData makes use of either the Embedded Object or the Embed Source data formats in *pDataObject* to create the object. For more information on these clipboard formats, see Chapter 7, "Data Transfer/Caching Interfaces and Functions." The main difference between these two formats is where the appropriate cache-initialization data lies. In the Embedded Object case, the source is an existing embedded object; the cache inside the object itself has the appropriate data. In the Embed Source case, it is the formats available in *pDataObject* other than Embed Source which should initialize the cache.

If the FileName format is present in the data transfer object, **OleCreateFromData** creates a package containing the indicated file. This format is placed on the clipboard when the user selects the File Copy To menu command.

If a package is not made, **OleCreateFromData** tries to create an object using the Embedded Object format if it is available and the Embed Source format if the Embedded Object format is not available.

If neither of these formats are available and the data transfer object supports the **IPersistStorage** interface, **OleCreateFromData** calls **IPersistStorage::Save** to ask the object to save itself.

OleCreateFromFile

HRESULT OleCreateFromFile(*rclsid, lpszFileName, riid, renderopt, pFormatetc, pClientSite, pStg, ppvObj***)**

REFCLSID *rclsid*
const char * *lpszFileName*
REFIID *riid*
unsigned long *renderopt*
LPFORMATETC *pFormatetc*
LPOLECLIENTSITE *pClientSite*
LPSTORAGE *pStg*
void * * *ppvObj*

OleCreateFromFile creates an embedded object of the indicated class from the contents of a named file. The newly created object is not shown to the user for editing.

Parameters

rclsid
Reserved for future use. Must be CLSID_NULL.

lpszFile
Specifies the full path name of the file from which the object should be initialized.

For information about the *riid*, *renderopt*, *pFormatetc*, *pClientSite*, *pStg*, and *ppvObj* parameters, see the section "Object Creation Parameters."

Return Values

Value	Meaning
S_OK	Embedded object successfully created.
STG_E _FILENOTFOUND	File not bound.
OLE_E _CANT_BINDTOSOURCE	Not able to bind to source.
STG_E _MEDIUMFULL	The medium is full.
DV_E_TYMED	Invalid TYMED.
DV_E_LINDEX	Invalid LINDEX.
DV_E _FORMATETC	Invalid FORMATETC structure.
E_OUTOFMEMORY	OLE libraries have not been properly initialized.

Comments

OleCreateFromFile is used in the Insert File operation of the Insert Object dialog box. If the ProgID in the Registration Database file contains the PackageOnFileDrop key; **OLeCreateFromFile** creates a package; otherwise, it creates an OLE 2 embedded object as appropriate for the class of the file (see **GetClassFile**). If an embedded object is created, **OleCreateFromFile** creates a file moniker for the file.

Unless it can manage with no conversion of representation, **OleCreateFromFile** calls **IPersistFile::Load** on a new instance of *rclsid* to open the file. It then calls **QueryInterface** to access **IPersistStorage** and calls **IPersistStorage::Save**(..., FALSE, TRUE) to indicate to the object that it should convert representations.

Where applicable, applications should call **OleCreateFromFSp** instead of **OleCreateFromFile**.

OleCreateFromFSp

HRESULT OleCreateFromFSp(*rclsid, pFSSpec, riid, renderopt, pFormatetc, pClientSite, pStg, ppvObj*)

REFCLSID *rclsid*
const FSSpec * *pFSSpec*
REFIID *riid*
unsigned long *renderopt*
LPFORMATETC *pFormatetc*
LPOLECLIENTSITE *pClientSite*
LPSTORAGE *pStg*
void * * *ppvObj*

OleCreateFromFSp creates an embedded object of the indicated class from the contents of a named file specification. The newly created object is not shown to the user for editing.

Parameters

rclsid
Reserved for future use; must be CLSID_NULL.

pFSSpec
Specifies the file specification from which the object should be initialized.

For information about the *riid*, *renderopt*, *pFormatetc*, *pClientSite*, *pStg*, and *ppvObj* parameters, see the section "Object Creation Parameters."

Return Values

Value	Meaning
S_OK	Embedded object successfully created.
STG_E_FILENOTFOUND	File specification not bound.
OLE_E_CANT_BINDTO-SOURCE	Not able to bind to source.
STG_E_MEDIUMFULL	The medium is full.
DV_E_TYMED	Invalid TYMED.

Value	Meaning
DV_E_LINDEX	Invalid LINDEX.
DV_E_FORMATETC	Invalid **FORMATETC** structure.
E_OUTOFMEMORY	OLE libraries have not been properly initialized.

Comments

OleCreateFromFSp is used in the Insert File operation of the Insert Object dialog box. It creates either a package (if the ProgID in the Registration Database file contains the PackageOnFileDrop key) or an OLE 2 embedded object as appropriate for the class of the file specification (see **GetClassFile**). If an embedded object is created, **OleCreateFromFSp** creates a file moniker for the file specification.

Unless it can manage with no conversion of representation, **OleCreateFromFSp** calls **IPersistFile::Load** on a new instance of *rclsid* to open the file. It then calls **QueryInterface** to access **IPersistStorage** and calls **IPersistStorage::Save**(..., FALSE, TRUE) to indicate to the object that it should convert representations.

OleCreateLink

HRESULT OleCreateLink(*pmk, riid, renderopt, pFormatetc, pClientSite, pStg, ppvObj*)
LPMONIKER *pmk*
REFIID *riid*
unsigned long *renderopt*
LPFORMATETC *pFormatetc*
LPOLECLIENTSITE *pClientSite*
LPSTORAGE *pStg*
void * * *ppvObj*

OleCreateLink creates an OLE compound-document link object. The source of the link is initialized with *pmk*.

Parameters

pmk
Points to an **IMoniker** interface instance indicating the linked object's source.

For information about the *riid, renderopt, pFormatetc, pClientSite, pStg,* and *ppvObj* parameters, see the section "Object Creation Parameters."

Return Values

Value	Meaning
S_OK	The compound-document link object was created successfully.
OLE_E_CANT_BINDTO-SOURCE	Not able to bind to source. Binding is necessary to get cache's initialization data.

Comments

When a container creates a linked object, it should assign a moniker to the newly-created link and inform the link object of the moniker by calling **IOleObject::SetMoniker** (OLEWHICHMK_OBJREL, ...).

If the container doesn't already have a moniker, it should get one from its client site by calling **IOleClientSite::GetMoniker** (OLEGETMONIKER_FORCEASSIGN, ...). Once obtained, the container should inform the link of this moniker by calling **IOleObject::SetMoniker** (OLEWHICHMK_CONTAINER, ...).

In the event that the client site fails to give a moniker to the link's container, the container should assign a moniker to the link object that is relative to the link's container. This moniker is needed for link tracking to work. All link objects need to have monikers assigned to generate relative moniker paths.

OleCreateLinkFromData

HRESULT OleCreateLinkFromData(*pDataObject, riid, renderopt, pFormatetc, pClientSite, pStg, ppvObj***)**

LPDATAOBJECT *pDataObject*
REFIID *riid*
unsigned long *renderopt*
LPFORMATETC *pFormatetc*
LPOLECLIENTSITE *pClientSite*
LPSTORAGE *pStg*
void * * *ppvObj*

OleCreateLinkFromData creates a linked object from a data transfer object retrieved either from the clipboard or as part of a drag and drop operation.

Parameters

pDataObject
Points to the data transfer object from which the linked object is to be created.

For information about the *riid, renderopt, pFormatetc, pClientSite, pStg,* and *ppvObj* parameters, see the section "Object Creation Parameters."

Return Values

Value	Meaning
S_OK	The linked object was created successfully.
CLIPBRD_E_CANT_OPEN	Not able to open the clipboard.
OLE_E_CANT_GETMONIKER	Not able to extract object's moniker.
OLE_E_CANT_BINDTO-SOURCE	Not able to bind to source. Binding is necessary to get cache's initialization data.

Comments

OleCreateLinkFromData works similar to **OleCreateFromData** in that it creates a compound document object from a data transfer object. However, where **OleCreateFromData** uses the Embedded Object or Embed Source formats from the data transfer object, **OleCreateLinkFromData** uses the Link Source format. From the perspective of cache initialization, the Link Source format behaves like Embed Source.

If the FileName format is available, **OleCreateLinkFromData** creates a package containing a link to the indicated file. If a package cannot be made, **OleCreateLinkFromData** looks for the Link Source format with which to create a linked object.

See Also **OleCreateLink**

OleCreateLinkToFile

HRESULT OleCreateLinkToFile(*lpszFileName, riid, renderopt, pFormatetc, pClientSite, pStg, ppvObj***)**
const char * *lpszFileName*
REFIID *riid*
unsigned long *renderopt*
LPFORMATETC *pFormatetc*
LPOLECLIENTSITE *pClientSite*
LPSTORAGE *pStg*
void * * *ppvObj*

OleCreateLinkToFile creates an object that is linked to a file.

Parameters

lpszFileName
Points to the source file to be linked to.

For information about the *riid, renderopt, pFormatetc, pClientSite, pStg,* and *ppvObj* parameters, see the section "Object Creation Parameters."

Return Values

Value	Meaning
S_OK	The object was created successfully.
STG_E_FILENOTFOUND	File name is invalid.
OLE_E_CANT_BINDTO-SOURCE	Not able to bind to source.

Where appropriate, applications should call **OleCreateLinkToFSp** instead of **OleCreateLinkToFile**.

OleCreateLinkToFSp

HRESULT OleCreateLinkToFSp(*pFSSpec, riid, renderopt, pFormatetc, pClientSite, pStg, ppvObj***)**
const FSSpec * *pFSSpec*
REFIID *riid*
unsigned long *renderopt*
LPFORMATETC *pFormatetc*
LPOLECLIENTSITE *pClientSite*
LPSTORAGE *pStg*
void * * *ppvObj*

OleCreateLinkToFSp creates an object that is linked to a file specification.

Parameters

pFSSpec
Points to the file specification that is to be linked to.

For information about the *riid, renderopt, pFormatetc, pClientSite, pStg,* and *ppvObj* parameters, see the section "Object Creation Parameters."

Return Values

Value	Meaning
S_OK	The object was created successfully.
STG_E_FILENOTFOUND	File specification is invalid.
OLE_E_CANT_BINDTO-SOURCE	Not able to bind to source.

OleCreateStaticFromData

HRESULT OleCreateStaticFromData(*pDataObject, riid, renderopt, pFormatetc, pClientSite, pStg, ppvObj***)**

LPDATAOBJECT *pDataObject*
REFIID *riid*
unsigned long *renderopt*
LPFORMATETC *pFormatetc*
LPOLECLIENTSITE *pClientSite*
LPSTORAGE *pStg*
void * * *ppvObj*

OleCreateStaticFromData creates a static object from a data transfer object.

Parameters

pDataObject
Points to the data transfer object from which the object is to be created.

For information about the *riid, renderopt, pFormatetc, pClientSite, pStg,* and *ppvObj* parameters, see the section "Object Creation Parameters." It is an error to pass OLERENDER_NONE and OLERENDER_ASIS in *renderopt*.

Return Values

Value	Meaning
S_OK	The static object was created successfully.

Comments

Any object that provides an **IDataObject** interface can be converted to a static object using **OleCreateStaticFromData**. **OleCreateStaticFromData** is useful in implementing the Convert To Picture option for a link.

Static objects can be created only if the source supports the OLE rendered format: PICT.

Static objects can be pasted from the clipboard using **OleCreateStaticFromData**. **OleQueryCreateFromData** will return OLE_S_STATIC if PICT is present and an OLE format is not present. But **OleCreateFromData** will not automatically create the static object in this case, if the container wants to paste a static object it should call **OleCreateStaticFromData**.

The new static object is of class CLSID_StaticMetafile. The static object will set the OLEMISC_STATIC and OLE_CANTLINKINSIDE bits returned from **IOleObject::GetMiscStatus**. The static object will have the aspect DVASPECT_CONTENT and a *lindex* of -1.

The *pDataObject* will still be valid after **OleCreateStaticFromData** returns. It is the caller's reponsibility to free *pDataObject*; OLE does not release it.

There cannot be more than one presentation stream in a static object.

Note The OLESTREAM<->IStorage conversion API functions also convert static objects.

See Also **OleCreateFromData**

OleQueryCreateFromData

HRESULT OleQueryCreateFromData(*pDataObject***)**
LPDATAOBJECT *pDataObject*

OleQueryCreateFromData checks whether a container application can create an embedded object from the given data transfer object.

Parameters

pDataObject
Points to the data transfer object that will be queried.

Return Values

Value	Meaning
S_OK	Formats that support embedded object creation are present.
S_FALSE	No formats are present that support either embedded or static object creation.
OLE_S_STATIC	Formats that support static object creation are present.

Comments

Containers should use **OleQueryCreateFromData** with the data transfer object retrieved with **OleGetClipboard** as part of the process of deciding to enable or disable their Edit/Paste or Edit/Paste Special... commands. **OleCreateFromData** or **OleCreateStaticFromData** is used to actually create the object.

OleQueryCreateFromData tests for the presence of the following formats in the data object:

Embedded Object
Embed Source
cfFileName
CF_METAFILEPICT

OleQueryCreateFromData returns OLE_S_STATIC when CF_METAFILEPICT is available.

OleQueryCreateFromData does not test for the presence of these formats on the clipboard; it looks for the specified formats in the data transfer object. A successful return from **OleQueryCreateFromData** does not guarantee a subsequent successful return from **OleCreateFromData** or **OleCreateStaticFromData**.

OleQueryCreateAll

unsigned long OleQueryCreateAll(*lpSrcDataObj, pdwResult***)**
LPDATAOBJECT *lpSrcDataObj*
unsigned long * *pdwResult*

OleQueryCreateAll checks whether a container application can create an embedded or linked object using the contents on the clipboard.

Parameters

lpSrcDataObj
Points to the data transfer object that will be queried.

pdwResult
On return, pointer to a value indicating the type of object that can be created.

Return Values

Value	Meaning
OLE_CREATE_EMBED	Format that supports creating an embedded object present.
OLE_CREATE_STATIC	Formats that support static object creation are present.
OLE_CREATE_LINK	Format that supports creating a linking object present.

Comments

OleQueryCreateAll is a function that wraps the calls to **OleQueryCreateFromData** and **OleGetClipboard**. Applications should call **OleQueryCreateAll** to determine if they should enable or disable their Edit/Paste or Edit/Paste Special... commands.

If the clipboard supports the creating of an object, **OleCreateFromData**, **OleCreateStaticFromData**, or **OleCreateLinkFromData** can be used to actually create the object.

OleQueryLinkFromData

HRESULT OleQueryLinkFromData(*pDataObject***)**
LPDATAOBJECT *pDataObject*

OleQueryLinkFromData determines whether a linked object can be created from the data transfer object.

Parameters

pDataObject
Points to the data transfer object that is to be created.

Return Values

Value	Meaning
S_OK	Formats that support linked object creation are present.
S_FALSE	Formats that support embedded object creation are not present.

OLE Initialization Functions

The following functions are used to manage OLE 2:

```
unsigned long OleBuildVersion();
HRESULT OleInitialize(LPMALLOC pMalloc);
void OleUninitialize(void);
HRESULT InitOleManager(long dwflags);
unsigned long UninitOleManager(void);
unsigned long IsOleManagerRunning (void);
unsigned long OleInitDBCSCountry(int iCntry);
```

For more information, see the ole2.h header file.

OleBuildVersion

unsigned long OleBuildVersion()

OleBuildVersion returns the major and the minor version number of the OLE default handler.

Return Values

Value	Meaning
unsigned long	The 16 high-order bits are the major build number; the 16 low-order bits are the minor build number.

Comments

Applications can be compiled to run against only one released major build version of the OLE library while they are using any of the incremental minor build versions.

With any given release of OLE there is a file called OLE*x*VER.H, which contains the major and minor build versions, defined as "rmm" and "rup." To get the build versions, applications call **OleBuildVersion**, which returns the major and minor build version numbers from this file. It is unlikely that the major build version would change between releases, but applications should still ensure compatibility by calling **OleBuildVersion**.

If the major version number is different than that expected by the application, the application must not call **OleInitialize**.

OleBuildVersion will always be the very first function that an application calls in the OLE 2 library.

In the following example, **OleBuildVersion** returns the major and minor build vesions of the OLE libraries; the application compares these values against the defined constants to determine if it is OK to initialize the libraries.

```
#define rmm     21
#define rup     373

unsigned long dwBuildVersion = OleBuildVersion();

// fail if different major version or older minor version.
if (HIWORD(dwBuildVersion) != rmm || LOWORD(dwBuildVersion) < rup)
    return ResultFromScode(E_FAIL);         //Do not initialize OLE
else
    OleInitialize(NULL);
```

See Also **OleInitialize**, **CoBuildVersion**

OleInitialize

HRESULT OleInitialize(*pMalloc*)
LPMALLOC *pMalloc*

OleInitialize initializes the OLE library so that it can be used.

Parameters

pMalloc
Points to the memory allocator that is to be used for task memory by the OLE library and by object handlers. To use the OLE implementation of **IMalloc**, pass NULL as this parameter.

Return Values

Value	Meaning
S_OK	The library was initialized successfully.
S_FALSE	OLE library is already initialized; *pMalloc* not used.
OLE_E _WRONGCOMPOBJ	COMPOBJ.DLL is the wrong version for OLE 2.
E_OUTOFMEMORY	Out of memory.
E_UNEXPECTED	An unexpected error occurred.

Comments

With the exception of **OleBuildVersion**, **OleInitialize** must be called by applications before any other function in the OLE library.

Calls to **OleInitialize** must be balanced by corresponding calls to **OleUninitialize**. Normally, **OleInitialize** is called only once by the process that wants to use the OLE library. In some instances (for example, two independent pieces of code written as DLLs) there may be competing calls to **OleInitialize**; in these cases, only the first successful call to **OleInitialize** will initialize the library and only its corresponding balanced call to **OleUninitialize** will uninitialize the library.

OleInitialize will return S_FALSE if the library has already been initialized. An application must not call **OleUninitialize** if the corresponding call to **OleInitialize** did not return S_OK; therefore, applications should set a flag after a successful initialization and test the value of the flag before closing or reinitializing the libraries. Only the application that initialized the libraries can unitialize them.

OleInitialize follows the normal reference counting rules described earlier in the description of the **IUnknown** interface. Since **OleInitialize** retains the *pMalloc* pointer beyond the duration of the call, it calls *pMalloc*->**AddRef**. Applications can release this pointer by calling *pMalloc*->**Release**.

See Also

OleUninitialize, **CoInitialize**

OleUninitialize

void OleUninitialize()

OleUninitialize uninitializes the OLE library, freeing any resources that it maintains.

Comments

OleUninitialize should be called at application shutdown, as the last call made to the OLE library. **OleUninitialize** internally calls **CoUninitialize** to uninitialize the Component Object Library.

Calls to **OleUninitialize** must be balanced with a previous corresponding call to **OleInitialize**; only the **OleUninitialize** call that corresponds to the **OleInitialize** call that actually did the initialization will uninitialize the library.

See Also

OleInitialize, CoUninitialize

InitOleManager

HRESULT InitOleManager(*dwflags***)**
long *dwflags*

InitOleManager initializes Microsoft OLE Extension, which must be running in order to expose the OLE libraries.

Parameters

dwflags
Specifies a flag used to control how the application is initialized; the flag value is taken from the **OLEMANAGER** enumeration. For more information, see the following comments.

Return Values

Value	Meaning
S_OK	Microsoft OLE Extension was initialized successfully.
S_FALSE	An error occurred while trying to initialize Microsoft OLE Extension.

Comments

InitOleManager must be called by your application during its startup routine; this starts Microsoft OLE Extension, which exposes the OLE libraries to your application.

Note **InitOleManager** patches the **ExitToShell**, **Launch**, **Chain**, **LoadSeg**, and **Unloadseg** traps. **UninitOleManager** restores these traps to the values set when **InitOleManager** was called. An application that wants to patch over these traps must take care not to interfere with the OLE patches.

An application that patches one of these traps before calling **InitOleManager** must not unpatch the trap until after **UninitOleManager** has been called (otherwise, the application will undo the traps set by OLE). If an application patches a trap after **InitOleManager** is called, it must recognize that **UninitOleManager** will undo the patch (that is, the patch will be restored to the value it was at before **InitOleManager** was called). Finally, if an application patches **Loadseg** or **Unloadseg** after **InitOleManager** has been called, it should check to see whether the patch being called is for OLE.

Calls to **InitOleManager** must be balanced by corresponding calls to **UninitOleManager**. Normally, **InitOleManager** is called only once by the process that wants to start OLE. In some instances, an application is used with add-in applications. In these cases, the add-in application will usually call **InitOleManager**, passing in OLEMGR_BIND_NORMAL in *dwflags*. Specifying OLEMGR_NO_ADDREF for *dwflags* does not result in a reference count being placed on Microsoft OLE Extension; this frees your application from having to call **UninitOleManager**.

On being called, **InitOleManager** performs the following steps as part of initializing OLE:

1. If it is not already running, starts Microsoft OLE Extension. If Microsoft OLE Extension is already running, this step is a no-op.
2. Registers application context information.
3. Sets up a table of API pointers (if **InitOleManager** is called by an add-in application, this step is the only step that is performed).

To stop Microsoft OLE Extension, the host application must call **UninitOleManager**.

The *dwflags* parameter takes its value from the **OLEMANAGER** enumeration, which is defined in ole2.h as follows:

```
typedef enum tagOLEMANAGER
{
    OLEMGR_BIND_NORMAL   = 0,
    OLEMGR_BIND_IF_THERE = 1,
    OLEMGR_NO_ADDREF     = 2,
    OLEMGR_FORCELONG     = 2147483647
} OLEMANAGER;
```

OLEMANAGER values have the following meaning:

Value	Meaning
OLEMGR_BIND_NORMAL	Used to indicate a normal application, launch, bind, and Addref.
OLEMGR_BIND_IF_THERE	Used to indicate that the application only wants to bind if Microsoft OLE Extension is already running(useful only for mini-servers).
OLEMGR_NO_ADDREF	This flag does not reference count Microsoft OLE Extension; the application will bind only if Microsoft OLE Extension is running (useful only for add-in applications).

See Also **UninitOleManager**

UninitOleManager

unsigned long UninitOleManager()

UninitOleManager uninitializes Microsoft OLE Extension, the special OLE initialization extension.

Return Values

Value	Meaning
unsigned long	Specifies the reference count on Microsoft OLE Extension.

Comments

UninitOleManager must be called at application shutdown. When called by an add-in application, **UninitOleManager** is a no-op.

Calls to **UninitManager** must be balanced with a previous corresponding call to **InitOleManager**; only the **UninitOleManager** call that corresponds to the **InitOleManager** call that started Microsoft OLE Extension will shut down the application.

When **UninitOleManager** is called by the last application using it (that is, the one that holds a valid reference count on the object), Microsoft OLE Extension shuts down.

See Also **InitOleManager**

IsOleManagerRunning

unsigned long IsOleManagerRunning()

IsOleManager indicates whether Microsoft OLE Extension is running.

Return Values

Value	Meaning
TRUE	Microsoft OLE Extension is running.
FALSE	Microsoft OLE Extension is not running.

OleInitDBCSCountry

unsigned long OleInitDBCSCountry(*iCntry***)**
int *iCntry*

OleInitDBCSCountry initalizes the double-byte character set for the country specified by *iCntry*.

Parameters

iCntry
Specifies the ID for the country in which the character set is to be initialized: 81 = Japan, 82 = Korea, 86 = KANJII, and 0 = no character set(default).

Return Values

Value	Meaning
unsigned long	0 = the function completed successfully; any other value indicates an error.

Apple Event Functions

This section describes the OLE functions used to handle the events that OLE generates during clipboard and interprocess communication operations.

Note While an application can call these functions directly, there is no need to since **OleInitialize** calls them as part of initializing the OLE libraries.

```
OSerror OleProcessDdeAE (AppleEvent * paevt, AppleEvent * preply, long refcon);
OSerror OleProcessLrpcAE (AppleEvent * paevt, AppleEvent * preply, long refcon);
OSerror OleProcessClipboardAE(AppleEvent * paevt, AppleEvent * preply, long refcon);
```

OleProcessDdeAE

OSErr OleProcessDdeAE (*paevt*, *preply*, *refcon*)
AppleEvent * *paevt*
AppleEvent * *preply*
long *refcon*

OleProcessDdeAE handles DDE class Apple events.

Parameters

paevt
Points to the Apple event to handle.

preply
Points to the reply Apple event.

refcon
Specifies the reference constant stored in the Apple event dispatch table.

Return Values

Value	Meaning
System error	In all cases where function did not return successfully.

Comments

To install **OleProcessDdeAE** in the system Apple event dispatch table, OLE applications call **AEInstallEventHandler**. **OleProcessDdeAE** must be installed after the more specific DDE event handlers.

OleProcessDdeAE replaces the OLE 1 functions **OleTryClientAE** and **OleTryServerAE**.

OleProcessLrpcAE

OSErr OleProcessLrpcAE (*paevt*, *preply*, *refcon*)
AppleEvent * *paevt*
AppleEvent * *preply*
long *refcon*

OleProcessLrpcAE handles LRPC class Apple events.

Parameters

paevt
Points to the Apple event to handle.

preply
Points to the reply Apple event.

refcon
Specifies the reference constant stored in the Apple event dispatch table.

Return Values

Value	Meaning
System error	In all cases where function did not return successfully.

Comments

To install **OleProcessLrpcAE** in the system Apple event dispatch table, OLE applications call **AEInstallEventHandler**.

OleProcessLrpcAE must be installed after the more specific DDE event handlers.

OleProcessClipboardAE

OSErr OleProcessClipboardAE(*paevt, preply, refcon***)**
AppleEvent * *paevt*
AppleEvent * *preply*
long *refcon*

OleProcessClipboardAE handles DDE class RNCF type Apple events that are generated by the OLE clipboard.

Parameters

paevt
Points to the Apple event to handle.

preply
Points to the reply Apple event.

refcon
Specifies the reference constant stored in the Apple event dispatch table.

Return Values

Value	Meaning
System error	In all cases where function did not return successfully.
-1	**AEGetParamPtr** failed.

Comments

To install **OleProcessClipboardAE** in the system Apple event dispatch table, OLE applications call **AEInstallEventHandler**. When a RNCF event is received, **OleProcessClipboardAE** is automatically called.

OleProcessClipboardAE calls the window procedure to retrieve a handle to the requested data. The handle is passed back to the caller in *paevt*.

CHAPTER 7

Data Transfer/Caching Interfaces and Functions

Overview of Data and Presentation Transfer

OLE's mechanism of transferring data and presentation is usable in a wide range of situations, particularly with those related to compound documents. Data can be copied to the clipboard or dragged and then pasted or dropped into the same document, a different document, or a different application.

Delayed rendering, a technique whereby data is not actually transferred until it is needed for rendering, is an integral part of data transfer. Only information about the impending transfer, such as data formats and mediums, is initially made available at copy or cut time. A source application creates a data transfer object that holds a copy of the selected data and exposes methods for retrieving the data and receiving change notifications.

When a paste occurs, the receiving application makes a call to get the actual data from the source application. The receiving application can request both the data format and the medium across which the data should be transferred. The receiving application's ability to select formats and mediums at run time allows objects to be transferred in the most efficient manner. A large object can be transferred using a storage object or a file, for example, while a smaller object can be transferred as a **hGlobal** by using the clipboard.

OLE supports the caching of presentation data in the container's storage so that a compound document object can be shown in its container without running the object's application. Multiple presentations can also be cached; the container can choose to maintain presentations for multiple target devices, such as the screen and the printer.

Data Structures and Enumerations

This section discusses the data structures and enumerations that play a central role in the transfer and caching of data and presentation information.

The **FORMATETC** structure is a generalized clipboard format, enhanced to encompass a target device, the aspect (view) of the data, and a storage medium. Where one might expect to find a clipboard format, a **FORMATETC** data structure is used instead.

The **STGMEDIUM** structure is a generalized global memory handle commonly used to pass one body of code to another. Where one would expect to find a global memory handle involved in a data transfer, OLE uses a **STGMEDIUM** structure in its place.

The **DVTARGETDEVICE** structure contains information about a target device.

The **ADVF** enumeration is a set of advisory flags that specifies values for controlling advisory connections and caching.

FORMATETC Data Structure

The **FORMATETC** structure is used by the data and presentation interfaces as the means for passing information. For example, in **IDataObject::GetData** a **FORMATETC** structure is used to indicate exactly what kind of data the caller is requesting. For more information on the **IDataObject** interface, see "IDataObject Interface," later in this chapter.

The **FORMATETC** data structure is defined in dvobj.h as follows:

```
typedef struct FARSTRUCT tagFORMATETC
{
    unsigned long       cfFormat;
    DVTARGETDEVICE *    ptd;
    unsigned long       dwAspect;
    long                lindex;
    unsigned long       tymed;
} FORMATETC, * LPFORMATETC;
```

The *cfFormat* member indicates the particular clipboard format of interest. There are three types of formats recognized by OLE:

- standard interchange formats, such as CF_TEXT,
- private application formats understood only by the application offering the format, or by
- other applications similar in functionality or OLE formats.

The OLE formats are used to create linked or embedded objects and are described in the following sections.

The *ptd* member points to a **DVTARGETDEVICE** data structure containing information about the target device for which the data is being composed. A NULL value is used whenever the data format is insensitive to the target device or when the caller doesn't care what device is used. In the latter case, if the data requires a target device, the object should pick an appropriate default device (often the display for visual objects). Data obtained from an object with a NULL target device (especially when the data format is insensitive to the device) can be thought of as an alternate form of the native representation of the object: a representation that can be used for data interchange. The resulting data is usually the same as it would be if the user chose the Save As command from the File menu and selected an interchange format.

The *dwAspect* member enables the caller to request multiple aspects, roles, or views of the object using a single clipboard format. Most data and presentation transfer and caching methods pass aspect information. For example, a caller might request an object's iconic picture, using the metafile clipboard format to retrieve it.

Values for *dwAspect* are taken from the **DVASPECT** enumeration, which is defined in dvobj.h as follows:

```
typedef enum tagDVASPECT {
    DVASPECT_CONTENT        = 1,
    DVASPECT_THUMBNAIL      = 2,
    DVASPECT_ICON           = 4,
    DVASPECT_DOCPRINT       = 8,
    } DVASPECT;
```

Even though **DVASPECT** values are individual flag bits, *dwAspect* can only represent one value. That is, *dwAspect* cannot contain the result of **DVASPECT** values that have been or-ed together.

DVASPECT values have the following meaning:

Values for DVASPECT	Meaning
DVASPECT_CONTENT	Provides a representation so the object can be displayed as an embedded object inside its container; this is the most common value for compound document objects. It is appropriate to use DVASPECT_CONTENT to get a presentation of the embedded object for rendering either on the screen or on a printer; DVASPECT_DOCPRINT, by contrast, indicates the look of the object as though it were printed.
DVASPECT_THUMBNAIL	Provides a thumbnail representation so that the object can be displayed in a browsing tool. The thumbnail is approximately a 20 by 20 pixel representation.
DVASPECT_ICON	Provides an iconic representation of the object.
DVASPECT_DOCPRINT	Represents the object as though it were printed using the Print command from the File menu. The described data represents a sequence of pages.

The *lindex* member represents the part of the aspect that is of interest. The value of *lindex* depends on the value of *dwAspect*. If *dwAspect* is either DVASPECT_THUMBNAIL or DVASPECT_ICON, *lindex* is ignored. If *dwAspect* is DVASPECT_CONTENT or DVASPECT_DOCPRINT, *lindex* must be -1 which indicates that the entire view is of interest and is the only value that is currently valid.

The *tymed* member indicates the means by which data is conveyed in a particular data transfer operation. In addition to being passed through global memory, data can be passed either through a disk file or an instance of one of the OLE storage-related interfaces.

Each clipboard format has a natural expression as either a *flat* format or a *structured*, hierarchical format. All standard formats, such as text, are expressed as flat formats. The OLE embedded object formats, Embedded Object and Embed Source, transfer data using the structured format. There are three types of medium that are used to transfer those formats designated as flat formats: hglobal, stream, and file; and a single type of structured media: storage.

It is always appropriate to ask for a particular format on either a flat or a structured medium, as appropriate for the natural expression of the format. Additionally, it is plausible to ask that a format whose natural expression is a structured format be provided on a flat format: the structured-to-flat mapping is provided by the compound file implementation of the structured storage model. However, it is not appropriate to ask for a flat format on a structured medium. For example, text format cannot be passed on TYMED_ISTORAGE.

Valid values for *tymed* are taken from the **TYMED** enumeration, which is defined in dvobj.h. These values may be or-ed together to represent a composite value.

```
typedef enum tagTYMED
{
    TYMED_HGLOBAL  = 1,
    TYMED_FILE     = 2,
    TYMED_ISTREAM  = 4,
    TYMED_ISTORAGE = 8,
    TYMED_GDI      = 16,                //Not used on Macintosh; for
                                        //compatiblity with Windows
    TYMED_MFPICT   = 32,
    TYMED_NULL     = 0,
} TYMED;
```

The **TYMED** values have specific meanings and required release behavior. However, for any of the **TYMED** values, if *pUnkForRelease* is non-NULL, *pUnkForRelease*->**Release** is always called. The following table describes each of the **TYMED** values and their mechanisms for release:

Value	Meaning	Release Mechanism
TYMED_HGLOBAL	Passes the data in a global memory handle. All global handles must be accessible directly by OLE and other applications.	**DisposeHandle** (*hGlobal*)
TYMED_FILE	Passes the data in the contents of a file on the disk.	**FSPClose** (*hFile*)
TYMED_ISTREAM	Passes the data using an instance of the **IStream** interface. The passed data is available through calls to the **IStream::Read**.	*pStm*-> **Release**()
TYMED_ISTORAGE	Passes the data using an instance of the **IStorage** interface; the passed data are the streams and storage objects nested beneath the **IStorage**.	*pStg*->**Release**()
TYMED_MFPICT	Passes the data in a global memory handle. All global handles must be accessible directly by OLE and other applications.	**DisposeHandle** (*hGlobal*)
TYMED_NULL	This is not actually a medium; it indicates that no data is being passed.	

STGMEDIUM Data Structure

The **STGMEDIUM** structure describes a medium of transfer and is defined in dvobj.h as follows:

```
typedef struct tagSTGMEDIUM {
    unsigned long       tymed;
    union
    {
    Handle      hGlobal;
    char *      lpszFileName;
    LPSTREAM    pstm;
    LPSTORAGE   pstg;
    };
    LPUNKNOWN   pUnkForRelease;
    } STGMEDIUM;
```

A **STGMEDIUM** structure is a tagged union whose *tymed* member corresponds to the **TYMED** enumeration. Each type of medium specified in **FORMATETC**::*tymed* has a matching **STGMEDIUM** *tymed* member through which occurrences of that medium are passed.

STGMEDIUM can be set to NULL by setting the *tymed* member to TYMED_NULL.

The *pUnkForRelease* member is used to provide flexibility of medium ownership. It is helpful to have the following ownership scenario choices:

- The callee owns the medium, freeing all resources when finished.
- The callee does not own the medium and informs the caller when finished so that resources can then be freed.

The provider of the medium indicates its choice of ownership scenarios in the value it provides in *pUnkForRelease*. A NULL value indicates that the receiving body of code owns and can free the medium. A non-NULL pointer specifies that **ReleaseStgMedium**can always be called to free the medium. For a detailed explanation of how storage mediums are freed and *pUnkForRelease* is used, see the description of **ReleaseStgMedium** later in this chapter.

DVTARGETDEVICE Data Structure

The **DVTARGETDEVICE** data structure, used to describe a target device, is defined in dvobj.h as follows:

```
typedef struct tagDVTARGETDEVICE {
    unsigned long   tdSize;
//Following fields are for Windows compatibility
    unsigned short  tdDriverNameOffset;
    unsigned short  tdDeviceNameOffset;
    unsigned short  tdPortNameOffset;
    unsigned short  tdExtDevmodeOffset;
    unsigned char   tdWinData[1];
    unsigned char   byAlign;
//Following fields are for use on Macintosh
    long            dwSizeX;
    long            dwSizeY;
    short           wDpiX;
    short           wDpiY;
    short           wColorDepth;
    short           wFlags;
    short           wMisc;
    unsigned char   tdData[1];
}DVTARGETDEVICE;
```

The following table describes these members:

DVTARGETDEVICE Member	Meaning
tdSize	Specifies the size of **DVTARGETDEVICE** structure in bytes. The initial size is included so that the structure can be copied more easily.
tdDriverNameOffset	Secifies the offset from the beginning of the **DVTARGETDEVICE** structure to the device driver name; must be NULL-terminated (a NULL device or port name can be specified by appropriate offset fields to zero).
tdDeviceNameOffset	Specifies the offset from the beginning of the **DVTARGETDEVICE** structure to the device name; must be NULL-terminated.
tdPortNameOffset	Specifies the offset from the beginning of the **DVTARGETDEVICE** structure to the port name;must be NULL-terminated.
tdExtDevmodeOffset	Specifies the offset from the beginning of the **DVTARGETDEVICE** structure to the **DEVMODE** structure (retrieved by calling **ExtDeviceMode**.)
tdWinData[1]	Specifies an array of bytes containing data for the target device. It is not necessary to include empty strings in *tdWinData*.
byAlign	Used internally for byte alignment.
dwSizeX	Specifies the maximum width in pixels.
dwSizeY	Specifies the maximum height in pixels.
wDpiX	Specifies the horizontal dots per inch.
wDpiY	Specifies the vertical dots per inch.
wColorDepth	Specifies the color depth (for example, 1==black and white, 8 = = 256 colors).
wFlags	Specifies characteristics for the target device; values are taken from the **TDFLAGS** enumeration: TD_PRINTER, TD_POSTSCRIPT, or TD_GX.
wMisc	Specifies the offset to an application-specific data; most often this value is NULL.
tdData	Specifies an array of bytes containing data for the target device. It is not necessary to include empty strings in *tdData*.

ADVF Enumeration

The values defined in the **ADVF** enumeration are used to specify information about data and/or view advisories and cache connections.

The valid values for **ADVF**, which can be or-ed together to form a composite value, are defined in dvobj.h as follows:

```
typedef enum tagADVF
{
    ADVF_NODATA = 1,
    ADVF_PRIMEFIRST = 2,
    ADVF_ONLYONCE = 4,
    ADVF_DATAONSTOP = 64,
    ADVFCACHE_NOHANDLER = 8,
    ADVFCACHE_FORCEBUILTIN = 16,
    ADVFCACHE_ONSAVE = 32,
} ADVF;
```

Depending on the method in which the **ADVF** value is being used, the values may have different meanings. Some of the methods use only a subset of the values while other methods use all of them.

ADVF_NODATA, when passed to **IDataObject::DAdvise**, is a request to avoid sending data with subsequent **IAdviseSink::OnDataChange** calls. TYMED_NULL is passed as the storage medium. The recipient of the data change notification can later retrieve the latest data by calling **IDataObject::GetData**. ADVF_NODATA however, is just a request. The data object may choose to provide the data anyway, especially when more than one advisory connection has been made specifying the same **FORMATETC** data structure.

IViewObject::SetAdvise returns E_INVALIDARG if ADVF_NODATA is passed to it.

When ADVF_NODATA is passed to **IOleCache::Cache**, it is an indication that the cache should not be updated by changes made to the running object. Instead, the container will update the cache by explicitly calling **IOleCache::SetData**. This situation typically occurs when the iconic aspect of an object is being cached.

ADVF_PRIMEFIRST requests that a data or view change notification be sent or the cache updated immediately without waiting for a change in the current data or view.

ADVF_ONLYONCE automatically deletes the advisory connection after sending one data or view notification. The advisory sink receives only one **IAdviseSink** call. A nonzero connection ID is returned if the connection is established so the caller can use it to delete the connection. For data change notifications, the combination of ADVF_ONLYONCE | ADVF_PRIMEFIRST provides, in effect, an asynchronous **IDataObject::GetData** call.

When used with caching, ADVF_ONLYONCE updates the cache one time only, on receipt of the first OnDataChange notification. After the update is complete, the advisory connection between the object and the cache is disconnected.

ADVF_DATAONSTOP is meaningful for data change notifications only when ADVF_NODATA is also given. This value indicates that just before the advisory connection shuts down, a call to **IAdviseSink::OnDataChange** should be made that provides the data with it. Without this value, by the time an **OnDataChange** call without data reaches the sink, the source might have completed its shut down and the data might not be accessible. Sinks that specify this value should, in **OnDataChange**, accept data if it is being passed because they may not get another chance to retrieve it.

For cache connections, ADVF_DATAONSTOP updates the cache as part of object closure. ADVF_DATAONSTOP is not applicable to view change notifications.

ADVFCACHE_NOHANDLER, ADVFCACHE_FORCEBUILTIN, and ADVFCACHE_ONSAVE are applicable only to the caching methods. The ADVFCACHE_NOHANDLER value is reserved for future use.

ADVFCACHE_FORCEBUILTIN forcefully caches data that requires only code shipped with OLE or the underlying operating system to be present in order to produce it with **IDataObject::GetData** or **IViewObject::Draw**, as appropriate. By specifying this value, the container can ensure that the data can be retrieved even when the object or handler code is not available. This value is used by DLL object applications and object handlers that perform the drawing of their objects. ADVFCACHE_FORCEBUILTIN instructs OLE to cache presentation data to ensure that there is a presentation in the cache.

ADVFCACHE_ONSAVE updates the cached representation only when the object containing the cache is saved. The cache is also updated when the OLE object transitions from the running state back to the loaded state (because a subsequent save operation would require re-running the object).

TDFLAGS Enumeration

The **TDFLAGS** enumeration is used to define characteristics of the target device; these values are supplied in the wFlags member of **DVTARGETDEVICE** structure.

The enumeration is defined in dvobj.h as follows:

```
typedef enum tagTDFLAGS
{
    TD_PRINTER = 1           //if set, target device describes a printer
    TD_POSTSCRIPT = 2        //if set, target device has postscript
    TD_GX = 4                //if set, target device has GX
}TDFLAGS;
```

OLE Clipboard Formats

There are three types of formats that are made available by using the **FORMATETC** structure when an application copies to the clipboard. They include the following:

- Standard PICT Macintosh format.
- Private formats understood only by the application offering the format or by other applications that are similar in functionality.
- OLE-defined formats.

Of interest here are the OLE-defined formats which are used to describe data that can become an embedded or linked compound document object. The format that best represents the data selection is made available first. This intentional ordering encourages a receiving application to use the first format if possible.

OLE defines six data formats. The formats with the term "Source" in their name are used to create embedded or linked objects; the Embedded Object format can be used to create either object type. The "Descriptor" formats are used to describe the data selection on the clipboard and are made available in conjunction with the other formats. These formats are summarized below and described in detail in subsequent sections:

OLE-Defined Formats	Purpose
Embed Source(EMBS)	Creates an embedded object from an object application's native data.
Link Source(LNKS)	Creates a standard new linked object.
Custom Link Source(CLNK)	Creates a custom new linked object.
Embedded Object (EMBO)	Creates an embedded or linked object from a container's existing embedded object.
Object Descriptor(OBJD)	Describes the data being transferred and is made available with all transfers.
Link Source Descriptor (LKSD)	Describes the link being transferred in the link source.

Embed Source Format

The embed source format (EMBS) is offered when the data selection can be the source of a new embedded object in a container. Embed source data is arranged exactly like it is in the normal persistent representation of an embedded object. Only the normal native data of the object is placed inside the transferred **IStorage**; presentations of the object are not to be passed.

When an embedded object is created for the first time, as is the case with Embed Source, the formats available with the data transfer object can be used to initialize the cache for the newly created embedded object. When the transfer operation is done using the clipboard, **OleSetClipboard** can also offer these other formats to non-OLE-aware applications.

Link Source Format

The link source format (LNKS) is offered when the data selection can be the source of a new linked object in a container. Link Source data contains a class identifier (CLSID) and a moniker intended to represent the link source.

Data in Link Source format is always passed on a flat storage medium. This means that a medium of type TYMED_ISTORAGE is never appropriate. The contents of the medium are a serialized CLSID immediately followed by the serialized data of the moniker. The CLSID is retrievable with **ReadClassStm**, and the moniker can be deserialized with **IPersistStream::Load**. A link can be created from the resulting moniker using **OleCreateLink**.

The cache in the new linked object is initialized with the formats available only from the data transfer object.

Custom Link Source Format

A custom link source format (CLNK) is offered by applications that implement a custom link object to fully or partially replace the default link object provided by OLE. Applications may want to use a custom link object for their objects that have special rendering needs.

A custom link object is a DLL object and is registered as an INPROC_SERVER in the Registration Database file. Custom link objects implement the following interfaces:

Interface	Usage
IPersistStorage	Compound document storage.
IDataObject	Data transfer objects.
IOleCache2	Compound document cache support.
IViewObject2	Compound document view support.
IRunnableObject	Required by all in-process objects.
IExternalConnection	Required by all in-process objects.
IOleLink	Compound document link management.
IOleObject	Compound document object support.

The typical custom link object used for special rendering will implement **IPersistStorage**, **IDataObject**, **IOleCache2**, and **IViewObject2** and then aggregate OLE's standard link object implementation for the remaining interfaces.

To use a custom link object, objects must register a special key in the Registration Database file:

```
HKEY_CLASSES_ROOT\CLSID\{...}\UseCustomLink
```

When the Link Source format is available and a user initiates a paste link, the link source application is asked whether or not it supports Custom Link Source. If Custom Link Source is supported, the link source application writes the CLSID of the custom link object into a specified **IStorage**. When the linked object is instantiated, the CLSID is read from the storage and passed to **CoCreateInstance**, which uses it to create the custom link object. The moniker passed with the Link Source data is given to the custom link object so it can bind the newly created linked object when necessary.

Embedded Object Format

The embedded object format (EMBO) is offered when the data selection is an embedded object and indicates that either a linked or embedded object can be created. The embedded object should be first in the list of formats that are made available.

The embedded object data is arranged exactly like the embed source data. To create an embedded object from the embedded object format, a receiving application copies the contents of the data selection's storage object into a new storage object. Before a copy can be safely done, it is necessary to check whether the object has changed since it was last saved. If it has, the object can be saved directly into the new storage. If no change has been made, the method **IStorage::CopyTo** can be called to copy the contents from the original storage to the new storage. The following code illustrates this logic:

```
lpObject->QueryInterface(IID_IPersistStorage, &lpPersistStorage);
if (lpPersistStorage->IsDirty() == NOERROR)  {
    OleSave(lpPersistStorage, lpNewStorage, FALSE);
    lpPersistStorage->SaveCompleted(lpNewStorage);
}
else  {
    lpPersistStorage->CopyTo(lpNewStorage);
}
```

The main difference between embed source and embedded object lies in the way that the cache for the new compound document object is initialized. When an embedded object is created for the first time, as is the case with embed source, only the formats available with the data transfer object can be used to initialize the cache for the newly created embedded object. With the embedded object format, the presentations in the cache of the embedded object itself are available as well.

Object Descriptor Format

The object descriptor format (OBJD) is offered whenever data is copied. Object descriptor data is made available in an instance of an **OBJECTDESCRIPTOR** data structure.

The **OBJECTDESCRIPTOR** structure is defined in ole2.h and consists of the following elements:

```
typedef struct tagOBJECTDESCRIPTOR
{
    unsigned long       cbSize;
    CLSID               clsid;
    unsigned long       dwDrawAspect;
    SIZEL               sizel;
    unsigned long       dwOutline;
    POINTL              pointl;
    unsigned long       dwStatus;
    unsigned long       dwFullUserTypeName;
    unsigned long       dwSrcOfCopy;
    unsigned long       dwExtra;   //Must Be NULL
}OBJECTDESCRIPTOR;
```

OBJECTDESCRIPTOR members have the following meanings:

OBJECTDESCRIPTOR Member	Description
cbSize	Specifies the size of the **OBJECTDESCRIPTOR** structure in bytes.
clsid	Used to obtain the icon for the 'DisplayAsIcon' option in the Paste Special dialog and is applicable only if the Embed Source or Embedded Object formats are offered. If neither of these formats are offered, the value of *clsid* should be CLSID_NULL.
dwDrawAspect	The value of this field is typically DVASPECT_CONTENT or DVASPECT_ICON. If the source application did not draw the object originally, the *dwDrawAspect* field contains a zero value (which is not the same as DVASPECT_CONTENT).

OBJECTDESCRIPTOR Member	Description
sizel	Contains the true extents of the object (in pixels), available through a call to **IOleObject::GetExtent**. Setting the *sizel* field is optional; its value can be (0, 0) for applications that do not draw the object being transferred.

dwOutline	Offset from beginning of structure to region describing outline of object Like *sizel*, this is only defined for drawable objects; otherwise, it is zero. To turn this data at this offset into a region handle, allocate a handle the size of the first word of the region data and then copy those *n* bytes into the handle (including the first word):
	`// ptr to region data`
	`char *p = ((char*) pOD) +`
	`   pOD->dwOutline;`
	`short size = *(short *) p;`
	`h = NewHandle(size);`
	`BlockMove(p, *h, size);`

pointl	Specifies the offset in pixel units from the upper-left corner of the object where a drag operation was initiated. This field is only meaningful for a drag and drop transfer operation. The value is (0,0) for other transfer situations, such as a clipboard copy and paste.
dwStatus	Contains miscellaneous status flags for the object. These flags are defined by the OLEMISC enumeration and are returned by calling **IOleObject::GetMiscStatus**.
dwFullUserTypeName	Specifies the offset from the beginning of the data structure to the null-terminated string that specifies the full user type name of the object. The value is 0 if the string is not present.

OBJECTDESCRIPTOR Member	Description
dwSrcOfCopy	Specifies the offset from the beginning of the data structure to the null-terminated string that specifies the source of the transfer. *dwSrcOfCopy* is typically implemented as the display name of the temporary moniker that identifies the data source. The value for *dwSrcOfCopy* is displayed in the Source line of the Paste Special dialog. A zero value indicates that the string is not present. If *dwSrcOfCopy* is zero, the string 'Unknown Source' is displayed in the Paste Special dialog.
dwExtra	Reserved field; must be NULL.

Link Source Descriptor Format

Like the object descriptor format, the link source descriptor format (LKSD) contains information about the source of a compound document object. Link source descriptor is always offered when lLink source is offered. The same data is included for both formats. However, with link source descriptor, the value of *dwSrcOfCopy* can represent either a pseudo object in the source application, referred to as an *outside link*, or the running embedded object, referred to as an *inside link*. For example, consider the case in which a word processor links to a drawing that is a linked object within a spreadsheet program. If the new link is an *inside link*, the draw program is launched to edit the drawing when a word processor user double-clicks. The link source is the original object application used to create the drawing. If the new link is an *outside link*, the spreadsheet program becomes the link source and is used for editing.

When a link is copied, the source field will show the display name of the link source and the list box in the Paste dialog will show "Linked <*object full type* >. The result text and image will not be changed since they typically apply to both linking or embedding. It is the responsibility of the copying application to add the "Linked" to the full user type name given in the link source descriptor data.

Copying Data to the Clipboard

Applications that support clipboard copy typically have a standard set of formats they always offer and another set to offer selectively, depending on the data being copied. This standard set of formats is application-specific. For example, a pure container that does not support linking to its embedded objects would offer a different set of formats than an object application that supports linking to pseudo objects. Applications that are to maintain compatibility with OLE 1 must support the PICT format.

The following table suggests possible format offerings by application type. In all cases, except for the container copying native data or multiple compound document objects, it is assumed that the data selection can be the source of a linked object. The placement of Picture relative to the other formats in the table is somewhat arbitrary. It is up to the application to determine where Picture belongs. Otherwise, the ordering is intentional. Containers that do not draw their objects (use them pictorially) do not need to offer a picture format.

Type of Application	Data Selection	Clipboard Formats
Container application	single compound document object	High Fidelity application-specific formats Embedded Object Object Descriptor Picture Low Fidelity application-specific formats Link Source (inside or outside moniker) Link Source Descriptor (inside or outside moniker)
Container application	native data or multiple compound document objects	High Fidelity application-specific formats Picture Low Fidelity application-specific
Object application	native data	High Fidelity application-specific formats Embedded Source Object Descriptor Picture Low Fidelity application-specific formats Link Source (outside moniker) Link Source Descriptor (outside moniker)
Container/object application	single compound document object	High Fidelity application-specific formats Embedded Object Object Descriptor Picture Low Fidelity application-specific formats Link Source (inside or outside moniker) Link Source Descriptor (inside or outside moniker)
Container/object application	native data or multiple compound document objects	High Fidelity application-specific formats Embed Source Object Descriptor Picture Low Fidelity application-specific formats Link Source (outside moniker) Link Source Descriptor (outside moniker)

A consideration when offering Link Source for an embedded object in an unsaved container document is whether the object is running or merely loaded. If the object is not running, and a link is created before the container document is saved, no

OnRename notification will be sent when the document is saved. Thus, the link will be broken. To ensure that links are valid whenever possible, containers should only permit linking to data in saved documents.

A few conditions can change the set of offered formats. Link Source and Link Source Descriptor should be removed from the data transfer object if either a moniker cannot be provided to represent the data selection, or, in the case of a copy, the data has changed since the copy was initiated. If the data selection is a single embedded object in a container, Embedded Object, Object Descriptor, and the formats provided by the loaded object are dynamically added to the list of offered formats.

Pasting Data From the Clipboard

An application implementing paste operations retrieves the data transfer object from the clipboard and looks for an acceptable format among the list of formats that are available. If the first acceptable format is one that the application can edit, the selection is typically treated as data that is native to the application and a linked or embedded object is not created, thus avoiding the extra overhead involved in compound document object creation. For example, if the data selection is a paragraph from a word processor application that offers text format as its first available format and the receiving application is also a word processor, the receiving application can integrate the paragraph directly into its document. A user will be able to edit the pasted data in the same way as the rest of the document.

If only PICT is available, a static object can be created from the data by calling **OleCreateStaticFromData**. Static objects are pictures for which OLE provides a compound document object wrapping, making it possible for containers to treat them as though they were linked or embedded objects. A static object has the class ID, CLSID_StaticMetafile and the aspect DVASPECT_CONTENT. Static objects cannot be edited.

Special consideration is involved if the selected format is a private one that transfers with a storage object. The receiving container cannot copy the data directly from the source storage object into the destination document because substorage and stream objects used to hold private data cannot be opened twice. However, if the selected data is local to the receiving container, it can simply be copied directly from the source document into the destination document. It is only the nonlocal case that requires an alternate method of transfer.

In order for the container to take advantage of the direct copy optimization in the local case, the container must have a way to determine whether it placed the original data on the clipboard. If a data transfer object exists (assuming the application creates one as part of its copy operation), its **IDataObject** interface pointer can be compared with the **IDataObject** interface pointer retrieved with

OleGetClipboard or **IDropTarget::DragEnter**. If these pointers are the same, it is safe to assume that the copied data and the new embedded object are from the same container.

To copy data from one storage object into another storage object in the nonlocal case, a container application can create a temporary document. The data is loaded from the source storage object and copied into the temporary document. The contents of the temporary document are then copied into the real container document and the temporary document is destroyed.

IDataObject Interface

The **IDataObject** interface plays the key role in the transferring and caching of data and presentations. The interface contains the methods that retrieve, store, and enumerate data and handle data change notifications. All applications that transfer data implement **IDataObject** regardless of whether they are containers or object applications. All applications that receive data use **IDataObject**.

IDataObject contains the following methods:

```
DECLARE_INTERFACE_(IDataObject, IUnknown)
{
  // *** IUnknown methods ***
 HRESULT QueryInterface (REFIID riid, void * * ppvObj);
 unsigned long AddRef () ;
 unsigned long  Release ();

  // *** IDataObject methods ***
 HRESULT GetData (LPFORMATETC pFormatetc, LPSTGMEDIUM pmedium);
 HRESULT GetDataHere (LPFORMATETC pFormatetc, LPSTGMEDIUM pmedium);
 HRESULT QueryGetData (LPFORMATETC pFormatetc );
 HRESULT GetCanonicalFormatEtc (LPFORMATETC pFormatetc, LPFORMATETC pFormatetcOut);
 HRESULT SetData (LPFORMATETC pFormatetc, STGMEDIUM * pmedium, unsigned long fRelease);
 HRESULT EnumFormatEtc (unsigned long dwDirection, LPENUMFORMATETC FAR* ppenumFormatetc );
 HRESULT DAdvise (FORMATETC * pFormatetc, unsigned long advf,
     LPADVISESINK pAdvise, unsigned long * pdwConnection);
 HRESULT DUnadvise (unsigned long dwConnection);
 HRESULT EnumDAdvise (LPENUMSTATDATA * ppenumAdvise );
};
```

For more information, see the dvobj.h header file.

IDataObject::GetData

HRESULT IDataObject::GetData(*pFormatetc, pmedium*)
LPFORMATETC *pFormatetc*
LPSTGMEDIUM *pmedium*

IDataObject::GetData retrieves data in a specified format using a specified storage medium.

Parameters

pFormatetc
Points to the format to use for returning the data.

pmedium
Points to the storage medium to use for returning the data. This is the storage medium provided by the callee.

Return Values

Value	Meaning
S_OK	Data was successfully retrieved and placed in the storage medium provided.
E_INVALIDARG	One or more arguments are invalid.
E_OUTOFMEMORY	Ran out of memory.
E_UNEXPECTED	A relatively catastrophic failure.
DV_E_LINDEX	Invalid value for *lindex*; currently, only -1 is supported.
DV_E_FORMATETC	Invalid value for *pFormatetc*.
DV_E_TYMED	Invalid *tymed* value.
DV_E_DVASPECT	Invalid *dwAspect* value.
OLE_E_NOTRUNNING	Object application is not running.
DATA_E_FORMATETC	Cannot support the requested media.

Comments

It is valid to ask **IDataObject::GetData** to return data in a specified format on one of a specified group of mediums. Multiple mediums can be specified by OR-ing together the *tymed* values in the **FORMATETC** structure. The callee allocates the medium and decides how the resources associated with that medium are to be released. **IDataObject::GetData** determines the best medium, given its selection, and attempts to transfer the data. Only one medium can be returned. If this initial transfer fails, **IDataObject::GetData** might try one of the other mediums specified before returning an error.

Conceptually, the *pmedium* parameter is an out parameter, implying that the caller allocates the **STGMEDIUM** structure and the callee fills it in. The callee determines who is responsible for releasing the medium's resources and sets *pmedium->pUnkForRelease* to the appropriate value.

Supporting transfer of data with the storage medium requires special handling. Because it is not possible to transfer ownership of a root **IStorage** object from one process to another, the callee must retain ownership of the data by setting the *pUnkForRelease* field in the **STGMEDIUM** structure passed in by the caller. Alternatively, callers should consider using **IDataObject::GetDataHere** because it is more efficient.

Data transferred across a stream extends from position zero of the stream pointer through to the position immediately before the current stream pointer (the stream pointer position upon exit).

See Also

IDataObject::SetData, **IDataObject::GetDataHere**, **IEnumFORMATETC**, **ReleaseStgMedium**

IDataObject::GetDataHere

HRESULT IDataObject::GetDataHere(*pFormatetc*, *pmedium***)**
LPFORMATETC *pFormatetc*
LPSTGMEDIUM *pmedium*

IDataObject::GetDataHere retrieves data in a specified format using a storage medium provided by the caller.

Parameters

pFormatetc
Points to the format to use for returning the data.

pmedium
Points to the storage medium to use for returning the data. This is the storage medium provided by the caller.

Return Values

Value	Meaning
S_OK	Data was successfully retrieved and placed in the storage medium provided.
E_INVALIDARG	One or more arguments are invalid.
E_OUTOFMEMORY	Ran out of memory.
E_UNEXPECTED	A relatively catastrophic failure.
DV_E_LINDEX	Invalid value for *lindex*; currently only -1 is supported.
DV_E_FORMATETC	Invalid **FORMATETC** structure pointed to by *pFormatetc*.
DV_E_TYMED	Invalid *tymed* value.
DV_E_DVASPECT	Invalid *dwAspect* value.

Value	Meaning
OLE_E_NOTRUNNING	Object application is not running.
DATA_E_FORMATETC	Cannot support the requested media.
STG_E_MEDIUMFULL	The caller-provided medium is not large enough.

Comments

IDataObject::GetDataHere is like **IDataObject::GetData** except that the caller allocates the medium across which the data is to be transferred. **IDataObject::GetDataHere** is called when the clipboard selection or data being dragged is an embedded object.

When the transfer medium is a stream, assumptions are made about where the data is being returned and the position of the stream's seek pointer. In a **IDataObject::GetData** call, the data returned is from stream position zero through just before the current seek pointer of the stream (the position on exit). For **IDataObject::GetDataHere**, the data returned is from the stream position on entry through just before the position on exit.

The callee must fill in the actual medium provided by the caller in the **hGlobal** case. That is, the callee cannot allocate a new **hGlobal**; it must put the data in the medium provided by the caller. The caller always sets the field *pmedium->tymed* to the value of *pFormatetc->tymed* because *pFormatetc->tymed* can only indicate one medium.

See Also

IDataObject::GetData

IDataObject::QueryGetData

HRESULT IDataObject::QueryGetData(*pFormatetc***)**
LPFORMATETC *pFormatetc*

IDataObject::QueryGetData determines whether a call to **IDataObject::GetData** would succeed if it were passed *pFormatetc*.

Parameters

pFormatetc
Points to the format to use for transferring data.

Return Values

Value	Meaning
S_OK	Data in the specified format would be successfully returned.
DATA_E_FORMATETC	Data in the specified format would not be successfully returned.
E_INVALIDARG	One or more arguments are invalid.
E_OUTOFMEMORY	Ran out of memory.
E_UNEXPECTED	An unexpected failure occurred.

Value	Meaning
DV_E_LINDEX	Invalid value for *lindex*; currently only -1 is supported.
DV_E_FORMATETC	Invalid **FORMATETC** structure.
DV_E_TYMED	Invalid *tymed* value.
DV_E_DVASPECT	Invalid *dwAspect* value.
OLE_E_NOTRUNNING	Object application is not running.

See Also

IDataObject::GetData, **FORMATETC** data structure

IDataObject::GetCanonicalFormatEtc

HRESULT IDataObject::GetCanonicalFormatEtc(*pFormatetc*, *pFormatetcOut***)**
LPFORMATETC *pFormatetc*
LPFORMATETC *pFormatetcOut*

IDataObject::GetCanonicalFormatEtc communicates to the caller which **FORMATETC** data structure produced the same output data.

Parameters

pFormatetc
Points to the format and medium in which the caller wants to obtain the returned data.

pFormatetcOut
Points to where to return the clearest equivalent of *pFormatetc*.

Return Values

Value	Meaning
S_OK	The returned **FORMATETC** structure is different than the one that was passed.
E_INVALIDARG	One or more arguments are invalid.
E_OUTOFMEMORY	Ran out of memory.
E_UNEXPECTED	A relatively catastrophic failure.
DATA_S _SAMEFORMATETC	The **FORMATETC** structures are the same and no value needs to be put in *pFormatetcOut*.
DV_E_LINDEX	Invalid value for *lindex*; currently, only -1 is supported.
DV_E_FORMATETC	Invalid **FORMATETC** structure.
OLE_E _NOTRUNNING	Object application is not running.

Comments

Often, a given data object returns the same data for more than one requested **FORMATETC** structure. This is especially true for target devices. The returned data is often insensitive to the particular target device in question. To enable callers to prevent caching duplicate sets of data, **IDataObject::GetCanonicalFormatEtc** provides the means by which objects can indicate to the caller which **FORMATETC** structures produce the same results.

The callee should pick a canonical representative of the set of **FORMATETC** structures equivalent to the one passed by the caller in *pFormatetc* and return that through *pFormatetcOut*. *pFormatetcOut* is allocated by the caller and filled in by the callee. The *tymed* member of both **FORMATETC** structure pointers (*pFormatetc->tymed* and *pFormatecOut->tymed*) is not significant and should be ignored.

The simplest implementation of **IDataObject::GetCanonicalFormatEtc** returns DATA_S_SAMEFORMATETC and sets *pFormatetcOut->ptd* to NULL. This type of implementation implies that the callee, usually a more sophisticated application, is sensitive to target devices.

IDataObject::SetData

HRESULT IDataObject::SetData(*pFormatetc, pmedium, fRelease***)**
LPFORMATETC *pFormatetc*
LPSTGMEDIUM *pmedium*
unsigned long *fRelease*

IDataObject::SetData sends data in a specified format.

Parameters

pFormatetc
Points to the format to use when interpreting the data contained in the storage medium.

pmedium
Points to the storage medium (an in parameter only) containing the actual data.

fRelease
Indicates who has ownership of the storage medium after completing the method. If TRUE, the callee takes ownership, freeing the medium after it has been used. If FALSE, the caller retains ownership and the callee uses the storage medium for the duration of the call only.

Return Values

Value	Meaning
S_OK	Data was successfully used.
E_INVALIDARG	One or more arguments are invalid.
E_OUTOFMEMORY	Ran out of memory.
E_UNEXPECTED	A relatively catastrophic failure.
DV_E_LINDEX	Currently only *lindex* -1 is supported. Passing any other lindex results in an error.
DV_E_FORMATETC	Invalid FORMATETC structure.

Value	Meaning
DV_E_TYMED	Invalid *tymed* value.
DV_E_DVASPECT	Invalid *dwAspect* value.
OLE_E _NOTRUNNING	Object application is not running.

Comments

The callee does not take ownership of the data until it has successfully used it. That is, DATA_E_FORMATETC or another error code is not returned. When the callee does take ownership, it must free the medium by calling **ReleaseStgMedium**.

See Also

IDataObject::GetData, **ReleaseStgMedium**

IDataObject::EnumFormatEtc

HRESULT IDataObject::EnumFormatEtc(*dwDirection*, *ppenumFormatetc* **)**
unsigned long *dwDirection*
LPENUMFORMATETC * *ppenumFormatetc*

IDataObject::EnumFormatEtc enumerates the formats that can be used to store data obtained with **IDataObject::GetData** or sent with **IDataObject::SetData**.

Parameters

dwDirection
Indicates the set of formats to be enumerated; valid values are taken from the enumeration **DATADIR.** For more information, see the following comments.

ppenumFormatetc
Points to where to return the instantiated enumerator.

Return Values

Value	Meaning
S_OK	Enumerator returned successfully.
E_INVALIDARG	One or more arguments are invalid.
E_OUTOFMEMORY	Ran out of memory.
E_NOTIMPL	The direction indicated by *dwDirection* is not supported.
OLE_S_USEREG	Request that OLE enumerate the formats from the Registration Database file.

Comments

The enumeration returned by **IDataObject::EnumFormatEtc** is not a guarantee of support because the formats can change over time. Accordingly, applications should treat the enumeration as a hint to the format types that can be passed.

IDataObject::EnumFormatEtc is called when one of the following actions occurs:

- An application calls **OleSetClipboard**. OLE must determine whether it is necessary to put OLE 1 compatibility formats on the clipboard.
- Data is being pasted from the clipboard or dropped. An application uses the first acceptable format.
- The Paste Special dialog box is displayed. The target application builds the list of formats from the **FORMATETC** entries.

Values for *dwDirection* are taken form the enumeration **DATADIR**, which is defined in dvobj.h as follows:

```
typedef enum tagDATADIR
{
    DATADIR_GET = 1,
    DATADIR_SET = 2,
} DATADIR;
```

Specifying DATADIR_GET for dwDirection enumerates formats that can be passed to **IDataObject::GetData**. DATADIR_SET enumerates formats that can be passed to **IDataObject::SetData**.

Formats can be registered statically in the Registration Database file or dynamically during application initialization. If an application has an unchanging list of formats and these formats are registered in the Registration Database file, it can ask OLE to enumerate the formats in the Registration Database file by calling **OleRegEnumFormatEtc** or by returning OLE_S_USEREG. OLE_S_USEREG instructs the default handler to call **OleRegEnumFormatEtc**. Object applications that are implemented as DLL object applications cannot return OLE_S_USEREG; they must call **OleRegEnumFormatEtc** directly.

Private formats can be enumerated for OLE 1 objects, if they are registered with the RequestDataFormats or SetDataFormats keys in the Registration Database file. Also, private formats can be enumerated for OLE 2 objects, if they are registered with the GetDataFormats or SetDataFormats keys.

For OLE 1 objects whose object applications do not have RequestDataFormats or SetDataFormats information registered in the Registration Database file, calling **IDataObject::EnumFormatEtc** with DATADIR_GET only enumerates the PICT format, regardless of whether they support other formats. Calling **IDataObject::EnumFormatEtc** with DATADIR_SET on such objects only enumerates Native, regardless of whether the object supports being set with other formats.

The **FORMATETC** structure returned by the enumeration usually indicates a NULL target device (*ptd*). This is appropriate because, unlike the other members of **FORMATETC**, the target device does not participate in the object's decision as to whether it can accept or provide the data in an **IDataObject::SetData** or **IDataObject::GetData** call, respectively.

FORMATETC::*tymed* often indicates that more than one kind of storage medium is acceptable.

See Also **IDataObject::SetData**, **IDataObject::GetData**, **OleRegEnumFormatEtc**

IDataObject::DAdvise

HRESULT IDataObject::DAdvise(*pFormatetc, advf, pAdvise, pdwConnection*)
FORMATETC * *pFormatetc*
unsigned long *advf*
LPADVISESINK *pAdvise*
unsigned long * *pdwConnection*

IDataObject::DAdvise creates a connection between the data transfer object and an advisory sink through which the sink can be informed when the object's data changes.

Parameters

pFormatetc
Points to the format to use when reporting changes to the specified sink.

advf
Contains a group of flags that specify information about the advisory connection; valid values are from the enumeration **ADVF**. For more information, see the section "ADVF Enumeration," earlier in this chapter.

pAdvise
Points to the advisory sink that should be informed of changes.

pdwConnection
Points to where to return the token that can later be passed to **IDataObject::DUnadvise** to remove an advisory connection.

Return Values

Value	Meaning
S_OK	The connection was successfully created.
E_INVALIDARG	One or more arguments are invalid.
E_OUTOFMEMORY	Ran out of memory.
E_UNEXPECTED	A relatively catastrophic failure.
DV_E_LINDEX	Invalid value for *lindex*; currently only -1 is supported.

Value	Meaning
DATA_E _FORMATETC	Cannot support the requested media.
OLE_E _ADVISENOTSUPPORTED	Advisory notifications are not supported.

Comments

Data transfer object implementations of **IDataObject** typically do not support advisory notifications and return OLE_E_ADVISENOTSUPPORTED from **IDataObject::DAdvise**.

By calling this method, callers register to be notified when data in the format and medium specified in *pFormatetc* changes. When a change occurs, a call is made to *pAdvise->OnDataChange*.

Applications that implement **IDataObject::DAdvise** can use the functionality provided in the **IDataAdviseHolder** interface. OLE supplies an **IDataAdviseHolder** implementation, accessible by calling **CreateDataAdviseHolder**.

If an advisory connection is successfully established, the object returns a nonzero value through *pdwConnection*; if a connection fails to be established, it returns zero. The caller can remove the established connection by passing the nonzero value of *pdwConnection* back to the object in a call to **IDataObject::DUnadvise**.

Containers of linked objects can set up advisory connections directly with the bound link source or indirectly via the standard OLE link object that manages the connection. Connections, set up through the OLE link object, are destroyed when the link object is deleted. Connections that are set up with the bound link source are not automatically deleted; the container must explicitly call **IDataObject::UnDAdvise** on the bound link source to delete it.

The OLE default link object creates a "wildcard advise" with the link source so that OLE can maintain the time-of-last change. This advise is specifically used to note the time that anything changed; OLE ignores all data formats that may have changed, noting just the time of last change. To allow wild card advises, the FORMATETC members should be set as follows before calling **IDataObject::DAdvise**:

```
cf == 0;
ptd == NULL;
dwAspect == -1;
lindex == -1
tymed == -1
```

The Advise flags should also include ADVF_NODATA.

Wildcard advises from OLE should always be accepted by applications.

See Also

IDataAdviseHolder interface, **IAdviseSink::OnDataChange**, **IDataObject::DUnadvise**

IDataObject::DUnadvise

HRESULT IDataObject::DUnadvise(*dwConnection*)
unsigned long *dwConnection*

IDataObject::DUnadvise deletes an advisory connection previously established by **IDataObject::DAdvise**.

Parameters

dwConnection
Specifies a nonzero value previously returned from **IDataObject::DAdvise**.

Return Values

Value	Meaning
S_OK	The connection was successfully deleted.
E_FAIL	The *pdwConnection* value does not indicate a valid connection.
E_OUTOFMEMORY	Ran out of memory.
OLE_E _ADVISENOTSUPPORTED	This **IDataObject** implementation does not support data advises.
OLE_E _NOCONNECTION	There is no connection for this connection identifier.

Comments

The *dwConnection* parameter is a nonzero value returned through *pdwConnection* in **IDataObject::DAdvise**. If this value does not actually indicate a valid connection, E_FAIL is returned.

If the advisory connection being deleted was initially set up using **IDataAdviseHolder::Advise**, **IDataAdviseHolder::Unadvise** should be called to delete it.

See Also

IDataObject::DAdvise

IDataObject::EnumDAdvise

HRESULT IDataObject::EnumDAdvise(*ppenumAdvise*)
LPENUMSTATDATA * *ppenumAdvise*

IDataObject::EnumDAdvise enumerates the advisory connections currently established on an object.

Parameters

ppenumAdvise
Points to where the new enumerator should be returned. NULL indicates there are no connections.

Return Values

Value	Meaning
S_OK	Enumerator returned successfully.
E_FAIL	Enumerator cannot be returned.
E_OUTOFMEMORY	Ran out of memory.
OLE_E _ADVISENOTSUPPORTED	Advisory notifications not supported.

Comments

The returned enumerator enumerates data stored in a **STATDATA** structure format.

The **STATDATA** structure is defined in dvobj.h as follows:

```
typedef struct tagSTATDATA
{
    FORMATETC       formatetc;
    unsigned long   advf;
    LPADVISESINK    pAdvSink;
    unsigned long   dwConnection;
} STATDATA;
```

While an enumeration is in progress, registering or revoking advisory connections on what is later enumerated is undefined. If there are no connections on the object, NULL is returned through *ppenumAdvise*.

CreateDataAdviseHolder

HRESULT CreateDataAdviseHolder(*ppDAHolder***)**
LPDATAADVISEHOLDER * *ppDAHolder*

CreateDataAdviseHolder returns an instance of the **IDataAdviseHolder** interface.

Parameters

ppDAHolder
Points to where to return the new interface instance.

Return Values

Value	Meaning
S_OK	**IDataAdviseHolder** instance successfully returned.
E_OUTOFMEMORY	**IDataAdviseHolder** instance could not be returned due to lack of memory.

Comments

The **IDataAdviseHolder** methods are used by objects that support data advisory connections to manage registration and notification; **IDataAdviseHolder** is described in the next section.

IDataAdviseHolder Interface

The **IDataAdviseHolder** interface is implemented by OLE and is used by object applications.The interface methods are used to keep track of the set of **IDataObject::DAdvise** calls and to send data change notifications when appropriate.

Object applications and handlers implementing **IDataObject::DAdvise**, **IDataObject::DUnadvise**, and **IDataObject::EnumDAdvise** can forward these calls to the corresponding methods in **IDataAdviseHolder**. The examples shown in the discussion of these methods illustrates how to do this.

IDataAdviseHolder contains the following methods:

```
DECLARE_INTERFACE_(IDataAdviseHolder, IUnknown)
{
  // *** IUnknown methods ***
  HRESULT QueryInterface (REFIID riid, void * * ppv);
  unsigned long AddRef () ;
  unsigned long Release ();

  // *** IDataAdviseHolder methods ***
  HRESULT Advise (LPDATAOBJECT pDataObject, FORMATETC * pFetc,
       unsigned long advf, LPADVISESINK pAdvise, unsigned long * pdwConnection);
  HRESULT Unadvise (unsigned long dwConnection);
  HRESULT EnumAdvise (LPENUMSTATDATA * ppenumAdvise);
  HRESULT SendOnDataChange (LPDATAOBJECT pDataObject, unsigned long dwReserved,
       unsigned long advf);
};
```

For more information, see the dvobj.h header file.

IDataAdviseHolder::Advise

HRESULT IDataAdviseHolder::Advise(*pDataObject, pFormatetc, advf, pAdvise, pdwConnection***)**
PDATAOBJECT *pDataObject*
LPFORMATETC * *pFormatetc*
unsigned long *advf*
LPADVISESINK *pAdvise*
unsigned long * *pdwConnection*

IDataAdviseHolder::Advise creates a connection between the data object and an advisory sink through which the sink can be informed when the object's data changes.

Parameters

pDataObject
Points to the source of the data.

pFormatetc
Points to the format to use when reporting changes to the specified sink.

advf
Contains a group of flags from the enumeration **ADVF** that specifies information about the advisory connection. For more information, see the description of the **ADVF** enumeration earlier in this chapter.

pAdvise
Points to the advisory sink that should be informed of changes.

pdwConnection
Points to where to return the token that can later be used to delete an advisory connection by passing it to **IDataAdviseHolder::Unadvise**.

Return Values

Value	Meaning
S_OK	The advisory connection was created.
E_INVALIDARG	One or more arguments are invalid.
DV_E_LINDEX	Invalid value for *lindex*; currently only -1 is supported.

Comments

Callers register to be notified when data in the format and medium specified in *pFormatetc* changes. A call is made to **IAdviseSink::OnDataChange** when a change occurs.

If an advisory connection is successfully established, the object returns a nonzero value through *pdwConnection.* If a connection fails to be established, it returns zero. The caller can delete the established connection by passing the nonzero value of *pdwConnection* back to the object in a call to **IDataAdviseHolder::Unadvise**.

See Also

IDataObject::DUnadvise, **CreateDataAdviseHolder**

IDataAdviseHolder::Unadvise

HRESULT IDataAdviseHolder::Unadvise(*dwConnection***)**
unsigned long *dwConnection*

IDataAdviseHolder::Unadvise deletes an advisory connection previously established by **IDataAdviseHolder::Advise**.

Parameters

dwConnection
Specifies a nonzero value previously returned from **IDataAdviseHolder::Advise**. If this value does not actually indicate a valid connection, E_FAIL is returned.

Return Values

Value	Meaning
S_OK	The previously established advisory connection was successfully deleted.
OLE_E_NOCONNECTION	The *dwConnection* parameter does not represent a valid connection.

IDataAdviseHolder::EnumAdvise

HRESULT IDataAdviseHolder::EnumAdvise(*ppenumAdvise* **)**
LPENUMSTATDATA * *ppenumAdvise*

IDataAdviseHolder::EnumAdvise enumerates the advisory connections currently established on an object.

Parameters

ppenumAdvise
Points to where the new enumerator should be returned. NULL indicates there are presently no connections.

Return Values

Value	Meaning
S_OK	Enumerator successfully returned.
E_OUTOFMEMORY	Enumerator could not be returned due to lack of memory.

Comments

While an enumeration is in progress, the effect of registering or revoking advisory connections on what is later enumerated is undefined. If there are no connections on the object, NULL is returned through *ppenumAdvise*.

IDataAdviseHolder::SendOnDataChange

HRESULT IDataAdviseHolder::SendOnDataChange(*pDataObject, dwReserved, advf***)**
LPDATAOBJECT *pDataObject*
unsigned long *dwReserved*
unsigned long *advf*

IDataAdviseHolder::SendOnDataChange calls **IAdviseSink::OnDataChange** for all advisory sinks currently registered with the data-advise holder whenever changes to the object occur.

Parameters

pDataObject
Points to the source of the data to be passed in the **IAdviseSink::OnDataChange** call(s). This is the object in which the data change has just occurred.

dwReserved
Reserved, must be zero.

advf
Contains a group of flags from the **ADVF** enumeration that specifies information about the notification to be sent. For more information, see the section "ADVF Enumeration," earlier in this chapter.

Return Values

Value	Meaning
S_OK	Data change notification successfully sent.
E_OUTOFMEMORY	Notification could not be sent due to lack of memory.

Comments

If the ADVF_NODATA flag is not specified when the advisory connection is initially set up, data is passed with the **IAdviseSink::OnDataChange** call. This data is obtained by calling **IDataObject::GetData**.

The value for *advf* is typically NULL. The only exception occurs when the object is shutting down and is sending the last data change notification for one or more clients that request only one data notification when the object shuts down. In this case, the value ADVF_DATAONSTOP should be passed for *advf*. None of the other ADVF flags are meaningful for **IDataAdviseHolder::SendOnDataChange**.

IEnumFORMATETC Interface

The **IEnumFORMATETC** interface enumerates arrays of **FORMATETC** data structures. Applications can implement **IEnumFORMATETC** for use in **IDataObject::EnumFormatEtc** or use the implementation provided in the OLE sample code.

IEnumFORMATETC is defined in dvobj.h as follows:

```
DECLARE_INTERFACE_(IEnumFORMATETC, IUnknown)
{
  // *** IUnknown methods ***
 HRESULT QueryInterface (REFIID riid, void * * ppvObj);
 unsigned long AddRef () ;
 unsigned long Release ();

  // *** IEnumFORMATETC methods ***
 HRESULT Next (unsigned long celt, FORMATETC * rgelt, unsigned long *pceltFetched);
 HRESULT Skip (unsigned long celt);
 HRESULT Reset();
 HRESULT Clone(IEnumFORMATETC ** ppenum);
};
```

For more information about enumerators in general, see the **IEnum*X*** interface in Chapter 5, "Component Object Interfaces and Functions."

The following data structure is the sample code supplied for the **IEnumFORMATETC** object. The first member is a pointer to the **IEnumFORMATETC** virtual function table. The other members keep track of the reference count on the interface, the current position within the enumeration, the total number of items available, and a **FORMATETC** structure pointer.

```
typedef struct tagOleStdEnumFmtEtc {
    IEnumFORMATETCVtbl * lpVtbl;
    unsigned long m_dwRefs;        /* reference count */
    unsigned long m_nIndex;        /* current index in list */
    unsigned long m_nCount;        /* how many items in list */
    LPFORMATETC m_lpEtc;           /* list of formatetc */
} OLESTDENUMFMTETC, * LPOLESTDENUMFMTETC;
```

The **OleStdEnumFmtEtc_Create** function in the sample code returns an **IEnumFORMATETC** interface pointer that can be used to enumerate through an object's array of format information. For an illustration of how this is done, see the code example under the description of **IDataObject::EnumFormatEtc**.

IEnumSTATDATA Interface

The **IEnumSTATDATA** interface enumerates through a set of data change notifications. Applications can implement **IEnumSTATDATA** for use in **IDataObject::EnumDAdvise** or use the implementation provided in **IDataAdviseHolder::EnumAdvise**.

IEnumSTATDATA is defined to enumerate types of **STATDATA** and is defined as follows:

```
DECLARE_INTERFACE_(IEnumSTATDATA, IUnknown)
{
  // *** IUnknown methods ***
 HRESULT QueryInterface (REFIID riid, void * * ppvObj);
 unsigned long AddRef () ;
 unsigned long Release ();

  // *** IEnumSTATDATA methods ***
 HRESULT Next (unsigned long celt, STATDATA * rgelt, unsigned long *pceltFetched);
 HRESULT Skip (unsigned long celt);
 HRESULT Reset();
 HRESULT Clone(IEnumSTATDATA ** ppenum);
};
```

For more information, see the dvobj.h header file.

For more information about enumerators in general, see the **IEnum*X*** interface in Chapter 5, "Component Object Interfaces and Functions."

IViewObject Interface

The **IViewObject** interface is similar to the **IDataObject** interface but operates in the context of drawing pictures instead of getting data. **IViewObject** supports the display and printing of data and the registration of view change notifications.

The **IViewObject** interface enables an object to be drawn on a caller-provided grafport. The caller can ask the object to compose a picture for a target device that is independent of the drawing grafport. As a result, the picture can be composed for one target device and drawn on another grafport. Different object representations can also be selected. For example, a caller can ask for an embedded object's content or iconic representation.

Unlike most interfaces, **IViewObject** is never accessed remotely.

The **IViewObject** interface contains the following methods:

```
DECLARE_INTERFACE_(IViewObject, IUnknown)
{
  // *** IUnknown methods ***
 HRESULT QueryInterface (REFIID riid, void * * ppvObj);
 unsigned long AddRef () ;
 unsigned long Release ();

  // *** IViewObject methods ***
 HRESULT Draw (unsigned long dwAspect, long lindex, void * pvAspect, DVTARGETDEVICE * ptd,
          GrafPtr pGrafTargetDev, GrafPtr pGrafDraw, LPCRECTL lprcBounds,
          LPCRECTL lprcWBounds, void *, unsigned long dwContinue);
 HRESULT GetColorSet (unsigned long dwAspect, long lindex, void * pvAspect,
          DVTARGETDEVICE * ptd, GrafPtr pGrafTargetDev, void * * ppColorSet);
 HRESULT Freeze (unsigned long dwAspect, long lindex, void * pvAspect, unsigned long * pdwFreeze);
 HRESULT Unfreeze (unsigned long dwFreeze);
 HRESULT SetAdvise (unsigned long dwAspect, unsigned long advf, LPADVISESINK pAdvise);
 HRESULT GetAdvise (unsigned long * pAspect, unsigned long * padvf, LPADVISESINK * ppAdvise);
};
```

For more information, see the dvobj.h header file.

IViewObject::Draw

HRESULT IViewObject::Draw(*dwAspect, lindex, pvAspect, ptd, pGrafTargetDev, pGrafDraw, lprcBounds, lprcWBounds, reserved, reserved*)

unsigned long *dwAspect*
long *lindex*
void * *pvAspect*
DVTARGETDEVICE * *ptd*
GrafPtr *pGrafTargetDev*
GrafPtr *pGrafDraw*
LPCRECTL *lprcBounds*
LPCRECTL *lprcWBounds*
unsigned long *reserved*
unsigned long *reserved*

IViewObject::Draw draws a pictorial representation of an object on a device context.

Parameters

dwAspect
Specifies the requested view of the object. This parameter contains only one value taken from the enumeration **DVASPECT**. For more information, see "DVASPECT Enumeration," earlier in this chapter.

lindex
Indicates the piece of the object that is of interest. Currently, only -1 is supported. Any other value results in an error.

pvAspect
Currently, this pointer must be NULL.

ptd
Points to the target device for which the picture should be rendered. If this value is NULL, the picture should be rendered for a default target device, usually a display device.

pGrafTargetDev
Specifies the information context on the target device indicated by *ptd*. This can be a device context, but is not necessarily. If *ptd* is NULL, *pGrafTargetDev* must also be NULL.

pGrafDraw
Specifies the GRAFPORT onto which the drawing should actually be done.

lprcBounds
Points to a **Rect** structure that indicates the rectangle (in local window coordinates) on which the object should be drawn. This parameter controls the positioning and stretching of the object.

lprcWBounds
On the Macintosh, must be NULL.

reserved
Reserved for future use; must be zero.

reserved
Reserved for future use; must be zero.

Return Values

Value	Meaning
S_OK	Object successfully drawn.
E_INVALIDARG	One or more arguments are invalid.
E_OUTOFMEMORY	Ran out of memory.
OLE_E_BLANK	No data to draw from.
E_ABORT	Draw operation aborted.
VIEW_E_DRAW	Error in drawing.
DV_E_LINDEX	Invalid value for *lindex*; currently only -1 is supported.
DV_E_DVASPECT	Invalid value for *dwAspect*.
OLE_E_INVALIDRECT	Invalid rectangle.

Comments

The *pGrafTargetDev* parameter is typically an information context on the *ptd* target device. Objects almost always need an information context for the target device. However, callers must be aware that it might be a full device context instead. Because callers usually have a device context available, the *pGrafTargetDev* parameter is passed by the caller for the convenience of the object.

For **IViewObject::Draw**, there is a relationship between the *dwAspect* value and the *lindex* and *lprcbounds* values. The *lprcbounds* value specifies the rectangle on *pGrafDraw* into which the drawing is to be mapped. For DVASPECT_THUMBNAIL, the object draws whatever it wants to draw, and it maps it into the space given in the best way. The client has no compositional control. Some objects might scale to fit while some might scale to fit but preserve aspect ratio. In addition, some might scale full width, but crop the bottom. For DVASPECT_ICON, the container can control the compositional size of the icon by using **IOleObject::SetExtent** and **IOleObject::GetExtent**, if the object supports **IOleObject**, or with **IViewObject2::GetExtent**. Otherwise, the compositional size of the icon is implicitly determined by the object itself and the container has no control over it.

IViewObject::GetColorSet

HRESULT IViewObject::GetColorSet(*dwAspect, lindex, pvAspect, ptd, pGrafTargetDev, ppColorSet*)
unsigned long *dwAspect*
long *lindex*
void * *pvAspect*
DVTARGETDEVICE * *ptd*
GrafPtr *pGrafTargetDev*
void * * *ppColorSet*

IViewObject::GetColorSet returns the set of colors that would be used by a call to **IViewObject::Draw** with the corresponding parameters. This method is not implemented in this release of OLE for the Macintosh.

Parameters

dwAspect
Specifies the requested view of the object. This parameter contains only one value taken from the enumeration **DVASPECT**. For more information, see "DVASPECT Enumeration,"earlier in this chapter.

lindex
Indicates the piece of the object that is of interest. Currently only -1 is supported. Any other value results in an error.

pvAspect
Currently, this pointer must be NULL.

ptd
Points to the target device for which the picture should be rendered. If this value is NULL, the picture should be rendered for a default target device, usually a display device.

pGrafTargetDev
Specifies the information context on the target device indicated by *ptd*. This parameter can be a device context, but is not necessarily. If *ptd* is NULL, *pGrafTargetDev* must also be NULL.

ppColorSet
Points to where to return the set of colors that would be used. If the object does not return the color set, NULL is returned.

Return Values

Value	Meaning
S_OK	Set of colors successfully returned.
S_FALSE	Set of colors is empty or the object does not care to give the information out.
E_INVALIDARG	One or more arguments are invalid.
E_OUTOFMEMORY	Ran out of memory.

Value	Meaning
E_UNEXPECTED	A relatively catastrophic failure.
DV_E_LINDEX	Invalid value for *lindex*; currently only -1 is supported.
DV_E_DVASPECT	Invalid value for *dwAspect*.

Comments

IViewObject::GetColorSet recursively queries any nested objects and returns a color set that represents the union of all colors requested. The color set eventually percolates to the top-level container that owns the window frame. This container can call **IViewObject::GetColorSet** on each of its embedded objects to obtain all the colors needed to draw the embedded objects. The container can use the color sets obtained in conjunction with the colors it needs to set the overall color palette.

IViewObject::Freeze

HRESULT IViewObject::Freeze(*dwAspect*, *lindex*, *pvAspect*, *pdwFreeze*)
unsigned long *dwAspect*
long *lindex*
void * *pvAspect*
unsigned long * *pdwFreeze*

IViewObject::Freeze informs an object that it should not change its drawn representation until a subsequent **IViewObject::Unfreeze** is called.

Parameters

dwAspect
Specifies the requested view of the object. This parameter contains only one value taken from the enumeration **DVASPECT**. For more information, see "DVASPECT Enumeration,"earlier in this chapter.

lindex
Indicates the piece of the object that is of interest. Currently only -1 is supported. Any other value results in an error.

pvAspect
Currently, this pointer must be NULL.

pdwFreeze
Points to where to return the key that is later passed to **IViewObject::Unfreeze**. This key is an index that the default cache uses to keep track of which object is frozen.

Return Values

Value	Meaning
S_OK	Presentation successfully frozen.
VIEW_S_ALREADYFROZEN	Presentation has already been frozen.

Value	Meaning
OLE_E_BLANK	Nothing in the cache.
DV_E_LINDEX	Invalid value for *lindex*; currently, only -1 is supported.
DV_E_DVASPECT	Invalid value for *dwAspect*.

Comments

After calling **IViewObject::Freeze**, successive calls to **IViewObject::Draw** (using the same parameters) produce the same picture, until **IViewObject::Unfreeze** is called. The most common use of this method is for banded printing.

While in a frozen state, view notifications are not sent. Pending view notifications are deferred to the subsequent call to **IViewObject::Unfreeze**.

See Also

IViewObject::Unfreeze

IViewObject::Unfreeze

HRESULT IViewObject::Unfreeze(*dwFreeze***)**
unsigned long *dwFreeze*

IViewObject::Unfreeze unfreezes a drawing previously frozen with **IViewObject::Freeze**.

Parameters

dwFreeze
Contains a key previously returned from **IViewObject::Freeze**. This key determines which object to unfreeze.

Return Values

Value	Meaning
S_OK	Drawing was successfully unfrozen.
OLE_E _NOCONNECTION	Error in the unfreezing process or the object is currently not frozen

See Also

IViewObject::Freeze

IViewObject::SetAdvise

HRESULT IViewObject::SetAdvise(*dwAspect, advf, pAdvise***)**
unsigned long *dwAspect*
unsigned long *advf*
LPADVISESINK *pAdvise*

IViewObject::SetAdvise sets up an advisory connection between the view object and an advisory sink through which the sink can be informed of changes made to an object's drawings.

Parameters

dwAspect
Specifies the view of the object for which the advisory connection is to be established. This parameter can contain only one value from the enumeration **DVASPECT**. For more information, see "DVASPECT Enumeration," earlier in this chapter.

advf
Contains a group of flags that specify information about the advisory connection; values are taken from the enumeration **ADVF**. For more information, see the section "ADVF Enumeration," earlier in this chapter.

pAdvise
Points to the advisory sink that is to be informed of changes. A NULL value deletes any existing advisory connection.

Return Values

Value	Meaning
S_OK	The advisory connection was successfully established.
E_INVALIDARG	One or more arguments are invalid.
E_OUTOFMEMORY	Ran out of memory.
OLE_E _ADVISENOTSUPPORTED	Advisory notifications are not supported.
DV_E_DVASPECT	Invalid value for *dwAspect*.

Comments

Callers register with this method to be notified when an object's view changes. When a change does occur, a call is made to *pAdvise*->**OnViewChange**.

At any time, a given **IViewObject** instance can support only one advisory connection. An existing advisory connection can be deleted by calling **IViewObject::SetAdvise** with *pAdvise* set to NULL.

See Also

IViewObject::GetAdvise, **IAdviseSink::OnDataChange**

IViewObject::GetAdvise

HRESULT IViewObject::GetAdvise(*pAspect*, *padvf*, *ppAdvise***)**
unsigned long * *pAspect*
unsigned long * *padvf*
LPADVISESINK * *ppAdvise*

IViewObject::GetAdvise retrieves the existing advisory connection, if any, on the object.

Parameters

pAspect
Points to where to return the most recent aspect of the object as returned by **IViewObject::SetAdvise**(*dwAspect*, ...). It can be NULL, indicating that the caller does not want this value returned.

padvf
Analogous to *pAspect*, but with respect to the *advf* parameter to **IViewObject::SetAdvise**. Can be NULL.

ppAdvise
Analogous to *pAspect*, but with respect to the *pAdvise* parameter to **IViewObject::SetAdvise**. Can be NULL.

Return Values

Value	Meaning
S_OK	The existing advisory connection was retrieved.
E_INVALIDARG	One or more arguments are invalid.
E_OUTOFMEMORY	Ran out of memory.

Comments

IViewObject::GetAdvise returns the values passed in the most recent call to **IViewObject::SetAdvise**.

See Also

IViewObject::SetAdvise

IViewObject2 Interface

The **IViewObject2** interface is implemented and used as an extension to the **IViewObject** interface implemented as implemented by DLL object applications and object handlers. A default implementation is provided with the OLE libraries. The interface is used by containers and object handlers to get the view extents of an object.

IViewObject2 contains the following methods:

```
DECLARE_INTERFACE_(IViewObject2, IViewObject)
{
  // *** IUnknown methods ***
  HRESULT QueryInterface (REFIID riid, void * * ppvObj);
  unsigned long AddRef () ;
  unsigned long Release ();

  // *** IViewObject methods ***
 HRESULT Draw (unsigned long dwAspect, long lindex, void * pvAspect, DVTARGETDEVICE  * ptd,
      GrafPtr pGrafTargetDev, GrafPtr pGrafDraw, LPCRECTL lprcBounds,
      LPCRECTL lprcWBounds, void *, unsigned long dwContinue);
 HRESULT GetColorSet (unsigned long dwAspect, long lindex, void * pvAspect,
      DVTARGETDEVICE * ptd, GrafPtr pGrafTargetDev, void * * ppColorSet);
 HRESULT Freeze (unsigned long dwAspect, long lindex, void * pvAspect, unsigned long * pdwFreeze);
 HRESULT Unfreeze (unsigned long dwFreeze);
 HRESULT SetAdvise (unsigned long dwAspect, unsigned long advf, LPADVISESINK pAdvise);
 HRESULT GetAdvise (unsigned long * pAspect, unsigned long * padvf, LPADVISESINK * ppAdvise);
```

```
    // *** IViewObject2 methods ***
    HRESULT GetExtent (unsigned long dwAspect, long lindex, DVTARGETDEVICE * ptd,
        LPSIZEL lpsizel);
};
```

For more information, see the dvobj.h header file.

IViewObject2::GetExtent

IViewObject2::GetExtent(*dwAspect*, *lindex*, *ptd*, *lpsizel*)
unsigned long *dwAspect*
unsigned long *lindex*
DVTARGETDEVICE *ptd*
LPSIZEL *lpsizel*

IViewObject2::GetExtent retrieves the view extent of an object, returning the size of the object in the cache.

Parameters

dwAspect
Specifies the requested view of the object. This parameter can contain only one value taken from the enumeration **DVASPECT**. For more information, see "DVASPECT Enumeration," earlier in this chapter.

lindex
Indicates the piece of the object that is of interest. Currently, only -1 is supported. Any other value results in an error.

ptd
Points to the target device for which the object's extent should be returned.

lpsizel
Points to where the object's extent is to be returned.

Return Values

Value	Meaning
S_OK	The object's extent was successfully returned.
OLE_E_BLANK	Appropriate cache is not available.
E_OUTOFMEMORY	Insufficient memory.

Comments

OLE provides a default implementation of **IViewObject2::GetExtent** that searches only the cache for the extent. This method is never remoted to the object application.

To prevent the object from being run if it isn't already running, containers call **IViewObject2::GetExtent** rather than **IOleObject::GetExtent** to determine the extents of the presentation to be drawn.

See Also

IOleObject::GetExtent

IOleCache Interface

The **IOleCache** interface enables objects to control what data gets cached inside an embedded object and to determine the data that will be available to the container when the object is not running or is unavailable.

The **IOleCache** interface is implemented by OLE and is used by container applications.

IOleCache contains the following methods:

```
DECLARE_INTERFACE_(IOleCache, IUnknown)
{
   // *** IUnknown methods ***
  HRESULT QueryInterface (REFIID riid, void * * ppvObj);
  unsigned long AddRef () ;
  unsigned long Release ();

   // *** IOleCache methods ***
  HRESULT Cache (LPFORMATETC pFormatetc, unsigned long advf, unsigned long * lpdwConnection);
  HRESULT Uncache (unsigned long dwConnection);
  HRESULT EnumCache (LPENUMSTATDATA * ppenumStatData);
  HRESULT InitCache (LPDATAOBJECT pDataObject);
  HRESULT SetData (LPFORMATETC pFormatetc, STGMEDIUM * pmedium, unsigned long fRelease);
};
```

For more information, see the dvobj.h header file.

IOleCache::Cache

HRESULT IOleCache::Cache(*pFormatetc, advf, lpdwConnection***)**
LPFORMATETC *pFormatetc*
unsigned long *advf*
unsigned long * *lpdwConnection*

IOleCache::Cache specifies the formats and other data to be cached inside an embedded object.

Parameters

pFormatetc
: Points to the data formats that are to be cached.

advf
: Contains a group of flags that specify information about the cache connection; values are taken from the enumeration **ADVF**. For more information, see "ADVF Enumeration," earlier in this chapter.

lpdwConnection
: Points to a returned token value that can later be used to turn caching off. The OLE implementation of caching always uses nonzero numbers for connection identifiers and does not return a value greater than or equal to 0x8000.

Return Values

Value	Meaning
S_OK	Requested data or view successfully cached.
E_INVALIDARG	One or more arguments are invalid.
E_OUTOFMEMORY	Ran out of memory.
E_UNEXPECTED	A relatively catastrophic failure.
CACHE_S_FORMATETC_ NOTSUPPORTED	Indicates the cache was created, but the object application does not support the specified format. Cache creation will succeed even if the format is not supported, allowing the caller to fill the cache. If the caller does not need to keep the cache, **IOleCache::UnCache** should be called.
CACHE_S_SAMECACHE	Indicates a cache already exists for the **FORMATETC** passed to **IOleCache::Cache.** In this case, the new advise flags are assigned to the cache, and the previously assigned connection identifier is returned. The new advise flags are assigned to the cache, and the previously assigned connection identifier are to be returned.
DV_E_LINDEX	Invalid value for *lindex*; currently only -1 is supported.
DV_E_TYMED	The value is not valid for *pFormatetc->tymed.*
DV_E_DVASPECT	The value is not valid for *pFormatetc->dwAspect.*
DV_E_CLIPFORMAT	The value is not valid for *pFormatetc->cfFormat.*
CO_E _NOTINITIALIZED	The cache's storage is not initialized.
DV_E _DVTARGETDEVICE	The value is not valid for *pFormatetc->ptd.*
OLE_E_STATIC	The cache is for static object and it already has a cache node.

Comments

IOleCache::Cache can specify either data caching by passing a valid data format in *pFormatetc* or view (presentation) caching by passing a zero data format in *pFormatetc* as follows:

```
pFormatetc->cfFormat == 0
```

With view caching, the object itself decides on the format to cache.

A custom object handler can choose not to store data in a given format. Instead, it can synthesize it on demand when requested.

IOleCache::Cache only accepts a subset of the values from the **ADVF** enumeration for *advf*; valid values for the *advf* parameter are:

ADVF_NODATA
ADVF_ONLYONCE
ADVF_PRIMEFIRST
ADVFCACHE_NOHANDLER
ADVFCACHE_FORCEBUILTIN
ADVFCACHE_ONSAVE

More detailed information about the **ADVF** enumeration can be found earlier in the section "ADVF Enumeration."

The *advf* value of ADVFCACHE_FORCEBUILTIN ensures that presentation data can be retrieved after the container document has been moved where the object application or object handler is not available.

When **IOleCache::Cache** is called with *pFormatetc->dwAspect* set to DVASPECT_CONTENT, *pFormatetc->lindex* set to -1, and *pFormatetc->ptd* set to NULL for static objects, no cache is created and *lpdwConnection* will be NULL. S_OK is returned, however, because the caching code is able to draw from the native data.

See Also **IOleCache::Uncache**

IOleCache::Uncache

HRESULT IOleCache::Uncache(*dwConnection***)**
unsigned long *dwConnection*

IOleCache::Uncache deletes a cache connection created with **IOleCache::Cache**.

Parameters

dwConnection
Contains the nonzero value previously returned through the *pdwConnection* parameter in a call to **IOleCache::Cache**.

Return Values

Value	Meaning
S_OK	The cache connection was deleted.
OLE_E_NOCONNECTION	No cache connection exists for *dwConnection*.

See Also **IOleCache::Cache**

IOleCache::EnumCache

HRESULT IOleCache::EnumCache(*ppenumStatData***)**
LPENUMSTATDATA * *ppenumStatData*

IOleCache::EnumCache enumerates presently established cache connections.

Parameters

ppenumStatData
Points to where to return the new enumerator. NULL is a legal value and indicates that there are currently no connections.

Return Values

Value	Meaning
S_OK	The cache enumerator successfully returned.
E_OUTOFMEMORY	The cache enumerator could not be returned due to lack of memory.

See Also

IOleCache::Cache

IOleCache::InitCache

HRESULT IOleCache::InitCache(*pDataObject***)**
LPDATAOBJECT *pDataObject*

IOleCache::InitCache fills the cache using the data provided by the data transfer object, *pDataObject*. The data transfer object is usually obtained from the clipboard or from a drag and drop operation.

Parameters

pDataObject
Points to the data transfer object from which the cache is to be initialized.

Return Values

Value	Meaning
S_OK	The cache was filled using the data provided.
E_INVALIDARG	The value is not valid for *pDataObject*.
E_OUTOFMEMORY	The cache could not be initialized due to lack of memory.
OLE_E_NOTRUNNING	The cache is not running.
CACHE_E_NOCACHE _UPDATED	Indicates none of the caches were updated.
CACHE_S_SOMECACHES _NOTUPDATED	Indicates only some of the existing caches were updated.

Comments

IOleCache::InitCache is usually called when an object is created with Embed Source or Link Source data, either by **OleCreateFromData**,

OleCreateLinkFromData or containers that do not use either of these helper functions.

Containers that do not use helper functions to create objects will usually want to use **IOleCache::Cache** to set up the cache entries which are then filled by calling **IOleCache::InitCache**.

See Also **IOleCache::Cache**

IOleCache::SetData

HRESULT IOleCache::SetData(*pFormatetc*, *pmedium*, *fRelease*)
LPFORMATETC *pFormatetc*
STGMEDIUM * *pmedium*
unsigned long *fRelease*

IOleCache::SetData fills the cache using the data contained in the storage medium.

Parameters

pFormatetc
Points to the format of the data being set.

pmedium
Points to the storage medium (an *in* parameter only) that contains the data.

fRelease
Indicates ownership of the storage medium after completion of the method. If TRUE, the callee takes ownership, freeing the medium when it is finished using it. When FALSE, the caller retains ownership and is responsible for freeing the medium. The callee can only use the storage medium for the duration of the call.

Return Values

Value	Meaning
S_OK	The cache was filled.
E_OUTOFMEMORY	Ran out of memory.
DV_E_LINDEX	The value is not valid for *pFormatetc->lindex*. Currently, only -1 is supported.
DV_E_FORMATETC	The **FORMATETC** structure is invalid.
DV_E_TYMED	The value is not valid for *pFormatetc->tymed*.
DV_E_DVASPECT	The value is not valid for *pFormatetc->dwAspect*.
OLE_E_BLANK	Uninitialized object.

Value	Meaning
DV_E_TARGETDEVICE	The object is static and *pFormatetc->ptd* is non-NULL.
STG_E_MEDIUMFULL	Medium is full.

Comments

IOleCache::SetData is usually called when an object is created from the clipboard or through a drag and drop operation and Embed Source data is used to create the object.

IOleCache::SetData is similiar to **IOleCache::InitCache**; the difference is that **IOleCache::SetData** initializes the cache using a single format and **IOleCache::InitCache** uses multiple formats.

See Also

IOleCache::Cache, **IOleCache::InitCache**

IOleCache2 Interface

The **IOleCache2** interface is an extension of the **IOleCache** interface that adds the ability for a client of an object to update each of the maintained caches. **IOleCache2** is implemented by OLE and used by containers and DLL object applications to update one or more caches created with **IOleCache::Cache**.

Even though a default implementation **IOleCache2** is provided with OLE, a DLL object application might need to provide its own implementation, depending on how it caches data.

IOleCache2 contains the following methods:

```
DECLARE_INTERFACE_(IOleCache2, IOleCache)
{
 // *** IUnknown methods ***
 HRESULT QueryInterface (REFIID riid, void * * ppvObj);
 unsigned long AddRef () ;
 unsigned long Release ();

 // *** IOleCache methods ***
 HRESULT Cache (LPFORMATETC pFormatetc, unsigned long advf,
      unsigned long * lpdwConnection);
 HRESULT Uncache (unsigned long dwConnection);
 HRESULT EnumCache (LPENUMSTATDATA * ppenumStatData);
 HRESULT InitCache (LPDATAOBJECT pDataObject);
 HRESULT SetData (LPFORMATETC pFormatetc, STGMEDIUM * pmedium, unsigned long fRelease);

 // *** IOleCache2 methods ***
 HRESULT UpdateCache (LPDATAOBJECT pDataObject, unsigned long grfUpdf, void * pReserved);
 HRESULT DiscardCache (unsigned long dwDiscardOptions);
};
```

For more information, see the dvobj.h header file.

IOleCache2::UpdateCache

HRESULT IOleCache2::UpdateCache(*pDataObject*, *dwgrfUpdf*, *pReserved***)**
LPDATAOBJECT *pDataObject*
unsigned long *dwgrfUpdt*
void * *pReserved*

IOleCache2::UpdateCache updates the cache(s) according to the value of the *grfUpdt* parameter.

Parameters

pDataObject
Points to the object that is the source for updating the cache; can be NULL.

dwgrfUpdt
Specifies the type of cache to update; see the following comments.

pReserved
Reserved parameter; must be NULL.

Return Values

Value	Meaning
S_OK	The cache(s) were updated according to the value specified in *dwgrfUpdt*.
E_OUTOFMEMORY	Out of memory.
E_INVALIDARG	One or more arguments are invalid.
E_UNEXPECTED	An unexpected error occurred.
OLE_E _NOTRUNNING	The specified *pDataObject* is not running.
CACHE_E _NOCACHE_UPDATED	None of the caches were updated.
CACHE_S_SOMECACHES _NOTUPDATED	Some of the caches were updated.

Comments

IOleCache2::UpdateCache can be called by containers or DLL object applications requiring more control over caching. This method is used when the caches need to be updated without updating the object.

The *pDataObject* points to the source for updating the cache(s). Typically, non-NULL values are passed by handlers and DLL object applications. Containers most often pass a NULL *pDataObject*, in which case, the source is obtained from the running object.

The *dwgrfUpdt* parameter controls the caches that get updated. The value is obtained by combining values from the following table:

Cache Control Values	Description
UPDFCACHE _NODATACACHE	Updates caches created by using ADVF_NODATA in the call to **IOleCache::Cache**.
UPDFCACHE _ONSAVECACHE	Updates caches created by using ADVFCACHE_ONSAVE in the call to **IOleCache::Cache**.
UPDFCACHE _ONSTOPCACHE	Updates caches created by using ADVFCACHE_ONSTOP in the call to **IOleCache::Cache**.
UPDFCACHE _NORMALCACHE	Dynamically updates the caches (as is normally done when the object sends out OnDataChange notices).
UPDFCACHE _IFBLANK	Updates the cache if blank, regardless of any other flag specified.
UPDFCACHE _ONLYIFBLANK	Updates only caches that are blank.
UPDFCACHE_ IFBLANKOR-ONSAVECACHE	The equivalent of UPDFCACHE_IFBLANK | UPDFCACHE_ONSAVECACHE.
UPDFCACHE_ALL	Updates all caches.
UPDFCACHE_ ALLBUTNO-DATACACHE	Updates all caches except those created with ADVF_NODATA in the call to **IOleCache::Cache**.

See Also **IOleCache**, **IOleCacheControl**

IOleCache2::DiscardCache

HRESULT IOleCache2::DiscardCache(*dwDiscardOptions*)
unsigned long *dwDiscardOptions*

IOleCache2::DiscardCache flushes the cache(s) that are in memory. The cache will satisfy subsequent **IDataObject::GetData** calls by reverting to disk-based data.

Parameters

dwDiscardOptions
Indicates whether data is to be saved prior to the discard. Valid values are from the enumeration **DISCARDCACHE**. For more information, see the following comments.

Return Values

Value	Meaning
S_OK	The cache(s) were discarded according to the value specified in *dwDiscardOptions*.
OLE_E _NOSTORAGE	There is no storage available for saving the dirty data in the cache.

Comments

IOleCache2::DiscardCache is useful for low memory conditions.

dwDiscardOptions takes its values from the **DISCARDCACHE** enumeration, which is defined in dvobj.h as follows:

```
typedef enum tagDISCARDCACHE {
    DISCARDCACHE_SAVEIFDIRTY     = 0
    DISCARDCACHE_NOSAVE          = 1
} DISCARDCACHE;
```

DISCARDCACHE values have the following meaning:

DISCARDCACHE Values	Meaning
DISCARDCACHE _SAVEIFDIRTY	Indicates that all of the dirty data in the cache(s) should be saved before the discard occurs. Containers that have drawn a large object and need to free up memory may want to specify DISCARDCACHE_SAVEIFDIRTY so that the newest presentation is saved for the next time the object must be drawn.
DISCARDCACHE _NOSAVE	Indicates that no save is necessary. Containers that have activated an embedded object, made some changes, and then called **IOleObject::Close**(OLECLOSE_NOSAVE) to rollback the changes may want to specify this option to ensure that the native and presentation data are not out of sync.

See Also

IOleCache, **IOleCacheControl**

IOleCacheControl Interface

The **IOleCacheControl** interface is used almost exclusively by object handlers or DLL object applications as the means by which the cache part of the handler is connected to the running object's **IDataObject** implementation. This allows the cache to receive notifications from the running object. Containers have no need for this interface; they should use **IRunnableObject** or **OleRun** instead.

IOleCacheControl contains the following methods:

```
DECLARE_INTERFACE_(IOleCacheControl, IUnknown)
{
   // *** IUnknown methods ***
   HRESULT QueryInterface (REFIID riid, void * * ppvObj);
   unsigned long AddRef () ;
   unsigned long  Release ();

   // *** IOleCacheControl methods ***
   HRESULT OnRun (LPDATAOBJECT pDataObject);
   HRESULT OnStop ();
};
```

For more information, see the dvobj.h header file.

IOleCacheControl::OnRun

HRESULT IOleCacheControl::OnRun(*pDataObject*)
LPDATAOBJECT *pDataObject*

IOleCacheControl::OnRun notifies the cache that the compound document object that is its data source has entered its running state.

Parameters

pDataObject
Points to the object that is entering the running state.

Return Values

Value	Meaning
S_OK	The cache was notified and *pDataObject* is valid.
E_OUTOFMEMORY	Out of memory.
E_INVALIDARG	One or more invalid arguments.
E_UNEXPECTED	An unexpected error occurred.

Comments

When **IOleCacheControl::OnRun** is called, the cache sets up advisory notifications as necessary. If the cache is already running, **IOleCacheControl::OnRun** returns S_OK.

Some DLL object applications might use the cache in a passive manner and not call **IOleCacheControl::OnRun**. These applications will need to call **IOleCache2::UpdateCache**, **IOleCache::InitCache**, or **IOleCache::SetData** to fill the cache when necessary to ensure that the cache gets updated.

IOleCacheControl::OnRun does not create a reference count on *pDataObject.* It is the responsibility of the caller of **OleRun** to ensure that the lifetime of *pDataObject* lasts until **IOleCacheControl::OnStop** is called.

Calling **IOleCacheControl::OnRun** creates a data advisory sink between the running object and the cache. The sink is destroyed when **IOleCacheControl::OnStop** is called.

See Also **IOleCacheControl::OnStop**, **OleRun**, **IOleCache2::UpdateCache**

IOleCacheControl::OnStop

HRESULT IOleCacheControl::OnStop()

IOleCacheControl::OnStop notifies the cache that it should terminate any existing connection previously given to it by using **IOleCacheControl::OnRun**. No indication is given as to whether a connection existed or not.

Return Values

Value	Meaning
S_OK	The cache was notified and the advise sink was successfully removed.
E_OUTOFMEMORY	Out of memory.
E_UNEXPECTED	An unexpected error occurred.

Comments The data advisory sink between the running object and the cache is destroyed as part of calling **IOleCacheControl::OnStop**.

See Also **IOleCacheControl::OnRun**

Clipboard Functions

The following functions are used in conjunction with clipboard and other data transfer operations.

```
HRESULT OleSetClipboard(LPDATAOBJECT pDataObject);
HRESULT OleSetClipboardEx(LPDATAOBJECT pDataObject);
HRESULT OleGetClipboard(LPDATAOBJECT * pDataObject);
HRESULT OleFlushClipboard(void);
HRESULT OleIsCurrentClipboard(LPDATAOBJECT pDataObject);
```

For more information, see the ole2.h header file.

OleSetClipboard

HRESULT OleSetClipboard(*pDataObject*)
LPDATAOBJECT *pDataObject*

OleSetClipboard puts the indicated **IDataObject** instance on the clipboard.

Parameters

pDataObject
Points to an **IDataObject** instance from which the data to be presented to the clipboard can be obtained. This parameter can be NULL, in which case the clipboard is emptied.

Return Values

Value	Meaning
S_OK	*pDataObject* was placed on the clipboard.
CLIPBRD_E _CANT_OPEN	Cannot open the clipboard.
CLIPBRD_E _CANT_EMPTY	Cannot empty the clipboard.
CLIPBRD_E _CANT_CLOSE	Cannot close the clipboard.

Comments

Any **IDataObject** formats that are offered on a global handle medium (TYMED_HGLOBAL or TYMED_MFPICT) and formatted with a NULL target device are offered on the clipboard using delayed rendering. The formats necessary for OLE 1 compatibility are synthesized from the OLE 2 formats that are present and put on the clipboard.

The clipboard is emptied before any data is made available. If the clipboard is currently open by another application, **OleSetClipboard** fails.

Passing NULL for *pDataObject* is legal and it empties the clipboard. If the contents of the clipboard are the result of a previous **OleSetClipboard** call and the clipboard is released, the *pDataObject* that was passed to the previous call is released. The clipboard owner should use this as a signal that the data it previously offered is no longer on the clipboard.

OleSetClipboard returns CLIPBRD_E_CANT_OPEN when called by a background process unless the background process owns the clipboard data object and calls **OleSetClipboard**(NULL).

Note If an application needs to leave data on the clipboard after shutting down, it can call **OleSetClipboard** (NULL) and then use the normal clipboard mechanisms for putting data on the clipboard. Calling **OleFlushClipboard** is another option; for more information, see the description of **OleFlushClipboard**.

See Also

OleGetClipboard

OleSetClipboardEx

HRESULT OleSetClipboardEx(*pDataObject*)
LPDATAOBJECT *pDataObject*

OleSetClipboardEx puts the OLE data formats from the indicated **IDataObject** instance on the clipboard.

Parameters

pDataObject
Points to an **IDataObject** instance from which the data to be presented to the clipboard can be obtained. This parameter can be NULL, in which case the clipboard is emptied.

Return Values

Value	Meaning
S_OK	*pDataObject* was placed on the clipboard.
CLIPBRD _E_CANT_OPEN	Cannot open the clipboard.
CLIPBRD _E_CANT_EMPTY	Cannot empty the clipboard.
CLIPBRD _E_CANT_CLOSE	Cannot close the clipboard.

Comments

OleSetClipboardEx is similar in functionality to **OleSetClipboard** except that **OleSetClipboardEx** only puts the OLE data formats on the clipboard.

The formats necessary for OLE 1 compatibility are synthesized from the OLE 2 formats that are present and put on the clipboard.

The clipboard is emptied before any data is made available. If the clipboard is currently open by another application, **OleSetClipboardEx** fails.

Passing NULL for *pDataObject* is legal and it empties the clipboard. If the contents of the clipboard are the result of a previous **OleSetClipboardEx** call and the clipboard is released, the *pDataObject* that was passed to the previous call is released. The clipboard owner should use this as a signal that the data previously offered on the clipboard is no longer available.

Note If an application needs to leave data on the clipboard after shutting down, it can call **OleSetClipboardEx** (NULL) and then use the normal clipboard mechanisms for putting data on the clipboard. Calling **OleFlushClipboard** is another option; for more information, see the description of **OleFlushClipboard**.

See Also

OleSetClipboard, **OleGetClipboard**

OleGetClipboard

HRESULT OleGetClipboard(*pDataObject*)
LPDATAOBJECT * *pDataObject*

OleGetClipboard retrieves the instance of the **IDataObject** from the clipboard that was placed there by using **OleSetClipboard**.

Parameters

pDataObject
Points to where to return the **IDataObject** instance. NULL is only returned in *pDataObject* if **OleGetClipboard** returns S_FALSE.

Return Values

Value	Meaning
S_OK	The **IDataObject** instance was successfully retrieved.
S_FALSE	Another object owns the clipboard.
E_OUTOFMEMORY	Ran out of memory.
CLIPBRD _E_BAD_DATA	Cannot get the contents of *pDataObject* from clipboard. The data on the clipboard is invalid.
CLIPBRD _E_CANT_OPEN	Cannot open the clipboard; often returned when a background process tries to open the clipboard.
CLIPBRD _E_CANT_CLOSE	Cannot close the clipboard.

Comments

If no instance of **IDataObject** exists on the clipboard, **OleGetClipboard** returns an OLE-provided instance of **IDataObject** that wraps the contents of the clipboard. **OleGetClipboard** also transforms OLE 1 clipboard format data into the representation expected by an OLE 2 caller.

The original **IDataObject** instance is not actually returned. Instead, **OleGetClipboard** returns an OLE-provided **IDataObject** implementation that forwards everything to the original except release and accords it special treatment. This allows **OleGetClipboard** to know when its caller is done with the **IDataObject** instance it returns through *pDataObject*.

OleGetClipboard allows only one client at a time to access the clipboard. No other client can access it until the first client has released it. To call either **OleSetClipboard** or **OleFlushClipboard**, access to the clipboard must first be obtained with a call to **OleGetClipboard**. Callers of **OleGetClipboard** should only hold on to the returned **IDataObject** for a very short time. It consumes resources in the application that offered it.

See Also

OleSetClipboard, **OleFlushClipboard**

OleFlushClipboard

HRESULT OleFlushClipboard()

OleFlushClipboard carries out the clipboard shutdown sequence, removing the **IDataObject** instance.

Return Values

Value	Meaning
S_OK	The clipboard has been flushed.
CLIPBRD _E_CANT_OPEN	Cannot open the clipboard.
CLIPBRD _E_CANT_CLOSE	Cannot close the clipboard.

Comments

OleFlushClipboard empties the clipboard as does **OleSetClipboard**(NULL). The difference is that **OleFlushClipboard** leaves all memory-based formats offered by the data transfer object, including the OLE 1 compatibility formats, on the clipboard so that they are available after application shutdown.

Applications should call **OleSetClipboard**(NULL) if there is either no need to leave data on the clipboard after shutdown or if data will be placed on the clipboard using the standard clipboard API functions. Applications should call **OleFlushClipboard** to enable pasting and paste-linking of OLE objects after shutdown.

To invoke **OleFlushClipboard**, the caller must first have obtained access to the clipboard by calling **OleGetClipboard**. After the flush, the **IDataObject** returned from **OleGetClipboard** is invalid for anything but a release operation (**IUnknown::Release**).

See Also

OleGetClipboard

OleIsCurrentClipboard

HRESULT OleIsCurrentClipboard(*pDataObject***)**
LPDATAOBJECT *pDataObject*

OleIsCurrentClipboard determines whether the *pDataObject* put on the clipboard by the caller using **OleSetClipboard**(*pDataObject*) is still on the clipboard.

Parameters

pDataObject
Points to an **IDataObject** instance.

Return Values

Value	Meaning
S_OK	Indicates that *pDataObject* is currently on the clipboard and the caller is the owner of the clipboard.

Value	Meaning
S_FALSE	Indicates that *pDataObject* is not on the clipboard.

See Also **OleSetClipboard**, **OleGetClipboard**

Data Transfer, Caching, and Drawing Functions

The following functions are used in conjunction with drawing and caching operations.

HRESULT OleDraw (LPUNKNOWN pUnk, unsigned long dwAspect, GrafPtr pGrafDraw, LPCRECT lprcBounds);
HRESULT OleDuplicateData (Handle hSrc, unsigned long cfFormat, unsigned short uiFlags);
HRESULT CreateDataCache (LPUNKNOWN pUnk, REFCLSID rclsid, REFIID riid, void ** ppvObj);
HRESULT ReleaseStgMedium (STGMEDIUM pmedium);

OleDraw

HRESULT OleDraw(*pUnk*, *dwAspect*, *pGrafDraw*, *lprcBounds***)**
LPUNKNOWN *pUnk*
unsigned long *dwAspect*
GrafPtr *pDraw*
LPCRECT *lprcBounds*

OleDraw is a helper function that can be used to draw objects.

Parameters

pUnk
Points to the object that is to be drawn.

dwAspect
Contains a value taken from the enumeration **DVASPECT**. For more information, see "DVASPECT Enumeration," earlier in this chapter.

pGrafDraw
Specifies the GrafPtr onto which the drawing should actually be done.

lprcBounds
Points to a **Rect** structure (in local window coordinates) that indicates the rectangle on which the object should be drawn. This parameter controls the positioning and stretching of the object.

Return Values

Value	Meaning
S_OK	Object was successfully drawn.
E_INVALIDARG	One or more arguments are invalid.
E_OUTOFMEMORY	Ran out of memory.
OLE_E_BLANK	There is no data to draw from.

Value	Meaning
E_ABORT	The draw operation was aborted.
VIEW_E_DRAW	An error occurred in drawing.
OLE_E _INVALIDRECT	The rectangle is invalid.
DV_E _NOIVIEWOBJECT	The object doesn't support the **IViewObject** interface.

Comments

OleDraw calls *pUnk*->**QueryInterface**, asking for **IViewObject**, converts the **Rect** structure to a **Rectl** structure, and then calls **IViewObject::Draw** as follows:

```
lpViewObj->Draw(dwAspect,-1,0,0,0,pGrafDraw,&rectl,0,0,0);
```

See Also

IViewObject::Draw

OleDuplicateData

Handle OleDuplicateData(*hSrc*, *cfFormat*, *uiFlags***)**
Handle *hSrc*
unsigned long *cfFormat*
unsigned short *uiFlags*

OleDuplicateData is a helper function that duplicates global memory and returns a new handle of the same type.

Parameters

hSrc
Specifies the handle of the source data.

cfFormat
Specifies the clipboard format of the source data.

uiFlags
Specifies the flags to be used in global memory allocation. If the value of *uiFlags* is NULL, GMEM_MOVEABLE is used as a default.

Return Values

Value	Meaning
Handle to the duplicated data.	Data was successfully duplicated.
NULL	Error duplicating data.

Comments

All formats are duplicated byte-wise; *hSrc* must be a global memory handle.

CreateDataCache

HRESULT CreateDataCache(*pUnk,rclsid, riid, ppvObj)*
LPUNKNOWN *pUnk*
REFCLSID *rclsid*
REFIID *riid*
void ** *ppvObj*

CreateDataCache creates a cache object and returns a pointer to the interface identified by *riid*.

Parameters

pUnk
Specifies the controlling unknown if this cache object is to be instantiated as part of an aggregate. Can be NULL, indicating that no aggregation will occur.

rclsid
Specifies the CLSID that is used *only* to generate default icon labels; most often, this will be CLSID_NULL.

riid
Specifies the IID that the caller is to use to communicate with the newly created cache, typically, this is **IID_IOleCache**. Callers can also request **IID_IDataObject**, **IID_IViewObject**, and **IID_IPersistStorage**.

ppvObj
Pointer to where to return the cache object.

Return Values

Value	Meaning
S_OK	A new instance of the OLE provided cache implementation was returned.
E_INVALIDARG	One or more arguments are invalid.
E_OUTOFMEMORY	Ran out of memory.
E_NOINTERFACE	The interface represented by *iid* is not supported by the object; *ppvObj* is set to NULL.

Comments

The returned object supports **IOleCache**, **IOleCache2**, and **IOleCacheControl** for controlling the cache, **IPersistStorage** for reading and writing to persistent storage, **IDataObject** without advise support, **IViewObject**, and **IViewObject2**. **CreateDataCache** can be used with DLL object applications and handlers that do not use the OLE default handler as an aggregate object.

Typically, **CreateDataCache** is called only by DLL object applications to obtain a default cache implementation.

See Also

IOleCache, **IDataObject**, **IPersistStorage**

ReleaseStgMedium

void ReleaseStgMedium(*pmedium*)
LPSTGMEDIUM *pmedium*

ReleaseStgMedium frees the specified storage medium.

Parameters

pmedium
Points to the storage medium that is to be freed.

Comments

After this call, the storage medium is invalid and can no longer be used.

Sometimes the original provider of the medium wishes to maintain control of the freeing of the medium. If this is the case and the medium is TYMED_HGLOBAL, or TYMED_MFPICT, **ReleaseStgMedium** does nothing. If the medium is TYMED_FILE, **ReleaseStgMedium** does nothing to the actual disk file. The file name string, however, is freed using the standard memory management mechanism. For TYMED_ISTREAM, **ReleaseStgMedium** calls **IStream::Release**; for TYMED_ISTORAGE, **IStorage::Release** is called. Following all these actions, *pmedium->pUnkForRelease->***Release** is invoked.

If the receiver of the medium is to free it, as is indicated by *pUnkForRelease* being set to NULL, **ReleaseStgMedium** does the following:

Medium	ReleaseStgMedium Action
TYMED _HGLOBAL	Calls **GlobalFree** on the handle.
TYMED _MFPICT	Calls **GlobalFree** on the handle.
TYMED _FILE	Frees the disk file by deleting it. Frees the file name string by using the standard memory management paradigm.
TYMED _ISTREAM	Calls **IStream::Release**.
TYMED _ISTORAGE	Calls **IStorage::Release**.

Icon Extraction Functions

The following functions, defined in ole2.h, are used to manipulate iconic representations of objects:

```
PicHandle OleGetIconOfFile (char * lpszPath, unsigned long fUseFileAsLabel);
PicHandle OleGetIconOfFSp (FSSpec * pFSSpec, unsigned long fUseFileAsLabel);
PicHandle OleGetIconOfClass (REFCLSID rclsid, char * lpszLabel, unsigned long fUseTypeAsLabel);
PicHandle OlePictFromIconAndLabel (PicHandle hIcon, char * lpszLabel, OleIconSource * pIconSource);
PicHandle OleGetIconFromIconSuite (Handle hSuite, char * lpszLabel,OleIconSource * pIconSource);
```

OleIconSource Data Structure

The **OleIconSource** structure is used with the **OlePictFromIconAndLabel** and **OleGetIconFromIconSuite** functions. The structure is also used with the icon functions included in the OLE SDK sample UI library.

The sample UI library contains the **OleUIPictExtractIconSource** function, which can be used to determine the source of a particular OLE icon PICT. **OleUIPictExtractIconSource** returns a structure of type **OleIconSource**, which is defined in macdef.h as follows:

```
typedef enum {  FileAndResIDMethod,
                CreatorAndIndexMethod,
                CreatorAndTypeMethod,
                SystemResIDMethod
} IconRetrievalMethod;

typedef struct {
    IconRetrievalMethod method;
    union {
        struct {
            char    szPathname[OLEICON_CCHPATHMAX];
            long    lFileID;
            short   sResID;
        } FileAndResIDStruct;

        struct {
            OSType  lCreator;
            short   sIndex;
        } CreatorAndIndexStruct;

        struct {
        OSType lCreator;
        OSType lType;
        } CreatorAndTypeStruct;

        struct {
            short sResID;
        } SystemResIDStruct;
    } IconSourceUnion;
}OleIconSource;
```

The **OleIconSource** structure describes how an icon can be accessed. The icon creation procedures follow one of four methods to obtain an icon from which they construct an icon PICT. To access these icons, the user uses the **OleIconSource** data structure which is bundled with the icon PICT at the time of its construction.

The **OleIconSource** data structure is a union of four different structures. The structure contained within a particular **OleIconSource** data structure is determined by the value of the "method" member of the structure. Based on the "method" member, an icon can be directly accessed as follows:

- **FileAndResIDMethod**
  The data provided in this instance includes a *filename*, a *file id* and a *resource id*. Using the *filename*, a resource file should be opened using **HOpenResFile**, for example. Once a resource has been opened, the *resource id* should be used with the procedure **GetIconSuite** to obtain an icon suite for the icon PICT from which the **OleIconSource** structure was obtained.
- **CreatorAndIndexMethod**
  The data provided is a *creator signature* and a numeric *index*. The *creator signature* should be used with **PBDTGetAppl** in order to obtain the filename of the application which contains the icon. As above **HOpenResFile** is used along with the filename to open a resource. The *index* is used with **Get1IndResource** to obtain the icon from the application.
- **CreatorAndTypeMethod**
  In this instance the **OleIconSource** structure provides a *creator signature* and a *file type*. The procedure **PBDTGetIcon** should be used with these pieces of data to obtain the required icon . This icon corresponds to a file of the type provided by the application possessing the given creator signature.
- **SystemResIDMethod**
  In the event that no suitable icon can be obtained by the icon creation procedures, a "vanilla document" icon PICT is created and returned to the user. In this situation the sole piece of data required to obtain this generic icon is a system *resource id*. This *resource id* is used in a call to **GetIconSuite** to obtain an icon suite corresponding to the icon pict from which the **OleIconSource** was obtained.

Macintosh Icon Picture Formats

The **PicHandle** returned by the procedures **OleGetIconOfFile**, **OleGetIconOfFSp**, **OleGetIconOfClass**, **OleGetIconFromIconSuite**, **OlePictFromIconAndLabel** references **QuickDraw** pictures which adhere to the following format:

```
< ICONSUITE PicComment >
```

contains the bit patterns for the different icon PICTS which comprise an icon suite for an icon. In the **OleUIPictIconDraw** function (included in the sample UI library), an icon suite is reconstructed from this comment and used to render the icon with the most appropriate color depth for the video device.

```
< ICONONLY PicComment >
```

contains no useful information, but simply delimits the icon picture commands from the remainder of the OLE2 icon PICT. The **OleUIPictExtractIcon** function in the sample UI library uses this comment to determine which **QuickDraw** commands describe the icon of an "icon and label" icon PICT.

```
< ICONLABEL PicComment >
```

contains a character array which stores the label for the icon. The procedure **OleUIPictExtractLabel** in the sample UI library intercepts this comment and extracts the label from it.

```
< ICONSOURCE PicComment >
```

contains an **OleIconSource** structure which describes the method by which the icon was obtained. From this structure, the user may directly access the icon.

Note that a particular OLE2 icon PICT may contain only a subset of the above format. In particular, if the icon in question was produced by **OleUIPictExtractIcon**, the icon PICT would contain those elements up to and include the <ICONONLY PicComment>. Also, icon PICTs obtained from **OlePictFromIconAndLabel** where NULL was passed for one or both of *pszLabel* and *pIconSource* would lack the <ICONLABEL PicComment> and <ICONSOURCE PicComment> respectively.

OleGetIconOfFile

Handle OleGetIconOfFile(*lpszPath, fUseFileAsLabel*)
char * *lpszPath*
unsigned long *fUseFileAsLabel*

OleGetIconOfFile obtains an icon for the file whose filename is specified in *lpszPath.*

Parameters

lpszPath
Specifies the pathname of the file; the filename pointed to by *lpszPath* must be fully specified.

fUseFileAsLabel
TRUE indicates that a label containing the filename (no path) should be attached to the icon. FALSE indicates no filename is to be attached; see the following comments.

Return Values

Value	Meaning
PicHandle	Contains a handle to the Icon PICT generated.
NULL	Unable to generate an icon PICT.

Comments

Where appropriate, applications should call **OleGetIconOfFSp** instead of **OleGetIconOfFile**.

The retrieved icon is combined with a label which is constructed as follows:

- If *fUseFileAsLabel* is TRUE, the filename (no pathname) is appended to the icon as the label. Otherwise, the Registration Database file is consulted for the AuxUserType2 which corresponds to the CLSID of the file for which the icon is being retrieved.
- If AuxUserType2 is found in the Registration Database file, it is used as the label.
- Finally, if neither of these methods yields a label, the string found in the Registration Database file under \Software\Microsoft\OLE2\DefaultIconLabel is appended to the icon.

For more information about the format of the PICT returned to the caller, see the section, "Macintosh Icon Picture Formats."

OleGetIconOfFSp

PicHandle OleGetIconOfFSp(*pFSSpec*, *fUseFileAsLabel*)
FSSpec * *pFSSpec*
unsigned long *fUseFileAsLabel*

OleGetIconOfFSp is used to return the icon from the FSSpec pointed to by *pFSSpec*.

Parameters

pFSSpec
Points to the FSSpec from which the icon is to be obtained.

fUseFileAsLabel
FALSE indicates the FSSpec given in *pFSSpec* is used as the icon label; TRUE indicates either the AuxUserType2 corresponding to the CLSID or the MainUserType for the CLSID is used as the label.

Return Values

Value	Meaning
PicHandle	Contains the handle to the FSSPec containing the icon.
NULL	Icon was not found.

Comments

OleGetIconOfFSp is identical to **OleGetIconOfFile** except that it uses the FSSpec structure pointed to by *pFSSpec* to identify the file for which the icon is to be retrieved. Otherwise,the same heuristic is used to obtain the icon.

OleGetIconOfClass

PicHandle OleGetIconOfClass(*rclsid*, *lpszLabel*, *fUseTypeAsLabel*)
REFCLSID *rclsid*
char * *lpszLabel*
unsigned long *fUseTypeAsLabel*

Parameters

rclsid
Specifies the CLSID of the object from which the icon is to be extracted.

lpszLabel
Specifies a label that is to be associated with the icon. May be NULL.

fUseTypeAsLabel
FALSE indicates the label given in *lpszLabel* is used as the icon label; TRUE indicates either the AuxUserType2 corresponding to the CLSID or the MainUserType for the CLSID is used as the label.

Return Values

Value	Meaning
PicHandle	Contains a handle to the icon PICT generated.
NULL	Unable to generate an icon PICT.

OlePictFromIconAndLabel

PicHandle OlePictFromIconAndLabel(*hPict*, *lpszLabel*, *pIconSource*)
PicHandle *hPict*
char * *lpszLabel*
OleIconSource * *pIconSource*

OlePictFromIconAndLabel creates and returns an icon PICT constructed from the **OleIconSource** structure provided by the user.

Parameters

hPict
Specifies the handle to the icon.

lpszLabel
Points to a label that is to be associated with the icon; may be NULL.

pIconSource
Points to the **OleIconSource**; may be NULL. For more information, see the section, "OleIconSource Data Structure," earlier in this chapter.

Return Values

Value	Meaning
PicHandle	Contains a handle to the icon PICT generated.
NULL	Unable to generate an icon PICT.

Comments

The PICT referenced by the handle *hPict* will be scaled into the 32x32 pixel space centered above the icon label.

If a label is supplied in *lpszLabel*, then it is appended to the bottom of the icon PICT. Similarly, if an **OleIconSource** structure is supplied, it too is included in the OLE2 icon PICT returned. If all three procedure arguments are non-NULL, the icon PICT returned from this routine is of the same internal format as that returned by the other **OleGetIcon*** routines.

If either *lpszLabel* or *pIconSource* are NULL, then that information will be absent from the OLE2 icon PICT. Hence, calling **OleUIPictExtractIconLabel** or **OleUIPictExtractSource** (included in the sample UI library) on the icon PICT returned from this routine will return NULL if the corresponding parameters were not specified in the call to this routine.

OleGetIconFromIconSuite

PicHandle OleGetIconFromIconSuite(*hSuite*, *lpszLabel*, *pIconSource*)
Handle *hSuite*
char * *lpszLabel*
OleIconSource * *pIconSource*;

OleGetIconFromIconSuite constructs and returns an icon PICT from the icon suite supplied by the caller.

Parameters

hSuite
Specifies the handle to the icon suite from which the icon is to be obtained.

lpszlabel
Points to the label that is to be associated with the icon; may be NULL.

pIconSource
Points to the **OleIconSource** data structure; may be NULL. For more information, see the section, "OleIconSource Data Structure," earlier in this chapter.

Return Values

Value	Meaning
PicHandle	Contains a handle to the icon PICT generated.
NULL	Unable to generate an icon PICT.

Comments

An icon suite is a convenient way to manipulate an icon family (group of icons sharing the same resource ID's but different resource types (color depth)). This procedure extracts the best color depth icon and places it in the returned icon PICT. In addition, the entire icon suite is encoded within the icon PICT. **OleUIPictIconDraw** (included in the sample UI library) extracts the icon suite and uses it to render the icon.

If a label is supplied in *lpszLabel*, then it is appended to the bottom of the icon PICT. Similarly, if an **OleIconSource** structure is supplied, it too is included in the OLE2 icon PICT returned. If all three procedure arguments are specified (non-NULL), the icon PICT returned from this routine is of the same internal format as those return from the other **OleGetIcon*** routines.

If either *lpszLabel* or *pIconSource* are NULL, then that information will be absent from the OLE2 icon PICT. Hence, calling **OleUIPictExtractIconLabel** or **OleUIPictExtractSource** (included in the sample UI library) on the icon PICT returned from this routine will return NULL if the corresponding parameters were not specified in the call to this routine.

CHAPTER 8

Linking Interfaces and Functions

This chapter describes the interfaces and functions that enable linking to occur. Implementation for most of these interfaces are provided by OLE; therefore, you will not need to write your own implementation.

The following table provides a brief summary of the interfaces that support linking.

Interface Name	Implemented By	Used By
IMoniker	OLE	Used by OLE to manage the binding of monikers to their sources.
IEnum-Moniker	OLE	Used by OLE, certain containers, and object applications to enumerate items that are monikers.
IOleLink	OLE	Used by containers to manage monikers inside of links and to manage the link's update options.
IBindCtx	OLE	Used by OLE to accumulate the set of objects that are bound during an operation and that should be released when the operation is completed.
IRunning-ObjectTable	OLE	Used by OLE and object applications to access the running object table.
IParse-DisplayName	Containers and object applications	Used by OLE to transform the display name of an object into a moniker.

What is a Moniker

OLE 2 uses a mechanism known as a moniker for linking and naming. A moniker is a conceptual handle to a link at its source and can be stored with the linked object's consumer. A moniker's main operation is to bind, or connect, to the object to which it points. The binding process invokes whatever algorithms are necessary to locate and run the link source object.

Two types of monikers are stored for each linked object: one that represents the absolute path to the link source and one that provides a relative path. When a linked object is activated, the relative moniker is used first to bind to the link source; the absolute moniker is used only if the relative one fails.

Using a relative moniker in addition to the absolute moniker supports the following link tracking situations:

- The link source and the link consumer (the linked object) have been copied or moved but retain the same relative structure, such as two documents in the same directory. Another case is a link between two objects, both embedded in a third document. In these situations, the relative moniker succeeds in binding.
- The link source does not move, but the link consumer does move, and in such a way that the relative structure is not maintained. In this case, the relative moniker fails to bind, but the absolute moniker does bind.

Monikers and Linked Objects

The distinction between an embedded and linked object is where the native representation of the object is persistently stored. An embedded object's native data is stored inside the container document, which also contains the presentation of the object. A linked object's native data is not kept with the linked object itself, but is kept with the source of the data, also known as the link source.

Compound document applications can support different levels of linking. Object applications can support linking to file-based documents, as well as linking to ranges of items (pseudo objects) in the document.

Applications that support linking must create and register a file moniker for their documents. Existing documents typically use the filename for the file moniker; new documents create a unique, temporary name that is replaced when the document is saved. To create the file moniker, applications call **CreateFileMoniker**, passing it the moniker name and where to return the pointer to the **IMoniker** instance.

File monikers for existing documents are registered in the running object table, a global table that stores information about running link sources. Registering a document's file moniker ensures that the document can be accessed by its linking container(s). When a container attempts to bind to the linked object, the moniker within the linked object first checks the running object table to see whether the object is already running. If the moniker for the object is registered, the container is connected to the running instance of the object; otherwise, the object handler is loaded and the object is placed in the running state.

Applications that support linking to documents that have not yet been saved will register the new document's temporary moniker. Applications must be aware that linking to unsaved documents can cause broken links if the container closes before the new document is saved and a permanent file moniker registered.

Note Registering a file moniker in the running object table results in a weak reference lock being put on the document object. Although this lock is not strong enough to hold the document alive should the user decide to close the document, the object should still revoke the moniker's registration as part of its close routine.

IMoniker Interface

The **IMoniker** interface is typically implemented and used by OLE. However, advanced applications that do not organize their data in files, such as database-oriented applications, may need to implement a new moniker type.

IMoniker contains the following methods:

```
DECLARE_INTERFACE_(IMoniker, IPersistStream)
{
 // *** IUnknown methods ***
 HRESULT QueryInterface (REFIID riid, void * * ppvObj);
 unsigned long AddRef ();
 unsigned long Release ();

  // *** IPersist methods ***
 HRESULT GetClassID)(LPCLSID lpClassID);

  // *** IPersistStream methods ***
 HRESULT IsDirty ();
 HRESULT Load (LPSTREAM pStm);
 HRESULT Save (LPSTREAM pStm, unsigned long fClearDirty);
 HRESULT GetSizeMax (ULARGE_INTEGER * pcbSize);

  // *** IMoniker methods ***
 HRESULT BindToObject (LPBC pbc, LPMONIKER pmkToLeft, REFIID riidResult, void * * ppvResult);
 HRESULT BindToStorage (LPBC pbc, LPMONIKER pmkToLeft, REFIID riid, void * * ppvObj);
 HRESULT Reduce (LPBC pbc, unsigned long dwReduceHowFar, LPMONIKER * ppmkToLeft,
          LPMONIKER * ppmkReduced);
 HRESULT ComposeWith (LPMONIKER pmkRight, unsigned long fOnlyIfNotGeneric,
          LPMONIKER * ppmkComposite);
 HRESULT Enum (unsigned long fForward, LPENUMMONIKER * ppenumMoniker);
 HRESULT IsEqual (LPMONIKER pmkOtherMoniker);
 HRESULT Hash (unsigned long * pdwHash);
 HRESULT IsRunning (LPBC pbc, LPMONIKER pmkToLeft, LPMONIKER pmkNewlyRunning);
 HRESULT GetTimeOfLastChange (LPBC pbc, LPMONIKER pmkToLeft, FILETIME * pfiletime);
 HRESULT Inverse (LPMONIKER * ppmk);
```

```
    HRESULT CommonPrefixWith (LPMONIKER pmkOther, LPMONIKER * ppmkPrefix);
    HRESULT RelativePathTo (LPMONIKER pmkOther, LPMONIKER *
    HRESULT GetDisplayName (LPBC pbc, LPMONIKER pmkToLeft, ppmkRelPath);
            char * * lplpszDisplayName);
    HRESULT ParseDisplayName (LPBC pbc, LPMONIKER pmkToLeft,
            char * lpszDisplayName, unsigned long * pchEaten, LPMONIKER * ppmkOut);
    HRESULT IsSystemMoniker (unsigned long * pdwMksys);
};
```

For more information, see the moniker.h header file.

The **IMoniker** interface contains methods to control and access monikers. Different classes of monikers can exist. Currently OLE supports these classes: generic composite, file, item, pointer, and anti- monikers. Supporting a moniker class means providing a unique implementation of the **IMoniker** interface for that class.

Generic composite (or simply composite) monikers are a sequenced collection of other monikers. In general, each type of moniker is designed to be part of a composite moniker that specifies the complete path to an object. The composition is generic in that it has no knowledge of the pieces involved other than that they are monikers.

Each moniker class can store arbitrary data in its persistent representation and can run arbitrary code at binding time. If there is an identifiable piece of persistent storage in which the object is stored, **IMoniker::BindToStorage** can be used to gain access to it. Many objects (all OLE embedded objects, for example) have such identifiable storage. Others, such as the objects that are the ranges on a spreadsheet, do not.

The most basic method in the **IMoniker** interface is **IMoniker::BindToObject**, which binds a moniker to the object to which it points. **IMoniker::BindToObject** runs whatever algorithm is necessary to locate the object and returns a pointer to a specified interface type to the caller.

Most monikers have a textual representation that is meaningful to the user and can be retrieved with **IMoniker::GetDisplayName**. The API function **MkParseDisplayName** turns a textual display name into the appropriate moniker. Using this function is usually as expensive as actually binding to the object.

Monikers can compare themselves to other monikers using **IMoniker::IsEqual**. A hash value useful for storing monikers in lookup tables is available through **IMoniker::Hash**. The earliest time after which the object that the moniker points to is known not to have changed can be obtained with **IMoniker::GetTimeOfLastChange**.

An application can request to rewrite a moniker into an equivalent moniker by calling **IMoniker::Reduce**. This method returns a new moniker that binds to the same object, but does so in a more efficient way.

Pointers to instances of the **IMoniker** interface can be marshaled to other processes, just as with any other interface pointer. Many monikers cannot be changed once they have been created, nor do they maintain an object state outside themselves. Item monikers are an example of a class of such monikers. These monikers, which can be replicated any time, usually support custom marshaling (see **IMarshal** interface) so they can serialize and deserialize themselves in the destination context. For more information about serialization, see "IPersistStream".

IMoniker::BindToObject

HRESULT IMoniker::BindToObject(*pbc*, *pmkToLeft*, *riid*, *ppvObj***)**
LPBC *pbc*
LPMONIKER *pmkToLeft*
REFIID *riid*
void * * *ppvObj*

IMoniker::BindToObject locates and loads the object referenced by a given moniker.

Parameters

pbc
Points to an instance of the **IBindCtx** interface, which is used in moniker binding operations.

pmkToLeft
Points to the moniker of the object to the left of this moniker.

riid
Identifies the interface by which the caller wants to connect to the object.

ppvObj
On a successful return, points to the instantiated object, unless BIND_JUSTTESTEXISTENCE was specified in the binding options. If BIND_JUSTTESTEXISTENCE was specified, NULL can be returned instead.

Return Values

Value	Meaning
S_OK	The binding operation was successful.
MK_E_NOOBJECT	An object, possibly intermediate, could not be found during an operation such as binding or parsing a display name.
MK_E_EXCEEDED-DEADLINE	The process was not completed within the time limit specified by the bind context.

Value	Meaning
MK_E_CONNECT-MANUALLY	During some process (binding, parsing a display name, and so on) OLE was unable to connect to a network device. The application receiving this error should call **IBindCtx::GetObjectParam** with the key "ConnectManually" to retrieve the moniker of the network device, get the display name, and put up a dialog box asking the user for a password, and so on.
MK_E_INTERMEDIATE INTERFACENOT-SUPPORTED	An object was found but did not support an interface required for an operation. (During binding, for example, a container is expected to support the **IOleItemContainer** interface, and during parsing of display names a container is expected to support the **IParseDisplayName** interface.)
E_UNEXPECTED	An unexpected error occurred.
E_OUTOFMEMORY	Out of memory.
STG_E_ACCESS-DENIED	Unable to access the storage object.
IOleItemContainer::Get-Object	Binding to a moniker containing an item moniker can return any of the errors associated with this function.

Comments

Because each type of OLE moniker is designed to be part of a composite moniker, any given piece has a prefix of the composite to its left, and a suffix of the composite to its right. If **IMoniker::BindToObject** is called on a given piece, most often it requires the services of the object indicated by the prefix to its left. An item moniker, for example, requires the **IOleItemContainer** interface of the object to its left.

The bind context contains a time limit in which the caller wants the binding process to be completed. If the process is not completed within the specified time, it fails and returns MK_E_EXCEEDEDDEADLINE. The moniker of the object for which the deadline was exceeded can be retrieved by calling **IBindCtx::GetObjectParam** with the keys ExceededDeadline, ExceededDeadline1, ExceededDeadline2, and so on. (This capability is not often used with **IMoniker::BindToObject**; it is more often used with other **IMoniker** methods such as **IMoniker::GetTimeOfLastChange**.)

The running object table is accessible from the bind context using the **IBindCtx::GetRunningObjectTable** method.

Note Binding to the right of the present piece of a composite moniker may involve binding to other objects. Consequently, binding a moniker can be an expensive operation since the composite moniker often needs to start object applications and open files. To avoid loading the object and releasing it, then loading it again later, **IMoniker::BindToObject** can use the bind context passed through the *pbc* parameter until the binding process is complete. For more information on bind contexts, see the section, "IBindCtx Interface."

See Also

IBindCtx::GetBindOptions, **IBindCtx::GetRunningObjectTable**, **IBindCtx::RegisterObjectBound**, **IMoniker::GetTimeOfLastChange**

IMoniker::BindToStorage

HRESULT IMoniker::BindToStorage(*pbc, pmkToLeft, riid, ppvObj*)
LPBC *pbc*
LPMONIKER *pmkToLeft*
REFIID *riid*
void * * *ppvObj*

IMoniker::BindToStorage returns access to the persistent storage of the receiver (that is, the location that contains the presentation of the information) by using the specified interface, rather than access to the object itself.

Parameters

pbc
Points to an instance of the **IBindCtx** interface.

pmkToLeft
Points to the moniker of the object to the left of this moniker.

riid
Identifies the interface to bind to the persistent storage. Common interfaces passed here include **IStorage**, **IStream**, and **ILockBytes**.

ppvObj
Points to where the instantiated storage is placed. NULL can be returned if BIND_JUSTTESTEXISTENCE was specified in the binding options.

Return Values

Value	Meaning
S_OK	The binding operation was successful.
MK_E_NOSTORAGE	An attempt was made to access or bind to the storage of an object that does not have storage.
MK_E_EXCEEDED-DEADLINE	The process was not completed within the time specified by the bind context.

Value	Meaning
MK_E_CONNECT-MANUALLY	During some process (binding, parsing a display name, and so on), OLE was unable to connect to a network device. For more information, see **IMoniker::BindToObject**.
MK_E_INTERMEDIATE INTERFACE-NOTSUPPORTED	An object was found but did not support an interface required for an operation. (For example, during binding, a container is expected to support the **IOleItemContainer** interface, and during parsing of display names a container is expected to support the **IParseDisplayName** interface.)
E_OUTOFMEMORY	Out of memory.
STG_E_ACCESS-DENIED	Unable to access the storage object.
IOleItemContainer::GetObject	Binding to a moniker containing an item moniker can return any of the errors associated with this function.

Comments

Shown below is a composite moniker that refers to a spreadsheet object (item moniker) embedded in a word processing document (file moniker):

```
[Macole:Foo:Bar.Doc] [SummaryTable]
```

Calling **IMoniker::BindToObject** on this composite lets the caller communicate with the spreadsheet; calling **IMoniker::BindToStorage** lets the caller communicate with the **IStorage** instance in which it resides.

IMoniker::BindToStorage is usually called during the right-to-left recursion process of **IMoniker::BindToObject** when it has been invoked on a generic composite moniker. Sometimes, monikers at the tail of the composite don't require access to the object on their left; they merely require access to its persistent storage. These monikers can be bound more efficiently by not binding to the objects of the monikers to their left.

Some objects do not have an identifiable piece of storage. Attempting to call **IMoniker::BindToStorage** on a moniker with this type of object(s) fails with the error MK_E_NOSTORAGE.

Using the bind context in **IMoniker::BindToStorage** is the same as in **IMoniker::BindToObject**.

See Also

IMoniker::BindToObject

IMoniker::Reduce

HRESULT IMoniker::Reduce(*pbc, dwReduceHowFar, ppmkToLeft, ppmkReduced*)
LPBC *pbc*
unsigned long *dwReduceHowFar*
LPMONIKER * *ppmkToLeft*
LPMONIKER * *ppmkReduced*

IMoniker::Reduce returns a more efficient or equally efficient moniker that refers to the same object.

Parameters

pbc
Points to the bind context to use.

dwReduceHowFar
Specifies how this moniker should be reduced; valid values are taken from the enumeration **MKRREDUCE**. For more information, see the following comments.

ppmkToLeft
On entry, *ppmkToLeft* points to the moniker that prefixes this one within the composite, that is, the moniker to the left of the current moniker. On exit, the pointer will be NULL or non-NULL. Non-NULL indicates that the previous prefix should be disregarded and the moniker returned through *ppmkToLeft* used as the prefix in its place (this is not usual). NULL indicates that the prefix should not be replaced. Most monikers will NULL out this parameter before returning. *ppmkToLeft* is an in/out parameter. It must be released before NULLING out. For more information on in/out parameters, see the discussion of parameter types in the section on "Memory Management" in Chapter 1 "Architectural Overview."

ppmkReduced
Points (on exit) to the reduced form of the moniker; it can be NULL.

Return Values

Value	Meaning
S_OK	The reduction of the moniker was successful.
MK_S_REDUCED _TO_SELF	The **IMoniker::Reduce** operation output is the same as the input, and further calls to reduce will have no effect.
MK_E_EXCEEDED-DEADLINE	The process was not completed within the time specified by the bind context.
E_UNEXPECTED	An unexpected error occurred.
E_OUTOFMEMORY	Out of memory.

Comments

Most monikers simply reduce to themselves (because they cannot be reduced any further). A moniker that reduces to itself passes itself through *ppmkReduced* and then returns MK_S_REDUCED_TO_SELF. A moniker that reduces to nothing should pass NULL through *ppmkReduced* and return S_OK.

Reducing a moniker that is a composite of other monikers returns the composite of the reduced pieces.

The *dwReduceHowFar* parameter controls the reduction process. Values for *dwReduceHowFar* are taken from the **MKRREDUCE** enumeration, which is defined in moniker.h as follows:

```
typedef enum tagMKRREDUCE {
    MKRREDUCE_ONE          = 3<<16,
    MKRREDUCE_TOUSER       = 2<<16,
    MKRREDUCE_THROUGUSER = 1<<16,
    MKRREDUCE_ALL          = 0
    } MKRREDUCE;
```

MKRREDUCE values have the following meanings:

Value	Meaning
MKRREDUCE_ONE	Performs only one reduction step on the moniker. In general, the caller must have specific knowledge about the particular kind of moniker to be able to take advantage of this option.
MKRREDUCE_TOUSER	Reduce the moniker to a form that the user identifies as a persistent object. If no such point exists, this option should be treated as MKRREDUCE_ALL.
MKRREDUCE_THROUGHUSER	Reduce the moniker to where any further reduction would prevent the user from identifying it as a persistent object. Often, this is the same stage as MKRREDUCE_TOUSER.
MKRREDUCE_ALL	Reduce the moniker until it is reduced to itself.

Being able to programmatically reduce a moniker to a display name recognizable to the user is an important aspect of moniker reduction. Paths in the file system, bookmarks in word-processing documents, and range names in spreadsheets are all examples of user identities. In contrast, a macro or an alias encapsulated in a moniker is not a user identity.

The bind context parameter is used as it is in **IMoniker::BindToObject**. Implementations of **IMoniker::Reduce** should note the time limit imposed by the caller and the reporting of the object moniker which, had it been running, would have allowed the reduction to progress further. For more information, see the "IBindCtx Interface" elsewhere in this chapter.

See Also **IBindCtx Interface**, **IMoniker::BindToObject**

IMoniker::ComposeWith

HRESULT IMoniker::ComposeWith(*pmkRight, fOnlyIfNotGeneric, ppmkComposite***)**
LPMONIKER *pmkRight*
unsigned long *fOnlyIfNotGeneric*
LPMONIKER * *ppmkComposite*

IMoniker::ComposeWith returns a new composite moniker formed from the moniker on the left and the moniker pointed to by *pmkRight*. This operation uses the pieces of the path to an object to form the full path.

Parameters

pmkRight
Points to the moniker to compose onto the end of the *pmkComposite*.

fOnlyIfNotGeneric
Controls what should be done in the case where using a generic composite is the way to form a composite.

ppmkComposite
Points (on exit) to the resulting composite moniker, which may be NULL.

Return Values

Value	Meaning
S_OK	The composite moniker was returned successfully.
MK_E_NEED-GENERIC	This error is returned when **IMoniker::ComposeWith** is called with *fOnlyIfNotGeneric* equal to TRUE, but the moniker only supports generic composition.
E_OUTOFMEMORY	Out of memory.
E_UNEXPECTED	An unexpected error occurred.

Comments

There are two kinds of composite monikers: those that know nothing about their pieces other than that they are monikers, and those that know more. The former is often referred to as a *generic composite moniker*. A generic composite moniker is a moniker made up of other simpler monikers stored in a left-to-right order. An example of the latter type of moniker might be the result of composing a file moniker containing a relative path onto the end of another file moniker. The result could be a new file moniker containing the complete path.

Applications can call the **CreateGenericComposite**function to create a generic composite moniker. Non-generic composite monikers can collapse a path within a storage domain to a more efficient representation in a subsequent **IMoniker::Reduce** operation. However, none of the monikers provided by OLE are capable of this.

In general, each moniker class should have a set of special monikers (possibly empty) that can be composed onto the end of a moniker of a given class in a nongeneric way. The moniker class understands enough of the semantics of these special monikers to realize they are more than just monikers. Each **IMoniker::ComposeWith** implementation examines *pmkRight* to see whether the moniker is such a moniker, special for this implementation. Often, *pmkRight* is asked for the moniker's class, but other possibilities exist, such as using **QueryInterface**. A common case of such special monikers are anti monikers.

If *pmkRight* is special, the **IMoniker::ComposeWith** implementation does whatever is appropriate for that special case. If not, *fOnlyIfNotGeneric* controls what should occur. If *fOnlyIfNotGeneric* is true, NULL should be passed back through *ppmkComposite* and the status, MK_E_NEEDGENERIC, returned. If *fOnlyIfNotGeneric* is FALSE, a generic composite should be returned using **CreateGenericComposite**. Most callers should set *fOnlyIfNotGeneric* to FALSE.

In any situation where *pmkRight* completely negates the receiver (that is, irrespective of *fOnlyIfNotGeneric*), and the resulting composite is empty, NULL should be passed back through *ppmkComposite* and the status S_OK returned.

The pieces of a moniker that have been composed together can be enumerated using **IMoniker::Enum**. On a generic composite, this enumerates the monikers contained within it. On other monikers, the particular pieces returned are implementation specific.

Composition of monikers is an associative operation. That is, if A, B, and C are monikers, then

$(A \circ B) \circ C$

is always equal to

$A \circ (B \circ C)$

where $\circ$ represents the composition operation. Each implementation of **IMoniker::ComposeWith** must maintain this invariant.

IMoniker::Enum

HRESULT IMoniker::Enum(*fForward*, *ppenumMoniker***)**
unsigned long *fForward*
LPENUMMONIKER * *ppenumMoniker*

IMoniker::Enum enumerates the composite pieces of a generic composite moniker.

Parameters

fForward
Specifies the enumeration order. A value of TRUE enumerates the monikers in the normal order; FALSE causes a reverse enumeration order.

ppenumMoniker
Points (on exit) to the returned enumerator. Can be NULL to indicate there is nothing to enumerate.

Return Values

Value	Meaning
S_OK	The enumerator was returned successfully.
E_OUTOFMEMORY	Out of memory.
E_UNEXPECTED	An unexpected error occurred.

Comments

IMoniker::Enum operates differently with different moniker classes. For example, enumerating a file moniker might enumerate the internally stored path into its components, even though they are not stored internally as separate monikers. If the moniker has no discernible internal structure, it simply passes back NULL through *ppenumMoniker* instead of an enumerator.

The returned enumeration is of the type **IEnumMoniker**, defined as:

```
typedef Enum<IMoniker*> IEnumMoniker;
```

This is shorthand for:

```
interface IEnumMoniker : IUnknown
{
  virtual SCODE Next(unsigned long celt, IMoniker* rgelt,
    unsigned long * pceltFetched) = 0;
  virtual SCODE Skip(unsigned long celt) = 0;
  virtual SCODE Reset() = 0;
  virtual SCODE Clone(IEnumMoniker** ppenumMoniker) = 0;
};
```

See Also

IEnumX Interface

IMoniker::IsEqual

HRESULT IMoniker::IsEqual(*pmkOther***)**
LPMONIKER * *pmkOther*

IMoniker::IsEqual compares two monikers and indicates whether they are equal.

Parameters

pmkOther
Points to the moniker to use for comparison.

Return Values

Value	Meaning
S_OK	The two monikers are alike.
S_FALSE	The two monikers are not alike.

Comments

IMoniker::IsEqual is used to implement the running object table.

The moniker entries in the running object table indicate which objects are running, providing a way for link consumers to connect to the appropriate running object.

Two monikers that can compare as equal in either order must also hash to the same value. Thus, Implementations of **IMoniker::IsEqual** and **IMoniker::Hash** are closely related and must always be written together.

See Also **IMoniker::Hash**

IMoniker::Hash

HRESULT IMoniker::Hash(*pdwHash*)
unsigned long * *pdwHash*

IMoniker::Hash returns a 32-bit integer associated with this moniker.

Parameters

pdwHash
Points to where to return the hash value.

Return Values

Value	Meaning
S_OK	The integer was returned successfully.

Comments

The returned integer can be used to maintain tables of monikers. The moniker can be hashed to determine a hash bucket in the table, then compared against all the monikers in the hash bucket by calling **IMoniker::IsEqual**. Two monikers that compare as equal in either order hash to the same value.

Implementations of **IMoniker::IsEqual** and **IMoniker::Hash** are closely related and must always be written together.

The value returned by **IMoniker::Hash** is invariant under marshaling: if a moniker is marshaled to a new context, **IMoniker::Hash** invoked on the unmarshaled moniker in the new context returns the same value as **IMoniker::Hash** invoked on the original moniker. This is the only way that a global table of monikers such as the running object table can be maintained in shared space, yet accessed from many processes. Thus, implementations of **IMoniker::Hash** should not rely on the memory address of the moniker, but only its internal state.

See Also **IMoniker::IsEqual**

IMoniker::IsRunning

HRESULT IMoniker::IsRunning(*pbc, pmkToLeft, pmkNewlyRunning*)
LPBC * *pbc*
LPMONIKER * *pmkToLeft*
LPMONIKER * *pmkNewlyRunning*

IMoniker::IsRunning determines whether the specified moniker is running.

Parameters

pbc
Points to the usual bind context.

pmkToLeft
Points to the moniker to the left of this one in the composite in which it is found.

pmkNewlyRunning
If non-NULL, this is the moniker most recently added to the running object table; applications can assume that without this moniker in the running object table, **IMoniker::IsRunning** would return S_FALSE. Can be NULL.

Return Values

Value	Meaning
S_OK	The moniker is running.
S_FALSE	The moniker is not running.
E_UNEXPECTED	An unexpected error occurred.

Comments

This moniker gains access to the running object table, which is used to determine if the object is running, by calling **IBindCtx::GetRunningObjectTable**. *pmkToLeft* is the moniker to the left of this object in the generic composite in which it is found, if any. *pmkNewlyRunning*, if non-NULL, is the moniker that has most recently been added to the running object table.

IMoniker::IsRunning will return S_FALSE if *pmkNewlyRunning* is not in the running object table. Thus, the only way this moniker can now be running is if the newly running moniker is running. This allows for some n^2 to n reductions in algorithms that use monikers. Implementations of this method in various kinds of moniker classes are roughly as follows:

Generic composite moniker implementation:

```
if (pmkToLeft != NULL)
    return (pmkToLeft->ComposeWith(this))->IsRunning(pbc, NULL,
            pmkNewlyRunning);
if (pmkNewlyRunning != NULL) {
    if (pmkNewlyRunning->IsEqual(this) == NOERROR)
        return NOERROR;
}
else if (pRunningObjectTable -> IsRunning(this) == NOERROR)
    return NOERROR;

// otherwise, forward it on to my last element.
return this->Last()->IsRunning(pbc, this->AllButLast(),
    pmkNewlyRunning);
```

Some moniker classes have a wild card entry that matches only those object that are currently running: This is specifically the behavior of item monikers.

```
if (pmkToLeft == NULL) {
    if (pmkNewlyRunning != NULL) {
        if (pmkNewlyRunning->IsEqual(this) == NOERROR)
            return NOERROR;
        if (pmkNewlyRunning->IsEqual(wild card moniker) !=
            NOERROR)
            return ResultFromScode(S_FALSE);
        goto TestBind:
        return pRunningObjetTable -> IsRunning;
    }
}
if (pmkToLeft->ComposeWith(my wild card moniker)->IsRunning
        (pbc, NULL, pmkNewlyRunning) != NOERROR)
    return ResultFromScode(S_FALSE);

TestBind:
    // In general, connect to the container and ask if object
    // is running. The use of IOleItemContainer is specific to
    // item monikers, but the theme is a general one.
    IOleItemContainer *pcont;
    pmkToLeft->BindToObject(pbc, NULL, IID_IOleItemContainer,
        &pcont);
    return pcont->IsRunning(szItemString);
```

For moniker classes that support a wild card entry that always matches any instance of the moniker class (all instances of the moniker class with the same moniker to their left are deemed to be running if the wild card is present):

```
if (pmkToLeft == NULL) {
    if (pmkNewlyRunning != NULL)
        return pmkNewlyRunning->IsEqual(this) == NOERROR ||
        pmkNewlyRunning->IsEqual(my wild card moniker) == NOERROR
    if (pRunningObjectTable->IsRunning(this) == NOERROR)
        return NOERROR;
    return pRunningObjectTable->IsRunning(my wild card moniker);
}
else
    return pmkToLeft->ComposeWith(my wild card moniker)->IsRunning
        (pbc, NULL, pmkNewlyRunning);
```

For moniker classes that do not support wildcard matching:

```
if (pmkToLeft == NULL) {
    if (pmkNewlyRunning != NULL)
        return pmkNewlyRunning->IsEqual(this);
    else
        return pRunningObjectTable->IsRunning(this);
else
    return ResultFromScode(S_FALSE);
```

IMoniker::GetTimeOfLastChange

HRESULT IMoniker::GetTimeOfLastChange(*pbc, pmkToLeft, pFileTime***)**
LPBC *pbc*
LPMONIKER *pmkToLeft*
FILETIME * *pFileTime*

IMoniker::GetTimeOfLastChange provides date and time information needed to determine if a linked or embedded object containing linked objects, is up to date.

pbc
Points to the bind context to be used for this operation.

pmkToLeft
Points to the moniker to the left of this one in the composite in which it is found.

pFileTime
Points to where to return the time of the last change.

Return Values

Value	Meaning
S_OK	The date/time information was returned successfully.
MK_E_EXCEEDED-DEADLINE	The process was not completed within the time specified by the bind context.
MK_E_CONNECT-MANUALLY	During some process (binding, parsing a display name, and so on.) OLE was unable to connect to a network device. For more information, see **IMoniker::BindToObject**.
MK_E_UNAVAIL-ABLE	The time of the change is unavailable, and will not be available no matter what deadline is used.
E_UNEXPECTED	An unexpected error occurred.

Comments

If all the objects in a document are not up-to-date, the user should be prompted to update them. Updating out-of-date objects causes them to bind and retrieve a new presentation. **IMoniker::GetTimeOfLastChange** does not bind to the object to determine whether it is out of date. Instead, it returns the best available answer based on the time-of-last-change information for objects already running.

Many monikers point to an object contained in the object denoted by the moniker to the left. Implementations of **IMoniker::GetTimeOfLastChange** can often take advantage of the fact that objects cannot have changed at a date later than the object in which they are contained. That is, these monikers can simply forward the call onto the moniker to their left.

The returned time of change is reported using a **FILETIME** data structure. The time is indicated in units of 100 nanoseconds allowing the times of fast-changing data to be recorded with precision. For information about converting between

Macintosh date and time structures and OLE's **FILETIME** structure, see the descriptions of the **CoMacDateTimeToFileTime** and **CoFileTimeToMacDateTime** functions.

If the time of last change is unavailable, for example, because the deadline was exceeded, then a time of FILETIME_MAX should be passed back. If the deadline was exceeded, then the status MK_E_EXCEEDEDDEADLINE should be returned. If the time of change is unavailable, and would not be available no matter what deadline were used, then MK_E_UNAVAILABLE should be returned; otherwise, S_OK should be returned.

If *pmkToLeft* is NULL, **IMoniker::GetTimeOfLastChange** should first check for a recorded change-time in the running object table with **IRunningObjectTable::GetTimeOfLastChange** before proceeding with other strategies. Moniker classes that support wild cards must consider exactly what gets put in the running object table and look for the appropriate item because generic composite monikers know nothing of wild cards, they may even need to do that in the non-NULL *pmkToLeft* case.

See Also

IMoniker::IsRunning, **IRunningObjectTable** Interface

IMoniker::Inverse

HRESULT IMoniker::Inverse(*ppmk***)**
LPMONIKER * *ppmk*

IMoniker::Inverse returns a moniker that destroys itself when it is composed to the end of another moniker.

Parameters

ppmk
Points to where to return the inverse moniker.

Return Values

Value	Meaning
S_OK	The inverse moniker has been returned successfully.
MK_E_NOINVERSE	A moniker class that does not have inverses was asked for one.
E_OUTOFMEMORY	Out of memory.

Comments

IMoniker::Inverse is needed in implementations of the **IMoniker::RelativePathTo** method, which is important for supporting monikers that track object movement.

IMoniker::Inverse is an abstract generalization of the "::" operation in Macintosh file systems. For example, a file moniker representing the path "a:b:c:d" would have as its inverse a moniker containing the path ":::::", because "a:b:c:d" composed with ":::::" yields nothing.

The inverse of a moniker does not destroy just that particular moniker, but all monikers with a similar structure. Thus, the inverse of a generic composite moniker is the reverse composite, or the inverse of its pieces. Nongeneric composite monikers (such as the preceding file moniker example) also have nontrivial inverses. However, there are many kinds of monikers whose inverse is trivial. As the moniker adds one more piece to an existing structure; its inverse is a moniker with the last piece of the existing structure removed. A moniker that removes the last piece of a generic moniker when it is composed onto the end of that generic moniker is called an anti moniker. An OLE-provided implementation of an anti moniker can be created by calling the **CreateAntiMoniker** helper function. A moniker with no internal structure can return an anti moniker as its inverse.

Not all monikers have inverses. The inverse of an anti moniker, for example, does not exist. Neither do the inverses of most monikers that are themselves inverses. Objects inside objects denoted by monikers without inverse, cannot have relative paths to other objects outside.

See Also **CreateAntiMoniker**, **IMoniker::RelativePathTo**

IMoniker::CommonPrefixWith

HRESULT IMoniker::CommonPrefixWith(*pmkOther*, *ppmkPrefix*)
LPMONIKER *pmkOther*
LPMONIKER * *ppmkPrefix*

IMoniker::CommonPrefixWith returns the longest common prefix that the receiver shares with the moniker pointed to by *pmkOther*.

pmkOther
Points to the (other) moniker whose common prefix is to be returned.

ppmkPrefix
Points to where to return the common prefix moniker. If the common prefix does not exist, NULL is returned.

Return Values

Value	Meaning
S_OK	The common prefix exists but is neither the receiver nor *pmkOther*.
MK_S_NOPREFIX	No common prefix exists.
MK_S_HIM	The other moniker is the prefix of the receiver moniker.
MK_S_US	The two monikers (the receiver and the other moniker) are equal.
MK_S_ME	The receiver moniker (the moniker whose **CommonPrefixWith** method is called) is a prefix of the other moniker.

Value	Meaning
MK_E_NOT-BINDABLE	**IMoniker::CommonPrefixWith** was called on a relative moniker. The moniker cannot be bound to something until it is composed with a container moniker.
E_OUTOFMEMORY	Out of memory.

This functionality is useful in constructing relative paths and in performing some of the calculations on monikers needed by the Edit/Links... dialog box.

IMoniker::CommonPrefixWith should only be called on absolute monikers; for example, a file moniker that starts with a volume name, followed by items. It should not be called on relative monikers.

IMoniker::RelativePathTo

HRESULT IMoniker::RelativePathTo(*pmkOther*, *ppmkRelPath*)
LPMONIKER *pmkOther*
LPMONIKER **ppmkRelPath*

IMoniker::RelativePathTo returns the relative path to a moniker that will yield *pmkOther* when composed onto the end of this moniker, or a moniker with a similar structure.

Parameters

pmkOther
Points to the moniker to which a relative path should be taken.

ppmkRelPath
Points to where to return the relative path; cannot be NULL.

Return Values

Value	Meaning
S_OK	A meaningful relative path has been returned.
MK_S_HIM	The only form of the relative path is the other moniker.
MK_E_NOTBINDABLE	**IMoniker::RelativePathTo** was called on a relative moniker. The moniker cannot be bound to something until it is composed with a container moniker.
E_OUTOFMEMORY	Out of memory.
E_UNEXPECTED	An unexpected error occurred.

Comments

Conceptually, implementations of **IMoniker::RelativePathTo** determine the longest prefix that the receiver and *pmkOther* have in common. This breaks the receiver and *pmkOther* into two parts each, say (P,T_{me}) and (P,T_{him}) respectively, where P is the maximal common prefix. The correct relative path result is then:

$T_{me}^{-1} \circ T_{him}$

That is, inverse (T_{me}) $\circ$ T_{him}.

For any given implementation of **IMoniker::RelativePathTo**, the same *pmkOther* monikers are usually treated in a special manner, as they would be with **IMoniker::ComposeWith**. For example, file monikers might treat other file monikers in a special manner in both cases.

IMoniker::RelativePathTo should be called only on absolute monikers; for example, a file moniker that starts with a volume name, followed by items. It should not be called on relative monikers.

See Also **IMoniker::GetDisplayName**

IMoniker::GetDisplayName

HRESULT IMoniker::GetDisplayName(*pbc*, *pmkToLeft*, *lplpszDisplayName***)**
LPBC *pbc*
LPMONIKER *pmkToLeft*
char * * *lplpszDisplayName*

IMoniker::GetDisplayName returns the current display name for this moniker. If none exists, it is NULL.

Parameters

pbc
Points to the bind context for this operation.

pmkToLeft
Points to the moniker to the left of this one in the composite in which it is found. Most monikers do not require this when calling **IMoniker::GetDisplayName**.

lplpszDisplayName
Points (on exit) to the current display name for this moniker. It is NULL if the moniker does not have a display name or if the time limit was exceeded.

Return Values

Value	Meaning
S_OK	The display name was returned successfully.
MK_E_EXCEEDED-DEADLINE	The process was not completed within the time specified by the bind context. The moniker of the object of which the deadline was exceeded can be retrieved
E_OUTOFMEMORY	Out of memory.
E_NOTIMPL	There is no display name.

Comments

To obtain the current display name of a moniker, **IMoniker::GetDisplayName** may have to access the storage of the object to which it refers, if not the object itself, which can be an expensive operation. As with other **IMoniker** methods, the *pbc* parameter specifies, as part of the overall bind context, a time limit within which the operation should be completed or fail, returning MK_E_EXCEEDEDDEADLINE if it is unable to do so.

Callers have the tendency to cache and use the last successful result obtained when they do not have quick access to the display name of a moniker (the standard implementation of OLE link does this).

Display names should be thought of as an annotation on the moniker that helps distinguish one moniker from another. Although rare, there might be more than one moniker with the same display name.

There is no guarantee that a display name obtained from a moniker will parse back into that moniker when calling **MkParseDisplayName** with it, though failure to do so also is rare.

A moniker that is a prefix of another has a display name that is a (string) prefix of the display name of the second moniker.

Monikers that are designed to be part of a generic composite must include any preceding delimiter as part of their display name. Many monikers take a parameter for this delimiter in their instance creation functions.

See Also

MkParseDisplayName

IMoniker::ParseDisplayName

HRESULT IMoniker::ParseDisplayName(*pbc, pmkToLeft, lpszDisplayName, pchEaten, ppmkOut***)**
LPBC *pbc*
LPMONIKER *pmkToLeft*
char * *lpszDisplayName*
unsigned long* *pchEaten*
LPMONIKER * *ppmkOut*

IMoniker::ParseDisplayName parses a composite moniker's remaining display name.

Parameters

pbc
Points to the bind context that is to be used to accumulate bound objects.

pmkToLeft
Points to the moniker to the left of this one in the so-far-parsed display name.

lpszDisplayName
Points to the display name to be parsed.

pchEaten
Points to the number of characters of the input name this parse consumed.

ppmkOut
Points to the resulting moniker.

Return Values

Value	Meaning
S_OK	The parse operation was completed successfully.
MK_E_SYNTAX	An error in the syntax of a filename was encountered while parsing a display name or while creating a file moniker.
E_OUTOFMEMORY	Out of memory.
E_UNEXPECTED	An unexpected error occurred.
IMoniker::BindToObject errors.	Parsing display names may cause binding. Thus, any error associated with this function may be returned.

Comments

The *lpszDisplayName* parameter is the yet-to-be-parsed tail of the display name. The **IMoniker::ParseDisplayName** function parses as much of the remaining tail as is appropriate for a display name within the object identified by `(pmkToLeft ° (the receiver))` and returns the corresponding moniker. The main loop of **MkParseDisplayName** finds the next moniker piece by calling **IMoniker::ParseDisplayName** and passing NULL through *pmkToLeft*. If the moniker that has been parsed to this point is a generic composite, the composite forwards this information onto its last piece, passing the prefix of the composite to the left of the piece in *pmkToLeft*.

Some moniker classes are able to parse their display names themselves because they are designed to designate only certain kinds of objects. Other monikers will need to bind to the object that they designate to do the parsing. These objects should not be released by **IMoniker::ParseDisplayName**, but instead should be transferred to the bind context for later release.

If a syntax error occurs, NULL is returned through *ppmkOut*. The number of characters that were successfully parsed in the display name is returned through *pchEaten*.

See Also

MkParseDisplayName

IMoniker::IsSystemMoniker

HRESULT IMoniker::IsSystemMoniker(*pdwMksys***)**
unsigned long * *pdwMksys*

IMoniker::IsSystemMoniker determines whether this moniker is a type of moniker whose implementation semantics are conceptually important to the binding process.

Parameters

pdwMksys
Points to where to return the enumerated moniker type. Valid values are taken from the enumeration **MKSYS**; may not be NULL.

Return Values

Value	Meaning
S_OK	The moniker is a system moniker.
S_FALSE	The moniker is not a system moniker.

Comments

The values returned through *pdwMksys* are taken from the **MKSYS** enumeration, which is defined in moniker.h as follows:

```
typedef enum tagMKSYS {
    MKSYS_NONE = 0,
    MKSYS_GENERICCOMPOSITE = 1,
    MKSYS_FILEMONIKER      = 2,
    MKSYS_ANTIMONIKER      = 3,
    MKSYS_ITEMMONIKER      = 4,
    MKSYS_POINTMONIKER     = 5,
    } MKSYS;
```

All user implementations of this method should simply return MKSYS_NONE through the *pdwMksys* parameter.

Note New values to the **MKSYS** enumeration may be defined in the future; therefore, callers of **IMoniker::IsSystemMoniker** should explicitly test against the return values that they care about and not assume that the returned value is one of the values listed here.

IParseDisplayName Interface

The **IParseDisplayName** interface is used to transform the display name of an object into a moniker. The interface is implemented by container and object applications and is used by OLE.

IParseDisplayName contains the following method:

```
DECLARE_INTERFACE_(IParseDisplayName, IUnknown)
{
  // *** IUnknown methods ***
  HRESULT QueryInterface (REFIID riid, void * * ppvObj);
  unsigned long AddRef ();
  unsigned long Release ();

  // *** IParseDisplayName method ***
  HRESULT ParseDisplayName (LPBC pbc, char * lpszDisplayName,
           unsigned long * pchEaten, LPMONIKER * ppmkOut);
};
```

For more information, see the ole2.h header file.

IParseDisplayName::ParseDisplayName

HRESULT IParseDisplayName::ParseDisplayName(*pbc*, *lpszDisplayName*, *pchEaten*, *ppmkOut*)
LPBC *pbc*
char * *lpszDisplayName*
unsigned long * *pchEaten*
LPMONIKER * *ppmkOut*

IParseDisplayName::ParseDisplayName parses an object's display name into a moniker to the object.

Parameters

pbc
Points to the bind context to be used to accumulate bound objects.

lpszDisplayName
Points to the display name to be parsed.

pchEaten
Points to the number of characters parsed from the display name.

ppmkOut
Points to the resulting moniker; NULL on error.

Return Values

Value	Meaning
S_OK	The parse operation was successful.
MK_E_SYNTAX	An error in the syntax of a filename was encountered while parsing a display name or while creating a moniker.
MK_E_NOOBJECT	Some, possibly intermediate, object could not be found during some operation, such as binding or parsing a display name.

Value	Meaning
MK_E_INTERMEDIATE-INTERFACENOTSUPPORTED	An object was found but did not support an interface required for an operation. For example, during binding, a container is expected to support the **IOleItemContainer** interface, and during parsing of display names a container is expected to support the **IParseDisplayName** interface.
E_UNEXPECTED	Failure of unknown cause.
E_OUTOFMEMORY	Out of memory.
IMoniker::BindToObject errors.	MK_E_EXCEEDEDDEADLINE and MK_E_CONNECTMANUALLY.

Comments

The *lpszDisplayName* parameter is the yet-to-be-parsed tail of the display name.

If a syntax error occurs, NULL should be returned through *ppmkOut*. The number of characters that were successfully parsed should be returned through *pchEaten*.

See Also

MkParseDisplayName

IBindCtx Interface

The **IBindCtx** interface, typically implemented and used by OLE, is passed to many of the moniker management operations. The primary purpose of the **IBindCtx** instance is to accumulate the set of objects that get bound during an operation, but that should be released when the operation is complete. This is particularly useful in binding generic composite monikers because using the bind context in this way avoids binding an object and releasing it, only to have it bound again when the operation moves to another piece of the composite.

Additionally, the bind context passes a group of parameters that do not change as an operation moves from one piece of a generic composite to another. Some of the binding options have a related return value in certain error conditions; the bind context provides the means by which they can be returned. The bind context is also the only means through which moniker operations should access contextual information about their environment.

All calls that query or set the state of the environment are funneled through the bind context. (Doing this allows for future enhancements that can dynamically modify binding behavior.) In OLE 2, the most important piece of contextual information that moniker operations need to access is the running object table. Monikers should always access this table indirectly through **IBindCtx::GetRunningObjectTable**, rather than using the API function **GetRunningObjectTable**.

The **IBindCtx** interface allows for future extensions to the passed-in contextual information in the form of the ability to maintain a string-keyed table of objects. For more information, see **IBindCtx::RegisterObjectParam**.

The **IBindCtx** interface contains the following methods:

```
DECLARE_INTERFACE_(IBindCtx, IUnknown)
{
  // *** IUnknown methods ***
 HRESULT QueryInterface (REFIID riid, void * * ppvObj);
 unsigned long AddRef ();
 unsigned long Release ();

  // *** IBindCtx methods ***
 HRESULT RegisterObjectBound (LPUNKNOWN pUnk);
 HRESULT RevokeObjectBound (LPUNKNOWN pUnk);
 HRESULT ReleaseBoundObjects ();

 HRESULT SetBindOptions (LPBIND_OPTS pbindopts);
 HRESULT GetBindOptions (LPBIND_OPTS pbindopts);
 HRESULT GetRunningObjectTable (LPRUNNINGOBJECTTABLE * pprot);
 HRESULT RegisterObjectParam (char * lpszKey, LPUNKNOWN pUnk);
 HRESULT GetObjectParam (char * lpszKey, LPUNKNOWN * ppUnk);
 HRESULT EnumObjectParam (LPENUMSTRING * ppenumString);
 HRESULT RevokeObjectParam (char * lpszKey);
};
```

For more information, see the moniker.h header file.

IBindCtx::RegisterObjectBound

HRESULT IBindCtx::RegisterObjectBound(*pUnk*)
LPUNKNOWN *pUnk*

IBindCtx::RegisterObjectBound registers an object as needing to be released when the moniker binding operation has been completed.

pUnk
Points to the object being registered as needing to be released.

Return Values

Value	Meaning
S_OK	The object was registered successfully.
E_INVALIDARG	One or more arguments are invalid.
E_UNEXPECTED	An unexpected error occurred.

Comments

A call to **IBindCtx::RegisterObjectBound** causes the bind context to create an additional reference to the passed-in object (with **IUnknown::AddRef**). The caller must still release its own copy of the pointer.

Calling **IBindCtx::RegisterObjectBound** twice with the same object requires two calls to **IBindCtx::RevokeObjectBound** to completely remove the registration of the object within the bind context.

See Also **IBindCtx::RevokeObjectBound**

IBindCtx::RevokeObjectBound

HRESULT RevokeObjectBound(*pUnk***)**
LPUNKNOWN *pUnk*

IBindCtx::RevokeObjectBound removes an object previously registered in the bind context.

pUnk
Points to the object that is to be removed from the bind context.

Return Values

Value	Meaning
S_OK	The object was removed successfully.
MK_E_NOTBOUND	**IBindCtx::RevokeObjectBound** was called for an object that was not registered by **IBindCtx::RegisterObjectBound**.
E_OUTOFMEMORY	Out of memory.
E_INVALIDARG	One or more arguments are invalid.

Comments

The **IBindCtx::RevokeObjectBound** function undoes the effect of **IBindCtx::RegisterObjectBound** by removing one occurrence of the object from the registered set in the bind context.

Applications usually release objects as a set by calling **IBindCtx::ReleaseBoundObjects** and do not typically call **IBindCtx::RevokeObjectBound**.

See Also **IBindCtx::RegisterObjectBound**, **IBindCtx::ReleaseBoundObjects**

IBindCtx::ReleaseBoundObjects

HRESULT IBindCtx::ReleaseBoundObjects()

IBindCtx::ReleaseBoundObjects releases all objects currently registered in the bind context.

Return Values

Value	Meaning
S_OK	The objects were released successfully.

Holding a bind context without calling **IBindCtx::ReleaseBoundObjects** prevents the reference count from going to zero for all objects bound during the binding process. This includes OLE item containers and the link sources themselves.

IBindCtx::SetBindOptions

HRESULT IBindCtx::SetBindOptions(*pbindopts*)
LPBIND_OPTS *pbindopts*

IBindCtx::SetBindOptions stores a block of bind options in the bind context so they can be used in moniker operations using the same bind context.

pbindopts
Points to a structure of binding options to store in the bind context (caller-supplied **BIND_OPTS** structure). These can be retrieved later with **IBindCtx::GetBindOptions**.

Return Values

Value	Meaning
S_OK	The parameters were stored successfully.
E_OUTOFMEMORY	Out of memory.

Comments

Using **IBindCtx::SetBindOptions** to store a block of data is an alternative to passing parameters to a function. Because bind options are common to most **IMoniker** methods and the bind options do not change as the binding progresses, it is more efficient to store the block of bind options with **IBindCtx::SetBindOptions** than to pass the options to each **IMoniker** method.

The *pbindOpts* parameter points to a **BIND_OPTS** structure, which is defined in moniker.h as follows:

```
typedef struct tagBIND_OPTS {
    unsigned long   cbStruct;       // size in bytes of BIND_OPTS.
    unsigned long   grfFlags;
    unsigned long   grfMode;
    unsigned long   dwTickCountDeadline;
} BIND_OPTS;
```

BIND_OPTS members have the following meaning:

Member	Description
cbStruct	Specifies the size, in bytes, of the BIND_OPTS structure.
grfFlags	Contains a group of Boolean flags. Legal values that can be or-ed together are taken from the enumeration **BINDFLAGS**. Moniker implementations should ignore any bits in this field that they do not understand.

Member	Description
grfMode	Contains a group of flags that indicates the caller's intended use for the object received from the associated moniker binding operation. Constants for this member are taken from the **STGM** enumeration. When applied to a **IMoniker::BindToObject** operation, the most significant flag values are: STGM_READ, STGM_WRITE, and STGM_READWRITE. Some binding operations may make use of other flags, particularly STGM_DELETEONRELEASE or STGM_CREATE, but such cases would be quite esoteric. When applied to the **IMoniker::BindToStorage** operation, most STGM values are potentially useful. The default value for *grfMode* is STGM_READWRITE.
dwTickCountDeadline	Indicates when the caller wants the operation to be completed. This parameter lets the caller limit the execution time of an operation when it is more important that the operation perform quickly rather than accurately. This capability is most often used with **IMoniker::GetTimeOfLastChange**, though it can be usefully applied to other operations as well.

dwTickCountDeadline is a 32-bit unsigned time value in milliseconds on the local clock maintained by the **TickCount** function. A value of zero indicates "no deadline;" however, because zero is also a valid return value from **TickCount**, callers should handle this case. Callers should also handle clock wrapping cases; if the value in this variable is less than the current time by more than 231 milliseconds, it should be interpreted as indicating a time in the future of its indicated value plus 232 milliseconds.

Typical deadlines will allow for a few hundred milliseconds of execution. Each function should try to complete its operation by this time on the clock, or fail with the error MK_E_EXCEEDEDDEADLINE if it cannot. Functions are not required to be absolutely accurate in this regard, since it is almost impossible to predict how long execution might take (thus, callers cannot rely on the operation being completed by the deadline), but operations that exceed their deadline excessively will usually cause intolerable user delays in the operation of their callers. In practice, the use of deadlines is a heuristic that callers can impose on the execution of moniker operations.

If a moniker operation exceeds its deadline because one or more objects it uses are not running, and, if one of these had been running, the operation would have completed more of its execution, the monikers of these objects should be recorded in the bind context. This is done by using **IBindCtx::RegisterObjectParam** under the parameter names "ExceededDeadline," "ExceededDeadline1," "ExceededDeadline2," and so on. Use the first name in this series that is currently unused because it gives the caller some knowledge of when to try the operation again.

The enumeration **BINDFLAGS**, which contains the legal values for the bit field *grfFlags* in the **BIND_OPTS** structure, is defined in moniker.h as follows:

```
typedef enum tagBINDFLAGS{
    BIND_MAYBOTHERUSER = 1,
    BIND_JUSTTESTEXISTENCE = 2,
} BINDFLAGS;
```

BINDFLAGS members have the following meanings.

Value	Meaning
BINDFLAGS_MAYBOTHERUSER	If present, this sort of interaction is permitted. If not present, the operation to which the bind context containing this parameter is applied should not interact with the user in any way, such as by asking for a password for a network volume that needs mounting. If prohibited from interacting with the user when it otherwise would, an operation can elect to use a different algorithm that does not require user interaction, or it can fail with the error MK_MUSTBOTHERUSER.

Value	Meaning
BINDFLAGS_JUSTTESTEXISTENCE	If present, this value indicates that the caller of the moniker operation to which this flag is being applied is not actually interested in having the operation carried out, but only in learning whether the operation could have been carried out had this flag not been specified. For example, this flag lets the caller indicate only an interest in finding out whether an object actually exists by using this flag in a **IMoniker::BindToObject** call. Moniker implementations can ignore this possible optimization and carry out the operation in full. Callers must be able to deal with both cases. See individual routine descriptions for details of exactly what status is returned.

IBindCtx::GetBindOptions

HRESULT IBindCtx::GetBindOptions(*pbindopts***)**
LPBIND_OPTS * *pbindopts*

IBindCtx::GetBindOptions returns the current binding options stored in this bind context.

Parameters

pbindopts
Points to the structure of binding options to be filled in (the caller-supplied **BIND_OPTS** structure).

Return Values

Value	Meaning
S_OK	The binding options were returned successfully.
E_INVALIDARG	One or more arguments are invalid. For example, the size is not correct or parameter not readable.

Comments

The caller must correctly set the *cbStruct* member in the **BIND_OPTS** structure before calling **IBindCtx::GetBindOptions**.

The stored parameters can be retrieved with **IBindCtx::GetBindOptions**. Using a block of parameters is an alternative way to pass parameters that are common to **IMoniker** operations and that do not change as the operation moves from one piece of a generic composite to another.

See Also

IBindCtx::SetBindOptions

IBindCtx::GetRunningObjectTable

HRESULT IBindCtx::GetRunningObjectTable(*pprot***)**
LPRUNNINGOBJECTTABLE * *pprot*

IBindCtx::GetRunningObjectTable returns access to the running object table relevant to this binding process.

Parameters

pprot
Points to where to return the running object table.

Return Values

Value	Meaning
S_OK	The pointer was returned successfully.
E_UNEXPECTED	An unexpected error occurred.

Comments

Moniker implementations should get access to the running object table by using **IBindCtx::GetRunningObjectTable**, rather than the API **GetRunningObjectTable**.

The appropriate running object table is determined implicitly when the bind context is created.

See Also

GetRunningObjectTable

IBindCtx::RegisterObjectParam

HRESULT IBindCtx::RegisterObjectParam(*lpszKey, pUnk***)**
char * *lpszKey*
LPUNKNOWN *pUnk*

IBindCtx::RegisterObjectParam registers an object pointer in an internally maintained table of object pointers.

Parameters

lpszKey
Points to the name under which the object is being registered.

pUnk
Points to the object to be registered.

Return Values

Value	Meaning
S_OK	The object was registered successfully.
E_OUTOFMEMORY	Out of memory.

Comments

IBindCtx::RegisterObjectParam registers the object under the name specified in the *lpszKey* parameter. The table of pointers is used to pass contextual information to the binding process. String keys are compared on a case-sensitive basis.

Like **IBindCtx::RegisterObjectBound**, **IBindCtx::RegisterObjectParam** creates an additional reference to the passed-in object using **IUnknown::AddRef**.

Calling **IBindCtx::RegisterObjectParam** a second time with a different object (using the same *lpszKey*), replaces the object stored in the first call to the method.

See Also **IBindCtx::RegisterObjectBound**

IBindCtx::GetObjectParam

HRESULT IBindCtx::GetObjectParam(*lpszKey, ppUnk*)
char * *lpszKey*
LPUNKNOWN * *ppUnk*

IBindCtx::GetObjectParam finds the specified object pointer in the internally maintained table of contextual object pointers and returns the corresponding object, if one exists.

Parameters

lpszKey
Points to the key under which to look for an object.

ppUnk
Points to where to return the object's interface pointer. NULL is returned on failure.

Return Values

Value	Meaning
S_OK	The object was returned successfully.
E_OUTOFMEMORY	Out of memory.

See Also **IBindCtx::EnumObjectParam**

IBindCtx::EnumObjectParam

HRESULT IBindCtx::EnumObjectParam(*ppenumString*)
LPENMSTRING * *ppenumString*

IBindCtx::EnumObjectParam returns an enumeration of the internally maintained table of contextual object pointers.

Parameters

ppenumString
Points to where to return the string enumerator.

Return Values

Value	Meaning
S_OK	The enumerator was returned successfully.
E_OUTOFMEMORY	Out of memory.

IBindCtx::RevokeObjectParam

HRESULT IBindCtx::RevokeObjectParam(*lpszKey*)
char * *lpszKey*

IBindCtx::RevokeObjectParam revokes the registration of the object currently found under this key in the internally maintained table of contextual object pointers, if any such key is currently registered.

Parameters

lpszKey
Points to the key whose registration is to be revoked.

Return Values

Value	Meaning
S_OK	The object registration was revoked successfully.
E_FAIL	Key not present.

See Also

IBindCtx::RegisterObjectParam

IEnumMoniker Interface

The **IEnumMoniker** interface is implemented by OLE and used by OLE, object applications, and certain containers to enumerate through items that are monikers. It is used specifically in the implementation of **IRunningObjectTable::EnumRunning**.

The **IEnumMoniker** interface contains the following methods, as do all enumerators:

```
DECLARE_INTERFACE_(IEnumMoniker, IUnknown)
{
   // *** IUnknown methods ***
  HRESULT QueryInterface (REFIID riid, void * * ppvObj);
  unsigned long AddRef ();
  unsigned long Release ();

   // *** IEnumMoniker methods ***
  HRESULT Next (unsigned long celt, LPMONIKER * rgelt, unsigned long * pceltFetched);
  HRESULT Skip (unsigned long celt);
  HRESULT Reset ();
  HRESULT Clone (IEnumMoniker * * ppenum);
};
```

For more information about enumerators in general, see **IEnum*X*** in Chapter 5, "Component Object Interfaces and Functions."

IOleLink Interface

The main architectural difference, from a container's perspective, between an embedded object and a linked object is that the linked object supports the **IOleLink** interface. **IOleLink** contains functionality by which the moniker inside the linked object and the linked object's update options are manipulated. OLE provides an implementation of **IOleLink** that is used by containers.

The **IOleLink** interface contains the following methods:

```
DECLARE_INTERFACE_(IOleLink, IUnknown)
{
  // *** IUnknown methods ***
 HRESULT QueryInterface (REFIID riid, void * * ppvObj);
 unsigned long AddRef ();
 unsigned long Release ();

  // *** IOleLink methods ***
 HRESULT SetUpdateOptions (unsigned long dwUpdateOpt);
 HRESULT GetUpdateOptions (unsigned long * pdwUpdateOpt);
 HRESULT SetSourceMoniker (LPMONIKER pmk, REFCLSID rclsid);
 HRESULT GetSourceMoniker (LPMONIKER * ppmk);
 HRESULT SetSourceDisplayName (const char * lpszDisplayName);
 HRESULT GetSourceDisplayName (char * * lplpszDisplayName);
 HRESULT BindToSource (unsigned long bindflags, LPBINDCTX pbc);
 HRESULT BindIfRunning ();
 HRESULT GetBoundSource (LPUNKNOWN * ppUnk);
 HRESULT UnbindSource ();
 HRESULT Update (LPBINDCTX pbc);
};
```

For more information, see the ole2.h header file.

IOleLink::SetUpdateOptions

HRESULT IOleLink::SetUpdateOptions(*dwUpdateOpt*)
unsigned long *dwUpdateOpt*

IOleLink::SetUpdateOptions sets the link update options for the linked object.

Parameters

dwUpdateOpt
Specifies when the data and/or presentation cache on the link consumer is updated; valid values are taken from the enumeration **OLEUPDATE**. For more information, see the following comments.

Return Values

Value	Meaning
S_OK	The operation was completed successfully.
E_INVALIDARG	One or more arguments are invalid.

Comments

Values for *dwUpdateOpt* are taken from the enumeration **OLEUPDATE**, defined in ole2.h as follows:

```
typedef enum tagOLEUPDATE {
    OLEUPDATE_ALWAYS     = 1,
    OLEUPDATE_ONCALL     = 3,
    } OLEUPDATE;
```

OLEUPDATE values are used as follows:

Value	Purpose
OLEUDPATE_ALWAYS	Update the link object whenever possible. This option supports the Automatic link-update option in the Links dialog box.
OLEUPDATE_ONCALL	Update the link object only when the **IOleObject::Update** member function is called. This option supports the Manual link-update option in the Links dialog box.

IOleLink::GetUpdateOptions

HRESULT IOleLink::GetUpdateOptions(*pdwUpdateOpt*)
unsigned long * *pdwUpdateOpt*

IOleLink::GetUpdateOptions retrieves link update options previously set with **IOleLink::SetUpdateOptions**.

Parameters

pdwUpdateOpt
Points to where to return the flags taken from the **OLEUPDATE** enumeration; for more information, see **IOleLink::SetUpdateOptions**.

Return Values

Value	Meaning
S_OK	The function was completed successfully.

IOleLink::SetSourceMoniker

HRESULT IOleLink::SetSourceMoniker(*pmk, rclsid*)
LPMONIKER *pmk*
REFCLSID *rclsid*

IOleLink::SetSourceMoniker stores a moniker that indicates the source of the link inside of the linked object.

Parameters

pmk
Points to the new moniker; may be NULL.

rclsid
Specifies the CLSID of the moniker.

Return Values

Value	Meaning
S_OK	The operation was completed successfully.

Comments

The stored moniker becomes part of the persistent state of the object. Setting the source moniker also allows an application to set the expected class of the object without binding to it. In order to support link source tracking, linked objects also store a relative moniker, which is computed as

```
pmkContainer->RelativePathTo(pmkLinkSource)
```

When a linked object is in the running state (the source moniker has been bound and connected), it registers to receive rename notifications from its link source. When a notification is received, the linked object updates its source moniker to the new name. It registers itself for notifications to handle situations in which a link is made to a newly created document that has never been saved. For example, newly created spreadsheets are named "SHEET1," "SHEET2," and so on. Only when they are saved for the first time do they acquire a persistent identity that is appropriate to store in the links to them. As long as the source document is saved before its link consumer is closed, the linked object will be able to track the source of the link.

The NULL option is used for the Cancel Link option of the Edit Links dialog box to indicate a static link. A static link continues to load and draw out of its cache, but cannot implement other verbs because the connection to its link source has been broken.

IOleLink::GetSourceMoniker

HRESULT IOleLink::GetSourceMoniker(*ppmk***)**
LPMONIKER * *ppmk*

IOleLink::GetSourceMoniker retrieves the moniker for the current link source.

Parameters

ppmk
Points to the address where the moniker currently in the link should be placed.

Return Values

Value	Meaning
S_OK	The operation was completed successfully.
MK_E_UNAVAILABLE	The moniker is unavailable, and would not be available no matter what deadlines were used.

IOleLink::SetSourceDisplayName

HRESULT IOleLink::SetSourceDisplayName(*lpszDisplayName***)**
const char * *lpszDisplayName*

IOleLink::SetSourceDisplayName parses a linked object's display name into a moniker, and stores the moniker in the linked object.

Parameters

lpszDisplayName
The display name of the new link source; may not be NULL.

Return Values

Value	Meaning
S_OK	The operation was completed successfully.
MK_E_SYNTAX	An error in the syntax of a filename was encountered while parsing a display name or creating a file moniker.
E_OUTOFMEMORY	Out of memory.

Comments

Monikers used to indicate the source of linked objects have a display name that can be shown to the user in dialog boxes. Display names can be parsed into monikers using the **MkParseDisplayName** function. Most often, the location of a link source is provided directly in a moniker, such as the moniker passed through the clipboard in a Copy/Paste Link operation. Less frequently, the moniker originates in a textual form, such as in the text box of a dialog. Before they can be stored as the source of a linked object, monikers originating in textual form need to be parsed.

If the caller is to do the parsing, it calls **MkParseUserName** and then passes the returned moniker to **IOleLink::SetSourceMoniker**. To let the linked object do the parsing, the caller should call **IOleLink::SetSourceDisplayName**. In this case, the display name is parsed and the resulting moniker stored in its place before the linked object needs to be bound for the first time.

See Also

MkParseDisplayName

IOleLink::GetSourceDisplayName

HRESULT IOleLink::GetSourceDisplayName(*lplpszDisplayName***)**
char * * *lplpszDisplayName*

IOleLink::GetSourceDisplayName retrieves the display name of the linked object's source.

Parameters

lplpszDisplayName
Points to where to return the name of the link source; cannot be NULL.

Return Values

Value	Meaning
S_OK	The operation completed successfully.
MK_E_EXCEEDEDDEADLINE	During some process (binding, parsing a display name, etc.) a deadline was exceeded.
E_OUTOFMEMORY	Out of memory.
E_UNEXPECTED	An unexpected error occurred.

Comments

The display name of a linked object's moniker can be obtained from its source moniker using **IMoniker::GetDisplayName**. However, the display name might either be unavailable or might not be obtained quickly enough to suit the caller because it could require that object applications be run. So that a reasonable representation of the link source is always available to the callers, linked objects keep a cache of their source's display name, which is updated each time the linked object connects to its source.

See Also

IMoniker::GetDisplayName

IOleLink::BindToSource

HRESULT IOleLink::BindToSource(*bindflags, pbc***)**
unsigned long *bindflags*
LPBINDCTX *pbc*

IOleLink::BindToSource binds the moniker contained within the linked object.

Parameters

bindflags
Controls the behavior of the binding operation using values taken from the enumeration **OLELINKBIND**. For more information, see the following comments.

pbc
Points to the bind context.

Return Values

Value	Meaning
S_OK	The binding operation was successful.
MK_E_NOOBJECT	An object, possibly intermediate, could not be found during an operation such as binding or parsing a display name.
MK_E_EXCEEDED-DEADLINE	The process was not completed within the time specified by the bind context.

Value	Meaning
MK_E_CONNECT-MANUALLY	During some process (binding, parsing a display name, and so on.) OLE was unable to connect to a network device. The application receiving this error should call **IBindCtx::GetObjectParam** with the key "ConnectManually" to retrieve the moniker of the network device, get the display name, and put up a dialog box asking the user for a password, and so on.
MK_E_INTERMEDIATE INTERFACENOT-SUPPORTED	An object was found but it did not support an interface required for an operation. During binding, for example, a container is expected to support the **IOleItemContainer** interface, and during parsing of display names a container is expected to support the **IParseDisplayName** interface.)
E_NOINTERFACE	Interface not supported.
E_OUTOFMEMORY	Out of memory.
OLE_E_CLASSDIFF	The bind operation failed because the class is different than the last time the object was successfully bound.
STG_E_ACCESS-DENIED	Incorrect permission for accessing this storage object.
E_UNEXPECTED	Failure of unknown cause.
IMoniker::Bind-ToObject errors.	All **IMoniker::BindToObject** errors.

Comments

When a user activates a linked object and the object application must be located, **IOleLink::BindToSource** is invoked to connect the object to the object application. If the object cannot be found, MK_E_NOOBJECT is returned.

The time limit specified in the bind context identifies the amount of time within which the binding operation must be completed. A value of zero specifies an infinite time. For more information, see the **BIND_OPTS** structure in the description for **IBindCtx::SetBindOptions**.

When binding a linked object, the current class of the link source might not be the same as it was when the linked object tried to connect. For example, the class of a link to a Lotus spreadsheet object that the user subsequently converted (using the Convert dialog) to an Excel sheet would now be different.

The *bindflags* parameter controls the behavior of the binding operation. It contains values taken from the enumeration **OLELINKBIND**, which is defined in ole2.h as follows.

```
typedef enum tagOLELINKBIND {
    OLELINKBIND_EVENIFCLASSDIFF = 1,
    } OLELINKBIND:
```

If OLELINKBIND_EVENIFCLASSDIFF is not provided, **IOleLink::BindToSource** returns OLE_E_CLASSDIFF when the class is different than when the linked object was last successfully bound.

If OLELINKBIND_EVENIFCLASSDIFF is given, the bind process proceeds even if the class has changed.

See Also **IBindCtx::SetBindOptions**

IOleLink::BindIfRunning

HRESULT IOleLink::BindIfRunning()

IOleLink::BindIfRunning binds the link to the link source, using **IOleLink::BindToSource**(NULL, NULL), if the link source is currently running.

Return Values

Value	Meaning
S_OK	The link was bound to the link source.

Comments **IOleLink::BindIfRunning** tries only the relative moniker in the running object table, when both a relative and absolute moniker are present. It tries the absolute moniker only if no relative moniker is present, otherwise it fails.

See Also **IOleLink::BindToSource**

IOleLink::GetBoundSource

HRESULT IOleLink::GetBoundSource(*ppUnk*)
LPUNKNOWN * *ppUnk*

IOleLink::GetBoundSource retrieves the object to which this link source is currently connected, if any source is present.

Parameters

ppUnk
Points to where to return the currently-connected source of this object. It cannot be NULL. If no source is currently connected, NULL is returned.

Return Values

Value	Meaning
S_OK	The object was retrieved successfully.

Value	Meaning
E_FAIL	No link source is currently connected.
E_UNEXPECTED	An unexpected error occurred.

Comments

If there is no source currently connected, then **IOleLink::GetBoundSource** returns E_FAIL and NULL is returned through **ppUnk*.

IOleLink::UnbindSource

HRESULT IOleLink::UnbindSource()

IOleLink::UnbindSource unbinds a currently linked object from the link source.

Return Values

Value	Meaning
S_OK	The unbind operation was completed successfully.

IOleObject::Close calls **IOleLink::UnbindSource** for linked objects.

See Also

IOleObject::Close, **IOleLink::BindToSource**

IOleLink::Update

IOleLink::Update(*pbc***)**
LPBINDCTX *pbc*

IOleLink::Update updates a linked object with the latest data from the link source. This function finds the link source if necessary and gets a new presentation from the source. This process may require the running of one or more object applications.

Parameters

pbc
Points to the bind context to be used for the update.

Return Values

Value	Meaning
S_OK	All caches updated successfully.
CACHE_E_NOCACHE _UPDATED	The bind operation worked but no caches were updated.
CACHE_S_SOMECACHES _NOTUPDATED	The bind operation worked but not all caches were updated.
MK_E_NOOBJECT	The bind operation failed. Some, possibly intermediate, object could not be found during an operation such as binding or parsing a display name.
MK_E_EXCEEDEDDEADLINE	The bind operation failed so the process was not completed within the time specified by the bind context.

Value	Meaning
MK_E_CONNECTMANUALLY	The bind operation failed. OLE was unable to connect to a network device. The application receiving this error should call **IBindCtx::GetObjectParam** with the key "ConnectManually" to retrieve the moniker of the network device, get the display name, and put up a dialog box asking the user for a password, and so on.
MK_E_INTERMEDIATE-INTERFACENOT-SUPPORTED	The bind operation failed. An object was found but did not support an interface required for binding. A container is expected to support the **IOleItemContainer** interface, and during parsing of display names a container is expected to support the **IParseDisplayName** interface.
E_NOINTERFACE	Interface not supported. The bind operation failed.
E_OUTOFMEMORY	Out of memory. The bind operation failed.
OLE_E_CLASSDIFF	The bind operation failed because the class is different from the last time the object was successfully bound.
STG_E_ACCESSDENIED	Incorrect permission for accessing this storage object.
OLE_E_CANT_BINDTO-SOURCE	Unable to bind to the source.
E_UNEXPECTED	An unexpected error occurred; the bind operation failed.

Comments

IOleLink::Update ensures that the linked object has the latest data from the link source. This function is useful for automatic links, when the link is not bound, and for all cases involving manual links.

The *pbc* parameter is used when the linked object has to bind to the link source. The link source is locked for the duration of the update. This method does not call **IOleObject::Update** on the link source; it just gets the necessary data by using **IDataObject::GetData**.

IRunningObjectTable Interface

The **IRunningObjectTable** interface provides access to the running object table, a globally accessible lookup table that keeps track of the objects that are currently running on the workstation. When a container tries to bind to a running object, it looks in the running object table to determine whether an instance is currently running. If there is already an instance of that object running, the container binds to that it instead of loading the object a second time. The table contains a series of data pairs, of the form:

```
(pmk, pUnk)
```

The *pmk* element points to the moniker that, if successfully bound, connects to the running object. The *pUnk* element points to the available running object's implementation of **IUnknown**. During the binding process, monikers consult the *pmk* entries in the running object table to see whether an object is already running.

Clients of objects access the running object table by calling **GetRunningObjectTable** or **IBindCtx::GetRunningObjectTable,** which return an instance of the **IRunningObjectTable** interface.

The **IRunningObjectTable** interface, implemented by OLE and used by OLE and object applications, contains the following methods:

```
DECLARE_INTERFACE_(IRunningObjectTable, IUnknown)
{
  // *** IUnknown methods ***
 HRESULT QueryInterface (REFIID riid, void * * ppvObj);
 unsigned long AddRef ();
 unsigned long Release ();

  // *** IRunningObjectTable methods ***
 HRESULT Register (unsigned long grfFlags, LPUNKNOWN pUnk, LPMONIKER pmk,
      unsigned long * * pdwRegister);
 HRESULT Revoke (unsigned long dwRegister);
 HRESULT IsRunning (LPMONIKER pmk);
 HRESULT GetObject (LPMONIKER pmk, LPUNKNOWN * ppUnk);
 HRESULT NoteChangeTime (unsigned long dwRegister, FILETIME * pFiletime);
 HRESULT GetTimeOfLastChange (LPMONIKER pmk, FILETIME * pFileTime);
 HRESULT EnumRunning (LPENUMMONIKER * ppenumMoniker );
};
```

For more information, see the moniker.h header file.

IRunningObjectTable::Register

HRESULT IRunningObjectTable(*grfFlags, pUnk, pmk, pdwRegister***)**
unsigned long *grfFlags*
LPUNKNOWN *pUnk*
LPMONIKER *pmk*
unsigned long * *pdwRegister*

IRunningObjectTable::Register registers a running object in the running object table.

Parameters

grfFlags
Specifies the strength or weakness of the registration. Zero specifies a weak registration and one specifies strong registration. A weak registration enables objects to be connected to and released only once. A strong registration enables multiple clients to connect to and release an active object multiple times. Strong registrations can be specified using the constant ROTFLAGS_REGISTRATIONKEEPSALIVE = 1.

pUnk
Points to the object that has just entered the running state.

pmk
Points to the moniker that is to bind to the newly running object.

pdwRegister
Points to where to return a value that can later be used to revoke the registration. It cannot be NULL. Zero is never returned as a valid registration value, so, unless **IRunningObjectTable::Register** fails, **pdwRegister* is never NULL on exit.

Return Values

Value	Meaning
S_OK	The object was registered successfully.
MK_S_MONIKER-ALREADYREGISTERED	An attempt was made to register a given *pmk* a second time.
E_OUTOFMEMORY	Out of memory.
E_INVALIDARG	One or more arguments are invalid.
E_UNEXPECTED	An unexpected error occurred.

Comments

If the moniker pointed to by *pmk* is bound to during registration, the object pointed to by *pUnk* should be used as the result of the bind operation (with an appropriate **QueryInterface**).

The moniker *pmk* should be fully reduced before registration. For information on reducing monikers, see **IMoniker::Reduce** described earlier. If an object is known by more than one fully reduced moniker, it should register itself under all such monikers.

OLE compound document objects should call **IRunningObjectTable::Register** as soon as the following conditions are all true simultaneously:

1. The object is in the running state.
2. The object knows its full moniker (see the description for **IOleObject::SetMoniker**).
   A. A moniker has been assigned to the object that is relative to the object's container (this is part of the persistent state of the object).

B. The object knows the current moniker of its container, which is almost always obtained by the container calling **IOleObject::SetMoniker**.

3. There is any possibility that a link is made to the object or something that it contains exists.

OLE objects register themselves as running by using their full moniker (see also **IOleObject::GetMoniker**). Generally, if a link has ever been made to an object, the object must assume that the link might still exist. For example, the consumer of the link might be on a floppy disk somewhere and later reappear. (The exceptions are rare situations where a link is created but almost immediately destroyed before the link source is saved.)

Attempting to register an object under the same moniker returns MK_S_MONIKERALREADYREGISTERED. In most cases, the application revokes the pending registration (in some rare cases, multiple objects may want to register under the same moniker).

With a weak registration only, the registration entry becomes invalid as soon as the last external connection to the object is released. Presumably the object will release itself as a result of the loss of connections. In the process of doing so, it revokes its registration. Objects that register themselves should always revoke their registration by calling **IRunningObjectTable::Revoke**.

See Also **IRunningObjectTable::Revoke**, **IOleObject::SetMoniker**

IRunningObjectTable::Revoke

HRESULT IRunningObjectTable::Revoke(*dwRegister***)**
unsigned long *dwRegister*

IRunningObjectTable::Revoke revokes an object's registration from the running object table.

Parameters

dwRegister
Specifies a value previously returned from **IRunningObjectTable::Register**.

Return Values

Value	Meaning
S_OK	The object registration has been successfully undone.
E_INVALIDARG	The object is not registered as running.
E_UNEXPECTED	An unexpected error occurred.

Comments **IRunningObjectTable::Revoke** revokes a registration, presumably because the object is about to quit running.

Whenever any of the conditions that put an object in the running state cease to be true, the object should revoke its registration(s).

See Also

IRunningObjectTable::Register

IRunningObjectTable::IsRunning

HRESULT IRunningObjectTable::IsRunning(*pmk***)**
LPMONIKER *pmk*

IRunningObjectTable::IsRunning determines whether an object with this moniker is currently registered as running.

Parameters

pmk
Points to the moniker to compare against entries in the running object table to determine whether the object is running.

Return Values

Value	Meaning
S_OK	The object is registered as running.
S_FALSE	The object is not registered as running.

Comments

In general, **IRunningObjectTable::IsRunning** should only be called by implementations of **IMoniker::IsRunning**. Clients of monikers should invoke this on their monikers rather than asking the running object table directly.

The running object table compares monikers by sending **IMoniker::IsEqual** to the monikers already in the table with *pmk* on the right as an argument.

See Also

IMoniker::IsEqual

IRunningObjectTable::GetObject

HRESULT IRunningObjectTable::GetObject(*pmk*, *ppUnk***)**
LPMONIKER *pmk*
LPUNKNOWN * *ppUnk*

IRunningObjectTable::GetObject returns the running object designated by *pmk*.

Parameters

pmk
Points to the moniker of the object to return.

ppUnk
Points to where to return the pointer to the object. A NULL value indicates the object is not registered.

Return Values

Value	Meaning
S_OK	The object has been successfully returned.
MK_E_UNAVAILABLE	The object is not registered as running.

Comments

Moniker implementations use **IRunningObjectTable::GetObject** to determine whether an object is already running and, if so, to get the pointer to the object.

The running object table compares monikers by sending **IMoniker::IsEqual** to the monikers already in the table with *pmk* on the right as an argument.

See Also

IMoniker::IsEqual

IRunningObjectTable::NoteChangeTime

HRESULT IRunningObjectTable::NoteChangeTime(*dwRegister, pFiletime***)**
unsigned long *dwRegister*
FILETIME * *pFiletime*

IRunningObjectTable::NoteChangeTime makes a note of the time that a particular object changed so that **IMoniker::GetTimeOfLastChange** can report an appropriate time-of-last-change.

Parameters

dwRegister
Identifies which object has changed. This is the value returned by the **IRunningObjectTable::Register** call. When an object is registered in the running object table (using **IRunningObjectTable::Register**), a *dwRegister* value is returned that is used to identify that object in other running object table methods. Here it is used to denote which object has changed.

pFiletime
Points (on entry) to the time at which the object changed.

Return Values

Value	Meaning
S_OK	The change of time has been successfully noted.
E_INVALIDARG	One or more invalid arguments.

Comments

For each object, OLE needs to know a time past which the object has not changed. This is used, for example, to determine whether links are up to date. While an object is on disk, this time comes from the file time stamp, but when the object is in the running state, the change times are recorded in the running object table. When an object application changes an object, it should call this method with the file time corresponding to the current instant, which can be retrieved by calling **CoFileTimeNow**.

See Also

CoFileTimeNow, **IRunningObjectTable::Register**

IRunningObjectTable::GetTimeOfLastChange

HRESULT IRunningObjectTable::GetTimeOfLastChange(*pmk, pFiletime***)**
LPMONIKER *pmk*
FILETIME * *pFiletime*

IRunningObjectTable::GetTimeOfLastChange reports the time of change recorded for the given moniker.

Parameters

pmk
Points to the moniker whose time of last change is being checked.

pFiletime
On exit, points to the time at which the object last changed.

Return Values

Value	Meaning
S_OK	The time of change has been successfully reported.
MK_E_UNAVAILABLE	Either no time has been recorded for the moniker, or the object is not registered as running.

Comments

When invoked with *pmkToLeft* = NULL, **IMoniker::GetTimeOfLastChange** calls **IRunningObjectTable::GetTimeOfLastChange** as its first task.

The running object table compares monikers by sending **IMoniker::IsEqual** to the monikers already in the table with *pmk* on the right as an argument.

IRunningObjectTable::GetTimeOfLastChange is not typically used by applications. Applications instead call **IMoniker::GetTimeOfLastChange**.

In most cases, if the object is registered in the running object table, the answer is the same, but in some cases, such as when the moniker contains wild card items, **IMoniker::GetTimeOfLastChange** returns the correct result while **IRunningObjectTable::GetTimeOfLastChange** might fail to find the moniker in the running object table.

IMoniker::GetTimeOfLastChange also returns the correct result when the object is passive (on disk).

See Also

IMoniker::IsEqual, **IMoniker::GetTimeOfLastChange**, **IRunningObjectTable::NoteChangeTime**

IRunningObjectTable::EnumRunning

HRESULT IRunningObjectTable::EnumRunning(*ppenumMoniker*)
LPENUMMONIKER * *ppenumMoniker*

IRunningObjectTable::EnumRunning allows applications to enumerate the monikers of all the objects registered as running in the running object table.

Parameters

ppenumMoniker
Points to the location that is to receive the pointer to the returned moniker enumerator.

Return Values

Value	Meaning
S_OK	Enumerator successfully returned.
E_OUTOFMEMORY	Out of memory.

Comments

The monikers that have been passed to **IRunningObjectTable::Register** are enumerated. The returned enumerator is of type **IEnumMoniker**. For more information, see the description of **IEnumMoniker** in this chapter.

Linking Functions

The following functions support linking operations:

```
HRESULT BindMoniker(LPMONIKER pmk, unsigned long grfOpt, REFIID riid, void * * ppvObj);
 HRESULT CreateAntiMoniker(LPMONIKER * ppmk);
 HRESULT CreateBindCtx(unsigned long dwReserved, LPBC * ppbc);
 HRESULT CreateFileMoniker(char * lpszPathName, LPMONIKER * ppmk);
 HRESULT CreateFileMonikerFSp(const FSSpec *pSpec, LPMONIKER * ppmk);
 HRESULT CreateItemMoniker(char * lpszDelim, char * lpszItem, LPMONIKER * ppmk);
 HRESULT CreatePointerMoniker(LPUNKNOWN pUnk, LPMONIKER * ppmk);
 HRESULT CreateGenericComposite(LPMONIKER pmkFirst, LPMONIKER pmkRest,
     LPMONIKER * ppmkComposite);
 HRESULT GetRunningObjectTable(unsigned long dwReserved, LPRUNNINGOBJECTTABLE * pprot);
 HRESULT MkParseDisplayName(LPBC pbc, char * szUserName, unsigned long * pchEaten,
     LPMONIKER * ppmk);
 HRESULT MkParseDisplayNameMac (LBPC pbc, char * szDisplayName,  short vRefNum, long DirID,
     unsigned long * pchEaten, LPLPMONIKER ppmk)
 HRESULT MonikerRelativePathTo(LPMONIKER pmkSrc, LPMONIKER pmkDest, LPMONIKER * ppmkRelPath,
     unsigned long fCalledFromMethod);
 HRESULT MonikerCommonPrefixWith(LPMONIKER pmkThis, LPMONIKER pmkOther,
     LPMONIKER * ppmkCommon);
HRESULT MkGetMacNetInfo(IMoniker* pmk, char** pszZoneName, char** pszServerName)
```

For more information, see the moniker.h header file.

BindMoniker

HRESULT BindMoniker(*pmk, grfOpt, riid, ppvObj***)**
LPMONIKER *pmk*
unsigned long *grfOpt*
REFIID *riid*
void * * *ppvObj*

BindMoniker binds a moniker with the specified interface and returns the result.

Parameters

pmk
Points to the moniker that is to be bound.

grfOpt
Reserved for future use; must be zero.

riid
Identifies the interface to connect to the object.

ppvObj
Points to the address to place the resulting object.

Return Values

Value	Meaning
S_OK	The bind operation was successful.
MK_E_NOOBJECT	Some, possibly intermediate, object could not be found during some operation, such as binding or parsing a display name.
E_OUTOFMEMORY	Out of memory.
IMoniker::BindToObject errors.	All **IMoniker::BindToObject** errors.

BindMoniker is a helper function that packages the following functionality:

```
IBindCtx pbc;
CreateBindCtx(0, &pbc);
pmk->BindToObject(pbc, NULL, riid, ppvObj);
pbc->Release();
```

See Also

IMoniker::BindToObject

CreateAntiMoniker

HRESULT CreateAntiMoniker(*ppmk***)**
LPMONIKER * *ppmk*

CreateAntiMoniker creates and returns a new anti moniker.

Parameters

ppmk
Pointer to where to return the new anti moniker.

Return Values

Value	Meaning
S_OK	The anti moniker was created successfully.
E_OUTOFMEMORY	Out of memory.

Comments An anti moniker is a moniker that when composed onto the end of a generic moniker removes the last piece. Anti monikers provide no functional use; they exist solely to support implementations of the **IMoniker::Inverse** method.

See Also **IMoniker::Inverse**

CreateBindCtx

HRESULT CreateBindCtx(*dwReserved, ppbc***)**
unsigned long *dwReserved*
LPPBC * *ppbc*

CreateBindCtx allocates and initializes a new bind context using an OLE-supplied implementation.

Parameters

dwReserved
Reserved for future use; must be zero.

ppbc
Points to where to store the new bind context.

Return Values

Value	Meaning
S_OK	The bind context was allocated and initialized successfully.
E_OUTOFMEMORY	Out of memory.

The default values for the following members of the **BIND_OPTS** structure in the newly created bind context are:

```
grfFlags = 0
grfMode = STGM_READWRITE
dwTickCountDeadline = 0
```

CreateFileMoniker

HRESULT CreateFileMoniker(*lpszPathName, ppmk***)**
char * *lpszPathName*
LPMONIKER * *ppmk*

CreateFileMoniker creates a moniker from a path name.

Parameters

lpszPathName
Points to the path of the needed file.

ppmk
Points to the newly created moniker.

Return Values

Value	Meaning
S_OK	The moniker was created successfully.
MK_E_SYNTAX	An error in the syntax of a path was encountered while creating a moniker.
E_OUTOFMEMORY	Out of memory.

Comments

The path can be absolute or relative. In the latter case, the resulting moniker will need to be composed onto another file moniker before it can be bound. In either case, it is often necessary to compose other monikers onto the end of this moniker in order to access the subpieces of the document stored in the file.

Where applicable, applications should call **CreateFileMonikerFSp** instead of **CreateFileMoniker**.

CreateFileMonikerFSp

HRESULT CreateFileMoniker(*pFSSpec, ppmk***)**
const FSSpec * *pFSSpec*
LPMONIKER * *ppmk*

CreateFileMonikerFsp creates a moniker from a file specification.

Parameters

pFSSpec
Points to the file specification from which to create the moniker.

ppmk
Points to the newly created moniker.

Return Values

Value	Meaning
S_OK	The moniker was created successfully.
MK_E_SYNTAX	An error in syntax occurred while creating a moniker.
E_OUTOFMEMORY	Out of memory.

CreateItemMoniker

HRESULT CreateItemMoniker(*lpszDelim, lpszItem, ppmk***)**
char * *lpszDelim*
char * *lpszItem*
LPMONIKER * *ppmk*

CreateItemMoniker allocates and returns a new item moniker.

Parameters

lpszDelim
Points to a string that will prefix *lpszItem* in the display name of this moniker. Often an exclamation mark: "!".

lpszItem
Points to the item name to pass to **IOleItemContainer::GetObject**.

ppmk
Points to where to put the new item moniker.

Return Values

Value	Meaning
S_OK	The moniker was created successfully.
E_OUTOFMEMORY	Out of memory.

Comments

The resulting moniker will be composed onto the end of a second moniker that binds to an object supporting the **IOleItemContainer** interface. When bound, the resulting composite moniker extracts the object of the indicated name from within the object container.

The *lpszItem* parameter is the item name that will later be passed to **IOleItemContainer::GetObject**. The *lpszDelim* parameter is simply another string that can prefix *lpszItem* in the display name of the item moniker.

See Also

IOleItemContainer::GetObject

CreatePointerMoniker

HRESULT CreatePointerMoniker(*pUnk, ppmk***)**
LPUNKNOWN *pUnk*
LPMONIKER * *ppmk*

CreatePointerMoniker creates a pointer moniker from the specified interface pointer.

Parameters

pUnk
Points to an instance of the **IUnknown** interface from which the pointer moniker will be created.

ppmk
Points to the location that will contain a pointer to the new pointer moniker.

Return Values

Value	Meaning
S_OK	The pointer moniker was created successfully.
E_UNEXPECTED	An unexpected error occurred.
E_OUTOFMEMORY	Out of memory.

Comments

A pointer moniker is essentially a wrapping of a pointer so that it can be passed to those interfaces that require monikers. The result of binding a pointer moniker is the pointer itself. Pointer monikers cannot be loaded and saved.

Think of pointers as a referencing mechanism into the "active space," that is, a process's memory. Most moniker implementations are, by contrast, references into "passive space," that is, the representation of an object on disk. Pointer monikers provide a means by which a given use of a moniker can transparently reference either active or passive space. **IMoniker** methods treat pointer monikers slightly differently, as described in the following table.

IMoniker Method	Treatment of Pointer Moniker
BindToObject	Turns into a **QueryInterface** on the pointer.
BindToStorage	Returns MK_E_NOSTORAGE.
Reduce	Reduces the moniker to itself.
ComposeWith	Always does a generic composition.
Enum	Returns NULL.
IsSystemMoniker	Returns MKSYS_POINTERMONIKER.
IsEqual	Uses the identity test paradigm on pointers after first checking the other moniker for the right class.
Hash	Returns a constant.
GetTimeOfLastChange	Returns MK_E_UNAVAILABLE.
Inverse	Returns an anti moniker.
RelativePathTo	Returns the other moniker.
GetDisplayName	Returns NULL.
ParseDisplayName	Binds to the *punk* pointer using the **IParseDisplayName** interface and works from there.

Instances of pointer monikers refuse to be serialized; that is, **IPersistStream::Save** will return an error. These monikers can, however, be marshaled to a different process; internally, OLE marshals and unmarshals the pointer using the standard paradigm for marshaling interface pointers.

CreateGenericComposite

HRESULT CreateGenericComposite(*pmkFirst, pmkRest, ppmkComposite*)
LPMONIKER *pmkFirst*
LPMONIKER *pmkRest*
LPMONIKER * *ppmkComposite*

CreateGenericComposite allocates and returns a new composite moniker.

Parameters

pmkFirst
Points to the first element(s) in the new composite; cannot be NULL. *pmkFirst* can point to any type of moniker, including a generic composite.

pmkRest
Points to the last element(s) in the new composite; cannot be NULL. *pmkRest* can point to any type of moniker, including a generic composite.

ppmkComposite
Points to where to return the new composite.

Return Values

Value	Meaning
S_OK	The composite moniker was allocated successfully.
E_OUTOFMEMORY	Out of memory.

Comments

Most monikers are a composite, that is, made up of other moniker pieces, and referred to as a generic composite moniker. All generic composite monikers are instances of the GenericCompositeMoniker class, whose implementation is provided with OLE.

The OLE-provided implementations of the **IMoniker::Reduce** and **IMoniker::BindToObject** methods for the **GenericCompositeMoniker** class manage the interactions between the various elements of the composite and, as a consequence, define the semantics of binding to the moniker.

Generic composite monikers of size zero or of size one are never exposed outside of OLE's internal GenericCompositeMoniker method implementations. From a client perspective, a generic composite moniker always contains at least two elements.

Generic composites get flattened into their component pieces before being put into the new composite.

CreateGenericComposite will be called by implementations of **IMoniker::ComposeWith** when they need to do a generic compose operation.

See Also

IMoniker::ComposeWith

GetRunningObjectTable

HRESULT GetRunningObjectTable(*dwReserved*, *pprot***)**
LPRUNNINGOBJECTTABLE * *pprot*

GetRunningObjectTable returns a pointer to the running object table for the caller's context.

Parameters

pprot
Points to where to return the running object table pointer.

Return Values

Value	Meaning
S_OK	The operation completed successfully.

MkParseDisplayName

HRESULT MkParseDisplayName(*pbc, szUserName, pchEaten, ppmk***)**
LPBC *pbc*
char * *szUserName,*
unsigned long * *pchEaten*
LPMONIKER * *ppmk*

Given a string, **MkParseDisplayName** returns a moniker of the object that *szUserName* refers to. This operation is known as parsing.

Parameters

pbc
Points to the bind context in which to accumulate bound objects.

szUserName
Points to the display name to be parsed.

pchEaten
Points, on exit, to the number of characters of the display name that were successfully parsed.

ppmk
Points to the resulting moniker.

Return Values

Value	Meaning
S_OK	The parse operation was successful and the moniker was created.
MK_E_SYNTAX	An error in the syntax of a filename was encountered while parsing a display name or while creating a moniker.
E_OUTOFMEMORY	Out of memory.
IParseDisplayName errors.	Any **IParseDisplayName** errors.

Comments

When a display name is parsed into a moniker, it is resolved into its component moniker pieces.

If a syntax error occurs, the number of successfully parsed characters is returned in *pchEaten* and NULL is returned through *ppmk*. Otherwise, the value returned through *pchEaten* indicates the size of the display name.

In general, parsing a display name is as expensive as binding to the object that it refers to because various name space managers need to be connected to by the parsing mechanism. Objects are not released by the parsing operation itself, but are instead handed over to the passed-in bind context. Thus, if the moniker resulting from the parse is immediately bound using this bind context, the redundant loading of objects is minimized.

Most compound document links are created by a user selecting Copy followed by Paste Link rather than by typing in the name of the link source. This link is created programmatically with no need for an intermediate form that is a human-readable textual representation. The primary use of **MkParseDisplayName** lies instead in textual programming languages that permit remote references as syntactic elements. The expression language of a spreadsheet is a good example of such a language. **MkParseDisplayName** is also used in the implementation of the standard Edit Links dialog. The parsing process is an inductive one, an initial step gets the process going, then an inductive step is repeatedly applied. At any point after the beginning of the parse, a certain prefix of *szUserName* has been parsed into a moniker, and a suffix of the display name remains not understood. This is illustrated in Figure 8.1.

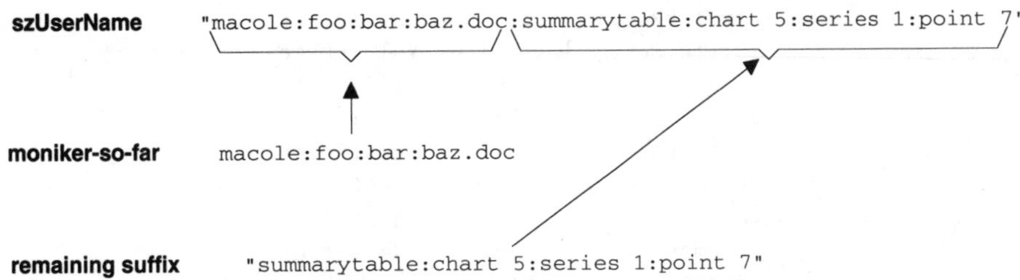

Figure 8.1 Intermediate stage in parsing a display name into a moniker

The inductive step, using **IMoniker::ParseDisplayName**, asks the moniker-so-far to parse as much of the remaining suffix as needed and to return the corresponding moniker and the new suffix. The moniker is composed onto the end of the existing moniker-so-far, and the process repeats. Implementations of **IMoniker::ParseDisplayName** vary in exactly where the knowledge of how to carry out the parsing is kept. Some monikers are only used in particular kinds of containers. It is likely that these monikers know the legal display name syntax within the objects that they denote, and can carry out the processes completely within **IMoniker::ParseDisplayName**.

Most commonly, however, the moniker-so-far is generic, meaning that it is not specific to one kind of container, and thus cannot know the legal syntax for the elements within the container.

Generic monikers employ the following strategy to carry out parsing. First, the moniker connects to the class of object that it currently denotes, asking for the **IParseDisplayName** interface (see the **CoGetClassObject** function). If that succeeds, it then uses the obtained interface pointer to attempt to carry out the parse. If the class refuses to handle the parse, then the moniker binds to the object it denotes, asking again for **IParseDisplayName**. If this fails, the parse is aborted. The effect is that ultimately an object gets to be in control of the syntax of the elements it contains.

Certain objects can carry out parsing more efficiently by having a moniker or their class do the parsing on their behalf. Notice that the OLE 2 parsing machinery knows nothing of the legal syntax of display names (with the exception of the initial parsing step (see the following code sample). It is beneficial to the user that display names in different contexts not have unnecessarily different syntax. While some rare circumstances call for special purpose syntax, it is recommended that the syntax for display names be the same as that of the native file system syntax. Most importantly, the delimiters used to separate one part of the display name from the next should be the same ones used by the native file system. It is less important that the piece of the path between the delimiters conform to the syntax of the file system, though this is recommended unless there are clear reasons to do otherwise.

The recommended syntax for display names under the Macintosh is:

```
displayName      ::=     initialPart [path]
initialPart      ::=     VolumeName
path             ::=     delim pathPiece
delim            ::=     ':' | !
pathPiece        ::=     identifier
volume name      ::=     identifier
volumen name     ::=     identifier
volumen name     ::=     identifier
identifier       ::=     (any character but a delim)*
```

To accommodate existing practice, the parsing process should treat an exclamation mark as a delimiter. However, in **IMoniker::GetDisplayName**, such exclamation marks should be converted to the normal ":" delimiter. Unless there is a good reason for doing so, applications should use only the characters listed above for delimiters.

Monikers and objects that have implementations on more than one platform, such as file monikers, should always parse according to the syntax of the platform on which they are currently running. When asked for their display name, monikers should also show delimiters appropriate to the platform on which they are currently running, even if they were originally created on a different platform. Users should always see delimiters appropriate for the host platform.

In order to accommodate monikers that are not file monikers or composite monikers that begin with a file moniker, the moniker must begin with an '@' sign followed by a ProgID. Following the ProgID can be anything that would normally follow a filename.

For example, consider the string"@Realtime:MSFT," where "Realtime" is a ProgID registered in the Registration Database file. To parse the string, the parsing code first looks for a file named "@Realtime" in the current directory (note that '@'is a legal filename character). If that fails, the parser looks for the ProgID "Realtime" in the Registration Database file. If found, it looks up the CLSID and then tries the **IParseDisplayName** interface first from the class factory. Should the parse of the class factory fail, the parser creates an instance of the class and tries to get the **IParseDisplayName** interface. If one of these succeeds, the full string, "@Realtime:MSFT" is passed to the **ParseDisplayName** method and a moniker is returned.

The initial step of the parsing process needs to determine the initial moniker-so-far. **MkParseDisplayName** knows the syntax that the display name of a moniker can legally begin with, and it uses this knowledge to choose the initial moniker. In OLE 2, this syntax is fixed because a legal display name must begin with a filename. However, that filename can be drive absolute, drive relative or working-directory relative.

The initial moniker is determined by trying the following strategies, in order, and using the first to succeed.

1. All prefixes of *szDisplayName* that consist solely of valid filename characters are consulted as file monikers in the running object table. This is attempted in order to support documents that are as yet unsaved.
2. The maximal prefix of *szDisplayName*, which consists solely of valid filename characters, is checked to see if an OLE1 document is registered by that name (this results in one or two DDE broadcasts). In this case, the returned moniker is an internal moniker provided by the OLE 1 compatibility layer of OLE 2.
3. The file system is consulted to check whether a prefix of *szDisplayName* matches an existing file. If so, the filename may be drive absolute, drive relative, or working-directory relative. This is the common case.
4. If the initial character of *szDisplayName* is an "@," the longest string immediately following it that conforms to the legal ProgID syntax is determined. This is converted to a CLSID with **CLSIDFromProgID**. If this is an OLE 2 class, the class object is so designated and an instance of it is asked in turn for

the **IParseDisplayName** interface. The resulting **IParseDisplayName** interface is then given the whole string to parse, starting with the "@." If the CLSID is an OLE1 class, then the string following the ProgID is considered an OLE 1 / DDE filename-item-syntax-link designator.

See Also **IMoniker::ParseDisplayName**, **GetDisplayName, MkParseDisplayNameMac**

MkParseDisplayNameMac

HRESULT MkParseDisplayNameMac (*pbc*, *szDisplayName*, *vRefNum*, *dirID*, *pchEaten*, *ppmk*)
LPBC *pbc*
char * *szDisplayName*
short *vRefNum*
long *dirID*
unsigned long * *pchEaten*
LPLPMONIKER *ppmk*

MkParseDisplayNameMac works the same as **MkParseDisplayName**, with the exception that **MkParseDisplayNameMac** uses a volume reference and directory ID to determine the directory.

Parameters

pbc
Points to the bind context in which to accumulate bound objects.

szUserName
Points to the display name to be parsed.

vRefNum
Specifies a volume reference number.

dirID
Specifies a directory ID.

pchEaten
Points, on exit, to the number of characters of the display name that were successfully parsed.

ppmk
Points to the resulting moniker.

Return Values

Value	**Meaning**
S_OK	The parse operation was successful and the moniker was created.
MK_E_SYNTAX	An error in the syntax of a filename was encountered while parsing a display name or while creating a moniker.

Value	Meaning
E_OUTOFMEMORY	Out of memory.
IParseDisplayName errors.	Any **IParseDisplayName** errors.

Comments

As with **MkParseDisplayName**, one of the strategies used to determine the initial moniker is to consult the file system to check if a prefix of *szDisplayName* matches an existing file. If *szDisplayName* begins with a partial path, then *vRefNum* and *dirID* determine the directory in which the partial path is relative. If *vRefNum* and *dirID* are both 0, then the default volume and directory are used.

See Also

MkParseDisplayName

MonikerRelativePathTo

HRESULT MonikerRelativePathTo(*pmkSrc*, *pmkDest*, *ppmkRelPath, dwReserved***)**
LPIMONIKER *pmkSrc*
LPIMONIKER *pmkDest*
LPIMONIKER *ppmkRelPath*
unsigned long *dwReserved*

MonikerRelativePathTo creates a moniker specifying the relative path from *pmkSrc* to *pmkDest*.

Parameters

pmkSrc
The moniker pointing to the start of the relative path.

pmkDest
The moniker to be expressed relative to *pmkSrc*.

ppmkRelPath
The location to be filled with the relative moniker.

dwReserved
Reserved for future use, must be nonzero.

Return Values

Value	Meaning
S_OK	The parse operation was completed successfully.
MK_S_HIM	The other moniker is the prefix of the receiver moniker.
MK_E_NOT-BINDABLE	**MonikerRelativePathTo** was called on a relative moniker. The moniker cannot be bound to something until it is composed with a container moniker.
E_UNEXPECTED	An unexpected error occurred.
E_OUTOFMEMORY	Out of memory.

Comments

MonikerRelativePathTo is not called by any code except implementations of moniker classes and can be ignored unless you are implementing a new class of monikers.

When implementing a class of monikers, you should implement **IMoniker::RelativePathTo** as shown in the following pseudo code:

```
HRESULT CMyMoniker::RelativePathTo (
            IMoniker * pmkOther,
            IMoniker **ppmkRelPath  )
{
    Does pmkOther point to a moniker of a type treated as special
        by this class?
    If so, execute special case code.
    Otherwise,
        return MonikerRelativePathTo( this, pmkOther, ppmkRelPath,0);
}
```

This function is necessary to handle those cases where *pmkOther* points to a generic composite moniker.

MonikerRelativePathTo should only be called on absolute monikers, not on relative monikers. This means that a file moniker must start with a volume name and be followed by items.

See Also

IMoniker::RelativePathTo

MonikerCommonPrefixWith

HRESULT MonikerCommonPrefixWith(*pmkSrc*, *pmkDest*, *ppmkRelPath*)
LPMONIKER *pmkSrc*
LPMONIKER *pmkDest*
LPMONIKER * *ppmkRelPath*

MonikerCommonPrefixWith returns the longest common prefix that the moniker pointed to by *pmkSrc* shares with the moniker pointed to by *pmkDest*.

Parameters

pmkSrc
The starting moniker for computing the longest common prefix.

pmkDest
The other moniker to use for computing the longest common prefix.

ppmkRelPath
The place at which the moniker of the longest common prefix common to *pmkSrc* and *pmkDest* is to be returned. Cannot be NULL.

Return Values

Value	Meaning
S_OK	The prefix operation was completed successfully.
MK_S_HIM	The other moniker is the prefix of the receiver moniker.
MK_S_ME	The receiver moniker, the moniker whose **CommonPrefixWith** method is called, is a prefix of the other moniker.
MK_S_US	The receiver and the other moniker are equal.
MK_E_NOPREFIX	The monikers have no common prefix.
MK_E_NOT-BINDABLE	**MonikerCommonPrefixWith** was called on a relative moniker. The moniker cannot be bound to something until it is composed with a container moniker.
E_UNEXPECTED	An unexpected error occurred.
E_OUTOFMEMORY	Out of memory.

MonikerCommonPrefixWith is solely for the use of moniker implementors. Clients should instead compute the common prefix between two monikers using *pmkSrc*->**CommonPrefixWith**(*pmkDest, ppmkRelPath*).

Implementations of **IMoniker::CommonPrefixWith** call **MonikerCommonPrefixWith** as part of their internal processing. Such a method should first check whether the other moniker is a type it recognizes and handles in a special way. If not, it should call **MonikerCommonPrefixWith**, passing itself as *pmkSrc* and the other moniker as *pmkDest*. **MonikerCommonPrefixWith** will handle the generic composite cases correctly.

MonikerCommonPrefixWith should only be called on absolute monikers, that is, a file moniker that starts with a volume name, followed by items. It should not be called on relative monikers.

See Also

IMoniker::CommonPrefixWith

MkGetMacNetInfo

HRESULT MkGetMacNetInfo(*pmk*, *ppszZoneName*, *ppszServerName*)
IMoniker* *pmk*
char** *ppszZoneName*,
char** *ppszServerName*

MkGetMacNetInfo returns the name of the AppleTalk zone and network server from a moniker referencing a source located on an AppleShare volume.

Parameters

pmk
Points to the moniker that is to be used to locate the information.

ppszZoneName
On return, contains a pointer to a string containing the AppleTalk zone name; will be NULL if *pmk* does not point to an AppleShare volume.

ppszServerName
On return, contains a pointer to a string containing the name of the network server; will be NULL if *pmk* does not point to an AppleShare volume.

Return Values

Value	Meaning
S_OK	Function completed successfully.
E_FAIL	The *pmk* parameter is neither a file moniker nor a composite moniker beginning with a file moniker.
E_OUTOFMEMORY	Out of memory.
E_INVALIDARG	One or more arguments are invalid.

Comments

This function works for file monikers or composite monikers beginning with a file moniker.

CHAPTER 9

Persistent Storage Interfaces and Functions

This chapter describes the interfaces, functions, and helper functions that support OLE's storage model, the implementation of which is commonly referred to as *compound files*.

Summary of Storage Interfaces

The following table provides a brief summary of the interfaces that support OLE's storage model:

Interface	Implemented By	Use
IStorage	OLE	Analogous to folders, containers use IStorage to instantiate a folder-like collection of storage and stream objects in which an embedded object's native data is saved. Object applications are given a valid *pStg* for embedded objects while an object is in the running state.
IStream	OLE	Container and object applications use to read and write the underlying bytes of data that comprise an **IStorage** object. **IStream** instances are analogous to files.
IRootStorage	OLE	Containers use to switch the underlying disk file that **IStorage** objects are being saved to.

Interface	Implemented By	Use
ILockBytes	OLE	Generally, used only by OLE to manipulate the byte array that underlies a compound file.
IEnumSTATSTG	OLE	Used to enumerate **IStorage** objects. An instance of the enumeration is available by calling **IStorage::EnumElements**.
IPersist	Object handlers and object applications	Used to obtain an object's CLSID. The base interface from which the three other persistence-related interfaces derive: **IPersistStorage**, **IPersistStream**, and **IPersistFile**.
IPersistStorage	Object handlers and object applications	Used by containers to read and write a compound document object's native data to and from its **IStorage**.
IPersistStream	OLE	Used by containers to save and reload objects stored in a simple serial stream rather than in an **IStorage** object (such as a moniker).
IPersistFile	Object applications; optionally implemented by container applications to support linking to embedded and file-based objects.	Used by OLE to load an outer-level document object residing in a file, as opposed to one that is embedded inside a compound document.

Note Any of the storage-related interfaces or API functions can return an OSErr system error code. If a system error is returned, information about the error is contained within the FACILITY_STORAGE facility field of the returned status code and can be extracted using the SCODE_FACILITY macro. For more information, see the section "Error Handling Functions and Macros," in Chapter 5, Component Object Interfaces and Functions.

OLE Storage Model

Overview to Structured Storage

Objects are saved to their containing documents using an instance of the **IStorage** interface passed to the object by its container. Usually, the container opens a child storage object within its own **IStorage** instance. Each **IStorage** instance can contain many levels of nested storage objects (objects contained within objects). Having obtained an **IStorage** instance for itself by calling **IStorage::CreateStorage**, an object has the streams and substorages available for saving its data.

An object can use as many streams as needed to save its native data. In addition to the native data stream, OLE uses one or more streams to store information about the object, including the object's cached presentation, identifying information about the object application, and link connectivity information. (This information is later used to load an object into memory using the **OleLoad** function and to convert objects from one type to another.)

To better understand the concept of storing objects, consider the word processing document shown in Figure 9.1. The document contains an embedded worksheet object, which in turn has a chart embedded in it.

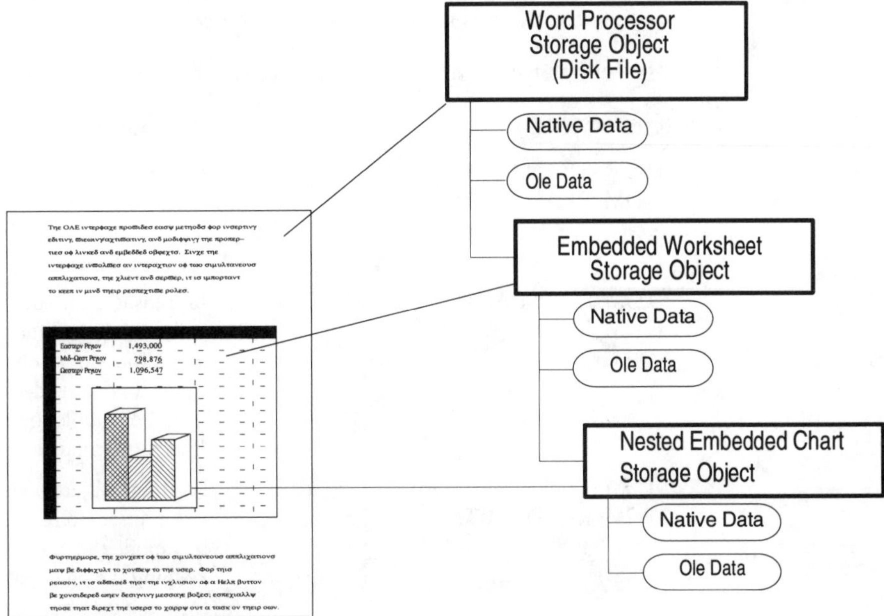

Figure 9.1 Word processing document with nested levels of objects

The word processing document is saved and opened as the outermost root storage object. The embedded worksheet and chart objects are saved as child storage objects. Inside these storage objects, stream objects are created in which the object's actual native data is saved (streams are also created for saving OLE information about each object).

Once an application has obtained a valid **IStorage** instance (by calling the **StgCreateDocfileFSp** or **StgOpenStorageFSp** functions), the needed data streams are created by calling **IStorage::CreateStream**. From this root storage object, child storages can be created to save the document's contained objects. These child storage elements are created by calling **IStorage::CreateStorage**

To open an existing storage object, applications call the **IStorage::OpenStorage** function. Child storage objects and their collective streams can be arbitrarily nested to any level in an open root storage object.

Note Child storage objects and streams must always be opened in STGM_SHARE_EXCLUSIVE access mode.

It is the container application's responsibility to open the **IStorage** instances for its embedded objects in the appropriate access mode. Most often, this is transacted read-write/deny-write mode, but the exact choice depends on how the container is allocating the storage object. The object and OLE must be free to read from and write to the streams inside the storage object.

The following access modes are available when opening storage objects:

Access Mode	Purpose
STGM_TRANSACTED | STGM_READWRITE	Using this mode, an object can freely write to its **IStorage** instance. OLE takes care of the transaction, freeing the container from the task. This is the most common mode.
STGM_TRANSACTED | STGM_READ | STGM_SHARE_DENY_WRITE	In transacted mode, write permissions are enforced at the time of the commit operation, not as changes are being made. Thus, this mode does not prevent the object from being able to write freely to its **IStorage** instance.
STGM_DIRECT | STGM_READWRITE	From the object's view, this mode behaves like transacted read and write. However, in this mode the container is responsible for keeping the changes to the object separate from the original version of the object when the container was loaded (and to which the object should revert if the container is closed without saving).

Although an embedded object can freely write to its own storage object, it cannot commit or revert changes. Because of this, the container is responsible for committing changes to its root storage object. This is done by calling **IStorage:Commit** on the open storage object.

An OLE object's **IStorage** instance can be put into one of three states, as described in the following table:

Storage State	Description
Normal	Upon being created or loaded into memory, all OLE 2 embedded objects are given an **IStorage** instance they hold while they are either loaded or running. While in the running state, objects are free to write or "scribble" into their open **IStorage** instance. Unless **IPersistStorage::Save** or **IPersistStorage::HandsOffStorage** is called on the object, this is the normal, default state for an object.
No Scribble	The state of an object between the time **IPersistStorage::Save** finishes and **IPersistStorage::SaveCompleted** is called. In no-scribble mode, the object can read from its storage, but it cannot write to it until **IPersistStorage:: SaveCompleted** is called, which puts the object back in normal state.
Hands Off	The state of an object when **IPersistStorage::HandsOffStorage** is called on the object. The object is unable to read or write to its storage until **IPersistStorage::SaveCompleted** is called, which puts the object and any of its child storages back in the normal state. There are two variations to the hands off state, hands off from normal and hands off after save, as described in the following sections.

Figure 9.2 shows the storage state transitions. Unmarked transitions are illegal.

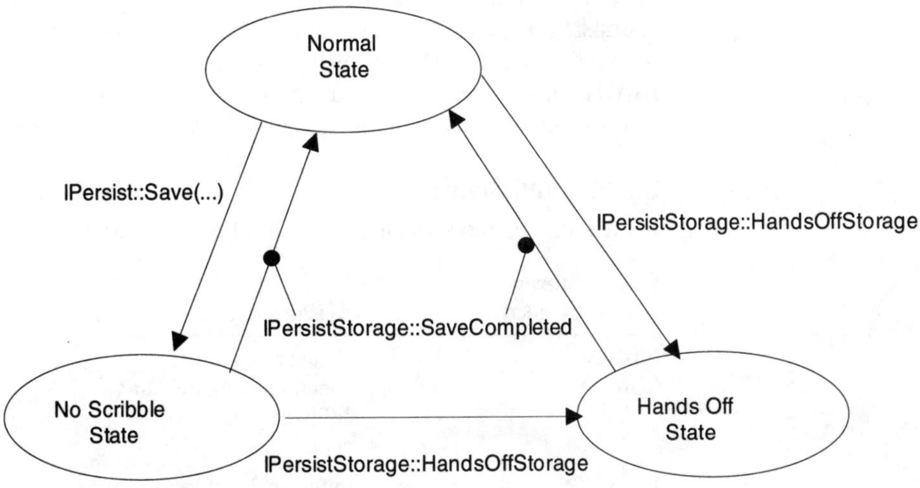

Figure 9.2 Transitions between the OLE storage states

The object should not clear its dirty bit if **IPersistStorage::HandsOffStorage** is called prior to **IPersistStorage::Save** and **IPersistStorage::SaveCompleted** being called.

To ensure that the object is saved correctly, the following steps should be followed (for more information, see **IPersistStorage::SaveCompleted**, later in this chapter):

1. In the application's initialization code, create the following variables:

```
m_fSaveWithSameAsLoad = FALSE
m_fNoScribbleMode = FALSE;
```

2. In the **IPersistStorage::Save** code, set the variables to the following values:

```
m_fSaveWithSameAsLoad = fSameAsLoad
m_fNoScribbleMode = TRUE;
```

3. In the **IPersistStorage::SaveCompleted** code, compare the object's **IStorage** pointer to *m_fSaveWithSameAsLoad* and then clear the dirty bit as appropriate:

```
if (pStg != NULL || m_fSaveWithSameAsLoad)
{
    if (m_fNoScribbleMode) {
        clear dirty bit
        send on save
    }
    m_fSaveWithSameAsLoad = FALSE;
}
m_fNoScribbleMode = FALSE;
```

The following tables describe the storage states and the transitions as various **IPersistStorage** methods are called. The state is not changed if an error occurs. Notice the relationship between clearing the dirty flag and calling **IAdviseSink::OnSave** to send notifications to connected advise sinks: the object calls **OnSave** precisely at the moment when it transitions from dirty to non-dirty.

Uninitialized State

In the uninitialized state, the object has been created, but not yet initialized.

IPersistStorage Method Called	Action to Take	State Entered
InitNew (*pStg*)	Create a new object containing default data as defined by the object application.	Normal
Load (*pStg*)	Initialize the object from the data found in *pStg*.	Normal

IPersistStorage Method Called	Action to Take	State Entered
GetClassID	Return the error: E_UNEXPECTED.	Uninitialized
Other **IPersistStorage** methods	Return the error: E_UNEXPECTED.	Uninitialized

Normal State

In the normal state, the object has been initialized and has a valid pointer to its **IStorage**. In this state, the object can freely read from and write to its storage. This is the default state for an embedded object, and is the state in which the object is found except when it is uninitialized or is undergoing a save operation.

IPersistStorage Method Called	Action to Take	State Entered
Save(*pStgSave*, TRUE)	Recursively save any dirty embeddings. Write data as appropriate into *pStgSave*. This call is used in the low memory save sequence and must not fail for lack of memory.	No scribble
Save(*pStgNew*, FALSE)	Recursively save any dirty embeddings. Write data as appropriate into *pStgNew*.	No scribble
HandsOffStorage	Recursively invoke **HandsOffStorage** on any loaded embeddings. Release *pStgCur* and any storage elements opened from there.	Hands off from normal
SaveCompleted	Return the error: E_UNEXPECTED. No other change of state.	Normal
InitNew or **Load**	Return the error: E_UNEXPECTED. No other change of state.	Normal
Other **IPersistStorage** methods	Return the error: E_UNEXPECTED.	Uninitialized

No Scribble State

In the no scribble state, the object has a valid **IStorage** and can read from it, but is not allowed to write to it. The primary reason for the existence of this state is to give the object's container a chance to save the object's data. Most containers just call **IStorage::Commit**, but some, such as databases, use other techniques for saving.

This state is parameterized by a Boolean value, *fSavedToCurrentStorage*, that indicates whether the object was saved into *pStgCur* or a separate **IStorage**. This is used to control the clearing of the dirty flag on error.

IPersistStorage Method Called	Action to Take	State Entered
SaveCompleted(NULL)	If *fSavedToCurrentStorage* is TRUE, then if the dirty flag is set, clear it and call **IAdviseSink::OnSave** to notify connected advise sinks.	Normal
SaveCompleted(*pStgNew*)	Do the equivalent of **HandsOffStorage** followed by **SaveCompleted**(*pStgNew*).	Normal or hands off after save; see below.
HandsOffStorage	Recurse on any loaded embeddings. Release *pStgCur* and any subelements opened.	Hands off after save
Save	This transition indicates a bug on the container's part: it has erroneously omitted an intervening call to **SaveCompleted**. The object can either fail (E_UNEXPECTED) or carry out the save a second time and succeed.	No scribble
InitNew or **Load**	Return the error: E_UNEXPECTED.	No scribble
Other **IPersistStorage** methods	Return the error: E_UNEXPECTED.	Uninitialized

Hands-Off State

In the hands off state, the object just saved its internal state into a storage, and was then told not to access its internal storage (this happens in the low memory save sequence). When the object eventually gets back a new storage, it is guaranteed to get back a storage containing exactly the bits that were just saved.

IPersistStorage Method Called	Action to Take	State Entered
SaveCompleted(*pStgNew*)	(Re)open the streams and storages needed. The bits in *pStgNew* are guaranteed to be the same as those last saved. Notice that if Save(*pStgSave*, false), were used, bits in *pStgNew* are different than those in the *pStgCur* being held and that was revoked in **HandsOffStorage**. If this function is successful, then if the dirty flag is set, clear it and call **IAdviseSink::OnSave** to notify connected advise sinks.	Normal, if able to reconnect to the new storage. Otherwise, if unsuccessful , fail with E_OUTOFMEMORY and remain in hands off after save.
SaveCompleted(NULL)	Return the error: E_INVALIDARG or E_UNEXPECTED.	Hands off after save
HandsOffStorage	Return the error: E_UNEXPECTED.	Hands off after save
Save	Return the error: E_UNEXPECTED.	Hands off after save
InitNew or **Load**	Return the error: E_UNEXPECTED.	Hands off after save
Other **IPersistStorage** methods	Return the error: E_UNEXPECTED.	Uninitialized

Hands Off From Normal State

In the hands off from normal state, the container temporarily prevents the object from accessing its storage until the container is done with it. When the container releases the storage back to the object, it returns a storage with exactly the same bits as were there when the object was in the hands off mode. Thus, the object does not need to completely reinitialize its internal state. Instead, the object can simply reconnect to the new storage by opening the appropriate streams and/or storages.

IPersistStorage Method Called	Action to Take	State Entered
SaveCompleted(*pStgNew*)	*pStgNew* is the new replacement **IStorage** for the one revoked by **HandsOffStorage**. The bits in the storage are guaranteed to be the same as those that were in the revoked storage. (Re)open the streams and storages needed. Do not clear the dirty flag even if this function is successful. Do not call **IAdviseSink::OnSave**.	If able to reconnect to new storage, enter normal(*pStgNew*). If unsuccessful, (for example, unable to reopen data streams) fail (E_OUTOFMEMORY, and so on) and remain in hands off from normal.
SaveCompleted(NULL)	Error: E_INVALIDARG or E_UNEXPECTED.	Hands off from normal
HandsOffStorage	Error: E_UNEXPECTED.	Hands off from normal
Save	Error: E_UNEXPECTED.	Hands off from normal
InitNew or **Load**	Error: E_UNEXPECTED.	Hands off after save
Other **IPersistStorage** methods	Error: E_UNEXPECTED.	Uninitialized

Storage Objects on the Macintosh

Compound files (OLE's implementation of **IStorage** objects) are contained within the data fork of a Macintosh file. Macintosh compound files are byte-swapped so that they are byte equivalent to Intel platforms (little Endian).

An applications native data is not byte-swapped or modified in any way. An application that has platform-specific native data should be able to convert between formats. If conversion is possible, the application must have the same class identifier (CLSID) on both platforms. If conversion is not possible, an application must specify a unique CLSID for each platform.

Storage and stream objects on the Macintosh can be given names up to 32 characters in length.

A set of API functions provide a Macintosh-specific interface to the storage. For example, whereas a Windows OLE developer calls **StgCreateDocfile** to create a root level storage object, the Macintosh OLE developer has a choice of calls. Either **StgCreateDocfileFSp**, **StgCreateDocfileMac**, or **StgCreateDocfile** can be called for the same functionality.

Saving Objects to Storage

To save its contained embeddings, an object's top-level container performs the following tasks:

1. Call **OleSave** on the **IStorage** object of each immediate embedded object, passing the **IStorage** object a pointer to where the object is to be saved. The object then recursively calls **OleSave** on any of its nested embeddings.

   OleSave first calls the **WriteClassStg** function to save the object's CLSID before calling the object handler's **IPersistStorage::Save** method. (Usually, the object handler is the OLE-provided default handler.) The object handler's implementation of the **IPersistStorage::Save** first saves the object's presentation cache and then calls the object's **IPersistStorage::Save** method to save the object's native data.

   Finally, **OleSave** calls **IStorage::Commit** on the **IStorage** object to commit the changes back one level to the transaction state of the root **IStorage** object.

2. After **OleSave** returns, the top-level container must call **IPersistStorage::SaveCompleted** on the immediate embedded objects to return them and any of their nested embeddings to the normal storage mode. Unless this is done, the object is left in the no-scribble mode it entered when **OleSave** called **IPersistStorage::Save**.

Note **IPersistStorage::SaveCompleted** is always called on the **IStorage** object containing the object. It is a call that recurses to all currently loaded or running embedded objects. Should **IPersistStorage::SaveCompleted** fail, the object(s) does not return to normal storage mode. In this case, the container should back out any changes that have been committed and try instead to save the object following the recommendations for saving an object in low-memory situations. For more information, see "Saving Objects in Low Memory," later in this chapter.

Saving a linked object is not different from saving an embedded object. To save a linked object that is not loaded or running, the **IStorage::CopyTo** method can be used. When an object is in the loaded or running state, **OleSave** should be called because it saves all changes.

Static objects are saved into a stream called CONTENTS.

The **OleSave** and **IPersistStorage::Save** functions use the *fSameAsLoad* flag to determine whether the storage object that the object is being saved to is the same one from which the object was loaded. The value of *fSameAsLoad* can be combined with the value of the *pStg* passed to these functions to determine the routine being used to save the compound document, as shown in the following table:

Value of *fSameAsLoad*	Value of *pStg* passed to IPersistStorage:: SaveCompleted	Save Routine to call
TRUE	NULL	File Save
FALSE	*pStg*	File Save As
FALSE	NULL	File Save Copy As

A container should save both the document's native data stream and any information on behalf of the compound document object, including the following data:

Data Saved on Behalf of a Compound Document Object	Description
szStgName	Stores the name of object's persistent **IStorage** element.
fMonikerAssigned	Keeps track of whether or not a moniker was assigned to the compound document object.
dwDrawAspect	Determines how to display the object when it is later loaded into memory: as an embedded object, a thumbnail representation (appropriate for browsing tools), an iconic representation, or as a sequence of pages (as if the object had been printed).

Storage Access Mode Flags

Overview

All storage objects and their contained streams can be created and opened in one or more access modes. The access modes for a given object are specified using a collection of flags divided into groups according to use. These flags are defined as follows in storage.h:

```
/* creation */
#define STGM_CREATE
#define STGM_CONVERT
#define STGM_FAILIFTHERE

/* temporary creation */
#define STGM_DELETEONRELEASE

/* transaction support */
```

```
#define STGM_DIRECT
#define STGM_TRANSACTED

/* access permissions */
#define STGM_READ
#define STGM_WRITE
STGM_READWRITE

/* File sharing privileges*/
#define STGM_SHARE_DENY_NONE      //Applicable only for shared volumes
#define STGM_SHARE_DENY_READ      //Applicable only for shared volumes
#define STGM_SHARE_DENY_WRITE     //Applicable only for shared volumes
#define STGM_SHARE_EXCLUSIVE      //Applicable only for shared volumes

/* priority access */
#define STGM_PRIORITY
```

Transaction support for storage and stream objects can be combined with the ability to read and/or write to the objects and to deny others the right to do the same. When new storage or stream objects are created or existing objects are opened, the correct flags for creation, permissions, sharing, and transaction support are specified. Flags for temporary file creation and priority mode are also an option.

The flags are or-ed together, usually in the *grfMode* parameter, which is passed to methods in the **IStorage** and **IStream** interfaces.

Only one value from each of the six groups of flags can be specified at any one time. For example, the following is a common combination of flags for a storage object opened in transacted mode with full read/write capabilities. Others are forbidden from writing to the storage object to protect its integrity.

```
STGM_TRANSACTED | STGM_READWRITE | STGM_SHARE_DENY_WRITE
```

Storage Creation Flags

STGM_CREATE, STGM_CONVERT, and STGM_FAILIFTHERE specify the action to take when trying to create a new storage or stream object when an object by the specified name already exists. Only one of these flags can be used in a given creation call. STGM_FAILIFTHERE is the default.

None of the flags should be passed to calls that open existing storage or stream objects.

STGM_CREATE

The STGM_CREATE flag is applicable only to the creation of storage objects. The flag is used in three situations:

- When an application is trying to create a storage object on a disk where a file of that name already exists.
- Inside another storage object where one of the data streams already has the specified name.
- Inside an **ILockBytes** instance.

STGM_CREATE indicates an existing storage object should be removed before the new one replaces it. A new object is always created when this flag is specified.

STGM_CONVERT

STGM_CONVERT allows the creation to proceed while preserving existing data. The old data is saved to a stream named CONTENTS containing the same data that was in the old **IStorage**, **IStream**, or **ILockBytes** instance. In the **IStorage** and **ILockBytes** cases, the data flattening to a stream is done regardless of whether the existing file or **ILockBytes** currently contains a layered storage object.

STGM_FAILIFTHERE

STGM_FAILIFTHERE causes the create operation to fail if an existing object with the specified name exists. In this case, STG_E_FILEALREADYEXISTS is returned.

STGM_FAILIFTHERE applies to both storage and stream objects.

Temporary Storage Creation Flag

The STGM_DELETEONRELEASE flag indicates that the underlying file is to be automatically destroyed when the root storage object is released. This capability is most useful for creating temporary files.

Transaction Flags

OLE's structured storage model support compound files being opened in both transacted and direct mode. In transacted mode, all changes are buffered and the buffered changes are written to disk or discarded only when an explicit commit or revert request occurs. A snapshot copy of the compound file is made so the original version of the file can be maintained.

In direct mode, no such buffering occurs and every change is followed by an automatic commit. The contents of a compound file opened in direct mode are only guaranteed to be in a valid state after **Release** or **IStorage::Commit** has been called and before a subsequent write operation.

Direct mode STGM_DIRECT is the default access mode, and is implied by the absence of STGM_TRANSACTED.

STGM_DIRECT

STGM_DIRECT is always specified for stream objects. STGM_TRANSACTED is not supported by OLE for stream objects.

For root storage objects, direct mode is only supported in the following combinations of access permissions flags:

- `STGM_READ | STGM_SHARE_EXCLUSIVE | STGM_READWRITE | STGM_SHARE_DENY_WRITE`
- `STGM_PRIORITY | STGM_READ`

STGM_TRANSACTED

The transaction for each open object is nested in the transaction for its parent storage object. Therefore, committing changes at the child level is dependent on committing changes in the parent and a commit of the root storage object (top-level parent) is necessary before changes to an object are actually written to disk. The changes percolate upward: inner objects publish changes to the transaction of the next object outwards. Outermost objects publish changes permanently into the file system.

Transacted mode is not required on the parent storage object in order to use transacted on a contained object.

The scope of changes that are buffered in transacted mode is very broad. A storage or stream object can be opened, have arbitrary changes made to it, and then have the changes reverted, preserving the object as it was when it was first opened. The creation and destruction of elements within a storage object is scoped by its transaction.

STGM_PRIORITY

The STGM_PRIORITY flag allows a storage object to be opened so that a subsequent copy operation can be done at reduced cost. STGM_PRIORITY allows an application to read certain streams from storage before opening the storage object in a mode that would require a snapshot copy to be made.

Priority mode has exclusive access to the committed version of the storage object. While a compound file is open in priority mode, no other opening of the compound file can commit changes, even one that was opened before the priority mode opening. Therefore, applications should keep storage objects open in priority mode for as short a time as possible.

Calling **StgOpenStorage** with a non-NULL *ppStgOpen* parameter takes a storage object currently open in priority mode to normal operating mode, without the possibility of losing access to the file to another process during an otherwise-necessary close and reopen operation.

When using STGM_PRIORITY, the following rules apply:

- STGM_DIRECT and STGM_READ must be specified with STGM_PRIORITY.
- STGM_WRITE and STGM_READWRITE must not be specified.

Access Permission Flags

The access permission flags specify the degree of access applications have to an object as well as the access others have. The following are general rules regarding permissions:

- Children of storage objects opened in direct mode must have permissions at least as restrictive as those of the parent.
- Children of storage objects opened in transacted mode can have any permissions.
- Storage objects opened in transacted, read-only (STGM_READ) mode are modifiable but the changes cannot be committed.
- Either write permissions or transacted mode is needed on a parent storage in order to open a child storage or stream with write permission.

STGM_READ

When applied to a stream object, STGM_READ enables applications to successfully call **IStream::Read**. If STGM_READ is omitted, **IStream::Read** will return an error.

When applied to a storage object, STGM_READ allows the enumeration of the storage object's elements and enables applications to open these elements in read mode. Parents of storage objects to be opened in read mode must also have been opened in read mode; otherwise, an error is returned.

STGM_WRITE

STGM_WRITE enables an object to commit changes to the storage. Specifically, unless this flag has been given, **IStorage::Commit** and **IStream::Commit** will fail. An open object whose changes cannot be committed can save its changes by copying the storage or stream with **IStorage::CopyTo** or **IStream::CopyTo**.

In direct mode, changes are committed after every change operation. Thus, write permissions are needed to call any function that causes a change. On streams, this includes **IStream::Write** and **IStream::SetSize**.

If a storage object is opened in direct mode without write permission and a stream within it is opened in direct mode but without write permission, writing to the stream fails because it causes an implicit commit to be made on the storage. Similarly, trying to create or destroy a contained element in this storage object also causes an implicit commit, resulting in an error.

File Sharing Privileges

STGM_READWRITE

STGM_READWRITE is the logical combination of the STGM_READ and STGM_WRITE. However, the defined value of STGM_READWRITE is not equal to (STGM_READ | STGM_WRITE).

STGM_SHARE_DENY_READ

When successfully applied to a root storage object, the STGM_SHARE_DENY_READ flag prevents others from opening the object in read mode. The open call fails and returns an error if the object is presently open in deny-read mode.

STGM_SHARE_DENY_READ is most useful when opening root storage objects. Deny modes on inner elements are still useful if some component is coordinating the opening of these inner elements, such as might happen in a Copy/Paste operation.

Opening a parent storage object with STGM_SHARE_DENY_READ applies only to that opening, not the entire global network-wide set of openings of the parent.

Deny modes are most useful when applied to the opening of a root storage object. Deny modes on inner elements are still useful if some component is coordinating the opening of these inner elements, such as might happen in the implementation of Copy/Paste. STGM_SHARE_DENY_WRITE is also important in avoiding snapshot copy operations.

STGM_SHARE_DENY_WRITE

When successfully applied to either a storage or a stream object, the STGM_SHARE_DENY_WRITE flag prevents subsequent openings of the object from specifying write mode. The open call fails and returns an error if the storage or stream is presently open in write mode. For information about the interaction of this flag with nested openings, see the earlier discussion about STGM_SHARE_DENY_READ.

STGM_SHARE_DENY_WRITE can be used to avoid unnecessary snapshot copy operations. Attempting to open a compound file storage object without specifying STGM_SHARE_DENY_WRITE is expensive because a snapshot copy of the storage object must be created.

For applications that have an "all in memory" model of dealing with persistent storage, the expense of the snapshot copy can be reduced by specifying STGM_PRIORITY. STGM_PRIORITY allows applications to read some of the elements before use and excluding them from the snapshot copy.

STGM_SHARE_EXCLUSIVE

STGM_SHARE_EXCLUSIVE is the logical combination of the STGM_SHARE_DENY_READ and STGM_SHARE_DENY_WRITE. All child storage or stream objects must be opened with STGM_SHARE_EXCLUSIVE.

Writable child storage objects, stream objects, and root storage objects can only be opened using STGM_SHARE_EXCLUSIVE.

STGM_SHARE_DENY_NONE

STGM_SHARE_DENY_NONE indicates that neither read access nor write access should be denied to subsequent openings. This is the default sharing mode and if no STGM_SHARE_* flag is explicitly given, STGM_SHARE_DENY_NONE is implied.

Storage Naming Conventions

When opening a root **IStorage** object, the storage-related functions take an FSP name as a parameter and when working with other storage objects, the functions may take a string name to specify a particular element of interest within some container. Depending on which component actually stores these names, different conventions and restrictions apply. The two components of relevant interest are the underlying file system and implementations of storage objects.

Names of root storage objects are actual names of files in the underlying file system. Thus, they obey the conventions and restrictions the file system imposes. Filename strings passed to storage-related functions are passed on uninterpreted and unchanged to the file system.

Names of elements contained within storage objects are managed by the implementation of the particular storage object. All implementations of storage objects must support element names 32 characters in length (including the NULL terminator). Some implementations might choose to support longer names. Whether the storage object does any case conversion is implementation defined. As a result, applications that define element names must choose names that are acceptable in either situation. OLE compound files support names up to 32 characters in length. Notably, they do not do case conversion.

The following naming conventions apply to elements inside an **IStorage** instance:

- Element names cannot contain the character ":". To maintain cross-platform compatibility, the characters "\", "/", ".", "..", and "!" should not be used.

In addition, the name space in an **IStorage** instance is partitioned into different areas of ownership. Different pieces of code can create elements in each area of the name space.

- Element names beginning with characters other than \0x01 through \0x1F (decimal 1 through decimal 31) are for use by the embedded object stored in the **IStorage** instance. Conversely, the embedded object must not use element names beginning with these characters.
- Element names beginning with a \0x01 and \0x02 are for the exclusive use of the OLE libraries.
- Element names beginning with a \0x03 are for the exclusive use of the container in which the object is embedded. The container can use this space to persistently store information associated with the object.
- Element names beginning with a \0x04 are for the exclusive use of the structured storage implementation. For example, they are useful if the implementation supports interfaces besides IStorage that need persistent state.
- All other names beginning with \0x05 through \0x1F are reserved for future use by the system.

String Name Block (SNB)

A string name block (SNB) is a pointer to an array of pointers to strings, that ends in a NULL pointer. SNB is defined as:

```
typedef LPSTR *SNB;
```

String name blocks are used to exclude particular contained storages or streams in storage object open calls.

STATSTG Structure

The **STATSTG** structure is used with **IEnumSTATSTG::Next** and the **Stat** methods in **IStorage**, **IStream**, and **ILockBytes**.

The **STATSTG** data structure is defined in storage.h:

```
typedef struct tagSTATSTG{
    FSSpec * pspec;
    char  * pwcsName;
    unsigned long type;
    ULARGE_INTEGER cbSize;
    FILETIME mtime;
    FILETIME ctime;
    FILETIME atime;
    unsigned long grfMode;
    unsigned long grfLocksSupported;
    CLSID clsid;
    unsigned long grfStateBits;
    unsigned long Reserved;
} STATSTG;
```

The *pspec* member is a pointer to an FSSpec that corresponds to the root level storage. It's value is valid only for a root level storage call to **IStorage::Stat**, where the STATFLAG argument (*grfStatFlag*) is STATFLAG_DEFAULT. For all other cases, *pspec* is NULL.

The *pwcsName* member is the name of the storage element. *pwcsName* is allocated and filled in by the callee and later freed by the caller. The following code illustrates how to free *pwcsName* using the standard allocator:

```
LPMALLOC pMalloc;
CoGetMalloc(MEMCTX_TASK, &pMalloc);
pMalloc->Free(statstg.pwcsName);
pMalloc->Release();
```

In some cases, such as when a name does not exist for a byte array, NULL is returned in *pwcsName*.

The *type* member identifies the type of the element. Legal values are found in the enumeration **STGTY**:

```
typedef enum tagSTGTY
{
    STGTY_STORAGE   = 1,     //Storage object
    STGTY_STREAM    = 2, `   //Stream object
    STGTY_LOCKBYTES = 3,     //Byte array object
} STGTY;
```

The *cbSize* member is the size of the element. It is the byte count for stream objects and byte arrays, and it is undefined for storage objects.

The next three members provide the date and time information. The modification date and time is returned in *mtime,* the creation date and time is returned in *ctime,* and the closest approximation of the time of last access is returned in *atime.*

The modification time differs depending on whether the storage element uses transacted or direct mode. Transacted mode elements return the time of the last commit operation invoked on the element. Direct mode elements return the later of the following:

- The time of the last explicit commit operation invoked on the element (using **IStorage::Commit** or **IStream::Commit**). In direct mode, committing changes has the effect of flushing the buffer.
- The time of the last release operation (using **IStorage::Release** or **IStream::Release**) in a situation where changes have been made because the stream or storage was opened or the last set of changes were committed. In this case, the release operation internally does a flush of the buffers.

In the compound file implementation, the time returned in *atime* is the same as *mtime* for internal elements. Whatever is supported in the underlying file system or exposed by **ILockBytes::Stat** for root elements is the same as *mtime.*

The *grfMode* member is the mode in which the element was opened. It is valid only on **Stat** method calls.

The *grfLocksSupported* member is a group of Boolean flags relevant only for stream objects and byte arrays. For each lock type, *grfLocksSupported* indicates whether a call to **IStream::LockRegion** or **ILockBytes::LockRegion** will ever be worthwhile.

Legal values for *grfLocksSupported* are combinations of values from the enumeration **LOCKTYPE**, which is defined in storage.h as follows:

```
typedef enum tagLOCKTYPE
{
    LOCK_WRITE      = 1,
    LOCK_EXCLUSIVE  = 2,
    LOCK_ONLYONCE   = 4
} LOCKTYPE;
```

LOCKTYPE values have the following meaning:

Value	Meaning
LOCK_WRITE	If the lock is granted, reading the specified region of the stream can be done by calling **IStream::Read** from any opening of this stream. Attempts to write to this region from any opening of this stream other than the one to which the lock was granted returns the error STG_E_ACCESSDENIED.
LOCK_EXCLUSIVE	Attempts to read or write this stream by other stream openings return the error STG_E_ACCESSDENIED.
LOCK_ONLYONCE	If the lock is granted, no other lock can be obtained on the bytes in the given region. Usually this lock type is an alias for some other lock type and other semantics can occur as a side effect. The underlying implementation can use the appropriate file system primitive to accomplish the lock.

For each flag, a FALSE (zero) value indicates that the specified type of write locking is not supported. A TRUE value indicates write locking can be supported, but there is no guarantee. Any other value returns the error STG_E_INVALIDFUNCTION.

The *clsid* member is relevant only for storage objects and represents the CLSID associated with the storage, if any. The *clsid* is CLSID_NULL for newly created storages.

The *grfStateBits* member is relevant only for storage objects and is the value most recently set with **IStorage::SetStateBits**.

The *Reserved* member is reserved for future use.

IEnumSTATSTG Interface

The **IEnumSTATSTG** interface enumerates items of type **STATSTG**. An instance of the **IEnumSTATSTG** interface is returned by calling **IStorage::EnumElements**.

The **IEnumSTATSTG** interface contains the following methods, as do all enumerators:

```
DECLARE_INTERFACE_(IEnumSTATSTG, IUnknown)
{
...
 HRESULT Next (unsigned long celt, STATSTG * rgelt, unsigned long *pceltFetched);
 HRESULT Skip (unsigned long celt);
 HRESULT Reset ();
 HRESULT Clone (IENUMSTATSTG * * ppenumStatStg);
};
```

For more information, see the storage.h header file.

For more information on enumerator objects in general, see **IEnum*X*** in Chapter 5, "Component Object Interfaces and Functions."

IStorage Interface

The **IStorage** interface contains the following methods:

```
DECLARE_INTERFACE_(IStorage, IUnknown)
{
  // *** IUnknown methods ***
 HRESULT QueryInterface ( REFIID riid, void * * ppvObj);
 unsigned long AddRef ();
 unsigned long Release ();

  // *** IStorage methods ***
 HRESULT CreateStream (const char * pwcsName, unsigned long grfMode,
      unsigned long dwReserved1, unsigned long dwReserved2, LPSTREAM * ppStm);
 HRESULT OpenStream (const char * pwcsName, void *pReserved1, unsigned long grfMode,
      unsigned long dwReserved2, LPSTREAM * ppStm);
 HRESULT CreateStorage (const char * pwcsName, unsigned long grfMode,
      unsigned long dwReserved1, unsigned long dwReserved2, LPSTORAGE * ppStg);
 HRESULT OpenStorage (const char * pwcsName, LPSTORAGE  *ppStg, unsigned long grfMode,
      SNB snbExclude, unsigned long dwReserved, LPSTORAGE * ppStg);
 HRESULT CopyTo (unsigned long dwCiidExclude, IID const *rgiidExclude, SNB snbExclude,
      LPSTORAGE * pStgDest);
 HRESULT MoveElementTo (const char * lpszName, LPSTORAGE  *pStgDest,
      char const * lpszNewName, unsigned long grfFlags);
 HRESULT Commit (unsigned long grfCommitFlags);
 HRESULT Revert ();
```

```
    HRESULT EnumElements (unsigned long dwReserved1, void *pReserved2,
        unsigned long dwReserved3, LPENUMSTATSTG * ppenumStatStg);
    HRESULT DestroyElement (const char * pwcsName);
    HRESULT RenameElement (const char * pwcsOldName, const char * pwcsNewName);
    HRESULT SetElementTimes (const char *lpszName, FILETIME const *pctime,
        FILETIME const *patime, FILETIME const *pmtime);
    HRESULT SetClass (REFCLSID rclsid);
    HRESULT SetStateBits (unsigned long grfStateBits, unsigned long grfMask);
    HRESULT Stat (STATSTG *pStatStg, unsigned long grfStatFlag);
};
```

For more information, see the storage.h header file.

The **IStorage** interface is implemented by OLE and is used by containers to instantiate a directory-like collection of storage and stream objects in which an embedded object's native data is saved. An application can also save its native data to **IStorage**. For an overview of saving application documents, see Chapter 3, "Programming Considerations."

The **IStorage** interface contains methods for managing root storage objects, child storage objects, and stream objects. **IStorage** instance pointers can be marshaled to other processes, just as any other interface pointer can. When an **IStorage** interface pointer is remoted to a process that has shared memory access with the original process, the custom marshaling facilities of OLE are used to create a remote version of the original object. This remote version does not need to communicate with the original process to carry out its functions.

An OLE application must release any owned **IStorage** instance pointers regardless of whether a higher-level storage obejct has caused the pointers to become invalid. This is necessary to deallocate memory. When a parent storage object releases its last reference or reverts, all child storage objects are invalidated.

IStorage::Release is used to close an open storage object, making the object invalid. In addition, **Release** reverts any logical uncommitted changes to the storage.

Notice that **IStorage::Release** does not return any error status that might arise from the cleanup. Applications that care about errors during cleanup should explicitly call **IStorage::Revert** or **IStorage::Commit** as appropriate before calling **Release**. This is similar to closing file handles in traditional file systems because once the file close has been attempted, no reasonable error handling is possible.

See **IUnknown::Release** for possible return values.

IStorage::CreateStream

HRESULT IStorage::CreateStream (*pwcsName*, *grfMode*, *dwReserved1*, *dwReserved2*, *ppStm*)
const char * *pwcsName*
unsigned long *grfMode*
unsigned long *dwReserved1*
unsigned long *dwReserved2*
LPSTREAM * *ppStm*

IStorage::CreateStream creates and immediately opens a new stream object contained in this storage object.

Parameters

pwcsName
Points to the name by which the newly created stream can later be reopened.

grfMode
Defines the access mode to use when opening the newly created stream. For more information, see the following comments.

dwReserved1
Reserved for future use; must be set to zero by the caller. However, to ensure future compatibility, the callee must not explicitly test for zero.

dwReserved2
Reserved for future use; must be set to zero by the caller. However, to ensure future compatibility, the callee must not explicitly test for zero.

ppStm
Points to where the opened **IStream** interface is returned (**ppStm*). Valid only if the operation is successful. This parameter is NULL if there is an error.

Return Values

Value	Meaning
S_OK	The stream was created successfully.
STG_E_ACCESSDENIED	Insufficient permissions to create stream.
STG_E_FILEALREADYEXISTS	The stream with the specified name already exists and *grfMode* is set to STGM_FAILIFTHERE.
STG_TOOMANY-OPENFILES	There are too many open files.
STG_E_INSUFFICIENTMEMORY	Out of memory.
STG_E_INVALIDFLAG	Unsupported value(s) specified in *grfMode*.
STG_E_INVALIDPOINTER	A bad pointer was passed in.
STG_E_INVALIDPARAMETER	Invalid parameter.

Value	Meaning
STG_E _REVERTED	The object has been invalidated by a revert operation above it in the transaction tree.
STG_E _INVALIDNAME	Invalid value for *pwcsName*.

Comments

If *pwcsName* specifies a stream that does not exist, **IStorage::CreateStream** creates a new stream. If a stream already exists with the name specified in *pwcsName*, the STGM_CREATE or STGM_FAILIFTHERE access modes (defined by the *grfMode* parameter) indicate how to create the stream. If STGM_CREATE is specified, any existing stream is destroyed and then replaced with a newly created stream. If STGM_FAILIFTHERE is specified, the method fails and returns the error STG_E_FILEALREADYEXISTS.

Any destruction and creation of the stream is subject to the transaction mode of the parent storage.

All elements within a storage object, including both streams and other storage objects, are kept in the same name space.

See Also

IStorage::OpenStream

IStorage::OpenStream

HRESULT IStorage::OpenStream(*pwcsName*, *pReserved1*, *grfMode*, *dwReserved2*, *ppStm*)
const char * *pwcsName*
void * *pReserved1*
unsigned long *grfMode*
unsigned long *dwReserved2*
LPSTREAM * *ppStm*

IStorage::OpenStream opens an existing named stream according to the access mode *grfMode*.

Parameters

pwcsName
Points to the name of the stream to open.

pReserved1
Reserved for future use; must be set to NULL by the caller. However, the callee should ignore the value.

grfMode
Defines the access mode to use when opening the stream. For more information, see the following comments.

dwReserved2
Reserved for future use; must be set to zero by the caller. However, the callee should ignore the value.

ppStm
Points to where the opened stream is returned (**ppStm*). Valid only if the operation is successful. *ppStm* is NULL if there is an error.

Return Values

Value	Meaning
S_OK	The stream was opened successfully.
STG_E_ACCESSDENIED	Insufficient permissions to open the stream.
STG_E_FILENOTFOUND	The stream with specified name does not exist.
STG_E_INSUFFICIENTMEMORY	Out of memory.
STG_E_INVALIDFLAG	Unsupported value(s) specified in *grfMode*.
STG_E_INVALIDNAME	Invalid name.
STG_E_INVALIDPOINTER	Invalid pointer.
STG_E_INVALIDPARAMETER	Invalid parameter.
STG_E_REVERTED	The object has been invalidated by a revert operation above it in the transaction tree.

Comments

The permissions on this storage object impose some restrictions on the permissions that can be given in *grfMode*. For more information about permissions, see "Storage Access Mode Flags," earlier in this chapter.

Opening streams in transacted mode is not supported by OLE. Opening the same stream more than once from the same storage instance is also not supported. This behavior is enforced by requiring the caller of **IStorage::OpenStream** to specify STGM_SHARE_EXCLUSIVE in *grfMode*. The call fails with STG_E_INVALIDFUNCTION if these flags are not specified.

OLE's compound file implementation does not support passing STG_DELETEONRELEASE to **IStorage::OpenStream**, although other implementations of **IStorage** might have this capability.

See Also

IStorage::CreateStream

IStorage::CreateStorage

HRESULT IStorage::CreateStorage(*pwcsName, grfMode, dwReserved1, dwReserved2, ppStg***)**
const char * *pwcsName*
unsigned long *grfMode*
unsigned long *dwReserved1*
unsigned long *dwReserved2*
LPSTORAGE * *ppStg*

IStorage::CreateStorage creates and opens a new storage object within this storage object.

Parameters

pwcsName
Points to the name by which the newly created storage can later be (re)opened.

grfMode
Defines the access mode to use when opening the newly created storage object.

dwReserved1
Reserved for future use; must be set to zero by the caller. However, to ensure future compatibility, the callee must not explicitly test for zero.

dwReserved2
Reserved for future use; must be set to zero by the caller. However, to ensure future compatibility, the callee must not explicitly test for zero.

ppStg
Points to where the opened storage is returned (**ppStg*). Valid only if the operation is successful. This parameter is NULL if there is an error.

Return Values

Value	Meaning
S_OK	The storage object was created successfully.
STG_E_ACCESSDENIED	Insufficient permissions to create storage object.
STG_E_FILEALREADYEXISTS	The specified file already exists.
STG_E_TOOMANYOPENFILES	Too many files are open.
STG_S_CONVERTED	The existing stream with the specified name was replaced with a new storage object containing a single stream called CONTENTS.
STG_E_INSUFFICIENTMEMORY	Out of memory.
STG_E_REVERTED	The object has been invalidated by a revert operation above it in the transaction tree.
STG_E_INVALIDFLAG	Invalid flag value(s) were specified in *grfMode*.
STG_E_INVALIDNAME	Invalid name.
STG_E_INVALIDPOINTER	Invalid pointer.
STG_E_INVALIDPARAMETER	Invalid parameter.

Comments

If a storage object does not exist with the name specified by *pwcsName*, it is created. If a storage object already exists with the name specified by *pwcsName*, the following values for *grfMode* indicate how to proceed:

Storage Access Flag	Meaning
STGM _CREATE	If a storage object with the specified name already exists, remove it and replace it with a new storage object.

Storage Access Flag	Meaning
STGM _CONVERT	If such an element exists, and is a stream, the stream is to be replaced with a new storage object that contains one stream named "CONTENTS". This stream contains exactly the data that was in the old stream before the conversion.
STGM _FAILIFTHERE	Do not create a new storage object if one already exists; return STG_E_FILEALREADYEXISTS.
STGM _DELETEONRELEASE	Delete the root storage object when it receives it final release.

See Also **IStorage::OpenStorage**

IStorage::OpenStorage

HRESULT IStorage::OpenStorage(*pwcsName*, *pstgPriority*, *grfMode*, *snbExclude*, *dwReserved*, *ppStg*)
const char * *pwcsName*
LPSTORAGE *pstgPriority*
unsigned long *grfMode*
SNB *snbExclude*
unsigned long *dwReserved*
LPSTORAGE * *ppStg*

IStorage::OpenStorage opens an existing storage object contained within this storage object according to the access mode *grfMode*.

Parameters

pwcsName
Points to the name of the storage element to open. The *pwcsName* parameter is ignored if *ppStg* is non-NULL. I this case, the name of the element is taken from *ppStg*.

pstgPriority
Typically NULL. A non-NULL value points to a previous opening of the storage object, usually one that was opened in priority-mode. When *pstgPriority* is non-NULL, the container should close and reopen the storage object without admitting the possibility that some concurrent process could steal away access permissions already obtained.

grfMode
Defines the access mode to use when opening the storage object; see the following comments.

snbExclude

Specifies a non-NULL value that points to a block of stream names in this **IStorage** instance which are to be emptied as the storage is opened. This exclusion happens independently of a snapshot copy. Can be NULL.

For more information on *snbExclude* and the *pstgPriority* parameters, see the **StgOpenStorage** function.

dwReserved

Reserved for future use; must be zero.

ppStg

Points to where the opened **IStorage** instance is returned. Valid only if the operation is successful. This parameter is NULL if there is an error.

Return Values

Value	Meaning
S_OK	The storage object was opened successfully.
STG_E_ACCESSDENIED	Insufficient permissions to open **IStorage** object.
STG_E_FILENOTFOUND	The storage object with the specified *pwcsName* does not exist.
STG_E_INSUFFICIENTMEMORY	Out of memory.
STG_E_REVERTED	The object has been invalidated by a revert operation above it in the transaction tree.
STG_E_INVALIDFLAG	Invalid flag value(s) specified in *grfMode.*
STG_E_INVALIDNAME	Invalid name.
STG_E_INVALIDPOINTER	Invalid pointer.
STG_E_INVALIDPARAMETER	Invalid parameter.

Comments

After the function returns, the storage object contained in *pstgPriority* is invalid, and can no longer be used. Use the one in *ppStg* instead.

The compound file implementation of storage objects does not support including STGM_PRIORITY in *grfMode*; that is, it does not support opening non-root storage objects in priority mode. For more information on access permissions, see the warning in the description of STGM_SHARE_DENY_WRITE related to opening a storage object read and/or write mode without specifying DENY_WRITE.

Root storage objects can be opened with STGM_DELETEONRELEASE, in which case the object is destroyed when it receives its final release. This is useful for creating temporary storage objects.

The compound file implementation does not support simultaneous openings of a storage object from the same open storage instance. This behavior is enforced by requiring the caller to specify STGM_SHARE_EXCLUSIVE in *grfMode*. **IStorage::OpenStorage** fails with the error STG_E_INVALIDFUNCTION if this flag is not specified.

See Also

StgOpenStorage

IStorage::CopyTo

HRESULT IStorage::CopyTo(*ciidExclude*, *rgiidExclude*, *snbExclude*, *pStgDest***)**
unsigned long *ciidExclude*
IID const * *rgiidExclude*
SNB *snbExclude*
LPSTORAGE *pStgDest*

IStorage::CopyTo copies the entire contents of an open storage object into the storage object *pStgDest*.

Parameters

ciidExclude
Specifies the number of elements in the array pointed to by *rgiidExclude*. If *rgiidExclude* is NULL, *ciidExclude* is ignored.

rgiidExclude
Specifies an array of interface identifiers the caller takes responsibility for copying from the source to the destination. It can be NULL, indicating that all other objects are to be copied. If non-NULL, an array length of zero indicates that no other objects are to be copied, only the state exposed by the storage object.

snbExclude
Points to a block of named elements in this storage that are not to be copied to the destination. It can be NULL. If IID_IStorage is the *rgiidExclude* array, this parameter is ignored.

pStgDest
Points to the open storage object where this open storage object is to be copied.

Return Values

Value	Meaning
S_OK	The storage object was successfully copied.
STG_S_DESTLACKSINTERFACE	The destination lacks an interface of the source object requested to be copied.
STG_E_ACCESSDENIED	The destination storage object is a child of the source storage object.
STG_E_MEDIUMFULL	The storage medium is full; cannot create new storage object.
STG_E_TOOMANYOPENFILES	Too many open files.

Value	Meaning
STG_E_INSUFFICIENTMEMORY	Out of memory.
STG_E_INVALIDPOINTER	Invalid pointer.
STG_E_INVALIDPARAMETER	Invalid parameter.

Comments

The *pStgDest* parameter can be a different implementation of the **IStorage** interface than the source. Thus, **IStorage::CopyTo** can only use the publicly available functionality of *pStgDest*.

If *pStgDest* is transacted, it can be reverted by calling **IStorage::Revert**.

The copy operation merges elements contained in the source storage with those already present in the destination. The copy process is recursive, invoking **IStorage::CopyTo** and **IStream::CopyTo** on the elements nested inside the source. If an attempt is made to copy a stream on top of an existing stream with the same name, the existing destination stream is first removed and then replaced with the source stream. Attempting to copy a storage on top of an existing destination storage does not remove the existing storage. Thus, after the copy operation, the storage contains older elements if they were not replaced by newer ones.

If the destination storage is a (transitive) child of the source, **IStorage::CopyTo** fails and returns STG_E_ACCESSDENIED.

The *rgiidExclude* parameter specifies an array of interface identifiers the caller knows about and does not want copied from source to destination. Presumably, the caller takes care of copying the state behind these interfaces. It is not an error for this array to include an interface this storage does not support; such interfaces are simply ignored. The **IStorage** interface is explicitly allowed to be in this array. In the event the destination lacks an interface of the source that was requested to be copied, this does not affect the other interfaces copied and STG_S_DESTLACKSINTERFACE is returned.

The *snbExclude* parameter specifies a block of named elements of the storage the caller wants excluded from the copy operation. Elements of these names are not created or otherwise touched in the destination.

A consequence of these rules is that:

```
pStg->CopyTo(0, 0, 0, pStgDest)
```

copies everything possible from the source to the destination. This is the most commonly used form of this operation.

See Also

IStorage::MoveElementTo, **IStorage::Revert**

IStorage::MoveElementTo

HRESULT IStorage::MoveElementTo(*lpszName*, *pStgDest*, *lpszNewName*, *grfFlags***)**
const char * *lpszName*
LPSTORAGE *pStgDest*
const char * *lpszNewName*
unsigned long *grfFlags*

IStorage::MoveElementTo moves a storage object to the indicated new destination container.

Parameters

lpszName
Points to the name of the element of this storage to be moved.

pStgDest
Points to the destination container into which the element is to be placed.

lpszNewName
Points to the new name to give to the element in its new container.

grfFlags
Specifies how the move is to happen. Values are taken from the enumeration **STGMOVE**. For more information, see the following comments.

Return Values

Value	Meaning
S_OK	The storage element was moved successfully.
STG_E _ACCESSDENIED	Insufficient permissions.
STG_E _FILENOTFOUND	The element could not be found.
STG_E _FILEALREADYEXISTS	The specified file already exists.
STG_E _INSUFFICIENTMEMORY	Out of memory.
STG_E _TOOMANYOPENFILES	Too many open files.
STG_E _REVERTED	The object has been invalidated by a revert operation above it in the transaction tree.
STG_E _INVALIDNAME	Invalid name.
STG_E _INVALIDPOINTER	Invalid pointer.

Value	Meaning
STG_E _INVALIDPARAMETER	Invalid parameter.
STG_E _INVALIDFLAG	Invalid flag.

Comments

Unless both this storage and the destination storage have some special knowledge about each other's implementation (for example, they could be different instances of the *same* implementation), then **IStorage::MoveElementTo** is similar to an **IStorage::CopyTo** on the indicated element, followed by a removal of the original element.

The *grfFlags* parameter controls how the move is to happen. Its values are taken from the enumeration **STGMOVE**, which is defined in storage.h as follows:

```
typedef enum tagSTGMOVE {
STGMOVE_MOVE = 0,
STGMOVE_COPY = 1,
} STGMOVE;
```

STGMOVE flags have the following meanings:

Value	Meaning
STGMOVE_MOVE	Carry out the move operation, as expected.
STGMOVE_COPY	Carry out the first part of the move operation but do not remove the original element. With this flag, the behavior resulting from copying an element on top of itself (that is, *pStgDest* is the same as the source **IStorage,** and *lpszNewName* = *lpszName*) is undefined.

See Also **IStorage::CopyTo**

IStorage::Commit

HRESULT IStorage::Commit(*grfCommitFlags*)
unsigned long *grfCommitFlags*

IStorage::Commit commits any changes made to a storage object since it was opened or last committed to persistent storage.

Parameters

grfCommitFlags
Controls how the object is to be committed to storage; values are taken from the enumeration **STGC**. For more information, see the following comments.

Return Values

Value	Meaning
S_OK	The Commit operation was successful.
STG_E_NOTCURRENT	Another opening of the storage object has committed changes. Indicates the possibility of overwriting changes.
STG_E_MEDIUMFULL	No space left on device to commit.
STG_E _TOOMANYOPENFILES	Too many open files.
STG_E_REVERTED	The object has been invalidated by a revert operation above it in the transaction tree.
STG_E_INVALIDFLAG	Invalid flag.
STG_E _INVALIDPARAMETER	Invalid parameter.

Comments

Calling **IStorage::Commit** has no effect if the storage object was opened in direct mode, except when invoked on a direct mode root storage object, it ensures that any internal memory buffers have been written out to disk (or to the underlying **ILockBytes**, as appropriate).

In transacted mode, **IStorage::Commit** causes the changes that have been made since the storage object was opened or since the last commit was done to be permanently reflected in the object's persistent image. The commit is subject to the transaction of the object's parent storage. If the parent reverts at a later time, the changes currently being committed are rolled back.

Calling **IStorage::Commit** has no effect on currently-opened storages or streams in this object. Changes to these nested storages and streams are not automatically committed but they are still valid and can be used. Committing involves informing the parent storage of the changes the object is currently informed about. Thus, this object has to be informed of changes from inner transactions before it can publish changes to its parent.

The *grfCommitFlags* parameter consists of the or-ing of elements from the enumeration **STGC**, which is defined in storage.h as follows:

```
typedef enum tagSTGC
{
    STGC_DEFAULT                              = 0,
    STGC_OVERWRITE                            = 1,
    STGC_ONLYIFCURRENT                        = 2,
    STGC_DANGEROUSLYCOMMITMERELYTODISKCACHE   = 4
} STGC;
```

STGY values have the following meaning:

Value	Meaning
STGC_DEFAULT	Allows new data to overwrite the old data, reducing space requirements.
STGC_OVERWRITE	Prevents multiple users of a storage object from overwriting the other's changes.
STGC_ONLYIFCURRENT	Commits changes only if no one has made changes since the last time this user opened the storage or committed. If other changes have been made, STG_E_NOTCURRENT is returned. If the caller chooses to overwrite the changes, **IStorage::Commit** can be called with *grfCommitFlags* set to STGC_DEFAULT.
STGC_DANGEROUSLY-COMMITMERELYTO-DISKCACHE	Commits the changes, but does not save them to the disk cache.

The caller can specify STGC_DEFAULT or any combination of the other elements. STGC_OVERWRITE is not recommended for normal operation, but it could be useful in the following situations:

- A commit was tried and STG_E_MEDIUMFULL was returned.
- The user has somehow specified a willingness to risk overwriting the old data.
- A low memory save sequence is being used to end up with a smaller file.

The commit operation obtains all the disk space it needs before attempting to store the new data, whether or not STGC_OVERWRITE is specified. If space requirements prohibit the save, the old data will be intact, including all uncommitted changes. However, if the commit fails due to reasons other than lack of disk space and STGC_OVERWRITE was specified, it is possible that neither the old nor the new version of the data will be intact.

When committing root storage objects, care must be taken to ensure that the operation is successfully completed or that, when failing, the old committed contents of the storage are still intact. In the OLE compound file implementation, unless *grfCommitFlags* is set to STGC_OVERWRITE, a two-phase commit process is used. First, all new data is written to unused space in the underlying file, growing it as necessary. Once this has been successfully completed, a table in the file is updated using a single sector write to indicate the new data is to be used in place of the old. The old data becomes free space, to be used at the next commit.

If the storage object was opened with some of its elements excluded, the caller is responsible for rewriting them before calling **IStorage::Commit**. The storage must have been opened in write mode in order for the commit to succeed.

Unless multiple simultaneous writers on the same storage object are prohibited, applications usually specify at least STGC_ONLYIFCURRENT in *grfCommitFlags* to prevent the changes made by one writer from inadvertently overwriting the changes made by another.

See Also **IStorage::Revert**, **IStream::Commit**

IStorage::Revert

HRESULT IStorage::Revert()

IStorage::Revert discards all changes made in or made visible to this storage object by nested commits since the storage object was opened or last committed.

Return Values

Value	Meaning
S_OK	The revert operation was successful.
STG_E_INSUFFICIENT-MEMORY	The revert operation failed due to lack of memory.
STG_E_TOOMANY-OPENFILES	Too many open files.
STG_E_REVERTED	The object has been invalidated by a revert operation above it in the transaction tree.

Comments

After **IStorage::Revert** finishes, any existing elements that were opened from the reverted storage object are invalid and can no longer be used. The error STG_E_REVERTED is returned on all calls except **IStorage::Release** using these openings.

Because commits happen implicitly and immediately, calling **IStorage::Revert** on a storage opened in direct mode only invalidates any child openings.

IStorage::EnumElements

HRESULT IStorage::EnumElements(*dwReserved1*, *pReserved2*, *dwReserved3*, *ppenumStatStg***)**
unsigned long *dwReserved1*
void * *pReserved2*
unsigned long *dwReserved3*
LPENUMSTATSTG * *ppenumStatStg*

IStorage::EnumElements enumerates the elements immediately contained within this storage object.

Parameters

dwReserved1
Reserved for future use; must be zero.

pReserved2
Reserved for future use; must be NULL.

dwReserved3
Reserved for future use; must be zero.

ppenumStatStg
Points to where to return the enumerator from which the elements of this storage can be obtained; NULL if there is an error. See the description of **IEnumSTATSTG** later in this chapter.

Return Values

Value	Meaning
S_OK	The enumeration was successful.
STG_E_INSUFFICIENTMEMORY	The enumeration failed due to lack of memory.
E_OUTOFMEMORY	The enumeration failed due to lack of memory.
STG_E_REVERTED	The object has been invalidated by a revert operation above it in the transaction tree.
STG_E_INVALIDPOINTER	Invalid pointer.
STG_E_INVALIDPARAMETER	Invalid parameter.

Comments

The storage object must be opened in read mode to allow the enumeration of its elements.

The order in which the elements are enumerated and whether the enumerator is a snapshot or always reflects the current state of the storage on which it was opened (not necessarily the state at which the enumerator was initialized), depends on the storage implementation. The OLE compound file implementation makes a snapshot.

See Also

IEnumSTATSTG

IStorage::DestroyElement

HRESULT IStorage::DestroyElement(*pwcsName***)**
const char * *pwcsName*

IStorage::DestroyElement removes an element from this storage, subject to the transaction mode in which the storage object was opened.

Parameters

pwcsName
Points to the element to remove.

Return Values

Value	Meaning
S_OK	The element was successfully removed.
STG_E_ACCESSDENIED	Insufficient permissions.
STG_E_FILENOTFOUND	The element could not be found.

Value	Meaning
STG_E_TOOMANYOPENFILES	Too many open files.
STG_E_INSUFFICIENTMEMORY	Out of memory.
STG_E_REVERTED	The object has been invalidated by a revert operation above it in the transaction tree.
STG_E_INVALIDPOINTER	Invalid pointer.
STG_E_INVALIDNAME	Invalid name.
STG_E_INVALID-PARAMETER	Invalid parameter.

Comments

The existing open instance of this element from this parent instance becomes invalid after **IStorage::DestroyElement** is called.

IStorage::RenameElement

HRESULT IStorage::RenameElement(*pwcsOldName*, *pwcsNewName***)**
const char * *pwcsOldName*
const char * *pwcsNewName*

IStorage::RenameElement renames an element contained in storage, subject to the transaction state of the storage object.

Parameters

pwcsOldName
Points to the old name of the element.

pwcsNewName
Points to the new name of the element.

Return Values

Value	Meaning
S_OK	The element was successfully renamed.
STG_E_ACCESSDENIED	The element named *pwcsNewName* already exists.
STG_E_FILENOTFOUND	The element could not be found.
STG_E_FILEALREADYEXISTS	The specified file already exists.
STG_E_TOOMANYOPENFILES	Too many open files.
STG_E_INSUFFICIENT-MEMORY	Not enough memory to rename the element.
STG_E_REVERTED	The object has been invalidated by a revert operation above it in the transaction tree.
STG_E_INVALIDPOINTER	Invalid pointer.

Value	Meaning
STG_E_INVALIDNAME	Invalid name.
STG_E_INVALIDPARAMETER	Invalid parameter.

Comments

A storage element cannot be renamed while it is open.

IStorage::RenameElement is not guaranteed to work in low memory conditions.

IStorage::SetElementTimes

HRESULT IStorage::SetElementTimes(*lpszName*, *pctime*, *patime*, *pmtime***)**
const char * *lpszName*
FILETIME const * *pctime*
FILETIME const * *patime*
FILETIME const * *pmtime*

IStorage::SetElementTimes sets the modification, access, and creation times of the indicated element of this storage object.

Parameters

lpszName
Points to the name of the element to change.

pctime
Points to the new creation time.

patime
Points to the new access time.

pmtime
Points to the new modification time.

Return Values

Value	Meaning
S_OK	The time values were successfully set.
STG_E_ACCESSDENIED	The element named *pwcsNewName* already exists.
STG_E_FILENOTFOUND	The element could not be found.
STG_E_FILEALREADYEXISTS	The specified file already exists.
STG_E_TOOMANYOPENFILES	Too many open files.
STG_E_INSUFFICIENTMEMORY	Not enough memory to rename the element.
STG_E_REVERTED	The object has been invalidated by a revert operation above it in the transaction tree.

Value	Meaning
STG_E_INVALIDPOINTER	Invalid pointer.
STG_E_INVALIDNAME	Invalid name.
STG_E_INVALIDPARAMETER	Invalid parameter.

Comments

Each of the time value parameters can be NULL, indicating that no modification should occur.

It is possible that one or more of these time values are not supported by the underlying file system. **IStorage::SetElementTimes** sets the times that can be set and ignores the rest.

The compound file implementation maintains modification and change times for internal storage objects. For root storage objects, whatever is supported by the underlying file system (or **ILockBytes**) is used. The compound file implementation does not maintain any time stamps for internal streams. Unsupported time stamps are reported as zero, enabling the caller to test for support.

IStorage::SetClass

HRESULT IStorage::SetClass(*rclsid***)**
REFCLSID *rclsid*

IStorage::SetClass persistently stores the object's CLSID.

Parameter

rclsid
Specifies the CLSID to be associated with this storage object.

Return Values

Value	Meaning
S_OK	The CLSID was successfully stored.
STG_E _ACCESSDENIED	Unable to access the storage object.
STG_E _REVERTED	The object has been invalidated by a revert operation above it in the transaction tree.
STG_E _MEDIUMFULL	Not enough space was left on device to complete the operation.

Comments

The current CLSID for a storage object can be retrieved with **IStorage::Stat**. When initially created, storage objects have an associated CLSID of CLSID_NULL.

See Also

IStorage::Stat

IStorage::SetStateBits

HRESULT IStorage::SetStateBits(*grfStateBits*, *grfMask***)**
unsigned long *grfStateBits*
unsigned long *grfMask*

IStorage::SetStateBits stores up to 32 bits of state information in this storage object.

Parameters

dwgrfStateBits
Specifies the new values of the bits to set. No legal values are defined for these bits; they are all reserved for future use and must not be used by applications.

dwgrfMask
Specifies a binary mask indicating which bits in *dwgrfStateBits* are significant in this call.

Return Values

Value	Meaning
S_OK	The state was successfully set.
STG_E _ACCESSDENIED	The caller cannot change state information.
STG_E _INVALIDFLAG	Invalid flag specified in *dwgrfStateBits* or *dwgrfMask*.
STG_E _INVALIDPARAMETER	Invalid parameter.

Comments

The current value of this state is retrievable with **IStorage::Stat**. When a storage object is initially created, this state value is zero.

See Also

IStorage::Stat

IStorage::Stat

HRESULT IStorage::Stat(*pStatStg*, *grfStatFlag***)**
LPSTATSTG *pStatStg*
unsigned long *grfStatFlag*

IStorage::Stat returns statistics about this open storage object.

Parameters

pStatStg
Points to a **STATSTG** structure filled in by the callee with the statistics of this storage object.

grfStatFlag
Controls the level of statistics returned about the storage object. Values are taken from the **STATFLAG** enumeration**.** For more information, see the following comments.

Return Values

Value	Meaning
S_OK	The statistics were successfully returned.
STG_E_ACCESS-DENIED	The storage object cannot be accessed.
STG_E_INSUFFICIENT-MEMORY	Not enough memory to rename the element.
STG_E_REVERTED	The object has been invalidated by a revert operation above it in the transaction tree.
STG_E_INVALID-FLAG	Invalid flag specified in *dwgrfStatflag*.
STG_E_INVALID-POINTER	Invalid pointer.

Comments

With *grfStatFlag* set to STATFLAG_NONAME, *pStatStg->pwcsName* is not returned (that is, it is returned as NULL), thus saving an alloc/free operation.

The *grfStatFlag* values are taken from the enumeration **STATFLAG**, which is defined in storage.h as follows:

```
typedef enum tagSTATFLAG
{
    STATFLAG_DEFAULT = 0,
    STATFLAG_NONAME    = 1
} STATFLAG;
```

See Also

ReadClassStg, **IEnumSTATSTG**

IStream Interface

The **IStream** interface contains the following methods:

```
DECLARE_INTERFACE_(IStream, IUnknown)
{
  // *** IUnknown methods ***
 HRESULT QueryInterface (REFIID riid, void * * ppvObj);
 unsigned long AddRef () ;
 unsigned long Release ();

  // *** IStream methods ***
 HRESULT Read (void *pv, unsigned long cb, unsigned long *pcbRead);
 HRESULT Write (void *pv, unsigned long cb, unsigned long *pcbWritten);
 HRESULT Seek (LARGE_INTEGER dlibMove, unsigned long dwOrigin,
      ULARGE_INTEGER *plibNewPosition);
 HRESULT SetSize (ULARGE_INTEGER libNewSize);
 HRESULT CopyTo (LPSTREAM pStm, ULARGE_INTEGER cb,
      ULARGE_INTEGER *pcbRead, ULARGE_INTEGER *pcbWritten);
```

```
    HRESULT Commit (unsigned long dwCommitFlags);
    HRESULT Revert ();
    HRESULT LockRegion (ULARGE_INTEGER libOffset, ULARGE_INTEGER cb,
        unsigned long dwLockType);
    HRESULT UnlockRegion (ULARGE_INTEGER libOffset, ULARGE_INTEGER cb,
        unsigned long dwLockType);
    HRESULT Stat (STATSTG *pStatStg, unsigned long grfStatFlag);
    HRESULT Clone)(LPSTREAM * ppStm);
};
```

For more information, see the storage.h header file.

The **IStream** interface is implemented by OLE and used by containers to read and write the underlying bytes of data comprising an **IStorage** object.

Stream objects are analogous to files. **IStream** is the interface to which the stream elements of a storage object conform.

The **IStream** interface supports streams up to 2^{64} bytes in length and it requires a 64-bit value to represent their seek pointers. OLE compound files can only support streams up to 2^{32} bytes in length and, therefore, read and write operations (using **IStream::Read** and **IStream::Write**, respectively) are always limited to 2^{32} bytes at a time.

Pointers to instances of the **IStream** interface can be marshaled to other processes, just as any other interface pointer can. When the destination is another process that has shared memory access with the original process, the compound file implementation of **IStream** uses OLE's custom marshaling facilities to create a remote version of the original stream. This stream does not need to communicate with the original process to carry out its functions. The remote version of a stream shares the same seek pointer as the original stream. However, if this functionality is not needed, **IStream::Clone** can be called to create a clone of the stream, which is then passed to the remote process.

Releasing an **IStream** instance invalidates the stream and, as a result, the stream can no longer be used for any operations.

IStream::Read

HRESULT IStream::Read(*pv*, *cb*, *pcbRead***)**
void * *pv*
unsigned long *cb*
unsigned long * *pcbRead*

IStream::Read reads data from the stream starting at the current seek pointer.

Parameters

pv
Points to the buffer into which the stream data should be stored.

cb
Specifies the number of bytes of data to read from the stream.

pcbRead
Points (after the call) to the number of bytes actually read from the stream. It can be NULL, indicating the caller is not interested in this value.

Return Values

Value	Meaning
S_OK	The data was successfully read from the stream.
S_FALSE	The data could not be read from the stream.
STG_E_ACCESSDENIED	Insufficient access.
STG_E_REVERTED	The object has been invalidated by a revert operation above it in the transaction tree.
STG_E_WRITEFAULT	Disk error during a write operation.
STG_E_INVALIDPOINTER	A bad pointer was passed in for *pv* or *pcbRead*.
Other errors.	Any **ILockBytes** or system errors.

Comments

To read from the stream, STGM_READ mode is required on the stream. The number of bytes actually read is returned in *pcbRead*, even if an error is returned. The seek pointer is adjusted for the number of bytes actually read.

If the end of the stream was reached during the read, the number of bytes read might be fewer than requested. In this case, an error is not returned and the number of bytes actually read is merely returned through *pcbRead*.

Some implementations might choose to return S_FALSE instead of S_OK when fewer than the requested number of bytes are returned. Callers must be prepared to deal with this (typically, by comparing **pcbRead* on exit against the number of bytes requested for the read.)

See Also

IStream::Write

IStream::Write

HRESULT IStream::Write(*pv*, *cb*, *pcbWritten***)**
void const * *pv*
unsigned long *cb*
unsigned long * *pcbWritten*

IStream::Write attempts to write *cb* bytes from the buffer pointed to by *pv* into the stream starting at the current seek pointer.

Parameters

pv
Points to the buffer containing the data to be written to the stream.

cb
Defines the number of bytes of data to write into the stream.

pcbWritten
After the call, points to the number of bytes actually written into the stream. It can be NULL, indicating the caller is not interested in this value.

Return Values

Value	Meaning
S_OK	The data was successfully written into the stream.
STG_E _MEDIUMFULL	No space left on device.
STG_E _ACCESSDENIED	Insufficient access.
STG_E _CANTSAVE	Data cannot be written for reasons other than no access or space.
STG_E _INVALIDPOINTER	A bad pointer was passed in for *pv* or *pcbWritten*.
STG_E _REVERTED	The object has been invalidated by a revert operation above it in the transaction tree.
STG_E _WRITEFAULT	Disk error during a write operation.
Other errors.	Any **ILockBytes** or system errors.

Comments

Writing a count of zero bytes is always a no-op. For a non-zero byte-count, if the seek pointer is currently past the end of the stream, the size of the stream is increased so the seek pointer can be reached. The fill bytes written to the stream are not initialized to any particular value.

In the compound file implementation, stream objects are not sparse. Any fill bytes are eventually allocated on the disk and assigned to the stream.

The number of bytes actually written is always returned in *pcbWritten*, even if an error is returned. The seek pointer is adjusted for the number of bytes actually written.

See Also

IStream::Read

IStream::Seek

HRESULT IStream::Seek(*dlibMove, dwOrigin, plibNewPosition*)
LARGE_INTEGER *dlibMove*
unsigned long *dwOrigin*
ULARGE_INTEGER * *plibNewPosition*

IStream::Seek adjusts the location of the seek pointer on the stream.

Parameters

dlibMove
Specifies the displacement to be added to the location indicated by *dwOrigin*. If *dwOrigin* is STREAM_SEEK_SET, this is interpreted as an unsigned value rather than a signed value.

dwOrigin
Specifies the seek mode; the origin with respect to which *dlibMove* should be interpreted. Valid values are taken from the enumeration **STREAM_SEEK.** For more information, see the following comments.

plibNewPosition
Points (after this call is completed) to the beginning of the stream. It can be NULL, indicating the caller is not interested in this value.

Return Values

Value	Meaning
S_OK	The seek pointer has been successfully adjusted.
STG_E _INVALIDPOINTER	A bad pointer was passed in for *plibNewPosition*.
STG_E _INVALIDFUNCTION	*dwOrigin* contains invalid value.
STG_E _REVERTED	The object has been invalidated by a revert operation above it in the transaction tree.
STG_E _WRITEFAULT	Disk error during a write operation.
Other errors.	Any **ILockBytes** or system errors.

Comments

It is an error to seek before the beginning of the stream but not an error to seek past the end of the stream. Seeking past the end of the stream is useful for subsequent writes, because the stream will be extended at that time to the seek position immediately before the write is done.

The *dwOrigin* parameter takes its values from the enumeration **STREAM_SEEK**, which is defined in storage.h as follows:

```
typedef enum tagSTREAM_SEEK
{
    STREAM_SEEK_SET = 0,
    STREAM_SEEK_CUR = 1,
    STREAM_SEEK_END = 2
} STREAM_SEEK;
```

STREAM_SEEK values have the following meanings:

Value	Meaning
STREAM_SEEK _SET	Sets the seek position relative to the beginning of the stream; *dlibMove* is the new seek position.
STREAM_SEEK _CUR	Sets the seek position relative to the current position of the stream; *dlibMove* is the (signed) displacement to be made.
STREAM_SEEK _END	Sets the seek position relative to the current end of the stream; *dlibMove* is the (signed) displacement to be made.

Calling **IStream::Seek** with *dlibMove* set to zero and *dwOrigin* set to STREAM_SEEK CUR returns the current seek position through *plibNewPosition*.

IStream::SetSize

HRESULT IStream::SetSize(*libNewSize***)**
ULARGE_INTEGER *libNewSize*

IStream::SetSize changes the size of the stream.

Parameters

libNewSize
Specifies the new size of the stream.

Return Values

Value	Meaning
S_OK	The stream size was successfully changed.
STG_E_MEDIUMFULL	Lack of space prohibited change of stream size.
STG_E _INVALIDFUNCTION	High unsigned long of *libNewSize* != 0.
STG_E _REVERTED	The object has been invalidated by a revert operation above it in the transaction tree.
STG_E _WRITEFAULT	Disk error during a write operation.
Other errors.	Any **ILockBytes** or system errors.

Comments

The seek pointer is not affected by the change in stream size. If *libNewSize* is larger than the current stream size, the stream is extended with fill bytes of undefined value, much as is done in an **IStream::Write** call if the seek pointer is past the current end-of-stream. If *libNewSize* is smaller than the current stream, the stream is truncated to the indicated size.

In most stream implementations, calling **IStream::SetSize** is an effective way of trying to obtain a large chunk of contiguous space. However, no guarantee is made that the space will be contiguous.

See Also

IStream::Write

IStream::CopyTo

HRESULT IStream::CopyTo(*pStm, cb, pcbRead, pcbWritten***)**
LPSTREAM *pStm*
ULARGE_INTEGER *cb*
ULARGE_INTEGER * *pcbRead*
ULARGE_INTEGER * *pcbWritten*

IStream::CopyTo copies data from one stream to another stream, starting at the current seek pointer in each stream.

Parameters

pStm
Points to the stream into which the data should be copied (*lpstm* can be a clone of the source stream).

cb
Specifies the number of bytes to read from the source stream.

pcbRead
Contains the number of bytes actually read from the source stream. It can be NULL, indicating the caller is not interested in this value.

pcbWritten
Contains the number of bytes actually written into the destination stream. It can be NULL, indicating the caller is not interested in this value.

Return Values

Value	Meaning
S_OK	The stream was successfully copied.
STG_E_MEDIUMFULL	Lack of space prohibited copy.
STG_E_INSUFFICIENTMEMORY	Out of memory.
STG_E_INVALIDPOINTER	A bad pointer for *pstm*, *pcbRead*, or *pcbWritten*.
STG_E_READFAULT	Disk error during read.
STG_E_REVERTED	The object has been invalidated by a revert operation above it in the transaction tree.

Value	Meaning
STG_E_WRITEFAULT	Disk error during a write operation.
Other errors.	Any **ILockBytes** or system errors. Can also return any error codes from **IStream**::**Read**, **IStream::Write**, and **IStream::Seek**.

Comments

IStream::CopyTo is equivalent to reading *cb* bytes into memory using **IStream::Read** and then immediately writing them to the destination stream using **IStream::Write**. Copying a stream onto a clone of itself can always be done in a safe manner.

Setting *cb* to its maximum large-integer value causes the remainder of the source stream to be copied.

The number of bytes actually read or written is always returned in *pcbRead* and *pcbWritten* respectively. The seek pointer in each stream instance is adjusted for the number of bytes read or written.

If **IStream::CopyTo** returns an error, no assumptions can be made about the seek positions of either the source or destination streams and the values in *pcbRead* and *pcbWritten is* not meaningful. One result of this is that if **IStream::CopyTo** returns successfully, *pcbRead* and *pcbWritten* are equal.

See Also

IStream::Read, **IStream::Write**

IStream::Commit

HRESULT IStream::Commit(*grfCommitFlags***)**
unsigned long *grfCommitFlags*

IStream::Commit commits any changes made to the storage object containing the stream.

Parameters

grfCommitFlags
Controls how the object is to be committed to storage. The *grfCommitFlags* parameter consists of the or-ing of elements from the enumeration **STGC**. For more information about *grfCommitFlags* , see "**IStorage::Commit**" earlier in this chapter.

Return Values

Value	Meaning
S_OK	The stream was successfully committed.
STG_E _MEDIUMFULL	The commit failed due to lack of space on device.
STG_E _REVERTED	The object has been invalidated by a revert operation above it in the transaction tree.

Value	Meaning
STG_E _WRITEFAULT	Disk error during a write operation.
Other errors.	Any **ILockBytes** or system errors.

Comments

OLE does not support stream objects being opened in transacted mode. Therefore, calling **IStream::Commit** in transacted mode is a no-op.

However, for other implementations, **IStream::Commit** causes the changes made to this stream since it was opened or last committed to be permanently reflected in the persistent image of the stream. This is subject to any transaction of the parent storage object of the stream. That parent can still cancel changes by calling **IStream::Revert** at a later time.

In direct mode, **IStream::Commit** ensures that any memory buffers have been flushed out to the stream's underlying open storage instance. This is much like a "flush" call in traditional file systems.

In compound files, **IStream** instances are only available inside **IStorage** instances. Thus, the open parent storage also needs to be flushed and committed.

See Also

IStorage::Commit

IStream::Revert

HRESULT IStream::Revert()

IStream::Revert discards all changes made to the stream since it was opened or last committed in transacted mode. In direct mode, **IStream::Revert** is a no-op.

Return Values

Value	Meaning
S_OK	The stream was successfully reverted.
STG_E_REVERTED	The object has been invalidated by a revert operation above it in the transaction tree.
STG_E_WRITEFAULT	Disk error during a write operation.
Other errors.	Any **ILockBytes** or system errors.

Comment

OLE does not support stream objects being opened in transacted mode. Accordingly, most applications will have no need to call this method.

IStream::LockRegion

HRESULT IStream::LockRegion(*libOffset*, *cb*, *dwLockType*)
ULARGE_INTEGER *libOffset*
ULARGE_INTEGER *cb*
unsigned long *dwLockType*

IStream::LockRegion locks a range of bytes in the stream. This method is *not* supported in the current release of OLE.

Parameters

libOffset
Specifies the beginning of the region to lock.

cb
Specifies the length of the region to be locked, in bytes.

dwLockType
Specifies the kind of lock being requested; values are taken from the enumeration **LOCKTYPE**. For more information on **LOCKTYPE**, see the section "STATSTG Structure," earlier in this chapter.

Return Values

Value	Meaning
S_OK	The range of bytes was successfully locked
STG_E_INVALIDFUNCTION	The function is not supported in this release.
STG_E_LOCKVIOLATION	Requested lock is supported, but cannot be presently granted because of an existing lock.

Comments

Range locking is not supported by compound files so calling **IStream::LockRegion** is a no-op. It might or might not be supported by other implementations.

The range of bytes begins with the byte at the offset *libOffset*, and extends for *cb* bytes toward the end of the stream. The specified range of bytes can extend past the current end of the stream.

Three types of locking can be supported: locking to exclude other writers, locking to exclude other readers or writers, and locking that allows only one requestor to obtain a lock on the given range, which is usually an alias for one of the other two lock types. A given stream instance might support either of the first two types, or both.

For information on how a caller can determine whether locking is supported; see the discussion of **IStream::Stat** and its parameter block, **STATSTG**.

Any region locked with **IStream::LockRegion** must later be explicitly unlocked by calling **IStream::UnlockRegion** with exactly the same values for *libOffset*, *cb*, and *dwLockType*. Two adjacent regions cannot be locked separately and then unlocked with a single unlock call.

All locks on a stream must be explicitly unlocked before the stream is released.

See Also **IStream::Stat**, **IStream::UnlockRegion**

IStream::UnlockRegion

HRESULT IStream::UnlockRegion(*libOffset, cb, dwLockType*)
ULARGE_INTEGER *libOffset*
ULARGE_INTEGER *cb*
unsigned long *dwLockType*

IStream::UnlockRegion unlocks a region of the stream previously locked with **IStream::LockRegion**. This method is *not* supported in the current release of OLE.

Parameter

libOffset
Specifies the beginning of the region to unlock.

cb
Specifies the length of the region to be locked, in bytes.

dwLockType
Specifies the kind of lock being released; values are taken from the enumeration **LOCKTYPE**. For more information on **LOCKTYPE**, see the section "STATSTG Structure," earlier in this chapter.

Return Values

Value	Meaning
S_OK	The requested unlock was granted.
STG_E_LOCK-VIOLATION	The requested unlock cannot be granted.
STG_E_INVALID-FUNCTION	The function is not supported in this release.

Comments Any locked region must be explicitly unlocked using **IStream::UnlockRegion**, with exactly the same *libOffset*, *cb*, and *dwLockType* parameters specified as in the original **IStream::LockRegion** call. Two adjacent regions cannot be locked separately and then unlocked with a single unlock call.

See Also **IStream::LockRegion**

IStream::Stat

HRESULT IStream::Stat(*pStatStg, grfStatFlag***)**
LPSTATSTG *pStatStg*
unsigned long *grfStatFlag*

IStream::Stat returns relevant statistics concerning this open stream.

Parameters

pStatStg
Points to a **STATSTG** structure filled with the statistics of this open stream.

grfStatFlag
Controls the level of statistics returned about this open stream object; values are taken from the enumeration **STATFLAG**. For more information on **STATFLAG**, see the discussion of **IStorage::Stat** earlier in this chapter.

Return Values

Value	Meaning
S_OK	The statistics were successfully returned.
STG_E_INSUFFICIENT-MEMORY	The stream could not be accessed due to lack of memory.
STG_E _INVALIDFLAG	A bad flag was passed into *grfStatFlag*.
STG_E _INVALIDPOINTER	A bad pointer was passed in for *pStatStg*.
STG_E_REVERTED	The object has been invalidated by a revert operation above it in the transaction tree.
STG_E _WRITEFAULT	Disk error during a write operation.
Other errors.	Any **ILockBytes** or system errors.

See Also

IStorage::Stat, **IEnumSTATSTG**

IStream::Clone

HRESULT IStream::Clone(*ppStm***)**
LPSTREAM * *ppStm*

IStream::Clone returns a new stream object that is a clone of this stream.

Parameters

ppStm
Points to where the new stream should be returned.

Return Values

Value	Meaning
S_OK	The stream was successfully copied.
STG_E_INSUFFICIENT-MEMORY	The stream could not be copied due to lack of memory.
STG_E_INVALIDPOINTER	A bad pointer was passed in for *ppStm*.

Value	Meaning
STG_E_REVERTED	The object has been invalidated by a revert operation above it in the transaction tree.
STG_E_WRITEFAULT	Disk error during a write operation.
E_OUTOFMEMORY	The stream could not be copied due to lack of memory.
Other errors.	Any **ILockBytes** or system errors.

Comments

The new stream objects sees the same underlying stream data as does the original stream. Writes made through one instance are immediately visible through the other.

Byte range locking is shared between the streams and a clone is not treated as "foreign" with respect to byte range locking. However, the cloned stream *does* have a seek pointer that is independent of the original. The initial setting of the seek pointer in the cloned stream is the same as the current setting of the seek pointer in the original at the time of the clone operation.

IRootStorage Interface

The **IRootStorage** interface is implemented by OLE and is used by containers to switch the underlying disk file that storage objects are being saved to.

IRootStorage contains the following method:

```
DECLARE_INTERFACE_(IRootStorage, IUnknown)
{
   // *** IUnknown methods ***
  HRESULT QueryInterface (REFIID riid, void * * ppvObj);
  unsigned long AddRef ();
  unsigned long Release ();

   // *** IRootStorage methods ***
  HRESULT SwitchToFile (char * lpstrFile);
};
```

For more information, see the storage.h header file.

IRootStorage::SwitchToFile

HRESULT IRootStorage::SwitchToFile(*lpstrFile***)**
char * *lpstrFile*

IRootStorage::SwitchToFile makes a copy of the file underlying this storage object in the file indicated by *lpstrFile*.

Parameters

lpstrFile
Specifies the filename of the new base file.

Return Values

Value	Meaning
S_OK	The file was successfully copied.
STG_E _INVALIDPARAMETER	One or more invalid arguments.
STG_E _MEDIUMFULL	The storage medium is full.
STG_E _ACCESSDENIED	Insufficient permissions to access the storage.
STG_E _REVERTED	The object has been invalidated by a revert operation above it the transaction tree.
STG_E _INVALIDPOINTER	A bad pointer was passed in for *lpstrFile*.
STG_E _FILEALREADYEXISTS	The file specified by *lpstrFile* already exists.
System errors.	Any **ILockBytes** or system errors.

Comments

It is illegal to call **IRootStorage::SwitchToFile** if this storage object or anything contained within it has been marshaled to another process. As a consequence, any embedded objects contained within the object owning this storage must be put in the hands off storage mode before calling this function.

IRootStorage::SwitchToFile associates the storage object with this new file rather than with its current file, including any uncommitted changes.

IRootStorage::SwitchToFile does not consume any additional memory or file handles.

See Also

IPersistStorage::HandsOffStorage

ILockBytes Interface

The **ILockBytes** interface is implemented and used by OLE to manipulate the actual byte array underlying a root compound file.

This implementation of **ILockBytes** can be used when the byte array is a real disk file, as is often the case. Some OLE containers are "database-like," meaning they store objects in places other than disk files. These containers can write their own **ILockBytes** implementation to direct data into their file system, or data store.

ILockBytes differs from **IStream** in that it has no seek pointer. Offsets are provided as part of the method call, rather than by an explicit seek pointer. However, some of the **ILockBytes** methods behave the same as in their **IStream** counterpart, such as the **SetSize**, **LockRegion**, and **UnlockRegion** methods.

Compound files use region locking to negotiate permissions when several copies of OLE on remote systems contend for the same storage object. When the compound file implementation of either **IStorage** or **IStream** is being marshaled to another process, the underlying **ILockBytes** interface pointer is marshaled to the same destination process. This marshaling is typically done by the default remoting mechanism. At the destination, a proxy **ILockBytes** instance is created whose function implementations call back to the original **ILockBytes** instance.

To make remote access more efficient, **ILockBytes** implementors should consider implementing custom marshaling using OLE's marshaling support. For more information, see the **IMarshal** interface.

The **ILockBytes** interface contains the following methods:

```
DECLARE_INTERFACE_(ILockBytes, IUnknown)
{
  // *** IUnknown methods ***
 HRESULT QueryInterface (REFIID riid, void * * ppvObj);
 unsigned long AddRef ();
 unsigned long Release ();

  // *** ILockBytes methods ***
 HRESULT ReadAt (ULARGE_INTEGER ulOffset, VOID *pv, unsigned long cb,
      unsigned long *pcbRead);
 HRESULT WriteAt (ULARGE_INTEGER ulOffset, VOID *pv, unsigned long cb,
      unsigned long *pcbWritten);
 HRESULT Flush ();
 HRESULT SetSize (ULARGE_INTEGER cb);
 HRESULT LockRegion (ULARGE_INTEGER libOffset, ULARGE_INTEGER cb,
      unsigned long dwLockType);
 HRESULT UnlockRegion (ULARGE_INTEGER libOffset, ULARGE_INTEGER cb,
      unsigned long dwLockType);
 HRESULT Stat (STATSTG *pStatStg, unsigned long grfStatFlag);
};
```

For more information, see the storage.h header file.

ILockBytes::ReadAt

HRESULT ILockBytes::ReadAt(*ulOffset, pv, cb, pcbRead***)**
ULARGE_INTEGER *ulOffset*
void HUGEP * *pv*
unsigned long *cb*
unsigned long * *pcbRead*

ILockBytes::ReadAt reads a specified number of bytes from the **ILockBytes** byte array starting at a specified position.

Parameters

ulOffset
Specifies the offset in the byte array at which to begin reading.

pv
Points to the buffer into which the data should be read.

cb
Specifies the number of bytes to read.

pcbRead
Specifies (after the call) the number of bytes actually read. The caller can set *pcbRead* to NULL, indicating this value is not of interest. The *pcbRead* parameter is zero if there is an error.

Return Values

Value	Meaning
S_OK	Some or all of the data requested was read.
STG_E_ACCESS-DENIED	The data could not be read due to insufficient access to the byte array.
E_FAIL	The data could not be read for reasons other than insufficient access.
STG_E_INVALID-HANDLE	An invalid floppy change has been made.
System errors.	Any system error.

Comments

The number of bytes actually read is always returned in *pcbRead*, even if an error is returned.

The number of bytes actually read might be less than requested if the end of the byte array is reached during the read operation.

See Also

ILockBytes::WriteAt

ILockBytes::WriteAt

HRESULT ILockBytes::WriteAt(*ulOffset, pv, cb, pcbWritten***)**
ULARGE_INTEGER *ulOffset*
VOID const HUGEP * *pv*
unsigned long *cb*
unsigned long * *pcbWritten*

ILockBytes::WriteAt writes data to the byte array.

Parameters

ulOffset
Specifies the offset in the byte array at which to begin writing the data.

pv
Points to the buffer containing the data to be written.

cb
Specifies the number of bytes to write.

pcbWritten
Specifies (after the call) the number of bytes actually read. The caller can set *pcbWritten* to NULL, indicating this value is not of interest. The *pcbWritten* parameter is zero if there is an error.

Return Values

Value	Meaning
S_OK	Some or all of the data requested was written.
STG_E_ACCESS-DENIED	The data could not be written due to insufficient access to the byte array.
E_FAIL	The data could not be written for reasons other than insufficient access.
STG_E_MEDIUMFULL	The disk is full.
STG_E_INVALIDHANDLE	An invalid floppy change has been made.
System errors.	Any system error.

Comments

If the offset specified by *ulOffset* is past the end of the byte array, **ILockBytes::WriteAt** first increases the size of the byte array, filling it with bytes of an undefined value. This is not done if *cb* is zero, because writing a count of zero bytes is always a no-op.

The number of bytes actually written is returned in *pcbWritten*, even if an error is returned.

See Also

ILockBytes::ReadAt

ILockBytes::Flush

HRESULT ILockBytes::Flush()

ILockBytes::Flush ensures that any internal buffers maintained by the **ILockBytes** implementation are written out to the backing store.

Return Values

Value	Meaning
S_OK	The flush operation was successful.
STG_E _ACCESSDENIED	The data could not be written due to insufficient access to the backing store.
STG_E_MEDIUMFULL	The data could not be written due to insufficient space on the medium.
E_FAIL	The data could not be written for reasons other than insufficient access or no space left.
STG_E_TOOMANY-FILESOPEN	Under certain circumstances, **Flush** does a dump-and-close to flush. This can lead to STG_E_TOOMANYFILESOPEN if there are no file handles available.
STG_E _INVALIDHANDLE	An invalid floppy change has been made.
System errors.	Any system error.

Comments

ILockBytes::Flush is used by the OLE compound file implementation during a transacted commit operation to protect against loss of data.

See Also

IStorage::Commit

ILockBytes::SetSize

HRESULT ILockBytes::SetSize(*cb***)**
ULARGE_INTEGER *cb*

ILockBytes::SetSize changes the size of the byte array.

Parameters

cb
Specifies the new size of the byte array.

Return Values

Value	Meaning
S_OK	The size of the byte array was successfully changed.
STG_E _MEDIUMFULL	Data could not be written due to insufficient space on the storage medium.
STG_E _ACCESSDENIED	Insufficient permissions to byte array.

Value	Meaning
E_FAIL	The size of the byte array could not be changed due to miscellaneous errors.
STG_E _INVALIDHANDLE	An invalid floppy change has been made.
System errors.	Any system error.

Comments

If the new size is larger than the current size of the byte array, **ILockBytes::SetSize** first extends the size of the byte array, filling it with bytes of an undefined value. If *cb* is smaller than the current size of the byte array, the array is truncated to the indicated size.

ILockBytes::LockRegion

HRESULT ILockBytes::LockRegion(*libOffset*, *cb*, *dwLockType*)
ULARGE_INTEGER *libOffset*
ULARGE_INTEGER *cb*
unsigned long *dwLockType*

ILockBytes::LockRegion locks a range of bytes in the byte array.

Parameters

libOffset
Specifies the beginning of the region to lock.

cb
Specifies the number of bytes to lock.

dwLockType
Specifies the type of lock access; valid values are taken from the enumeration LOCKTYPE. For more information, see the section "STATSTG Structure" earlier in this chapter.

Return Values

Value	Meaning
S_OK	The requested lock was granted.
STG_E _LOCKVIOLATION	The requested lock is supported, but cannot be presently granted because of an existing lock.
STG_E _INVALIDFUNCTION	Invalid value for *dwLockType*.
STG_E _SHAREREQUIRED	The 16-bit file implementation can return STG_E_SHAREREQUIRED if it is unable to lock because no sharing support is loaded.
STG_E _INVALIDHANDLE	An invalid floppy change has been made.
System errors.	Any system error.

Comments

The *libOffset* parameter specifies the beginning of the lock range, extending *cb* bytes towards the end of the array. The range of bytes can extend past the current end of the array.

Region locking is optional for **ILockBytes** implementors. Whether region locking is supported depends on how the storage objects constructed on top of the byte array are used. If it can be known that, at any one time, only one storage object is to be opened on the storage behind the byte array, region locking can be ignored. However, if the **ILockBytes** is built on top of a disk file, multiple simultaneous openings of a storage object are possible and region locking is needed to coordinate these accesses.

The lock type is specified by *dwLockType*. A given **ILockBytes** instance might support one or all types. OLE's compound file implementation only supports LOCK_ONLYONCE.

For information on how a caller can determine whether locking is supported; see **ILockBytes::Stat** and its parameter block **STATSTG**.

See Also

IStream::LockRegion, **ILockBytes::UnlockRegion**

ILockBytes::UnlockRegion

HRESULT ILockBytes::UnlockRegion(*libOffset*, *cb*, *dwLockType***)**
ULARGE_INTEGER *libOffset*
ULARGE_INTEGER *cb*
unsigned long *dwLockType*

ILockBytes::UnlockRegion unlocks a region previously locked with **ILockBytes::LockRegion**.

Parameters

libOffset
Specifies the beginning of the region to unlock.

cb
Specifies the number of bytes to unlock.

dwLockType
Specifies the type of lock access; valid values are taken from the enumeration **LOCKTYPE**. For more information, see the section "STATSTG Structure," earlier in this chapter.

Return Values

Value	Meaning
S_OK	The requested unlock was granted.
STG_E _LOCKVIOLATION	The requested unlock cannot be granted.
STG_E _INVALIDFUNCTION	Invalid value for *dwLockType*.

Value	Meaning
STG_E _INVALIDHANDLE	An invalid floppy change has been made.
System errors.	Any system error.

Comments Any locked region must be explicitly unlocked using **ILockBytes::UnlockRegion**, using exactly the same *libOffset*, *cb*, and *dwLockType* parameters that were specified in the original **ILockBytes::LockRegion** call.

Two adjacent regions cannot be locked separately and then unlocked with a single unlock call.

See Also **ILockBytes::LockRegion**

ILockBytes::Stat

HRESULT ILockBytes::Stat(*pStatStg, grfStatFlag***)**
LPSTATSTG *pStatStg*
unsigned long *grfStatFlag*

ILockBytes::Stat returns relevant statistics about this byte array.

Parameters

pStatStg
Points to a **STATSTG** structure filled with statistics about this byte array; will be zero if an error occurs. For more information, see the section "STATSTG Structure," earlier in this chapter.

grfStatFlag
Specifies the level of statistics to return for this object; valid values are taken from the enumeration **STATFLAG**. For more information, see **IStorage::Stat**, described earlier in this chapter.

Return Values

Value	Meaning
S_OK	Stat operation was successful.
STG_E _ACCESSDENIED	Statistics cannot be returned because access to the byte array cannot be granted.
E_OUTOFMEMORY	Memory not available for stat operation.
E_FAIL	Stat operation did not succeed due to errors other than lack of access or available memory.
STG_E _INSUFFICIENTMEMORY	The name cannot be allocated.
STG_E _UNKNOWN	The file time cannot be converted to FILETIME format.

Value	Meaning
STG_E _INVALIDHANDLE	An invalid floppy change has been made.
System errors.	Any system error.

Comments

The **ILockBytes::Stat** call is used by the compound file implementation to respond to an **IStorage::Stat** call invoked on a root storage object.

If no reasonably interpretable name for the **ILockBytes** exists, this function should return NULL in *pStatStg->pwcsName*.

See Also

IEnumSTATSTG Interface

IPersist Interface

The **IPersist** interface is the base interface from which the **IPersistStorage**, **IPersistStream**, and **IPersistFile** interfaces are derived. **IPersist** is implemented by object applications and used by container applications to get the CLSID associated with an object.

IPersist consists of the following method:

```
DECLARE_INTERFACE_(IPersistStorage, IPersist)
{
  // *** IUnknown methods ***
 HRESULT QueryInterface (REFIID riid, void * * ppvObj);
 unsigned long AddRef ();
 unsigned long Release ();

  // *** IPersist methods ***
 HRESULT GetClassID (LPCLSID pclsid);
};
```

For more information, see the ole2.h header file.

IPersist::GetClassID

HRESULT IPersist::GetClassID(*pclsid*)
pclsid

IPersist::GetClassID returns a document object's CLSID.

Parameter

pclsid
Points to where to return the CLSID.

Return Values

Value	Meaning
S_OK	The CLSID was successfully returned.
E_FAIL	The CLSID could not be returned.

Comments

The returned CLSID can be used to locate and dynamically load object-specific code into the caller's context.

IPersistFile Interface

The **IPersistFile** interface is implemented by object applications and optionally by container applications to support linking to embedded and file-based objects.

IPersistFile permits applications to load and save documents stored in disk files (as opposed to objects stored in **IStorage** instances). Because the information needed to open a file varies from one application to another, the application is responsible for opening the file.

Generally, **IPersistFile** is used to bind a linked object. In the container's case, this would be a link to an embedded object.

IPersistFile contains the following methods; the non-FSP functions should delegate to the FSP implementations.

```
DECLARE_INTERFACE_(IPersistFile, IPersist)
{
   // *** IUnknown methods ***
  HRESULT QueryInterface (REFIID riid, void * * ppvObj);
  unsigned long AddRef ();
  unsigned long Release ();

   // *** IPersist methods ***
  HRESULT GetClassID (LPCLSID pclsid);

   // *** IPersistFile methods ***
  HRESULT IsDirty ();
  HRESULT Load (const char * lpszFileName, unsigned long grfMode);
  HRESULT Save (const char * lpszFileName, unsigned long fRemember);
  HRESULT SaveCompleted (const char * lpszFileName);
  HRESULT GetCurFile (char * * lplpszFileName);
  HRESULT LoadFSP (const FSSpec *pFSSpec, unsigned long grfMode);
  HRESULT SaveFSP (const FSSpec * pFSSpec, unsigned long fRemember);
  HRESULT SaveCompletedFSP (const FSSpec * pFSSpec);
  HRESULT GetCurFSP (FSSpec * pFSSpec);
};
```

For more information, see the ole2.h header file.

IPersistFile::IsDirty

HRESULT IPersistFile::IsDirty()

IPersistFile::IsDirty checks a document object for changes since it was last saved.

Return Values

Value	Meaning
S_OK	The object has changed.
S_FALSE	The object has not changed.

Comments

The dirty flag is conditionally cleared in **IPersistFile::Save**. A simple object with no contained objects simply checks its dirty flag. A container with one or more contained objects needs to maintain an internal dirty flag that reflects any one object being dirty.

In practice, recursive polling is not needed in the **IsDirty** method; rather, a container can keep its internal dirty flag up to date by the appropriate use of **IAdviseSink::OnDataChange** notifications.

See Also

IPersistFile::Save

IPersistFile::Load

HRESULT IPersistFile::Load(*lpszFileName*, *grfMode***)**
const char * *lpszFileName*
unsigned long *grfMode*

IPersistFile::Load loads the document object contained in the given filename.

Parameters

lpszFileName
Points to the absolute path of the file to open.

grfMode
Specifies the storage access mode with which the caller intends to use the file; for a description of valid values, see "Access Permission Flags" earlier in this chapter.

Return Values

IPersistFile::Load can return any of the error codes that begin with STG_E, in addition to the following codes:

Value	Meaning
S_OK	The document was successfully loaded.
E_FAIL	The document could not be loaded.
E_OUTOFMEMORY	There is not enough memory to load the document.

Comments

The filename must be an absolute path. **IPersistFile::Load** is an initialization function only and it does not show the loaded document to the user.

The *grfMode* values express only the intent that the caller has in opening the file. The application can add more restrictive permissions as necessary. Zero is a valid value; the object should interpret the request as though the user opened the file using default values.

IPersistFile::Load is called by the File Moniker implementation of **IMoniker::BindToObject**.

See Also **IMoniker::BindToObject**

IPersistFile::Save

HRESULT IPersistFile::Save(*lpszFileName, fRemember***)**
const char * *lpszFileName*
unsigned long *fRemember*

IPersistFile::Save saves a copy of the object to the indicated filename.

Parameters

lpszFileName
Points to the file in which the document should be saved.

fRemember
Determines which disk file the document is to be logically associated with after the call is completed. Valid only if *lpszFileName* is non-NULL.

Return Values

IPersistFile::Save can return any of the error codes beginning with STG_E in addition to the following codes.

Value	Meaning
S_OK	The file was successfully saved.
E_FAIL	The file could not be saved.

Comments

The *lpszFileName* parameter can be NULL, indicating that a simple "File Save" operation is requested to the now-current filename. A non-NULL value indicates either a "File Save As" or a "File Save Copy As" operation. In this case, the full path of the destination file is specified in the *lpszFileName* parameter.

The *fRemember* parameter determines whether a "Save As" or a "Save Copy As" operation is requested by the user. If *fRemember* is TRUE, the file pointed to by *lpszFileName* should become the current working copy of the document ("Save As"). FALSE indicates that after completing the **IPersistFile::Save** call, the working copy should be whatever it was before **IPersistFile::Save** was called ("Save Copy As").

If, upon exiting, the saved file is the current working copy, the internal dirty flag maintained by the object should be cleared and the container must call **IPersistFile::SaveCompleted** at some later time when it is done with the data in the file.

Whenever a file is saved with a new name, the object should send a rename notification (call **IAdviseSink::OnRename**) to its existing advisory connections.

Some clients of objects might find calling **IPersistFile::Save** useful for programmatically manipulating documents. OLE does not call **IPersistFile::Save**.

See Also **IPersistFile::SaveCompleted**

IPersistFile::SaveCompleted

HRESULT IPersistFile::SaveCompleted(*lpszFileName***)**
const char * *lpszFileName*

IPersistFile::SaveCompleted indicates the caller has saved the file with a call to **IPersistFile::Save** and is finished working with it.

Parameters

lpszFileName
Points to the filename in which the document was saved.

Return Values

Value	Meaning
S_OK	S_OK is returned in all cases.

See Also **IAdviseSink::OnSave**, **IPersistFile::Save**

IPersistFile::GetCurFile

HRESULT IPersistFile::GetCurFile(*lplpszFileName***)**
char * * *lplpszFileName*

IPersistFile::GetCurFile returns either the absolute path of the document's currently-associated file, or the default filename prompt, if there is no currently-associated file.

Parameters

lplpszFileName
Points to where to return the current path or the default save prompt of the document, as appropriate.

Return Values

Value	Meaning
S_OK	The return value is a pathname.
S_FALSE	The return value is the save prompt.
E_OUTOFMEMORY	Not enough memory to successfully return a value.
E_FAIL	Failure due to reasons other than insufficient memory.

IPersistFile::LoadFSP

HRESULT IPersistFile::LoadFSP(*pFSSpec*, *grfMode***)**
const FSSpec * *pFSSpec*
unsigned long *grfMode*

IPersistFile::LoadFSP loads the document object contained in the given file specification.

Parameters

pFSSpec
Points to the file specification to open.

grfMode
Specifies the storage access mode with which the caller intends to use the file; for a description of valid values, see "Access Permission Flags" earlier in this chapter.

Return Values

IPersistFile::LoadFSP can return any of the error codes that begin with STG_E, in addition to the following:

Value	Meaning
S_OK	The document was successfully loaded.
E_FAIL	The document could not be loaded.
E_OUTOFMEMORY	There is not enough memory to load the document.

Comments

IPersistFile::LoadFSP is an initialization function only and it does not show the loaded document to the user.

The *grfMode* values express only the intent that the caller has in opening the file. The application can add more restrictive permissions as necessary. Zero is a valid value; the object should interpret the request as though the user opened the file using default values.

See Also

IPersistFile::SaveFSP, **IPersistFile::GetCurFSP**

IPersistFile::SaveFSP

HRESULT IPersistFile::SaveFSP(*pFSSpec*, *fRemember***)**
const FSSpec * *pFSSpec*
unsigned long *fRemember*

IPersistFile::SaveFSP saves the document object contained in the given file specification.

Parameters

pFSSpec
Points to the file specification in which the object is to be saved.

fRemember
Determines which file specification the document is to be logically associated with after the call is completed. Valid only if *pFSSpec* is non-NULL.

Return Values

IPersistFileFSP::Save can return any of the error codes beginning with STG_E in addition to the following codes.

Value	Meaning
S_OK	The document was successfully saved.
E_FAIL	The document could not be saved.

Comments

The *pFSSpec* parameter can be NULL, indicating that a simple "File Save" operation is requested to the now-current file specification. A non-NULL value indicates either a "File Save As" or a "File Save Copy As" operation. In this case, the destination file specification is in the *pFSSpec* parameter.

The *fRemember* parameter determines whether a "Save As" or a "Save Copy As" operation is requested by the user. If *fRemember* is TRUE, the file specification pointed to by *pFSSpec* should become the current working copy of the document ("Save As"). FALSE indicates that after completing the **IPersistFileFSP::Save** call, the working copy should be whatever it was before **IPersistFileFSP::Save** was called ("Save Copy As").

If, upon exiting, the saved file specification is the current working copy, the internal dirty flag maintained by the object should be cleared and the container must call **IPersistFile::SaveCompletedFSP** at some later time when it is done with the data in the file specification.

Whenever a file specification is saved with a new name, the object should send a rename notification (call **IAdviseSink::OnRename**) to its existing advisory connections.

Some clients of objects might find calling **IPersistFile::SaveFSP** useful for programmatically manipulating documents. OLE does not call **IPersistFileFSP::Save**.

See Also

IPeristFile::LoadFSP, **IPersistFile::GetCurFSP**, **IPersistFile::SaveCompletedFSP**

IPersistFile::SaveCompletedFSP

HRESULT IPersistFile::SaveCompletedFSP(*pFSSpec*)
const FSSpec * *pFSSpec*

IPersistFile::SaveCompletedFSP indicates the caller has saved the file specification with a call to **IPersistFile::SaveFSP** and is finished working with it.

Parameters

pFSSpec
Points to the file specification in which the document was saved.

Return Values

Value	Meaning
S_OK	S_OK is returned in all cases.

See Also

IAdviseSink::OnSave, **IPersistFile::SaveFSP**

IPersistFile::GetCurFSP

HRESULT IPersistFile::GetCurFSP(*pFSSpec*)
FSSpec * *pFSSpec*

IPersistFile::GetCurFSP returns either the name of the file specification currently associated with the object or the default file name prompt, if there is no currently-associated file specification.

Parameters

pFSSpec
Points to where to return the name of the file specification.

Return Values

Value	Meaning
S_OK	The return value is a valid file specification.
S_FALSE	The return value is the save prompt.
E_OUTOFMEMORY	Not enough memory to successfully return a value.
E_FAIL	Failure due to reasons other than insufficient memory.

IPersistStorage Interface

The **IPersistStorage** interface is implemented by object applications and/or object handlers. The interface's methods are used by OLE and container applications to manipulate an object's storage.

IPersistStorage contains the following methods:

```
DECLARE_INTERFACE_(IPersistStorage, IPersist)
{
  // *** IUnknown methods ***
  HRESULT QueryInterface (REFIID riid, void * * ppvObj);
  unsigned long AddRef ();
  unsigned long Release ();

  // *** IPersist methods ***
  HRESULT GetClassID (LPCLSID pclsid);

  // *** IPersistStorage methods ***
  HRESULT IsDirty ();
  HRESULT InitNew (LPSTORAGE pStg);
  HRESULT Load (LPSTORAGE pStg);
  HRESULT Save (LPSTORAGE pStgSave, unsigned long fSameAsLoad);
  HRESULT SaveCompleted (LPSTORAGE pStgNew);
  HRESULT HandsOffStorage ();
};
```

For more information, see the ole2.h header file.

IPersistStorage::IsDirty

HRESULT IPersistStorage::IsDirty()

IPersistStorage::IsDirty checks an object for changes since it was last saved.

Return Values

Value	Meaning
S_OK	The object has changed since the last save.
S_FALSE	The object has not changed since the last save.
E_OUTOFMEMORY	Memory constraints prohibit the successful determination of whether the object has changed.
E_FAIL	It is not possible to determine whether or not the object has changed due to errors other than lack of memory.

Comments

Logically, the same sort of recursive calls to currently loaded objects must be done as in **IPersistStorage::Save**. Thus, an object is dirty if it or any of its contained objects are dirty. In practice, recursive polling is not needed in the **IsDirty** method. Rather, a container can keep its internal dirty flag up to date by the appropriate use of **IAdviseSink::OnDataChange** notifications.

The dirty flag must be conditionally cleared in the subsequent call to **IPersistStorage::Save**.

IPersistStorage::InitNew

HRESULT IPersistStorage::InitNew(*pStg***)**
LPSTORAGE *pStg*

IPersistStorage::InitNew initializes the specified storage object.

Parameters

pStg
Points to the **IStorage** instance to initialize.

Return Values

Value	Meaning
S_OK	The new **IStorage** instance successfully returned.
CO_E _ALREADYINITIALIZED	This **IStorage** instance has already been initialized.
E_OUTOFMEMORY	Memory constraints prohibit the successful initialization of the **IStorage** instance.
E_FAIL	The **IStorage** instance could not be initialized due to errors other than lack of memory.

Comments

An object that uses **IPersistStorage** must have access to a valid **IStorage** instance at all times while it is running. This includes the time just after the object has been created but before it has been made persistent. The object's container must provide the object with access to an **IStorage** instance during this time by calling **IPersistStorage::InitNew**. Depending on the container's state, a temporary file might need to be created for this purpose.

If the object wants to retain the **IStorage** instance, it must call **IUnknown::AddRef** to increment its reference count.

See Also

IUnknown::AddRef

IPersistStorage::Load

HRESULT IPersistStorage::Load(*pStg***)**
LPSTORAGE *pStg*

IPersistStorage::Load loads an object into memory or in the running state, depending on whether the container or object handler calls the method.

Parameters

pStg
Points to the **IStorage** instance from which to load or run the object.

Return Values

Value	Meaning
S_OK	The object was loaded successfully.
CO_E_ALREADYINITIALIZED	The object was already loaded.

Value	Meaning
E_OUTOFMEMORY	Memory constraints prohibit the object from loading.
E_FAIL	The object could not be loaded due to errors other than lack of memory.
IStorage errors	Can also return any of the error codes from **IStorage** methods.

Comments

When **IPersistStorage::Load** is called by the container on the object handler, **Load** places the object in the loaded state. When **IPersistStorage::Load** is called by the object handler, **Load** places the object in the running state.

The **IStorage** instance passed in *pStg* contains the persistent representation of the object created when **IPersistStorage::Save** was called. The object should load whatever state information it needs. The object handler and/or object can hold onto the open **IStorage** instance while it is in the loaded or running state.

See Also

IPersistStorage::Save

IPersistStorage::Save

HRESULT IPersistStorage::Save(*pStgSave*, *fSameAsLoad***)**
LPSTORAGE *pStgSave*
unsigned long *fSameAsLoad*

IPersistStorage::Save saves an object to storage, including any nested objects.

Parameters

pStgSave
Points to the **IStorage** instance in which the object is to be saved.

fSameAsLoad
Indicates whether *pStgSave* is the same **IStorage** instance from which the object was loaded or just created.

Return Values

Value	Meaning
S_OK	The object was loaded successfully.
STG_E_MEDIUMFULL	The object could not be saved due to lack of disk space.
E_FAIL	The object could not be saved due to errors other than lack of memory.

Comments

If *fSameAsLoad* is TRUE, the object writes incremental changes to *pStgSave*. If *fSameAsLoad* is FALSE, the caller is either cloning the object or responding to a Save As request and the object must copy all of its state to the new storage. Any state information from the object's old storage (the storage from which the object was loaded) must also be saved.

IPersistStorage::Save saves any currently-loaded nested objects within the object by recursively calling **OleSave** or **IStorage::CopyTo**. Nonloaded nested objects do not need to have anything done to them (*fSameAsLoad* is TRUE) or they can be handled by copying their storage objects (*fSameAsLoad* is FALSE).

The object should not call **IStorage::Commit** on *pStgSave*. It is the responsibility of the caller to deal with the newly-saved changes. Often, the caller is using the transaction support, so it is appropriate to commit the changes with **IStorage::Commit**. The object should not write its CLSID to *pStgSave* because this too is to be done by the caller.

After the save, it is the callee's responsibility to put the object in the no scribble state. This temporarily revokes the object's right to write to its **IStorage** until **IPersistStorage::SaveCompleted** is called. When **SaveCompleted** is called, the object should, if necessary, clear the dirty flag reported by **IPersistStorage::IsDirty**. Because the storage is off limits between the time **Save** is completed and **SaveCompleted** is called, the caller of **Save** should call **SaveCompleted** as quickly as possible.

If *pStgSave* is not the current storage for the object (*fSameAsLoad* is FALSE) when the function exits, *pStgSave* can no longer be used.

Implementations of **IPersistStorage::Save** generally call **WriteFmtUserTypeStg** internally.

See Also

OleSave, **IStorage::CopyTo**, **IStorage::Commit**

IPersistStorage::SaveCompleted

HRESULT IPersistStorage::SaveCompleted(*pStgNew*)
LPSTORAGE *pStgNew*

IPersistStorage::SaveCompleted terminates both the no scribble and the hands off mode, returning the object to normal storage mode.

Parameter

pStgNew
Points to the **IStorage** instance in which the object was saved. It is NULL in no scribble storage mode and is never NULL in hands off storage mode.

Return Values

Value	Meaning
S_OK	Normal storage mode was re-entered successfully.
E_OUTOFMEMORY	The required streams cannot be opened. The container is left in the hands off state.
E_UNEXPECTED	Neither **IPersistStorage::Save** nor **IPersistStorage::HandOffStorage** was previously called.

Value	Meaning
E_INVALIDARG	**IPersistStorage::HandOffStorage** was called previously and *pStgNew* is NULL.
E_FAIL	The object could not be saved due to errors other than lack of memory.

Comments

In the hands off storage state, *pStgNew* is never NULL. If the current mode is hands off, the data in *pStgNew* depends on how the mode was entered:

- If the hands off state was entered from the normal state, *pStgNew* is the replacement for the one revoked by **IPersistStorage::HandsOffStorage**. The bits in *pStgNew* are the same as those that were in the revoked storage.
- If the hands off state was entered from the no scribble state, the bits in *pStgNew* are the same as those last saved. If **IPersistStorage::Save**(*pStgSave*, FALSE) was used, the bits in *pStgNew* are different than the ones in the **IStorage** instance being held onto and that was revoked in **IPersistStorage::HandsOffStorage**.

In the no scribble state, *pStgNew* might or might not be NULL. If it is NULL, the object is allowed to scribble to the storage it has. If it is non-NULL, the object should internally simulate receiving a call to **HandsOffStorage**, then proceed as in that case. Containers must be prepared for objects that refuse to do this (meaning, return an error, such as E_UNEXPECTED) and take responsibility for calling **HandsOffStorage** themselves.

As with **IPersistStorage::Save** and **IPersistStorage::HandsOffStorage**, **SaveCompleted** is a call that recurses to all currently loaded or running nested objects.

If **SaveCompleted** returns an error, the object should not return to the normal storage state. It should act as though **IPersistStorage::SaveCompleted** was never called in order to give the container the opportunity to try an alternate save strategy. **IOleObject::Close** can be called if necessary.

When **IPersistStorage::SaveCompleted** is called, often the object will clear the dirty flag reported by **IPersistStorage::IsDirty**. For more information on the various states an object can be in during a save operation and the effect it has on **SaveCompleted**, see the section "Overview to Structured Storage " earlier in this chapter.

See Also

IPersistStorage::IsDirty, **IPersistStorage::Save**

IPersistStorage::HandsOffStorage

HRESULT IPersistStorage::HandsOffStorage()

IPersistStorage::HandsOffStorage causes the object to release its storage object and enter the hands off storage state.

Return Values

Value	Meaning
S_OK	S_OK is returned in all cases.

Comments

Object applications must provide a working implementation of **HandsOffStorage** to ensure that Save As scenarios work properly.

The hands off storage state is terminated when **IPersistStorage::SaveCompleted** is called. **SaveCompleted** passes a pointer to the storage object taking the place of the one released in **HandsOffStorage**.

IPersistStorage::HandsOffStorage is called from either the no scribble or the normal storage state. Between the time **HandsOffStorage** is called to initiate hands off storage state and **IPersistStorage::SaveCompleted** is called to terminate it, callers cannot expect the object to respond in any predictable manner.

See Also

IPersistStorage::SaveCompleted

IPersistStream Interface

The **IPersistStream** interface is implemented and used by OLE to support persistent objects that use a simple serial stream for their storage needs (monikers are an example of objects that use **IPersistStream**). Containers might have a need to implement this interface in support of new moniker types.

Unlike the **IStorage** instances used in the implementation of **IPersistStorage**, the **IStream** instances used in **IPersistStream** are valid only during the call in which they are passed; the object *cannot* retain them after the call completes.

The **IPersistStream** interface contains the following methods:

```
DECLARE_INTERFACE_(IPersistStream, IPersist)
{
  // *** IUnknown methods ***
 HRESULT QueryInterface (REFIID riid, void * * ppvObj);
 unsigned long AddRef ();
 unsigned long Release ();

  // *** IPersist methods ***
 HRESULT GetClassID (LPCLSID pclsid);

  // *** IPersistStream methods ***
```

```
    HRESULT IsDirty ();
    HRESULT Load (LPSTREAM pStm);
    HRESULT Save ( PSTREAM pStm, unsigned long fClearDirty);
    HRESULT GetSizeMax (ULARGE_INTEGER * pcbSize);
};
```

For more information, see the ole2.h header file.

IPersistStream::IsDirty

HRESULT IPersistStream::IsDirty()

IPersistStream::IsDirty checks an object for changes since it was last saved.

Return Values

Value	Meaning
S_OK	The object has changed since the last save.
S_FALSE	The object has not changed since the last save.
E_OUTOFMEMORY	Memory constraints prohibit the successful determination of whether the object has changed.
E_FAIL	It was not possible to determine whether or not the object has changed due to errors other than lack of memory.

Comments

Calling **IPersistStream::IsDirty** determines whether any changes have occurred to an object that requires **IPersistStream::Save** being called to avoid losing information.

The dirty flag is conditionally cleared in the implementation of **IPersistStream::Save**.

See Also

IPersistStream::Save

IPersistStream::Load

HRESULT IPersistStream::Load(*pStm***)**
LPSTREAM *pStm*

IPersistStream::Load initializes an object previously stored with **IPersistStream::Save**.

Parameters

pStm
Points to the stream from which the object should load itself.

Return Values

Value	Meaning
S_OK	The object was successfully loaded.
E_FAIL	The object was not successfully loaded.

Value	Meaning
E_OUTOFMEMORY	Memory constraints prohibit the successful loading of the object.

Comments

On entry, the stream is logically positioned just as it was in the call to **IPersistStream::Save**. The **IPersistStream::Load** method can both read and seek data from the stream but it cannot write to the stream.

Upon returning, the stream should be left in the same position as it was on exit from the call to **IPersistStream::Save**, which is just past the end of the data.

See Also

IPersistStream::Save

IPersistStream::Save

HRESULT IPersistStream::Save(*pStm*, *fClearDirty***)**
LPSTREAM *pStm*
unsigned long *fClearDirty*

IPersistStream::Save saves the state of an object to the indicated stream.

Parameters

pStm
Points to the stream into which the object should be stored.

fClearDirty
Specifies whether or not the object's dirty flag should be cleared; TRUE clears the internal dirty flag after the save operation and FALSE leaves it alone.

Return Values

Value	Meaning
S_OK	Stream was successfully saved.
STG _E_MEDIUMFULL	**IStream::Write** returned STG_E_MEDIUMFULL.
STG _E_CANTSAVE	**IStream::Write** returned STG_E_CANTSAVE or if the object cannot currently be serialized.

Comments

The object does not write its CLSID to the stream because this is done by the caller. This permits the caller, in appropriate situations, to more efficiently store homogeneous collections of objects.

On entry, the stream is positioned to where the object should write its data, at which point the object can immediately invoke **IStream::Write** calls. The object can read and seek about in the stream, but the object must not seek the stream before the position at which it was on function entry. On exiting from this function, the stream should be positioned immediately past all the persistent data of the object.

If the object contains other objects that cannot be serialized, the object itself cannot be serialized. **IPersistStream::Save** returns STG_E_CANTSAVE and the position of the seek pointer is undefined.

See Also **IPersistStream::Load**, **IStream::Write**

IPersistStream::GetSizeMax

HRESULT IPersistStream::GetSizeMax(*pcbSize***)**
ULARGE_INTEGER * *pcbSize*

IPersistStream::GetSizeMax determines an upper boundary for the size of the stream that would be needed to save this object with **IPersistStream::Save**.

Parameters

pcbSize
Points to where to return the size boundary.

Return Values

Value	Meaning
S_OK	The size was successfully returned.

Comments The returned value can be used to set buffer sizes for immediate and subsequent calls to **IPersistStream::Save**. This value must be a conservative estimate of the size required because the caller of **IPersistStream::Save** can choose to provide a non-growable buffer.

See Also **IPersistStream::Save**

Storage Creation Functions

This section describes the OLE API functions used to create **IStorage**, **IStream**, and **ILockBytes** objects.

The following functions are defined in storage.h:

```
CreateILockBytesOnHGlobal (Handle hGlobal, unsigned long fDeleteOnRelease,
     LPLOCKBYTES * ppLkbyt);
CreateStreamOnHGlobal (Handle hGlobal, unsigned long fDeleteOnRelease, LPSTREAM * ppStm);
StgCreateDocfile(const char * pwcsName, unsigned long grfMode, unsigned long dwReserved,
     LPSTORAGE  *ppStgOpen);
StgCreateDocfileOnILockBytes(LPLOCKBYTES pLkbyt, unsigned long grfMode,
     unsigned long dwReserved, LPSTORAGE *ppStgOpen);
```

The following functions are defined in macapi.h:

```
OSErr OleMakeFsspec (short vRefNum, long dirlD, const char * szFileName, fSSpecPtr pFSSpec);
OSErr OleFullPathFromFSSpec(FSSpecPtr pFSSpec, char * szFileName, unsigned long pcb);
StgCreateDocfileFSp(const FSSpec * pFSSpec,OSType creator, OSType fileType, ScriptCode scriptTag,
    unsigned long grfMode, unsigned long reserved, IStorage * * ppstgOpen);
StgCreateDocfileMac(const char * szFileName,short vRefNum, OSType creator,
    unsigned long grfMode, unsigned long reserved, IStorage * * ppstgOpen);
```

StgCreateDocfileFSp

StgCreateDocfileMac

OleMakeFSSpec

OSErr OleMakeFSSpec(*vRefNum, dirID, szFileName, pFSSpec***)**
short *vRefNum*
long *dirID*
const char * *szFileName*
FSSpecPtr *pFSSpec*

OleMakeFSSpec creates a FSSpec from a null-terminated pathname.

Parameters

vRefNum
Specifies the volume reference number.

dirID
Specifies the parent directory ID.

szFileName
Specifies the null-terminated pathname from which to create the FSSpec.

pFSSpec
On return, points to the newly created FSSpec.

Return Values

Value	Meaning
NoErr(0)	The function completed successfully.
fnfErr(-43)	The file or directory does not exist.

Comments

OleMakeFSSpec works similar to the Macintosh **FSMakeFSSpec** function except that it puts no limit on the size of *szFileName*. Note that *szFileName* is a null-terminated string.

See Also

OleFullPathFromFSSpec

OleFullPathFromFSSpec

OSErr OleFullPathFromFSSpec(*pFSSpec, szFileName, pcb***)**
FSSpecPtr *pFSSpec*
char * *szFileName*
unsigned long * *pcb*

Given a FSSpec, **OleFullPathFromFSSpec** creates creates a null-terminated pathname.

Parameters

pFSSpec
Pointer to the FSSpec.

szFileName
Points to the buffer that contains the newly created pathname.

pcb
Specifies the size of the *szFileName* buffer passed in.

Return Values

Value	Meaning
NoErr(0)	The function completed successfully.
fnfErr(-43)	The file or directory does not exist.

See Also

OleMakeFSSpec

CreateILockBytesOnHGlobal

HRESULT CreateILockBytesOnHGlobal(*hGlobal, fDeleteOnRelease, ppStm***)**
Handle *hGlobal*
unsigned long *fDeleteOnRelease*
LPLOCKBYTES * *ppLkbyt*

CreateILockBytesOnHGlobal returns an OLE-provided instance of the **ILockBytes** interface.

Parameters

hGlobal
Contains the memory handle previously allocated by **GlobalAlloc**. The handle must have been allocated as moveable and nondiscardable. If the handle is to be shared between processes, it must also have been allocated as shared. New handles should be allocated with a size of zero. If *hGlobal* is NULL, **CreateILockBytesOnHGlobal** internally allocates a new shared memory block.

fDeleteOnRelease
Indicates whether the underlying handle for this stream should be automatically freed when the stream is released.

ppLkbyt
Points to where to put the newly created **ILockBytes** instance.

Return Values

Value	Meaning
S_OK	The **ILockBytes** instance was created successfully.
E_INVALIDARG	An invalid value was specified for *hGlobal.*
E_OUTOFMEMORY	Not enough memory to create an **ILockBytes** instance.

Comments

The returned **ILockBytes** instance can be the basis for a compound file. A call to **StgCreateDocfileOnILockBytes** builds a compound file on top of the **ILockBytes**. The memory block is grown as needed.

The current contents of the memory block are undisturbed by the creation of the **ILockBytes**. The caller can use **StgOpenStorageOnILockBytes** to reopen a previously existing storage object already contained in the memory block.

Note Freeing the handle that **GetHGlobalFromILockBytes** returns invalidates the **ILockBytes** instance. Therefore, *ppLkbyt*->**Release** must be called before freeing the handle.

See Also

StgOpenStorageOnILockBytes

CreateStreamOnHGlobal

HRESULT CreateStreamOnHGlobal(*hGlobal*, *fDeleteOnRelease*, *ppStm*)
Handle *hGlobal*
unsigned long *fDeleteOnRelease*
LPSTREAM * *ppStm*

CreateStreamOnHGlobal returns an OLE-provided **IStream** instance where data is stored inside a global memory handle.

Parameters

hGlobal
Contains the memory handle allocated by **NewHandle**. The handle must have been allocated as moveable and nondiscardable. New handles should be allocated with a size of zero. If *hGlobal* is NULL, **CreateStreamOnHGlobal** internally allocates such a shared new memory block.

fDeleteOnRelease
Specifies whether the handle to the memory is automatically freed when the stream is released.

ppStm
Points to where to return the stream. It cannot be NULL.

Return Values

Value	Meaning
S_OK	The stream was successfully created.
E_OUTOFMEMORY	The stream could not be created due to lack of memory.
E_INVALIDARG	Invalid value for one of the parameters.

Comments

The returned stream supports both reading and writing, is not transacted, and does not support locking. The initial contents of the stream are the current contents of the memory block provided in *hGlobal*. If *hGlobal* is NULL, **CreateStreamOnHGlobal** internally allocates a handle. The current contents of the memory block, therefore, are undisturbed by the creation of the stream and the user can call **CreateStreamOnHGlobal** to open a stream on an existing memory block.

The initial size of the stream is the size of the memory handle. Because of allocation granularity rounding, this is not necessarily the same size as the handle originally allocated. If the logical size of the stream is important, the caller should follow the call to **CreateStreamOnHGlobal** with a call to **IStream::SetSize**.

See Also

GlobalSize, **IStream::SetSize**

StgCreateDocfile

HRESULT StgCreateDocfile(*pwcsName*, *grfMode*, *dwReserved*, *ppStgOpen***)**
const char * *pwcsName*
unsigned long *grfMode*
unsigned long *dwReserved*
IStorageFAR* * *ppStgOpen*

StgCreateDocfile creates a new root compound file in the file system.

Parameters

pwcsName
Points to the pathname of the compound file to create. Passed uninterpreted to the file system. This can be a relative name or NULL. If NULL, a temporary compound file is allocated with a unique name.

grfMode
Specifies the access mode to use when opening the new compound file. For more information, see the following comments.

dwReserved
Reserved for future use; must be zero.

ppStgOpen
If the operation is successful, it points to where the opened storage object is placed (**ppStgOpen*).

Return Values

Value	Meaning
S_OK	The compound file was successfully created.
STG_E_ACCESSDENIED	The calling process does not have sufficient access. Attempt to open file with conflicting permissions to a simultaneous open.
STG_E_FILEALREADY-EXISTS	The compound file already exists and *grfMode* is set to STGM_FAILIFTHERE.
STG_S_CONVERTED	The compound file was successfully converted to Storage format.
STG_E _INSUFFICIENTMEMORY	Out of memory.
STG_E _INVALIDNAME	Bad name in *pwcsName*.
STG_E_INVALIDPOINTER	Bad pointer in *pwcsName* or *ppStgOpen*.
STG_E_INVALIDFLAG	Bad flag combination in *grfMode*.
STG_E _TOOMANYOPENFILES	Out of file handles.
File System Errors	Any file system error.

Comments

Where applicable, applications should call **StgCreateDocfileFSp** instead of **StgCreateDocfile**.

The name of the open compound file can be retrieved by calling **IStorage::Stat**.

StgCreateDocfile creates the file if it does not exist. If it does exist, the use of the STGM_CREATE, STGM_CONVERT, and STGM_FAILIFTHERE flags in *grfMode* indicate how to proceed:

Flag Values for *grfMode*	Meaning
STGM_CREATE	If the compound file exists, destroy it and replace it with the new name *pwcsName*.
STGM_CONVERT	If the compound file exists, replace it with the new file *pwcsName*, saving any data in the old file to a stream named **CONTENTS** in the new compound file. This stream contains the same data that was in the old file before the conversion.

Flag Values for *grfMode*	Meaning
STGM _DELETEONRELEASE	Indicates that the compound file is to be automatically destroyed when it is released. This capability is most useful with temporary files.
STGM _FAILIFTHERE	If the compound file exists, fail and return STG_E_FILEALREADYEXISTS.

If the compound file is opened in transacted mode (*grfMode* specifies STGM_TRANSACTED) and a file with this name already exists, the existing file is not altered until all outstanding changes are committed. If the calling process lacks write access to the existing file (because of access control in the file system), *grfMode* can only specify STGM_READ and *not* STGM_WRITE or STGM_READWRITE. The resulting new open compound file can still be written to, but a commit operation will fail (in transacted mode, write permissions are enforced at commit time).

If *grfMode* specifies STGM_TRANSACTED and no file yet exists with the name specified by *pwcsName*, the file is created immediately. In an access controlled file system, the caller must have write permissions in the file system directory in which the compound file is created.

The absence of STGM_TRANSACTED in *grfMode* indicates the file is to be created and opened in direct access mode. Any existing file is destroyed before creating the new file.

StgCreateDocfile can be used to create a temporary compound file by passing a NULL value for *pwcsName*. However, these files are temporary only in the sense that they have a system-provided unique name, which is meaningless to the user.

The caller is responsible for deleting the temporary file when finished with it, unless STGM_DELETEONRELEASE was specified for *grfMode*.

See Also **StgCreateDocFileOnILockBytes**

StgCreateDocfileFSp

HRESULT StgCreateDocfileFSp(*pFSSpec, creator, filetype, scriptTag, grfMode, reserved, ppstgOpen***)**
const FSSpec* *pFSSpec*
OSType *creator*
OSType *filetype*
ScriptCode *scriptTag*
unsigned long *grfMode*
unsigned long *reserved*
IStorage * * *ppstgOpen*

StgCreateDocfileFSp creates a new root compound file in the file system using the file system specification record provided.

Parameters

pFSSpec
Points to the file system specification record that identifies the compound file to create.

creator
Signature resource that identifies the compound files creator.

filetype
Signature resource that identifies the type of the compound file.

scriptTag
Specifies the script system to use when displaying the compound file's name.

grfMode
Specifies the access mode to use when opening the new compound file.

reserved
Reserved for future use; must be zero.

ppstgOpen
If the operation is successful, then *ppstgOpen* points to where the opened storage object is placed (**ppstgOpen*).

Return Values

Value	When Returned
S_OK	Compound file created successfully.
STG_E _INVALIDPARAMETER	The *reserved* parameter has not been set to zero.
STG_E _INVALIDFLAG	An invalid flag has been set in *grfMode*.
STG_E _FILEALREADYEXISTS	The STG_FAILIFTHERE flag has been set in *grfMode* and the file already exists.

Comments

Applications should call **StgCreateDocfileFSp** when they are using the DLL version of the OLE libraries. Applications using the static version of the OLE libraries should call **StaticStgCreateDocfileFSp**. For more information, see the section, "Static and DLL Versions of OLE Functions," in Appendix D, "OLE 2 for the Macintosh: How It Differs from OLE 2 for Windows."

StgCreateDocfileFSp creates a new root compound file, opens it according to the access mode specified in *grfMode* and returns a pointer to the open **IStorage** object through *ppstgOpen*.

StgCreateDocfileFSp creates the file if it does not exist; or if it does exist, then the flags specified in *grfMode* indicate how to proceed. The following tables describes the common flags:

Flag	Description
STGM_CREATE	If the compound file already exists, destroy it and replace it with the new file.
STGM_CONVERT	If the compound file exists, then replace it with the new file, saving any data in the old file to a stream named **CONTENTS** in the new compound file. This stream contains the same data that was in the old file before the conversion.
STGM _DELETEONRELEASE	Indicates that the newly created **IStorage** is to be automatically destroyed when it is released. This capability is most useful with temporary files.
STGM _FAILIFTHERE	If the compound file specified by *pspec* already exists, then fail and return the error STG_E_FILEALREADYEXISTS.

Comments

If the compound file is opened in transacted mode (*grfMode* set to STGM_TRANSACTED) and a file with this name already exists, then the existing file is not altered until all outstanding changes are committed.

If the calling process lacks write access to the existing file (because of access control in the file system), then *grfMode* may only specify STGM_READ. STGM_WRITE or STGM_READWRITE. The resulting new open **IStorage** can still be written to, but a commit operation will fail (in transacted mode, write permissions are enforced at commit time).

If *grfMode* specifies STGM_TRANSACTED and no file yet exists with the name specified by *pspec*, then the file is created immediately. In an access controlled file system, the caller must have write permissions in the file system directory in which the compound file is created.

The absence of STGM_TRANSACTED in *grfMode* indicates the file is to be created and opened in direct access mode; any existing file is destroyed before the new file is created.

See Also StgCreateDocfileMac

StgCreateDocfileMac

HRESULT StgCreateDocfileMac(*szFileName, vRefNum, creator, filetype, grfMode, reserved, ppstgOpen***)**
const char * *szFileName*
short *vRefNum*
OSType *creator*
OSType *filetype*
unsigned long *grfMode*
unsigned long *reserved*
IStorage * * *ppstgOpen*

StgCreateDocfileMac creates a new root compound file in the file system with the specified file name.

Parameters

szFileName
Points to the path name of the compound file to create. If NULL, a temporary compound file is allocated with a unique name. The name of an open compound file can be retrieved by calling **IStorage::Stat**.

vRefNum
Specifies the reference number for the disk volume.

creator
Signature resource that specifies the compound files creator.

filetype
Signature resource that specifies the type of the compound file.

grfMode
Specifies the access mode to use when opening the new compound file.

reserved
Reserved for future use; must be zero.

ppstgOpen
If the operation is successful, then *ppstgOpen* points to where the opened storage object is placed (**ppstgOpen*).

Return Values

Value	When Returned
S_OK	Compound file created successfully.
STG_E _INVALIDPARAMETER	The *reserved* parameter has not been set to zero.

Value	When Returned
STG_E _INVALIDFLAG	An invalid flag has been set in *grfMode*.
STG_E _FILEALREADYEXISTS	The STG_FAILIFTHERE flag has been set in *grfMode* and the file already exists.

Comments

Where applicable, applications should call **StgCreateDocfileFSp** instead of **StgCreateDocfileMac**.

Applications should call **StgCreateDocfileMac** when they are using the DLL version of the OLE libraries. Applications using the static version of the OLE libraries should call **StaticStgCreateDocfileMac**. For more information, see the section, "Static and DLL Versions of OLE Functions," in Appendix D, "OLE 2 for the Macintosh: How It Differs from OLE 2 for Windows."

StgCreateDocfileMac creates a file in the same manner as **StgCreateDocfileFSp**. **StgCreateDocfileMac** can be used to create a temporary compound file by passing a NULL value for *szFileName*; these files are temporary only in the sense that they have a system-provided unique name, which may be meaningless to the user.

Unless *grfMode* specifies STGM_DELETEONRELEASE, the caller is responsible for deleting the temporary file when finished with it.

See Also

StgCreateDocfileFSp

StgCreateDocfileOnILockBytes

HRESULT StgCreateDocfileOnILockBytes(*pLkbyt*, *grfMode*, *dwReserved*, *ppStgOpen***)**
LPLOCKBYTES *pLkbyt*
unsigned long *grfMode*
unsigned long *dwReserved*
LPSTORAGE * *ppStgOpen*

StgCreateDocfileOnILockBytes creates and opens a new compound file on top of an **ILockBytes** instance provided by the caller.

Parameters

pLkbyt
Points to the underlying byte array on which to create a compound file.

grfMode
Specifies the access mode to use when opening the new compound file. For more information, see the following comments.

dwReserved
Reserved for future use; must be zero.

ppStgOpen
If the operation is successful, This parameter points to where the opened storage object is placed (**ppStgOpen*).

Return Values

Value	Meaning
S_OK	The compound file was successfully created.
STG_E _ACCESSDENIED	The calling process does not have sufficient access. Attempt to open **ILockBytes** with conflicting permissions to a simultaneous open.
STG_E _FILEALREADYEXISTS	The compound file already exists and *grfMode* is set to STGM_FAILIFTHERE.
STG_S _CONVERTED	The compound file was successfully converted. The original **ILockBytes** was successfully converted to **IStorage** format.
STG_E _INSUFFICIENTMEMORY	Out of memory.
STG_E _INVALIDPOINTER	A bad pointer was in *pLkbyt* or *ppStgOpen*.
STG_E _INVALIDFLAG	A bad flag combination in *grfMode*.
STG_E _TOOMANYOPENFILES	Out of file handles.
File System Errors	Any file system error.
ILockBytes Errors	Any **ILockBytes** error.

Comments

StgCreateDocfileOnILockBytes can be used to store a document in a relational database. The byte array indicated by *pLkbyt* is used for the underlying storage in place of a disk file.

StgCreateDocfileOnILockBytes has almost exactly the same semantics as **StgCreateDocfile**. For more information, see the discussion of **StgCreateDocfile**.

The newly created compound file is opened according to the access modes in *grfMode*. For conversion purposes, the file is always considered to already exist. As a result, it is not useful to use the STGM_FAILIFTHERE value, because it always causes an error to be returned. However, STGM_CREATE and STGM_CONVERT are both still useful.

The ability to build a compound file on top of an **ILockBytes** instance is provided to support having the data (underneath an **IStorage** and **IStream** tree structure) live in persistent space, space that does not ultimately reside in the file system. Given this capability, there is nothing preventing a document that *is* stored in a file from using this facility. For example, a container might do this to minimize the impact on its file format caused by adopting OLE. However, it is recommended that OLE documents adopt the **IStorage** interface for their own outer-level storage. This has the following advantages:

- The storage structure of the document is the same as its storage structure when it is an embedded object, reducing the number of cases the application needs to handle.
- Outside tools can be written to access the embeddings and links within the document without special knowledge of the document's file format. An example of such a tool is a copy utility that copies a whole a web of linked documents. It needs access to the contained links to determine the extent of the web.
- The **IStorage** instance addresses the problem of how to commit the changes to the file. An application using the **ILockBytes** byte array must handle these issues itself.
- Future file systems will likely implement **IStorage** and **IStream** as their native abstractions, rather than layer on top of a byte array as is done in compound files. Such a file system could be built so documents using the **IStorage** interface as their outer level containment structure would get an automatic efficiency gain by having the layering flattened when files are saved on the new file system.

See Also **StgCreateDocfile**

Storage Query Functions

This section describes the OLE API functions used to test whether a file represents a valid storage object or if a pointer to an **ILockBytes** instance contains a storage object.

The following functions are described in storage.h:

```
StgIsStorageFile (const char * pwcsName);
StgIsStorageILockBytes (LPLOCKBYTES pLkbyt);
```

The following functions are described in macapi.H:

```
StgIsStorageFileFSp (const FSSpec *, pFSSpec);
StgIsStorageFileMac (const char * szFileName, short vRefNum);
```

StgIsStorageFile

HRESULT StgIsStorageFile(*pwcsName***)**
const char Far* *pwcsName*

StgIsStorageFile determines whether a particular disk file contains a storage object.

Parameter

pwcsName
Points to the name of the disk file be examined. The *pwcsName* parameter is passed uninterpreted to the underlying file system.

Return Values

Value	Meaning
S_OK	The file contains an **IStorage**.
S_FALSE	The file does not contain an **IStorage** object.
STG_E _INVALIDFILENAME	A bad name was passed in.
STG_E _FILENOTFOUND	The *pwcsName* parameter could not be determined.
File System Errors	Any file system error.

Comment

Where applicable, applications should call **StgIsStorageFileFSp** instead of **StgIsStorageFile**.

At the beginning of the disk file underlying an **IStorage** object is a signature distinguishing the storage object from other file formats. The **StgIsStorageFile** function is useful to applications whose documents use a disk file format that might or might not use storage objects.

StgIsStorageILockBytes can be used in a similar manner, testing an **ILockBytes** byte array to see whether it contains an **IStorage** object.

See Also

StgIsStorageILockBytes

StgIsStorageFileFSp

HRESULT StgIsStorageFileFSp (*pFSSpec*)
const FSSpec* *pFSSpec*

StgIsStorageFileFSp determines if a particular disk file, identified by the specified file system specification record, contains a storage object.

Parameter

pFSSpec
File system specification record that identifies the disk file that is be examined.

Return Values

Value	When Returned
S_TRUE	File system specification record contains a storage object.
S_FALSE	File system specification record does not contain a storage object.
STG_E_UNKNOWN	It was not possible to determine whether or not the file system specification record contains a storage object.
System errors	May return any OsErr system errors.

Comments

Applications should call **StgIsStorageFileFSp** when they are using the DLL version of the OLE libraries. Applications using the static version of the OLE libraries should call **StaticStgIsStorageFileFSp**. For more information, see the section, "Static and DLL Versions of OLE Functions," in Appendix D, "OLE 2 for the Macintosh: How It Differs from OLE 2 for Windows."

See Also

StgIsStorageILockBytes, **StgIsStorageFileMac**

StgIsStorageFileMac

HRESULT StgIsStorageFileMac (*szFileName, vRefNum*)
const char * *szFileName*
short *vRefNum*

StgIsStorageFileMac determines if a particular disk file contains a storage object.

Parameter

szFileName
Points to the name of the disk file that is be examined; *szFileName* is passed uninterpreted to the underlying file system.

vRefNum
Specifies the volume reference number that identifies the disk volume.

Return Values

Value	When Returned
S_TRUE	File contains a storage object.
S_FALSE	File does not contain a storage object.

Value	When Returned
STG_E_UNKNOWN	It was not possible to determine whether or not the file contains a storage object.
System errors	May return any OsErr system errors.

Comment

Where applicable, applications should call **StgIsStorageFileFSp** instead of **StgIsStorageFileMac**.

Applications should call **StgIsStorageFileMac** when they are using the DLL version of the OLE libraries. Applications using the static version of the OLE libraries should call **StaticStgIsStorageFileFSp**. For more information, see the section, "Static and DLL Versions of OLE Functions," in Appendix D, "OLE 2 for the Macintosh: How It Differs from OLE 2 for Windows."

StgIsStorageFileMac is useful to applications whose documents use a disk file format that may or may not use storage objects. At the beginning of the disk file that underlies a storage object is a signature that distinguishes the file format of a storage object from other file formats.

The **StgIsStorageILockBytes** and **StgIsStorageFileFSp** functions can be used in a similar manner, testing an **ILockBytes** byte array or a file system specification record to see if they contain a storage object.

See Also

StgIsStorageILockBytes, **StgIsStorageFileFSp**

StgIsStorageILockBytes

HRESULT StgIsStorageILockBytes(*pLkbyt***)**
LPLOCKBYTES *pLkbyt*

StgIsStorageILockBytes determines whether or not a given **ILockBytes** byte array contains a storage object.

Parameters

pLkbyt
Points to the **ILockBytes** byte array to be examined.

Return Values

Value	Meaning
S_OK	The *pLkbyt* parameter contains an **IStorage** object.
S_FALSE	The *pLkbyt* parameter does not contain an **IStorage** object.

Comment

At the beginning of the **ILockBytes** byte array underlying a storage object is a signature distinguishing an **IStorage** object from other file formats. **StgIsStorageILockBytes** is useful to applications whose documents use an **ILockBytes** byte array format that might or might not use storage objects.

StgIsStorageFile can be used in a similar manner, testing a disk file to see whether it contains a storage object.

See Also **StgIsStorageFile**

Input/Output Storage Functions

This section describes the functions used to support the retrieval of data from an **IStorage**, **IStream**, or **ILockBytes** object or the saving of data to objects of those types.

The following functions are defined in storage.h:

```
HRESULT GetClassFile (const char * szFilename, LPCLSID pclsid);
HRESULT GetClassFSp(const FSSpec * pFSSpec, CLSID * pclsid);
HRESULT GetHGlobalFromILockBytes (LPLOCKBYTES pLkbyt, Handle * phglobal);
HRESULT GetHGlobalFromStream (LPSTREAM pstm, Handle * phglobal);
HRESULT ReadClassStg(LPSTORAGE pStg, LPCLSID pclsid);
HRESULT ReadClassStm(LPSTREAM pStm, LPCLSID pclsid);
HRESULT ReadFmtUserTypeStg (LPSTORAGE pStg, unsigned long * pcf, char * * ppszUserType);
HRESULT StgOpenStorage(const char * pwcsName, LPSTORAGE ppStg, unsigned long grfMode,
    SNB snbExclude, unsigned long dwReserved, LPSTORAGE  *ppStgOpen);
HRESULT StgOpenStorageOnILockBytes(LPLOCKBYTES pLkbyt, LPSTORAGE ppStg,
    unsigned long grfMode, SNB snbExclude, unsigned long dwReserved, LPSTORAGE  *ppStgOpen);
HRESULT StgSetTimes(char const * lpszName, FILETIME const * pctime,
    FILETIME const * patime, FILETIME const * pmtime);
HRESULT WriteClassStg(LPSTORAGE pStg, REFCLSID rclsid);
HRESULT WriteClassStm(LPSTREAM pStm, REFCLSID rclsid);
HRESULT WriteFmtUserTypeStg (LPSTORAGE pStg, unsigned long cf, char * pszUserType);
```

The following functions are defined in macapi.H:

```
HRESULT ReadOle1FmtProgIDStgMac(IStorage* pstg, char** ppszOle1ProgID);
HRESULT StgOpenStorageFSp (const FSSpec * pFSSpec, IStorage * pStgPriority, unsigned long grfMode,
    SNB snbExclude, unsigned long reserved, IStorage * * ppStgOpen);
HRESULT StgOpenStorageMac (const char *pszFileName, short vRefNum, IStorage * pStgPriority,
    const unsigned long grfMode, SNB snbExclude, unsigned long reserved,
    IStorage * * ppStgOpen);
HRESULT StgSetTimesMac (const char * lpszName, short vRefNum, long dirID, const FILETIME * pctime,
    const FILETIME * patime, const FILETIME * pmtime);
HRESULT StgSetTimesFSp (const FSSpec * pFSSpec, const FILETIME * pctime, const FILETIME * patime,
    const FILETIME * pmtime);
HRESULT StgGetFrefFromIStorage (const IStorage * pStg, short * pFRefNum);
HRESULT StgGetFSpFromIStorage (const IStorage * pStg, FSSpec * pFSSpec);
HRESULT WriteOle1FmtProgIDStgMac(IStorage* pstg, const char* pszOle1ProgID);
```

GetClassFile

HRESULT GetClassFile(*lpszFileName, pclsid***)**
const char * *lpszFileName*
LPCLSID *pclsid*

GetClassFile returns the CLSID associated with the given filename.

Parameters

szFileName
Points to the filename from which the CLSID is to be retrieved.

pclsid
Points to where to return the CLSID.

Return Values

Value	Meaning
S_OK	The CLSID was successfully returned.
MK_E_CANTOPENFILE	Unable to open the specified file name.
MK_E_INVALIDEXTENSION	The specified extension in the Registration Database file is invalid.
System errors	Any system error.

Comments

Where applicable, applications should call **GetClassFSp** instead of **GetClassFile**.

GetClassFile locates the CLSID for the code that can work with the specified file. For example, when a link to a file-based document is activated, the file moniker uses the returned CLSID to locate the link source's application.

The following strategies are used to determine the appropriate CLSID:

1. If the file is an OLE compound file, **GetClassFile** internally calls **ReadClassStg** to get and return the CLSID saved with **IStorage::SetClass**.
2. The file creator and file type (as indicated by the Finder Info) are used as a key to the Registration Database file. If a CLSID value is found under that key, then **GetClassFile** returns that value as the CLSID.
3. As a last resort, **GetClassFile** tries to use a three letter file extension to find a file's class.
4. If none of the above methods work, **GetClassFile** returns MK_E_INVALIDEXTENSION.

For information on registering information in the Registration Database file, see Chapter 4, "Registering Object Applications."

See Also

IStorage::SetClass, **ReadClassStg**, **WriteClassStg**

GetClassFSp

HRESULT GetClassFSp(*pFSSpec, pclsid***)**
const FSSpec * *pFSSpec*
CLSID * *pclsid*

GetClassFSp returns the CLSID associated with the given file specification.

Parameters

pFSSpec
Points to the file specification from which the CLSID is to be retrieved.

pclsid
Points to where to return the CLSID.

Return Values

Value	Meaning
S_OK	The CLSID was successfully returned.
MK_E_ CANTOPENFILE	Unable to open the specified file specification.
MK_E_ INVALIDEXTENSION	The specified extension in the Registration Database file is invalid.
System errors	Any system error.

Comments

GetClassFSp locates the CLSID for the code that can work with the specified file specification. For example, when a link to a file-specification-based document is activated, the file moniker uses the returned CLSID to locate the link source's application.

The following strategies are used to determine the appropriate CLSID:

1. If the file specification is an OLE compound file, **GetClassFSp** internally calls **ReadClassStg** to get and return the CLSID saved with **IStorage::SetClass**.
2. The file creator and file type (as indicated by the Finder Info) are used as a key to the Registration Database file. If a CLSID value is found under that key, then **GetClassFSp** returns that value as the CLSID.
3. If the file specification is not a storage object, **GetClassFSp** attempts to match various bits in the data fork of the file specification against a pattern.
4. As a last resort, **GetClassFSp** tries to use a three letter file extension to find a file's class.
5. If none of the above methods works, **GetClassFSp** returns MK_E_INVALIDEXTENSION.

See Also

GetClassFile

GetHGlobalFromILockBytes

HRESULT GetHGlobalFromILockBytes(*pLkbyt*, *phglobal***)**
LPLOCKBYTES *pLkbyt*
Handle * *phglobal*

GetHGlobalFromILockBytes returns a global memory handle to an **ILockBytes** instance created using **CreateILockBytesOnHGlobal**.

Parameters

pLkbyt
Points to the **ILockBytes** instance for which the handle is being returned.

phglobal
Points to the current memory handle used by this **ILockBytes** instance.

Return Values

Value	Meaning
S_OK	The handle was returned successfully.
E_INVALIDARG	Invalid value specified for *pLkbyt*. It can also indicate that the **ILockBytes** passed in is not one created by **CreateILockBytesOnHGlobal**.
System errors	Any system error.

Comments

The handle returned might be different from the original handle due to the need for handle resizing. The contents of the returned memory can be written to a clean disk file, and opened as a storage object using **StgOpenStorage**.

See Also

StgOpenStorage

GetHGlobalFromStream

HRESULT GetHGlobalFromStream(*pStm*, *phglobal***)**
LPSTREAM *pStm*
Handle * *phglobal*

GetHGlobalFromStream returns a global memory handle to a stream created using **CreateStreamOnHGlobal**.

Parameters

pStm
Points to the stream created by **CreateStreamOnHGlobal**.

phglobal
Points to the current memory handle used by this stream.

Return Values

Value	Meaning
S_OK	The handle was successfully returned.
E_INVALIDARG	Invalid value for *pstm*. In addition to the usual E_INVALIDARG cases, if the **IStream** passed in is not one created by **CreateStreamOnHGlobal**.

Value	Meaning
System errors	Any system error.

Comments The returned handle might be different than the original handle.

See Also **CreateStreamOnHGlobal**

ReadClassStg

HRESULT ReadClassStg(*pStg, pclsid***)**
LPSTORAGE *pStg*
LPCLSID *pclsid*

ReadClassStg returns the CLSID retrieved from a previous call to **IStorage::Stat**.

Parameters

pStg
Points to the **IStorage** instance containing the CLSID to be returned.

pclsid
Points to where to return the CLSID. May return CLSID_NULL.

Return Values

Value	Meaning
S_OK	The CLSID was returned successfully.
E_OUTOFMEMORY	The CLSID could not be returned due to lack of memory.
IStorage::Stat errors.	Can also return any of the error codes from **IStorage::Stat**.
System errors	Any system error.

See Also **OleLoad, WriteClassStg**

ReadClassStm

HRESULT ReadClassStm(*pStm, pclsid***)**
LPSTREAM *pStm*
CLSID * *pclsid*

ReadClassStm returns an object's CLSID from the stream.

Parameters

pStm
Points to the stream from which the CLSID is to be read.

pclsid
Points to where to return the CLSID.

Return Values

Value	Meaning
S_OK	The CLSID was successfully returned.
STG_E _READFAULT	End of file was reached.
IStream::Read errors.	Can return any of the error codes from **IStream::Read**.
System errors	Any system error.

Comments

The returned CLSID must have been previously written to the stream with **WriteClassStm**.

Most applications do not call **ReadClassStm**. OLE calls it before making a call to an application's **IPersistStream::Load** implementation.

See Also

WriteClassStm, **ReadClassStg**, **WriteClassStg**

ReadFmtUserTypeStg

HRESULT ReadFmtUserTypeStg(*pStg*, *pcf*, *lplpszUserType***)**
LPSTORAGE *pStg*
unsigned long * *pcf*
char * * *lplpszUserType*

ReadFmtUserTypeStg returns the clipboard format and user type saved with **WriteFmtUserTypeStg**.

Parameters

pStg
Points to the object's **IStorage** instance from which the information is to be read.

pcf
Points to where to return the clipboard format. It can be NULL, indicating the format is of no interest to the caller.

lplpszUserType
Points to where to return the user type. It can be NULL, indicating the user type is of no interest to the caller.

Return Values

Value	Meaning
S_OK	The information was read successfully.
E_OUTOFMEMORY	Out of memory.
E_FAIL	**WriteFmtUserTypeStg** was never called on the object.
IStream::Read errors.	Can return any of the error codes from **IStream::Read**.

Comments

WriteClassStg must have been previously called before calling **ReadFmtUserTypeStg**.

The *lplpszUserType* pointer is allocated and filled in by the callee and later freed by the caller. The following code illustrates how to free *lplpszUserType* using the standard allocator, **CoGetMalloc**:

```
LPMALLOC pMalloc;
CoGetMalloc(MEMCTX_TASK, &pMalloc);
pMalloc->Free(lplpszUserType);
pMalloc->Release();
```

See Also

WriteFmtUserTypeStg, **CoGetMalloc**

ReadOle1FmtProgIDStgMac

HRESULT ReadOle1FmtProgIDStgMac(*pstg*, *ppszOle1ProgID*)
IStorage* *pstg*
char** *ppszOle1ProgID*

ReadOle1FmtProgIDStgMac reads the ProgID of the OLE1 object application to define the layout of the native data stored in the "\1Ole10Native" stream of the storage containing the embedded OLE 1 object.

Parameters

pstg
Points to the storage object from which the data is to be read.

ppszOle1FmtProgID
On return, points to the ProgID of the OLE 1 object application corresponding to the layout of the native data.

Return Values

Value	Meaning
E_FAIL	The tagged format of the storage is not OLE1.
May also return errors from **ReadFmtUserTypeStg**.	
System errors	Any system error.

Comments

WriteOle1FmtProgIDStgMac must have been previously called before calling **ReadOle1FmtProgIDStgMac**.

Calling **ReadFmtUserTypeStg**(*pstg*, *&cf*, ...) on a storage containing an OLE 1 embedded object whose native data is stored in the "\1Ole10Native" stream returns "cf = OLE1." In this case, **ReadOle1FmtProgIDStgMac**() returns the ProgID of the OLE 1 object application that corresponds to the layout of the native data found.

This differs from Windows, where **ReadFmtUserTypeStg**() returns "cf = <**RegisterClipboardFormat**(*Ole1ProgID*)>," and **GetClipboardFormatName**(*cf*) returns the ProgID.

The *pszOle1FmtProgID* pointer is allocated and filled in by the callee and later freed by the caller. The following code illustrates how to free *pszOle1FmtProgID* using the standard allocator, **CoGetMalloc**:

```
LPMALLOC pMalloc;
CoGetMalloc(MEMCTX_TASK, &pMalloc);
pMalloc->Free(pszOle1FmtProgID);
pMalloc->Release();
```

See Also **WriteOle1FmtProgIDStgMac**, **CoGetMalloc**

StgOpenStorage

HRESULT StgOpenStorage(*pwcsName, ppStg, grfMode, snbExclude, dwReserved, ppStgOpen*)
const char * *pwcsName*
LPSTORAGE *ppStg*
unsigned long *grfMode*
SNB *snbExclude*
unsigned long *dwReserved*
LPSTORAGE * *ppStgOpen*

StgOpenStorage opens an existing storage object in the file system.

Parameter

pwcsName
Points to the path of the storage object to open. If *ppStg* is non-NULL, *pwcsName* is ignored. In this case, the name is inferred from the location of *ppStg*.

ppStg
Points to a previous opening of a root storage object (usually, one that was opened in priority mode) or NULL, which is most often the case.

If *ppStg* is non-NULL, the storage object is closed and reopened according to *grfMode*. After **StgOpenStorage** returns, the **IStorage** instance contained in *ppStg* on function entry is invalid, and can no longer be used. The caller should use *ppStgOpen* instead.

grfMode
Specifies the access mode to use to open the storage object. For more information, see the following comments.

snbExclude
A non-NULL *snbExclude* points to a block of elements in this storage to be emptied as the storage is opened. This exclusion occurs independently of whether a snapshot copy happens on the open object. It can be NULL, indicating nothing is to be excluded.

dwReserved
Reserved for future use; must be zero.

ppStgOpen
If the operation is successful, *ppStgOpen* points to where the opened object is placed (**ppStgOpen*).

Return Values

Value	Meaning
S_OK	The storage object was successfully opened.
STG_ E_FILENOTFOUND	The file does not exist.
STG_E _ACCESSDENIED	Insufficient access to open file. Exclusions specified without read-write permissions or attempt to open file with conflicting permissions to a simultaneous open.
STG_E _FILEALREADYEXISTS	The file exists but is not a storage object.
STG_E _TOOMANYOPENFILES	Cannot open another file.
STG_E _INSUFFICIENTMEMORY	Out of memory.
STG_E _INVALIDNAME	Bad name in *pwcsName* or *snbExclude*.
STG_E _INVALIDPOINTER	Bad pointer in *snbExclude*, *pwcsName*, *ppStg*, or *ppStgOpen*.
STG_E _INVALIDFLAG	Bad flag combination in *grfMode*.
STG_E _INVALIDFUNCTION	STGM_DELETEONRELEASE specified in *grfMode*.
STG_E _TOOMANYOPENFILES	Out of file handles.
STG_E _OLDDLL	The DLL being used to open this Storage is a version prior to the one used to create it.
STG_E _OLDFORMAT	The storage being opened was created by the Beta 1 **IStorage** provider. This format is no longer supported.
System errors	Any system error.

Comments

Where applicable, applications should call **StgOpenStorageFSp** instead of **StgOpenStorage**.

Opening a storage object in read and/or write mode without denying write permission to others (*grfMode* set to STGM_SHARE_DENY_WRITE) can be expensive because **StgOpenStorage** must make a snapshot copy of the entire storage object.

Applications often try to open storage objects with the following access permissions:

```
STGM_READWRITE | STGM_SHARE_DENY_WRITE
        // transacted vs. direct mode omitted for exposition
```

If the call is successful, a snapshot copy need never be made. If it fails, the application can either revert to using STGM_READWRITE and have a snapshot copy made or use the following permissions:

```
STGM_READ | STGM_SHARE_DENY_WRITE
        // transacted vs. direct mode omitted for exposition
```

In the former case, the application should prompt the user before doing an expensive copy. In the latter case, if the call succeeds, a snapshot copy will not have been made because STGM_SHARE_DENY_WRITE was specified, denying others write access.

To reduce the expense of making a snapshot copy, applications can use priority mode (*grfMode* set to STGM_PRIORITY).

The *snbExclude* parameter specifies a set of element names in the storage object to be emptied as the storage object is opened. Streams are set to a length of zero and storage objects have all their elements removed. By excluding certain streams, the expense of making a snapshot copy can be significantly reduced. Almost always, this paradigm is used after first opening the storage object in priority mode, after which the now-excluded elements are read into memory. This earlier priority mode opening of the storage object should be passed through *ppStg* so the exclusion implied by priority mode is now removed. The caller is responsible for rewriting the contents of excluded items before committing. This technique is only useful for applications whose documents do not require constant access to their storage while they are active.

See Also **StgOpenStorageOnILockBytes**

StgOpenStorageFSp

HRESULT StgOpenStorageFSp(*pFSSpec, pstgPriority, grfMode, snbExclude, reserved, ppstgOpen***)**
const FSSpec * *pSpec*
IStorage * *pstgPriority*
const unsigned long *grfMode*
SNB *snbExclude*
unsigned long *reserved*
IStorage * * *ppstgOpen*

StgOpenStorageFSp opens an existing storage object in the file system.

Parameter

pFSSpec
Points to the file system specification record that identifies the storage object to open.

pstgPriority
Most often NULL. A non-NULL *pstgPriority* points to a previous opening of a root storage object, most often one that was opened in priority-mode.

grfMode
Specifies the access mode to use to open the storage object.

snbExclude
A non-NULL *snbExclude* points to a block of elements in this storage that are to be emptied as the object is opened. This exclusion occurs independent of whether a snapshot copy happens on the open. May be NULL.

reserved
Reserved for future use; must be zero.

ppstgOpen
If the operation is successful, then *ppstgOpen* points to where the opened storage is placed (**ppstgOpen*).

Return Values

Value	When Returned
S_TRUE	File contains a storage object.
S_FALSE	File does not contain a storage object.
STG_E_UNKNOWN	It was not possible to determine whether or not the file contains a storage object.
System errors	Any system error.

Comments

Applications should call **StgOpenStorageFSp** when they are using the DLL version of the OLE libraries. Applications using the static version of the OLE libraries should call **StaticStgOpenStorageFSp**. For more information, see the section, "Static and DLL Versions of OLE Functions," in Appendix D, "OLE 2 for the Macintosh: How It Differs from OLE 2 for Windows."

If *pstgPriority* is non-NULL, the container should close the storage object and reopen it according to *grfMode*. When **StgOpenStorageFSp** returns, the container should use the storage object contained in *ppstgOpen* because *pstgPriority* is no longer valid.

Opening a storage object in read and/or write mode without denying write permission to others (*grfMode* specifies STGM_SHARE_DENY_WRITE) can be expensive since **StgOpenStorageMac** must make a snapshot of the entire storage object. (For more information on opening a storage object with the STGM_SHARE_DENY_WRITE flag, see "Access Permission Flags" earlier in this chapter.

Applications will often try to open storage objects with one of the following sets of permissions (transacted vs. direct mode is omitted for exposition) to avoid making a snapshot copy:

```
STGM_READWRITE | STGM_SHARE_DENY_WRITE or
STGM_READ | STGM_SHARE_DENY_WRITE
```

If the open fails, the application can revert to opening the storage object using STGM_READWRITE and accepting the overhead involved in the snapshot copy. However, the application should prompt the user before beginning the copy.

To reduce the expense of making a snapshot copy, applications can open storage objects in priority mode (*grfMode* specifies STGM_PRIORITY) or use *snbExclude* to exclude certain streams or storages from the open process. The *snbExclude* parameter specifies a set of element names in this storage object that are to be emptied as the storage object is opened: streams are set to a length of zero; storage objects will have all of their elements removed.

This paradigm will typically be used after first opening the storage object in priority mode, then completely reading the now-excluded elements into memory. This earlier priority mode opening of the storage object should be passed through *pStgPriority* to remove the exclusion implied by priority mode.

The calling application is responsible for rewriting the contents of excluded items before committing. This technique is only useful for applications whose documents do not require constant access to their storage while they are active.

See Also **StgOpenStorageMac**

StgOpenStorageMac

HRESULT StgOpenStorageMac(*pszFileName, vRefNum, pstgPriority, grfMode, snbExclude, reserved, ppstgOpen*)

const char * *pszFileName*
short *vRefNum*
IStorage * *pstgPriority*
const unsigned long *grfMode*
SNB *snbExclude*
unsigned long *reserved*
IStorage * * *ppstgOpen*

StgOpenStorageMac opens an existing storage object in the file system.

Parameters

pszFileName
Points to the path name of the storage object to open. *pszFileName* is ignored if *pstgPriority* is non-NULL; in this case, the name is inferred from the location of *pstgPriority*.

vRefNum
Specifies the volume reference number that identifies the disk volume.

pstgPriority
A non-NULL value points to a previous opening of a root storage object, most often one that was opened in priority-mode. Most often NULL.

grfMode
Specifies the access mode to use to open the storage object.

snbExclude
A non-NULL *snbExclude* points to a block of elements in this storage that are to be emptied when the storage is opened. This exclusion occurs independent of whether a snapshot copy happens on the open. May be NULL.

reserved
Reserved for future use; must be zero.

ppstgOpen
If the operation is successful, then *ppstgOpen* points to where the opened storage is placed (**ppstgOpen*).

Return Values

Value	When Returned
S_OK	Storage object successfully opened.
STG_E_FILENOTFOUND	File name specified in *pszFileName* does not exist.

Value	When Returned
STG_E_FILEALREADYEXISTS	File name specified in *pszFileName* is not a storage object.
System errors	Any system error.

Comments

Where applicable, applications should call **StgOpenStorageFSp** instead of **StgOpenStorageMac**.

Applications should call **StgOpenStorageMac** when they are using the DLL version of the OLE libraries. Applications using the static version of the OLE libraries should call **StaticStgOpenStorageMac**. For more information, see the section, "Static and DLL Versions of OLE Functions," in Appendix D, "OLE 2 for the Macintosh: How It Differs from OLE 2 for Windows."

If *pstgPriority* is non-NULL, the container should close the storage object and reopen it according to *grfMode*. When **StgOpenStorageMac** returns, the container should use the storage contained in *ppstgOpen* because *pstgPriority* is no longer valid.

For more information, refer to the description of **StgOpenStorageFSp**.

See Also

StgOpenStorageFSp

StgOpenStorageOnILockBytes

HRESULT StgOpenStorageOnILockBytes (*pLkbyt, ppStg, grfMode, snbExclude, dwReserved, ppStgOpen***)**
LPLOCKBYTES *pLkbyt*
LPSTORAGE *ppStg*
unsigned long *grfMode*
SNB *snbExclude*
unsigned long *dwReserved*
LPSTORAGE * *ppStgOpen*

StgOpenStorageOnILockBytes opens an existing storage object that does not reside in a disk file, but instead lives in an **ILockBytes** instance provided by the caller.

Parameters

pLkbyt
Points to the underlying byte array that contains the storage object in which the compound file lives.

ppStg
Most often NULL. A non-NULL *ppStg* points to a previous opening of a root storage object, most often one that was opened in priority-mode.

grfMode
Specifies the access mode to use to open the storage object; see **StgOpenStorage** earlier in this chapter.

snbExclude
A non-NULL *snbExclude* points to a block of elements in this storage to be emptied as the object is opened. This exclusion occurs independently of whether a snapshot copy happens on the open storage object. It can be NULL, indicating nothing is to be excluded.

dwReserved
Reserved for future use; must be zero.

ppStgOpen
If the operation is successful, the *ppStgOpen* parameter points to where the opened storage is placed (**ppStgOpen*).

Return Values

Value	Meaning
S_OK	**IStorage** object successfully opened.
STG_E _FILENOTFOUND	Byte array does not contain a storage object.
STG_E _ACCESSDENIED	Insufficient access. Exclusions specified without read-write permissions or attempt to open file with conflicting permissions to a simultaneous open.
STG_E_TOOMANY-OPENFILES	Cannot open another file.
E_OUTOFMEMORY	Not enough memory to open **IStorage** object.
STG_E _INSUFFICIENTMEMORY	Out of memory.
STG_E_INVALIDNAME	Bad name in *snbExclude*.
STG_E_INVALIDPOINTER	Bad pointer in *snbExclude*, *pLkbyt*, *ppStg*, or *ppStgOpen*.
STG_E_INVALIDFLAG	Bad flag combination in *grfMode*.
STG_E_INVALID-FUNCTION	STGM_DELETEONRELEASE specified in *grfMode*.
STG_E _TOOMANYOPENFILES	Out of file handles.
STG_E_OLDDLL	The DLL being used to open this storage is a version prior to the one used to create it.
STG_E_OLDFORMAT	The storage being opened was created by the Beta 1 **IStorage** provider. This format is no longer supported.

Value	Meaning
System errors	Any system error.
ILockBytes Errors	Any **ILockBytes** error.

Comments

The storage object must have been previously created by calling **StgCreateDocfileOnILockBytes**. If *pLkbyt* currently contains an **IStorage**, that object is opened according to the access modes in *grfMode* and returned through *ppStgOpen*.

The semantics of **StgOpenStorageOnILockBytes** are almost exactly the same as those of **StgOpenStorage**.

See Also

StgOpenStorage

StgSetTimes

HRESULT StgSetTimes(*lpszName*, *pctime*, *patime*, *pmtime***)**
char const * *lpszName*
FILETIME const * *pctime*
FILETIME const * *patime*
FILETIME const * *pmtime*

StgSetTimes sets the creation, access, and modification times of the indicated file, if supported by the underlying file system.

Parameters

lpszName
Points to the name of the file to change.

pctime
Points to the new creation time.

patime
Points to the new access time.

pmtime
Points to the new modification time.

Return Values

Value	Meaning
S_OK	Time values successfully set.
STG_E_FILENOTFOUND	Element does not exist.
STG_E_INVALIDNAME	Bad name passed in *lpszName*, or a file system error.
STG_E_ACCESSDENIED	Insufficient permissions to access storage.
System errors	Any system error.

Comments

Where applicable, applications should call **StgSetTimesFSp** instead of **StgSetTimes**.

Each of the time value parameters can be NULL, indicating no modification should occur.

It is possible that one or more of these time values are not supported by the underlying file system. **IStorage::SetElementTimes** sets the times that can be set and ignores the rest.

StgSetTimesMac

HRESULT StgSetTimesMac (*lpszName, vRefNum, dirID, pcTime, patime, pmtime*)
const char * *szFileName*
short *vRefNum*
long *dir ID*
const FILETIME * *pctime*
const FILETIME * *patime*
const FILETIME * *pmtime*

StgSetTimesMac sets the creation, access, and modification times of the indicated file.

Parameter

lpszName
Points to the name of the disk file on which the time is to be set; *szFileName* is passed uninterpreted to the underlying file system.

vRefNum
Specifies the volume reference number that identifies the disk volume.

dirID
Specifies the parent directory ID of the disk volume; can be zero.

pctime
Points to the new creation time.

patime
Points to the new access time.

pmtime
Points to the new modification time.

Return Values

Value	Meaning
S_OK	Time values successfully set.
STG_E_FILENOTFOUND	Element does not exist.
STG_E_INVALIDNAME	Bad name passed in *lpszName*, or a file system error.

Value	Meaning
STG_E_ACCESSDENIED	Insufficient permissions to access storage.
System errors	Any system error.

Comment

Where applicable, applications should call **StgSetTimesFSp** instead of **StgSetTimesMac**.

Applications should call **StgSetTimesMac** when they are using the DLL version of the OLE libraries. Applications using the static version of the OLE libraries should call **StaticStgSetTimesMac**. For more information, see the section, "Static and DLL Versions of OLE Functions," in Appendix D, "OLE 2 for the Macintosh: How It Differs from OLE 2 for Windows."

Except for taking a volume reference and a parent directory ID, this function is functionally equivalent to **StgSetTimes**.

StgSetTimesFSp

HRESULT StgSetTimesFSp (*lpszName, pcTime, patime, pmtime*)
const FSSpec * *szName*
const FILETIME * *pctime*
const FILETIME * *patime*
const FILETIME * *pmtime*

StgSetTimesFSp sets the creation, access, and modification times of the file specification.

Parameter

lpszName
Points to the name of the file specification on which the time is to be set; *szFileName* is passed uninterpreted to the underlying file system.

pctime
Points to the new creation time.

patime
Points to the new access time.

pmtime
Points to the new modification time.

Return Values

Value	Meaning
S_OK	Time values successfully set.
STG_E_FILENOTFOUND	Element does not exist.
STG_E_INVALIDNAME	Bad fsspec passed in *pFSSpec*, or a file system error.

Value	Meaning
STG_E_ACCESSDENIED	Insufficient permissions to access storage.
System errors	Any system error.

Comment

Applications should call **StgSetTimesFSp** when they are using the DLL version of the OLE libraries. Applications using the static version of the OLE libraries should call **StaticStgSetTimesFSp**. For more information, see the section, "Static and DLL Versions of OLE Functions," in Appendix D, "OLE 2 for the Macintosh: How It Differs from OLE 2 for Windows."

For optimum use with file specifications and volume names on the Macintosh, applications should use (in this order) the following functions: **StgSetTimesFSp**, **StgSetTimesMac**, or **StgSetTimes**.

WriteClassStg

HRESULT WriteClassStg(*pStg*, *rclsid*)
LPSTORAGE *pStg*
REFCLSID *rclsid*

WriteClassStg writes the specified CLSID to the specified **IStorage** instance.

Parameters

pStg
Points to the object's **IStorage** instance.

rclsid
Points to the CLSID to be stored with the object.

Return Values

Value	Meaning
S_OK	CLSID returned successfully.
STG_E_MEDIUMFULL	CLSID could not be set due to lack of memory.
IStorage::SetClass errors.	Can return any of the error codes from **IStorage::SetClass**.
System errors	Any system error.

Comments

Containers typically call **WriteClassStg** before calling **IPersistStorage::Save**.

See Also

OleSave, **ReadClassStg**

WriteClassStm

HRESULT WriteClassStm(*pStm, clsid***)**
LPSTREAM *pStm*
REFCLSID *rclsid*

WriteClassStm writes the indicated CLSID to the stream.

Parameters

pStm
Points to the stream into which the CLSID is to be written.

clsid
Specifies the CLSID to write to the stream.

Return Values

Value	Meaning
S_OK	CLSID successfully written.
STG_E_MEDIUMFULL	No space left on device.
IStream::Write errors.	Can also return any of the error codes from **IStream::Write**.
System errors	Any system error.

Comments

WriteClassStm writes the CLSID in a way that it can be retrieved by **ReadClassStm**.

Most applications do not call **WriteClassStm**. OLE calls it before making a call to an application's **IPersistStream::Save** implementation.

See Also

ReadClassStm, **WriteClassStg**, **ReadClassStg**

WriteFmtUserTypeStg

HRESULT WriteFmtUserTypeStg(*pStg, cFormat, lpszUserType***)**
LPSTORAGE *pStg*
unsigned long *cFormat*
char * *lpszUserType*

WriteFmtUserTypeStg writes the specified clipboard format and current user type to the specified **IStorage** instance.

Parameters

pStg
Points to the **IStorage** instance where the information is to be written.

cFormat
Specifies the clipboard format that describes the structure of the native area of the **IStorage** instance. The format tag includes the policy for the names of streams and substorages within this storage and rules for interpreting data within those streams.

lpszUserType
Points to the object's current user type. It cannot be NULL. This is the type returned by **IOleObject::GetUserType**. If this function is transported to a remote machine where the object class does not exist, this persistently stored user type can be shown to the user in dialog boxes.

Return Values

Value	Meaning
S_OK	The information was written successfully.
STG_E_MEDIUMFULL	Information could not be written due to lack of space on the storage medium.
System errors	Any system error.
IStream::Write errors.	

Comments

WriteClassStg must be called before calling **WriteFmtUserTypeStg**.

WriteFmtUserTypeStg must be called in an object's implementation of **IPersistStorage::Save** and by document-level objects that use structured storage for their persistent representation in their save sequence.

To read the information saved, applications call **ReadFmtUserTypeStg**.

See Also

WriteClassStg, **IPersistStorage::Save**, **ReadFmtUserTypeStg**

WriteOle1FmtProgIDStgMac

HRESULT WriteOle1FmtProgIDStgMac(*pstg*, *pszOle1ProgID*)
IStorage* *pstg*
const char* *pszOle1ProgID*

WriteOle1FmtProgIDStgMac writes to storage the ProgID of the OLE 1 object application to define the layout of the native data stored in the "\1Ole10Native" stream of a storage containing an embedded OLE 1 object.

Parameters

pstg
Points to the storage object where the ProgID is to be written.

szOle1FmtProgID
Contains the ProgID of the OLE 1 object application that corresponds to the layout of the native data. If NULL, then the previously stored OLe1FmtProgID is removed.

Return Values

Value	Meaning
E_FAIL	The tagged format is not OLE1.
May also return errors from **ReadFmtUserTypeStg** and **IStream::Write**.	
System errors	Any system error.

Comments

WriteOle1FmtProgIDStgMac is provided for completeness. If an application wants to directly save an object in the OLE 1 format of an OLE 1 object application (rarely done, if ever), it would write the appropriate native data in the "\1Ole10Native" stream, call **WriteFmtUserTypeStg**(*pstg*, '*OLE1*', ...), and then call **WriteOle1FmtProgIDStgMac**(*pstg*, *szOle1FmtProgID*).

ReadOle1FmtProgIDStgMac is called to read the ProgID written by **WriteOleFmtProgIDStgMac**.

See Also

ReadOle1FmtProgIDStgMac

StgGetFRefFromIStorage

HRESULT StgGetFRefFromIStorage(*pStg, pFRefNum)*
const IStorage * *pStg;*
short * *pFRefNum*;

StgGetFRefFromIStorage returns a file reference number that identifies the specified storage object.

Parameters

pStg
Points to the storage object that is to be examined.

pFRefNum
Points to the file reference number that is returned.

Return Values

Value	When Returned
S_OK	Successful conversion.
STG_E_INVALIDPOINTER	Either *pSpec* or *pStg* is NULL.
STG_E_INVALIDARG	*pStg* does not point to a root storage object.
System errors	Any system error.

Comment

Applications should call **StgGetFRefFromIStorage** when they are using the DLL version of the OLE libraries. Applications using the static version of the OLE libraries should call **StaticStgGetFRefFromIStorage**. For more information, see the section, "Static and DLL Versions of OLE Functions," in Appendix D, "OLE 2 for the Macintosh: How It Differs from OLE 2 for Windows."

StgGetFRefFromIStorage only works with pointers that point to root storage objects.

See Also **StgGetFSpFromIStorage**

StgGetFSpFromIStorage

HRESULT StgGetFSpFromIStorage(*pStg, pFSSpec*)
const ISTORAGE * *pStg;*
FSSpec * *pFSSpec*;

StgGetFSpFromIStorage returns a file system specification record that identifies the specified storage object.

Parameters

pStg
Points to the storage object that is to be examined.

pFSSpec
Points to the file system specification record that is returned.

Return Values

Value	When Returned
S_OK	Successful conversion.
STG_E_INVALIDPOINTER	Either *pSpec* or *pStg* is NULL.
STG_E_INVALIDARG	*pStg* does not point to a root storage object.
System errors	Any system error.

Comment

Applications should call **StgGetFSpFromIStorage** when they are using the DLL version of the OLE libraries. Applications using the static version of the OLE libraries should call **StaticStgGetFSpFromIStorage**. For more information, see the section, "Static and DLL Versions of OLE Functions," in Appendix D, "OLE 2 for the Macintosh: How It Differs from OLE 2 for Windows."

StgGetFSpFromIStorage only works with pointers that point to root storage objects.

See Also **StgGetFRefFromIStorage**

Compound Document Storage Functions

The helper functions described in this section support the loading of storages and streams and the saving of data to those storages and streams.

The following functions are defined in ole2.h:

```
OleLoad(LPSTORAGE pStg, REFIID riid, LPOLECLIENTSITE pClientSite, void * * ppvObj);
 OleLoadFromStream( LPSTREAM pStm, REFIID riid, void * * ppvObj);
 OleSave(LPPERSISTSTORAGE pPS, LPSTORAGE pStg, unsigned long fSameAsLoad);
 OleSaveToStream( LPPERSISTSTREAM pPStm, LPSTREAM pStm );
```

OleLoad

HRESULT OleLoad (*pStg, riid, pClientSite, ppvObj*)
LPSTORAGE *pStg*
REFIID *riid*
LPOLECLIENTSITE *pClientSite*
**void * * ** *ppvObj*

OleLoad loads an embedded or linked object into memory.

Parameters

pStg
Points to the **IStorage** instance from which to load the object.

riid
Identifies the interface to use when talking to the object.

pClientSite
Points to the object's client site.

ppvObj
Points to the newly loaded object.

Return Values

Value	Meaning
S_OK	Object loaded successfully.
E_OUTOFMEMORY	Object could not be loaded due to lack of memory.
E_NOINTERFACE	Object does not supported the specified interface.
IPersistStorage::Load errors.	

Comments

OLE containers load objects into memory by calling the **OleLoad** function. When calling **OleLoad**, the application passes in a pointer to the open **IStorage** object in which the object's data is stored. This is usually a child storage object to the container's root **IStorage** object. Using the OLE information stored with the object, the object handler (usually, the default handler) attempts to load the object. On completion of the **OleLoad** function, the object is said to be in the loaded state, its object application is not running.

Some applications load all of the document's native data. Containers often defer loading the document's contained objects until required to do so. For example, until an object is scrolled into view and needs to be drawn, it does not need to be loaded.

OleLoad does the following steps as part of its functionality:

1. Checks to see whether an auto-conversion of the object is necessary (see **OleDoAutoConvert**).
2. Gets the CLSID from the open **IStorage** by calling **IStorage::Stat**.
3. Calls **CoCreateInstance** to create an instance of the handler. If the handler code is not available, the default handler is used (see **OleCreateDefaultHandler**).
4. Calls **QueryInterface**, asking for **IPersistStorage**. If successful, **IPersistStorage::Load** (or **IPersistStorage::InitNew**) is invoked.
5. Calls **IOleObject::SetClientSite**(*pClientSite*) to inform the object of its client site.
6. Queries and returns the interface identified by *riid*.

See Also

ReadClassStg, **IClassFactory::CreateInstance**, **IPersistStorage::Load**

OleLoadFromStream

HRESULT OleLoadFromStream(*pStm, riid, ppvObj*)
LPSTREAM *pStm*
REFIID *riid*
void ** *ppvObj*

OleLoadFromStream loads an object from the stream.

Parameter

pStm
Points to the stream from which the object is to be loaded.

riid
Specifies the interface that the caller wants to use to talk to the object.

ppvObj
Points to where to return the object.

Return Values

Value	Meaning
S_OK	Object successfully loaded.
E_OUTOFMEMORY	Out of memory.
E_NOINTERFACE	Interface not supported.
ReadClassStream errors.	Can return any of the error codes from **ReadClassStream**.

Value	Meaning
CoCreateIntance errors.	Can return any of the error codes from **CoCreateInstance**.
IPersistStream::Load errors.	Can return any of the error codes from **IPersistStream::Load**.

Comments

OleLoadFromStream can be used to load an object that supports the **IPersistStream** interface. The CLSID of the object must immediately precede the object's data in the stream.

If the CLSID for the stream is CLSID_NULL, *ppvObj* is set to NULL.

See Also

OleSaveToStream

OleSave

HRESULT OleSave (*pPS*, *pStg*, *fSameAsLoad*)
LPPERSISTSTORAGE *pPS*
LPSTORAGE *pStg*
unsigned long *fSameAsLoad*

OleSave saves an object opened in transacted mode into the storage object pointed to by *pStg*.

Parameters

pPS
Points to the object to be saved.

pStg
Points to the destination storage object.

fSameAsLoad
Indicates whether or not *pStg* is the same storage object from which the object was loaded or created; TRUE indicates that the storage is the same and FALSE indicates a different storage object.

Return Values

Value	Meaning
S_OK	Object was successfully saved.
STG_E_MEDIUMFULL	Object could not be saved due to lack of disk space.
IPersistStorage::Save errors	Can return any of the error codes from **IPersistStorage::Save**.

Comments

OleSave handles the common scenario in which an object uses the compound file implementation for its storage and is open in transacted mode. More customized or sophisticated scenarios can be handled with the **IPersistStorage** and **IStorage** interfaces directly.

OleSave does the following:

1. Calls **IPersist::GetClassID** to get the CLSID.
2. Writes the CLSID to the storage object.
3. Calls **IPersistStorage::Save** to save the object.
4. If there were no errors on the save, calls **IStorage::Commit** to commit the changes.

Static objects are saved into a stream called CONTENTS.

See Also **IStorage Interface, IPersistStorage Interface**

OleSaveToStream

HRESULT OleSaveToStream(*pPStm, pStm***)**
LPPERSISTSTREAM *pPStm*
LPSTREAM *pStm*

OleSaveToStream saves an object to the stream.

Parameters

pPStm
Points to the object to be saved to the stream, preceded by its serialized CLSID. It can be NULL, which has the effect of writing CLSID_NULL to the stream.

pStm
Points to the stream in which the object is to be saved.

Return Values

Value	Meaning
S_OK	Object successfully saved.
STG_E_MEDIUMFULL	No space left on device.
WriteClassStm errors	Can return any of the error codes from **WriteClassStm**.
IPersistStream::Save errors	Can return any of the error codes from **IPerisistStream::Save**.

Comments

OleSaveToStream can be used to save an object that supports the **IPersistStream** interface. It does the following steps:

1. Calls **IPersistStream::GetClassID** to get the object's CLSID.
2. Writes the CLSID to the stream with **WriteClassStm**.
3. Calls **IPersistStream::Save** with *fClearDirty* set to TRUE.

See Also **OleLoadFromStream**

CHAPTER 10

Drag and Drop Interfaces and Functions

An OLE drag and drop operation allows for the transfer of data within a document, between documents, or between applications. Drag and drop provides the same functionality as the OLE clipboard copy and paste but adds visual feedback and eliminates the need for menus. In fact, if an application supports clipboard copy and paste, little extra is needed to support drag and drop.

During an OLE drag and drop operation, there are three separate pieces of code used:

Drag and Drop Code	Implementation
IDropSource interface	Implemented by the object containing the dragged data, referred to as the drag source.
IDropTarget interface	Implemented by the object that might potentially accept the drop, referred to as the drop target.
DoDragDrop function	Implemented by OLE and used to initiate a drag and drop operation. Once the operation is in progress, it facilitates communication between the drag source and the drag target.

The **IDropSource** and **IDropTarget** interfaces can be implemented in either a container or in an object application. The role of being a drop source or drop target is not limited to any one type of OLE application.

The OLE function, **DoDragDrop**, implements a loop that tracks mouse and keyboard movement until such time as the drag is canceled or a drop occurs. **DoDragDrop** is the key function in the drag and drop process, facilitating communication between the drag source and drop target.

During a drag and drop operation, there are three types of feedback that can be displayed to the user:

Type of Feedback	Description
Source feedback	Provided by the drag source, source feedback indicates the data is being dragged and does not change during the course of the drag. Typically, the data is highlighted to signal it has been selected.
Cursor feedback	Provided by the drag source, the cursor feedback indicates what happens if the mouse is released at any given moment. Feedback changes continually as the user moves the mouse and/or presses a modifier key. For example, if the mouse is moved into a window that cannot accept a drop, the cursor changes to the "not allowed" symbol.
Target feedback	Provided by the drop target, the target feedback indicates where the drop is to occur.

DROPEFFECT Enumeration

DoDragDrop and many of the drag and drop interface methods pass information about the effects that a drag source allows in a specific drag operation and the effect a potential drop will have on a target window. Valid drop effect values are the result of or-ing together values contained in the **DROPEFFECT** enumeration:

```
typedef enum tagDROPEFFECT{
    DROPEFFECT_NONE   = 0,        \\only lower three bits are significant
    DROPEFFECT_COPY   = 1,
    DROPEFFECT_MOVE   = 2,
    DROPEFFECT_LINK   = 4,
    DROPEFFECT_SCROLL = 0x80000000,
    }DROPEFFECT;
```

DROPEFFECT values have the following meaning:

DROPEFFECT Name	Value	Description
DROPEFFECT_NONE	0	Drop target cannot accept the data.
DROPEFFECT_COPY	1	Drop results in a copy. The original data is untouched by the drag source.
DROPEFFECT_MOVE	2	Drag source should remove the data.
DROPEFFECT_LINK	4	Drag source should create a link to the original data.
DROPEFFECT_SCROLL	0x80000000	Scrolling is about to start or is currently occurring in the target. This value is used in addition to the other values.

Presently, only 4 of the 32 bit positions in a **DROPEFFECT** have meaning. In the future, more interpretations for the bits will be added. Drop sources and drop targets should mask these values appropriately before comparing. They should never compare a **DROPEFFECT** against, say, DROPEFFECT_COPY by

```
if (dwDropEffect == DROPEFECT_COPY)...
```

Instead, the application should always mask for the value or values being sought:

```
if ((dwDropEffect & DROPEFFECT_COPY) == DROPEFFECT_COPY...
```

or

```
if (dwDropEffect & DROPEFFECT_COPY)...
```

Doing this allows new drop effects to be defined, while preserving backwards compatibility with existing code.

IDropSource Interface

The **IDropSource** interface is implemented by all applications containing data that can be dropped into another application.

IDropSource contains the following methods:

```
DECLARE_INTERFACE_(IDropSource, IUnknown)
{
   // *** IUnknown methods ***
  HRESULT QueryInterface (REFIID riid, void * * ppvObj);
  ULONG AddRef ();
  ULONG Release ();

   // *** IDropSource methods ***
  HRESULT QueryContinueDrag (unsigned long fEscapePressed, unsigned long grfKeyState);
  HRESULT GiveFeedback (unsigned long dwEffect);
};
```

For more information, see the ole2.h header file.

Drag Source Responsibilities

The drag source is responsible for the following tasks:

- Providing the drop target with a data transfer object that exposes the **IDataObject** and **IDropSource** interfaces.
- Generating pointer and source feedback.

- Determining when the drag has been canceled or a drop has occurred.
- Performing any action on the original data caused by the drop operation, such as deleting the data or creating a link to it.

The main task is creating a data transfer object that exposes the **IDataObject** and **IDropSource** interfaces. The drag source might or might not include a copy of the selected data. Including a copy of the selected data is not mandatory, but it safeguards against inadvertent changes and allows the clipboard operations code to be identical to the drag and drop code.

Creating the data transfer object is dependent on the set of clipboard formats supported and whether the drag source is a container or server. Many drag sources use the same type of object that is the source of the selected data. When doing so, however, it is important to be aware of the areas that are treated differently.

The following table lists the areas in which the data transfer object and data source object differ:

Data Transfer Object	Data Source Object
Invisible.	Visible.
Stores a pointer to the data source document.	Does not need to store a data source document pointer.
Stores a pointer to a temporary moniker for the data selection.	Does not need to store a temporary moniker pointer.
Exposes only **IDataObject** and **IDropSource**.	Exposes **IDataObject** and other interfaces needed for linking and embedding, such as **IOleObject**. **IDropSource** not exposed.
SetData, **Advise**, **Unadvise**, and **EnumAdvise** methods in **IDataObject** are not supported.	If drag source is a server, all **IDataObject** methods are supported. If drag source is a container, **SetData**, **Advise**, **Unadvise**, and **EnumAdvise** methods in **IDataObject** are not supported.
Embedded Object, Embed Source, and Link Source formats are offered.	Embedded Object, Embed Source, and Link Source formats are not offered.

For more information on creating a data transfer object, see Chapter 7, "Data Transfer/Caching Interfaces and Functions."

While a drag operation is in progress, the drag source is responsible for setting the cursor and, if appropriate, for providing additional source feedback to the user. The drag source cannot provide any feedback that tracks the mouse position other than by actually setting the real cursor. This rule must be enforced to avoid conflicts with the feedback provided by the drop target.

A drag source can also be a drag target. When dropping on itself, the source/target can provide target feedback to track the mouse position. In this case, however, it is the drop target tracking the mouse, not the source.

Based on the feedback offered by the drop target, the source sets an appropriate cursor. Drop sources should use a variation on the standard northwest-pointing arrow, as shown in Figure 10.1:

Figure 10.1 Default drag and drop cursors representing an illegal action and a move operation

For more information on the recommended user interface considerations for a drag and drop operation, see Chapter 2, "User Interface Guidelines."

Drag Distance and Delay Values

Dragging occurs when the drag cursor has been moved a specified minimum distance or a specified amount of time has passed since that distance was achieved. The default minimum distance, or radius, for cursor movement is two pixels, as defined by the constant DD_DEFDRAGMINDIST in ole2.h. The default drag delay time is equivalent to the system double-click time as defined by **GetDblTime**(). The drag delay value can be used when an application detects a mouse button down to determine when to begin the drag operation . When the cursor enters the region in which dragging can be done for the first time, the application can set an internal variable and compare that variable against the current value of **TickCount** while the cursor is in the region. The drag operation can begin if the cursor is still within the region in which dragging is allowed after this time interval expires.

The minimum distance setting is used when a mouse move is detected. When the cursor has entered the region in which dragging can be done, an application can examine each movement to determine whether the cursor position has changed sufficiently.

Generating Drag Feedback

IDropSource contains two methods, **QueryContinueDrag**, and **GiveFeedback**. **QueryContinueDrag** is called by **DoDragDrop** at the beginning of its loop to check whether the drag has been canceled, whether a drop is to occur, or whether the drag should continue.

The following table shows each state, listing the condition that determines the state and the designated return value.

User Action	Effect on Drag Operation	Return Value
ESC key is pressed	Cancel the drag	DRAGDROP_S_CANCEL
CMD-PERIOD (.) is pressed	Cancel the drag	DRAGDROP_S_CANCEL
Absence of the other two conditions.	Continue the drag	S_OK

For every mouse move, **DoDragDrop** calls the drop target's **IDropTarget::DragOver**, which sets the drop effect. **DoDragDrop** passes the drop effect to **IDropSource::GiveFeedback,** which sets the pointer according to the feedback value. The drag source can either set its pointers manually or return DRAGDROP_S_USEDEFAULTCURSORS to ask OLE to use standard pointers defined for drag and drop operations. The standard cursors include an arrow with a plus sign (+) to indicate the copy effect, and a circle with a diagonal line across it to indicate an attempt to drop in an invalid region.

Ending the Drop Operation

When **DoDragDrop** returns, either the drop has occurred or the operation was canceled. The drag source uses the HRESULT returned from **DoDragDrop** to determine what to do with the data: delete it or leave it as is. If the data is to be deleted, as is the case with a move operation, the drag source must disable the sending of any data change notifications until the delete operation has been completed.

IDropSource::QueryContinueDrag

HRESULT IDropSource::QueryContinueDrag(*fEscapePressed*, *grfKeyState***)**
unsigned long *fEscapePressed*
unsigned long *grfKeyState*

IDropSource::QueryContinueDrag determines whether a drag operation should continue.

Parameters

fEscapePressed
Specifies TRUE if ESC or CMD-PERIOD keys have been pressed by the user since the previous call to **IDropSource::QueryContinueDrag** (or the call to **DoDragDrop** if **IDropSource::QueryContinueDrag** has not been called); otherwise, specifies FALSE.

grfKeyState
Identifies the present state of the modifier keys on the keyboard.

Return Values

Value	Meaning
S_OK	The drag operation should continue.
DRAGDROP_S_DROP	The drop operation should occur.
DRAGDROP_S_CANCEL	The drop operation should be canceled.

Value	Meaning
E_OUTOFMEMORY	Out of memory.
E_UNEXPECTED	An unexpected error occurred.

Comments

To determine whether the drag operation should continue, **IDropSource::QueryContinueDrag** checks whether the mouse button has been released, causing a drop operation to occur, and/or whether the ESCAPE (or COMMAND-PERIOD) key has been hit, causing a cancel. The former case can be handled by examining the flags in the *grfKeyState* parameter, while the latter can be done by examining the *fEscapePressed* flag.

See Also

DoDragDrop

IDropSource::GiveFeedback

HRESULT IDropSource::GiveFeedback(*dwEffect***)**
unsigned long *dwEffect*

IDropSource::GiveFeedback enables a source application to provide feedback during a drag and drop operation.

Parameter

dwEffect
Specifies the **DROPEFFECT** value returned by the most recent call to **IDropTarget::DragEnter** or **IDropTarget::DragOver**. For a list of values, see the section "DROPEFFECT Enumeration," earlier in this chapter.

Return Values

Value	Meaning
S_OK	The function completed successfully.
DRAGDROP_S_USE-DEFAULTCURSORS	OLE should use the default pointer (cursor) to provide feedback to the user.
E_OUTOFMEMORY	Out of memory.
E_INVALIDARG	*dwEffect* is invalid.
E_UNEXPECTED	An unexpected error occurred.

Comments

IDropSource::GiveFeedback is called by **DoDragDrop** once for every time it calls **IDropTarget::DragEnter** or **IDropTarget::DragOver**. This action enables the drop source to provide appropriate feedback in the source data. Unless a new target is immediately entered (in which case the call is omitted), **IDropSource::GiveFeedback** is called with *dwEffect* set to DROPEFFECT_NONE when **IDropTarget::DragLeave** is called.

The *dwEffect* parameter can include DROPEFFECT_SCROLL, indicating the source may put up the drag-scrolling variation of the appropriate cursor.

OLE defines a set of recommended cursors that can be used for each of the different drop effects. For consistency across OLE applications, the drop source should use the recommended cursors. For more information on these cursors, see Chapter 2, "User Interface Guidelines."

IDropSource::GiveFeedback can return DRAGDROP_S_USEDEFAULTS, which causes **DoDragDrop** to put up the cursor appropriate for *dwEffect*. Other source feedback can be provided in addition to this standard feedback.

See Also **RegisterDragDrop**, **DoDragDrop**, **IDropTarget::DragLeave**, **IDropTarget::DragOver**

IDropTarget Interface

The **IDropTarget** interface is implemented by all applications that can accept dropped data. Every application window that can be a drop target registers as such by calling **RegisterDragDrop**, passing an **IDropTarget** interface pointer as an argument.

IDropTarget contains the following methods:

```
DECLARE_INTERFACE_(IDropTarget, IUnknown)
{
  // *** IUnknown methods ***
  HRESULT QueryInterface (REFIID riid, void * * ppvObj);
  ULONG AddRef ();
  ULONG Release ();

  // *** IDropTarget methods ***
  HRESULT DragEnter (LPDATAOBJECT pDataObject, unsigned long grfKeyState, POINTL pt,
      unsigned long * pdwEffect);
  HRESULT DragOver (unsigned long grfKeyState, POINTL pt, unsigned long * pdwEffect);
  HRESULT DragLeave ();
  HRESULT Drop (LPDATAOBJECT pDataObject, unsigned long grfKeyState, POINTL pt,
      unsigned long * pdwEffect);
};
```

For more information, see the ole2.h header file.

Drop Target Responsibilities

The drop target is responsible for the following tasks:

- Registering and revoking each drop target window.
- Determining what the effect on the drag source is at any given time.
- Implementing drag scrolling.

- Providing target feedback.
- Integrating the data if a drop occurs or if the drag is canceled.

Registering as a Drop Target

Before they can accept dropped data, applications that have implemented the **IDropTarget** interface must register their CLSID and object handler as potential drop targets in the Registration Database file . Applications must call **RegisterDragDrop** for every window that can accept dropped data.

Passed to **RegisterDragDrop** is a windowptr and a pointer to the **IDropTarget** interface. **RegisterDragDrop** creates a stream to hold the **IDropTarget** interface pointer so the interface can be remoted across processes to support drag and drop from one application to another.

Note Drop targets must be externally locked in memory by calling **CoLockObjectExternal**. This lock ensures that the drop target is not prematurely released during a drag and drop operation. However, for applications using the visible document object to expose the **IDropTarget** interface, an additional call to **CoLockObjectExternal** is not required, since objects visible to the user typically already have an external lock.

If **IDropTarget** is not exposed through an object visible to the user, a call to **CoLockObjectExternal**(...,TRUE,...) is necessary before **RegisterDragDrop** is called. To free the locked drop target, call **CoLockObjectExternal**(...,FALSE,...) before calling **RevokeDragDrop**. For more information on locking objects and applications in memory, see the **CoLockObjectExternal** function.

Typically, when the window is no longer available to accept drops, the drop target calls **RevokeDragDrop** to remove the registration. It is important to call **RevokeDragDrop** rather than rely on destroying the window to remove the registration. Neglecting to call **RevokeDragDrop** can result in a memory leak.

In the case where the desktop is registered as a drop target along with windows belonging to applications running on the desktop, revoking the application windows might not be sufficient to block a potential drop. If the desktop is still a valid registered drop target when the user drags across the application window, the cursor might reflect that a drop can be accepted. This is misleading to the user, who might think the data is to be dropped onto the application window when it is really to be dropped onto the desktop. To guard against this effect, application windows should stay registered and return an appropriate cursor when a drop cannot be accepted.

Determining Drop Effect Values

The drop target determines the effect of a potential drop in every **IDropTarget::DragEnter** and **IDropTarget::DragOver** call. **IDropTarget::DragEnter** is called when the mouse pointer initially enters the drop target window and is always called before **IDropTarget::Drop** or **IDropTarget::DragLeave** is called. **IDropTarget::DragOver** is called for every mouse move while the pointer is positioned over the drop target window. **DragLeave** is called when the pointer leaves the drop target window.

IDropTarget::DragEnter and **IDropTarget::DragOver** are passed parameters that identify the location of the mouse, the modifier key state, and a list of drop effects. **DragEnter** also receives a pointer to the data transfer object's **IDataObject** interface so it can enumerate the available formats. The drop target uses the list of available formats, the mouse pointer position, and the modifier key state to determine the appropriate drop effect value to return.

The modifier keys affect the result of the drop in the same document and when dragging an object between documents, as shown in the following table:

Key Combination	User-Visible Feedback	Drop Effect
OPTION + SHIFT	=	DROPEFFECT_LINK
OPTION	+	DROPEFFECT_COPY
No keys	None	DROPEFFECT_MOVE, when dragging within the same document, and DROPEFFECT_COPY, when dragging between two documents.

Another factor in determining the drop effect value is whether the drag source and drop target are in the same window. Areas in which data can be dropped may be different if the drop is local. For more information on the UI recommendations for dragging and dropping objects, see Chapter 2, "User Interface Guidelines."

Drag Scrolling and Related Values

Drag scrolling is supported solely by the drop target; however, the drag source is responsible for displaying the scroll pointer. Objects that want to support drag scrolling should register themselves in the normal way through **RegisterDragDrop**.

Scrolling occurs when the pointer has been in an area close to the window's edge for a specified time interval. There is a hot zone adjacent to the window's edge that triggers drag scrolling. The default size (inset width in pixels), drag delay time, and scroll interval are determined by the following constants, as defined in ole2.h:

```
#define DD_DEFSCROLLINSET 15        //inset width of hot zone in pixels
#define DD_DEFSCROLLDELAY 10        //drag scroll delay time
#define DD_DEFSCROLLINTERVAL 2      //drag scroll interval (speed)
```

When the pointer first enters the hot zone, the pointer changes to its drag-scrolling variation. The size and existence of the hot zone are controlled by the drop target. Some drop targets allow scrolling in both the horizontal and vertical directions while others allow only vertical scrolling.

As soon as the pointer enters the hot zone, the drop target informs the drag source that the pointer should change to its drag scrolling variation by returning DROPEFFECT_SCROLL, which is then passed to the drop source in **IDropSource::GiveFeedback**. As long as the pointer is in the hot zone, the drop target should keep returning DROPEFFECT_SCROLL.

The drop target determines the scroll delay time the pointer must remain in the hot zone before scrolling is to begin. Drop targets should set an internal variable when the hot zone is first entered and compare that variable against the current **TickCount** in each subsequent call to **IDropTarget::DragOver**.

Ending the Drag Operation

A particular drag operation is ended when either the user clicks outside of the drop target window or releases the mouse while inside the window. **DoDragDrop** calls **IDropTarget::DragLeave** in the first case, **IDropTarget::Drop** in the second case. The implementation of **IDropTarget::DragLeave** involves releasing the data transfer object and, if appropriate, killing the drag scrolling timer.

The tasks involved in a drop operation are similar to the tasks involved in a clipboard paste. Depending on the order and type of formats passed with the data transfer object, the data is integrated statically, as an embedded or linked object.

IDropTarget::DragEnter

HRESULT IDropTarget::DragEnter(*pDataObject*, *grfKeyState*, *pt*, *pdwEffect*)
LPDATAOBJECT *pDataObject*
unsigned long *grfKeyState*
POINTL *pt*
unsigned long * *pdwEffect*

IDropTarget::DragEnter determines whether the target window can accept the dragged object and what effect the dragged object will have on the target window.

Parameters

pDataObject
Points to an instance of the **IDataObject** interface, through which the dragged data is accessible.

grfKeyState
Specifies a combination of the MK_CONTROL, MK_SHIFT, MK_ALT, MK_LBUTTON, MK_MBUTTON, and MK_RBUTTON flags that identifies the present state of the keyboard modifier keys.

pt

Points to a structure containing the current mouse/cursor coordinates in screen coordinates.

pdwEffect

On entry, contains the *dwOKEffects* parameter originally passed to **DoDragDrop**. On exit, contains the effect of this drag operation, which is to be returned to the caller in **IDropSource::GiveFeedback**. The value for *pdwEffect* is from the **DROPEFFECT** enumeration. For a list of values, see the section "DROPEFFECT Enumeration," earlier in this chapter.

Return Values

Value	Meaning
S_OK	The function completed successfully.
E_OUTOFMEMORY	Out of memory.
E_INVALIDARG	One or more arguments are invalid.
E_UNEXPECTED	An unexpected error occurred.

Comments

During calls to **IDropTarget::DragEnter** and **IDropTarget::DragOver**, the target should provide appropriate target feedback to the user. During a drop operation, as the mouse passes over the unobscured portion of the window associated with this drop target, **IDropTarget::DragEnter**, **IDropTarget::DragOver**, and **IDropTarget::DragLeave** are called as the mouse first enters, moves around within, then leaves each drop target.

The first time the mouse enters the screen region for a given target, **IDropTarget::DragEnter** is called. As long as the drag operation continues and the target remains the same, **IDropTarget::DragOver** is called. When the target changes or the drag operation is canceled, **IDropTarget::DragLeave** is called. When the drop finally happens, **IDropTarget::Drop** is called. **IDropTarget::Drop** is never called without first calling **IDropTarget::DragEnter** on the given drop target.

IDropTarget::DragEnter determines whether the dragged object is acceptable by examining the clipboard formats available for the object, the values pointed to by the *pdwEffect* parameter, and the state of the modifier keys, as indicated in the *grfKeyState* parameter. If the dragged object can be dropped, **IDropTarget::DragEnter** determines the corresponding effect on the drop source.

The drop target indicates its decision through the *pdwEffect* parameter. The *pdwEffect* parameter is an or-ing together of values contained in the **DROPEFFECT** enumeration. Typically, DROPEFFECT_COPY is passed in *pdwEffect*, although DROPEFFECT_LINK can be passed to create a link to the source data. Whether the source allows the dragged data to be permanently moved from the source application is indicated by the presence or absence of DROPEFFECT_MOVE.

The value returned in *pdwEffect* is passed through the **DoDragDrop** function to **IDropSource::GiveFeedback** so the source can change the pointer appropriately and provide feedback to the user.

To provide appropriate target feedback, the drop target can pull data from *pDataObject*. (For example, a drop operation into a spreadsheet might want to know the size of the table being dropped is so it can highlight an appropriate set of cells.)

See Also **DoDragDrop**, **IDropSource::GiveFeedback**

IDropTarget::DragOver

HRESULT IDropTarget::DragOver(*grfKeyState*, *pt*, *pdwEffect***)**
unsigned long *grfKeyState*
POINTL *pt*
unsigned long * *pdwEffect*

IDropTarget::DragOver provides feedback to the user and to **DoDragDrop** about the state of the drag operation within a drop target application.

Parameters

grfKeyState
A combination of the MK_CONTROL, MK_SHIFT, MK_ALT, MK_LBUTTON, MK_MBUTTON, and MK_RBUTTON flags that identifies the present state of the keyboard modifier keys.

pt
Structure containing the current mouse/cursor coordinates in screen coordinates. For performance reasons, **IDropTarget::DragOver** should call **GetMouse** and not use the mouse/cursor coordinates contained within *pt*.

pdwEffect
On entry, contains the *dwOKEffects* parameter originally passed to **DoDragDrop**. On exit, contains the effect of this drag operation, which is to be returned to the caller in **IDropSource::GiveFeedback**. The value for *pdwEffect* is from the **DROPEFFECT** enumeration. For a list of values, see the section "DROPEFFECT Enumeration," earlier in this chapter.

Return Values

Value	Meaning
S_OK	State information returned successfully.
E_OUTOFMEMORY	Out of memory.
E_INVALIDARG	One or more arguments are invalid.
E_UNEXPECTED	An unexpected error occurred.

Comments

After the pointer initially enters the target window, **IDropTarget::DragOver** is called each time the pointer (mouse) moves until the drag operation is canceled or a drop occurs. For efficiency reasons, no clipboard data object is passed. The clipboard data object passed in the most recent call to **IDropTarget::DragEnter** is used.

IDropTarget::DragOver determines whether the dragged object is acceptable by examining the clipboard formats available for the object, the values pointed to by the *pdwEffect* parameter, and the state of the modifier keys, as indicated in the *grfKeyState* parameter. If the dragged object can be dropped, **IDropTarget::DragOver** determines the corresponding effect on the drag source application.

The target application indicates its decision through the *pdwEffect* parameter.

To provide appropriate target feedback, the drop target can pull data from *pDataObject* (as was passed in the most recent call to **IDropTarget::DropEnter**).

See Also

IDropTarget::DragEnter, **IDropSource::GiveFeedback**, **DoDragDrop**

IDropTarget::DragLeave

HRESULT IDropTarget::DragLeave()

IDropTarget::DragLeave causes the drop target to remove its feedback. This method is called when the mouse leaves the area of a given target while a drag is in progress or when the drag operation is canceled.

Return Values

Value	Meaning
S_OK	Drop target feedback was removed.
E_OUTOFMEMORY	Out of memory.

Comments

The data transfer object passed to the most recent call to **IDropTarget::DragEnter** is implied.

The drop target should remove any target feedback it currently has showing. If the drop target is currently holding on to the data transfer object passed to **IDropTarget::DragEnter**, it should release it at this time.

See Also

IDropTarget::DragEnter

IDropTarget::Drop

HRESULT IDropTarget::Drop(*pDataObject, grfKeyState, pt, pdwEffect***)**
LPDATAOBJECT *pDataObject*
unsigned long *grfKeyState*
POINTL *pt*
unsigned long * *pdwEffect*

IDropTarget::Drop drops the source data, indicated by *pDataObject*, on this target application.

Parameter

pDataObject
Points to an instance of the **IDataObject** interface, through which the data is accessible.

grfKeyState
Identifies the present state of the keyboard modifier keys; the value is a combination of the MK_CONTROL, MK_SHIFT, MK_ALT, MK_LBUTTON, MK_MBUTTON, and MK_RBUTTON flags.

pt
Structure containing the current mouse/cursor coordinates in screen coordinates.

pdwEffect
On entry, contains the *dwOKEffects* parameter originally passed to **DoDragDrop**. On exit, contains the effect of this drag operation, which is to be returned to the caller in **IDropSource::GiveFeedback**. The value for *pdwEffect* is from the **DROPEFFECT** enumeration. For a list of these values, see the section "DROPEFFECT Enumeration," earlier in this chapter.

Return Values

Value	Meaning
S_OK	The function completed successfully.
E_OUTOFMEMORY	Out of memory.
E_INVALIDARG	One or more arguments are invalid.
E_UNEXPECTED	An unexpected error occurred.

Comments

The data being dropped is accessible through *pDataObject*. The formats available through the **IDataObject** interface should be used in conjunction with the state of the modifier keys to determine the semantics of what should happen on the drop. Appropriate information is passed back through *pdwEffect*. The caller can only use *pDataObject* for the duration of this call.

By the time **IDropTarget::Drop** returns, the drop operation should have obtained everything it needs from *pDataObject*. After a successful drop, the drop target should take the foreground.

See Also

IDropTarget::DragEnter, **IDropSource::GiveFeedback**, **DoDragDrop**

Drag and Drop Functions

The following functions are used in drag and drop operations:

```
RegisterDragDrop(WindowPtr pWnd, LPDROPTARGET pDropTarget);
RevokeDragDrop(WindowPtr pWnd);
DoDragDrop(LPDATAOBJECT pDataObject, LPDROPSOURCE pDropSource, unsigned long dwEffect,
        unsigned long * pdwEffect);
```

For more information, see the compobj.h header file.

RegisterDragDrop

HRESULT RegisterDragDrop(*pWnd, pDropTarget***)**
WindowPtr *pWnd*
LPDROPTARGET *pDropTarget*

RegisterDragDrop registers an application window as being able to accept dropped objects. This function only registers the window specified by the *pWnd* parameter.

Parameter

pWnd
Specifies the WindowPtr to the window that is the target for the drop.

pDropTarget
Points to the **IDropTarget** implementation through which information about the *pWnd* is communicated while the drag and drop operation is in progress.

Return Values

Value	Meaning
S_OK	The application was registered successfully.
DRAGDROP_E_INVALIDHWND	Invalid WindowPtr.
DRAGDROP_E_ALREADYREGISTERED	The window has already been registered as a drop target or, if NULL is returned, there is an invalid WindowPtr for the window.

Comments

To accept drop operations, an application registers the applicable window(s) as a potential drop target. **RegisterDragDrop** must be called for each window capable of accepting dropped objects.

The *pDropTarget* parameter points to an instance of the **IDropTarget** interface, through which communication is made with the target application during a drag and drop operation. During a drag and drop operation, as the mouse passes over unobscured portions of the target window(s), **IDropTarget::DragOver** is called. When a drop operation actually occurs in a given window, **IDropTarget::Drop** is called.

See Also

RevokeDragDrop

RevokeDragDrop

HRESULT RevokeDragDrop(*pWnd***)**
WindowPtr *pWnd*

RevokeDragDrop revokes an application window previously registered for drag and drop operations.

Parameter

pWnd
Specifies the WindowPtr to the window that is the target for the drop.

Return Values

Value	Meaning
S_OK	Application window was revoked successfully.
DRAGDROP_E_INVALIDHWND	Invalid WindowPtr for the window.
DRAGDROP_E_NOTREGISTERED	An attempt was made to revoke a drop target that has not been registered.
E_OUTOFMEMORY	Out of memory.

Comments

To revoke a window's ability to accept dropped objects, an application calls **RevokeDragDrop** on the window previously registered with **RegisterDragDrop**.

If an application wants to ensure that an object is kept alive during a call to **RevokeDragDrop**, it should preserve the lock count of the object by calling **CoLockObjectExternal**, which guarantees the object will be available after the **RevokeDragDrop** call:

```
CoLockObjectExternal(pUnk, TRUE, FALSE);
RevokeDragDrop(pWnd);
CoLockObjectExternal(pUnk, FALSE, FALSE);
```

See Also

RegisterDragDrop

DoDragDrop

HRESULT DoDragDrop(*pDataObject, pDropSource, dwEffect, pdwEffect***)**
LPDATAOBJECT *pDataObject*
LPDROPSOURCE *pDropSource*
unsigned long *dwEffect*
unsigned long * *pdwEffect*

DoDragDrop initiates a drag and drop operation and facilitates communication between the drop source and the drop target.

Parameters

pDataObject
Points to an instance of the **IDataObject** interface, which provides the data being dragged.

pDropSource
Points to an instance of the **IDropSource** interface, which is used to communicate with the source during the drag operation.

dwEffect
Determines the effects the drag source allows in the drag operation. Most significant is whether it permits a move. Values are from the **DROPEFFECT** enumeration. For a list of values, see the section "DROPEFFECT Enumeration," earlier in this chapter.

pdwEffect
Points to a value that indicates how the drag operation affected the source data. The *pdwEffect* parameter is set only if the operation is not canceled.

Return Values

Value	Meaning
S_OK	The drop operation was initiated successfully.
DRAGDROP_S_CANCEL	The drop operation was canceled.
E_OUTOFMEMORY	Out of memory.
E_UNSPEC	An unexpected error occurred.
DRAGDROP_S_DROP	The drop operation was successful.

Comments

When a user starts to drag data, the drag source calls **DoDragDrop**, passing it pointers to the data transfer object's **IDataObject** and **IDropSource** interfaces and a place holder for a value indicating the effect of a potential drop. When the mouse pointer passes over a window that is a registered drop target, **DoDragDrop** calls **IDropTarget::DragEnter**.

The modifier key state, location of the mouse, and the **IDataObject** interface pointer are passed as parameters to **IDropTarget::DragEnter**. This information is used by **IDropTarget::DragEnter** to return a value that represents what the effect of a drop would be on the drag source. From the perspective of the drag source, the result is that the data is either removed or unchanged. For a list of valid drop effects, see the section "DROPEFFECT Enumeration," earlier in this chapter.

For each iteration of its loop, **DoDragDrop** calls **IDropSource::QueryContinueDrag** to check whether to continue or cancel the drag. The return value from **IDropSource::QueryContinueDrag** determines which **IDropTarget** method is called next.

IDropSource::QueryContinueDrag Return Value	Resulting Interface Method Call(s)
DRAGDROP_S_CANCEL	**IDropTarget::DragLeave**
DRAGDROP_S_DROP	**IDropTarget::Drop**
S_OK	**IDropTarget::DragOver** **IDropSource::GiveFeedback**

IDropTarget::DragOver and **IDropSource::GiveFeedback** are paired so that as the mouse moves across the drop target, the user is given the most up-to-date feedback on the mouse's position. **DoDragDrop** continues to loop until such time that the user cancels the drag or drops the data. Depending on the user action, **IDropSource::GiveFeedback** returns DRAGDROP_S_CANCEL for a canceled drag and DRAGDROP_S_DROP for a successful drop.

The values for *pdwEffect* and *dwOKEffect* are based on an or-ing of the values in the **DROPEFFECT** enumeration. The *pdwEffect* parameter determines the effect the drag and drop operation had on the source data. Typically, DROPEFFECT_COPY is passed in *dwEffect*, although DROPEFFECT_LINK can be passed to create a link to the source data. The presence or absence of DROPEFFECT_MOVE indicates whether the source allows the dragged data to be permanently moved from the source application.

See Also **IDropSource::GiveFeedback**

CHAPTER 11

In-Place Activation Interfaces and Functions

This chapter describes the OLE interfaces and API functions that support in-place activation under the Macintosh operating system.

In-Place Activation:Programing Considerations

This section describes some considerations for implementing in-place activation.

Hierarchical Menu Ranges

The recommended ranges for hierarchical menus during an in-place activation session are 0 - 200 for object applications and 201 and above for container applications.

Activating Objects while Background Utilities Are Running

In-place activation UI will be disrupted when utilities that have an option to hide background applications have that option enabled. Most noticeably, you will not be able to see the container document. Applications should take the appropriate steps to ensure that they do not in-place activate under these conditions.

Container not Receiving Low-Level Events

When clicking in the content region of the container's frame window, the object application needs to send the low-level event on to the container. Often, the container will not get these events, usually because of one the following problems:

- Object application did not send the low-level event or sent the event to the wrong process serial number (see **OleSendLowLevelEvent**).
- The container did not register to receive the low-level event (see **OleSendLowLevelEvent**).
- The container did not fill in the signature field in the **OLEINPLACEFRAMEINFO** data structure.

In-Place Object Documents not Clipped to Container's Window

During an in-place session, if the object appliction's windows do not appear to be clipped properly to the container documents, the object application is most likely passing the wrong window pointer to **OleClipWindows**. Furthermore, **OleClipWindows** checks the state of the visible bit of the window before subclassing it; if the window is invisible, **OleClipWindows** does nothing in order to avoid improperly clipping the hidden window.

Hide Others Application Menu Option

While in-place active and UIVisible, the object application must detect and gracefully handle the user selecting "Hide Others" from the system application menu. If the object application detects that the user has selected Hide Others while it is UIVisible, it must call **SetFrontProcess** using the container's ProcessSerialNumber. This will cause the container to UIDeactivate the in-place session.

UI Deactivating a Session

When deactivating a UI-active in-place session, there are two scenarios that need to be considered in order to determine how the container application retakes the foreground position:

- If the container application caused the UIDeactivate, either as the result of receiving a user Content click or receiving a Resume event while already UIVisible, the container must retake the foreground in the **IOleInPlaceSite::OnUIDeactivate** method.
- If the UI-active session was ended by the user pressing the ESC key, then the object application must bring the container application to the foreground by calling SetFrontProcess with the container's ProcessSerialNumber. This will cause the container to receive a Resume event resulting in an UIDeactivate (see preceding bullet).

Failure to follow these steps can result in an indeterminate state.

Click in Scroll Bars Causes UI Deactivate

During an in-place session, if the user clicks outside of the in-place object's immediate window area, the container must properly handle the mouse down event, not "blindly" processing low-level event content clicks without checking the mouse position. For example, should the user click on the scroll bars, the container must not do a complete UI deactivation without checking the mouse position. In this case, the click, while outside the in-place window, has no cause to terminate the in-place session.

In-Place Object UI Deactivates After Taking the Foreground

After receiving an **IOleInPlaceActiveObject::OnDocWindowActivate** or **IOleInPlaceActiveObject::OnDocWindowActivate** call, the object application needs to take the foreground position and resume the in-place session. A problem during this scenario is that upon taking the foreground position, the in-place object immediately UI deactivates, terminating the in-place session.

This problem can be caused by the object application hiding its in-place window before calling **IOleInPlaceSite::OnUIVisible**(FALSE) which results in the container application retaking the foreground.

Because the object application hid its window right before the container took the foreground, the object application did not get the DocDeactivate event. As a result, the object application gets the DocDeactivate event when it resumes the foreground position which is improper.

Handling Floating Windows

A Macintosh OLE object application must correctly handle floating windows when active in place. If the floating windows aren't handled correctly, the object application won't receive mouse clicks when the cursor is over the structure region of the container window (except when over the inplace object window).

There are two ways an object application can handle floating windows; however, the first method is recommended. (If the application has no floating windows, then it can simply pass the *app1Evt* on to **OleSendLowLevelEvent** without calling **FindWindow**).

1. When an app1Evt arrives, the object appliction can call **FindWindow** with its position and, if the click occurred in a floating window, change the event to a mouseDown and handle it as it normally does. Otherwise, the object application can pass it on to the container via **OleSendLowLevelEvent**.
2. The structure region of all floating object windows can be subtracted from the *hFrameRgn* before it is passed into **OleSetInPlaceRects** (the *hFrameRgn* should be saved first). Then, whenever a floating window is moved, the object application can retrieve the previous *hFrameRgn*, subtract the current *strucRgns* from it, and again call **OleSetInPlaceRects**.

In-Place Data Structures

This section describes the data structures used with the in-place activation interfaces and functions.

BORDERWIDTHS

The **BORDERWIDTHS** structure contains four integer widths for determining border space on the frame- and document-level windows for displaying toolbars and optional frame adornments.

```
typedef RECT    BORDERWIDTHS;
typedef LPRECT  LPBORDERWIDTHS;
typedef LPCRECT LPCBORDERWIDTHS;
```

Each member of the structure is the width in pixels being requested or set for the top, left, bottom, and right sides of the window, as shown in Figure 11.1:

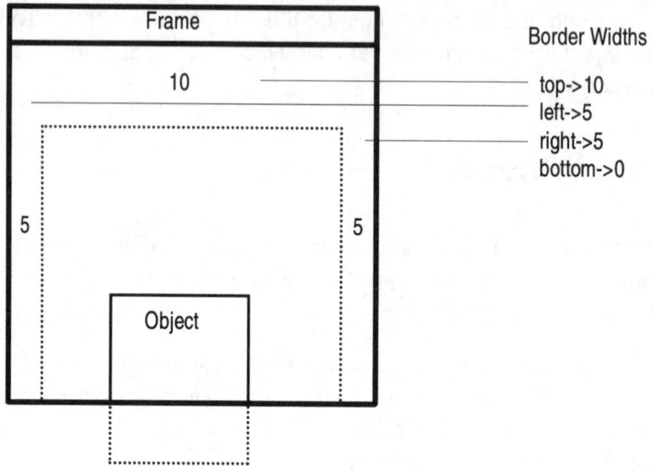

Figure 11.1 Negotiating space for frame adornments

To negotiate space, the object fills in the **BORDERWIDTHS** structure and passes it to **RequestBorderSpace** and **SetBorderSpace** methods on the frame or document interface, depending on where the space is being requested.

OLEINPLACEFRAMEINFO

The **OLEINPLACEFRAMEINFO** structure provides data needed by an object application to communicate with a container while an object is active in place. The structure is defined as follows:

```
typedef struct FARSTRUCT tagOIFI //OleInPlaceFrameInfo
{
    long            recordlength;
    long            version;
    WindowPtr       frameWindow;
    OSType          signature;
```

```
    long                refcon;
    ProcessSerialNumber psn;
    Handle              hCmdKeys;
    short               numCmds;
    short               growHandles;
    short               dragConstraint;
    Boolean             fAdjustMenus;
    Boolean             unused;
}OLEINPLACEFRAMEINFO, * LPOLEINPLACEFRAMEINFO;
```

The container fills in the structure when the object application calls the container's **IOleInPlaceSite::GetWindowContext** method.

The **OLEINPLACEFRAMEINFO** members have the following meaning:

OLEINPLACEFRAMEINFO Member	Meaning
recordLength	Indicates the size of the **OLEINPLACEFRAMEINFO** structure *(sizeof(OLEINPLACEFRAMEINFO))*.
version	Specifies the version of the **OLEINPLACEFRAMEINFO** structure that is currently being used. For this release, 1.
frameWindow	Specifies the pointer to the in-place container's document window.
signature	Specifies the creator signature of the in-place container.
refcon	Application-specific field.
psn	Specifies the in-place container's process serial number.
hCmdKeys	Reserved; must be NULL.
numCmds	Reserved; must be NULL.
growHandles	Specifies which of the in-place container's grow handles the object application is allowed to use during an in-place session. 0 = noConstraint, 1 = hAxisOnly, 2 = vAxisOnly, and 3 = noAxis.
dragConstraint	Specifies the drag constraints placed on the an in-place object by the container; 0 = noConstraint, 1 = hAxisOnly, 2 = vAxisOnly, and 3 = noAxis.

OLEINPLACEFRAMEINFO Member	Meaning
fAdjustMenus	Boolean value set by the container(TRUE) to indicate whether or not the container wants to receive **AdjustMenus** calls from the object application during an in-place session.
unused	Reserved for future use; must be FALSE.

OleMBarRec Data Structure

The **OleMBarRec** structure is used to construct the composite menu bar shared by the object and container applications during an in-place session. The structure contains data that is private to OLE; however the handle to this structure must be passed in various methods and API functions.

```
typedef struct {
    //private date
} OleMBarRec, OleMBarPtr, **OleMBarhandle
```

IOleWindow Interface

The **IOleWindow** interface is implemented and used by both container and object applications. The **IOleWindow** interface contains methods that allow an application to obtain the handle to the various windows participating in in-place activation and also to enter and exit context-sensitive help mode.

All other in-place activation interfaces are derived from the **IOleWindow** interface.

IOleWindow contains the following methods:

```
DECLARE_INTERFACE_(IOleWindow, IUnknown)
{
   // *** IUnknown methods ***
  HRESULT QueryInterface (REFIID riid, void * * ppvObj);
  unsigned long AddRef ();
  unsigned long Release ();

   // *** IOleWindow methods ***
  HRESULT GetWindow (WindowPtr * ppWnd);
  HRESULT ContextSensitiveHelp (unsigned long fEnterMode);
};
```

For more information, see the ole2.h header file.

IOleWindow::GetWindow

HRESULT IOleWindow::GetWindow(*ppWnd*)
WindowPtr * *ppWnd*

IOleWindow::GetWindow returns the window pointer to one of the various windows participating in the in-place activation.

Parameter

ppWnd
Points to where to return the window pointer.

Return Values

Value	Meaning
S_OK	The window pointer was successfully returned.
E_INVALIDARG	One or more invalid arguments.
E_UNEXPECTED	An unexpected error happened.
E_FAIL	There is no window pointer currently attached to this object.

IOleWindow::ContextSensitiveHelp

HRESULT IOleWindow::ContextSensitiveHelp(*fEnterMode*)
unsigned long *fEnterMode*

IOleWindow::ContextSensitiveHelp determines whether the context-sensitive help mode should be entered during an in-place activation session. This method is currently not supported on the Macintosh.

Parameter

fEnterMode
Specifies TRUE if help mode should be entered; FALSE if it should be exited.

Return Values

Value	Meaning
S_OK	The help mode was entered or exited successfully, depending on the value passed in *fEnterMode*.
E_UNEXPECTED	An unexpected error happened.

Comments

Applications can invoke context-sensitive help in either of the following user situations:

- SHIFT+F1 is pressed, then a topic is clicked on.
- F1 is pressed when a menu item is selected.

When SHIFT+F1 is used, either the frame or the active object can receive the keystrokes. If the container's frame receives the keystroke, it calls its containing document's **IOleWindow::ContextSensitiveHelp** with *fEnterMode* TRUE. This propagates the help state to all of its in-place objects so they can correctly handle the mouse click or WM_COMMAND.

If an active object receives the SHIFT+F1 keystroke, it calls the container's **IOleInPlaceSite::ContextSensitiveHelp** with *fEnterMode* TRUE, which then recursively calls each of its in-place sites until there are no more to be notified. The container then calls its document's or frame's **ContextSensitiveHelp** method with *fEnterMode* TRUE.

When in context-sensitive help mode, an object that receives the mouse click can either:

- Ignore the click if it does not support context-sensitive help, or
- Tell all the other objects to exit context-sensitive help mode (**ContextSensitiveHelp**(FALSE)) and then provide help for that context.

An object in context-sensitive help mode that receives a WM_COMMAND should tell all the other in-place objects to exit context-sensitive help mode and then provide help for the command.

If a container application is to support context-sensitive help on menu items, it must provide its own message filter so that can intercept the F1 key.

If the object is not UI visible, it should fail the call to **IOleWindow::ContextSensitiveHelp** and return E_FAIL.

IOleInPlaceObject Interface

The **IOleInPlaceObject** interface is implemented by object applications and is used by containers to activate and deactivate an in-place object. A pointer to the **IOleInPlaceObject** interface can be obtained by calling **QueryInterface** on the **IOleObject** interface.The **IOleInPlaceObject** interface contains the following methods:

```
DECLARE_INTERFACE_(IOleInPlaceObject, IOleWindow)
{
  // *** IUnknown methods ***
 HRESULT QueryInterface (REFIID riid, void * * ppvObj);
 unsigned long AddRef ();
 unsigned long Release ();

  // *** IOleWindow methods ***
 HRESULT GetWindow (WindowPtr * ppWnd);
 HRESULT ContextSensitiveHelp (unsigned long fEnterMode);
```

```
    // *** IOleInPlaceObject methods ***
    HRESULT InPlaceDeactivate ();
    HRESULT UIDeactivate ();
    HRESULT SetObjectRects (LPCRECT lprcPosRect, RgnHandle clipRgn,
        RgnHandle, frameRgn, RgnHandle cliRgn);
    HRESULT ReactivateAndUndo ();
};
```

For more information, see the ole2.h header file.

IOleInPlaceObject::InPlaceDeactivate

HRESULT IOleInPlaceObject::InPlaceDeactivate()

IOleInPlaceObject::InPlaceDeactivate deactivates an active in-place object and discards the object's undo state.

Return Values

Value	Meaning
S_OK	The object was successfully deactivated.
E_UNEXPECTED	An unexpected error happened.

Comments

On return from **IOleInPlaceObject::InPlaceDeactivate**, the object discards its undo state. The object application should not shut down immediately after this call. Instead, it should wait for an explicit call to **IOleObject::Close** or for the object's reference count to reach zero.

If the in-place user interface is still visible during the call to **InPlaceDeactivate**, the object application should call its own **IOleInPlaceObject::UIDeactivate** method to hide the user interface. The in-place user interface can be optionally destroyed during calls to **IOleInPlaceObject::UIDeactivate** and **IOleInPlaceObject::InPlaceDeactivate**. If the user interface has not already been destroyed when the container calls **IOleObject::Close**, the user interface must be destroyed during the call to **IOleObject::Close**.

During the call to **IOleObject::Close**, the object should check to see whether it is still in-place active. If so, it should call **InPlaceDeactivate**.

See Also

IOleInPlaceSite::OnInPlaceDeactivate, **IOleObject::Close**

IOleInPlaceObject::UIDeactivate

HRESULT IOleInPlaceObject::UIDeactivate()

IOleInPlaceObject::UIDeactivate deactivates and removes the user interface that supports in-place activation.

Return Values

Value	Meaning
S_OK	The in-place UI was deactivated and removed.
E_UNEXPECTED	An unexpected error happened.

Comments

Resources such as menus and windows can be either cleaned up or kept around in a hidden state until **IOleInPlaceObject::InPlaceDeactivate** or **IOleObject::Close** is called to completely deactivate the object. On deactivating the in-place object's user interface, the object is left in a ready state for quick reactivation. The object stays in this state until the undo state of the document changes. The container should then call **IOleInPlaceObject::InPlaceDeactivate** to tell the object to discard its undo state.

If the container has called **IOleInPlaceObject::UIDeactivate**, it should later call the **IOleInPlaceObject::InPlaceDeactivate** method to properly clean up resources. The container can assume that stopping or releasing the object cleans up resources if necessary. The object must be prepared to do so if **IOleInPlaceObject::InPlaceDeactivate** has not been called at these points.

In its implementation of this method, an object application must:

1. Call **OleUnsetInPlaceWindow**.
2. Call both **IOleInPlaceUIWindow::SetActiveObject** and **IOleInPlaceFrame::SetActiveObject** passing in NULL to deactivate the object.
3. Release the **IOleInPlaceUIWindow** and **IOleInPlaceFrame** pointers and set them to NULL.
4. Call **IOleInPlaceSite::OnUIDeactivate**. If the container caused the in-place session to end, then it must take the foreground.
5. Restore its menu bar.

See Also **IOleInPlaceObject::InPlaceDeactivate**, **IOleInPlaceSite::OnUIDeactivate**, **IOleInPlaceObject::ReactivateAndUndo**, **IOleObject::Close**

IOleInPlaceObject::SetObjectRects

HRESULT IOleInPlaceObject::SetObjectRects(*lprcPosRect, clipRgn, frameRgn, cliRgn* **)**
LPCRECT *lprcPosRect*
RgnHandle *clipRgn*
RgnHandle *frameRgn*
RgnHandle *cliRgn*

IOleInPlaceObject::SetObjectRects indicates how much of the in-place object is visible.

Parameters

lprcPosRect
Points to the rectangle containing the global coordinates of the in-place object.

clipRgn
Specifies the clipping area within the container's window.

frameRgn
Specifies the entire structure region of the containing window (strucRgn).

cliRgn
Contains the union of all structure regions in the container application's windows.

Return Values

Value	Meaning
S_OK	Operation was successful.
E_INVALIDARG	One or more invalid arguments.
E_UNEXPECTED	An unexpected error happened.

Comments

The in-place container calls **IOleInPlaceObject::SetObjectRects** whenever an operation occurs that results in the in-place *lprcPosRect*, *clipRgn*, *frameRgn*, or *cliRgn* changing (for example, moving, sizing, or scrolling the container windows).

The object must always be assured that when it is about to call **OleSetInPlaceRects** it has the correct information from the container. During an in-place session, the container is responsible for moving the containing document and the object application is responsible for moving the in-place window to the containing document. There must be communication between the container and object application to ensure that if one moves the other follows.

If the object is not UI visible, it should fail the call to **IOleInPlaceObject::SetObjectRects** and return E_FAIL.

To ensure proper clipping, the object should call **OleSetParentRgns**, **OleSizeObjectWindow**, and **OleSetInPlaceRects**, in this order.

Note Object must not replace the call to **OleSizeObjectWindow** with a call to **OleMoveWindow**. **OleSizeObjectWindow** performs both the move and size of the window, which is needed for proper behavior.

Figure 11.2 shows a diagram outlining the *lprcPosRect*, *clipRgn*, *cliRgn*, and *frameRgn* areas. Notice that the *cliRgn* is the union of all frame regions, including any inactive frames in the background.

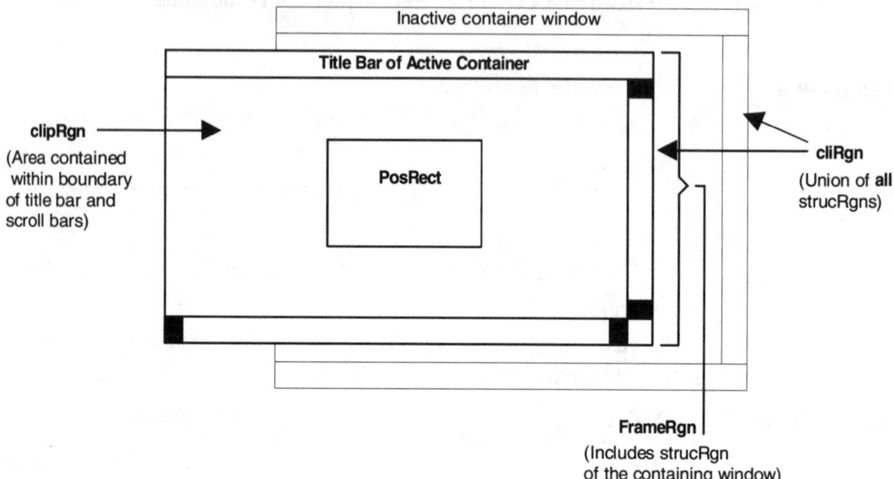

Figure 11.2 In-place container region areas

It is possible for *clipRect* to change without the *lprcPosRect* changing. The size of an in-place object's rectangle is always calculated in pixels.

See Also **IOleInPlaceSite::OnPosRectChange, OleSetInPlaceRects**

IOleInPlaceObject::ReactivateAndUndo

HRESULT IOleInPlaceObject::ReactivateAndUndo()

IOleInPlaceObject::ReactivateAndUndo reactivates a previously deactivated object, undoing the last state of the object.

Return Values

Value	Meaning
S_OK	The object was successfully reactivated.

Value	Meaning
E_NOTUNDOABLE	Called when the undo state is not available.
E_UNEXPECTED	An unexpected error happened.

Comments

If the user chooses the Undo command before the undo state of the object is lost, the object's immediate container calls **IOleInPlaceObject::ReactivateAndUndo** to activate the user interface, carry out the Undo operation, and return the object to the active state.

IOleInPlaceActiveObject Interface

The **IOleInPlaceActiveObject** interface is implemented by object applications to provide a direct channel of communication between the in-place object and the frame and document interfaces. The container uses the interface methods to manipulate an object while it is active in place.The **IOleInPlaceActiveObject** interface contains the following methods:

```
DECLARE_INTERFACE_(IOleInPlaceActiveObject, IOleWindow)
{
   // *** IUnknown methods ***
  HRESULT QueryInterface (REFIID riid, void * * ppvObj);
  unsigned long AddRef ();
  unsigned long Release ();

   // *** IOleWindow methods ***
  HRESULT GetWindow (WindowPtr * ppWnd);
  HRESULT ContextSensitiveHelp (unsigned long fEnterMode);

   // *** IOleInPlaceActiveObject methods ***
  HRESULT TranslateAccelerator (EventRecord * pEvt);
  HRESULT OnFrameWindowActivate (unsigned long fActivate);
  HRESULT OnDocWindowActivate (unsigned long fActivate);
  HRESULT ResizeBorder (LPCRECT lprectBorder, LPOLEINPLACEUIWINDOW lpUIWindow,
        unsigned long fFrameWindow);
  HRESULT EnableModeless (unsigned long fEnable);
};
```

For more information, see the ole2.h header file.

IOleInPlaceActiveObject::TranslateAccelerator

HRESULT IOleInPlaceActiveObject::TranslateAccelerator(*lpEvt***)**
EventRecord * *lpEvt*

IOleInPlaceActiveObject::TranslateAccelerator translates events from the active object's event queue. This method is used only with DLL object applications, which currently are not supported on the Macintosh.

Parameter

lpEvt
Points to the event that might need to be translated.

Return Values

Value	Meaning
S_OK	The event was translated successfully.
S_FALSE	The event was not translated.
E_INVALIDARG	One or more invalid arguments.
E_UNEXPECTED	An unexpected error happened.

Comments

IOleInPlaceActiveObject::TranslateAccelerator is called by the container's message loop when an embedded object is active in place. While active in place, an active object always has the first chance at translating the messages. Therefore, **IOleInPlaceActiveObject::TranslateAccelerator** should be called before any other translation. The container should apply its own translation only if this function returns S_FALSE.

The **IOleInPlaceActiveObject::TranslateAccelerator** function is only invoked for an object created by a DLL object application. An object created by an object application gets keystrokes from its own message pump so the container does not get those messages.

If the container calls **IOleInPlaceActiveObject::TranslateAccelerator** for an object that is not created by a DLL object application, the default object handler returns S_FALSE.

IOleInPlaceActiveObject::OnFrameWindowActivate

HRESULT IOleInPlaceActiveObject::OnFrameWindowActivate(*fActivate*)
unsigned long *fActivate*

IOleInPlaceActiveObject::OnFrameWindowActivate notifies the object when the top-level in-place container application suspends or resumes.

Parameter

fActivate
Indicates whether the container is suspending or resuming. A value of TRUE indicates the application is resuming while a value of FALSE indicates the application is pausing.

Return Values

Value	Meaning
S_OK	The method completed successfully.

Comments

IOleInPlaceActiveObject::OnFrameWindowActivate is called when the container is either being resumed or suspended and the object is the current active object for the frame.

If the object application is becoming active (*fActivate*==TRUE), then it must make itself the foreground application and shows its UI. Otherwise, the object application must remove its in-place UI.

See Also

IOleInPlaceSite::OnUIVisible

IOleInPlaceActiveObject::OnDocWindowActivate

HRESULT IOleInPlaceActiveObject::OnDocWindowActivate(*fActivate*)
unsigned long *fActivate*

IOleInPlaceActiveObject::OnDocWindowActivate notifies the active in-place object when the container's document window gains or loses activation.

Parameter

fActivate
Indicates the state of the container's in-place document window. It is TRUE if the window is activating; FALSE if it is deactivating.

Return Values

Value	Meaning
S_OK	The method completed successfully.

Comments

IOleInPlaceActiveObject::OnDocWindowActivate is called when the container's in-place document window is activated or deactivated and the object is the current active object for the document.

If the the object application is becoming active (*fActivate*==TRUE), then it must make itself the foreground process and show its UI. Otherwise, the object application must remove its in-place UI.

If activating, the object should install frame-level tools (including the shared composite menu and/or optional toolbars and frame adornments), and take focus. When deactivating, the object should remove the frame-level tools, but not call **IOleInPlaceUIWindow::SetBorderSpace** (NULL).

IOleInPlaceActiveObject::ResizeBorder

HRESULT IOleInPlaceActiveObject::ResizeBorder(*lprectBorder, lpUIWindow, fFrameWindow*)
LPCRECT *lprectBorder*
LPOLEINPPLACEWINDOW *lpUIWindow*
unsigned long *fFrameWindow*

IOleInPlaceActiveObject::ResizeBorder is called to alert the object that it needs to resize its border space.

Parameters

lprectBorder
Points to a **Rect** structure containing the new outer rectangle within which the object can request border space for its tools.

lpUIWindow
Points to the frame or document object whose border has changed.

fFrameWindow
A value of TRUE indicates the frame object is calling this method; otherwise, it is FALSE.

Return Values

Value	Meaning
S_OK	The method completed successfully.
E_INVALIDARG	One or more invalid arguments.
E_UNEXPECTED	An unexpected error happened.

Comments

The **IOleInPlaceActiveObject::ResizeBorder** function is called by the top-level container's document or frame object when the border space allocated to the in-place object should change. Because the active in-place object is unaware of whether the frame or document object has changed, **IOleInPlaceActiveObject::ResizeBorder** needs to be passed the pointer to the object's **IOleInPlaceUIWindow** interface.

In most cases, the resize just requires the object to grow, shrink, or scale the frame adornments. However, for more complicated adornments, the object might need to renegotiate the border space with calls to **IOleInPlaceUIWindow::RequestBorderSpace** and **IOleInPlaceUIWindow::SetBorderSpace**.

If the object is not UI visible, it should fail the call to **IOleInPlaceObject::ResizebBorder** and return E_FAIL.

See Also

IOleInPlaceUIWindow::GetBorder

IOleInPlaceActiveObject::EnableModeless

HRESULT IOleInPlaceActiveObject::EnableModeless(*fEnable***)**
unsigned long *fEnable*

IOleInPlaceActiveObject::EnableModeless is called to enable or disable modeless dialog boxes when the container creates or destroys a modal dialog.

Parameter

fEnable
A value of TRUE enables modeless dialog windows; a value of FALSE disables them.

Return Values

Value	Meaning
S_OK	The method completed successfully.

Comments

Calls to **IOleInPlaceActiveObject::EnableModeless**(FALSE) must be balanced with corresponding calls to **EnableModeless**(TRUE).

IOleInPlaceActiveObject::EnableModeless is called by the top-level container to enable and disable modeless dialogs that the object displays. To display a modal dialog, the container first calls the **IOleInPlaceActiveObject::EnableModeless** method, specifying FALSE to disable the object's modeless dialog windows. After completion, the container calls **IOleInPlaceActiveObject::EnableModeless** (TRUE) to re-enable the object's modeless dialog boxes.

Before returning from **IOleInPlaceActiveObject::EnableModeless**(*fEnable*), an object application must first call **OleMaskMouse**(*fEnable*) so that normal mouse processing will occur when the container tries to put up a modal dialog; the mouse processing will be masked again when the request has been withdrawn. After *fEnable* = FALSE has been done, the container application must bring the object application to the foreground (via SetFrontProcess), if appropriate.

Notice that when *fEnable* is FALSE, the container is the background application; after the return of this method call, it must make itself the foreground application in order to display its modal dialog. When *fEnable* is FALSE, the object application should ignore the next Suspend event.

See Also **IOleInPlaceFrame::EnableModeless**

IOleInPlaceUIWindow Interface

The **IOleInPlaceUIWindow** interface is implemented by container applications and is used by object applications to negotiate border space on the document or frame object.

The **IOleInPlaceUIWindow** interface contains the following methods:

```
DECLARE_INTERFACE_(IOleInPlaceUIWindow, IOleWindow)
{
  // *** IUnknown methods ***
  HRESULT QueryInterface (REFIID riid, void * * ppvObj);
  unsigned long AddRef ();
  unsigned long Release ();

  // *** IOleWindow methods ***
  HRESULT GetWindow (WindowPtr * ppWnd);
  HRESULT ContextSensitiveHelp (unsigned long fEnterMode);

  // *** IOleInPlaceUIWindow methods ***
  HRESULT GetBorder (Rect * lprectBorder);
  HRESULT RequestBorderSpace (LPCBORDERWIDTHS lpborderwidths);
  HRESULT SetBorderSpace (LPCBORDERWIDTHS lpborderwidths);
  HRESULT SetActiveObject (LPOLEINPLACEACTIVEOBJECT lpActiveObject,
       const char * lpszObjName);
};
```

For more information, see the ole2.h header file.

IOleInPlaceUIWindow::GetBorder

HRESULT IOleInPlaceUIWindow::GetBorder(*lprectBorder***)**
Rect * *lprectBorder*

IOleInPlaceUIWindow::GetBorder returns a **Rect** structure in which the object can put toolbars and similar controls while an object is active in place.

Parameter

lprectBorder
Points to a **Rect** structure where the outer rectangle is to be returned. The **Rect** structure is relative to the window being represented by the interface.

Return Values

Value	Meaning
S_OK	The rectangle was successfully returned.
E_NOTOOLSPACE	The object cannot install toolbars in this object.
E_INVALIDARG	One or more invalid arguments.
E_UNEXPECTED	An unexpected error happened.

Comments

The **IOleInPlaceUIWindow::GetBorder** function, when called on a document or frame window object, returns the outer rectangle where the object can put toolbars or similar controls. If the object is to install these tools, it should negotiate space for the tools within this rectangle using **IOleInPlaceUIWindow::RequestBorderSpace** and then call **IOleInPlaceUIWindow::SetBorderSpace** to get this space allocated.

See Also

IOleInPlaceUIWindow::RequestBorderSpace, **IOleInPlaceUIWindow::SetBorderSpace**

IOleInPlaceUIWindow::RequestBorderSpace

HRESULT IOleInPlaceUIWindow::RequestBorderSpace(*lpborderwidths***)**
LPCBORDERWIDTHS *lpborderwidths*

IOleInPlaceUIWindow::RequestBorderSpace determines whether tools can be installed around the object's window frame while the object is active in place.

Parameter

lpborderwidths
Points to a **BORDERWIDTHS** structure containing the requested widths (in pixels) needed on each side of the window for the tools.

Return Values

Value	Meaning
S_OK	The requested space could be allocated to the object.
E_NOTOOLSPACE	The object cannot install toolbars in this window object, or there is insufficient space to install the toolbars.

Value	Meaning
E_INVALIDARG	One or more invalid arguments (for example, an invalid pointer or parameter).
E_UNEXPECTED	An unexpected error happened.

Comments

The object calls **IOleInPlaceUIWindow::RequestBorderSpace** to ask if tools can be installed inside the window frame. These tools would be allocated between the rectangle returned by **IOleInPlaceUIWindow::GetBorder** and the **BORDERWIDTHS** structure specified in the argument to this call.

The space for the tools is not actually allocated to the object until it calls **IOleInPlaceUIWindow::SetBorderSpace**, allowing the object to negotiate for space (such as while dragging toolbars around), but deferring the moving of tools until the action is completed.

If the object wants to install these tools, it should pass the width in pixels that is to be used on each side. For example, if the object wanted 10 pixels on the top, 0 pixels on the bottom, and 5 pixels on the left and right sides, it would pass the following **BORDERWIDTHS** structure to **IOleInPlaceUIWindow::RequestBorderSpace**:

```
lpbw->top       = 10
lpbw->bottom    =  0
lpbw->lLeft     =  5
lpbw->right     =  5
```

For more information on negotiating border space, see the description of the **BORDERWIDTHS** structure earlier in this chapter.

See Also

IOleInPlaceUIWindow::GetBorder, **IOleInPlaceUIWindow::SetBorderSpace**

IOleInPlaceUIWindow::SetBorderSpace

HRESULT IOleInPlaceUIWindow::SetBorderSpace(*lpborderwidths***)**
LPCBORDERWIDTHS *lpborderwidths*

IOleInPlaceUIWindow::SetBorderSpace allocates space for the border requested in the call to the **IOleInPlaceUIWindow::RequestBorderSpace** method.

Parameter

lpborderwidths
Points to a **BORDERWIDTHS** structure containing the requested width (in pixels) of the tools. It can be NULL, indicating the object does not need any space.

Return Values

Value	Meaning
S_OK	The requested space has been allocated to the object.

Value	Meaning
OLE_E_INVALIDRECT	The rectangle does not lie within that returned by **IOleInPlaceUIWindow::GetBorder**.
E_INVALIDARG	One or more invalid arguments.
E_UNEXPECTED	An unexpected error happened.

Comments

The object calls the **IOleInPlaceUIWindow::SetBorderSpace** method to allocate the space on the border.

The **BORDERWIDTHS** structure used in this call generally would have been passed in a previous call to **IOleInPlaceUIWindow::RequestBorderSpace**, which must have returned S_OK.

If an object needs to renegotiate space on the border, it can just call **SetBorderSpace** again with the new widths. If the call to **SetBorderSpace** fails, the object can do a full negotiation for border space with calls to **GetBorder**, **RequestBorderSpace**, and **SetBorderSpace**.

See Also

IOleInPlaceUIWindow::GetBorder, **IOleInPlaceUIWindow::RequestBorderSpace**

IOleInPlaceUIWindow::SetActiveObject

HRESULT IOleInPlaceUIWindow::SetActiveObject (*lpActiveObject, lpszObjName*)
LPOLEINPLACEACTIVEOBJECT *lpActiveObject*
const char * *lpszObjName*

IOleInPlaceUIWindow::SetActiveObject is called by the object to provide each of the frame and document objects a direct channel of communication with the active in-place object.

Parameters

lpActiveObject
Points to the active in-place object's **IOleInPlaceActiveObject** interface.

lpszObjName
Points to a string containing the object title.

Return Values

Value	Meaning
S_OK	The method completed successfully.
E_INVALIDARG	One or more invalid arguments.
E_UNEXPECTED	An unexpected error happened.

Comments

When deactivating, the object calls **IOleInPlaceUIWindow::SetActiveObject**, passing NULL for the *lpActiveObject* and *lpszObjName* parameters.

Since the container is receiving the new **IOleInPlaceActiveObject** pointer, it must release the old one and AddRef the new one.

IOleInPlaceFrame Interface

The **IOleInPlaceFrame** interface is implemented by container applications and is used by object applications to control the display and placement of the composite menu, keystroke accelerator translation, context-sensitive help mode, and modeless dialog boxes.

On the Macintosh, the in-place frame space is the desk top primary screen Rect, which contains the menu bar. The space at the top of the Rect must be greater than the height of the menu bar.

The **IOleInPlaceFrame** interface contains the following methods:

```
DECLARE_INTERFACE_(IOleInPlaceFrame, IOleInPlaceUIWindow)
{
  // *** IUnknown methods ***
  HRESULT QueryInterface (REFIID riid, void * * ppvObj);
  unsigned long AddRef ();
  unsigned long Release ();

  // *** IOleWindow methods ***
  HRESULT GetWindow (WindowPtr * ppWnd);
  HRESULT ContextSensitiveHelp (unsigned long fEnterMode);

  // *** IOleInPlaceUIWindow methods ***
  HRESULT GetBorder (Rect * lprectBorder);
  HRESULT RequestBorderSpace (LPCBORDERWIDTHS lpborderwidths);
  HRESULT SetBorderSpace (LPCBORDERWIDTHS lpborderwidths);
  HRESULT SetActiveObject (LPOLEINPLACEACTIVEOBJECT lpActiveObject, const char * lpszObjName);

  // *** IOleInPlaceFrame methods ***
  HRESULT InsertMenus (OleMBarHandle hOleMBar);
  HRESULT AdjustMenus (OleMBarHandle hOleMBar);
  HRESULT RemoveMenus (OleMBarHandle hOleMBar);
  HRESULT SetStatusText (const char * lpszStatusText);
  HRESULT EnableModeless (unsigned long fEnable);
  HRESULT TranslateAccelerator (EventRecord * lpEvent, long ID);
};
```

For more information, see the ole2.h header file.

IOleInPlaceFrame::InsertMenus

HRESULT IOleInPlaceFrame::InsertMenus(*hOleMBar*)
OleMBarHandle *hOleMBar*

IOleInPlaceFrame::InsertMenus is called by the object application to allow the container to insert its menu groups in the composite menu that is to be used during the in-place session.

Parameters

hOleMBar
Specifies a handle to the empty composite menu that will be used during the in-place session.

Return Values

Value	Meaning
S_OK	The method completed successfully.
E_INVALIDARG	One or more invalid arguments.
E_UNEXPECTED	An unexpected error happened.

Comments

The object application asks the container to add its menus to the menu specified in *hOleMBar*. The container should provide the same menu handles that it uses in its normal menu bar by calling **OleAddMBarMenu**(*hOleMBar*, ...,...).

After inserting its menus, the container must call **OlePatchGetMHandle**((*OleMBarHandle*)*hOleMBar*).

See Also

OleAddMBarMenu, **IOleInPlaceFrame::AdjustMenus**, **IOleInPlaceFrame::RemoveMenus**

IOleInPlaceFrame::AdjustMenus

HRESULT IOleInPlaceFrame::AdjustMenus(*hOleMBar*)
OleMBarHandle *hOleMBar*

IOleInPlaceFrame::AdjustMenus is called by the object application to give the in-place container a chance to modify its menus. A container indicates its desire to to have the opportunity to adjust its menus by setting the *fAdjustMenus* member of **OLEINPLACEFRAMEINFO** to TRUE.

Parameters

hOleMBar
Specifies a handle to the composite menu.

Return Values

Value	Meaning
S_OK	The method completed successfully.
E_INVALIDARG	One or more invalid arguments.
E_UNEXPECTED	An unexpected error happened.

Comments

The object application, as part of its own menu setup, calls **IOleInPlaceFrame::AdjustMenus** to ask the container to setup its menus. The container indicates its willingness to have this method called by setting the *fAdjustMenus* field to TRUE in the **OLEINPLACEFRAMEINFO** structure.

The container should always implement this method to simply do its normal menu setup. It may, however, return S_OK without doing anything, if its menus do not need periodic updating.

To eliminate the LRPC cost of menu setup for the object application, the container should be coded in such a way as to not depend on this method being called (set the *fAdjustMenus* to FALSE in the **OLEINPLACEFRAMEINFO** structure) Assuming the state of its menus does not arbitrarily change over time, the container application can best ensure up-to-date menus by adjusting them in its **IOleInPlaceSite::OnUIActivate**, **IOleInPlaceSite::OnUIVisible**, **IOleInPlaceFrame::InsertMenus** and **IOleInPlaceFrame::TranslateAccelerator** methods.

See Also **IOleInPlaceFrame::InsertMenus**, **IOleInPlaceFrame::RemoveMenus**

IOleInPlaceFrame::RemoveMenus

HRESULT IOleInPlaceFrame::RemoveMenus(*hOleMBar***)**
OleMBarHandle *hOleMBar*

IOleInPlaceFrame::RemoveMenus is called by the object application to tell the contain● to remove the OLE menu patching. The container does this by calling **OleUnpatchGetMHandle**((*OleMBarHandle*)(*hOleMBar*).

Parameter

hOleMBar
Specifies a handle to the in-place composite menu which was constructed by calls to **IOleInPlaceFrame::InsertMenus**.

Return Values

Value	Meaning
S_OK	The method completed successfully.
E_INVALIDARG	One or more invalid arguments.
E_UNEXPECTED	An unexpected error happened.

See Also **IOleInPlaceFrame::InsertMenus**, **IOleInPlaceFrame::AdjustMenus**

IOleInPlaceFrame::SetStatusText

HRESULT IOleInPlaceFrame::SetStatusText(*lpszStatusText***)**
const char * *lpszStatusText*

IOleInPlaceFrame::SetStatusText sets and displays status text about the in-place object in the container's frame status line.

Parameter

lpszStatusText
Points to a null-terminated character string containing the message to display.

Return Values

Value	Meaning
S_OK	The text was displayed.
S_TRUNCATED	Some text was displayed but the message was too long.
E_INVALIDARG	One or more invalid arguments.
E_UNEXPECTED	An unexpected error happened.
E_FAIL	The text could not be displayed.

Comments

The object calls **IOleInPlaceFrame::SetStatusText** to ask the frame to display object text in the frame's status line, if it has one. Because the status line is owned by the container's frame, calling **IOleInPlaceFrame::SetStatusText** is the only way an object can display status information. If the container refuses the object's request, the object application can negotiate for border space to display its own status window.

IOleInPlaceFrame::EnableModeless

HRESULT IOleInPlaceFrame::EnableModeless(*fEnable***)**
unsigned long *fEnable*

IOleInPlaceFrame::EnableModeless enables or disables a frame's modeless dialog boxes.

Parameter

fEnable
Specifies whether the modeless dialogs are to be enabled (TRUE) or disabled (FALSE).

Return Values

Value	Meaning
S_OK	The dialog was either enabled or disabled successfully, depending on the value for *fEnable*.
E_UNEXPECTED	An unexpected error happened.

Comments

IOleInPlaceFrame::EnableModeless is called by the active in-place object when it is about to display or remove one of its modal dialogs. This gives the container the opportunity to hide or show its scroll bars.

See Also

IOleInPlaceActiveObject::EnableModeless

IOleInPlaceFrame::TranslateAccelerator

HRESULT IOleInPlaceFrame::TranslateAccelerator(*lpEvent, ID*)
EventRecord * *lpEvent*
long *ID*

IOleInPlaceFrame::TranslateAccelerator translates menu selections and accelerator keystrokes intended for the container's frame while an object is active in place.

Parameters

lpEvent
Points to an EventRecord structure containing the action that triggered the accelerator.

ID
Contains the command identifier value corresponding to the menuID. The highword of the ID contains the hashed menu ID and the lowword value contains the menu item. A value of zero indicates a key stroke sequence not associated with a menu.

Return Values

Value	Meaning
S_OK	The keystroke was used.
S_FALSE	The keystroke was not used.
E_INVALIDARG	One or more invalid arguments.
E_UNEXPECTED	An unexpected error happened.

Comments

All key events that are not handled by the object application are remoted to the container via this method. If the *ID* is zero, the EventRecord will contain the key stroke; otherwise, the container passes the highword of the *ID* to **OleUnhashMenuID** and this result can be passed to the default menu processing.

Note If the accelerator specifies an operation that causes the container to quit, the container must be coded to quit after returning from **IOleInPlaceFrame::TranslateAccelerator**.

See Also

OleUnhashMenuID

IOleInPlaceSite Interface

The **IOleInPlaceSite** interface is implemented by container applications and is used by object applications to interact with the object's in-place client site.

The **IOleInPlaceSite** interface pointer is obtained by calling **QueryInterface** on the object's **IOleClientSite** interface.

The **IOleInPlaceSite** interface contains the following methods:

```
DECLARE_INTERFACE_(IOleInPlaceSite, IOleWindow)
{
// *** IUnknown methods ***
HRESULT QueryInterface (REFIID riid, void * * ppvObj);
unsigned long AddRef ();
unsigned long Release ();

// *** IOleWindow methods ***
HRESULT GetWindow (WindowPtr * ppWnd);
HRESULT ContextSensitiveHelp (unsigned long fEnterMode);

// *** IOleInPlaceSite methods ***
HRESULT CanInPlaceActivate ();
HRESULT OnInPlaceActivate ();
HRESULT OnUIActivate ();
HRESULT OnUIVisible(unsigned long visible);
HRESULT GetObjectRects (Rect * lprcPosRect, RgnHandle, clipRgn, RgnHandle, frameRgn, RgnHandle cliRgn);
HRESULT GetWindowContext (LPOLEINPLACEFRAME * lplpFrame, LPOLEINPLACEUIWINDOW * lplpDoc,
        Rect * lprcPosRect, RgnHandle, clipRgn, RgnHandle, frameRgn, RgnHandle cliRgn,
        LPINPLACEFRAMEINFO lpFrameInfo);
HRESULT Scroll (long scrollExtent);
HRESULT OnUIDeactivate (unsigned long fUndoable);
HRESULT OnInPlaceDeactivate ();
HRESULT DiscardUndoState ();
HRESULT DeactivateAndUndo ();
HRESULT OnPosRectChange (LPCRECT lprcPosRect);
};
```

For more information, see the ole2.h header file.

IOleInPlaceSite::CanInPlaceActivate

HRESULT IOleInPlaceSite::CanInPlaceActivate()

IOleInPlaceSite::CanInPlaceActivate is called by the object to determine whether the container can activate the object in place.

Return Values

Value	Meaning
S_OK	The container allows in-place activation for this object.
S_FALSE	The container does not allow in-place activation for this object.
E_UNEXPECTED	An unexpected error happened.

Comments

IOleInPlaceSite::CanInPlaceActivate is called by the object when this object wants to activate in place. This method allows the container application to accept or refuse the activation request.

Only objects being displayed as DVASPECT_CONTENT can be activated in-place.

IOleInPlaceSite::OnInPlaceActivate

HRESULT IOleInPlaceSite::OnInPlaceActivate()

IOleInPlaceSite::OnInPlaceActivate notifies the container that one of its objects is being activated in place.

Return Values

Value	Meaning
S_OK	The container allows the in-place activation.
E_UNEXPECTED	An unexpected error happened.

Comments

IOleInPlaceSite::OnInPlaceActivate is called by the object from an in-active state. The container should note that the object is becoming active.

A container that supports linking to embedded objects must properly manage the running of its in-place objects when they are UI inactive and running in the hidden state. To reactivate the in-place object quickly, a container should not call **IOleObject::Close** until the container's **IOleInPlaceSite::DeactivateAndUndo** method is called. To safeguard against the object being left in an unstable state should a linking client do a silent update, the container should call **OleLockRunning** to lock the object in the running state. This prevents the hidden in-place object from shutting down before it can be saved in its container.

IOleInPlaceSite::OnUIActivate

HRESULT IOleInPlaceSite::OnUIActivate()

IOleInPlaceSite::OnUIActivate notifies the container that the object is about to be activated in-place and that the object application is about to bring itself to the foreground.

Return Values

Value	Meaning
S_OK	The container allows the in-place activation.
E_NOT_FRONT_PROCESS	The container is not the front process.
E_UNEXPECTED	An unexpected error happened.

Comments

Upon being notified by the object of the impending in-place activation, the container must ignore the next Suspend event.

IOleInPlaceSite::OnUIActivate is called by the in-place object just prior to bringing itself to the foreground. The container should remove any user interface associated with its own activation. If the container is itself an embedded object, it should remove its document-level user interface.

If there is already an object active in place in the same document, the container should call **IOleInPlaceObject::UIDeactivate** before calling **OnUIDeactivate**.

If the container is not the foreground process, it should return E_NOT_FRONT_PROCESS. This will happen if the user has switched to a third application; consequently, the object application will not go fully UI visible.

See Also

IOleInPlaceObject::UIDeactivate

IOleInPlaceSite::OnUIVisible

HRESULT IOleInPlaceSite::OnUIVisible(unsigned long *visible*)
unsigned long *visible*

IOleInPlaceSite::OnUIVisible is called by the object when it is taking the foreground as part of becoming in-place active.

Parameters

visible
Specifies whether the object application's UI is to be made visible (TRUE) or hidden (FALSE).

Return Codes

Value	Meaning
S_OK	The container allows the in-place activation.
E_NOT_FRONT_PROCESS	The container is not the front process.
E_UNEXPECTED	An unexpected error happened.

Comments

On the Macintosh, object applications are not child windows of the containing document (as they are under Windows). They make themselves appear to be so by overlapping the containing document via the **IOleInPlaceSite::SetObjectRects** and **IOleInPlaceSite::OnPosRectChange** methods.

Once the user decides to suspend an in-place session (for example, by selecting a third application), the object application loses focus and must hide its in-place UI since it cannot maintain its foreground windowing position. So while Windows has two states to deal with, InPlaceActive and UIActive, Macintosh object applications include a third state, UIVisible.

If the container is not the foreground process, it should return E_NOT_FRONT_PROCESS.

The object application calls **IOleInPlaceSite::OnUIVisible**(TRUE) immediately before bringing itself to the foreground. The object application must check for an error condition before coming to the foreground.

IOleInPlaceSite::GetObjectRects

HRESULT IOleInPlaceSite::GetObjectRects(*lprcPosRect, clipRgn, frameRgn, cliRgn***)**
Rect * *lprcPosRec*
RgnHandle *clipRgn*
RgnHandle *frameRgn*
RgnHandle *cliRgn*

IOleInPlaceSite::GetObjectRects returns the position area of the container application's containing window.

Parameters

lprcPosRect
Points to the rectangle containing the global coordinates of the in-place object.

clipRgn
Specifies the clipping area within the container's window.

frameRgn
Specifies the entire structure region of the containing window (strucRgn).

cliRgn
Contains the union of all structure regions in the container application's windows.

Return Values

Value	Meaning
S_OK	The method completed successfully.
E_INVALIDARG	One or more invalid arguments.
E_UNEXPECTED	An unexpected error happened.

Comments

Objects call this method when they need to adjust the position area of the containing window. For more information on the area coordinates of these parameters, see **IOleInPlaceObject::SetObjectRects**.

Before calling this method, the rgnhandles must have been allocated by the object application.

IOleInPlaceSite::GetWindowContext

HRESULT IOleInPlaceSite::GetWindowContext(*lplpFrame, lplpDoc, lprcPosRect, clipRgn, frameRgn, cliRgn, lpFrameInfo*)

LPOLEINPLACEFRAME * *lplpFrame*
LPOLINPLACEUIWINDOW * *lplpDoc*
Rect * *lprcPosRec*
RgnHandle *clipRgn*
RgnHandle *frameRgn*
RgnHandle *cliRgn*
LPOLEINPLACEFRAMEINFO *lpFrameInfo*

IOleInPlaceSite::GetWindowContext enables the in-place object to retrieve the window interfaces that form the window object hierarchy, and the position in the parent window where the object's in-place activation window should be placed.

Parameters

lplpFrame
Points to where the pointer to the frame interface is to be returned.

lplpDoc
Points to where the pointer to the document window interface is to be returned.

lprcPosRect
Points to the rectangle containing the global coordinates of the in-place object.

clipRgn
Specifies the clipping area within the container's window.

frameRgn
Specifies the entire structure region of the containing window (strucRgn).

cliRgn
Contains the union of all structure regions in the container application's windows.

lpFrameInfo
Points to an instance of the **OLEINPLACEFRAMEINFO** structure that the container is to fill in with appropriate data.

Return Values

Value	Meaning
S_OK	The method completed successfully.
E_INVALIDARG	One or more invalid arguments.
E_UNEXPECTED	An unexpected error happened.

Comments

Before calling this method, the rgnhandles must have been allocated by the object application.

For more information on the area coordinates of these parameters, see **IOleInPlaceObject::SetObjectRects**.

When an object is going in-place active, it calls **IOleInPlaceSite::GetWindowContext** from its container.

The container AddRefs and returns the **IOleInPlaceFrame** and **IOleInPlaceUIWindow** pointers. Since this routine Add Refs the pointers, the object application must balance calls to it with an equal number of release calls.

See Also **IOleInPlaceObject::SetObjectRects**

IOleInPlaceSite::Scroll

HRESULT IOleInPlaceSite::Scroll(*scrollExtent***)**
long *scrollExtent*

IOleInPlaceSite::Scroll is called by an in-place object to tell the container to scroll the object by the number of pixels specified by *scrollExtent*.

Parameter

scrollExtent
Contains the number of pixels by which to scroll in the *X* and *Y* directions. Positive *X* values mean to move *X* pixels to the left (scroll to the right). The highword contains the horizontal scroll direction and the lowword contains the vertical scroll position. The values are signed to indicate the direction of the scroll.

Return Values

Value	Meaning
S_OK	The method completed successfully.
E_INVALIDARG	One or more invalid arguments.
E_UNEXPECTED	An unexpected error happened.

Comments As a result of scrolling, the in-place object's position and clipping region may change. If this happens, the container should call IOleInPlaceObject::SetObjectRects to provide the new information.

See Also **IOleInPlaceObject::SetObjectRects**

IOleInPlaceSite::OnUIDeactivate

HRESULT IOleInPlaceSite::OnUIDeactivate(*fUndoable***)**
unsigned long *fUndoable*

On deactivation, **IOleInPlaceSite::OnUIDeactivate** notifies the container that the UI-active in-place session has ended.

Parameter

fUndoable
Specifies whether the object can undo changes. It is TRUE if the object can undo, FALSE if it cannot.

Return Values

Value	Meaning
S_OK	The method completed successfully.
E_UNEXPECTED	An unexpected error happened.

Comments

IOleInPlaceSite::OnUIDeactivate is called by the site's in-place object when it is deactivating. If the container caused the UIDeactivate, it must resinstall its user interface and take the foreground.

The object indicates whether it can undo changes through the *fUndoable* flag. If the object can undo changes, the container can (by the user invoking the Edit Undo command) call the **IOleInPlaceObject::ReactivateAndUndo** method to undo the changes.

See Also

IOleInPlaceObject::ReactivateAndUndo

IOleInPlaceSite::OnInPlaceDeactivate

HRESULT IOleInPlaceSite::OnInPlaceDeactivate()

IOleInPlaceSite::OnInPlaceDeactivate notifies the container that the object is no longer active in place.

Return Values

Value	Meaning
S_OK	The method completed successfully.
E_UNEXPECTED	An unexpected error happened.

Comments

IOleInPlaceSite::OnInPlaceDeactivate is called by an in-place object when it is fully deactivated. This method gives the container a chance to run code pertinent to the object's deactivation. In particular, **IOleInPlaceSite::OnInPlaceDeactivate** is called as a result of **IOleInPlaceObject::InPlaceDeactivate** being called. Calling **IOleInPlaceSite::OnInPlaceDeactivate** indicates that the object can no longer support Undo.

If the container is holding pointers to the **IOleInPlaceObject** and **IOleInPlaceActiveObject** interface implementation, it should release them after the **IOleInPlaceSite::OnInPlaceDeactivate** call.

See Also

IOleInPlaceObject::InPlaceDeactivate

IOleInPlaceSite::DiscardUndoState

HRESULT IOleInPlaceSite::DiscardUndoState()

IOleInPlaceSite::DiscardUndoState is called by the active object while performing some action that would discard the Undo state of the object. **IOleInPlaceSite::DiscardUndoState** tells the container to discard its Undo state.

Return Values

Value	Meaning
S_OK	The method completed successfully.
E_UNEXPECTED	An unexpected error happened.

Comments

If an object is activated in place and the object application maintains only one level of undo stack, there is no need to have more than one entry on the undo stack. That is, once a change has been made to the active object that invalidates its Undo state saved by the container, there is no need to maintain this Undo state in the container. The in-place object calls **IOleInPlaceSite::DiscardUndoState** to notify the container to discard the object's last saved Undo state.

IOleInPlaceSite::DeactivateAndUndo

HRESULT IOleInPlaceSite::DeactivateAndUndo()

IOleInPlaceSite::DeactivateAndUndo is called by the active object when the user invokes Undo in a state just after activating the object.

Return Values

Value	Meaning
S_OK	The method completed successfully.
E_UNEXPECTED	An unexpected error happened.

Comments

Upon completion of this call, the container should call **IOleInPlaceObject::UIDeactivate** to remove the user interface for the object, activate itself, and Undo.

IOleInPlaceSite::OnPosRectChange

HRESULT IOleInPlaceSite::OnPosRectChange(*lprcPosRect***)**
LPCRECT *lprcPosRect*

IOleInPlaceSite::OnPosRectChange is called by an in-place object when the object's extents have changed.

Parameter

lprcPosRect
Points to the rectangle containing the position of the in-place object in the client coordinates of its parent window.

Return Values

Value	Meaning
S_OK	The method completed successfully.
E_INVALIDARG	One or more invalid arguments.
E_UNEXPECTED	An unexpected error happened.

Comments

It is through the container's **IOleInPlaceSite::OnPosRectChange** method that the object application tells the container that the in-place object window position or size has changed.

In response to this information, the container recalculates the regions the same way it did in the **IOleInPlaceSite::GetWindowContext** method and then calls **IOleInPlaceObject::SetObjectRects** which triggers the object application to give OLE the correct information with a call to **OleSetInPlaceRects**. The container may adjust the *PosRect* to suit its needs before calling **IOleInPlaceObject::SetObjectRects**.

See Also

IOleInPlaceObject::SetObjectRects

In-Place Activation Functions

The following functions, defined in ole2.h, are used to support in-place activation:

```
HRESULT OleSendLowLevelEvent(ProcessSerialNumber * ppsn, EventRecord * pevt);
HRESULT OleSendLLE OSType sig, EventRecord * lpEvent);
HRESULT OleNewMBar(OleMBarHandle * phOleMBar);
HRESULT OleDisposeMBar(OleMBarHandle hOleMBar);
HRESULT OleInsertMenus(OleMBarHandle hOleMBar, short beforeID1, short beforeID3, short beforeID5);
HRESULT OleHashMenuID (short * pmenuID);
HRESULT OleUnhashMenuID(short * pmenuID);
HRESULT OlePatchGetMHandle(OleMBarHandle hOleMBar);
HRESULT OleUnpatchGetMHandle(OleMBarHandle hOleMBar);
HRESULT OleAddMBarMenu(OleMBarHandle hOleMBar, MenuHandle hMenu, short group);
HRESULT OleSetINFrontOf(ProcessSerialNumber * PPsn);
HRESULT OleSetInPlaceWindow(WindowPtr pWndObject, LPOLEINPLACEFRAMEINFO lpFrameInfo);
HRESULT OleUnSetInPlaceWindow(unsigned long fInvalidate);
HRESULT OleClipWindows(WindowPtr pWndClip);
HRESULT OleClipwindow (WindowPtr pWndClip);
HRESULT OleUnclipWindow(WindowPtr pWndClip);
void OleMoveWindow(WindowPtr pWnd, short hPosition, short vPosition, Boolean fActivate);
void OleDragParentWindow(WindowPtr pWnd, Point startPt, const Rect * pLimitRect);
long OleDragObjectWindow(WindowPtr pWnd, Point startPt, const Rect * pLimitRect, const Rect * pSlopRect,
    short constrain, ProcPtr actionProc);
void OleSizeParentWindow (WindowPtr pWnd, short hPosition, short vPosition, Boolean fUpdate);
void OleSizeObjectWindow (WindowPtr pWnd, const Rect * prcNewBounds, Boolean fUpdate);
long OleZoomParentWindow(WindowPtr pWnd short wPart, Boolean fMakeFront);
long OleGrowParentWindow(WindowPtr pWnd, Point pt, const Rect * prcMinMax);
long OleGrowObjectWindow(WindowPtr pWnd, Point pt, const Rect * prcMinMax, Rect * prcNewBounds);
```

```
short OleWhichGrowHandle(WindowPtr pWnd, Point pt);
HRESULT OleGetCursor(CursPtr pCursor, WindowPtr pWndObject);
HRESULT OleSetCursor(CursPtr pCursor, WindowPtr pWndParent);
HRESULT OleUpdateCursor(WindowPtr pWndObject);
HRESULT OleSetInPlaceRects(RgnHandle posRgn, RgnHandle clipRgn, RgnHandle frameRgn,
    RgnHandle cliRgn, long reserved);
HRESULT OleSetParentRgns(RgnHandle clipRgn, RgnHandle frameRgn,
    RgnHandle cliRgn);
HRESULT OleMaskMouse(Boolean fEnable);
```

OleSendLowLevelEvent

HRESULT OleSendLowLevelEvent(*ppsn*, *lpEvent*)
ProcessSerialNumber *ppsn*
EventRecord * *lpEvent*

OleSendLowLevelEvent is called by the in-place object to send mouseDown events to the container while it is active in place.

Parameters

ppsn
Specifies the container's process serial number.

lpEvent
Points to the event that is to be sent.

Return Values

Value	Meaning
S_OK	The function completed successfully.
E_FAIL	An unexplained error occurred.
E_INVALIDARG	One or more invalid arguments.

Comments

As shown in Figure 11.3, any time a mouse click is made outside the *PosRgn* but inside the *frameRgn* (indicated by the shaded grey area), the object application will receive an app1Evt.

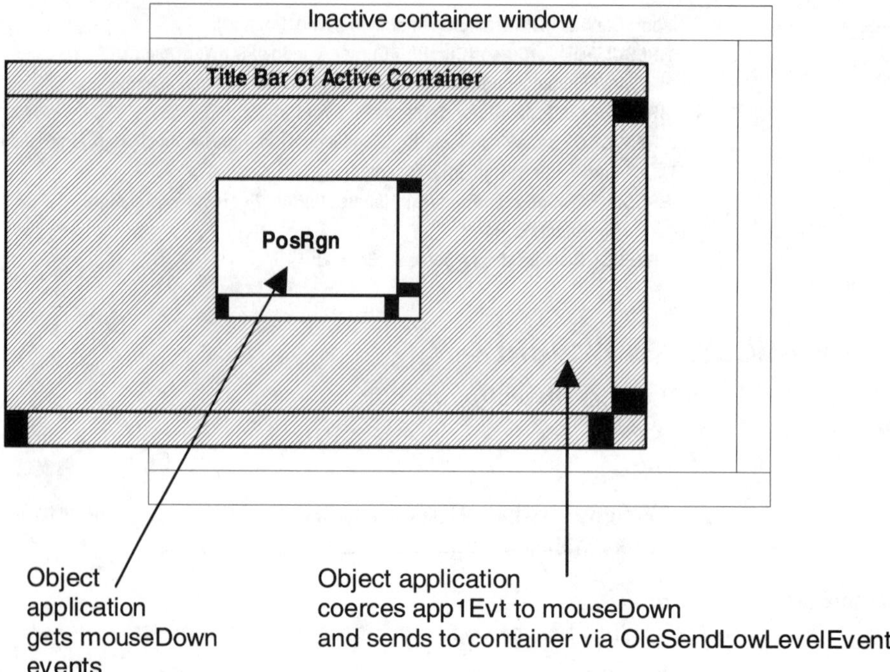

Figure 11.3 Handling of mouse-down events during an in-place session

In its menu processing code, the object application must change the *event->what* field to a mouseDown event and call **OleSendLowLevelEvent**, passing in the container's process serial number and event (this is the only way that the container will get the mouseDown event):

```
event.what = mouseDown;
OleSendLowLevelEvent(ppsn, &event);
```

To receive mouseDown events, the mouse masking must be on; see **OleMaskMouse**. In addition, the container must have also installed the OLE 2 event as shown below:

```
myErr = AEInstallEventHandler('OLE2', 'EVNT', //Handler for low-level
                                               //wrapper
        (EventHandlerProcPtr) RemoteLowLevelEvt, 0, false);

RemoteLowLevelEvt(AppleEvent theAppEvt, AppleEvent reply,
    long HandlerRefCon)
{
OSErr    myErr;
long     cb;
DescTypedescType;
EventRecord theEvent;
```

```
    if (noErr != AEGetKeyPtr(&theAppEvt, keyDirectObject, typeWildCard,
         &descType, (Ptr)&theEvent, sizeof(theEvent), &cb)) )
    {
        return myErr;
    }

    DoEvent(&theEvent);      //Process Event
    return noErr;
}
```

See Also **OleMaskMouse**

OleSendLLE

HRESULT OleSendLLE(*sig*, *lpEvent*)
OSType *sig*
EventRecord * *lpEvent*

The functionality offered by **OleSendLLE** has been superceded by **OLESendLowLevelEvent**; applications should call **OleSendLowLevelEvent** in place of **OleSendLLE**.

Parameters

sig
Specifies the container's creator signature.

lpEvent
Points to the event that is to be sent.

Return Values

Value	Meaning
S_OK	The function completed successfully.
E_FAIL	An unexplained error occurred.
E_INVALIDARG	One or more invalid arguments.

OleNewMBar

HRESULT OleNewMBar(*phOleMBar*)
OleMBarHandle * *phOleMBar*

OleNewMBar is called by the in-place object to allocate the composite menu bar.

Parameters

phOleMBar
Upon successful return, contains the handle to the composite menu bar.

Return Values

Value	Meaning
S_OK	The function completed successfully.
E_OUTOFMEMORY	Out of memory.

OleDisposeMBar

HRESULT OleDisposeMBar(*hOleMBar*)
OleMBarHandle *hOleMBar*

OleDisposeMBar is called by the object to free the composite menu bar.

Parameters

hOleMBar
Specifies the handle to the composite menu bar.

Return Values

Value	Meaning
S_OK	The function completed successfully.
E_INVALIDARG	One or more invalid argumemts.

OleInsertMenus

HRESULT OleInsertMenus (*hOleMBar*, *beforeID1*, *beforeID3*, *beforeID5*)
OleMBarHandle *hOleMBar*
short *beforeID1*
short *beforeID3*
short *beforeID5*

OleInsertMenus is called by the object to insert the object's and container's menus into the composite menu bar.

Parameters

hOleMBar
Specifies the handle to the composite menu bar.

beforeID1
Specifies the menu ID before which the group 0 menu is inserted in the menu bar.

beforeID3
Specifies the menu ID before which the group 2 menu is inserted in the menu bar.

beforeID5
Specifies the menu ID before which the group 4 menu is inserted in the menu bar.

Return Values

Value	Meaning
S_OK	The function completed successfully.
E_FAIL	An unexplained error occurred.

Comments

The object application must call **OleInsertMenus** whenever it is going to display the composite menu bar.

Before calling **OleInsertMenus**, the object application first allocates *hOleMBar* and call **IOleInPlaceFrame::InsertMenus** to give the container a chance to add its menus to the composite menu bar. The object application then saves its menu bar and deletes any menu it doesn't want as part of the composite menu.

The parameters to **OleInsertMenus** specify where the different groups of container menus go. Each group of menus is inserted before the menu whose menu ID equals *beforeID#*. The *beforeID1* parameter specifies before which object application menu the container's group 0 menus go. The *beforeID3* parameter specifies before which object application menu the container's group 2 menus go and the *beforeID5* parameter specifies before which object application menu the container's group 4 menus go. In other words, the container's group 0 menus (which are usually only "File") are usually placed before the object applications "Edit" menu; therefore, the Edit menu ID is the second parameter to **OleInsertMenus**.

A zero value in any of the *beforeID#* parameters results in the object application putting the specified menu group at the end of its menus. If a menu is already in the menu bar, **OleInsertMenus** does nothing. To update the composite menu bar, applications must call **DrawMenuBar**.

OleHashMenuID

HRESULT OleHashMenuID(*pMenuID*)
short * *pMenuID*

OleHashMenuID, when called called by the container, will report the hash value of the specified menu ID if, and only if, the menu has been hashed.

Parameters

pMenuID
Specifies the menu ID that is to be hashed. If the *menuID* is currently hashed, then on return, *pMenuID* will contain the hashed value.

Return Values

Value	Meaning
S_OK	S_OK returned in all cases.

Comments

The menuID will not be changed if the corresponding in *pMenuID* has not been hashed.

OleUnhashMenuID

HRESULT OleUnhashMenuID(*pMenuID*)
short * *pMenuID*

OleUnhashMenuID, when called by the container, returns the unhashed *menuID*, if it has been hashed. Otherwise, the menu ID is left unchanged.

Parameters

pMenuID
Specifies the menu ID that is to be unhashed. If the menu ID was not hashed, then on return, *pMenuld* will have the same value it did when **OleUnhashMenuID** was called.

Return Values

Value	Meaning
S_OK	S_OK is returned in all cases.

Comments

In its default menu processing routine, any non-NULL menu commands which the object application does not understand must be forwarded to the container for processing via **IOleInPlaceFrame::TranslateAccelerator**. Before attempting to act upon the menu, the container calls **OleUnhashMenuID**.

See Also

IOleInPlaceFrame::TranslateAccelerator

OlePatchGetMHandle

HRESULT OlePatchGetMHandle(*hOleMBar*)
OleMBarHandle *hOleMBar*

OlePatchGetMHandle is called by the container application to patch **GetMHandle** within the application's trapped dispatch table.

Parameters

hOleMBar
Specifies the handle to the composite menu bar.

Return Values

Value	Meaning
S_OK	The function completed successfully.
E_OUTOFMEMORY	Out of memory.

Comments

Calls to **OlePatchGetMHandle** must be balanced with calls to **OleUnpatchGetMHandle**.

The *menuIDs* in *hOleMBar* will be hashed to a range between 15000-17000. OLE applications should not assign menuIDs within this range.

The container calls **OlePatchGetMHandle** in the **IOleInPlaceFrame::InsertMenus** code after the repeated **OleAddMBarMenu** calls.

See Also

OleAddMBarMenu, **IOleInPlaceFrame::InsertMenus**

OleUnpatchGetMHandle

HRESULT OleUnpatchGetMHandle(*hOleMBar*)
OleMBarHandle *hOleMBar*

OleUnpatchGetMHandle is called by the container application to unhash menus and to remove the **GetMHandle** patch previously established with **OlePatchGetMHandle**.

Parameters

hOleMBar
Specifies the handle to the composite menu bar.

Return Values

Value	Meaning
S_OK	The function completed successfully.

Comments

Menus are unhashed and the patch to **GetMHandle** is removed if, and only if, there are no more unbalanced calls to **OlePatchGetMHandle**.

The container calls **OleUnpatchGetMHandle** in the **IOleInPlaceFrame::RemoveMenus** code.

Note Because a trapped patch is being removed, the application must ensure that it has not patched **GetMHandle** during the lifetime of the OLE patch.

OleAddMBarMenu

HRESULT OleAddMBarMenu(*hOleMBar*, *hMenu*, *group*)
OleMBarHandle *hOleMBar*
MenuHandle *hMenu*
short *group*

OleAddMBarMenu adds the container application's menu to the in-place composite menu bar.

Parameters

hOleMBar
Specifies the handle to the composite menu bar.

hMenu
Specifies the handle to the menu that is being added to the composite menu bar.

group
Specifies the menu group.

Return Values

Value	Meaning
S_OK	The function completed successfully.
E_OUTOFMEMORY	Out of memory.

Value	Meaning
OLE_E_WRONG_MENU	A NULL value was passed in for *hOleMBar*.
E_FAIL	An unexplained error occurred.

Comments

In its **IOleInPlaceFrame::InsertMenus** method, the container calls **OleAddMBarHandle** once for each menu it wants to add to the composite menu bar.

The *group* parameter specifies the menu group. The container can specify menus to be added to group 0, 2, 4 or -1, where -1 denotes a hierarchical menu. Applications should check the menu ID for validity before inserting.

```
MenuHandle hMenu;
hMenu = GetMHandle(mFile);
Assert(hMenu)
if(hMenu)
{
    OleAddMBarMenu(hOleMBar,hMenu, 0);
}
```

OleSetInFrontOf

HRESULT OleSetInFrontOf(*pPsn*)
ProcessSerialNumber * *pPsn*

OleSetInFrontOf is called by the object application to bring the object to the foreground during an in-place activation.

Parameters

pPsn
Points to the container's process serial number.

Return Values

Value	Meaning
NOERROR	The function completed successfully.
E_UNSPEC	An unexpected error occurred.

Comments

Object applications must call **OleSetInFrontOf** immediately after calling **IOleInPlaceSite::OnUIActivate** or **IOleInPlaceSite::OnUIVisible**(TRUE) to bring the in-place object to the foreground. If **OleSetInFrontOf** returns NOERROR, the in-place session was initiated successfully. If **OleSetInFrontOf** returns any value other than NOERROR, the object should suspend in-place activation and call **IOleInPlaceSite::OnUIVisible**(FALSE).

OleSetInPlaceWindow

HRESULT OleSetInPlaceWindow(*pWndObject, lpFrameInfo*)
WindowPtr *pWndObject*
LPOLEINPLACEFRAMEINFO *lpFrameInfo*

OleSetInPlaceWindow is called by the object application to inform the OLE libraries which window is serving the in-place object.

Parameters

pWndObject
Specifies the in-place object's window.

lpFrameInfo
Points to an instance of the **OLEINPLACEFRAMEINFO** structure.

growHandles

Return Values

Value	Meaning
S_OK	The function completed successfully.
E_INVALIDARG	One or more invalid arguments.
E_OUTOFMEMORY	Out of memory.
OLE_E_IPBUSY	Another in-place UI-visible session still exists.

Comments

This is the official request to begin in-place activation. The object application calls **OleSetInPlaceWindow** to tell OLE which object application window is servicing the in-place object. This function will install a new window definition procedure (**wdef**) for this window.

OleSetInPlaceWindow must be called before calling **OleClipWindows**.

If **OleSetInPlaceWindow** returns OLE_E_IPBUSY, this means another object application is UI visible. In this case, the object application may enter a **WaitNextEvent** loop and continue to call **OleSetInPlaceWindow** until it either succeeds or times out and chooses to open edit.

See Also

OleUnSetInPlaceWindow

OleUnSetInPlaceWindow

HRESULT OleUnSetInPlaceWindow(*fInvalidate*)
unsigned long *fInvalidate*

The object application calls **OleUnSetInPlaceWindow** to indicate that the in-place window should be unsubclassed and the clipped windows should be unclipped.

Parameters

fInvalidate
A value of TRUE indicates that OLE should invalidate the regions that were clipped to make the container look like it was foreground window. A value of FALSE indicates the container is taking the foreground and will cover these clipped areas when it takes the foreground. Typically, the object application sends TRUE for Suspend/Deactivate events and FALSE in all other situations.

Return Values

Value	Meaning
S_OK	The function completed successfully.
OLE_E_NOEXTENSION	The in-place extension was not installed.
OLE_E_VERSEXTENSION	Incorrect version of the in-place extension.

Comments

Applications should call **OleUnsetInPlaceWindow**(TRUE) whenever the container is not coming to the foreground after an in-place session is closed or suspended. Calling **OleUnsetInPlaceWindow** is the first step to exiting the UI visible state.

See Also

OleSetInPlaceWindow, **OleClipWindows**

OleClipWindows

HRESULT OleClipWindows(*pWndClip*)
WindowPtr *pWndClip*

OleClipWindows is called by the object application to clip all windows in its window list, starting from and including *pWndClip*.

Parameters

pWndClip
Specifies the in-place object's top-most document window.

Return Values

Value	Meaning
S_OK	The function completed successfully.
E_OUTOFMEMORY	The application ran out memory.
E_FAIL	An unexplained error occurred.

Comments

OleClipWindows must be called while the object application is in the background. The clipping applied to the windows by this function gives the appearance that the container is in the fromt of the object application, even though the object application is the foreground application.

For *pWndClip*, the object application specifies its top-most document window (the WindowList low-memory global can be used). Applications with floating windows must pass in their top-most non-floating window.

OleClipWindows checks the state of the visible bit of the window before subclassing it; if the window is invisible, **OleClipWindows** does nothing (in order to avoid improperly clipping the hidden window).

OleClipWindow

HRESULT OleClipWindow(*pWndClip*)
WindowPtr *pWndClip*

OleClipWindow is called by the object application to clip the window associated with *pWndClip*.

Parameters

pWndClip
Specifies the in-place object's window that is to be clipped.

Return Codes

Value	Meaning
S_OK	The function completed successfully.
E_OUTOFMEMORY	The application ran out memory.
E_FAIL	An unexplained error occurred.

Comments

OleClipWindow only clips the window associated with *pWndClip*. To clip all windows, starting with *pWndClip*, applications should call **OleClipWindows**.

See Also

OleClipWindows

OleUnclipWindow

HRESULT OleUnclipWindow(*pWndClip***)**
WndPtr *pWndClip*

OleUnclipWindow unclips the window associated with *pWndPtr*.

Parameters

pWndClip
Specifies the WndPtr to the window that is to be unclipped.

Return Values

Value	Meaning
S_OK	The function completed successfully.

Comments

OleUnclipWindow is useful during in-place sessions when you need to unclip a window and bring it forward (for example, dialogs).

OleMoveWindow

void OleMoveWindow(*pWnd,hposition, vposition, fActivate*)
WindowPtr *pWnd*
short *hposition*
short *vposition*
Boolean *fActivate*

OleMoveWindow is called by either the container or object application to move its window.

Parameters

pWnd
Specifies the in-place window that is to be moved.

hposition
Specifies the new horizontal position of the window.

vposition
Specifies the new veritical position of the window.

fActivate
A value of TRUE indicates that **OleMoveWindow** should make the window active (if it isn't already) and bring it to the foreground.

Return Values

Value	Meaning
S_OK	The function completed successfully.
OLE_E_NOEXTENSION	The in-place extension was not installed.
OLE_E_VERSEXTENSION	Incorrect version of the in-place extension.

Comments

OleMoveWindow moves the window to another part of the screeen, without affecting its size or plane.

OleDragParentWindow

void OleDragParentWindow(*pWnd, startPt, pLimitRect*)
WindowPtr *pWnd*
Point *startPt*
const Rect **pLimitRect*

OleDragParentWindow drags the in-place container window and object window.

Parameters

pWnd
Specifies the parent window to be dragged.

startPt
Specifies the mouse position in global coordinates, usually, *Event->where*.

pLimitRect
Points to bounding limits of the drag.

Return Values

Value	Meaning
S_OK	The function completed successfully.

Comments

Upon receiving a mouseDown event in the drag region of the *pWnd*, an in-place container calls **OleDragParentWindow** followed by a call to **IOleInPlaceObject::SetObjectRects**. **OleDragParentWindow** moves both the in-place container's and object application's windows.

See Also

IOleInPlaceObject::SetObjectRects

OleDragObjectWindow

long OleDragObjectWindow(*pWnd,startPt, pLimitRect, pSlopRect, constrain, actionProc*)
WindowPtr *pWnd*
Point *startPt*
const Rect * *pLimitRect*
const Rect * *pSlopRect*
short *constrain*
ProcPtr *actionProc*

OleDragObjectWindow is called by the object application to drag its in-place window within the container's in-place document.

Parameters

pWnd
Specifies the in-place object window that is to be dragged.

startPt
Specifies the current mouse position in global coordinates, usually *Event->where.*

pLimitRect
Points to the bounding limits of the drag.

pSlopRect
Points to the bounding limits for the feedback(for example, the size of the window).

constrain
Specifies the limits the container placed on the direction of the drag: 0 = noConstraint, 1 = hAxisOnly, 2 = vAxisOnly, and 3 = noAxis. The container indicates its willingness to have objects dragged into its containing document by setting the *dragConstraint* field in the **OLEINPLACEFRAMEINFO** data structure.

actionProc
Specifies a callback procedure to use while dragging; Most often NULL, meaning the system will handle it.

Return Values

Value	Meaning
long	0 indicates the object was dragged successfully within the constraints of the containing window; -1 indicates that the object application is trying to drag a non-in-place window while active in-place. Otherwise, the high word contains the vertical distance moved and the low word contains the horizontal distance moved. A value of 0x80008000 means the object window was released outside the *pSlopRect*.

Comments

An in-place object drags its in-place window by calling **OleDragObjectWindow** followed by a call to **IOleInPlaceSite::OnPosRectChange**.

For more information on dragging, see the Macintosh **DragGrayRgn** function.

See Also

IOleInPlaceSite::OnPosRectChange

OleSizeParentWindow

void OleSizeParentWindow(*pWnd,hposition, vposition, fUpdate*)
WindowPtr *pWnd*
short *hposition*
short *vposition*
Boolean *fUpdate*

OleSizeParentWindow sizes the container's in-place window and clips the inplace object's active window.

Parameters

pWnd
Specifies the container's in-place window.

hposition
Specifies the new horizontal size of the window.

vposition
Specifies the new vertical size of the window.

fUpdate
A value of TRUE indicates that **OleSizeParentWindow** will accumulate any newly created area of the content region into the update region. A value of FALSE indicates that the container is responsible for maintaining the update region.

Comments

The container calls **OleSizeParentWindow** followed by a call to **IOleInPlaceObject::SetObjectRects**.

See Also
IOleInPlaceObject::SetObjectRects

OleSizeObjectWindow

void OleSizeObjectWindow(*pWnd, prcNewBounds, fUpdate*)
WindowPtr *pWnd*
const Rect **prcNewBounds*
Boolean *fUpdate*

OleSizeObjectWindow moves and resizes the in-place object's window to effectively zoom the window.

Parameters

pWnd
Specifies the object window.

prcNewBounds
Specifies the new bounding rectangle of the window.

fUpdate
A value of TRUE indicates that **OleSizeObjectWindow** will accumulate any newly created area of the content region into the update region. A value of FALSE indicates that the object will be responsible for maintaining the update region.

Comments

The object application calls **OleSizeObjectWindow** when it needs to resize its in-place window.

OleZoomParentWindow

long OleZoomParentWindow(*pWnd, wPart, fMakeFront*)
WindowPtr *pWnd*
short *wPart*
Boolean *fMakeFront*

OleZoomParentWindow grows the in-place container window.

Parameters

pWnd
Specifies the parent window.

wPart
Specifies the new bounding rectangle of the window.

fMakeFront
A value of TRUE indicates that **OleZoomParentWindow** will accumulate any newly created area of the content region into the update region. A value of FALSE indicates that the object will be responsible for maintaining the update region.

Return Values

Value	Meaning
0	Always returns zero.

OleGrowParentWindow

long OleGrowParentWindow(*pWnd, pt, prcMinMax*)
WindowPtr *pWnd*
Point *pt*
const Rect * *prcMinMax*

OleGrowParentWindow grows the in-place container window.

Parameters

pWnd
Specifies the parent window.

pt
Specifies the current mouse position in global coordinates, usually *Event->where*.

prcMinMax
Specifies the minimum and maximum sizes allowed.

Return Values

Value	Meaning
growResult	A return value of 0 indicates that the size is the same as that of the current PosRgn. Otherwise, the high-order word is the new height of the window and the low-order word is the new width.

Comments

When there is a mouseDown event in the grow area of the in-place container's window, the container should call **OleGrowParentWindow** with *pt* equal to the point where the mouse button was pressed (in global coordinates, as stored in the where field of the EventRecord).

OleGrowParentWindow wraps the functionality offered by the Macintosh **GrowWindow** function.

OleGrowObjectWindow

long OleGrowObjectWindow(*pWnd, pt, prcMinMax, prcNewBounds*)
WindowPtr *pWnd*
Point *pt*
const Rect **prcMinMax*
Rect * *prcNewBounds*

OleGrowObjectWindow is called by the object application to grow its in-place window.

Parameters

pWnd
Specifies the in-place object's window.

pt
Specifies the current mouse position in global coordinates, usually, *Event->where*.

prcMinMax
Specifies the mimimum and maximum sizes allowed.

prcNewBounds
On return, contains the new dimensions of the window to pass to **OleSizeObjectWindow** and **OleSetInPlaceRects**.

Return Values

Value	Meaning
growResult	A return value of 0 indicates that the size is the same as that of the current *PosRgn*. Otherwise, the high-order word is the new height of the window and the low-order word is the new width.

Comments

When there is a mouseDown event in the grow area of the in-place container's window, the container should call **OleGrowObjectWindow** with *pt* equal to the point where the mouse button was pressed (in global coordinates, as stored in the where field of the EventRecord).

OleGrowObjectWindow wraps the functionality offered by the Macintosh **GrowWindow** function.

OleWhichGrowHandle

short OleWhichGrowHandle(*pWnd, pt*)
WindowPtr *pWnd*
Point *pt*

OleWhichGrowHandle determines if the mouse is over a grow handle and, if so, returns information.

Parameters

pWnd
Specifies the in-place object window.

pt
Specifies the global coordinates of the mouse, usually *Event->where*.

Return Values

Value	Meaning
0	The cursor is in the standard grow box.
1-8	Specifies the grow handle.
-1	The cursor is in the drag region but not in the grow region.
-2	The cursor is not over the in-place window.
-3	The window is not an in-place window.
-4	The in-place window is not UI visible.

Comments

OleWhichGrowHandle internally calls **FindWindow** to ensure that the window is visible.

Handles 1...8 are numbered from the top left to the bottom right, as shown in Figure 11.4:

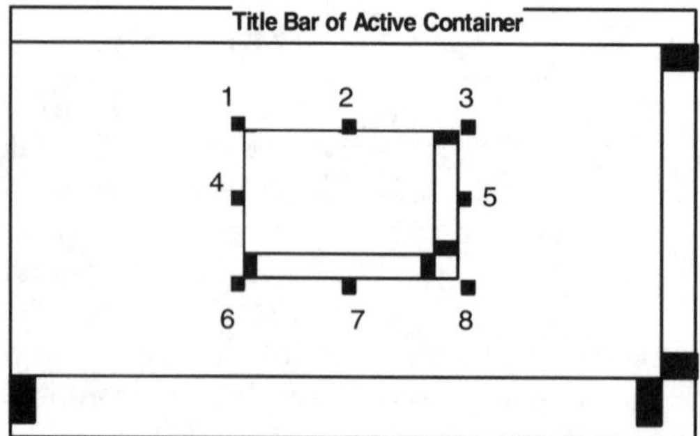

Figure 11.4 Numbering of grow handles

OleGetCursor

HRESULT OleGetCursor(*pCursor, pWndObject*)
CursPtr *pCursor*
WindowPtr *pWndObject*

OleGetCursor is called by the object application to get cursor information previously set by the container application.

Parameters

pCursor
On return, points to a 68-byte buffer where the container's Cursor record.

pWndObject
Pointer to the object application's in-place window.

Return Values

Value	Meaning
S_OK	The function completed successfully.
E_INVALIDARG	One or more invalid arguments.
E_FAIL	An unexplained error occurred.
OLE_E_NOEXTENSION	The in-place extension was not installed.
OLE_E_VERSEXTENSION	Incorrect version of the in-place extension.

Comments

During its idle processing, the object application should check the mouse cursor position and, if it is outside the cursor updating visible content area of the object window, either call **OleUpdateCursor** or **OleGetCursor** followed by **OleSetCursor**.

See Also

OleUpdateCursor, **OleSetCursor**

OleSetCursor

HRESULT OleSetCursor(*pCursor, pWndParent*)
CursPtr *pCursor*
WindowPtr *pWndParent*

OleSetCursor is optionally called by the container application in set cursor information at the time of the in-place session.

Parameters

pCursor
Points to a Cursor record containing the cursor pertinent to the current mouse location.

pWndParent
Pointer to the container application's in-place window.

Return Values

Value	Meaning
S_OK	The function completed successfully.
E_INVALIDARG	One or more invalid arguments.
E_FAIL	An unexplained error occurred.
OLE_E_NOEXTENSION	The in-place extension was not installed.
OLE_E_VERSEXTENSION	Incorrect version of the in-place extension.

Comments

If the container does not set up cursor information, the standard arrow is the default cursor.

If the windows specified in *pWndParent* is not the current in-place parent window, **OleSetCursor** does nothing.

OleUpdateCursor

HRESULT OleUpdateCursor(*pWndObject*)
WindowPtr *pWndObject*

OleUpdateCursor may be called by the object application to update the cursor while it is outside the visible content area of the object application window.

Parameters

pWndObject
Pointer to the object application's in-place window.

Return Values

Value	Meaning
S_OK	The function completed successfully.
E_INVALIDARG	One or more invalid arguments.
E_FAIL	An unexplained error occurred.
OLE_E_NOEXTENSION	The in-place extension was not installed.
OLE_E_VERSEXTENSION	Incorrect version of the in-place extension.

Comments

OleUpdateCursor is a helper function that wraps calls to **OleGetCursor**, **OleWhichGrowHandle**, and the **SetCursor** functions.

If the cursor is over a drag/resize area of the object window, the standard resize cursors will be drawn. If no cursor information was provided by the container and the cursor is outside the object application window (in the call to **OleSetCursor**), the standard arrow cursor is used.

If a callback is provided, the application can supply custom resize cursors.

OleSetInPlaceRects

OleSetInPlaceRects (*posRgn*, *clipRgn*, *frameRgn*, *cliRgn*, *reserved*)
RgnHandle *posRgn*
RgnHandle *clipRgn*
RgnHandle *frameRgn*
RgnHandle *cliRgn*
long *reserved*

OleSetInPlaceRects is called by the object application to instruct the OLE libraries on how to clip the object application window that is servicing the in-place session (specified in the call to **OleSetInPlaceWindow**).

Parameters

posRgn
Specifies the content region of the in-place object window after any object adornments have been added.

clipRgn
Specifies the clipping area within the container's immediate in-place window.

frameRgn
Specifies the entire strucRgn of the in-place object's containing window.

cliRgn
Contains the union of all strucRgns in the container application's windows.

reserved
Reserved for future use; must be NULL.

Return Values

Value	Meaning
S_OK	The function completed successfully.
E_INVALIDARG	One or more invalid arguments.
E_FAIL	An unexplained error occurred.
OLE_E_NOEXTENSION	The in-place extension was not installed.
OLE_E_VERSEXTENSION	Incorrect version of the in-place extension.

Comments

OleSetInPlaceRects typically gets called whenever the in-place object's window has changed size or position.

The *PosRgn* can be calculated in one of the following ways:

- If there are no adornments, the application simply calls **RectRgn**(*PosRect*).
- If adornments are present (such as scroll bars), the *PosRgn* must include the adornment area.
- If editing an irregular-shaped object, the *PosRgn* can be non-rectangular.

For a graphical illustration of the *PosRgn*, *clipRgn*, *frameRgn*, and *cliRgn*, see **IOleInPlaceObject::SetObjectRects**.

See Also **IOleInPlaceObject::SetObjectRects**, **IOleInPlaceSite::GetWindowContext**, **OleSetInPlaceWindow**

OleSetParentRgns

OleSetInPlaceRects (*clipRgn, frameRgn, cliRgn*)
RgnHandle *clipRgn*
RgnHandle *frameRgn*
RgnHandle *cliRgn*

OleSetParentRgns is called by the object application to instruct the OLE libraries on how to clip the object application window that is servicing the in-place session (specified in the call to **OleSetInPlaceWindow**).

Parameters

clipRgn
Specifies the clipping area within the container's immediate in-place window.

frameRgn
Specifies the entire strucRgn of the in-place object's containing window.

cliRgn
Contains the union of all strucRgns in the container application's windows.

Return Values

Value	Meaning
S_OK	The function completed successfully.
E_INVALIDARG	One or more invalid arguments.
E_FAIL	An unexplained error occurred.
OLE_E_NOEXTENSION	The in-place extension was not installed.
OLE_E_VERSEXTENSION	Incorrect version of the in-place extension.

Comments

So that the proper clipping regions are in place before moving or sizing the object window, the object application calls **OleSetParentRgns** in the **IOleInPlaceObject::SetObjectRects** method.

For a graphical illustration of the *clipRgn, frameRgn*, and *cliRgn*, see **IOleInPlaceObject::SetObjectRects**.

See Also **OleSetInPlaceRects, IOleInPlaceObject::SetObjectRects**, **IOleInPlaceSite::GetWindowContext**, **OleSetInPlaceWindow**

OleMaskMouse

OleMaskMouse(*fEnable*)
unsigned long *fEnable*

OleMaskMouse is called by the object application when it wants to enable or disable *mouseDown -> appl1Evnt* coercion.

Parameters

fEnable
Enables (TRUE) or disables (FALSE) the control of mouse click processing by OLE during an in-place session.

Return Codes

Value	Meaning
S_OK	The function completed successfully.
E_OUTOFMEMORY	Out of memory.
OLE_E_NOEXTENSION	The in-place extension was not installed.
OLE_E_VERSEXTENSION	Incorrect version of the in-place extension.

Comments

Calling **OleMaskMouse**(TRUE) causes OLE to intercept mouse clicks while over the in-place container window and to pass them on to the object application as app1Evnts.**OleMaskMouse**(FALSE) causes all mouse clicks to behave normally.

OleMaskMouse(FALSE) must be called before putting up any dialogs. **OleMaskMouse**(TRUE) must be called once the dialog has gone away.

OleMaskMouse(TRUE) is implicitly called in **OleSetInPlaceWindow** and **OleMaskMouse**(FALSE) is implicitly called in **OleUnSetInPlaceWindow**.

When **IOleInPlaceObject::EnableModeless** (*fEnable*) is called, the object application must call **OleMaskMouse**(*fEnable*). When the container wants to put up a modal dialog, the object application removes the mouse masking and re-enables the masking when the modal has been removed.

See Also

IOleInPlaceObject::EnableModeless

CHAPTER 12

Compatibility with OLE 1

This chapter discusses the issues that affect compatibility with OLE 1 applications and describes the API functions that promote compatibility.

Overview

Note In moving from OLE 1 to OLE 2, the following changes in terminology were made:

- The OLE 1 term "server application" has been changed to "object application."
- The OLE 1 term "client application" has been changed to "container application."

Compatibility implies that an OLE 1 container application can contain OLE 2 embedded and linked objects and that an OLE 1 object application can create objects to be embedded in and linked to by OLE 2 containers. OLE provides this capability by means of a built-in compatibility layer that includes a set of API functions for conversion.

Compatibility between OLE 2 and OLE 1 applications is achieved through the implementation of two special remoting objects, called a stub and proxy. The stub is instantiated on the object application's side of the process; the proxy is instantiated on the container application's side. These special stubs and proxies use DDE to communicate rather than LRPC. When an OLE 2 object makes a call to a function in an OLE 1 client application, for example, the stub intercepts the call and responds appropriately. For the most part, this response simulates the response that an OLE 2 object or container would make. However, in a few cases the behavior is different and special HRESULT values are returned.

All OLE applications must be prepared to receive and dispatch Apple events. OLE 1 applications deal with three types of DDE class events: EMBD, RNCF, and the default DDE type. Whereas all OLE 1 applications must handle the default DDE event; the EMBD and RNCF types are optional in certain cases. The EMBD type

DDE event is for object applications only; its purpose is to inform an application that it is being launched by OLE rather than by a user. The RNCF type DDE event is handled by applications supporting the Clipboard Application Protocol (CLAP).

OLE 2 applications must handle the three OLE 1 events plus a few others. The following table describes the OLE events for both OLE 1 and OLE 2 applications and the available handlers that applications install:

Class and Type	Description	OLE Handler
DDE/RNCF Apple event	Retrieves CLAP clipboard format	OleProcessClipboardAE
DDE/EMBD Apple event	Indicates that OLE started the application to service a linked or embedded object	None: Application installs handler that sets a flag to indicate method of startup
DDE/ typeWildCard Apple event	Processes DDE events	OleProcessDdeAE
OLE2/EVNT Apple event	Supports in-place activation	None: Application installs handler that forwards the event for normal processing
DgDp/chyz Apple event	Supports drag and drop	OleProcessDragDropAE
LRPC Apple event	Supports remoting	OleProcessLrpcHLE

Working with OLE 1 Containers

This section describes some of the known idiosyncrasies of working with OLE 1 containers.

- A successful call to **OleClientSite::GetContainer** returns a pointer to the container's **IOleContainer** interface. If the container does not support **IOleContainer**, OLE_E_NOT_SUPPORTED is returned. All OLE 1 clients fall in this category as do OLE 2 containers that do not support linking to their embedded objects.
- Calls to **IOleClientSite::ShowObject** to request to make the embedded or linked object visible, always returns OLE_E_NOT_SUPPORTED when called on an OLE 1 client. This method helps make the user model work smoothly; however, its failure does not effect OLE functionality.
- When an OLE 1 container contains an OLE 2 object and the object is activated or the OLE1 function **OleUpdate** is called, the aspect of the data returned will always be DVASPECT_CONTENT. This is because OLE 1 clients have no concept of a **FORMATETC** data structure. This situation may occur when an iconic OLE 2 object is pasted from an OLE 2 container into an OLE 1 container. When the object is first pasted, its presentation remains iconic. With the next update, however, the object's content picture is returned.

- OLE 1 clients can link to OLE 2 objects only if the link source:
- is represented by a file moniker or a generic composite moniker consisting of a file moniker and one item moniker.
- is not an embedded OLE 2 object.
- An OLE 1 container can contain an incompatible link when a linked object is pasted from an OLE 2 container into the OLE 1 container or when an OLE 2 container, to allow the OLE 1 version of the application access to its data, saves the data to an OLE 1 file. When the OLE 1 container loads the incompatible link, the link is converted to an embedded object and assigned the class name "Ole2Link." The OLE 1 container cannot connect to the link source. However, if the newly created embedded object is then pasted into an OLE 2 container using the clipboard or converted to an OLE 2 object using **OleConvertOLESTREAMToIStorage**, it will be converted back to its original state as an OLE 2 linked object.
- When the link source for an OLE 1 linked object changes its name, the link can remain intact only if the file moniker for the link source has changed. That is, if the link source is a range of cells within an OLE 2 spreadsheet application and the name of the file that contains the cell range changes, OLE will track the link. However, if the name of the cell range changes, the link will be broken.
- Pasting an OLE 2 linked object into an OLE 1 client document and then calling the OLE 1 function **OleCopyFromLink** to convert it to an embedded object will fail if the data transfer object provided by the link source does not support **IPersistStorage**. Creating an embedded object always requires native data and **IPersistStorage** provides access to native data.

Working with OLE 1 Object Applications

This section describes some of the known problems associated with trying to embed or link OLE 1 objects into OLE 2 containers.

- As is the case with OLE 2 objects, either **IPersistStorage::InitNew** or **IPersistStorage::Load** must be called to properly initialize a newly instantiated OLE 1 object before any other OLE calls are made. The **InitNew** method should be called to initialize a newly created object; the **Load** method should be called for existing objects. If one of the **OleCreate** helper functions or **OleLoad** is being used, these functions make the **IPersistStorage** call, thus eliminating the need to make the call directly.
- When an OLE 2 container with an OLE 1 embedded or linked object calls **IDataObject::GetData** or **IDataObject::GetDataHere**, the container can expect support for a smaller set of formats and storage media than would be supported for an OLE 2 object.

The following table lists the combinations that can be supported.

Tymed Formats	Data Formats
TYMED_MFPICT	PICT
TYMED_HGLOBAL	NATV and other OLE 1 object formats

For the aspect value of DVASPECT_ICON, only TYMED_MFPICT with CF_METAFILEPICT is supported. The icon returned from the **IDataObject::GetData** or **IDataObject::GetDataHere** call will always be the first icon (index 0) in the executable object application.

- Several methods typically called by containers have unique implementations for OLE 1. **IPersistStorage::IsDirty** is defined to return S_OK if the object has changed since its last save to persistent storage; S_FALSE if it has not changed.
- When an OLE 2 container with an OLE 1 embedded object calls **IPersistStorage::IsDirty**, the compatibility code always returns S_OK when the object is running because there is no way to determine if the object has in fact changed until the File Close or File Update command is selected. S_FALSE is returned when the object application is not running.
- An OLE 2 implementation of **IOleObject::IsUpToDate** can return either S_OK if the linked object is up-to-date, S_FALSE if it is not up-to-date, or OLE_E_UNAVAILABLE if the object cannot determine whether it is up-to-date. An OLE 1 implementation always returns either E_NOT_RUNNING if an object is in the loaded state, or S_FALSE, if the object application is running.
- The OLE 1 implementation of **IOleItemContainer::EnumObjects** always returns OLE_E_NOTSUPPORTED because it is not possible for an OLE 1 object application to enumerate its objects.
- **IOleObject::Close** takes a save option as a parameter that indicates whether the object should be saved before the close occurs. For OLE 2 objects, there are three possible save options: OLECLOSE_SAVEIFDIRTY, OLECLOSE_NOSAVE, and OLECLOSE_PROMPTSAVE. The OLE 1 implementation of **IOleObject::Close** treats OLECLOSE_PROMPTSAVE as equivalent to OLECLOSE_SAVEIFDIRTY because it is not possible to require an OLE 1 object application to prompt the user.
- OLE 2 containers cannot expect an OLE 1 object to activate in-place; all OLE 1 objects support activation in a separate, open window.
- OLE 1 object applications do not support linking to their embedded objects. It is up to OLE 2 containers with OLE 1 embedded objects to prevent a possible link from occurring. Containers can call **CoIsOle1Class** to determine at clipboard copy time if a data selection being copied is an OLE 1 object. If **CoIsOle1Class** returns TRUE, indicating that the selection is an OLE 1 object, the container should not offer the Link Source format. The Link Source format must be available for a linked object to be created.

- OLE 2 containers can store multiple presentations for an OLE 1 object. However, only the first presentation format is sent to the container when the OLE 1 object application closes. After that, the object application is in the process of closing down and cannot honor requests for any more formats. Therefore, only the first presentation cache will be updated. The rest will be out of date (perhaps blank) if the object has changed since the last update.
- OLE 1 object applications do not update the cache for every change to an embedded object; therefore, until the user selects the File Update command, an OLE 2 container cannot assume it is obtaining the latest data from the object application. By calling **IOleObject::Update,** the container can obtain the latest object data.
- An OLE 1 embedded (not linked) object does not notify its container that its data has changed until the user does a File Update or File Close. Therefore, if an OLE 2 container registers for a data change notification on an OLE 2 object in a particular format, it should be aware that it will not be notified immediately when the data changes.
- When an OLE 1 object is inserted into a container document and then closed without an update being invoked, a save will not occur and the correct streams for the object are not written into storage. Any subsequent loading of the object by the container will fail. To protect against this potential condition, containers that want data to be available after the object closes without updating can implement the following:

```
OleCreate();                          \\ to insert the object
OleRun();                             \\ if OLERENDER_NONE was
specified
IOleObject::Update();                 \\ to get snapshot of data
OleSave();
IOleObject::DoVerb();
```

Upgrading Applications

When an OLE 1 object application is being upgraded to an OLE 2 object application, several issues arise. A primary issue is whether the OLE 2 application will replace the OLE 1 application or both versions will coexist. If only the newer version will be available to the user, it is desirable to convert the objects from the older version automatically to the new version format. Objects can be converted on a global basis, where all objects of a specific class are converted, or on a more selective basis, where only some objects are converted. Conversion can be either automatic, under programmatic control, or under the control of a user. For more information on converting objects, see "Object Class Conversion and Emulation Functions in Chapter 5."

Being able to detect whether an object is from an OLE 1 object application is helpful for implementing conversion functionality. The OLE 2 implementation of **IPersistStorage::Load** can check for a stream named "\1Ole10Native." The "\1Ole10Native" stream contains an unsigned long header whose value is the length of the native data that follows. The existence of this stream indicates that the data is coming from an OLE 1 object application. Applications can check if a storage object contains an object in an OLE 1 format by calling **ReadFmtUserTypeStg** (*pStg*, *pcf*, *lplpszUserType*) and examining the contents of *pcfFormat.* This is where the OLE 1 class name would appear.

In **IPersistStorage::Save**, objects that are being permanently converted should be written back to storage in the new format and the "\1Ole10Native" stream should be deleted. The conversion bit in the storage should also be cleared once the conversion to the new format is complete.

To allow manual conversion of an old OLE 1 object to the new OLE 2 version, the OLE 2 object application must put the OLE 1 object application's ProgID (OLE 1 server class name) in the Registration Database file under CLSID\{...}\Conversion\Readable\Main. This entry indicates that the OLE 2 application is able to read its OLE 1 data format; the "clipboard format" of the OLE 1 data is the ProgID (that is, the class name) of the OLE 1 object.

To get a CLSID for an OLE 1 object application, **CLSIDFromProgId** or **CLSIDFromString** must be called. That is, an OLE 1 application cannot be assigned a CLSID from an OLE 2 application or by using a GUID from a range assigned by Microsoft. Because all OLE 1 CLSIDs are expected to fall in a specific range, OLE 1 CLSIDs are assigned with **CLSIDFromProgId**.

For information on the required Registration Database file entries for upgraded applications, see Chapter 4, "Registering Object Applications."

OLE 1 Compatibility Functions

The following API functions enable an application to determine whether an object class is from OLE 1 and support conversion between OLE 1 and OLE 2 storage formats.

CoIsOle1Class

unsigned long CoIsOle1Class(*rclsid***)**
REFCLSID *rclsid*

CoIsOle1Class determines whether a given CLSID represents an OLE 1 object.

Parameters

rclsid
Reference to the CLSID to check.

Return Values

Value	Meaning
S_TRUE	CLSID refers to an OLE 1 object.
S_FALSE	CLSID does not refer to an OLE 1 object.

Comments

CoIsOle1Class is useful for preventing linking to embedded OLE 1 objects within a container. Once a container has determined that copied data represents an embedded object, **CoIsOle1Class** can be called to determine whether the embedded object is an OLE 1 object.

If **CoIsOle1Class** returns S_TRUE, the container does not offer Link Source.

OleConvertIStorageToOLESTREAM

HRESULT OleConvertIStorageToOLESTREAM(*pStg*, *pOleStm***)**
LPSTORAGE* *pStg*
LPOLESTREAM *pOleStm*

OleConvertIStorageToOLESTREAM converts the storage of an OLE object from OLE 2 structured storage to OLE 1 storage.

Parameters

pStg
Points to the OLE 2 **IStorage** instance that is to be converted to an OLE 1 **OLESTREAM** storage.

pOleStm
Points to where to return the object's **OLESTREAM** object.

Return Values

Value	Meaning
CONVERT10_E_STG _NO_STD_STREAM	Object cannot be converted because its storage is missing a stream.
E_INVALIDARG	Invalid value for *pStg* or *pOleStm*.

Comment

OleConvertIStorageToOLESTREAM is useful for converting an OLE 2 document to the OLE 1 format. The OLESTREAM code implemented for OLE 1 must be available.

On entry, the stream pointed to by *pOleStm* should be created and positioned just as it would be for an OLE 1 **OleSaveToStream** call. On exit, the stream contains the persistent representation of the object using OLE 1 storage.

See Also

OleConvertOLESTREAMToIStorage

OleConvertIStorageToOLESTREAMEx

HRESULT OleConvertIStorageToOLESTREAMEx (*pStg, cfFormat, lWidth, lHeight, dwSize, pmedium, pOleStm*)

LPSTORAGE *pStg*
unsigned long *cfFormat*
long *lWidth*
long *lHeight*
unsigned long *dwSize*
LPSTGMEDIUM *pmedium*
LPOLESTREAM *pOleStm*

OleConvertIStorageToOLESTREAMEx converts the storage of an embedded object from OLE 2 structured storage to OLE 1 storage. This function differs from **OleConvertIStorageToOLESTREAM** in that the presentation data to be written to the OLE 1 storage is passed in.

Parameters

pStg
Points to the object's OLE 2 **IStorage** instance to be converted to an OLE 1 **OLESTREAM** storage.

cfFormat
Specifies the format of the presentation data. Can be NULL, in which case the *lWidth, lHeight, dwSize,* and *pmedium* parameters are ignored.

lWidth
Specifies the width of the object presentation data in pixels units.

lHeight
Specifies the height of the object presentation data in pixels.

dwSize
Specifies the size of the data to be converted, in bytes.

pmedium
Points to the **STGMEDIUM** structure for the serialized data to be converted.

pOleStm
Points to the object's **OLESTREAM** storage.

Return Values

Value	Meaning
S_OK	The conversion was completed successfully.
DV_E_STGMEDIUM	*pmedium->hGlobal* is NULL.
E_INVALIDARG	*dwSize* is NULL or *pStg* or *pOleStm* is invalid.
DV_E_TYMED	*pmedium->tymed* is not TYMED_HGLOBAL or TYMED_ISTREAM.

Comments

Since **OleConvertIStorageToOLESTREAMEx** can specify which presentation data to convert, it can be used by applications that do not use the OLE default caching resources but do use OLE's conversion resources.

The value of *pmedium->tymed* may only be TYMED_HGLOBAL or TYMED_ISTREAM. The medium will not be released by **OleConvertIStorageToOLESTREAMEx**.

See Also

OleConvertOLESTREAMToIStorageEx, **OleConvertIStorageToOLESTREAM**

OleConvertOLESTREAMToIStorage

HRESULT OleConvertOLESTREAMToIStorage(*pOleStm*, *pStg*, *ptd*)
LPOLESTREAM *pOleStm*
LPSTORAGE *pStg*
const DVTARGETDEVICE * *ptd*

OleConvertOLESTREAMToIStorage converts an OLE 1 **OLESTREAM** storage to OLE 2 structured storage.

pOleStm
Points to the OLE 1 **OLESTREAM** storage that is to be converted.

pStg
Points to where to return the OLE 2 **IStorage** instance of the object.

ptd
Points to a target device; can be NULL.

Return Values

Value	Meaning
CONVERT10_S_NO _PRESENTATION	Object either has no presentation data or uses native data for its presentation.
DV_E_DVTARGETDEVICE or DV_E_DVTARGET-DEVICE_SIZE	Invalid value for *ptd*.
E_INVALIDARG	Invalid value for *pOleStm*.

Comments

OleConvertOLESTREAMToIStorage can be used to convert an application document that supported OLE 1 to one that supports OLE 2. The *pOleStm* pointer contains the current OLE 1 persistent storage of the embedded object.

On entry, *pOleStm* should be created and positioned just as it would be for an **OleLoadFromStream** function call. On exit, *pOleStm* is positioned just as it would be on exit from **OleLoadFromStream**, and *pStg* now contains the uncommitted persistent representation of the object using the OLE 2 storage model.

For OLE 1 objects that use native data for their presentation, **OleConvertOLESTREAMToIStorage** returns CONVERT10_S_NO_PRESENTATION. Upon receiving this return value, callers should call **IOleObject::Update** to get the presentation data so that it can be written to storage.

The following steps illustrate the conversion process using C:

1. Create a root **IStorage** object by calling **StgCreateDocfile**(..., &*pStg*).
2. Open the OLE 1 file (using **FSopenDf** or another OLE 1 technique).
3. Using the OLE 1 procedure for reading files, read from the file until an OLE object is encountered.
4. Allocate an **IStorage** object from the root **IStorage** created in step 1:

```
pStg->lpVtbl->CreateStorage(...&pStgChild);
hRes = OleConvertOLESTREAMToIStorage(pOleStm, pStgChild);
hRes = OleLoad(pStgChild, &IID_IOleObject, pClientSite, ppvObj);
```

5. Repeat step 3 and 4 as often as is necessary until the file is completely read.

OleConvertOLESTREAMToIStorageEx

HRESULT OleConvertOLESTREAMToIStorageEx(*pOleStm, pStg, pcfFormat, plWidth, plHeight, pdwSize, pmedium***)**

LPOLESTREAM *pOleStm*
LPSTORAGE *pStg*
unsigned long * *pcfFormat*
long * *plWidth*
long * *plHeight*
unsigned long * *pdwSize*
LPSTGMEDIUM *pmedium*

OleConvertOLESTREAMToIStorageEx converts an OLE 1 **OLESTREAM** storage to OLE 2 structured storage.

Parameters

pOleStm
Points to the OLE 1 **OLESTREAM** storage for the object.

pStg
Points to the OLE 2 **IStorage** instance of the object.

pcfFormat
Points to where to return the format of the presentation data. May be NULL, indicating the absence of presentation data.

plWidth
Points to where to return the width value (in pixels) of the presentation data.

plHeight
Points to where to return the height value (in pixels) of the presentation data.

pdwSize
Points to where to return the size in bytes of the converted data.

pmedium
Points to where to return the **STGMEDIUM** structure for the converted serialized data.

Return Values

Value	Meaning
S_OK	The conversion was completed successfully.
DV_E_TYMEDI	The value of *pmedium->tymed* is not TYMED_ISTREAM or TYMED_NULL.

Comments

This function differs from **OleConvertOLESTREAMToIStorage** in that the presentation data that is read from **OLESTREAM** is passed out and the newly created **IStorage** does not contain a presentation stream.

Since **OleConvertOLESTREAMToIStorageEx** can specify which presentation data to convert, it can be used by applications that do not use OLE's default caching resources but do use the conversion resources.

The *tymed* member of **STGMEDIUM** can only be TYMED_NULL or TYMED_ISTREAM. If TYMED_NULL, then the data will be returned in a global handle through the *hGlobal* member of **STGMEDIUM,** otherwise data will be written into the *pstm* member of this structure.

See Also

OleConvertIStorageToOLESTREAMEx, OleConvertIStorageToOLESTREAM

CHAPTER 13

Concurrency Management

Overview

OLE applications must correctly handle user input while processing one or more calls from OLE or the operating system. OLE calls, when made between processes, fall into two categories:

- Synchronous calls
- Asynchronous notifications

Most of the communication that takes place within OLE is synchronous. When making synchronous calls, the caller waits for the reply before continuing and, if preferred, can receive incoming events while waiting. OLE enters into a modal loop to wait for the reply, receiving and dispatching other events in a controlled manner. On the Macintosh platform, OLE makes synchronous calls by posting an Apple Event.

To send asynchronous notifications, OLE uses Apple Events. There are five asynchronous methods defined in OLE:

- **IAdviseSink::OnDataChange**
- **IAdviseSink::OnViewChange**
- **IAdviseSink::OnRename**
- **IAdviseSink::OnSave**
- **IAdviseSink::OnClose**

When sending asynchronous notifications, the caller does not wait for the reply. While processing an asynchronous call, synchronous calls cannot be made. For example, a container application's implementation of **IAdviseSink::OnDataChange** cannot contain a call to **IPersistStorage::Save**.

Figure 13.1 shows a high-level view of the communication that occurs between a caller, OLE, and a callee when each of these types of calls are sent.

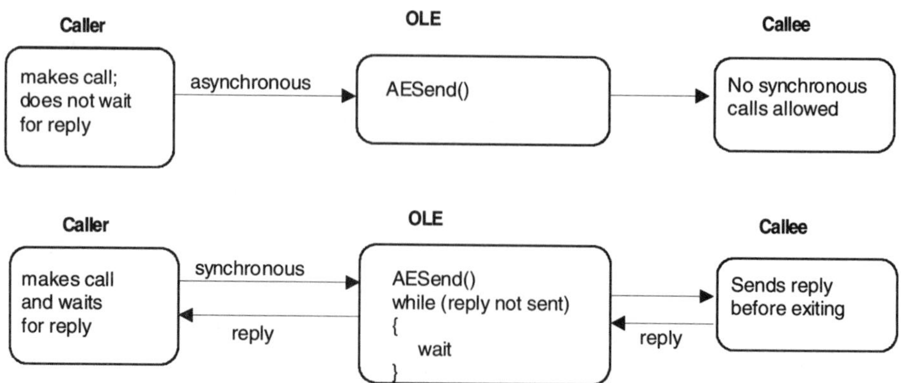

Figure 13.1 Communication between caller, OLE and callee

To minimize problems that can arise from asynchronous event processing, the majority of OLE method calls are synchronous. When an application makes a synchronous method call, OLE enters a modal wait loop that handles the required replies and dispatches incoming events to applications capable of processing them.

OLE manages method calls by assigning an identifier called a "logical thread ID." A new one is assigned when a user selects a menu command or when the application initiates a new OLE operation. Subsequent calls that relate to the initial OLE call are assigned the same logical thread ID as the initial call.

IMessageFilter Interface

Applications can selectively handle incoming or outgoing events while waiting for responses from synchronous calls by implementing the **IMessageFilter** interface. The ability to filter events is often useful when a dialog box is being displayed or a lengthy operation is in progress. Performance can be improved when applications handle some events and defer others.

IMessageFilter contains the following methods:

```
DECLARE_INTERFACE_(IMessageFilter, IUnknown)
{
  // *** IUnknown methods ***
 HRESULT QueryInterface (THIS_ REFIID riid, void * * ppvObj);
 unsigned long AddRef (THIS);
 unsigned long Release (THIS);

  // *** IMessageFilter methods ***
 unsigned long HandleInComingCall (THIS_unsigned long dwCallType, ProcessSerialNumber *pPSNCaller,
      unsigned long dwTickCount, LPINTERFACEINFO lpInterfaceInfo);
 unsigned long RetryRejectedCall (THIS_ProcessSerialNumber *pPSNCallee, unsigned long dwTickCount,
      unsigned long dwRejectType );
```

```
unsigned long MessagePending (THIS_ProcessSerialNumber *pPSNCallee, unsigned long dwTickCount,
    unsigned long dwPendingType);
};
```

For more information, see the compobj.h header file.

IMessageFilter::HandleIncomingCall

unsigned long IMessageFilter::HandleIncomingCall(*dwCallType, pPSNCaller, dwTickCount, lpInterfaceInfo*)

unsigned long *dwCallType*
ProcessSerialNumber **pPSNCaller*
unsigned long *dwTickCount*
LPINTERFACEINFO *lpInterfaceInfo*

IMessageFilter::HandleIncomingCall is called when an incoming OLE event is received. This method provides the application with a single entry point for all incoming calls.

Parameters

dwCallType
Indicates the kind of incoming call that has been received; valid values are from the enumeration **CALLTYPE.** For more information, see the following comments.

pPSNCaller
Points to the process serial number of the process that is calling this process.

dwTickCount
Specifies the elapsed tick count since the outgoing call was made if *dwCallType* is not CALLTYPE_TOPLEVEL. If *dwCallType* is CALLTYPE_TOPLEVEL, *dwTickCount* should be ignored.

lpInterfaceInfo
Points to an instance of the **INTERFACEINFO** data structure, which is used to describe the interface method that was called. For more information, see the following comments.

Return Values

Value	Meaning
SERVERCALL _ISHANDLED	The application might be able to process the call.
SERVERCALL _REJECTED	The application cannot handle the call due to an unforeseen problem.
SERVERCALL _RETRYLATER	The application cannot handle the call at this time. For example, an application might return this value when it is in a user-controlled modal state.

Comments

Depending on the application's current state, the call can be either accepted and processed or rejected (permanently or temporarily). The return value SERVERCALL_ISHANDLED indicates that the application might be able to process the call. Whether processing is successful might depend on the interface for which the call is destined. OLE rejects or processes the call, returning RPC_E_CALL_REJECTED if the call could not be processed.

IMessageFilter::HandleIncomingCall should not be used to hold off updates to objects during operations; **IViewObject::Freeze** should be used for that purpose. **IMessageFilter::HandleIncomingCall** can be used to set up the application's state so that the call can be processed in the future.

OLE's default processing for incoming calls is that all calls are dispatched, regardless of their logical thread ID.

The values for *dwCallType* are taken from the **CALLTYPE** enumeration, which is is defined in compobj.h as follows:

```
typedef enum tagCALLTYPE
{
    CALLTYPE_TOPLEVEL               = 1,
    CALLTYPE_NESTED                 = 2,
    CALLTYPE_ASYNC                  = 3,
    CALLTYPE_TOPLEVEL_CALLPENDING   = 4,
    CALLTYPE_ASYNC_CALLPENDING      = 5
    } CALLTYPE;
```

CALLTYPE values have the following meanings:

Value	Meaning
CALLTYPE _TOPLEVEL	A call has arrived with a new logical thread ID. The application is not currently waiting for a reply from an outgoing call. Calls of this type can be handled or rejected.
CALLTYPE _NESTED	A call has arrived with the same logical thread ID as that of an outgoing call for which the application is currently waiting for a reply. Calls of this type should always be handled.
CALLTYPE _ASYNC	An synchronous call has arrived; calls of this type cannot be rejected. OLE always delivers them.
CALLTYPE_TOPLEVEL _CALLPENDING	A call has arrived with a new logical thread ID. The application is currently waiting for a reply from an outgoing call. Calls of this type may be handled or rejected.

Value	Meaning
CALLTYPE_ASYNC _CALLPENDING	An asynchronous call has arrived with a new logical thread ID. The application is currently waiting for a reply from an outgoing call. Calls of this type cannot be rejected.

The *lpInterfaceInfo* parameter points to an instance of the structure **INTERFACEINFO**, which is defined in compobj.h as follows:

```
typedef struct tagINTERFACEINFO
{
    interface IUnknown   *pUnk;      //pointer to the object
    IID                  iid;        //interface id
    short                wMethod;    //interface method
} INTERFACEINFO, * LPINTERFACEINFO;
```

IMessageFilter::RetryRejectedCall

unsigned long IMessageFilter::RetryRejectedCall(*pPSNCallee*, *dwTickCount*, *dwRejectType*)
ProcessSerialNumber * *pPSNCallee*
unsigned long *dwTickCount*
unsigned long *dwRejectType*

IMessageFilter::RetryRejectedCall gives an application the chance to display a dialog box that the user can use to either retry a rejected call, or switch to the task identified by *pPSNCallee*.

Parameters

pPSNCallee
Points to the process serial number of the process that was called by this process.

dwTickCount
Specifies the number of elapsed ticks since the call was made.

dwRejectType
Specifies either SERVERCALL_REJECTED or SERVERCALL_RETRYLATER, as returned by the object application in **IMessageFilter::HandleInComingCall**.

Return Values

Value	Meaning
-1	The call should be canceled. OLE then returns RPC_E_CALL_CANCELLED from the original method call.
Value between 0 and 100	The call is to be retried immediately.
Value > 100	OLE will wait for this many milliseconds and then retry the call.

Comments

IMessageFilter::RetryRejectedCall is called by OLE immediately after it receives SERVERCALL_RETRYLATER or SERVERCALL_REJECTED from **IMessageFilter::HandleInComingCall**.

If an application task rejects a call, OLE checks to determine whether there are incoming calls (possibly from the application this task tried to call). If so, OLE processes the calls after checking the return from **IMessageFilter::HandleIncomingCall**. If not, the application is probably in a state where it cannot handle such calls, perhaps temporarily. **IMessageFilter::RetryRejectedCall** is called when the latter condition occurs.

Applications should silently retry calls that have returned SERVERCALL_RETRYLATER and show a dialog box only after a reasonable amount of time has passed, such as five seconds. The callee may momentarily be in a state where calls can be handled. This option to wait and retry is provided for special kinds of calling applications such as background tasks executing macros or scripts, so that they can retry in a nonintrusive way.

If, after a dialog box is displayed, the user chooses to cancel, the call will appear to fail with RPC_E_CALL_REJECTED.

See Also

IMessageFilter::HandleInComingCall

IMessageFilter::MessagePending

unsigned long IMessageFilter::MessagePending(*pPSNCallee*, *dwTickCount*, *dwPendingType***)**
ProcessSerialNumber * *pPSNCallee*
unsigned long *dwTickCount*
unsigned long *dwPendingType*

IMessageFilter::MessagePending is continually called while OLE is waiting for a reply to a remote call; this allows an application to process events appearing in the application's event queue.

Parameters

pPSNCallee
Points to the process serial number of the process that this process is calling.

dwTickCount
Specifies the elapsed time since the call was made. The value is calculated from the Macintosh function, **TickCount**.

dwPendingType
Indicates the type of call made during which an event was received. Valid values are from the enumeration **PENDINGTYPE.** For more information, see the following comments.

Return Values

Value	Meaning
PENDINGMSG _CANCELCALL	Cancel the outgoing call. This should be returned only under extreme conditions. Canceling a call that has not replied or been rejected can create orphan transactions and lose resources. OLE fails the original call and return RPC_E_CALL_CANCELLED.
PENDINGMSG _WAITNOPROCESS	Continue waiting for the reply and do not dispatch the event. Leaving events in the queue enables them to be processed normally if the outgoing call is completed.
PENDINGMSG _WAITDEFPROCESS	Reserved for future use. Applications should instead return PENDINGMSG_WAITNOPROCESS.

Comments

When an application makes a call causing an LRPC call, OLE enters a loop, waiting for a reply. While in this loop, OLE will continually call **IMessageFilter::MessagePending** (if the application has registered a message filter), allowing the application to process events (including NULL events) appearing in the calling application's queue.

The following rules apply to the implementation of **IMessageFilter::MessagePending**:

1. In **IMessageFilter::MessagePending**, the application *must* execute a **WaitNextEvent** call, passing in a sleep parameter to **WaitNextEvent** that is greater than zero.
2. To guarantee that "Urgent" events (that is, updateEvt, activateEvt, and osEvt events) are not lost, the call to **WaitNextEvent** should test for these types of events. If such an event is found, the application should process it as quickly as possible. An application should always handle an osEvt, even if this means just removing it from the queue.
3. The return value PENDINGMSG_WAITDEFPROCESS is meaningless. Applications should instead return PENDINGMSG_WAITNOPROCESS.
4. Since PENDINGMSG_WAITDEFPROCESS is meaningless, applications must act on UI events on their own by using **WaitNextEvent** to test for such events and handling them as appropriate (note that if the application refuses to handle such events, other applications may be blocked from receiving their UI events.)

Non-urgent Macintosh events that appear in the caller's queue should remain until sufficient time has passed. A two or three second delay is recommended to ensure that the events are probably not the result of the user typing ahead. If the amount of time has passed and the call has not been completed, the events should be flushed from the queue, and a dialog box displayed offering the user the choice to retry (keep waiting) or switch to the task identified by *pPSNCallee*. The object should not display the message until both the time out expires and a user event (for example, mouse down) has been received; this eliminates unnecessarily displaying the warning.

The above rule ensures that if calls are completed in a reasonable amount of time, "type ahead" will be treated correctly. Also, if the callee does not respond, type ahead is not misinterpreted and the user is able to act to solve the problem. For example, OLE 1 object applications can queue up requests without responding when they are in modal dialogs.

Handling input while waiting for an outgoing call to finish can introduce complications. The application should determine whether to process the event without interrupting the call, continue waiting, or cancel the operation.

When there is no response to the original OLE call, the application can cancel the call and recover the OLE object to a consistent state by calling **IStorage::Revert** on its storage. The object can be released when the container "shut downs." However, canceling a call can create orphaned operations and resource leaks. Canceling should be used only as a last resort. It is strongly recommended that applications not allow calls to be canceled.

Leaving events in the queue can cause the queue to fill.

The values for *dwPendingType* are taken from the enumeration **PENDINGTYPE**, which is defined in compobj.h as follows:

```
typedef enum tagPENDINGTYPE {
    PENDINGTYPE_TOPLEVEL     = 1,
    PENDINGTYPE_NESTED       = 2,
} PENDINGTYPE;
```

PENDINGTYPE values have the following meaning:

Value	Meaning
PENDINGTYPE _TOPLEVEL	The outgoing call is not nested within a call from another application.
PENDINGTYPE _NESTED	The outgoing call is nested within a call from another application.

See Also **IStorage::Revert**

CoRegisterMessageFilter

HRESULT CoRegisterMessageFilter(*lpMessageFilter* , *lplpMessageFilter***)**
LPMESSAGEFILTER *lpMessageFilter*
LPMESSAGEFILTER * *lplpMessageFilter*

CoRegisterMessageFilter registers with OLE the instance of an application's **IMessageFilter** interface to be used for handling concurrency issues. DLL object applications cannot register a message filter.

Parameters

lpMessageFilter
Points to the **IMessageFilter** interface supplied by the application. Can be NULL, indicating that the current **IMessageFilter** registration should be revoked.

lplpMessageFilter
Returns a pointer to the previously registered **IMessageFilter** instance. If NULL, indicates no previous **IMessageFilter** instance was registered.

Return Values

Value	Meaning
S_OK	**IMessageFilter** instance registered or revoked successfully.
S_FALSE	An error occurred while registering or revoking the **IMessageFilter** instance.

APPENDIX A

Object Handlers

Note The information in this section is subject to change.

Introduction

An object handler is nothing more than a piece of code that implements the interfaces expected by a container when an object is in its loaded state. OLE includes a default object handler.

The following types of object handlers are used with OLE:

Types of object handlers	Description
Default object handler	The default object handler provided with OLE is used to cache presentation data and to render objects using data from the OLE default data cache. In most cases, the default handler/cache provides the level of functionality needed for container applications.
Custom handler	A custom handler is typically used with the OLE default object handler and an object application to do special rendering. A custom handler can be written to supplement or replace some or all of the functionality offered by the OLE default object handler. Custom handlers are registered in the Registration Database file in place of the OLE2.DLL default object handler using the keyword **InprocHandler**.

Types of object handlers	Description
DLL object application	An object application can be written as a DLL to directly reside in the container's process space. DLL object applications replace not only the functionality of an object application, but that of the default object handler and/or custom object handler. DLL object applications are registered in the Registration Database file using the keyword **InprocServer**, which leads to their often being referred to as an *in-process server.*

OLE Default Object Handler

Note Object handlers provide services on behalf of OLE object applications while an object is in its loaded state, thus avoiding the process time of starting the object applications. The OLE default object handler is always used unless a custom handler or DLL object application is written and registered for an object class.

Figure A.1 shows a representation of the OLE default object handler and its aggregation of the default data cache. The illustration shows only the interface implementations exposed externally; internal implementations are not shown. For example, the data cache has internal implementations of **IDataObject** and **IPersistStorage** that are made available to the default handler through its aggregation with the cache.

As shown, the default handler is used as the intermediary between the container application and an object application. If the default handler is unable to handle a request by the container or the object needs to be put into its running state, the handler passes the call on to the object application for processing. Through the exposed **IOleClientSite** interface, the object application is able to obtain the services offered by the container application.

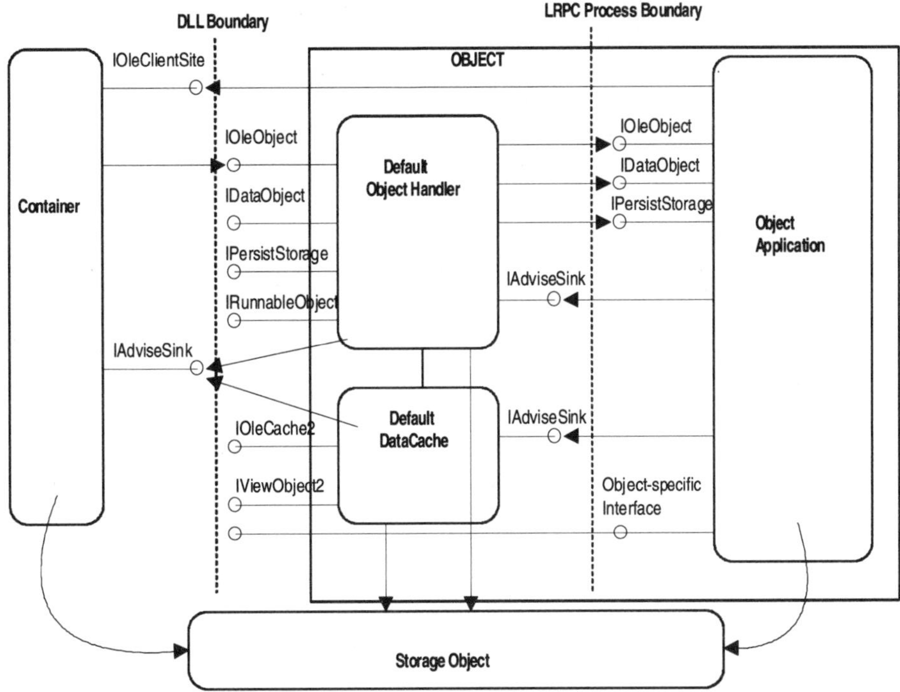

Figure A.1 OLE default object handler

The container makes interface method calls to what it interprets to be the object application. In reality, the calls are intercepted by the default object handler, which provides services on behalf of the object in its loaded state.

The OLE default handler and data cache are often thought of as being one object; in reality, they are two separate objects; the cache is aggregated with the handler. The default handler (through **IViewObject2**) is responsible for drawing the requested object using the data maintained in the data cache. Drawing is always done locally, never by remoting the call to the object application.

The object handler transparently converts the cached data for drawing purposes as the object is moved from one platform to another platform (for example, from the Macintosh to Windows). OLE, through its implementation of the **IOleCache2** interface, can convert between the presentation formats it knows about: PICTs on the Macintosh and metafiles, bitmaps and DIB on Windows.

The default handler is also responsible for transitioning the object from the loaded state to the running state and for keeping the data cache up to date against changes made to the running object. As an object enters its running state, the handler sets up appropriate advisory connections on the running object by passing an **IAdviseSink** of itself to the running object. When the object changes, **OnDataChange** is invoked on the handler's sink, at which point the handler updates the cache. After updating the cache, the handler sends **OnDataChange** and/or **OnViewChange** notifications to the advisory sink in the container.

Through the default handler, the following interface implementations are exposed for use by the container while an object is in its loaded state:

Default Handler's Interface Implementations	Purpose
IDataObject	Uses the cached presentation data to enumerate and retrieve data from the Registration Database file and to be notified when an object's data has changed.
IPersistStorage	Saves and loads presentation/data caches.
IViewObject2	Enables the container to render an object, using one of three standard data formats obtained from the object's cached data. These formats include metafile, bitmap, and DIB.
IOleObject	Enumerates the list of verbs (using entries from the Registration Database file) that the container makes available to the user for a given object. **IOleObject::DoVerb** puts the object into its running state.
IOleCache2	Caches, uncaches, and selectively updates an object's presentation data.

Interfaces Implemented by the Default Handler

The following sections describe the interfaces implemented by the default handler in order to clarify how the default handler works with an object in its loaded and running states.

IOleObject Interface

The default handler's implementation of the **IOleObject** interface is minimal in that only the **DoVerb** and **Update** methods put the object in the running state; the remainder of the **IOleObject** methods either return an HRESULT or save the information for future use.

The following table lists the **IOleObject** methods along with a description of how the default handler's implementation affects an object when it is in its loaded and running states.

IOleObject Method	Object in Loaded State	Object in Running State
Advise	Remembers and forwards to the object application at the appropriate time.	Remembers the **Advise** and delegates to the running object.
EnumAdvise	Enumerates the remembered advises.	Enumerates the remembered advises.
Unadvise	Delegates the call to the advise holder object in order to remove the advise from the list.	Delegates the call to the advise holder object in order to remove the advise from the list and tells the object to do an unadvise.
Close	Returns NOERROR. Containers can safely call **Close**, but it is meaningless while an object is in its loaded state.	Delegates the call to the running object.
DoVerb	Puts the object in its running state and delegates the call to the running object.	Delegates the call to the object.
EnumVerbs	Searches the verb entries in the Registration Database file to create the needed enumeration; returns NOERROR.	Delegates the call to the running object; if the object returns OLE_YES_USEREG, the object searches the Registration Database file.
GetClientSite	Returns the last **IOleClientSite** (as remembered by **SetClientSite**) and returns NOERROR.	Delegates the call to the running object.
GetClipboardData	Cannot be called unless the object is running; returns OLE_E_NOTRUNNING.	Delegates the call to the running object.
GetExtent	If available, returns the size of the requested aspect from the cache. Otherwise, returns NOERROR if aspect not found.	Delegates the call to the running object. A successful call returns to the container while an error forces object to get the extents from the cache.

IOleObject Method	Object in Loaded State	Object in Running State
GetMiscStatus	Searches the MiscStatus entries in the Registration Database file for the specified CLSID and returns NOERROR.	Delegates the call to the running object. If the object returns OLE_YES_USEREG, searches the Registration Database file.
GetMoniker	Calls **IOleClientSite::GetMoniker** if **SetClientSite** has been called with a valid **IOleClientSite** pointer. Otherwise, returns E_UNSPEC.	Calls **IOleClientSite::GetMoniker** if **SetClientSite** has been called with a valid **IOleClientSite** pointer. Otherwise, returns E_UNSPEC.
GetUserClassID	Returns the CLSID remembered from creation time and returns NOERROR.	
GetUserType	Retrieves a string from the CLSID's AuxUserType entry in the Registration Database file and returns NOERROR.	Delegates the call to the running object; if the object returns OLE_YES_USEREG, searches the Registration Database file.
InitFromData	Returns OLE_E_NOTRUNNING.	Delegates the call to the running object.
IsUpToDate	Returns OLE_E_NOTRUNNING.	Delegates the call to the running object.
SetClientSite	Save the **IOleClientSite** pointer for future use and returns NOERROR.	Remembers and delegates the call to the running object.
SetColorScheme	Returns OLE_E_NOTRUNNING.	Delegates the call to the running object.
SetExtent	Returns OLE_E_NOTRUNNING.	Delegates the call to the running object.

IOleObject Method	Object in Loaded State	Object in Running State
SetHostNames	Saves the string for future use and returns NOERROR.	Saves the string and delegates the call to the running object.
SetMoniker	Returns NOERROR (object can obtain later from object's client site.	Delegates the call to the running object.
Update	Runs and delegates the call to the object; if the object was not previously running, it stops the object after the update. Updates the OnSave caches.	Delegates the call to the running object. Updates the OnSave caches.

IDataObject Interface

The default handler's **IDataObject** implementation depends on what is in the cache. In the loaded state, the handler delegates **GetData**, **GetDataHere**, and **QueryGetData** method calls to the cache's **IDataObject** implementation.

The default handler's **IDataObject** implementation is as follows:

IDataObject Methods	Object in Loaded State	Object in Running State
DAdvise	Remembers and forwards to the object application at the appropriate time.	Remembers the **Advise** and delegates the call to the running object.
EnumDAdvise	Enumerates the remembered advises.	Enumerates the remembered advises.
DUnadvise	Delegates the call to the advise holder object in order to remove the advise from the list.	Delegates the call to the advise holder object in order to remove the advise from the list and tells the object to do an unadvise.
EnumFormatEtc	Creates an enumerator from the object's DataFormats and GetSet entries in the Registration Database file. The cache returns E_NOTIMPL.	Delegates the call to the running object; if the object returns OLE_YES_USEREG, searches the Registration Database file.
GetCanonicalFormatEtc	Returns OLE_E_NOTRUNNING.	Delegates the call to the running object.

IDataObject Methods	Object in Loaded State	Object in Running State
GetData	Calls the cache. If the data is not cached, the handler returns OLE_E_NOTRUNNING.	Calls the cache. If the data is not cached, the handler delegates the call to the running object and returns the data from the object. (A subsequent call to **IOleCache::Cache** is needed to cache the data.)
GetDataHere	Calls the cache. If the data is not cached, the handler returns OLE_E_NOTRUNNING.	Calls the cache. If the data is not cached, delegates the call to the running object and returns the data from the object.
QueryGetData	Calls the cache. If the data is not cached, the handler returns OLE_E_NOTRUNNING.	Calls the cache. If the data is not cached, delegates the call to the running object and returns the data from the object.
SetData	Returns OLE_E_NOTRUNNING.	Delegates the call to the running object.

IPersistStorage Interface

In the loaded state, the default handler (after performing some action) delegates all **IPersistStorage** method calls to the cache. The default handler never tries to run the object as the result of an **IPersistStorage** call; the handler works exclusively with the cached data and never with the object's native data.

The default handler's implementation of **IPersistStorage** works as follows for when an object is in both the loaded and running state:

IPersistStorage Methods	Object in Loaded State	Object in Running State
GetClassID	Returns the remembered CLSID or what is in the object's storage.	Delegates the call to the running object and then to the cache.
IsDirty	Delegates the call to the cache.	Delegates the call to the running object; if the object is dirty, it returns immediately. If the object is not dirty, it asks the cache if it is dirty, returning whatever from the cache.
InitNew	Increments the object's storage reference count and delegates the call to the cache.	Delegates the call to the running object and then to to the cache.

IPersistStorage Methods	Object in Loaded State	Object in Running State
Load	Increments the object's storage reference count and delegates the call to the cache.	Delegates the call to the running object and then to the cache.
Save	Saves the OLE private data stream and then delegates the call to the cache, which will write the presentation data stream.	Delegates the call to the running object and then to the cache.
SaveCompleted	Clears the internal state saved with the **Save** method and delegates the call to the cache.	Delegates the call to the running object and then to the cache.
HandsOffStorage	Releases the object's storage and delegates the call to the cache.	Delegates the call to the running object and then to the cache.

Interfaces Implemented by the Cache

This section describes the interfaces implemented by the OLE default data cache. The cache implements the **IPersistStorage**, **IDataObject**, **IViewObject2,** and **IOleCache2** interfaces, as described in the following sections.

IPersistStorage Interface

The following table describes the cache's **IPersistStorage** implementation and the effect of calling its methods on an object in both the loaded and running state:

IPersistStorage Methods	Object in Loaded State
GetClassID	Returns the CLSID passed to **OleCreateDefaultHandler**. **GetClassId** is not usually called because the default handler already knows the CLSID
IsDirty	Returns NOERROR if the cache is dirty; otherwise, it returns S_FALSE.
InitNew	Saves and increments the object's new storage reference count and returns NOERROR.
Load	Saves and increments the object's storage reference count. Does demand loading of the presentation streams available in the cache as required by the cache's implementation. Regardless of the running state of the object application, an error code may be returned.

IPersistStorage Methods	Object in Loaded State
Save	Saves all presentation data that have changed since the call to **Load** along with information about what was cached. Regardless of the running state of the object application, an error code may be returned.
SaveCompleted	Releases the storage pointer and returns NOERROR.
HandsOffStorage	Releases the storage pointer that the cache had previously remembered.

IDataObject Interface

The following table lists the cache's **IDataObject** implementation and the effect of calling its methods on an object in the loaded state. The cache does not make any **IDataObject** method calls on the object in its running state; in the running state, the cache delegates all calls to the default handler.

IDataObject Methods	Object in Loaded State
DAdvise	Returns OLE_E_ADVISENOTSUPPORTED.
EnumDAdvise	Returns OLE_E_ADVISENOTSUPPORTED.
DUnadvise	Returns OLE_E_NOCONNECTION.
EnumFormatEtc	Returns E_NOTIMPL.
GetCanonicalFormatEtc	Returns E_NOTIMPL.
GetData	Returns the data if the requested presentation was cached before this call, otherwise, returns OLE_E_BLANK. **GetData** supports TYMED_HGLOBAL, TYMED_METAPICT, and TYMED_GDI.
GetDataHere	Returns the data if the requested presentation was cached before this call, otherwise, returns OLE_E_BLANK. **GetDataHere** supports TYMED_ISTREAM and TYMED_HGLOBAL.
QueryGetData	If the requested **FORMATETC** was cached, then it returns NOERROR; otherwise, the cache returns S_FALSE or OLE_E_BLANK.
SetData	

IViewObject2 Interface

The cache's **IViewObject2** implementation is used to render objects using data from the cache. The cache tries to perform the requested action based on a presentation in the cache. At no time does the cache try to run the object application. If you plan to implement the **IViewObject2** interface in a handler, you must implement the entire interface method set. However, in your implementation you can delegate method calls as needed to the cache's **IViewObject**.

The cache's **IViewObject2** interface implementation is as follows when an object is in the loaded state (**IViewObject2** is an extension of **IViewObject**; as such, it inherits all of the **IViewObject** methods):

IViewObject2 Methods	Effect on Object in Loaded State
Draw	Attempts to draw the object using a presentation from the cache; otherwise, it returns OLE_E_BLANK.
GetColorSet	Tries to determine the color set from the Metafile or DIB in the cache. Returns OLE_E_BLANK if there is no presentation; otherwise, it returns NOERROR or S_FALSE, depending on the success of the method.
Freeze	Adds the aspect to an internal list that affects the behavior of **Draw** and returns NOERROR if successful. It returns OLE_E_BLANK if not. If this is a repeat request, it returns VIEW_S_ALREADY_FROZEN.
UnFreeze	Removes an entry from the internal list of frozen aspects and returns OLE_E_NOCONNECTION if the aspect was not frozen, otherwise, it returns NOERROR.
SetAdvise	Saves the **IAdviseSink** so that the cache itself will call its OnViewChange when the object application notifies the cache (through the cache's **IAdviseSink**). It returns NOERROR.
GetAdvise	Returns the last **IAdviseSink** and the last aspect from which the advise happened (from **SetAdvise**) and returns NOERROR.
GetExtent	Returns the view extents of an object using data from the cache.

IOleCache2 Interface

The cache only works with an object in its loaded state; when an object is in the running state, the cache delegates all calls to the default handler.

The following table summarizes the **IOleCache2** methods, and the effect that calling these methods has on an object in its loaded state. **IOleCache2** is an extension of **IOleCache** and, as such, it inherits all of the **IOleCache** methods.

IOleCache2 Methods	Effect on Object in the Loaded State
Cache	Tries to create a cache for the requested **FORMATETC**. Returns the cache connection ID and OLE_S_SAMECACHE if the **FORMATETC** is already cached. If the **FORMATETC** is already cached but a new set of Advise flags are passed in to **Cache**, then **Cache** overwrites the old Advise flags with the new ones before returning CACHE_S_SAMECACHE. (Note that these flags are advisory only. The cache may be updated more frequently, depending on the state of the running object.) In the running state, **Cache** checks to see if the object supports the specified **FORMATETC**. Even if the **FORMATETC** is not supported, the cache creates the cache node and returns CACHE_S_FORMATNOTSUPPORTED. There might be cases in which you get a cache connection ID of zero but no error. This implies that the **FORMATETC** is implicitly cached by the object as part of its native data and need not be explicitly cached (thus reducing storage space for the object).
UnCache	Invalidates the cache connection ID returned by **Cache**.
EnumCache	Returns an enumerator that enumerates all implicit and explicit cache nodes. For more information, see "Strategies for Caching Data," later in this appendix.
InitCache	Using the **IDataObject** as the source, **InitCache** updates each of the associated cache nodes. NOERROR is returned if one or more nodes are updated; otherwise, CACHE_S_NOTUPDATED is returned.
SetData	Using the **IDataObject** as its source, **SetData** determines whether there are any associated cache nodes that need to be updated.
UpdateCache	Selectively updates the various cache nodes according to the control flag(s) passed in to the method. Semantically, **UpdateCache** is similar to **InitCache**.

Strategies for Caching Data

The default cache supports two types of data caching: *implicit* and *explicit*. Implicit caching refers to when an object directly supports the data formats needed to render itself in the container, thus saving the overhead of storing these data formats in the object's storage. Explicit caching means that the data formats required to render the object are physically cached and saved with the object.

To illustrate the use of implicit caching, consider the case of a custom handler being used to render objects. In this case, the handler is able to render the object directly from the object's native data in storage. When the container asks the handler to cache the data format for an object, the handler first checks to see if the object supports the specified data format. If it does, the handler returns a cache connection ID of zero and returns CACHE_S_SAMECACHE. A connection ID of zero indicates that the object directly supports the data format and an explicit cache of the data format is not required. This behavior is always true for objects created by DLL object applications.

In contrast, there are only two cases that require an explicit cache of the data:

- The container asks to cache an iconic representation of the object (DVASPECT_ICON).
- The container specifies ADVFCACHE_FORCEBUILTIN to forcefully cache the data.

In these cases, the handler delegates the call to the default cache to explicitly create a cache node for the data format.The handler must remember the connection ID returned by **IOleCache::Cache** and support enumerating the connection ID in **IOleCache::EnumCache**.

Typically, handlers have an array of **STATDATA** data structures that they use for enumeration:

```
typedef struct tagSTATDATA
{
    FORMATETC formatetc;
    DWORD advf;
    IAdviseSink FAR* pAdvSink;
    DWORD dwconnection;
} STATDATA
```

The number of entries in the array will be equal to the number of **FORMATETC**s that the object supports. The array is initialized with the supported **FORMATETC**s and zero for connection IDs. An explicit cache against one of the supported **FORMATETC**s results in a nonzero cache connection ID being stored in the corresponding **STATDATA** entry. At load time, the explicit caches must be enumerated and the connection IDs stored in the appropriate location in the **STATDATA** array.

A handler that renders objects directly by using the object's native data does not use the cached representation for drawing—even if the handler is told to explicitly cache the presentation data (through ADVFCACHE_FORCEBUILTIN). Instead, it continues to draw using the native data from the object's storage.

Custom Object Handlers

A custom handler is simply a class-specific handler, something other than the default handler provided with OLE. Custom handlers typically implement one or more interfaces in a different manner than does the default handler. Most often the custom handler uses the features provided by the default handler, either through aggregation or delegation. Delegation can be done against an entire interface implementation or on an individual method basis. If the custom handler delegates based on methods, it must implement all of the methods in that interface. In almost all cases, a custom handler delegates caching to the OLE default cache.

Currently, a custom handler must aggregate the default handler, because this is the only means by which the object can be transitioned into and out of the running state. Figure A.2 shows a common integration point for a custom object handler, between the container application and the OLE default object handler. As shown, the custom handler acts like a filter between the container application and the default handler and object application. (The drawing shown is representative of how the sample object handler (shipped with the OLE SDK) is designed to work.

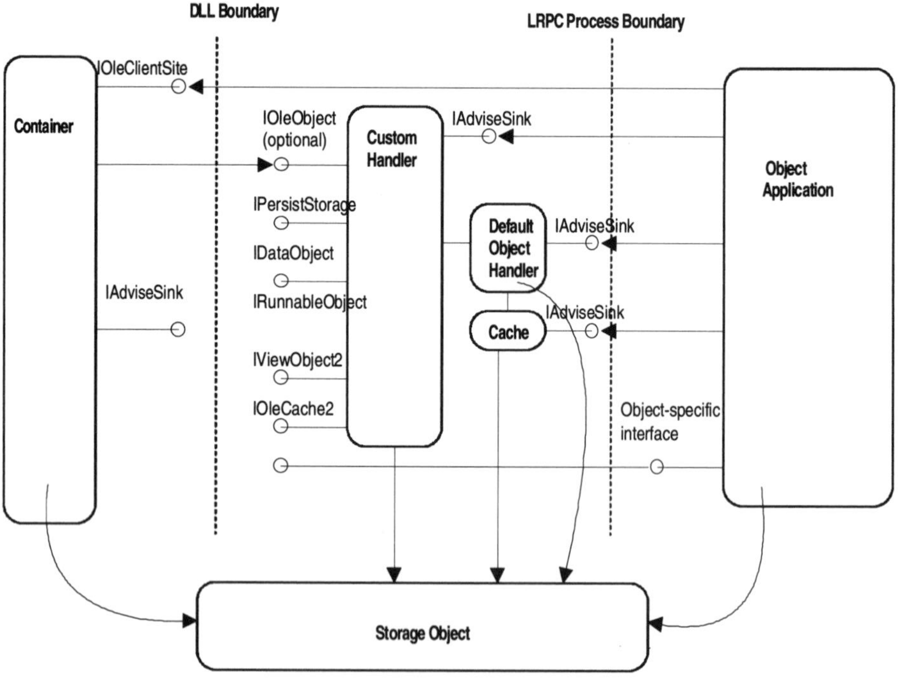

Figure A.2 Relationship between a custom handler and the default handler

More complex handlers can be created that not only replace the functionality offered by the default handler, but that of the object application also. In these cases, the handler is acting as a DLL object application. For more information on DLL object applications, see "DLL Object Applications," later in this appendix.

In general, it is unlikely that writing a custom handler to totally replace the functionality offered by the default object handler would be to your advantage. Before you set out to write an object handler, first determine your needs. As a first step, look at the support offered by the OLE default object handler and ask yourself what is needed beyond the support offered by the default handler.

Some of the reasons you might consider writing a custom object handler are listed below:

- Custom handlers can be written to handle data formats beyond the PICT, format supported by the default object handler.
- Custom handlers can be used for special resizing while an object is in its loaded state. The handler can be designed to trap the incoming **IOleObject::SetExtent** calls and use the object's native data to render the object instead of starting the object application.
- Custom handlers reside in the container application's process space and are much faster than object applications.
- Custom handlers provide very fast services for display and print operations; however, because they typically do not have a user interface, they are generally not suitable for tasks requiring an object to be in its running state (for example, editing). Because they often reduce or eliminate the need to run an object application; this makes certain tasks in container applications much faster.
- Custom handlers can support any class of object, as can the default object handler. An object handler also can be designed to work with only a specific class of object(s), as discussed later in this appendix.
- Custom handlers can support unique interface implementations; implementing them in a handler avoids the LPRC overhead associated with providing the **IMarshal** interface needed for marshaling the methods to and from an object application.
- Custom handlers lend themselves more readily to licensing for redistribution than do applications.

Rendering Handlers

Rendering handlers are the most common type of custom object handler. Rendering handlers provide better drawing functionality than that offered by the default handler and they save disk storage space. Because the object can draw directly from its native data, no data cache is needed.

Rendering handlers can be written to support both embedded and linked objects; this section describes supporting embedded objects. For information on rendering linked objects, see Chapter 7, "Data Transfer/Caching Interfaces and Functions."

Rendering Objects from Native Data

Rendering an object from its native data requires the object application to first write the data to storage. The handler then draws the object from the data in storage. This requires that the handler and object application coordinate the use of object's storage. Elements within a storage object must be opened in STGM_SHARE_EXCLUSIVE mode. Hence the storage cannot be opened by the object application and the handler at the same time.

The following list outlines the coordination of storage between the object application and the rendering handler:

- The handler sets up an ADVF_NODATA advise with the object application.
- The object application writes its data into the data streams and releases the streams before sending an **OnDataChange** to the handler. Note that the object must not commit the changes to storage.
- When the handler receives the **OnDataChange** notification, it generates an **OnViewChange** notification and sets a flag to indicate it needs to get the object's new extents in a subsequent call to **IViewObject2::GetExtent**.
- When the container calls **IViewObject::Draw** or **IDataObject::GetData**, the handler opens the stream, reads the data, and releases the stream immediately.

Interfaces Implemented by Rendering Handlers

A rendering handler needs to implement the **IPersistStorage**, **IOleCache2**, **IViewObject2**, and **IDataObject** interfaces. For a description of these interfaces and their role when implemented in a handler, see "Interfaces Implemented by the Default Handler," earlier in this appendix.

In addition, a rendering handler needs to implement the **IAdviseSink** interface as follows:

- The **IAdviseSink** must have a different object identity than the rendering handler, meaning that it must be implemented as a separate object.
- The handler and sink objects cannot share a common **QueryInterface** method.
- When **QueryInterface** is called on the sink, the sink must not return pointers to the handler object's interface implementations.
- The sink object typically supports only **IUnknown** and **IAdviseSink**. In the **IAdviseSink** implementation, only the OnDataChange method need be implemented; the remaining methods can be coded to return NOERROR. In the

OnDataChange method, the sink sets the flag indicating a need to get the new extents on the object and send the OnViewChange notification for the appropriate aspects to the container.

Writing a Custom Object Handler

Writing an object handler is fairly straightforward; the level and complexity of implementation is directly related to the functionality required. To write a custom object handler, you must do the following steps:

1. Implement the **IClassFactory** interface and the **DllGetClassObject** and **DllCanUnloadNow** functions.
2. Determine the additional OLE interfaces preferred for the object handler, then implement them into the handler's code.
3. Aggregate the OLE default handler with the custom object handler.
4. Register the object handler in the Registration Database file, using the key "InprocHandler."

In addition to these steps, all those common to any OLE application apply, including program initialization and termination, interface negotiation, object loading, and so forth, as discussed earlier in this book.

Required Interface Implementations

An object handler must implement the **IClassFactory** interface and **DllGetClassObject**. **IClassFactory** enables the object handler to create objects of a specific class while the exported **DllGetClassObject** function returns a pointer to the handler's **IClassFactory** interface implementation. In addition to these, you can implement any of the other OLE interfaces, depending on the level of functionality needed. Once implemented, an interface's methods are used just as they would be when interacting with the OLE default object handler or an object application. For example, you might include an implementation of the **IOleObject** interface, in which **DoVerb** executes certain verbs on behalf of the loaded object (for example, play) while delegating all other supported verbs to the object application. Or you could decide to implement a custom **IViewObject2** and **IOleCache2** to support data formats other than those supported by the default handler (PICT).

Note A custom object handler can instantiate any class of objects, just as the default object handler does. On the other hand, an object handler can be designed to work specifically with a certain class of object(s). This can be done by testing for a certain CLSID of an object and rejecting all others in the **IClassFactory::CreateInstance** implementation.

The following code example shows an implementation of the **DllGetClassObject** function and the **IClassFactory::CreateInstance** method. The implementation of

DllGetClassObject is quite simple: when the container application calls one of the OLE object-creation functions, OLE first searches in the Registration Database file for the keyword InprocHandler and loads the associated object handler into memory. When the object handler is loaded , OLE then calls **DllGetClassObject** to return an instance of the **IClassFactory** interface. OLE can then use the **IClassFactory** pointer to call **IClassFactory::CreateInstance** to instantiate the object for the container application.

```
STDAPI DllGetClassObject(REFCLSID rclsid, REFIID riid, LPVOID * ppv)
//-------------------------------------------------------------------
// Exported DLL initialization is run in context of running application
// -------------------------------------------------------------------
{
    HRESULT hRes;
    CClassFactory *pClassFactory = new CClassFactory(rclsid);
    if (pClassFactory != NULL) {
        hRes = pClassFactory->QueryInterface(riid, ppv);
        pClassFactory->Release(); //OK to release ptr since
                                  //container now responsible for
                                  //releasing the instantiated
                                  //class factory object
    }
    return hRes;
} //DLLGetClassObject()

CClassFactory::CClassFactory(REFCLSID rclsid)
{
    m_dwRefs = 1;
    m_ClsId = rclsid;


}   // CClassFactory()

CClassFactory::~CClassFactory()
{
}   // ~CClassFactory()

STDMETHODIMP CClassFactory::CreateInstance(IUnknown * pUnkOuter,
                                           REFIID riid,
                                           LPLPVOID ppunkObject)
{
    HRESULT hRes;
    CHandlerObject* pObject;

    if (ppunkObject)
    {
        *ppunkObject = NULL; //NULL-out return parameters
    }
```

```
    if (pUnkOuter != NULL)
    {
    //Custom handler doesn't support being an aggregate object (although
    //it aggregates the default handler)

        hRes = ResultFromScode(E_NOTIMPL);
        goto errReturn;
    }

    pObject = new CHandlerObject(NULL);  //create memory for object
    //Create object
    if ((hRes = pObject->CreateObject(m_ClsId,riid,ppunkObject)) != NOERROR)
    {
        delete pObject;
    }

    errReturn:
        return hRes;
}
```

Aggregating the OLE Default Object Handler

In writing a custom object handler, you must make the default object handler an aggregate object of your custom handler. By aggregating the default handler, you expose the features offered by the OLE default object handler, including the ability to cache the presentation data for an object and to launch the object application when an object needs to be put into its running state. In this way, you are still able to write only those interface implementations needed to support your class of object(s), while delegating other interface implementations to the default handler.

The custom handler processes all calls within its capabilities, delegating requests it does not support to the default object handler (such as cache updating). It can delegate either on a method-by-method basis or it can delegate on a complete interface implementation.

The default handler launches the object application when an object needs to be put in its running state. In the running state, calls from the object application to the container are first passed to the custom handler, which might process them, depending on in its interface implementations. Depending on the call, the container is then notified of changes made to an object.

To aggregate the default handler, the custom handler calls **OleCreateDefaultHandler**, passing in its CLSID (as registered in the Registration Database file) and a pointer to the **IUnknown** interface. The CLSID is used by the default handler to locate certain entries in the Registration Database file for that object, the **IUnknown** is the controlling Unknown which ensures that the custom handler always gets first chance at any call. After aggregating the default handler, the custom handler can call **QueryInterface** to get pointers to the default handler's interface implementations so it can later delegate calls to them.

The following example illustrates how to create a custom handler that aggregates the default handler. The application calls **OleCreateDefaultHandler** to instantiate a default handler. If the call is successful, the default handler's **QueryInterface** method is called to retrieve pointers to each of the interfaces to which the custom handler may delegate future calls.

```
HRESULT CHandlerObject::CreateObject(REFCLSID rclsid, REFIID riid,
                                     LPVOID * ppv)
//-----------------------------------------------------------------
// CreateObject:
//-----------------------------------------------------------------
{
    HRESULT hRes = ResultFromScode(E_FAIL);
    ULONG dwRefs;

    m_ClsId = rclsid;
    //Create instance of default handler as an aggregate object
    hRes = OleCreateDefaultHandler(m_ClsId, &m_Unknown, IID_IUnknown,
                                   (LPVOID *) &m_pDefHandler);
    if (hRes != NOERROR)
    {
        return hRes;
    }
    //Cache pointers to interfaces of default handler; note that these
    //are non-Addref'd pointers.
    hRes = m_pDefHandler->QueryInterface(IID_IOleObject,
                                         (LPVOID *)&m_pOleObject);
    if (hRes == NOERROR)
    {
    //OK to release because OleCreateDefaultHandler keeps object
    //alive
        dwRefs = m_pOleObject->Release();
    }

    hRes = m_pDefHandler->QueryInterface(IID_IDataObject,
                                         (LPVOID *)&m_pDataObject);
    if (hRes == NOERROR)
    {
        dwRefs = m_pDataObject->Release();
    }

    hRes = m_pDefHandler->QueryInterface(IID_IViewObject,
                                         (LPVOID *)&m_pViewObject);
    if (hRes == NOERROR)
    {
```

```
        dwRefs = m_pViewObject->Release();
    }

    hRes = m_pDefHandler->QueryInterface(IID_IOleCache,
                                         (LPVOID *)&m_pOleCache);
    if (hRes == NOERROR)
    {
        dwRefs = m_pOleCache->Release();
    }

    hRes = m_pDefHandler->QueryInterface(IID_IPersistStorage,
                                         (LPVOID *) &m_pPersistStorage);
    if (hRes == NOERROR)
    {
        dwRefs = m_pPersistStorage->Release();
    }
    //Get interface for whoever is creating the object
    if ((hRes = m_Unknown.QueryInterface(riid, ppv)) == NOERROR)
    {
        ULONG dwRefs = ((LPUNKNOWN)*ppv)->Release();
    }

    return hRes;

}
```

Registering Object Handlers

Object handlers must be registered in the Registration Database file. The registration process is the same as for registering object applications, except that the keyword "InprocHandler" is used as the registration key.

The Registration Database file contains, by default, the following entry set belonging to the OLE default handler, Def$DefFSet:

```
HKEY_CLASSES_ROOT\CLSID\{00000402-0000-0000-c000-000000000046}\InprocHandler =
OLE2:Def$DefFSet
```

To register a custom handler, this entry must be set to the CLSID the handler is associated with and the name of the DLL, as shown in the following entry (the entry shown is for an OLE sample object handler):

```
HKEY_CLASSES_ROOT\CLSID\{00000402-0000-0000-c000-000000000046}\InprocHandler = DBGHNDLR.DLL
```

Whenever a container application calls one of the OLE object-creation functions, OLE uses the CLSID specified for the object and the **InprocHandler** key to search the Registration Database file. If an object handler is found for the CLSID, it is loaded and initialized. Because handlers are usually designed to work with a particular object application, the Registration Database file entry should be included with the entries for the related object application.

For more information on registering object handlers, see Chapter 4, "Registering Object Applications."

Loading Object Handlers

Object handlers get loaded when the container application calls one of the following OLE object-creation functions or **IClassFactory::CreateInstance**:

OleCreate **OleCreateLink**

OleCreateLinkToFile **OleCreateFromData**

OleCreateLinkFromData **OleCreateFromFile**

OleLoad **CoCreateInstance**

CoGetClassObject

Once the object handler has been loaded, the container can call **QueryInterface** for any interface pointer, just as it usually does. If the custom object handler has implemented that interface, it returns a pointer to it; otherwise, it passes **QueryInterface** on to the default handler for processing.

Unloading Object Handlers

Object handlers, as DLLs, are controlled by the container process that instantiated them. This means that they remain in the container's process space until the container frees them, usually at application shutdown. To optimize the freeing of an object handler from memory, the object handler can optionally implement and export the **DllCanUnloadNow** function. Containers call **DllCanUnloadNow** to find out whether there are any existing instances of an object class remaining for which the object handler is responsible. If there are no objects loaded, **DllCanUnloadNow** returns TRUE, indicating that the handler can be safely freed from memory. To take advantage of this optimization, the container must call **CoFreeUnusedLibraries**.

Whether or not the object handler implemented **DllCanUnloadNow**, the object handler is forcefully unloaded when the container application calls **OleUninitialize** to uninitialize the OLE libraries. **DllCanUnloadNow** is optional and can be used to better manage memory resources.

DLL Object Applications

Overview

Figure A.3 shows how an object application can be implemented as a DLL object application. An object handler implemented in this manner always replaces the functionality offered by the OLE default handler and/or custom object handler. Obviously, process time is going to be much faster, given that there is no LRPC overhead or startup time. It's much easier to expose a new interface in a DLL object application because LRPC remoting is not required, hence there is no need to write custom marshaling code (see the **IMarshal** interface). The downside of a DLL object application is that it has full responsibility for an object, in any and all of its states.

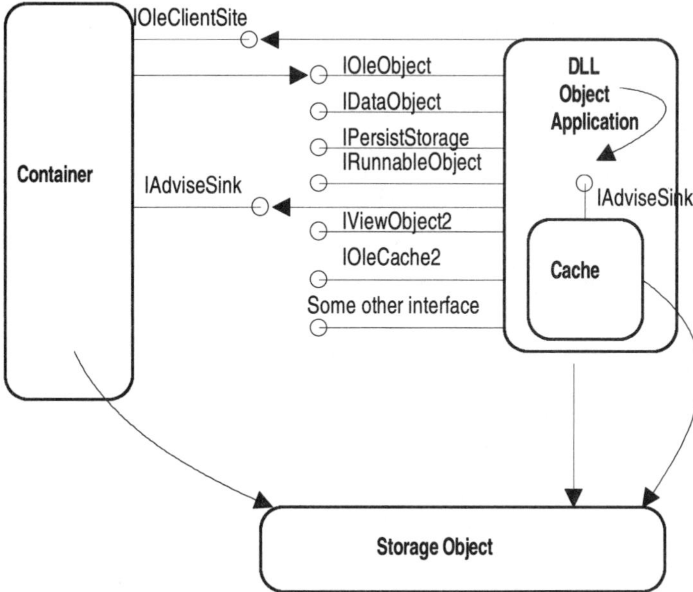

Figure A.3 Object application implemented as a DLL

While OLE provides a default data cache, DLL object applications must expose their own implementation of the **IOleCache2** interface, delegating method calls as needed to the default cache. Because a DLL object application replaces the default handler (which exposes the default cache), DLL object applications need to call the **CreateDataCache** function to get an instance of the default cache.

The following factors should be considered before writing a DLL object application.

- DLL object applications are responsible for handling an object in any and all of its states. This implies that a DLL object application has a user interface for editing objects.
- DLL object applications cannot register a message filter for handling concurrency issues (by using the **IMessageFilter** interface); only object applications can register message filters.
- DLL object applications are never "single use," they are always "multiple-use."
- Currently, the OLE libraries are not able to load a DLL object; therefore, DLL object applications cannot support links to file-based objects.
- DLL object applications are registered in the Registration Database file using the keyword **InprocServer**. Other than using the required keyword, register DLL object applications just as you would register a custom object handler (see "Registering Object Handlers," earlier in this appendix).
- The **DllCanUnloadNow** function can be implemented by the DLL object application and called by the container application to see whether there are any existing objects in memory for which the DLL object application is responsible. If there are no objects, the DLL object application can be safely freed.
- DLL object applications can be written to support any of the OLE interfaces, including those that handle in-place activation and drag and drop operations. Support of in-place activation implies there is a user interface.
- Currently, DLL object applications are not compatible with OLE 1 applications because there is no way for the OLE 1 application to load the OLE 2 DLL. One work around is to create a small stub that handles the loading and unloading of the OLE 2 DLL.
- Because object handlers do not have a message processing loop, they cannot perform background processing during idle message processing. However, the object handler can implement a timer loop during which it processes any background tasks to work around this problem.

Required Interfaces for DLL Object Applications

A DLL object application must implement all of the interfaces required of a custom handler as well as the **IExternalConnection**, **IRunnableObject**, and **IOleObject** interfaces. In addition, a DLL object application is free to implement any of the other OLE interfaces. Generally, a DLL object application implements at least **IDataObject** and **IPersistStorage**. DLL object applications typically don't implement the **IAdviseSink** interface.

The implementation of **IDataObject**, **IPersistStorage**, and **IOleObject** should be similar to that for an object application, with one exception: the handler's **IPersistStorage::Save** and **IOleObject::Update** methods need to call **IOleCache2::UpdateCache** to update all cache nodes created with ADVFCACHE_ONSAVE.

The **IOleCache2** implementation should be similar to that implemented for a rendering handler; for more information, see "Rendering Handlers," earlier in this appendix.

The following sections describe the implementation aspects behind the **IRunnableObject** and **IExternalConnection** interfaces. For information on the other interfaces required of a custom handler, see "Interfaces Implemented by the Default Handler," earlier in this appendix.

IRunnableObject Interface and DLL Object Applications

IRunnableObject is implemented by DLL object applications to transition the object in and out of the running state.

IRunnableObject Interface Methods	Object in Running State
GetRunningClass	Returns the object's CLSID.
Run	If the object is running, it returns NOERROR. Otherwise, the object sets the run flag to TRUE and registers itself in the Running Object Table.
IsRunning	Returns the run flag previously set in **Run**.
LockRunning	Calls **CoLockObjectExternal** to create or release an external connection to the object.
SetContainedObject	Returns NOERROR; can be ignored.

IExternalConnection Interface and Silent Updates to Linked Objects

The **IExternalConnection** interface must be implemented to support silent updates of linked objects.

IExternalConnection Interface Methods	Object in Running State
AddConnection	Creates an external connection to the running object.
ReleaseConnection	Releases an external connection previously created by **AddConnection** and, if this is the last connection to the object, closes the object.

APPENDIX B

Creating Distribution Disks

This appendix discusses the distribution of OLE applications. It lists the files that must be included on thedistribution disk(s) and describes special considerations for registering OLE object applications.

Disk Contents

In addition to the application-specific files you ship with your application, you must distribute the the Microsoft OLE Extension if your application is OLE 2 aware. When installing your application on the end user's system your setup program must copy the extension into the Extensions folder.

Installing Your Application

During installation, your setup program should register your OLE application in both the OLE 1 Embedding Preferences file and the OLE 2 Registration Database file. The setup program should verify the version number of Microsoft OLE Extension in the Extensions folder and, if necessary, install a newer version of it, if available.

During each startup operation, the application should verify and re-register all necessary information if any of the information is missing from the registration files.

For more information on registering OLE applications, see Chapter 4, "Registering Object Applications."

APPENDIX C

Data Structures and Enumerations

This appendix summarizes the data structures and enumerations used with the interfaces and functions described elsewhere in this book. The material is divided into two parts: Data Structures and Enumerations.

Data Structures

The following sections describe the data structures commonly used with many of the OLE interfaces and functions:

BIND_OPTS

The **BIND_OPTS** structure is application-defined and used with **IBindCtx::SetBindOptions** and **IBindCtx::GetBindOptions** to define the binding options for a given bind context.

BIND_OPTS is defined in moniker.h as follows:

```
typedef struct tagBIND_OPTS {
    unsigned long   cbStruct;       // size in bytes of BIND_OPTS.
    unsigned long   grfFlags;
    unsigned long   grfMode;
    unsigned long   dwTickCountDeadline;
} BIND_OPTS;
```

BIND_OPTS members have the following meaning:

Member	Description
cbStruct	Specifes the size, in bytes, of the BIND_OPTS structure.
grfFlags	Contains a group of Boolean flags. Legal values that can be or-ed together are taken from the enumeration **BINDFLAGS**. Moniker implementations should ignore any bits in this field that they do not understand.
grfMode	Contains a group of flags that indicates the caller's intended use for the object received from the associated moniker binding operation. Constants for this member are taken from the **STGM** enumeration. When applied to a **IMoniker::BindToObject** operation, the most significant flag values are: STGM_READ, STGM_WRITE, and STGM_READWRITE. Some binding operations may make use of other flags, particularly STGM_DELETEONRELEASE or STGM_CREATE, but such cases would be quite esoteric. When applied to the **IMoniker::BindToStorage** operation, most STGM values are potentially useful. The default value for *grfMode* is STGM_READWRITE | STGM_SHARE_EXCLUSIVE.
dwTickCountDeadline	A 32-bit unsigned time value in milliseconds on the local clock that indicates when the caller wants the operation to be completed. This parameter lets the caller limit the execution time of an operation when it is more important that the operation perform quickly rather than accurately. This capability is most often used with **IMoniker::GetTimeOfLastChange**, though it can be usefully applied to other operations as well.

BORDERWIDTHS

The **BORDERWIDTHS** structure contains four integer widths for determining border space on the frame- and document-level windows for displaying toolbars and optional frame adornments.

```
typedef RECT    BORDERWIDTHS;
typedef LPRECT  LPBORDERWIDTHS;
typedef LPCRECT LPCBORDERWIDTHS;
```

Each member of the structure is the width in pixels being requested or set for the top, bottom, left, and right sides of the window, as shown below:

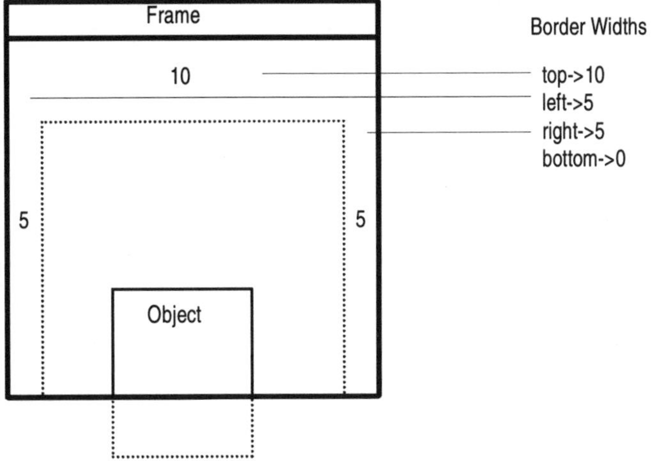

To negotiate space, the object fills in the **BORDERWIDTHS** structure and passes it to **RequestBorderSpace** and **SetBorderSpace** methods on the frame or document interface, depending on where the space is being requested.

DVTARGETDEVICE

The **DVTARGETDEVICE** data structure, used to describe a target device, is defined in dvobj.h as follows:

```
typedef struct tagDVTARGETDEVICE {
    unsigned long   tdSize;
//Following fields are for Windows compatibility
    unsigned short  tdDriverNameOffset;
    unsigned short  tdDeviceNameOffset;
    unsigned short  tdPortNameOffset;
    unsigned short  tdExtDevmodeOffset;
    unsigned char   tdWinData[1];
    unsigned char   byAlign;
```

```
//Following fields are for use on Macintosh
    long            dwSizeX;
    long            dwSizeY;
    short           wDpiX;
    short           wDpiY;
    short           wColorDepth;
    short           wFlags;
    short           wMisc;
    unsigned char   tdData[1];
}DVTARGETDEVICE;
```

The following table describes the **DVTARGETDEVICE** members:

DVTARGETDEVICE Member	Meaning
tdSize	Specifies the size of **DVTARGETDEVICE** structure in bytes. The initial size is included so that the structure can be copied more easily.
tdDriverNameOffset	Specifies the offset from the beginning of the **DVTARGETDEVICE** structure to the device driver name; must be NULL-terminated (a NULL device or port name can be specified by appropriate offset fields to zero).
tdDeviceNameOffset	Specifies the offset from the beginning of the **DVTARGETDEVICE** structure to the device name; must be NULL-terminated.
tdPortNameOffset	Specifies the offset from the beginning of the **DVTARGETDEVICE** structure to the port name; must be NULL-terminated.
tdExtDevmodeOffset	Specifies the offset from the beginning of the **DVTARGETDEVICE** structure to the **DEVMODE** structure (retrieved by calling ExtDeviceMode.)
tdWinData[1]	Specifies an array of bytes containing data for the target device. It is not necessary to include empty strings in *tdWinData*.
byAlign	Used internally for byte alignment.
dwSizeX	Specifies the maximum width in pixels.
dwSizeY	Specifies the maximum height in pixels.
wDpiX	Specifies the horizontal dots per inch.
wDpiY	Specifies the vertical dots per inch.
wColorDepth	Specifies the color depth (for example, 1==black and white, 8 = = 256 colors).

DVTARGETDEVICE Member	Meaning
wFlags	Specifies characteristics for the target device (for example, postscript).
wMisc	Specifies the offset to an application-specific data; most often this value is NULL.
tdData	Specifies an array of bytes containing data for the target device. It is not necessary to include empty strings in *tdData*.

FILETIME

The **FILETIME** data structure is a 64-bit value representing the number of 100-nanosecond intervals since January 1, 1601. The structure is used with the OLE functions **CoFileTimeToMacTime**, **CoFileTimeNow**, and **CoMacToFileTime**.

The **FILETIME** data structure is defined in compobj.h, as follows:

```
typedef struct FARSTRUCT tagFILETIME
{
    unsigned long dwLowDateTime;
    unsigned long dwHighDateTime;
} FILETIME;
```

FORMATETC

The **FORMATETC** structure is a generalized clipboard format, enhanced to encompass a target device, the aspect, or view of the data, and a storage medium. Where one might expect to find a clipboard format, a **FORMATETC** data structure is used instead.

The **FORMATETC** structure is used by the data and presentation interfaces as the means for passing information. For example, in **IDataObject::GetData** a **FORMATETC** structure is used to indicate exactly what kind of data the caller is requesting. For more information on the **IDataObject** interface, see "IDataObject Interface."

The **FORMATETC** data structure is defined in dvobj.h as follows:

```
typedef struct FARSTRUCT tagFORMATETC
{
    unsigned long       cfFormat;
    DVTARGETDEVICE *    ptd;
    unsigned long       dwAspect;
    long                lindex;
    unsigned long       tymed;
} FORMATETC, * LPFORMATETC;
```

The *cfFormat* member indicates the particular clipboard format of interest. There are three types of formats recognized by OLE:

- standard interchange formats, such as CF_TEXT,
- private application formats understood only by the application offering the format, or by
- other applications similar in functionality, or OLE formats.

The OLE formats are used to create linked or embedded objects and are described in the following sections.

The *ptd* member points to a **DVTARGETDEVICE** data structure containing information about the target device for which the data is being composed. A NULL value is used whenever the data format is insensitive to the target device or when the caller doesn't care what device is used. In the latter case, if the data requires a target device, the object should pick an appropriate default device (often the display for visual objects). Data obtained from an object with a NULL target device (especially when the data format is insensitive to the device) can be thought of as an alternate form of the native representation of the object: a representation that can be used for data interchange. The resulting data is usually the same as it would be if the user chose the Save As command from the File menu and selected an interchange format.

The *dwAspect* member enables the caller to request multiple aspects, roles, or views of the object using a single clipboard format. Most data and presentation transfer and caching methods pass aspect information. For example, a caller might request an object's iconic picture, using the metafile clipboard format to retrieve it.

Values for *dwAspect* are taken from the **DVASPECT** enumeration. Even though **DVASPECT** values are individual flag bits, *dwAspect* can only represent one value. That is, *dwAspect* cannot contain the result of **DVASPECT** values that have been or-ed together.

The *lindex* member represents the part of the aspect that is of interest. The value of *lindex* depends on the value of *dwAspect*. If *dwAspect* is either DVASPECT_THUMBNAIL or DVASPECT_ICON, *lindex* is ignored. If *dwAspect* is DVASPECT_CONTENT or DVASPECT_DOCPRINT, *lindex* must be -1 which indicates that the entire view is of interest and is the only value that is currently valid.

The *tymed* member indicates the means by which data is conveyed in a particular data transfer operation. In addition to being passed through global memory, data can be passed either through a disk file or an instance of one of the OLE storage-related interfaces.

Each clipboard format has a natural expression as either a *flat* format or a *structured*, hierarchical format. All standard formats, such as text, are expressed as flat formats. The OLE embedded object formats, Embedded Object and Embed Source, transfer data using the structured format. There are three types of media that are used to transfer those formats designated as flat formats: hglobal, stream, and file; and a single type of structured media: storage.

It is always appropriate to ask for a particular format on either a flat or a structured medium, as appropriate for the natural expression of the format. Additionally, it is plausible to ask that a format whose natural expression is a structured format be provided on a flat format: the structured-to-flat mapping is provided by the compound file implementation of the structured storage model. However, it is not appropriate to ask for a flat format on a structured medium. For example, text format cannot be passed on TYMED_ISTORAGE.

Valid values for *tymed* are taken from the **TYMED** enumeration. These values may be or-ed together to represent a composite value.

INTERFACEINFO

The **INTERFACEINFO** structure is used with **IMessageFilter::HandleIncomingCall** to describe the interface method that generated an incoming OLE event call.

INTERFACEINFO is defined in compobj.h as follows:

```
typedef struct tagINTERFACEINFO
{
    interface IUnknown   *pUnk;      //pointer to the object
    IID                  iid;        //interface id
    short                wMethod;    //interface method
} INTERFACEINFO, * LPINTERFACEINFO;
```

OBJECTDESCRIPTOR

An Object Descriptor format is offered whenever data is copied. This format is defined in an **OBJECTDESCRIPTOR** data structure.

OBJECTDESCRIPTOR is defined in ole2.h as follows:

```
typedef struct tagOBJECTDESCRIPTOR
{
    unsigned long        cbSize;
    CLSID                clsid;
    unsigned long        dwDrawAspect;
    SIZEL                sizel;
    unsigned long        dwOutline;
    POINTL               pointl;
    unsigned long        dwStatus;
```

```
    unsigned long       dwFullUserTypeName;
    unsigned long       dwSrcOfCopy;
    unsigned long       dwExtra; //MUST BE NULL
}OBJECTDESCRIPTOR;
```

OBJECTDESCRIPTOR values have the following meaning:

OBJECTDESCRIPTOR Member	Meaning
cbSize	Specifies the size of the **OBJECTDESCRIPTOR** structure in bytes.
clsid	Used to obtain the icon for the 'DisplayAsIcon' option in the Paste Special dialog and is applicable only if the Embed Source or Embedded Object formats are offered. If neither of these formats are offered, the value of *clsid* should be CLSID_NULL.
dwDrawAspect	The value of this field is typically DVASPECT_CONTENT or DVASPECT_ICON. If the source application did not draw the object originally, the *dwDrawAspect* field contains a zero value (which is not the same as DVASPECT_CONTENT).
sizel	Contains the true extents of the object (in pixels), available through a call to **IOleObject::GetExtent**. Setting the *sizel* field is optional; its value can be (0, 0) for applications that do not draw the object being transferred.

dwOutline	Offset from beginning of structure to region describing outline of object Like *sizel*, this is only defined for drawable objects; otherwise, it is zero. To turn this data at this offset into a region handle, allocate a handle the size of the first word of the region data and then copy those *n* bytes into the handle (including the first word):
	`// ptr to region data`
	`char *p = ((char*) pOD) +`
	`   pOD->dwOutline;`
	`short size = *(short *) p;`
	`h = NewHandle(size);`
	`BlockMove(p, *h, size);`

pointl
: Specifies the offset in pixel units from the upper-left corner of the object where a drag operation was initiated. This field is only meaningful for a drag and drop transfer operation. The value is (0,0) for other transfer situations, such as a clipboard copy and paste.

dwStatus
: Contains miscellaneous status flags for the object. These flags are defined by the OLEMISC enumeration and are returned by calling **IOleObject::GetMiscStatus**.

dwFullUserTypeName
: Specifies the offset from the beginning of the data structure to the null-terminated string that specifies the full user type name of the object. The value is zero if the string is not present.

dwSrcOfCopy
: Specifies the offset from the beginning of the data structure to the null-terminated string that specifies the source of the transfer. *dwSrcOfCopy* is typically implemented as the display name of the temporary moniker that identifies the data source. The value for *dwSrcOfCopy* is displayed in the Source line of the Paste Special dialog. A zero value indicates that the string is not present. If *dwSrcOfCopy* is zero, the string 'Unknown Source' is displayed in the Paste Special dialog.

dwExtra
: Reserved field; must be NULL.

OleIconSource

The **OleIconSource** structure is used with the **OlePictFromIconAndLabel** and **OleGetIconFromIconSuite** functions. The structure is also used with the icon functions included in the OLE SDK sample UI library.

The OLE SDK sample UI library contains the **OleUIPictExtractIconSource** procedure, which can be used to determine the source of a particular OLE icon PICT. **OleUIPictExtractIconSource** returns a structure of type **OleIconSource**, which is defined in macdef.h as follows:

```
typedef enum {  FileAndResIDMethod,
                CreatorAndIndexMethod,
                CreatorAndTypeMethod,
                SystemResIDMethod
} IconRetrievalMethod;
```

```
typedef struct {
    IconRetrievalMethod method;
    union {
        struct {
            char    szPathname[OLEICON_CCHPATHMAX];
            long    lFileID;
            short   sResID;
        } FileAndResIDStruct;

        struct {
            OSType  lCreator;
            short   sIndex;
        } CreatorAndIndexStruct;

        struct {
        OSType lCreator;
        OSType lType;
        } CreatorAndTypeStruct;

        struct {
            short sResID;
        } SystemResIDStruct;
    } IconSourceUnion;
}OleIconSource;
```

The **OleIconSource** structure describes how an icon can be accessed. The icon creation procedures follow one of four methods to obtain an icon from which they construct an icon PICT. To access these icons, the user uses the **OleIconSource** data structure which is bundled with the icon PICT at the time of its construction.

The **OleIconSource** data structure is a union of four different structures. The structure contained within a particular **OleIconSource** data structure is determined by the value of the "method" member of the structure. Based on the "method" member, an icon can be directly accessed as follows:

- **FileAndResIDMethod**

  The data provided in this instance includes a *filename*, a *file id* and a *resource id*. Using the *filename*, a resource file should be opened using **HOpenResFile**, for example. Once a resource has been opened, the *resource id* should be used with the procedure **GetIconSuite** to obtain an icon suite for the icon PICT from which the **OleIconSource** structure was obtained.

- **CreatorAndIndexMethod**

  The data provided is a *creator signature* and a numeric *index*. The *creator signature* should be used with **PBDTGetAppl** in order to obtain the filename of the application which contains the icon. As above **HOpenResFile** is used along with the filename to open a resource. The *index* is used with **Get1IndResource** to obtain the icon from the application.

- **CreatorAndTypeMethod**

  In this instance the **OleIconSource** structure provides a *creator signature* and a *file type*. The procedure **PBDTGetIcon** should be used with these pieces of data to obtain the required icon . This icon corresponds to a file of the type provided by the application possessing the given creator signature.

- **SystemResIDMethod**

  In the event that no suitable icon can be obtained by the icon creation procedures, a "vanilla document" icon PICT is created and returned to the user. In this situation the sole piece of data required to obtain this generic icon is a system *resource id*. This *resource id* is used in a call to **GetIconSuite** to obtain an icon suite corresponding to the icon pict from which the **OleIconSource** was obtained.

OLEINPLACEFRAMEINFO

The **OLEINPLACEFRAMEINFO** structure provides data needed by an object application in order to communicate with a container during an in-place session. The container is responsible for filling in the structure.

The structure is defined as follows:

```
typedef struct FARSTRUCT tagOIFI //OleInPlaceFrameInfo
{
    long                 recordlength;
    long                 version;
    WindowPtr            frameWindow;
    OSType               signature;
    long                 refcon;
    ProcessSerialNumber  psn;
    Handle               hCmdKeys;
    short                numCmds;
    short                growHandles;
    short                dragConstraint;
    Boolean              fAdjustMenus;
    Boolean              unused;
}OLEINPLACEFRAMEINFO, * LPOLEINPLACEFRAMEINFO;
```

The container fills in the structure when the object application calls the container's **IOleInPlaceSite::GetWindowContext** method.

The **OLEINPLACEFRAMEINFO** members have the following meaning:

OLEINPLACEFRAMEINFO Member	Meaning
recordLength	Indicates the size of the **OLEINPLACEFRAMEINFO** structure (*sizeof(OLEINPLACEFRAMEINFO)*).
version	Specifies the version of the **OLEINPLACEFRAMEINFO** structure that is currently being used. For this release, 1.
frameWindow	Specifies the pointer to the in-place container's document window.
signature	Specifies the creator signature of the in-place container.
refcon	Application-specific field.
psn	Specifies the in-place container's process serial number.
hCmdKeys	Reserved; must be NULL.
numCmds	Reserved; must be NULL.
growHandles	Specifies which of the in-place container's grow handles the object application is allowed to use during an in-place session. 0 = no constraints, 1 = haxisOnly, 2 = vaxisOnly, and 3 = no grow handles may be used.
dragConstraint	Specifies the drag constraints placed on the an in-place object by the container; 0 = no constraints, 1 = haxisOnly, 2 = vaxisOnly, and 3 = dragging not allowed.
fAdjustMenus	Boolean value set by the container(TRUE) to indicate whether or not the container wants to receive **AdjustMenus** calls from the object application during an in-place session.
unused	Reserved for future use; must be FALSE.

OleMBarRec

The **OleMBarRec** structure is used to construct the composite menu bar shared by the object and container applications during an in-place session. The structure contains data that is private to OLE; however the handle to this structure must be passed in various methods and API functions.

OleMBarRec is defined in ole2.h as follows:

```
typedef struct {
    //private date
} OleMBarRec, OleMBarPtr, **OleMBarhandle
```

OLEVERB

The **OLEVERB** enumeration is used with **IOleObject::EnumVerbs**.

OLEVERB is defined in ole2.h as follows:

```
typedef struct tagOLEVERB
{
    long            iVerb;
    char *          lpszVerbName;
    unsigned long   fuFlags;
    unsigned long   grfAttribs;
} OLEVERB;
```

OLEVERB members have the following meaning:

OLEVERB Member	Description
iVerb	Verb number being enumerated. If the object supports OLEIVERB_OPEN, OLEIVERB_SHOW and/or OLEIVERB_HIDE (or other predefined verb), these will be the first verbs enumerated, since they have the lowest verb numbers.
lpszVerbName	Name of the verb. On the Macintosh, the following metacharacters may be included: • ! which marks the menu item with the subsequent character • < which sets the character style of the item • (which disables the item The meta-characters / and ^ are not permitted.

fuFlags
On Windows, a group of flags taken from the flag constants beginning with MF_ defined in **AppendMenu**. Container should use these flags in building the object's verb menu. All flags defined in **AppendMenu** are supported except for:

- MF_BITMAP
- MF_OWNERDRAW
- MF_POPUP

grfAttribs
Group of flag bits taken from the enumeration OLEVERBATTRIB. OLEVERBATTRIB_NEVERDIRTIES indicates that the execution of this verb can never cause the object to become dirty and require saving to persistent storage.

OLEVERBATTRIB_ONCONTAINERMENU indicates that this verb should be placed on the container's menu of object verbs when the object is selected. OLEIVERB_HIDE, OLEIVERB_SHOW, and OLEIVERB_OPEN never have this value set.

STATDATA

The **STATDATA** structure is used with **IOleObject::EnumAdvise.**

STATDATA is defined in dvobj.h as follows:

```
typedef struct STRUCT tagSTATDATA
{
    FORMATETC        formatEtc;
    unsigned long    advf;
    LPADVISESINK     pAdvise;
    unsigned long    dwConnection;
} STATDATA;
```

STATSTG

The STATSTG structure is used with IEnumSTATSTG::Next, and the Stat methods in IStorage, IStream, and ILockBytes.

STATSTG is defined in storage.h as follows:

```
typedef struct tagSTATSTG{
    FSSpec * pspec;
    char  * pwcsName;
    unsigned long type;
    ULARGE_INTEGER cbSize;
    FILETIME mtime;
    FILETIME ctime;
    FILETIME atime;
    unsigned long grfMode;
    unsigned long grfLocksSupported;
    CLSID clsid;
    unsigned long grfStateBits;
    unsigned long Reserved;
} STATSTG;
```

STATSTG members have the following meaning:

Member	Description
pspec	Pointer to an FSSpec that corresponds to the root level storage. Its value is valid only for a root level storage call to **IStorage::Stat**, where the STATFLAG argument (*grfStatFlag*) is STATFLAG_DEFAULT. For all other cases, *pspec* is NULL.
pwcsName	Contains the name of the storage element. *pwcsName* is allocated and filled in by the callee and later freed by the caller.
type	Identifies the type of the element. Legal values are found in the **STGTY** enumeration.
cbSize	Specifies the size of the storage element. It is the byte count for stream objects and byte arrays, and it is undefined for storage objects.
mtime	Contains the date and time when the storage was last modified.
ctime	Contains the date and time when the storage was created.
atime	Contains the closest approximation of the time of last access.
grfMode	Specifies the mode in which the element was opened. It is valid only on **Stat** method calls.

grfLocksSupported	A group of Boolean flags relevant only for stream objects and byte arrays. For each lock type, *grfLocksSupported* indicates whether a call to **IStream::LockRegion** or **ILockBytes::LockRegion** will ever be worthwhile. Legal values for *grfLocksSupported* are combinations of values from the **LOCKTYPE** enumeration.
clsid	Relevant only for storage objects and represents the CLSID associated with the storage, if any. The *clsid* is CLSID_NULL for newly created storages.
grfStateBits	Relevant only for storage objects and is the value most recently set with **IStorage::SetStateBits**.
Reserved	Reserved for future use.

STGMEDIUM

The **STGMEDIUM** structure describes a medium of transfer for data objects.

STGMEDIUM is defined in dvobj.h as follows:

```
typedef struct tagSTGMEDIUM {
    unsigned long       tymed;
    union
    {
    Handle      hGlobal;
    char *      lpszFileName;
    LPSTREAM    pstm;
    LPSTORAGE   pstg;
    };
    LPUNKNOWN   pUnkForRelease;
    } STGMEDIUM;
```

A **STGMEDIUM** structure is a tagged union whose *tymed* member corresponds to the **TYMED** enumeration. Each type of medium specified in **FORMATETC**::*tymed* has a matching **STGMEDIUM** *tymed* member through which occurrences of that medium are passed.

STGMEDIUM can be set to NULL by setting the *tymed* member to TYMED_NULL.

The *pUnkForRelease* member is used to provide flexibility of medium ownership. It is helpful to have the following ownership scenario choices:

- The callee owns the medium, freeing all resources when finished.
- The callee does not own the medium and informs the caller when finished so that resources can then be freed.

The provider of the medium indicates its choice of ownership scenarios in the value it provides in *pUnkForRelease*. A NULL value indicates that the receiving body of code owns and can free the medium. A non-NULL pointer specifies that **ReleaseStgMedium**can always be called to free the medium. For a detailed explanation of how storage mediums are freed and *pUnkForRelease* is used, see the description of **ReleaseStgMedium**.

Enumerations

ADVF

The values defined in the **ADVF** enumeration are used to specify information about data and/or view advisories and cache connections.

ADVF is defined in dvobj.h as follows:

```
typedef enum tagADVF
{
    ADVF_NODATA                = 1,
    ADVF_PRIMEFIRST            = 2,
    ADVF_ONLYONCE              = 4,
    ADVF_DATAONSTOP            = 64,
    ADVFCACHE_NOHANDLER        = 8,
    ADVFCACHE_FORCEBUILTIN     = 16,
    ADVFCACHE_ONSAVE           = 32,
} ADVF;
```

The **ADVF** values can be or-ed together to form a composite value.

Depending on the method in which the **ADVF** value is being used, the values may have different meanings. Some of the methods use only a subset of the values while other methods use all of them.

ADVF_NODATA, when passed to **IDataObject::DAdvise**, is a request to avoid sending data with subsequent **IAdviseSink::OnDataChange** calls. TYMED_NULL is passed as the storage medium.

The recipient of the data change notification can later retrieve the latest data by calling **IDataObject::GetData**. ADVF_NODATA however, is just a request. The data object may choose to provide the data anyway, especially when more than one advisory connection has been made specifying the same **FORMATETC** data structure.

IViewObject::SetAdvise returns E_INVALIDARG if ADVF_NODATA is passed to it.

When ADVF_NODATA is passed to **IOleCache::Cache**, it is an indication that the cache should not be updated by changes made to the running object. Instead, the container will update the cache by explicitly calling **IOleCache::SetData**. This situation typically occurs when the iconic aspect of an object is being cached.

ADVF_PRIMEFIRST requests that a data or view change notification be sent or the cache updated immediately without waiting for a change in the current data or view.

ADVF_ONLYONCE automatically deletes the advisory connection after sending one data or view notification. The advisory sink receives only one **IAdviseSink** call. A nonzero connection ID is returned if the connection is established so the caller can use it to delete the connection. For data change notifications, the combination of ADVF_ONLYONCE | ADVF_PRIMEFIRST provides, in effect, an asynchronous **IDataObject::GetData** call.

When used with caching, ADVF_ONLYONCE updates the cache one time only, on receipt of the first OnDataChange notification. After the update is complete, the advisory connection between the object and the cache is disconnected.

ADVF_DATAONSTOP is meaningful for data change notifications only when ADVF_NODATA is also given. This value indicates that just before the advisory connection shuts down, a call to **IAdviseSink::OnDataChange** should be made that provides the data with it. Without this value, by the time an **OnDataChange** call without data reaches the sink, the source might have completed its shut down and the data might not be accessible. Sinks that specify this value should, in **OnDataChange**, accept data if it is being passed because they may not get another chance to retrieve it.

For cache connections, ADVF_DATAONSTOP updates the cache as part of object closure. ADVF_DATAONSTOP is not applicable to view change notifications.

ADVFCACHE_NOHANDLER, ADVFCACHE_FORCEBUILTIN, and ADVFCACHE_ONSAVE are applicable only to the caching methods. The ADVFCACHE_NOHANDLER value is reserved for future use.

ADVFCACHE_FORCEBUILTIN forcefully caches data that requires only code shipped with OLE or the underlying operating system to be present in order to produce it with **IDataObject::GetData** or **IViewObject ::Draw**, as appropriate. By specifying this value, the container can ensure that the data can be retrieved even when the object or handler code is not available. This value is used by DLL object applications and object handlers that perform the drawing of their objects. ADVFCACHE_FORCEBUILTIN instructs OLE to cache presentation data to ensure that there is a presentation in the cache.

ADVFCACHE_ONSAVE updates the cached representation only when the object containing the cache is saved. The cache is also updated when the OLE object transitions from the running state back to the loaded state (because a subsequent save operation would require rerunning the object).

BINDFLAGS

The **BINDFLAGS** enumeration contains the legal values for the bit field *grfFlags* in the **BIND_OPTS** structure.

BINDFLAGS is defined in moniker.h as follows:

```
typedef enum tagBINDFLAGS{
    BIND_MAYBOTHERUSER        = 1,
    BIND_JUSTTESTEXISTENCE    = 2,
} BINDFLAGS;
```

BINDFLAGS values have the following meanings.

Value	Meaning
BINDFLAGS _MAYBOTHERUSER	If present, this sort of interaction is permitted. If not present, the operation to which the bind context containing this parameter is applied should not interact with the user in any way, such as by asking for a password for a network volume that needs mounting. If prohibited from interacting with the user when it otherwise would, an operation can elect to use a different algorithm that does not require user interaction, or it can fail with the error MK_MUSTBOTHERUSER.
BINDFLAGS _JUSTTESTEXISTENCE	If present, this value indicates that the caller of the moniker operation to which this flag is being applied is not actually interested in having the operation carried out, but only in learning whether the operation could have been carried out had this flag not been specified. For example, this flag lets the caller indicate only an interest in finding out whether an object actually exists by using this flag in a **IMoniker::BindToObject** call. Moniker implementations can ignore this possible optimization and carry out the operation in full. Callers must be able to deal with both cases. See individual routine descriptions for details of exactly what status is returned.

BINDSPEED

The **BINDSPEED** enumeration is used with **IOleItemContainer::GetObject**.

BINDSPEED is defined in ole2.h as follows:

```
typedef enum tagBINDSPEED
{
    BINDSPEED_INDEFINITE = 1,
    BINDSPEED_MODERATE   = 2,
    BINDSPEED_IMMEDIATE  = 3,
} BINDSPEED;
```

BINDSPEED values have the following semantics:

Value	Meaning
BINDSPEED_INDEFINITE	Caller will wait indefinitely. BINDSPEED_INDEFINITE is specified if the speed needed in the bind context is zero.
BINDSPEED_MODERATE	Caller will wait a moderate amount of time. BINDSPEED_MODERATE is specified if the speed needed in the bind context is greater than 2500 milleseconds. BINDSPEED_MODERATE includes those objects indicated by BINDSPEED_IMMEDIATE, plus those objects that are always running when loaded. In this case, the designated object should be loaded, checked to see whether it is running and if so, it should be returned. Otherwise, MK_E_EXCEEEDEDDEADLINE should be returned.
BINDSPEED_IMMEDIATE	Caller will wait only a short time. If BINDSPEED_IMMEDIATE is specified, the object should be returned only if it is already running or if it is a pseudo-object. This is an object internal to the item container, such as a cell range in a spreadsheet or a character range in a word processor. Otherwise, MK_E_EXCEEEDEDDEADLINE should be returned.

CALLTYPE

The **CALLTYPE** enumeration is used with **IMessageFilter** interface methods.

CALLTYPE is defined in compobj.h as follows:

```
typedef enum tagCALLTYPE
{
    CALLTYPE_TOPLEVEL               = 1,
    CALLTYPE_NESTED                 = 2,
    CALLTYPE_ASYNC                  = 3,
    CALLTYPE_TOPLEVEL_CALLPENDING   = 4,
    CALLTYPE_ASYNC_CALLPENDING      = 5
    } CALLTYPE;
```

CALLTYPE values have the following meanings:

Value	**Meaning**
CALLTYPE_TOPLEVEL	A call has arrived with a new logical thread ID. The application is not currently waiting for a reply from an outgoing call. Calls of this type should always be handled.
CALLTYPE_NESTED	A call has arrived with the same logical thread ID as that of an outgoing call for which the application is currently waiting for a reply. Calls of this type can be handled or rejected.
CALLTYPE_ASYNC	An synchronous call has arrived; calls of this type *cannot* be rejected. OLE always delivers them.
CALLTYPE_TOPLEVEL _CALLPENDING	A call has arrived with a new logical thread ID. The application is currently waiting for a reply from an outgoing call. Calls of this type may be handled or rejected.
CALLTYPE_ASYNC _CALLPENDING	An asynchronous call has arrived with a new logical thread ID. The application is currently waiting for a reply from an outgoing call. Calls of this type cannot be rejected.

CLSCTX

Different pieces of code can be associated with one object class for use in different execution contexts. The context in which the caller is interested is passed to **CoGetClassObject** in the parameter *dwClsContext*. This parameter's value is a group of flags taken from the enumeration **CLSCTX**, which is defined in compobj.h as follows:

```
typedef enum tagCLSCTX
{
    CLSCTX_INPROC_SERVER      = 1
    CLSCTX_INPROC_HANDLER     = 2,
    CLSCTX_LOCAL_SERVER       = 4,
} CLSCTX;
```

CLSCTX contexts are tried in the order in which they are listed. Multiple values can be or-ed together, indicating that multiple contexts are acceptable to the caller; for example:

```
#define CLSCTX_INPROC (CLSCTX_INPROC_SERVER|CLSCTX_INPROC_HANDLER)
#define CLSCTX_SERVER (CLSCTX_INPROC_SERVER|CLSCTX_LOCAL_SERVER)
```

CLSCTX contexts are used as follows:

Object Class Context Values	Description
CLSCTX_INPROC _SERVER	The code that creates and manages objects of this class is loaded in the container's process space (runs in same process as caller).
CLSCTX_INPROC _HANDLER	The DLL code that implements container-side structures of this class (when instances of it are accessed remotely) is loaded in the container's process space (runs in same process as caller).
CLSCTX_LOCAL _SERVER	The EXE code that creates and manages objects of this class is loaded in a separate process space (runs on same machine but in a different process).

DATADIR

The **DATADIR** enumeration is used with the OLE function **OleRegEnumFormatEtc**.

DATADIR is defined in dvobj.h as follows:

```
typedef enum tagDATADIR
{
    DATADIR_GET      = 1,      //Enumerate those formats that can be
                               //passed to IDataObject::GetData
    DATADIR_SET      = 2,      //Enumerate those formats that can be
                               //passed to IDataObject::SetData
```

DISCARDCACHE

The **DISCARDCACHE** enumeration is used with **IOleCache2::DiscardCache** to define how to flush the cache.

DISCARDCACHE is defined in dvobj.h as follows:

```
typedef enum tagDISCARDCACHE {
    DISCARDCACHE_SAVEIFDIRTY    = 0
    DISCARDCACHE_NOSAVE         = 1
    } DISCARDCACHE;
```

DISCARDCACHE values have the following meaning:

DISCARDCACHE Values	Meaning
DISCARDCACHE _SAVEIFDIRTY	Indicates that all of the dirty data in the cache(s) should be saved before the discard occurs. Containers that have drawn a large object and need to free up memory may want to specify DISCARDCACHE_SAVEIFDIRTY so that the newest presentation is saved for the next time the object must be drawn.
DISCARDCACHE _NOSAVE	Indicates that no save is necessary. Containers that have activated an embedded object, made some changes, and then called **IOleObject::Close**(OLECLOSE_NOSAVE) to rollback the changes may want to specify this option to ensure that the native and presentation data are not out of sync.

DROPEFFECT

he OLE **DoDragDrop** function and many of the **IDRopSource** and **IDropTarget** interface methods pass information about the effects that a drag source allows in a specific drag operation and the effect a potential drop will have on a target window. Valid drop effect values are the result of or-ing together values contained in the **DROPEFFECT** enumeration:

```
typedef enum tagDROPEFFECT{
    DROPEFFECT_NONE         = 0,\\only lower three bits are significant
    DROPEFFECT_COPY         = 1,
    DROPEFFECT_MOVE         = 2,
    DROPEFFECT_LINK         = 4,
    DROPEFFECT_SCROLL       = 0x80000000,
    }DROPEFFECT;
```

DROPEFFECT values have the following meaning:

DROPEFFECT Name	Value	Description
DROPEFFECT _NONE	0	Drop target cannot accept the data.
DROPEFFECT _COPY	1	Drop results in a copy. The original data is untouched by the drag source.
DROPEFFECT _MOVE	2	Drag source should remove the data.
DROPEFFECT _LINK	4	Drag source should create a link to the original data.
DROPEFFECT _SCROLL	0x80000000	Scrolling is about to start or is currently occurring in the target. This value is used in addition to the other values.

Presently, only 4 of the 32 bit positions in a **DROPEFFECT** have meaning. In the future, more interpretations for the bits will be added. Drop sources and drop targets should carefully mask these values appropriately before comparing. They should never compare a **DROPEFFECT** against, say, DROPEFFECT_COPY by

```
if (dwDropEffect == DROPEFECT_COPY)...
```

Instead, the application should always mask for the value or values being sought:

```
if (dwDropEffect & DROPEFFECT_COPY) == DROPEFFECT_COPY...
```

or

```
if (dwDropEffect & DROPEFFECT_COPY)...
```

Doing this allows new drop effects to be defined, while preserving backwards compatibility with existing code.

DVASPECT

DVASPECT is defined in dvobj.h as follows:

```
typedef enum tagDVASPECT {
    DVASPECT_CONTENT         = 1,
    DVASPECT_THUMBNAIL       = 2,
    DVASPECT_ICON            = 4,
    DVASPECT_DOCPRINT        = 8,
    } DVASPECT;
```

DVASPECT values have the following meaning:

Values for DVASPECT	Meaning
DVASPECT _CONTENT	Provides a representation so the object can be displayed as an embedded object inside its container; this is the most common value for compound document objects. It is appropriate to use DVASPECT_CONTENT to get a presentation of the embedded object for rendering either on the screen or on a printer; DVASPECT_DOCPRINT, by contrast, indicates the look of the object as though it were printed.
DVASPECT _THUMBNAIL	Provides a thumbnail representation so that the object can be displayed in a browsing tool. The thumbnail is approximately a 120 by 120 pixel 6-color device-independent bitmap wrapped in a metafile.
DVASPECT _ICON	Provides an iconic representation of the object.
DVASPECT _DOCPRINT	Represents the object as though it were printed using the Print command from the File menu. The described data represents a sequence of pages.

EXTCONN

EXTCONN is used to define *extconn* parameters to the methods in the **IExternalConnection** interface. **EXTCONN** is defined in compobj.h as follows:

```
typedef enum tagEXTCONN
{
    //Strong connection on object; default
    EXTCONN_STRONG        = 0x0001,
}EXTCONN
```

LOCKTYPE

The **LOCKTYPE** enumeration is used to supply values for the *grfLocksSupported* field to the STATSTG data structure.

LOCKTYPE is defined in storage.h as follows:

```
typedef enum tagLOCKTYPE
{
    LOCK_WRITE      = 1,
    LOCK_EXCLUSIVE  = 2,
    LOCK_ONLYONCE   = 4
} LOCKTYPE;
```

LOCKTYPE values have the following meaning:

Value	Meaning
LOCK _WRITE	If the lock is granted, reading the specified region of the stream can be done by calling **IStream::Read** from any opening of this stream. Attempts to write to this region from any opening of this stream other than the one to which the lock was granted returns the error STG_E_ACCESSDENIED.
LOCK _EXCLUSIVE	Attempts to read or write this stream by other stream openings return the error STG_E_ACCESSDENIED.
LOCK _ONLYONCE	If the lock is granted, no other lock can be obtained on the bytes in the given region. Usually this lock type is an alias for some other lock type and other semantics can occur as a side effect. The underlying implementation can use the appropriate file system primitive to accomplish the lock.

MEMCTX

The **MEMCTX** enumeration is used with the OLE function **CoGetMalloc**, providing values for its *dwDestContext* parameter.

MEMCTX is defined in compobj.h as follows:

```
typedef enum tagMEMCTX
{
    MEMCTX_TASK         = 1,    //task (private) memory
    MEMCTX_SHARED       = 2,    //shared memory (between processes)
} MEMCTX;
```

MKRREDUCE

The **MKRREDUCE** enumeration contains values that specify how far to reduce a moniker with **IMoniker::Reduce**.

MKRREDUCE is defined in moniker.h as follows:

```
typedef enum tagMKRREDUCE {
    MKRREDUCE_ONE              = 3<<16,
    MKRREDUCE_TOUSER           = 2<<16,
    MKRREDUCE_THROUGUSER       = 1<<16,
    MKRREDUCE_ALL              = 0
    } MKRREDUCE;
```

MKRREDUCE values have the following meanings:

Value	Meaning
MKRREDUCE _ONE	Performs only one reduction step on the moniker. In general, the caller must have specific knowledge about the particular kind of moniker to be able to take advantage of this option.
MKRREDUCE _TOUSER	Reduces the moniker to a form that the user identifies as a persistent object. If no such point exists, this option should be treated as MKRREDUCE_ALL.
MKRREDUCE _THROUGHUSER	Reduces the moniker to where any further reduction would prevent the user from identifying it as a persistent object. Often, this is the same stage as MKRREDUCE_TOUSER.
MKRREDUCE _ALL	Reduces the moniker until it is reduced to itself.

MKSYS

The **MKSYS** enumeration contains values that are returned by **IMoniker::IsSystemMoniker**. These values indicate the type of a moniker.

MKSYS is defined in moniker.h as follows:

```
typedef enum tagMKSYS {
    MKSYS_NONE = 0,
    MKSYS_GENERICCOMPOSITE    = 1,
    MKSYS_FILEMONIKER         = 2,
    MKSYS_ANTIMONIKER         = 3,
    MKSYS_ITEMMONIKER         = 4,
    MKSYS_POINTMONIKER        = 5,
    } MKSYS;
```

MSHCTX

The **MSHCTX** enumeration is used in various **IMarshal** and **IStandardMarshal** interface methods to determine the destination context of the marshaling operation.

MSHCTX is defined in compobj.h as follows:

```
typedef enum tagMSHCTX
{
    MSHCTX_LOCAL         = 0,
    MSHCTX_NOSHAREDMEM    = 1,
} MSHCTX;
```

MSHCTX values have the following meanings:

Value	Description
MSHCTX _LOCAL	Unmarshaling context is local; it has shared memory access.
MSHCTX _NOSHAREDMEM	Unmarshaling context does not have shared memory access with the marshaling context.

MSHLFLAGS

The **MSHLFLAGS** enumeration is used with **IMarshall** and **IStandardMarshal** interface methods. **MSHLFLAGS** contains a group of flags that determine how the marshaling is to be done; **MSHFLAGS** is defined in compobj.h as follows:

```
typedef enum tagMSHLFLAGS
{
    MSHLFLAGS_NORMAL         = 0,
    MSHLFLAGS_TABLESTRONG    = 1,
    MSHLFLAGS_TABLEWEAK      = 2,
} MSHLFLAGS;
```

MSHLFLAGS flags have the following meanings:

Value	Description
MSHLFLAGS _NORMAL	Marshaling is done by passing an interface from one process to another. The marshaled-data-packet that results from the call will be transported to the other process, where it will be unmarshaled (see **CoUnmarshalInterface**). By means of this flag, the marshaled data packet is unmarshaled either one or zero times. If it is unmarshaled successfully, **CoReleaseMarshalData** is not called on the data packet; and any necessary processing is done in the unmarshal itself. If unmarshaling fails, or it is not attempted, only then is **IMarshal::ReleaseMarshalData** called on the data packet.
MSHLFLAGS _TABLESTRONG	Marshaling is happening because the data packet is to be stored in a globally accessible table from which it is to be unmarshaled zero, one, or more times. Further, the presence of the data packet in the table is to count as a reference on the marshaled interface. When removed from the table, it is the responsibility of the table implementor to call **CoReleaseMarshalData** on the data-packet.
MSHLFLAGS _TABLEWEAK	Marshaling is happening because the data packet is to be stored in a globally accessible table from which it is to be unmarshaled zero, one, or more times. However, the presence of the data packet in the table does not count as a reference on the marshaled interface. Destruction of the data packet is done by calling **CoReleasemarshalData**.

OLECLOSE

The **OLECLOSE** enumeration is used with **IOleObject::Close**. **OLECLOSE** is defined in ole2.h as follows:

```
typedef enum tagOLECLOSE
{
    OLECLOSE_SAVEIFDIRTY     = 0,
    OLECLOSE_NOSAVE          = 1,
    OLECLOSE_PROMPTSAVE      = 2,
} OLECLOSE;
```

OLECLOSE values have the following meaning:

Value	Meaning
OLECLOSE _SAVEIFDIRTY	Indicates that the object is always to be saved if it is dirty.
OLECLOSE _NOSAVE	Indicates that a save is not to occur whether the object is dirty or not.
OLECLOSE _PROMPTSAVE	Indicates that the user should determine whether the save should occur by being prompted with a message.

OLECONTF

The **OLECONTF** enumeration is used with **IOleContainer::EnumObjects**.

OLECONTF is defined in ole2.h as follows:

```
typedef enum tagOLECONTF
{
    OLECONTF_EMBEDDINGS          =  1,
    OLECONTF_LINKS               =  2,
    OLECONTF_OTHERS              =  4,
    OLECONTF_ONLYUSER            =  8,
    OLECONTF_ONLYIFRUNNING       = 16,
} OLECONTF;
```

OLECONTF values have following meanings:

Values	Meaning
OLECONTF _EMBEDDINGS	Enumerates the embedded objects in the container.
OLECONTF _LINKS	Enumerate the linked objects in the container.
OLECONTF _OTHER	Enumerates all objects in the container other than OLE compound document objects. If this flag is not given, pseudo objects in the container will be omitted.
OLECONTF _ONLYUSER	Enumerates only those objects the user is aware of. For example, hidden named-ranges in Microsoft Excel would not be enumerated using this value.
OLECONTF _ONLYIFRUNNING	Enumerates only the objects that are currently running inside this container.

OLEGETMONIKER

The **OLEGETMONIKER** enumeration is used with **IOleClientSite::GetMoniker** to specify a type of moniker.

OLEGETMONIKER is defined in ole2.h as follows:

```
typedef enum tagOLEGETMONIKER
{
    OLEGETMONIKER_ONLYIFTHERE        = 1,
    OLEGETMONIKER_FORCEASSIGN        = 2,
    OLEGETMONIKER_UNASSIGN           = 3,
    OLEGETMONIKER_TEMPFORUSER        = 4,
} OLEGETMONIKER;
```

OLEGETMONIKER values have the following meaning:

Value	Meaning
OLEGETMONIKER _ONLYIFTHERE	Returns a moniker only if one has previously been assigned.
OLEGETMONIKER _FORCEASSIGN	Returns an assigned moniker. Forced moniker assignment should be postponed until such time that a Paste Link actually occurs.
OLEGETMONIKER _UNASSIGN	Removes moniker assignment and returns NULL.
OLEGETMONIKER _TEMPFORUSER	Returns a temporary, unassigned moniker. This flag is used when a moniker is needed, for example, to represent data being copied to the clipboard at the time of the copy.

OLEGROWHANDLES

The **OLEGROWHANDLES** enumeration is used to support in-place activation.

OLEGROWHANDLES is defined in ole2.h, as follows:

```
typedef enum tagOLEGROWHANDLES
{
    oleNoGrow = 0,
    oleHorizGrow = 1,    // OR these bits together
    oleVertGrow = 2,
    oleHVHandle = 3
} OLEGROWHANDLES;
```

OLELINKBIND

The **OLELINKBIND** enumeration is used with **IOleLink::BindToSource**.

OLELINKBIND is defined in ole2.h as follows:

```
typedef enum tagOLELINKBIND {
    OLELINKBIND_EVENIFCLASSDIFF   = 1,
} OLELINKBIND:
```

OLEMANAGER

The **OLEMANANAGER** enumeration is used to specify values for the **InitOleManager** function; this enumeration is defined in ole2.h as follows:

```
typedef enum tagOLEMANAGER
{
    OLEMGR_BIND_NORMAL       = 0,
    OLEMGR_BIND_IF_THERE     = 1,
    OLEMGR_NO_ADDREF         = 2,
    OLEMGR_ASYNC             = 4,
    OLEMGR_FORCELONG         = 2147483647
} OLEMANAGER;
```

OLEMANAGER values have the following meaning:

Value	Meaning
OLEMGR_BIND_NORMAL	Used to indicate a normal application, launch, bind, and Addref.
OLEMGR_BIND_IF_THERE	Used to indicate that the application only wants to bind if Microsoft OLE Extension is already running(useful only for mini-servers).
OLEMGR_NO_ADDREF	This flag does not reference count Microsoft OLE Extension; the application will bind only if Microsoft OLE Extension is running (useful only for add-in applications).
OLEMGR_ASYNC	Reserved for future use.

OLEMISC

The **OLEMISC** enumeration is used with **IOleObject::GetMiscStatus**.

OLEMISC is defined in ole2.h:

```
typedef enum tagOLEMISC
{
    OLEMISC_RECOMPOSEONRESIZE               = 1,
    OLEMISC_ONLYICONIC                      = 2,
    OLEMISC_INSERTNOTREPLACE                = 4,
    OLEMISC_STATIC                          = 8,
    OLEMISC_CANTLINKINSIDE                  = 16,
    OLEMISC_CANLINKBYOLE1                   = 32,
    OLEMISC_ISLINKOBJECT                    = 64,
    OLEMISC_INSIDEOUT                       = 128,
    OLEMISC_ACTIVATEWHENVISABLE             = 256,
    OLEMISC_RENDERINGISDEVICEINDEPENDENT    = 512,
    } OLEMISC;
```

OLEMISC values have the following meaning:

Value	Description
OLEMISC _RECOMPOSEONRESIZE	If true, signifies that when the size the container allocates to the object changes, the object would like the opportunity to recompose its picture. When resize occurs, the object is likely to do something other than scale its picture. The container should force the object to run so it can call **IOleObject::GetExtent.**
OLEMISC _ONLYICONIC	This object has no useful content view other than its icon. From the user's perspective, the Display As Icon checkbox (in the Paste Special dialog box) for this object should always be checked. Note that such an object should still have a drawable content aspect; it will look the same as its icon view.
OLEMISC _INSERTNOTREPLACE	Indicates that this is the kind of object that when inserted into a document should be inserted beside the selection instead of replacing it. An object which linked itself to the selection with which it was initialized would set this bit. Containers should examine this bit after they have initialized the object with the selection. See **IOleObject::InitFromData**.
OLEMISC_STATIC	Indicates that this object is a static object. See **OleCreateStaticFromData**.

Value	Description
OLEMISC _CANTLINKINSIDE	Indicates that this is the kind of object that should not be the link source that when bound to runs the object. That is, if when the object is selected, its container wishes to offer the Link Source format in a data transfer, then the link, when bound, must connect to the outside of the object. The user would see the object selected in its container, not open for editing. Some objects that do not want to implement being the source of a link when they are embedded may want to set this bit.
OLEMISC _CANLINKBYOLE1	Indicates that this object can be linked to by OLE 1 containers. This bit is used in the *dwStatus* field of the OBJECTDESCRIPTOR structure transferred with the Object and Link Source Descriptor formats. An object can be linked by OLE 1 if it is not an embedded object or pseudo object contained within an embedded object.
OLEMISC _ISLINKOBJECT	This object is a link object. This bit is significant to OLE and is set by the OLE 2 link object; object applications have no need to set this bit.
OLEMISC _INSIDEOUT	This object is capable of activating in-place, without requiring installation of menus and toolbars to run. Several such objects can be active concurrently. Some containers, such as forms, may choose to activate such objects automatically.
OLEMISC_ACTIVATE-WHENVISIBLE	This bit is set only when OLEMISC_INSIDEOUT is set, and indicates that this object prefers to be activated whenever it is visible. Some containers may always ignore this hint.
OLEMISC_RENDERINGIS DEVICEINDEPENDENT	This object does not pay any attention to target devices. Its presention data will be the same in all cases.

OLEREG_KEYWORD

The **OLEREG_KEYWORD** enumeration is used with the OLE functions **OleregGetValue**, **OleregRemoveKey**, and **OleregSetValue** as part of reading and writing values to the OLE Registration Database file.

OLEREG_KEYWORD is defined in MacDef.H as follows:

```
typedef enum tagOLEREG_KEYWORD {
    OLEREG_ROOT,
    OLEREG_GENERIC,
    OLEREGSVR_CLASS,
    OLEREGSVR_HUMAN_READABLE,
    OLEREGSVR_EXTENSION,
    OLEREGSVR_FILE_TYPE =    OLEREGSVR_EXTENSION,
    OLEREGSVR_PROTOCOL,
    OLEREGSVR_SERVER,
    OLEREGSVR_SIGNATURE = OLEREGSVR_SERVER,
    OLEREGSVR_HANDLER,
    OLEREGSVR_VERB,
    OLEREGSVR_NET_DRIVE,

    //The Following keywords can only be used with OleregGetValue
    OLEREG_QUERY_ONLY = 2000,
    OLEREGSVR_CLASS_FROM_HUMAN_READABLE,
    OLEREGSVR_CLASS_FROM_EXTENSION,
    OLEREGSVR_CLASS_FROM_SIG =
    OLEREGSVR_CLASS_FROM_EXTENSION
} OLEREG_KEYWORD;
```

OLERENDER

The **OLERENDER** enumeration is used with the OLE object creation functions.

OLERENDER is defined in as follows:

```
typedef enum tagOLERENDER
{
     OLERENDER_NONE        = 0,
     OLERENDER_DRAW        = 1,
     OLERENDER_FORMAT      = 2,
     OLERENDER_ASIS        = 3
} OLERENDER;
```

OLERENDER values have the following meaning:

Value	Meaning
OLERENDER_NONE	The container is not requesting any local cache drawing or data retrieval capabilities in the object. *pFormatetc* is ignored for this option.
OLERENDER_DRAW	The container will draw the content of the object on the screen (a NULL target device) using **IViewObject::Draw**. The object determines the data formats that need to be cached. Only the *ptd* and *dwAspect* members of *pFormatetc* are significant, since the object may cache things differently depending on the parameter values. However, *pFormatetc* can legally be NULL here, in which case the object is to assume the display target device and the DVASPECT_CONTENT aspect.
OLERENDER_FORMAT	The container will pull one format from the object using **IDataObject::GetData**. The format of the data to be cached is passed in *pFormatetc*, which may not in this case be NULL.
OLERENDER_ASIS	The container is not requesting any local cache drawing or data retrieval capabilities in the object. *pFormatetc* is ignored for this option. The difference between this and OLERENDER_NONE is important in other helper functions such as **OleCreateFromData** and **OleCreateLinkFromData**.

The **STGMEDIUM** structure is a generalized global memory handle commonly used to pass one body of code to another. Where one would expect to find a global memory handle involved in a data transfer, OLE uses a **STGMEDIUM** structure in its place.

The **DVTARGETDEVICE** structure contains enough information about a Windows target device so that a handle to a device context (hDC) can be created using the Windows **CreateDC** function.

The **ADVF** enumeration is a set of advisory flags that specifies values for controlling advisory connections and caching.

OLEUPDATE

The **OLEUPDATE** enumeration contains values for controling when the data and/or presentation cache on the link consumer is updated. The enumeration is used with **IOleLink::SetUpdateOptions**.

OLEUPDATE is defined in ole2.h as follows:

```
typedef enum tagOLEUPDATE {
    OLEUPDATE_ALWAYS     = 1,
    OLEUPDATE_ONCALL     = 3,
    } OLEUPDATE;
```

OLEUPDATE values are used as follows:

Value	Purpose
OLEUDPATE_ALWAYS	Updatesthe link object whenever possible. This option supports the Automatic link-update option in the Links dialog box.
OLEUPDATE_ONCALL	Updates the link object only when the **IOleObject::Update** member function is called. This option supports the Manual link-update option in the Links dialog box.

OLEWHICHMK

The **OLEWHICHMK** enumeration is used with **IOleClientSite::GetMoniker** and **IOleObject::SetMoniker**, and **IOleObject::GetMoniker**.

OLEWHICHMK is defined in ole2.h as follows:

```
typedef enum tagOLEWHICHMK {
    OLEWHICHMK_CONTAINER      = 1,
    OLEWHICHMK_OBJREL         = 2,
    OLEWHICHMK_OBJFULL        = 3,
    }OLEWHICHMK;
```

OLEWHICHMK values have the following meaning:

Values	Meaning
OLEWHICHMK _CONTAINER	Returns the moniker belonging to the object's container, typically a file moniker.
OLEWHICHMK _OBJREL	Returns the object's moniker relative to the client site, typically an item moniker.
OLEWHICHMK _OBJFULL	Returns the object's full moniker, typically a composite moniker.

PENDINGTYPE

The **PENDINGTYPE** enumeration is used with **IMessageFilter::MessagePending** and is defined in compobj.h as follows:

```
typedef enum tagPENDINGTYPE {
    PENDINGTYPE_TOPLEVEL     = 1,
    PENDINGTYPE_NESTED       = 2,
} PENDINGTYPE;
```

PENDINGTYPE values have the following meaning:

Value	Meaning
PENDINGTYPE _TOPLEVEL	The outgoing call is not nested within a call from another application.
PENDINGTYPE _NESTED	The outgoing call is nested within a call from another application.

REGCLS

The **REGCLS** enumeration supplies values for the *flags* parameter to **CoRegisterClassObject**.

REGCLS is defined in compobj.h as follows:

```
typedef enum tagREGCLS {
    REGCLS_SINGLEUSE         = 0,
    REGCLS_MULTIPLEUSE       = 1,
    REGCLS_MULTI_SEPARATE    = 2,
    } REGCLS;
```

REGCLS values have the following meaning:

Value	Description
REGCLS _SINGLEUSE	Once a container has connected to the class object with **CoGetClassObject**, the class object should be removed from public view so that no other container applications can similarly connect to it. This flag is commonly given for single document interface (SDI) applications. Specifying this flag does not affect the responsibility of the object application to call **CoRevokeClassObject**; it must always call **CoRevokeClassObject** when it is done by using an object class.
REGCLS _MULTIPLEUSE	Enables multiple **CoGetClassObject** calls to connect to the same class object.

Value	Description
REGCLS _MULTI_SEPARATE	Similar to REGCLS_MULTIPLEUSE, except that REGCLS_MULTI_SEPARATE does not automatically register the class object as CLSCTX_INPROC_SERVER for a local server; instead it provides separate control over each context.

REGENUMPROGIDF

The **REGENUMPROGIDF** enumeration is used with **RegEnumProgID** to specify the status information returned for the given subkey in the OLE 2 Registration Database file.

REGENUMPROGIDF is defined in macdef.h:

```
typedef enum tagREGENUMPROGIDF
{
    REGENUMPROGIDF_ISPROGID   = 1;  //the returned subkey is a ProgID
    REGENUMPROGIDF_EMBPREF    = 2;  //the returned subkey came from the
                                    //Embedding Preferences folder
    REGENUMPROGIDF_INSERTABLE = 4;  //the returned subkey is an
                                    //insertable ProgID
} REGENUMPROGIDF;
```

REGENUMPROGIDF values have the following meaning:

Value	Meaning
REGENUMPROGIDF _ISPROGID	A subkey SUB is a ProgID if HKEY_CLASSES_ROOT\SUB has a CLSID subkey or a Protocol\StdFileEditing subkey, or SUB came from the OLE 1 Embedding Preferences file.
REGENUMPROGIDF _EMBPREF	This flag is set if the returned subkey is a ProgID from Embedding Preferences file. If this is returned, then the ProgID did not come from the Registration Database file, so an application should not look for subkeys/values of the ProgID in the Registration Database file. To enter the ProgID into the registration database (along with its appropriate OLE1 information from the Embedding Preferences file), the application calls **CLSIDFromProgID**(*szProgID*, *&clsid*).

Value	Meaning
REGENUMPROGIDF _INSERTABLE	A subkey SUB is insertable if HKEY_CLASSES_ROOT\SUB has a Insertable subkey or a Protocol\StdFileEditing, or SUB came from the OLE 1 Embedding Preferences file.

STATFLAG

The **STATFLAG** enumeration controls the level of statistics returned about the storage object using **IStorage::Stat**.

STATFLAG is defined in storage.h as follows:

```
typedef enum tagSTATFLAG
{
    STATFLAG_DEFAULT     = 0,
    STATFLAG_NONAME      = 1
} STATFLAG;
```

STGC

The **STGC** enumeration defines the type of commit operation that will be performed using **IStorage::Commit**.

STGC is defined in storage.h as follows:

```
typedef enum tagSTGC
{
    STGC_DEFAULT                               = 0,
    STGC_OVERWRITE                             = 1,
    STGC_ONLYIFCURRENT                         = 2,
    STGC_DANGEROUSLYCOMMITMERELYTODISKCACHE   = 4
} STGC;
```

STGY values have the following meaning:

Value	Meaning
STGC_OVERWRITE	Allows new data to overwrite the old data, reducing space requirements.
STGC_ONLYIF-CURRENT	Prevents multiple users of a storage object from overwriting the others' changes.

Value	Meaning
STGC_ONLYIF-CURRENT	Commits changes only if no one has made changes since the last time this user opened the storage or committed. If other changes have been made, STG_E_NOTCURRENT is returned. If the caller chooses to overwrite the changes, **IStorage::Commit** can be called with *grfCommitFlags* set to STGC_DEFAULT.
STGC_DANGEROUSLY-COMMITMERELY-TODISKCACHE	Commits the changes, but does not save them to the disk cache.

STGMOVE

The **STGMOVE** enumeration is used to define the type of move operation that is to be performed with **IStorage::MoveElementTo**.

STGMOVE is defined in storage.h as follows:

```
typedef enum tagSTGMOVE {
STGMOVE_MOVE          = 0,
STGMOVE_COPY          = 1,
} STGMOVE;
```

STGMOVE values have the following meanings:

Values for *grfFlags*	Meaning
STGMOVE_MOVE	Carries out the move operation, as expected.
STGMOVE_COPY	Carries out the first part of the move operation but do not remove the original element. With this flag, the behavior resulting from copying an element on top of itself (that is, *pStgDest* is the same as the source **IStorage,** and *lpszNewName* = *lpszName*) is undefined.

STGTY

The **STGTY** enumeration is used to define the type of storage medium: storage obejct, stream object, or byte-array object.

STGY is defined in storage.h as follows:

```
typedef enum tagSTGTY
{
    STGTY_STORAGE           = 1,    //Storage object
    STGTY_STREAM            = 2,    //Stream object
    STGTY_LOCKBYTES         = 3,    //Byte array object
} STGTY;
```

STREAM_SEEK

The **STREAM_SEEK** enumeration is used with **IStream::Seek** to specify the position within the stream at which to begin the seek operation.

STREAM_SEEK is defined in storage.h as follows:

```
typedef enum tagSTREAM_SEEK
{
    STREAM_SEEK_SET         = 0,
    STREAM_SEEK_CUR         = 1,
    STREAM_SEEK_END         = 2
} STREAM_SEEK;
```

STREAM_SEEK values have the following meaning:

Value	Meaning
STREAM_SEEK_SET	Sets the seek position relative to the beginning of the stream; *dlibMove* is the new seek position.
STREAM_SEEK_CUR	Sets the seek position relative to the current position of the stream; *dlibMove* is the (signed) displacement to be made.
STREAM_SEEK_END	Sets the seek position relative to the current end of the stream; *dlibMove* is the (signed) displacement to be made.

TDFLAGS

The **TDFLAGS** enumeration is used to define characteristics of the target device; these values are supplied in the wFlags member of **DVTARGETDEVICE** structure.

The enumeration is defined in dvobj.h as follows:

```
typedef enum tagTDFLAGS
{
    TD_PRINTER = 1          //if set, target device describes a printer
    TD_POSTSCRIPT = 2       //if set, target device has postscript
    TD_GX = 4               //if set, target device has GX
}TDFLAGS;
```

TYMED

The **TYMED** enumeration is defined in dvobj.h:

```
typedef enum tagTYMED
{
    TYMED_HGLOBAL       = 1,
    TYMED_FILE          = 2,
    TYMED_ISTREAM       = 4,
    TYMED_ISTORAGE      = 8,
    TYMED_GDI           = 16,  //Not used on Mac; for compatiblity
                               //with Windows
    TYMED_MFPICT        = 32,
    TYMED_NULL          = 0,
} TYMED;
```

The **TYMED** values have the following specific meanings and required release behavior. However, for any of the **TYMED** values, if *pUnkForRelease* is non-NULL, *pUnkForRelease*->**Release** is always called.

Value	Meaning	Release Mechanism
TYMED _HGLOBAL	Passes the data in a global memory handle. All global handles must be allocated with the GMEM_SHARE flag.	**GlobalFree**(*hGlobal*)
TYMED _FILE	Passes the data in the contents of a file on the disk.	**Close**(*hFile*)
TYMED _ISTREAM	Passes the data using an instance of the **IStream** interface. The passed data is available through calls to the **IStream::Read**.	*pStm*->**Release**()
TYMED _ISTORAGE	Passes the data using an instance of the **IStorage** interface; the passed data are the streams and storage objects nested beneath the **IStorage**.	*pStg*->**Release**()

Value	Meaning	Release Mechanism
TYMED _MFPICT	Passes the data in a global memory handle. All global handles must be allocated with the GMEM_SHARE flag.	**GlobalFree**(*hGlobal*)
TYMED _NULL	This is not actually a medium; it indicates that no data is being passed.	

USERCLASSTYPE

The **USERCLASSTYPE** enumeration is used with the OLE function **OleRegGetClassUserType** and **IOleObject::GetUserType**.

USERCLASSTYPE is defined in ole2.h as follows:

```
typedef enum tagUSERCLASSTYPE {
    USERCLASSTYPE_FULL       = 1,
    USERCLASSTYPE_SHORT      = 2,
    USERCLASSTYPE_APPNAME    = 3,
} USERCLASSTYPE;
```

USERCLASSTYPE values have the following meaning:

Value	Meaning
USERCLASSTYPE _FULL	Full type name of the class.
USERCLASSTYPE _SHORT	A short name (maximum of 15 characters) used for popup menus and the Links dialog box.
USERCLASSTYPE _APPNAME	The name of the application servicing the class and used in the Result text in dialogs.

APPENDIX D

OLE 2 for the Macintosh: How It Differs from OLE 2 for Windows

OLE 2 for the Macintosh is functionally identical to OLE for Windows. Applications implement and use the same set of interfaces to support the same set of features. API and helper functions are mostly applicable across platforms, with multiple versions provided to serve platform-specific needs.

The major differences between OLE for the Macintosh and OLE for Windows involve the packaging and installation of OLE, the user interface model, and the architecture in a few areas. Due to the user interface model differences, developers must consider several platform-specific issues when implementing visual editing (in-place activation). The registration database architecture differs; Macintosh developers use a set of API functions that mimic those provided by Windows to register their objects at run time. Interprocess communication is facilitated by Apple events, for which applications must register and be prepared to receive. Where appropriate, a set of Macintosh-specific API functions exist to make development in these areas of difference more similar to the Macintosh programming environment.

Minor differences involve issues of naming. OLE maps Windows-specific data types used in interface method and function calls to Macintosh-specific versions so that developers can use the appropriate term for their platform. The naming of clipboard formats is different, where on the Macintosh four character resource names are used. File Monikers specify paths according to platform.

Differences in Architecture

Whereas most areas of OLE are designed to work across platforms, a few areas necessitated an alternate approach due to operating system differences or constraints. These areas include the packaging of OLE, the registration database, interprocess communication, visual editing, and structured storage.

OLE Packaging

Unlike OLE for Windows, where OLE is packaged and released as a dynamic linked library, OLE for the Macintosh is packaged and released as an extension that must be started by your application in order to make OLE functionality available to your applications. The name of this extension is Microsoft OLE Extension and it must be installed into the System 7 Extensions folder.

To start Microsoft OLE Extension, your OLE application must call **InitOleManager**, typically during application startup. To stop Microsoft OLE Extension, call **UninitOleManager** as part of your application's shutdown sequence.

Once Microsoft OLE Extension is started and running, an application initializes the OLE libraries just as they do under Windows, by calling **OleInitialize** and/or **CoInitialize**.

Other than this difference in packaging, OLE for the Macintosh and OLE for Windows are functionally identical.

In-Place Activation

On the Macintosh, the implementation of in-place activation is different than on Windows. Besides the fundamental differences in architecture between the Macintosh and Windows that must be taken into consideration, there are many new APIs that support in-place activation.

For more information on implementing in-place activation, see Chapter 11, "In-Place Activation Interfaces and Functions."

Interprocess Communication

The interprocess communication used for OLE is built on high-level events, using shared memory in the system heap. Interprocess communication is restricted at present to the local machine.

Structured Storage

Compound files, the implementation of structured storage provided by OLE, is contained within the data fork of a Macintosh file. Macintosh compound files are byte-swapped so that they are byte equivalent on any file system.

A set of API functions are available to provide a Macintosh-specific interface to the storage. For example, whereas a Windows OLE developer calls **StgCreateDocfile** to create a root level storage object, the Macintosh OLE developer has a choice of calls. Either **StgCreateDocfileMac**, **StgCreateDocfileFSp**, or **StgCreateDocfile** can be called for the same functionality.

An applications file data is not byte-swapped or modified in any way. An application that has platform-specific native data should be able to convert between formats. If conversion is possible, the application must have the same class identifier (CLSID) on both platforms. If conversion is not possible, an application must specify a unique CLSID for each platform.

Storage and stream objects on the Macintosh can be given names up to 64 characters in length. However, to be compatible with the Windows environment, it is recommended that names do not exceed 32 characters.

Using Structured Storage

The Macintosh version of the STATSTG data structure used in **IStorage::Stat**, **IStream::Stat**, and **IStorage::EnumElements** has an additional member not included in the Windows version. The *pspec* member is a pointer to an FSSpec that corresponds to the root level storage. It has a valid value only for a root level storage call to **IStorage::Stat** where the STATFLAG argument (*grfStatFlag*) is STATFLAG_DEFAULT; *pspec* is NULL for all other cases.

Neither the *pspec* or *pwcsName* members of STATSTG should be freed by the caller in this release.

The declaration of STATSTG for the Macintosh appears below:

```
typedef struct FARSTRUCT tagSTATSTG
{
    FSSpec * pspec;
    char * pwcsName;
    DWORD type;
    ULARGE_INTEGER cbSize;
    FILETIME mtime;
    FILETIME ctime;
    FILETIME atime;
    DWORD grfMode;
    DWORD grfLocksSupported;
    CLSID clsid;
    DWORD grfStateBits;
    DWORD reserved;
} STATSTG;
```

After a reboot, it is possible for recovered files that have names beginning with *dftmp* to appear in the trash. Files that have creator signatures corresponding to applications that have died are temporary files created by these applications and may have recoverable data. Any other files may be thrown away.

Temporary files created when using structured storage are kept in an invisible folder called 'Temporary Items' on the root hard drive. To view its contents, use the following MPW command:

```
ls 'hd:temporary items'
```

Temporary storage files may end up in the trash in a recovered items folder after a reboot. Empty the trash to remove these files.

Concurrency

On the Macintosh, OLE applications *must* implement the **IMessageFilter** interface in order to manage concurrency-related issues. On startup, a Macintosh OLE application must register its **IMessageFilter** interface implementation so that it can correctly handle concurrency issues while it is involved in remoted calls (such as the processing of events while awaiting the reply to a remoted call).

To register an **IMessageFilter** interface implementation, an application calls **CoRegisterMessageFilter**. For more information on the **IMessageFilter** interface and concurrency issues, see Chapter 13, "Concurrency Management."

Differences in Implementation

This section describes the areas where implementation strategies differ between OLE for Windows and OLE for the Macintosh.

Object Design

Objects are designed differently depending on the development environment and language being used. One of the most important issues is the way in which objects are constructed using MPW C++. The compatibility of the MPW C++ virtual function table construction and the virtual function table construction by other C++ compilers is important.

The OLE C interface definitions have been developed so as to avoid potential virtual function table compatibility problems. MPW C creates virtual tables that have an additional *long* at the beginning before the first function pointer. Each function pointer is also a *long*.

Enumerations and Data Structures

All enumerations defined for the Macintosh version of OLE have an extra field, *_FORCELONG, which is used to force all fields to 32 bits. This field is not used for any other purpose.

OBJECTDESCRIPTOR

An Object Descriptor format is offered whenever data is copied. This format is defined in an **OBJECTDESCRIPTOR** data structure.

OBJECTDESCRIPTOR is defined in ole2.h as follows:

```
typedef struct tagOBJECTDESCRIPTOR
{
    unsigned long       cbSize;
    CLSID               clsid;
    unsigned long       dwDrawAspect;
    SIZEL               sizel;
    unsigned long       dwOutline;
    POINTL              pointl;
    unsigned long       dwStatus;
    unsigned long       dwFullUserTypeName;
    unsigned long       dwSrcOfCopy;
    unsigned long       dwExtra; //MUST BE NULL
}OBJECTDESCRIPTOR;
```

OBJECTDESCRIPTOR values have the following meaning:

OBJECTDESCRIPTOR Member	Description
cbSize	Specifies the size of the **OBJECTDESCRIPTOR** structure in bytes.
clsid	Used to obtain the icon for the 'DisplayAsIcon' option in the Paste Special dialog and is applicable only if the Embed Source or Embedded Object formats are offered. If neither of these formats are offered, the value of *clsid* should be CLSID_NULL.
dwDrawAspect	The value of this field is typically DVASPECT_CONTENT or DVASPECT_ICON. If the source application did not draw the object originally, the *dwDrawAspect* field contains a zero value (which is not the same as DVASPECT_CONTENT).
sizel	Contains the true extents of the object (in pixels), available through a call to **IOleObject::GetExtent**. Setting the *sizel* field is optional; its value can be (0, 0) for applications that do not draw the object being transferred.

OBJECTDESCRIPTOR Member	Description

dwOutline	Offset from beginning of structure to Region describing outline of object Like *sizel*, this is only defined for drawable objects; otherwise, it is zero. To turn this data at this offset into a region handle, allocate a handle the size of the first word of the region data and then copy those *n* bytes into the handle (including the first word):
	`// ptr to region data`
	`char *p = ((char*) pOD) +`
	`   pOD->dwOutline;`
	`short size = *(short *) p;`
	`h = NewHandle(size);`
	`BlockMove(p, *h, size);`

pointl	Specifies the offset in pixel units from the upper-left corner of the object where a drag operation was initiated. This field is only meaningful for a drag and drop transfer operation. The value is (0,0) for other transfer situations, such as a clipboard copy and paste.
dwStatus	Contains miscellaneous status flags for the object. These flags are defined by the OLEMISC enumeration and are returned by calling **IOleObject::GetMiscStatus**.
dwFullUserTypeName	Specifies the offset from the beginning of the data structure to the null-terminated string that specifies the full user type name of the object. The value is zero if the string is not present.
dwSrcOfCopy	Specifies the offset from the beginning of the data structure to the null-terminated string that specifies the source of the transfer. *dwSrcOfCopy* is typically implemented as the display name of the temporary moniker that identifies the data source. The value for *dwSrcOfCopy* is displayed in the Source line of the Paste Special dialog. A zero value indicates that the string is not present. If *dwSrcOfCopy* is zero, the string 'Unknown Source' is displayed in the Paste Special dialog.
dwExtra	Reserved field; must be NULL.

OLEINPLACEFRAMEINFO

The **OLEINPLACEFRAMEINFO** structure provides data needed by an object application in order to communicate with a container during an in-place session. The container is responsible for filling in the structure.

The structure is defined as follows:

```
typedef struct FARSTRUCT tagOIFI //OleInPlaceFrameInfo
{
    long                    recordlength;
    long                    version;
    WindowPtr               frameWindow;
    OSType                  signature;
    long                    refcon;
    ProcessSerialNumber     psn;
    Handle                  hCmdKeys;
    short                   numCmds;
    short                   growHandles;
    short                   dragConstraint;
    Boolean                 fAdjustMenus;
    Boolean                 unused;
} OLEINPLACEFRAMEINFO, FAR* LPOLEINPLACEFRAMEINFO;
```

The container fills in the structure when the object application calls the container's **IOleInPlaceSite::GetWindowContext** method.

The **OLEINPLACEFRAMEINFO** members have the following meaning:

OLEINPLACEFRAMEINFO Member	Meaning
recordLength	Indicates the size of the **OLEINPLACEFRAMEINFO** structure *(sizeof(OLEINPLACEFRAMEINFO))*.
version	Specifies the version of the **OLEINPLACEFRAMEINFO** structure that is currently being used. For this release, 1.
frameWindow	Specifies the pointer to the in-place container's document window.
signature	Specifies the creator signature of the in-place container.
refcon	Application-specific field.
psn	Specifies the in-place container's process serial number.
hCmdKeys	Reserved; must be NULL.
numCmds	Reserved; must be NULL.

OLEINPLACEFRAMEINFO Member	Meaning
growHandles	Specifies which of the in-place container's grow handles the object application is allowed to use during an in-place session. 0 = no constraints, 1 = haxisOnly, 2 = vaxisOnly, and 3 = no grow handles may be used.
dragConstraint	Specifies the drag constraints placed on the an in-place object by the container; 0 = no constraints, 1 = haxisOnly, 2 = vaxisOnly, and 3 = dragging not allowed.
fAdjustMenus	Boolean value set by the container(TRUE) to indicate whether or not the container wants to receive **AdjustMenus** calls from the object application during an in-place session.
unused	Reserved for future use; must be FALSE.

Data Types and Parameter Usage

The Windows environment includes an extensive collection of data types. Some of these data types have been redefined by OLE to better describe functionality in the OLE world and to facilitate portability between platforms. However, other data types do not apply solely to OLE; they are used across the spectrum of Windows applications. Therefore, it is necessary to take these Windows-specific types and provide an equivalent list of Macintosh-specific types.

The following table lists the data types used with OLE for Windows and their equivalent data type on the Macintosh platform:

Windows Data Type	Macintosh Data Type
LONG, HTASK, SIZE, HACCEL	long
BOOL, DWORD, *LPDWORD, ULONG, CLIPFORMAT	unsigned long
HANDLE, HWND, HGLOBAL, HMENU	Handle
BYTE	Byte
WORD, UINT	unsigned short
LPSTR, LPCSTR	char *
LPVOID	void *
HFILE	short
RECT, *LPRECT	Rect, Rect *

Windows Data Type	Macintosh Data Type
MSG, *LPMSG	EventRecord, EventRecord *
HDC	GrafPtr
LOGPALETTE	OLECOLORSCHEME
DC, IC	GrafPort
RECTL	Rect (where each coordinate is a *long*)

Application Initialization and Shutdown

On the Macintosh, an OLE application must register as an SLM client by calling the SLM function **InitLibraryManager**(*0, kCurrentZone, kNormalMemory)* in its initialization sequence. The application must always call **PPCInit** before calling **OleInitialize**. If **OleInitialize** is called first, the application will crash.

At shutdown time, an application call **CleanupLibraryManager**(*void*) to terminate the SLM session and **CloseAllLibraries** to close the OLE libraries.

Data Transfer Issues

OLE 2 for Windows can draw data using three different presentation formats: metafilepict, bitmap, and device-independent bitmap. At present, OLE 2 for the Macintosh draws data in one format: PICT.

OLE for the Macintosh uses four byte resource strings to represent clipboard formats. The following table lists the OLE-defined clipboard formats.

Format Name	Resource
cfPict	PICT
cfText	TEXT
cfOwnerLink	OLNK
cfObjectLink	OJLK
cfLink	LINK
cfNative	NATV
cfBinary	BINA
cfClap	CLAP
cfTransferDesc	TNAM
cfDataObject	DOBJ
cfEmbeddedObject	EMBO
cfEmbedSource	EMBS
cfLinkSource	LNKS

Format Name	Resource
cfOleDraw	DRAW
cfLinkSrcDescriptor	LKSD
cfObjectDescriptor	OBJD

OLE uses the CLAP format as a level of indirection to other formats.

Format Conversion

All cached metafile data is automatically converted to PICT; OLE notices that the data comes from a foreign platform and performs the conversion.

Monikers on the Macintosh

Monikers on the Macintosh use a colon (:) delimeter rather than the slash that is used in the Windows environment.

Event Handling

OLE applications must be prepared to receive and dispatch one special high level event and several Apple events. Applications must install their own handler for the DDE/EMBD and OLE2/EVNT events; OLE installs a handler for all other events. If an application wants to install its own handler to provide custom processing, this handler should include a call to the OLE handler for the particular event. The following table describes the OLE events and handlers:

Class and Type	Description	OLE Handler
DDE/RNCF Apple event	Retrieves CLAP clipboard format	OleProcessClipboardAE
DDE/EMBD Apple event	Indicates that OLE started the application to service a linked or embedded object.	None - application installs handler that sets a flag to indicate method of startup.
DDE/ typeWildCard Apple event	Processes DDE events	OleProcessDdeAE
OLE2/EVNT Apple event	Supports visual editing	None - application installs handler that forwards the event for normal processing.
LRPC high level event	Supports remoting	RemProcessLrpcHLE

An application's SIZE resource must be set up to specify certain components that allow OLE to function properly, such as the *canbackground* flag. Components of the SIZE resource add high-level event awareness to the application, allowing it to respond to both local and remote high-level events. OLE 2 does not require an application to respond to remote high-level events, but unless there is a specific reason not to respond, such as security, both flags should be set.

Miscellaneous Differences

In the Macintosh environment, the following strategies are used to implement **GetClassID**:

1. If the file is a storage object (call **StgIsStorageFile** to determine whether a file is a storage object), **GetClassFile** returns the CLSID that was written with **IStorage::SetClass**.
2. The file creator and file type as indicated by the Finder Info (in the FInfo type) are used as a registration database key. If a value is found under that key, then it is the CLSID that is used.

OleDuplicateData returns an unlocked, movable, nonpurgeable Macintosh handle.

Interface Differences

The following sections summarize the differences that exist between the OLE interface defined for Windows and those defined for the Macintosh.

IMessageFilter

All of the methods in the **IMessageFilter** include an additional parameter, which is defined as follows:

```
ProcessSerialNumber *pPSNCaller
```

This parameter points to the process serial number of the process that was called by or is calling another process.

IViewObject

The *pfnContinue* parameter to **IViewObject::Draw** is not used by OLE on the Macintosh.

IPersistFile

The following methods have been added to **IPersistFile** to support saving of objects to file specifications:

- **IPersistFile::LoadFSP**

  ```
  HRESULT LoadFSP (const FSSPEC * pSpec, unsigned long grfMode);
  ```

- **IPersistFile::SaveFSP**

  ```
  HRESULT SaveFSP (const FSSPEC * pSpec, unsigned long fRemember);
  ```

- **IPersistFile::SaveCompletedFSP**

  ```
  SaveCompletedFSP(const FSSPEC * pSpec);
  ```

- **IPersistFile::GetCurFSP**

  ```
  GetCurFSP (FSSPEC ** pSpec);
  ```

For more information, see the **IPersistFile** interface in Chapter 9, "Persistent Storage Interfaces and Functions."

IOleInPlaceObject

The **IOleInPlaceObject::SetObjectRects** interface is defined as follows for the Macintosh version of OLE:

```
HRESULT IOleInPlaceObject::SetObjectRects(lprcPosRect, clipRgn,
    frameRgn, cliRgn )
```

where

```
LPCRECT lprcPosRect //Points to the rect containing the position of
                    //the in-place object in the client coordinates
                    //of its parent window.
RgnHandle clipRgn   //clipping area within containing window
RgnHandle frameRgn  //entire structure rgn of containing window
RgnHandle cliRgn    //union of all structure rgns of all container
                    //app windows
```

For more information, see the **IOleInPlaceObject** interface in Chapter 11, "In-Place Activation Interfaces and Functions."

IOleInPlaceFrame

The **IOleInPlaceFrame** interface has the following changes:

- **IOleInPlaceFrame::InsertMenus** is implemented using just the *hmenuShared* parameter, as follows:

```
HRESULT InsertMenus (HMENU hmenuShared);
```

- The **IOleInPlaceFrame::SetMenu** method is not implemented.
- The *ID* parameter to **IOleInPlaceFrame::TranslateAccelerator** method is defined as a long, (rather than a WORD as in the Windows version of OLE):

```
HRESULT TranslateAccelerator (LPMSG lpmsg, long ID);
```

- A new method, **IOleInPlaceFrame::AdjustMenus**, has been added:

```
HRESULT AdjustMenus(HANDLE hmenuShared);
```

For more information, see the **IOleInPlaceFrame** interface in Chapter 11, "In-Place Activation Interfaces and Functions."

IOleInPlaceSite

The **IOleInPlaceSite** interface has the following changes:

- Two new methods, **IOleInPlaceSite::OnUIVisible** and **IOleInPlaceSite::GetObjectRects**, have been added:

```
HRESULT OnUIVisible (BOOL visible); // true if visibile

HRESULT GetObjectRects (LPRECT lprcPosRect,RgnHandle clipRgn,
    RgnHandle frameRgn,RgnHandle cliRgn);
```

- **IOleInPlaceSite::GetWindowContext** is implemented as follows:

```
HRESULT GetWindowContext (LPOLEINPLACEFRAME FAR* lplpFrame,
    LPOLEINPLACEUIWINDOW FAR* lplpDoc, Rect * lprcPosRect,
    RgnHandle clipRgn,RgnHandle frameRgnRgnHandle cliRgn,
    LPOLEINPLACEFRAMEINFO lpFrameInfo);
```

For more information, see the **IOleInPlaceSite** interface in Chapter 11, "In-Place Activation Interfaces and Functions."

API Function Differences

This section describes API functions that are different, new, or obsolete for the Macintosh version of OLE:

API Functions Not Supported

CoCreateGuid

The **CoCreateGuid** function, used to create unique CLSID values, is not supported on the Macintosh. To obtain a valid CLSID, post a message to Microsoft from Compuserve, as follows:

1. Logon to Compuserve.
2. Type **GO WINOBJ**
3. Post a message (public or private), requesting the number of CLSIDs needed. To validate the request, Microsoft requires your company's name, address, and telephone number.

Unless specified, a block of 250 values will be assigned per request.

In-Place Activation

The following API functions are used to support in-place activation under the Windows environment; they are not supported on the Macintosh:

IsAccelerator

OleTranslateAccelerator

OleCreateMenuDescriptor

OleSetMenuDescriptor

OleDestroyMenuDescriptor

These functions have been replaced with a new subset of API functions; for more information on these functions, see Chapter 11, "In-Place Activation Interfaces and Functions." **OleTranslateAccelerator** is supported in the UI library which ships with OLE.

Validation Functions

The following API functions, shipped with the Windows version of OLE, are not supported in OLE for the Macintosh:

IsValidIid

IsValidInterface

IsValidPtrIn

IsValidPtrOut

Static and DLL Versions of OLE Functions

There are three versions of the Macintosh-only OLE storage and registration database functions available; these different versions are used depending on whether or not the application is using the static or runtime version of the OLE libraries. To illustrate, consider the following definitions of the **StgIsStorageFileFSp** and **RegDeleteValue** functions:

```
HRESULT StgIsStorageFileFSp (const FSSpec *, pSpec);
HRESULT _StgIsStorageFileFSp (const FSSpec *, pSpec);
HRESULT StaticStgIsStorageFileFSp (const FSSpec *, pSpec);

HRESULT RegDeleteValue(HKEY hKey, const char * lpszValue);
HRESULT _RegDeleteValue(HKEY hKey, const char * lpszValue);
HRESULT StaticRegDeleteValue(HKEY hKey, const char * lpszValue);
```

Applications should call the first version of the function (for example, **StgIsStorageFileFSp** or **RegDeleteValue**) when they are using the run-time version of the shared OLE libraries. Applications using the static version of the OLE libraries should call the **Static*** version.

To determine at runtime which of these storage functions to call, applications use the _* version, which calls the appropriate function depending on the value of the externally defined constant **_bstatic**. If **_bstatic** is TRUE, the **Static*** version of the function is called; a value of FALSE results in the first version being called.

The registration functions use the external constant **_bregstatic** to determine which function to call at runtime.

Registration Database Functions Having Static and DLL Versions

The following registration database functions have both a runtime and a static version available for use on the Macintosh:

RegOpenKey	**RegCloseKey**
RegCreateKey	**RegDeleteKey**
RegEnumKey	**RegEnumProgID**
RegQueryValue	**RegQueryValueEx**
RegSetValue	**RegSetValueEx**
RegDeleteValue	**RegEnumValue**

Storage Functions Having Static and Runtime Versions

The following storage-related functions have both a runtime and a static version available for use on the Macintosh:

StgCreateDocfileMac	**StgCreateDocFileFSp**
StgOpenStorageMac	**StgOpenStorageFSp**
StgIsStorageFileMac	**StgIsStorageFileFSp**
StgSetTimesMac	**StgSetTimesFSp**
StgGetFSpFromIStorage	**StgGetFRefFromIStorage**

Enhanced Functions for Use on the Macintosh

The following OLE functions have enhanced versions that provide better functionality on the Macintosh. These functions have the suffix FSp, Mac, or FRef as shown in the following table. For optimum performance, applications should use the FSp version where applicable (followed by the Mac version, and then the regular OLE version).

OLE Function	Enhanced for Macintosh Function
OleGetIconOfFile	**OleGetIconOfFSp**
OleCreateFromFile	**OleCreateFromFSp**
OleCreateLinkToFile	**OleCreateLinkToFSp**
CreateFileMoniker	**CreateFileMonikerFSp**
StgCreateDocfile	**StgCreateDocfileFSp** **StgCreateDocfileMac**
StgOpenStorage	**StgOpenStorageFSp** **StgOpenStorageMac**
StgIsStorageFile	**StgIsStorageFileFSp** **StgIsStorageFileMac**
StgSetTimes	**StgSetTimesFSp** **StgSetTimesMac**
GetClassFile	**GetClassFSp**
No equivalent function	**StgGetFSPFromIStorage** **StgGetFRefFromIStorage**

New API Functions

Initialization

OLE for the Macintosh is packaged and released as an extension, which is called Microsoft OLE Extension. In order for your application to initialize and make calls to the OLE libraries, Microsoft OLE Extension must be started by your application, typically during its initialization.

The following functions are used to start and stop Microsoft OLE Extension:

InitOleManager

UninitOleManager

The following function initializes the double-byte character set for a specified country:

OleInitDBCSCountry

In-Place Activation

The following OLE functions support in-place activation of objects.

OleSendLowLevelEvent

OleNewMBar

OleInsertMenus

OleUnhashMenuID

OlePatchGetMHandle

OleUnpatchGetMHandle

OleAddMBarMenu

OleSetInFrontOf

OleSetInPlaceWindow

OleUnSetInPlaceWindow

OleClipWindows

OleClipWindow

OleUnclipWindow

OleMoveWindow

OleDragParentWindow

OleDragObjectWindow

OleSizeParentWindow

OleSizeObjectWindow

OleZoomParentWindow

OleGrowParentWindow

OleGrowObjectWindow

OleGetCursor

OleSetCursor

OleUpdateCursor

OleSetInPlaceRects

OleSetParentRgns

OleMaskMouse

OleDisposeMBar

OleWhichGrowHandle

Object Creation

The following new functions are supported with OLE for the Macintosh:

OleCreateLinkToFSp

OleCreateFromFSp

OleQueryCreateAll

FileTime Conversion

The following functions are the equivalent of **CoFileTimeToDosDateTime** and **CoDosDateTimeToFileTime** in OLE for Windows.

CoFileTimeToMacDateTime

CoMacDateTimeToFileTime

Clipboard

- **OleSetClipboardEx**

Apple Event Processing

The following functions are used to handle Apple Events for OLE.

OleProcessClipboardAE

OleProcessLrpcAE

OleProcessDdeAE

Icon Extraction

The following functions are used in the Macintosh version of OLE to support objects being represented as icons.

OleGetIconOfFSp

OlePictFromIconAndLabel

OleGetIconFromIconSuite

Storage Related

The following functions support tasks related to creating, opening, and saving OLE storage objects on the Macintosh:

OleMakeFSSpec

OleFullPathFromFSSpec

ReadOle1FmtProgIDStgMac

WriteOle1FmtProgIDStgMac

StgCreateDocfileMac

StgCreateDocfileFSp

StgOpenStorageMac

StgOpenStorageFSp

StgIsStorageFileMac

StgIsStorageFileFSp

StgSetTimesMac

StgSetTimesFSp

StgGetFSpFromIStorage

StgGetFRefFromIStorage

Registration Database

The following functions are new to OLE for the Macintosh and are used to manipulate entries in the OLE 2 Registration Database file:

RegCloseKey

RegCreateKey

RegDeleteKey

RegEnumKey

RegEnumProgID

RegFlush

RegInitialize

RegOpenKey

RegQueryValue

RegQueryValueEx

RegSetValue

RegDeleteValue

RegSetValueEx

RegEnumValue

Object Linking

The following functions are used to support the linking of objects:

CreateFileMonikerFSp

MkParseDisplayNameMac

MkGetMacNetInfo

Glossary

A

Activation The process of binding an object in order to put it into its running state. Also refers to invoking a particular operation on an object. *See Binding.*

Advisory sink An object that implements **IAdviseSink** and optionally **IAdviseSink2**; these interfaces enable the object to receive notifications of changes in the embedded object or link source.

Aggregate object A component object that is made up of one or more other component objects. One of the objects in the aggregate is designated the controlling unknown; this object has the implementation of **IUnknown** to which the other implementations forward their calls.

Aggregation A composition technique for implementing component objects whereby a new object can be built using one or more existing objects that support some or all of the new object's required interfaces.

Artificial reference counting The technique of incrementing an object's reference count to safeguard the object prior to making a potentially destructive function call. After the function returns, the reference count is decremented.

Asynchronous call A function call whereby the caller does not wait for the reply. OLE defines five asynchronous methods, all within the **IAdviseSink** interface: **OnDataChange**, **OnViewChange**, **OnRename**, **OnSave**, and **OnClose**.

Automation A way to manipulate an application's objects from outside the application to enable programmability.

B

Binding The process of getting an object into the running state so that operations supplied by the object's application (such as Edit and Play) can be invoked.

C

Cache An object provided by OLE that stores presentation data for embedded objects.

Cache initialization state The stage where an embedded object's cache is filled using the data formats provided on the clipboard or from a drag and drop operation.

Class Factory Table A task table that stores the registered class identifier (CLSID) of a class object. Every OLE object application (or container that allows linking to its embedded objects) must register a CLSID for each supported class of object. *See also Class identifier.*

Class identifier (CLSID) A unique identification tag associated with an OLE object. An object registers its CLSID in the registration database to enable clients to locate and load the executable code associated with the object(s).

Class object An object that implements the **IClassFactory** interface, allowing it to instantiate an instance of an object of a specific class. Object implementors implement one class object for each object class they support.

Client A component that is requesting services from another component. *See also Container.*

Client site The display site for an embedded or linked object within the compound document. The client site is used to provide positional and conceptual information about the object.

Component object An object that conforms to the component object model. Component objects implement and use the set of interfaces that support object interaction.

Composite moniker *See Generic composite moniker.*

Commit The act of persistently saving any changes made to an object since its storage was opened or since the last time changes were saved. *See also Revert.*

Component object model An object-oriented programming model that defines how objects interact within a single application or between applications.

Composite menu A shared menu bar composed of menu groups from both the in-place container and the in-place object application. The object application is responsible for installing and removing the menu from the container's frame window.

Compound document A document that contains data of different formats, such as sound clips, spreadsheets, text, and bitmaps, created by different applications. Compound documents are stored by container applications.

Compound document object A component object that is used specifically in compound documents. Compound document objects are either linked or embedded.

Compound file An OLE-provided implementation of the interfaces that support the structured storage model. Compound files are disk-based files and are sometimes referred to as *Docfiles.*

Container *See Container application.*

Container application An application that is the consumer of a compound document object. Container applications provide storage for the object, a site for display, and access to this display site.

Container/Object An application that has implemented OLE interfaces such that the application supports the features and capabilities of both a container and object application.

Container/Server *See Container/Object.*

D

Data transfer object An object that implements the **IDataObject** interface for the purpose of transferring data via the clipboard and drag and drop operations.

Default object handler An object handler that is provided with the OLE 2 SDK. The default object handler performs tasks on behalf of the loaded object, such as rendering an object from its cached state when the object is loaded into memory.

Direct access mode One of two access modes in which a storage object can be opened. In direct mode, all changes are immediately committed to the root storage object. *See also Transacted access mode.*

Docfile *See Compound file.*

Drag and drop The act of using the mouse, or other pointing device, to drag data from one window and drop it into the same window or another window.

E

Embedded object An compound document object that physically resides with the container, but is initially created and subsequently edited by its object application.

Explicit caching One of two ways an object can cache its presentation data; explicit caching requires the physical creation of the cache nodes needed to save the data formats of the object. *See also Implicit caching.*

F

File moniker An object that implements the **IMoniker** interface for the file class. Representing a file-based link source, a file moniker is a wrapper for a pathname in the native file system and is always the left-most part of a generic composite moniker. *See also Item moniker and Generic composite moniker.*

G

Global memory *See Shared application memory.*

Generic composite moniker An object that implements the **IMoniker** interface for the composite class. The generic composite moniker is a sequenced collection of other types of monikers, starting with a file moniker to provide the document-level pathname and continuing with one or more item monikers. *See also Item moniker and File moniker.*

H

Handler *See Object handler.*

Helper function A function that encapsulates functionality that is publicly available with the OLE SDK. That is, a caller can choose the implement the tasks included in the helper function or just call the helper function.

HRESULT An opaque result handle defined to be zero for a successful return from a function and non-zero if error or status information is to be returned. To convert an HRESULT into the more detailed SCODE, applications call **GetScode**(). *See SCODE.*

I

Implicit caching The "implied" caching of presentation data by an object that is capable of rendering itself using its native data. Cache nodes are not created with implicit caching. *See also Explicit caching.*

In parameter A parameter that is allocated, set, and freed by the caller of a function.

In/Out parameter A parameter that is initially allocated by the caller of a function and set, freed, and reallocated if necessary by the callee.

In-place editing *See In-place activation.*

In-place activation The ability to activate an object within the context of its container document and to associate a verb with that activation (for example, edit, play, change); not all applications support in-place activation. Sometimes referred to as in-place editing or visual editing (from a user's viewpoint).

In-process object application An object application that is run in the container's process space. Sometimes referred to as an in-process server.

Input synchronized call A function call whereby the callee must complete the call before yielding control. This ensures that focus management works correctly and that data entered by the user is processed appropriately. Many of the methods used for in-place activation are input synchronized:

Instance An in-memory instantiation of an object.

Instantiate The process of allocating and initializing an object's data structures in memory.

Interface A grouping of semantically related functions through which one application accesses the services of another. Interfaces are the binary standard for component object interaction.

Interface identifier (IID) A unique identification tag associated with each interface; applications use the IID to reference the interface in function calls.

Interface negotiation The process by which a server or container can query an object about a specified interface and have the object return a pointer to that interface if it is supported. *See also Reference counting.*

Item moniker An object that implements the **IMoniker** interface for the item class. Item monikers contain an application-defined string to represent a link source. *See also File moniker and Generic composite moniker.*

L

Link object A component object that is instantiated when a linked compound document object is created or loaded. The link object implements the IOleLink interface and is provided by OLE.

Linked object A compound document object whose source data physically resides where it was initially created. Only a moniker that represents the source data and the appropriate presentation data is kept with the compound document. Changes made to the link source are automatically reflected in the linked compound document object in the container(s).

Link source The data that is the source of a linked compound document object. A link source may be a file, an embedded object, or either a portion of a file or an embedded object (also called pseudo objects).

Loaded state The state of a compound document object after its data structures created by the object handler have been loaded into container memory. *See also Passive state and Running state.*

Local application memory Memory that is allocated by OLE (or an optional object handler) using an application-supplied memory allocator.

Local server An object application that is not run in the container's process space, but on the same machine as the the container application.

Lock OLE defines two types of locks that can be held on an object: *strong* and *weak*. A strong lock will keep an object in memory, a weak lock will not.

LRPC (Lightweight remote procedure call) OLE's RPC-based protocol for interprocess communication. LRPC is "lightweight" in that it handles communication between processes on one machine only.

M

Marshaling The processing of packaging and sending interface parameters across process boundaries.

Member function *See method.*

Method One of a group of semantically related functions that make up a specific interface, providing a specific service.

Mini server A mini server is a object application that cannot run stand-alone; it is always run from another application. An object created by a mini server is stored as part of the container document.

Moniker An object that implements the **IMoniker** interface and provides a conceptual handle to the source of a linked object. There are several types of moniker classes, each with a different implementation of IMoniker. *See also File moniker, Item moniker, and Generic composite moniker.*

Multiple Document Interface (MDI) Application An application that can support multiple documents from one application instance. MDI object applications can simultaneously service a user and one or more embedding containers. *See also Single Document Interface (SDI) application.*

Multiple object application An application that is capable of supporting more than one class of object; for example, a spreadsheet program might support charts, spreadsheets, and macros.

N

Nested object An object that is contained within another object; OLE objects can be arbitrarily nested to any level.

Native data Data provided by an object that is used to edit the object.

O

Object A unit of information that resides in a container's compound document and whose behavior is constant no matter where it is located; the object's behavior is defined by the object rather than by the compound document that holds it.

Object application An application that is capable of creating compound document objects that can then be embedded in, or linked to, by containers.

Object class A type of object that is registered in the registration database and that is serviced by a particular object application. *See Class object.*

Object handler A piece of object-specific code that is dynamically loaded into the address space of its container. Object handlers process requests for specific class or classes of objects, enabling single process communication rather than remote messaging.

Object state The description of the relationship between a compound document object in its container and the application responsible for the object's creation. There are three compound document object states: *passive*, *loaded*, and *running*.

Object type name A unique identification string that is stored as part of the information available for an object in the registration database—for example, Acme Drawing.

OLE An acronym for Object Linking and Embedding.

Out parameter A parameter that is allocated and set by the callee of a function and freed by the caller.

P

Passive state The state of a compound document object when it is in its stored state (on disk or in a database). The object is not selected or active. *See also Loaded state and Running state.*

Persistent storage Storage of a file or object in an **IStorage**-based medium such as a file system or database.

Primary verb The action associated with the most common, preferred operation users perform on an object; the primary verb is always defined as verb zero in the system registration database. An object's primary verb is executed by double-clicking on the object.

Presentation data Data provided by an object that is used to render the object on an output device.

Programmability The ability for an application to define a set of properties and commands and make them accessible to other applications. *See Automation.*

Proxy An interface-specific object that packages parameters for that interface in preparation for a remote method call. A proxy runs in the address space of the sender and communicates with a corresponding stub in the receiver's address space. *See also Stub, Marshaling, and Unmarshaling.*

Pseudo object A selection of data within a document or embedded object that can be the source for a compound document object.

R

Reference counting Keeping a count of each interface pointer instance to ensure that an object is not destroyed before all references to it are released.

Revert The act of discarding any change(s) made to an object since the last time the changes were committed or the object's storage was opened. *See Commit.*

Root IStorage object The outermost **IStorage** instance in a document; also called the root storage object. Compound document objects are always saved as children of a root **IStorage** object.

Running state The state of a compound document object when the object application is running and it is possible to edit the object, access its interfaces, and receive notification of changes. *See also Loaded state and Passive state.*

Running object table A globally accessible lookup table that is used to store running objects and their monikers. Registering an object in the running object table results in a reference count being made on behalf of the object; before the object can be destroyed, its moniker must be released from the running object table.

S

SCODE A unsigned long value that is used to pass detailed information to the caller of an interface method or API function. *See also HRESULT.*

Server *See object application.*

Shared application memory Memory that is primarily used between processes to optimize the data copying that occurs in LPRC calls.

Single Document Interface (SDI) Application An application that can support only one document at a time. Multiple instances of an SDI application must be started to service both an embedded object and a user. *See also Multiple Document Interface (MDI) application.*

Single object application An application that is capable of creating and manipulating one class of object. *See also Multiple object application.*

Stand-alone object application An object application that was implemented as an executable program.

State *See Loaded state, Passive state, and Running state.*

Static object A picture that is provided by a compound document object wrapping by OLE. This wrapping makes it possible for containers to treat static objects as though they were linked or embedded objects with one exception: they cannot be edited.

Storage object An object that implements the **IStorage** interface. The storage of a compound document object is always relative to a root **IStorage** object. *See also Root IStorage object.*

Stream object An object that implements the **IStream** interface. Objects can create as many data streams (**IStream** objects) as needed in which to save an object's data.

Structured storage model A specification that defines a hierarchical method of storing objects. OLE provides an implementation of the structured storage model called Compound Files. *See Compound file and Docfile.*

Stub An interface-specific object that unpackages the parameters for that interface marshaled across the process boundary and makes the required method call. The stub runs in the address space of the receiver and communicates with a corresponding proxy in the sender's address space. *See Proxy, Marshaling, and Unmarshaling.*

Synchronous call A function call whereby the caller waits for the reply before continuing. Most OLE interface methods are synchronous calls.

T

Transacted access mode One of two access modes in which a storage object can be opened. When opened in transacted mode, changes are stored in temporary buffers until the root **IStorage** object commits its changes.

U

Uniform data transfer A model for transferring data via the clipboard, drag and drop, or through automation. Objects conforming to the model implement the **IDataObject** interface. This model replaces DDE. *See Data transfer object.*

Unmarshaling The processing of unpackaging parameters that have been sent across process boundaries.

V

Virtual Table (VTBL) An array of function pointers that point to interface method implementations.

Visual Editing A marketing term that refers to the user being able to interact with a compound document object in the context of its container; the term most often used by developers is in-place activation. *See also In-place activation.*

Index

A

Access permission flags
  STGM_READ 526
  STGM_WRITE 527
Activate as
  option button 34
Activating linked objects 117
Activating objects 117
  IOleObject::DoVerb 117
  of different classes 270
Activation
  definition of 117
Active editor menu 65
Active object state 53
Active objects
  communicating with 673
  undo changes 60
Active state
  of an object 23
AddConnection method 217
AddRef method 206
AdjustMenus method 675
ADVF enumeration 382, 779
ADVF_NODATA 750
Advise method 123, 137, 296, 300, 334, 405
Advise notifications 116
  receiving 130
  registering for 124
  sending 129
  types of 123
Advisory connections 123, 300, 382, 780
  deleting 300, 335
  effects of registering 301
  effects of revoking 301
  enumerating 301, 335
  enumerating current 402, 406
  registering or revoking while enumerating 336
  setting up 737
  setting up between object and sink 334
  specifying information about 382, 779
Advisory notifications
  sending OnClose 147
Advisory sinks 301, 302
  deleting 402, 406
  registering for notification 334
  setting up 400, 405, 415
  updating 407
Aggregate objects
  reference counting 99
  references to 98
Aggregation
  creation of objects by 98
  of default object handler 753
Alloc method 213
Allocating memory 213
Anti moniker
  create 496
  defined 497
  return 496
API functions
  registration database 157
Apple events
  functions for handling 371
  processing 372, 373
Application disks 761
Application frame window
  hiding during shutdown 151
Application window
  creation of 105
  hiding during shutdown 156
Applications
  closing 148, 152, 155
  determining startup method 106
  implementation guidelines 103
  locking in memory 108
  registering as a drop target 641
  registering for drag and drop 113
  registering in database 157
  Registering information in database 166
  registering object classes 106
  registration database 157
    overwriting OLE 1 entries 173
  startup tasks 103
  upgrading from OLE 1 173
  verifying build version of OLE libraries 104
  verifying entries in the registration database 104
Arguments
  passing between processes 223
Artifical reference counting 99
Artificial reference counting
  definition of 200
Asynchronous notifications 382, 780
  and IAdviseSink 293
  types of 293
Asynchronous operations 116, 725
AutoTreatAs key 268

B

Back pointers 203
Balloon help messages 87
Base interface See IUnknown interface
Bind contexts
  allocate and initialize for a moniker 497
Bind options
  returning currently stored options 476
  storing blocks of 473
BIND_OPTS structure 473, 476, 763
BINDFLAGS enumeration See also BIND_OPTS, See BIND_OPTS structure
  defined 475, 781
BindIfRunning method 486
Binding
  a moniker to a specified interface 496
  definition of 26
  to monikers 120
Binding embedded objects 118
Binding generic composite monikers 122
Binding linked objects 119
Binding objects 117, 121
BindMoniker function 496
BINDSPEED enumeration 314, 782
BindToObject method 449
BindToSource
  IOleLink 327, 341
BindToSource method 484
BindToStorage method 451
Bitmaps 737, 738
Border space
  for in-place active objects 672
  IOleInPlaceUIWindow 670
BORDERWIDTHS structure 656, 672, 673, 765
  setting fields of 672

C

C nested data structures 90
C programming
  defining an interface method
    example of 90
  implementing VTBLs 90
C versus C++ 90
C++ programming
  defining an interface method
    example of 90
C++ versus C 90
Cache
  IOleCache 352
  purpose of 20
  updating 294
Cache advisories
  specifying information about 382, 779
Cache connection ID 746
  storing STATDATA array 747
Cache connections
  deleting 421
  enumerating 422
Cache data
  structures used for 375
Cache method 419
Cache node 747
Cache objects
  creation of 436
  deleting connections 421
  enumerating connections 422
  filling the cache 422, 423
  notifying cache of running state 428
  specifying data formats for 419
  terminating connections to 429
  updating the cache 425
CACHE_S_SAMECACHE 746
Caching data 746
Caching functions 434
Callbacks 123
Calls
  retry rejected (IMessageFilter) 729
  waiting to reply to 730
CALLTYPE enumeration 727, 783
CanInPlaceActivate method 680
CF_EMBEDDEDOBJECT
  description of 386
CF_LINKSOURCEDESCRIPTOR
  description of 389
CF_METAFILEPICT format 364
CF_OBJECTDESCRIPTOR
  description of 811
cfFileName format 364
Change notifications
  handling of 123
  receiving 130
  See Also notifications
  sending 129
Change source dialog 48
Changes
  checking objects for 582
  checking streams for 588
Class factory
  obtaining for a class 208
Class identifier
  returning 331
Class identifiers 11

Class objects
automatic conversion of 273
creating instance of 244
emulation of 272
functions that support 243
initializing 208
loading of 252
locating and loading 245
locking/unlocking reference counts 251
newly initialized
valid operations 208
no longer available notification 251
registering 106
registration of 248
retrieving from DLL object handler 261
Client site
identifying within container 317
obtaining pointers to 317
Clipboard
creating embedded object from 364
flushing 433
flushing of object data 154
functions that manage 429
OLE-defined formats 384
Clipboard data formats
CF_EMBEDEDOBJECT 386
CF_OBJECTDESCRIPTOR 769, 811
CLNK 385
EMBS 384
LNKS 385
OBJD 387
OLE-defined 384
order of 390
supported by types applications 390
Clipboard data object
closing 154
Clipboard format
CF_LINKSOURCEDESCRIPTOR 389
PICT 389
CLNK
description of 385
Clone method 222, 564
Close method 152, 154, 318
Close notifications 147
Closing an application
sequence of events 150, 155
Closing applications 148, 152, 155
safeguards 155
sending close notifications 147
Closing compound documents 145
Closing documents
checking for changes 145
Closing embedded objects 152
considerations 154
Closing loaded objects 146
Closing OLE libraries 156
Closing pseudo objects 146
CLSCTX enumeration 784
example of using 246
CLSID 158, 340
conversion to ProgID 160
database key 160, 161
for an storage object
obtaining 551
for document objects 574
registering of 106
verifying an OLE 1 object 719
CLSIDFromProgID 159
CLSIDFromProgID function 288
CLSIDFromString function 290
creating CLSIDs and IIDs 210
CLSIDs 11, 158
comparing values 288
conversion functions 286
converting 159
converting to strings 290
creating from a string 290
creating from ProgID 288
obtaining for a given file 607, 608
obtaining for object handlers 233
obtaining from Microsoft 209
writing to storage objects 624
writing to stream objects 625
CoBuildVersion function 262
CoCreateInstance function 116, 244, 352
CoCreateStandardMalloc function 264
CoDisconnectObject function 146, 255
CoFileTimeNow function 259
CoFileTimeToMacDateTime function 258
CoFreeAllLibraries function 257
CoFreeLibrary function 257
CoFreeUnusedLibraries
and optimizing unloading 756
CoFreeUnusedLibraries function 258
CoGetClassObject function 245
creating object classes 208
CoGetCurrentProcess function 263
CoGetMalloc 263
CoGetStandardMarshal function 236
use of 230
CoGetTreatAsClass function 272
CoInitialize
task allocator passed to 264
CoInitialize function 265
CoIsHandlerConnected function 256
CoIsOle1Class function 719
CoLoadLibrary function 256

CoLockObjectExternal 343
typical usage 252
use while closing application 253
CoLockObjectExternal function 113, 147, 148, 152, 156, 251, 311, 342, 347, 641
Color palette
specifying 339
Color sets
obtaining for IViewObject::Draw 413
CoMacDateTimeTofileTime function 259
CoMarshalHresult function 238
CoMarshalInterface function 239
Command keys 67
Commit method 133, 139, 141, 544, 560
Committing changes to storage 521
IStorage::Commit 521
Committing objects to storage 544
CommonPrefixWith method 463
Communicating with in-place active objects 673
Comound documents
moniker changes 137, 138
Complex handlers 749
Component object interfaces 199
Component Object Model
description of 2
Component Object Model library
closing and freeing resources 266
functions that support 261
initialization of 265
obtaining version numbers 262
Component objects
C nested structures 90
C++ multiple inheritance 97
C++ nested classes 91
declaration of 90
description of 2, 89
designing of 89
functions that support 243
ComposeWith method 455
Composite menu
adjusting 675
in-place activation 675
notifying container of changes 681
removing 676
Composite menu bar
adding container menus 695
allocating 691
freeing 692
inserting menus into 692
Composite monikers
allocate and return 501
parsing display names 466
returning 455
Compound document
and when notifications are generated 293
Compound document applications
levels of linking 446
Compound document interfaces 293
described 293
Compound document objects
and requests for more or less room 308
Functions supported 343
kinds of 445, 446
linked 15
methods for managing 316
notifying cache of running state 428
states of 23
traversing 306
Compound documents See Documents
checking for changes 145
closing 145
doing a full save operation 141
initializing the document structure 110
making visible to the user 113
naming of 132
opening 109
procedure for saving 141
registering for drag and drop 113
resetting dirty flag 138
saving 131
using File Save 138
saving changes in transacted mode 143
saving changes incrementally 143
saving to storage 134
saving to temporary files 138
setting the dirty flag 113
setting types of 111
storage functions 629
Compound file, description of 511
Compound files
creating on ILockBytes object 600
creation of 594
opening an instance of 613
Compound-document link object
creating 359
Concurrency
handling of 105
IMessageFilter interface 105
Concurrency issues
using IMessageFilter 725
Connecting links 122
Connections
advisory 300
Connections to objects
disconnecting remote 255

Constants
  DOCTYPE_EMBEDDED
    definition of 110
  DOCTYPE_FROMFILE
    definition of 110
  DOCTYPE_FROMSTG
    definition of 110
  DOCTYPE_NEW
    definition of 110
  DOCTYPE_UNKNOWN
    definition of 110
Container applications
  creating embedded object from clipboard 364
  definition of 20
  description of 13
  implementation of 103
  interfaces implemented by 20
  OnClose notifications 297
  registering to receive change notifications 295
  supporting in-place activation 680
  typical interface groupings 21
Container/object applications
  definition of 20
Containers
  activating objects in place 680
  implementing drag and drop 633
CONTENTS stream 521, 632
ContextSensitiveHelp method 659
Controlling unknown 99, 208
  in aggregate objects 98
  pointer to 99
Conversion
  of objects 717
  OLE 1 stream to OLE 2 storage 723
  OLE 2 storage to OLE 1 719, 720, 722
Conversion functions
  GUIDs, CLSIDs, and ProgIDs 286
Conversion of class objects
  automatic 273
Convert dialog 33
Convert dialog box 32
  implementing IStdMarshalInfo interface 233
Convert to
  option button 34
ConvertDlg function
  use during class conversion 269
Converting FILETIME structure 258
Converting Macintosh time to FILETIME structure 259
Converting object classes 266
Converting objects 32
Copying data
  directly from source to destination 391
Copying streams 564
CopyTo method 541, 559
CoRegisterClassObject
  locking/unlocking reference counts 109
CoRegisterClassObject function 248, 354
CoRegisterMessageFilter 105
CoRegisterMessageFilter function 733
CoReleaseMarshalData function 242
CoRevokeClassObject function 152, 156, 251
CoTreatAsClass function 272, 340
  use during class conversion 270
CoUninitialize 266
CoUninitialize function 266, 368
CoUnmarshalHresult function 238
CoUnmarshalInterface function 241, 247
CreateAntiMoniker function 496
CreateBindCtx function 497
CreateDataAdviseHolder 403
CreateDataAdviseHolder function 124
CreateDataCache 757
  and DLL object applications 757
CreateDataCache function 436
CreateFileMoniker function 446, 497
CreateFileMonikerFSp function 498
CreateGenericComposite function 501
CreateILockBytesOnHGlobal function 592
CreateInstance method 116, 210
CreateItemMoniker function 499
CreateOleAdviseHolder 300
CreateOleAdviseHolder function 124, 344
CreatePointerMoniker function 499
CreateStorage method 537
CreateStream method 134, 535
CreateStreamOnHGlobal function 593
Creating anti monikers 496
Creating File Monikers 111
Creating ILockBytes instance in memory 592
Creating IStream objects in memory 593
Creating Object
  Insert Object dialog 39
Creating object classes 207
Creating objects
  with helper functions 115
Creating user disks 761
Creation functions 756
Cursor information
  obtaining 707
  setting 707
  updating 708
Cursors
  changing during drag and drop 637
  drag and drop
    default 637
CurVer
  database key 163

Custom handlers 748
- acting as DLL object application 749
- aggregation 748
- aggregation of default handler 748
- and 751
- and DllCanUnloadNow 751
- and DllGetClassObject 751
- and IClassFactory 751
- and registering with InprocHandler keyword 751
- complex 749
- considerations for writing 749
- delegation 748
- delegation to default handler 753
- delegation to OLE default cache 748
- forced unloading 756
- installing 755
- reasons for writing 749
- registered in 735
- registering 755
- registration of 755
- rendering 749
- required interface implementations 751
- versus default handler 749
- writing 751

Custom marshaling
- and DLL object applications 757

Cut and paste operations
- using the clipboard 391

D

Dadvise method 123, 400
- example of 124

Data
- transferring 633

Data advisories
- specifying information about 382, 779

Data cache
- maintaining 330

Data caching
- cache connection ID 746
- explicit 746, 747
- forced 747
- implicit 746
- keeping cache current 737
- types of 746

Data caching functions 434

Data change notifications
- and calling object 294
- and containers 294
- and link objects 294
- and OLE cache 294
- registering for 294

Data drawing functions 434

Data formats
- enumerating for data storage 398
- for specfic target devices 376, 768
- order of on the clipboard 390
- specifying for cached objects 419
- specifying for transfer 397

Data notifications 116

Data objects
- placing on the clipboard 430, 431
- removing from on the clipboard 433
- retrieving from the clipboard 432
- verifying on the clipboard 433

Data retrieval
- from specific medium 393, 394

Data streams, opening 112

Data structures See Structures, See structures
- initialization of 105

Data transfer 394
- between processes 10
- from storage to memory 20
- structures used for 375

Data transfer model 77
- clipboard 77
- clipboard method 77
- cut and paste method 77
- description of 11
- drag and drop 77
- drag and drop method 81
- overview of 375

Data transfer object
- creating 636
- creation dependencies 636

Data transfer objects 360, 363
- and differences with data source object 636
- closing 154
- creating 636
- creating embedded object from 363
- creating linked objects from 365
- used to create static objects 362

DataAdviseHolder
- creation of 124

DATADIR enumeration 398, 784

DAvise method 137

DeactivateAndUndo method 687

Deactivating in-place objects 661, 685

Deactivation of in-place objects 686

Default cache 747

Default object handler 340, 735
- aggregation of 753
- aggregation of data cache 736
- and implementations of IOleObject::GetUserType 332
- and IOleObject::EnumVerbs 328
- and the data cache 737
- cached data vs object's native data 742

Default object handler *continued*
caching presentation data 735
conversion formats 737
converting cached data for drawing 737
create new instance of 352
creating new instance of 353
data cache aggregated with handler 737
drawing objects 737
exceptions to using 736
initializing new instance of 352
interface method calls intercepted by 737
keeping data cache current 737
obtaining services of container application 736
passing calls on to object applications 736
rendering objects 735
representation of 736
setting up advisory connections 737
transitioning objects to running state 737
used for 735
when used 736
DEFINE_GUID macro 210
Delegation
and custom handlers 753
DestroyElement method 548
Dialog box messages 84
Dialog boxes
Convert 32
Error 34
Help text for 34
DIB 737, 738
DidAlloc method 216
Differences
Architecture 807
OLE for Windows 807
Direct mode 133
Direct storage mode
description of 514
Dirty flag
for compound documents 113
resetting 138
setting for compound document 113
DISCARDCACHE enumeration 427, 785
DiscardUndoState method 687
Disconnecting remote processes 255
DisconnectObject method 232
Disks
distribution of OLE applications 761
Display name
parsing an object's display name into a moniker 469
retrieving 483
Display names
obtaining 465
parsing 466, 502, 506
parsing into monikers 483
Distribution disks 761
DLL initialization
functions that support 256
DLL object applications 339, 340
and data caching 757
and IOleCache2 757
and their responsibility for objects 757
considerations for writing 758
implementing 757
required interfaces for 758
requirement for calling CreateDataCache 757
translating events 666
DLL object class
functions that support 260
DLL object handler 261
DllCanUnloadNow 751, 756
and unloading handlers 756
DllCanUnloadNow function 260
DllGetClassObject 751
custom object handlers 751
DllGetClassObject function 261
DLLs
determining whether to unload 260
loading of 256
unloading from memory 260
unloading of 257
unloading those not used 258
Document objects
getting the CLSID 574
Document window
hiding during closing 146
Documents
closing 145
checking for changes 145
hiding the document window 146
taking control away from user 147
doing a full save operation 141
full save operations
in low memory 142
registering for drag and drop 113
resetting dirty flag 138
saving changes incrementally 143
saving in transacted mode 143
saving to temporary files 138
saving with file save 138
DoDragDrop function 633, 638, 649
key function in drag and drop process 633
tracking mouse and keyboard movement 633
Double-byte character set
initializing 371
DoVerb
IOleObject 351
invoking 326
DoVerb method 117, 325

Drag and drop
- cancelling feedback 646
- clipboard copy and paste 633
- description of 633
- determining scroll delay times 643
- dragging
  - delay values 637
- drop effects 634
- drop targets 638
- dropping the source data 647
- effects allowed by drag source 634
- functionality provided 633
- functions 647
- initiating operation 649
- invalid drop target pointer 81
- modifier keys 82
- pointer feedback 634
- providing feedback 645
- registering an application for 113
- registering as a drop target 648
- source feedback 634
- target feedback 634
- three pieces of code associated with 633
- transferring data 633
- types of feedback 634
- unregistering as a drop target 648

Drag and drop interfaces 633

Drag and drop method 81

Drag and drop operations
- drag feedback 637
- drag scrolling 642
  - changing time delay 642
  - default time delay 642
  - hotzone 642
- drag source responsibilities 635
- drop effect values 641
- drop target 641
- drop target responsibilities 640
- drop targets
  - revoking registration of 641
- quiting 638
- terminating 643
- valid pointers (cursors) 637

Drag operation
- feedback during 639

Drag operations 636
- continue or not 638

Drag pointer
- generating feedback with 637, 639

Drag scrolling
- determining values 642
- hot zone definition 643

Drag source
- and mouse tracking feedback 636
- as drag target 636
- conflicts with feefback from drop target 636
- effects allowed by 634
- responsibilities of 635
- responsible for 636

Drag target
- acceptance of drag object 643

DragEnter method 643

Dragged object
- determining acceptance of 643

Dragging
- defined 637
- delay values 637
- minimum distance 637
- minimum time 637

DragLeave method 643, 646

DragOver method 644, 645

Draw
- IViewObject 336

Draw method 410

Drawing functions 434

Drawing objects 410, 434

Drop effect
- determining values 641

Drop method 643, 647

Drop target
- effect of drag operation on 634
- indicating invalid region 638
- registering as 113, 641, 648
- removing feedback by 646
- responsibilities of 640
- revoking registration as 146
- support of drag scrolling 642
- unregistering as 648

Drop targets
- revoking registration of 641

DROPEFFECT enumeration 634, 645, 650, 786

Dropping data
- in drag and drop operation 647

DUnadvise method 402

Duplication
- of bitmaps 435
- of metafiles 435

DVASPECT Enumeration 295, 336, 377, 768, 787

DVASPECTenumeration 333

DVTARGETDEVICE structure 380, 765

E

Embed source format 360, 364
Embedded object 445, 446
  identifying client site within container 317
  transitioning to loaded state 318
Embedded object format 360, 364
Embedded objects 44, 340, 365
  activating 118
  and returning class identifier 331
  as containers 49
  binding of 118
  closing 152
  closing in an application 154
  committing changes to storage 515
  create from file 357
  create from file specification 358
  creating 351
  creating from clipboard 364
  creating from data transfer object 355, 363
  creation of 114
  definition of 14
  drag and drop operations 633
  in the running state 25
  indicating as contained in OLE container 343
  indicating contained as 347
  initializing 583
  initializing for use 583
  links to 120
  loading into memory 583
  returning CLSID for 340
  running the application 118
  updating 330
  with links to other objects 330
Embedding helper object
  creating 353
Embedding objects
  benefits of 14
EMBS
  description of 384
Emulating class objects 266
Emulating objects 33
EnableModeless method 669, 677
Enum method 456
EnumAdvise
  IOleObject 335
EnumAdvise method 301, 335, 406
EnumCache method 422
EnumDAdvise method 402
EnumElements method 547
Enumerating
  generic composites 456
  using IOleContainer interface 308
Enumerating items of type STATSTG 533
Enumerating objects
  IEnumX interface 219
Enumerations
  ADVF 382, 779
  BINDFLAGS 475, 781
  BINDSPEED 314, 782
  CALLTYPE 727, 783
  cloning of 222
  CLSCTX 246, 784
  DATADIR 398, 784
  DISCARDCACHE 427, 785
  DROPEFFECT 634, 645, 650, 786
  DVASPECT 295, 333, 336, 377, 768, 787
  EXTCONN 218, 787
  LOCKTYPE 532, 788
  MEMCTX 263, 788
  methods used for 219
  MKRREDUCE 789
  MKSYS 789
  MSHCTX 224, 790
  MSHLFLAGS 224, 790
  OLECLOSE 319, 791
  OLECONTF 310, 792
  OLEGETMONIKER 304, 793
  OLEGROWHANDLES 793
  OLELINKBIND 484, 486, 794
  OLEMANAGER 794
  OLEMISC 795
    defined 337
  OLEREG_KEYWORD 797
  OLERENDER 350, 797
  OLEUPDATE 481, 799
  OLEWHICHMK 304, 799
  OLWWHICHMK 322
  PENDINGTYPE 732, 800
  REGCLS 249, 800
  REGENUMPROGIDF 801
  resetting the sequence 222
  returning for object pointers 478
  skipping over elements 221
  specifying elements to return 220
  STATFLAG 553, 802
  STGC 545, 802
  STGMOVE 544, 803
  STGTY 531, 803
  STREAM_SEEK 558, 804
  TDFLAGS 383, 804
  TYMED 378, 787, 805
  USERCLASSTYPE 332, 806
Enumerator
  example of 220
Enumerator interfaces
  generic description of 219
Enumerator objects 219

EnumFormatEtc method 398
EnumObjectParam method 478
EnumObjects method 310
EnumRunning method 495
EnumVerbs
  IOleObject 326
EnumVerbs method 328
Error codes
  common to all interface methods 278
  conventions for defining 278
  example of handling 280
  functions that support 278
  handling of 278
  NOERROR 279
  S_FALSE 279
  S_OK 279
  status code
    code field 282
    context field 281
    facility field 282
    severity field 281
  structure of 281
Error reporting 9
Explicit caches
  enumerating at load time 747
Explicit caching 747
Explicit data caching 746
  iconic 747
EXTCONN enumeration 218, 787
Extents
  changing for active object 687
External connections
  releasing of 218
  strong reference locks and 343
External references
  checking for outstanding 98, 113, 152
  incrementing during application shutdown 155
  passing a count of 90
  to compound documents 111

F

FAILED macro
  description of 286
File extension key 163
File menu
  setting for compound documents 112
File moniker
  definition of 119
  revoking registration 146
File Monikers
  binding to 121
  change notifications 137
  creating 111, 446
  registering 111, 446
File New command 109, 112
File Open command 109, 112
File Quit command 112, 148, 154
File Save As command 132
  cancelling (undoing) 142
File Save command 112, 138
File Save Copy As command 132
File sharing privileges
  STGM_READWRITE 527
  STGM_SHARE_DENY_NONE 528
  STGM_SHARE_DENY_READ 527
  STGM_SHARE_DENY_WRITE 528
  STGM_SHARE_EXCLUSIVE 528
File specification objects
  obtaining name of 581
  saving of 581
File Specifications
  monikers created from 498
File type
  database key 163
File Update command 131
File-based objects
  checking for changes 576
  loading of 576
  obtaining pathnames 578
  saving of 577, 578
FileName format 361
Files
  copying storages 565
  obtaining CLSID for 607, 608
  required on the install disk 761
  setting date and time stamps 621, 622
  storage system for 11
  to include with applications 761
File-spec objects
  loading of 579
File-specification objects
  loading of 579
Filetime conversion
  functions that support 258
FILETIME structure 258, 531, 767
  converting 258
  creation of 259
FILETIME structure: 259
Flags
  resetting document's dirty flag 138
Flat data format
  definition of 378, 769
Flush method 570

FORMATETC 747
FORMATETC structure 376, 384, 767
  prevent caching duplicate sets of data 396
Formats
  CF_METAFILEPICT 364
  cfFileName 364
  Embed Object 360
  Embed source 360, 364
  Embedded Object 364
  FileName 361
  link source 360
Free method 214
Freeing memory 214
Freeze method 131, 414
Freezing presentation data 414
fSameAsLoad flag 521
  how to use 521
Functions
  apple-event 371
  BindMoniker 496
  caching 434
  calling at runtime 821
  clipboard 429
  CLSIDFromProgID 288
  CLSIDFromString 290
  CoBuildVersion 262
  CoCreateInstance 244
  CoCreateStandardMalloc 264
  CoFileTimeNow 259
  CoFileTimeToMacDateTime 258
  CoFreeAllLibraries 257
  CoFreeLibrary 257
  CoFreeUnusedLibraries 258
  CoGetClassObject 245
  CoGetCurrentProcess 263
  CoGetMalloc 263
  CoGetStandardMarshal 236
  CoGetTreatAsClass 272
  CoInitialize 265
  CoIsHandlerConnected 256
  CoIsOle1Class 719
  CoLoadLibrary 256
  CoLockObjectExternal 251
  CoMacDateTimeTofileTime 259
  CoMarshalHresult 238
  CoMarshalInterface 239
  component object 243
  component objects 199
  compound document 293
  compound document object 343
  compound document storage 629
  CoRegisterClassObject 248
  CoRegisterMessageFilter 733
  CoReleaseMarshalData 242
Functions *(continued)*
  CoRevokeClassObject 251
  CoTreatAsClass 272
  CoUninitialize 266
  CoUnmarshalHresult 238
  CoUnmarshalInterface 241
  CreateAntiMoniker 496
  CreateBindCtx 497
  CreateDataAdviseHolder 403
  CreateDataCache 436
  CreateFileMoniker 497
  CreateFileMonikerFSp 498
  CreateGenericComposite 501
  CreateILockBytesOnHGlobal 592
  CreateItemMoniker 499
  CreateOleAdviseHolder 344
  CreatePointerMoniker 499
  CreateStreamOnHGlobal 593
  creation 756
  custom marshaling 233
  differences from Windows version 820
  DLL initialization 256
  DLL object class functions 260
  DllCanUnloadNow 260
  DllGetClassObject 261
  DoDragDrop 649
  drag and drop 647
  drawing 434
  enhanced for the Macintosh 822
  error handling 278
  file time conversion 258
  GetClassFile 607, 608
  GetConvertStorage 277
  GetHGlobalFromILockBytes 609
  GetHGlobalFromStream 609
  GetRunningObjectTable 502
  GetScode 284
  icon extraction 437
  IIDFromString 291
  InitOleManager 368
  In-place activation 688
  IsEqualCLSID 288
  IsEqualGUID 287
  IsEqualIID 287
  IsOleManagerRunning 371
  linking 495
  MkGetMacNetInfo 510
  MkParseDisplayName 502
  MkParseDisplayNameMac 506
  MonikerCommonPrefixWith 508
  MonikerRelativePathTo 507
  new for the Macintosh 823
  not supported for in-place activation 820
  not supported on the Macintosh 820

Functions *(continued)*
object class conversion and emulation 266
object creation 348
OLE 2 registration database 176
OLE initialization 365
OLE library 261
OleAddMBarMenu 695
OleBuildVersion 365
OleClipWindow 699
OleClipWindows 698
OleConvertIStorageToOLESTREAM 719
OleConvertIStorageToOLESTREAMEx 720
OleConvertOLESTREAMToIStorage 722
OleConvertOLESTREAMToIStorageEx 723
OleCreate 351
OleCreateDefaultHandler 352
OleCreateEmbeddingHelper 353
OleCreateFromData 355
OleCreateFromFile 357
OleCreateFromFSp 358
OleCreateLink 359
OleCreateLinkFromData 360
OleCreateLinkToFile 361
OleCreateLinkToFSp 361
OleCreateStaticFromData 362
OleDisposeMBar 692
OleDoAutoConvert 273
OleDragObjectWindow 701
OleDragParentWindow 701
OleDraw 434
OleDuplicateData 435
OleFlushClipboard 433
OleFullPathFromFSSpec 592
OleGetAutoConvert function 274
OleGetClipboard 432
OleGetCursor 707
OleGetIconFromIconSuite 443
OleGetIconOfClass 442
OleGetIconOfFile 440, 441
OleGrowObjectWindow 705
OleGrowParentWindow 704
OleHashMenuID 693
OleInitDBCSCountry 371
OleInitialize 367
OleInsertMenus 692
OleIsCurrentClipboard 433
OleLoad 629
OleLoadFromStream 630
OleLockRunning 346
OleMakeFSSpec 591
OleMaskMouse 711
OleMoveWindow 700
OleNewMBar 691
OleNoteObjectVisible 347

Functions *(continued)*
OlePatchGetMHandle 694
OlePictFromIconAndLabel 442
OleProcessClipboardAE 373
OleProcessDdeAE 372
OleProcessLrpcAE 372
OleQueryCreateAll 364
OleQueryCreateFromData 363
OleQueryLinkFromData 365
OleregCloseRegistration 194
OleRegEnumFormatEtc 179
OleRegEnumVerbs 178
OleRegGetMiscStatus 177
OleRegGetUserType 177
OleregGetValue 194
OleregRemoveKey 197
OleregSetValue 196
OleRun 345
OleSave 521, 631
OleSaveToStream 632
OleSendLLE 691
OleSendLowLevelEvent 689
OleSetAutoConvert 275
OleSetClipboard 430, 431
OleSetContainedObject 347
OleSetCursor 707
OleSetInFrontOf 696
OleSetInPlaceRects 709
OleSetInPlaceWindow 697
OleSetParentRgns 710
OleSizeObjectWindow 703
OleSizeParentWindow 702
OleUnclipWindow 699
OleUnhashMenuID 693
OleUninitialize 368
OleUnpatchGetMHandle 695
OleUnSetInPlaceWindow 697
OleUpdateCursor 708
OleWhichGrowHandle 706
OleZoomParentWindow 704
ProgIDFromCLSID 289
PropagateResult 284
ReadClassStg 610
ReadClassStm 610
ReadFmtUserTypeStg 611
ReadOle1FmtProgIDStgMac 612
RegCloseKey 180
RegCreateKey 180
RegDeleteKey 181
RegDeleteValue 181
RegEnumKey 182
RegEnumProgID 183
RegEnumValue 185
RegFlush 187

Functions *(continued)*
RegInitialize 187
RegisterDragDrop 648
RegOpenKey 188
RegQueryValue 188
RegQueryValueEx 189
RegSetValue 190
RegSetValueEx 191
ReleaseStgMedium 437
ResultFromScode 285
RevokeDragDrop 648
SetConvertStg 276
static and runtime support for storage functions 822
StgCreateDocfile 594
StgCreateDocfileFSp 597
StgCreateDocfileMac 599
StgCreateDocfileOnILockBytes 600
StgGetFRefFromIStorage 627
StgGetFSpFromIStorage 628
StgIsStorageFile 603
StgIsStorageFileFSp 604
StgIsStorageFileMac 604
StgIsStorageILockBytes 605
StgOpenStorage 613
StgOpenStorageFSp 616
StgOpenStorageMac function 618
StgOpenStorageOnILockBytes 619
StgSetTimes 621
StgSetTimesFSp 623
StgSetTimesMac 622
Storage creation 590
storage input/output 606
string and CLSID conversion 286
StringFromCLSID 290
StringFromGUID2 292
StringFromIID 292
UninitOleManager 370
using static version 821
validation functions not supported 821
WriteClassStg 624
WriteClassStm 625
WriteFmtUserTypeStg 625
WriteOle1FmtProgIDStgMac 626
Functions that support OLE 1 719

G

Generic composite moniker
components of 119
definition of 119
Generic composite monikers
binding to 122
Generic composites
enumerating 456
Generic monikers
and anti monikers 497
GetAdvise method 416
GetBindOptions method 476
GetBorder method 671
GetBoundSource method 122, 486
GetCanonicalFormatEtc method 396
GetClassFile function 121, 357, 359, 607, 608
GetClassForHandler method 233
GetClassID method 574
GetClientSite method 317
GetClipboardData method 324
GetColorSet method 413
GetContainer method 306
GetConvertStorage function 277
GetCurFile method 578
GetCurFSP method 581
GetData method 393
GetDataHere method 394
GetDisplayName method 465
GetExtent
IOleObject 333
IViewObject2 333
GetExtent method 418
GetHGlobalFromILockBytes function 609
GetHGlobalFromStream function 609
GetMarshalSizeMax method 227
GetMHandle calls
patching 694
GetMHandle patches
removing 695
GetMiscStatus method 336
GetMoniker method 304, 322
GetObject method 121, 313, 492
GetObjectParam method 478
GetObjectRects method 683
GetObjectStorage method 315
GetRunningClass method 340
GetRunningObjectTable function 502
GetRunningObjectTable method 477
GetScode function 284
GetSize method 215
GetSizeMax method 590
GetSourceDisplayName method 483
GetSourceMoniker method 482
GetTimeOfLastChange method 461, 494
GetUnmarshalClass method 226
GetUpdateOptions method 481
GetUserClassID
IOleObject 332
GetUserClassID method 331
GetUserType method 331
GetWindow method 659
GetWindowContext method 684

GiveFeedback method 637, 639, 643
Grouping interfaces 101
Grow handles
  obtaining information about 706
Guidelines
  user interface 27
GUIDs
  comparing values 287
  conversion functions for 286
  converting to strings 292
  creation of 209
  defining with macro 210

H

HandleIncomingCall method 727
  description of 727
Handling messages 726
Hands off mode
  entering 587
Hands Off state
  termination of 585
Hands off storage state 515
Hands-off storage mode 139
HandsOffStorage method 139, 142
Hash method 458
Hashing
  menu IDs 693
HeapMinimize method 216
Help mode
  entering during in-place activation 659
Help text
  Convert dialog box 34
Helper functions
  using to create objects 115
Hglobal format
  left when flushing clipboard 433
HRESULT 738
HRESULT return value 9
HRESULTs
  definition of values 278
  generation of 284
  marshaling to a stream 238
  obtaining from SCODEs 285
  obtaining SCODE from 284
  unmarshaling from a stream 238

I

IAdviseSink 750, 758
  and default handler 737
  and DLL object applications 758
  OnClose 296
  OnDataChange 294
IAdviseSink *(continued)*
  OnRename 296
  OnSave 296
  OnViewChange 295
  registering for types of notification 293
IAdviseSink interface 123, 131, 293, 334
IAdviseSink::OnSave
  when to call 518
IAdviseSink2
  OnLinkSourceChange 298
IAdviseSink2 interface 297, 334
IBindCtx
  EnumObjectParam 478
  GetBindOptions 476
  GetObjectParam 478
  GetRunningObjectTable 477
  RegisterObjectBound 471
  RegisterObjectParam 477
  ReleaseBoundObjects 472
  RevokeObjectBound 472
  RevokeObjectParam 479
  SetBindOptions 473
IBindCtx interface 470
IClassFactory 751
  CreateInstance 210
  custom object handlers 751
  LockServer 212
IClassFactory interface 207, 353
  initialization of 105
IClassFactory objects
  destroying 152
Icon
  getting PICT icon 443
Icon extraction functions 437
Icon picture formats 439
Icons
  obtaining a handle to 440, 441
  obtaining a label for 442
IDataAdvise holder
  releasing 147
IDataAdviseHolder
  Advise 405
  EnumAdvise 406
  SendOnDataChange 407
  Unadvise 406
IDataAdviseHolder interface 124, 137, 404
  creating an instance of 403
IDataObject 741, 744, 750, 758
  and default handler implementations 738
  and DLL object applications 758
  and drag operations 636
  DAdvise 400
  DUnadvise 402
  EnumDAdvise 402

IDataObject *(continued)*
- EnumFormatEtc 398
- GetCanonicalFormatEtc 396
- GetData 393
- GetDataHere 394
- implemented by default object handler 741
- implemented by the cache 744
- instance on the clipboard 430, 431, 432
- instance removing from the clipboard 433
- instance verifying on the clipboard 433
- QueryGetData 395
- SetData 397

IDataObject interface 362, 392
- drag and drop operations 642

IDropSource
- exposing in drag operations 636
- GiveFeedback 639
- QueryContinueDrag 638
- where implemented 633

IDropSource interface 633, 635

IDropTarget
- DragEnter 643
- DragLeave 646
- DragOver 645
- Drop 647
- where implemented 633

IDropTarget interface 113, 633, 640

IEnumFORMATETC interface 408

IEnumMoniker
- IRunningObjectTable
- EnumRunning
- See Also enumerators

IEnumMoniker interface 479

IEnumOLEVERB interface 298

IEnumSTATDATA interface 409

IEnumSTATSTG interface 533

IEnumX
- Clone 222
- Next 220
- Reset 222
- Skip 221

IEnumX interface 219, 298

IExternalConnection 758
- AddConnection 217
- and DLL object applications 758
- ReleaseConnection 218

IExternalConnection interface 216, 759

IFactory::CreateInstance method
- creating object classes 208

IGetExtent method 333

IIDFromString function 291

IIDs
- converting to string 292
- creating from a string 291
- creation of 210

IIIDs
- comparing values 287

ILockBytes
- Flush 570
- LockRegion 571
- ReadAt 568
- SetSize 570
- Stat 573
- UnLockRegion 572
- WriteAt 569

ILockBytes byte arrays
- reading data from 568
- writing data to 569

ILockBytes interface 566

ILockBytes object
- obtaining memory handle 609
- OLE provided instance of 592

IMalloc
- Alloc 213
- DidAlloc 216
- Free 214
- GetSize 215
- HeapMinimize 216
- Realloc 214

IMalloc interface 213

IMalloc::Realloc
- size of memory allocations returned by 215

IMarshal 757
- DisconnectObject 232
- GetMarshalSizeMax 227
- GetUnmarshalClass 226
- MarshalInterface 229
- ReleaseMarshalData 231
- UnmarshalInterface 230

IMarshal interface 223, 449
- data structures 224

IMessageFilter
- HandleIncomingCall 727
- MessagePending 730
- RetryRejectedCall 729

IMessageFilter interface 726
- registering implementation of 105
- registering with OLE 733

IMoniker
- BindToObject 449
- BindToStorage 451
- CommonPrefixWith 463
- ComposeWith 455
- Enum 456
- GetDisplayName 465

IMoniker *(continued)*
GetTimeOfLastChange 461
Hash 458
Inverse 462
IsEqual 457
IsRunning 458
IsSystemMoniker 468
ParseDisplayName 466
Reduce 453
RelativePathTo 464
IMoniker interface 359, 447
basic operation in 448
description of 448
pointers to instances of 449
Implicit data caching 746
Inactive object state 50
Incoming calls
single entry point for 727
Incremental save operations 143
InitCache method 422
InitFromData method 322
Initializing document structures 110
Initializing embedded objects 583
Initializing new class objects
IPersistStorage::InitNew 208
IPersistStorage::Load 208
Initializing objects 112, 588
Initializing the interface VTBL data structures 105
Initnew method 116, 583
InitOleManager function 368
In-place activation
accelerator keystrokes
translating 678
activating objects with background utilities running 653
active object
visible portion of 663
active object made visible 671
active objects
resizing border space for tools 668
allocating border space 672
BORDERWIDTHS 765
changing extents 687
clicking in scroll bars 654
clipping objects to the container window 654
composite menu 675
container not receiving low-level events 653
deactivating UI 685
deactivation notification 686
displaying frame adornments 656, 765
displaying status text 676
displaying toolbars 656, 765
entering help mode 659
functions 688
handling floating windows 655
In-place activation *(continued)*
handling hierarchical menu ranges 653
handling mouseDown events 689, 711
hatch border 656, 765
hiding others application menu option 654
interacting with client site 679
interfaces and functions 653
IOleWindow interface 658
miscellaneous functions for 688
modeless dialogs 669, 677
notifications from container 668
notifying objects 680
objects
valid formats for activating 680
OLEINPLACEFRAMEINFO 773
programming considerations 653
querying containers for support 680
reactivating objects 664
removing composite menu 676
removing the user interface 662
requesting border space for tools 671
scrolling objects 685
structures 655
taking the foreground 682
toolbar space 671
toolbars 671
UI deactivating after taking the foreground 655
UI deactivating an in-place session 654
undoing active state 687
undoing changes 687
undoing changes made to object 664
In-place activation retrieving window interfaces 684
In-place activation:window pointers 659
In-place active objects
container loses activation 668
notifiying when container window changes 667
translating events 666
undoing state of 664
In-place container windows
growing 704
In-place object window
clipping 709, 710
dragging 701
In-place object windows
growing 705
sizing 703
In-place objects
bringing to the foreground 696
deactivating 661
menus for 681
position in the container window 683
position in the parent window 684
unclipping windows 697
window serving object 697

In-place windows
clipping 698, 699
dragging 701
moving 700
sizing 702
unclipping 699
InPlaceDeactivate method 661
In-process handlers
definition of 18
In-process servers
applications implemented as 16
definition of 16
InProcHandler 751, 755
database key 161
keyword 735
keyword used in registering custom handlers 755
InProcServer
database key 161
Input/output storage functions 606
Insert Object
dialog box 160
Insert Object dialog 39
recommended text 41
Insert Object dialog box 114, 159
Insertable
database key 160
InsertMenus method 675
Inside-out objects
description of 60
Install programs
converting object classes 267
Instantiation
definition of 25
Interface IDs
creating 209
Interface implementations
relationship between 102
Interface key
registration database 164
Interface pointers See Also Reference counting
as back pointers 203
as in-parameters 203
as local variables 203
as out-parameters 203
avoiding reference counting 200
decrementing the reference count of 206
incrementing the reference count of 206
keeping alive 199
making globally accessible 235
multiple from same IUnknown 200
optimizing reference counting 202
reference counting rules 200
See Also reference counting
separate reference counts 200
Interface pointers *(continued)*
storing marshaled 235
temporarily owned 200
Interface reference counters
required size of 206
INTERFACEINFO structure 769
Interfaces
base interface 6
benefits of grouping 102
communication across boundaries 18
component object 199
definition of 1
description of 4
determining for an object 204
differences from Windows version 817
IAdviseSink 293
IAdviseSink2 297
IBindCtx 470
IClassFactory 207
IDataAdviseHolder 404
IDataObject 392
IDropSource 635
IDropTarget 640
IEnumFORMATETC 408
IEnumMoniker 479
IEnumOLEVERB 298
IEnumSTATDATA 409
IEnumSTATSTG 533
IEnumX 219
IExternalConnection 216
ILockBytes 566
IMalloc 213
IMarshal 223
IMessageFilter 726
IMessageFilter differences from Windows version 817
IMoniker 447
implemented by container applications 20
implemented by object applications 22
initialization of 105
IOleAdviseHolder 299
IOleCache 419
IOleCache2 424
IOleCacheControl 427
IOleClientSite 303
IOleContainer 308
IOleInPlaceActiveObject 665
IOleInPlaceFrame differences from Windows version 819
IOleInPlaceFrameWindow 674
IOleInPlaceObject 660
IOleInPlaceObject differences from Windows version 818
IOleInPlaceSite 679
IOleInPlaceSite differences from Windows version 819
IOleInPlaceUIWindow 670
IOleItemContainer 312

Interfaces *(continued)*
IOleLink 480
IOleObject 316
IOleWindow 658
IParseDisplayName 468
IPersist 574
IPersistFile 575
IPersistFile differences from Windows version 818
IPersistStorage 581
IPersistStream 587
IRootStorage 565
IRunnableObject 339
IRunningObjectTable 488
IStdMarshalInfo 232
IStorage 533
IStream 553
IUnknown 199
IViewObject 409
IViewObject differences from Windows version 817
IViewObject2 417
keeping references to 6
Linking
description of 445
logical groupings of 101
marshaling of pointers to 233
negotiation between 6
obtaining pointers to 101
pointers to 6
reference counting 6
Inverse method 462
IOleAdviseHolder
Advise 300
EnumAdvise 301
returning instance of OLE provided implementation 344
SendOnClose 302
SendOnRename 301
SendOnSave 302
Unadvise 300
IOleAdviseHolder interface 124, 137, 299, 335, 344
IOleCache
Cache 352, 419
EnumCache 422
InitCache 422
SetData 423
Uncache 421
IOleCache interface 419
IOleCache2 750, 751
and default handler implementations 738
and the default object handler 737
custom object handlers 751
implemented by the default object handler 745
UpdateCache 425
IOleCache2 interface 424, 745
IOleCacheControl
OnRun 428
OnStop 429
IOleCacheControl interface 427
IOleClientSite
GetContainer 306
GetMoniker 304, 359
OnShowWindow 307
RequestNewObjectLayout 308
requirements for containers 303
SaveObject 303
ShowObject 307
IOleClientSite interface 303
IOleClientSite::GetContainer
value returned by OLE 1 714
IOleClientSite::ShowObject
value returned by OLE 1 714
IOleContainer 306
EnumOjbects 310
LockContainer 311, 340
IOleContainer interface 308
IOleInPlaceActiveObject
EnableModeless 669
OnDocWindowActivate 668
OnFrameWindowActivate 667
ResizeBorder 668
TranslateAccelerator 666
IOleInPlaceActiveObject interface 665
IOleInPlaceFrame
AdjustMenus 675
EnableModeless 677
InsertMenus 675
RemoveMenus 676
SetStatusText 676
TranslateAccelerator 678
IOleInPlaceFrame interface 674
IOleInPlaceObject
InPlaceDeactivate 661
ReactivateAndUndo 664
SetObjectRects 663
UIDeactivate 662
IOleInPlaceObject interface 660
IOleInPlaceSite
CanInPlaceActivate 680
DeactivateAndUndo 687
DiscardUndoState 687
GetObjectRects 683
GetWindowContext 684
OnInPlaceActivate 680
OnInPlaceDeactivate 686
OnPosRectChange 687
OnUIActivate 681

IOleInPlaceSite *(continued)*
OnUIDeactivate 685
OnUIVisible 682
Scroll 685
IOleInPlaceSite interface 679
IOleInPlaceUIWindow
GetBorder 671
RequestBorderSpace 671
SetActiveObject 673
SetBorderSpace 672
IOleInPlaceUIWindow interface 670
IOleItemContainer 308
GetObject 313
GetObjectStorage 315
IsRunning 316
IOleItemContainer interface 312
and item monikers 121
IOleLink
BindIfRunning 486
BindToSource 327, 341, 484
GetBoundSource 486
GetSourceDisplayName 483
GetSourceMoniker 482
GetUpdateOptions 481
SetSourceDisplayName 483
SetSourceMoniker 481
SetUpdateOptions 480
UnbindSource 487
Update 487
IOleLink interface 480
IOleLink::bindtosource 486
IOleObject 738, 751, 758
Advise 296, 297, 300, 334
and default handler implementations 738
and DLL object applications 758
Close 318
compound document object management 316
custom object handlers 751
DoVerb 307, 325, 351
invoking 326
EnumAdvise 335
EnumVerbs 326, 328
default handler implementation of 328
GetClientSite 306, 317
GetClipboardData 324
GetExtent 333
GetMiscStatus 323, 336
GetMoniker 322, 359
GetUserClassID 331, 332
GetUserType 331
implemented by default object handler 738
InitFromData 322
IsUpToDate 330
SetClientSite 317
IOleObject *(continued)*
SetColorScheme 339
SetExtent 333, 334
SetHostNames 318
SetMoniker 321, 359
Unadvise 335
UpDate 330
IOleObject interface 316
IOleObject::Close
OLE 1 implementation 716
IOleObject::Update
use during class conversion 269
IOleWindow
ContextSensitiveHelp 659
GetWindow 659
IOleWindow interface 658
IParseDisplayName
ParseDisplayName 469
IParseDisplayName interface 468
IPersist
GetClassID 331, 574
IPersist interface 574
base interface for persistent storage objects 574
IPersistFile
GetCurFile 578
GetCurFSP 581
IsDirty 576
Load 358, 359, 576
LoadFSP 579
Save 577
SaveCompleted 578
SaveCompletedFSP 581
SaveFSP 579
IPersistFile interface 575
IPersistStorage 742, 743, 750, 758
and default handler implementations 738
and DLL object applications 758
HandsOffStorage 587
implemented by default object handler 742
implemented by the cache 743
InitNew 583
IsDirty 582
Load 583
Save 356, 358, 359, 584
SaveCompleted 585
IPersistStorage interface 135, 139, 356, 358, 359, 581
IPersistStorage methods
Save
rules for calling 518
IPersistStorage methods::HandsOff
rules for calling 515
IPersistStorage::HandsOff
rules for calling 517, 518, 519

IPersistStorage::InitNew
  and OLE 1 objects 715
IPersistStorage::Load
  and OLE 1 objects 715
IPersistStorage::Save
  rules for calling 515, 517, 518, 519
IPersistStorage::SaveCompleted
  rules for calling 515, 517, 518, 519
IPersistStream
  GetSizeMax 590
  IsDirty 588
  Load 588
  Save 589
IPersistStream interface 587
IRootStorage
  SwitchToFile 565
IRootStorage interface 565
IRunnableObject 758
  and DLL object applications 758
  GetRunningClass 340
  IsRunning 341, 344
  LockRunning 342, 346
  Run 341, 345
  SetContainedObject 343, 348
IRunnableObject interface 339, 759
  and silent updates 339
  Run method 247
IRunningObjectTable
  EnumRunning 495
  GetObject 492
  GetTimeOfLastChange 494
  IsRunning 492
  NoteChangeTime 493
  Register 321, 489
  Revoke 491
IRunningObjectTable interface 147, 488
IsDirty method 576, 582, 588
IsEqual method 457
IsEqualCLSID function 288
IsEqualGUID function 287
IsEqualIID function 287
IsOleManagerRunning function 371
IsRunning method 122, 316, 341, 344, 458, 492
IsSystemMoniker method 468
IStdMarshalInfo
  GetClassForHandler 233
IStdMarshalInfo interface 232
IStorage 750
    Commit 521
  and caching data 746
  Commit 544
  CopyTo 541
  CreateStorage 537
  CreateStream 535
IStorage *(continued)*
  DestroyElement 548
  EnumElements 547
  MoveElementTo 543
  OpenStorage 539
  OpenStream 536
  RenameElement 549
  Revert 547
  SetClass 551
  SetElementTimes 550
  SetStateBits 552
  Stat 552
IStorage interface 294, 533
  releasing pointer to 534
IStorage objects 133
  saving data to 134
IStream
  Clone 564
  Commit 560
  CopyTo 559
  LockRegion 562
  Read 554
  Revert 561
  Seek 557
  SetSize 558
  Stat 564
  UnLockRegion 563
  Write 555
IStream interface 134, 294, 553
IStream object
  creating an instance of 535
  OLE provided instance of 593
IStream objects
  opening 112
  reading 112
  using to save data 134
IsUpToDate method 122, 330
Item containers
  determine if specified item in item container is running 316
Item moniker
  definition of 119
Item monikers
  allocating 499
  binding 312, 313
  binding to 121
  returning 499
IUnknown 753
  AddRef 206
  and aggregation of default handler 753
  OLE base interface 6
  QueryInterface 204
  Release 206

IUnknown interface 199
    initialization of 105
IViewObject 750
    Draw 336, 410
    Freeze 414
    GetAdvise 416
    GetColorSet 413
    SetAdvise 295, 333, 415
    Unfreeze 415
IViewObject interface 131, 409
IViewObject::Draw
    obtaining color sets for 413
IViewObject2 750, 751
    and default handler implementations 738
    and the default object handler 737
    custom object handlers 751
    GetExtent 333, 418
    implemented by the default object handler 745
IViewObject2 interface 417, 745

L

Libraries
    unloading of 257
Link consumer 446
Link objects 330
    and class identifier 331
    and OleRun function 345
    assigning monikers to newly created 359
    becoming out-of-date 330
    creating compound document 359
    creating from data transfer object 360
    definition of 19
    determining if can create from data transfer object 365
    getting update options 481
    keeping track of 19
Link source 345, 446
    binding link to 486
    bound 331
    cached copy 46
    change notifications for 298
    effects of updating 330
    informing of change events 334
    obtaining latest data from 487
    obtaining new presentations from 330
    retrieving current 482
    retrieving object link source is connected to 486
    storing 481
    unbinding object from 487
Link source format 360
Link tracking
    described 446
Link update options
    setting 480
Linked object 445, 446
    display name of source 483
    monikers stored in 483
    source of 481
    types 46
Linked objects 44, 446
    automatic updates 45
    binding moniker contained in 484
    binding of 119
    change source dialog 48
    definition of 13
    editing of 117
    in the running state 26
    maintaining 47
    manual updates 45
    monikers assigned 119
    multiple references 26
    parsing display names of 483
    relationship to object verbs 45
    running the application 119
    saving to storage 521
    unbinding 487
    updating 487
Linking
    types of 446
Linking files
    as embedded objects 115
Linking interfaces
    description of 445
Linking objects
    benefits of 14
    functions used 495
Links
    binding to link source 486
    closing to embedded objects 216
    determining the state of 122
    incompatible from OLE 1 715
    loss of in unsaved containers 390
    to embedded objects
        support by OLE 1 servers 716
    updating 145
    working with OLE 1 715
Links dialog 47
Links to embedded objects 26
LNKS
    description of 385
Load
    IPersistFile 358, 359
Load method 576, 583, 588
Loaded objects
    closing 146
Loaded state
    objects entering 25
    of an object 23

LoadFSP method 579
Loading data from streams 588
Loading libraries into memory 256
Loading objects
    into memory from storage 629
    into memory from streams 630
Loading objects from storage 112
Local servers
    definition of 16
LocalServer
    database key 161
Locating and loading class objects 245
LockContainer
    IOleContainer 340
LockContainer method 311
Locking data
    within a stream 562
Locking objects
    CoLockObjectExternal 251
LockRegion method 562, 571
LockRunning method 342, 346
LockServer method 212
LOCKTYPE enumeration 532, 788
logical thread ID 726
Low memory
    guaranteed operable methods 141
    saving objects in 140, 142
LPRC apple events
    processing 372
LRPC
    OLE's use of 10

M

MacFInfo key 171
Macros
    FAILED 286
    for status codes 285
    MAKE SCODE 286
    SCODE_CODE 285
    SCODE_FACILITY 285
    SCODE_SEVERITY 285
    SUCCEEDED 286
MAKE SCODE macro
    description of 286
Marshaling
    a reference of an object IID 229
    creating a proxy 226
    creating an instance of 236
    custom 235
    description of 234
    destroying previously marshaled data 231, 242
    determining memory bounds 227
    functions that support 233
Marshaling *(continued)*
    implemented by objects 235
    initialize newly created proxy 230
    interface parameters 10
    parameters/arguments 223
    steps for performing 240
Marshaling objects
    disconnecting from 232
Marshaling pointers
    support provided by OLE 233
MarshalInterface method 229
MEMCTX enumeration 263, 788
Memory
    allocation of 213
    controlling allocation of 7
    determining size of allocated 215
    loading objects from storage 629
    loading objects from streams 630
    local application task 7
    management of 7
    manangement of 213
    reallocation of 214
    releasing unused 216
    shared 7
Memory allocation
    application in control of 265
    determining IMalloc instance 216
    OLE-provided allocators 264
    retrieval of allocators 263
Memory handles
    for ILockBytes instance 609
    for stream objects 609
Menu
    active editor 65
    popup 67
    selected object 65
    workspace 63
Menu bar
    adding container menus 695
    allocating 691
    freeing 692
    inserting menus into 692
Menu IDs
    hashing values of 693
    unhashing 695
Menu selections
    translating 678
Menu summary 66
Menus
    adjusting 675
    composite 675, 676, 681
    for in-place active objects 675, 681
    replacing after in-place session 685
Message loops 725

MessagePending method 730
Messages
  controlled dispatching 725
  handling and deferring 726
  in the caller's queue 731
  to the user 84
Metafiles 737, 738
Mini servers
  definition of 22
MkGetMacNetInfo function 510
MkParseDisplayName function 502
MkParseDisplayNameMac function 506
MKRREDUCE enumeration 789
MKSYS enumeration 789
Modeless dialogs
  enabling and disabling 677
  enabling and disabling of 669
Modifier keys
  drag and drop 82
Moniker 304
  container's 304
  object's 304
  object's full moniker 304
MonikerCommonPrefixWith function 508
MonikerRelativePathTo function 507
Monikers
  32-bit integer associated with 458
  allocate and return new composite moniker 501
  allocating and returning new item monikers 499
  and absolute paths 446
  and lookup tables 448
  and relative paths 446, 507
  binding 484
  binding to 119, 121
  binding to specified interface 496
  comparing 457
  composite
    kinds of 455
  creating an anti moniker 496
  creating from file specification 498
  creating from path name 497
  defined 445
  definition of 19
  destroying 462
  determining if running 458
  enumerating 495
  file type 121
  generic composite 448
  generic type 122
  implementation semantics and importance to binding process 468
  item type 121
  link source 481
  main operation of 445
Monikers *(continued)*
  maintaining tables of 458
  new bind contexts for 497
  obtaining current display name for 465
  obtaining from display names 502, 506
  obtaining longest common prefix 463
  obtaining longest common shared prefix 508
  obtaining relative path to 464
  parsing an object's display into 469
  reducing 448, 453
  retrieving current link source for 482
  returning 304, 322
  returning an anti moniker 496
  returning AppleTalk zone 510
  stored by object handler 321
  syntax for 504
  textual representations of 448
  types of 19, 119
mouseDown events
  enabling or disabling 711
  handling during in-place session 689
MoveElementTo method 543
MSHCTX enumeration 224, 233, 790
MSHLFLAGS enumeration 224, 790
Multiple inheritance
  C++ 97

N

Name change notifications 296
Naming documents 132
Native data
  clipboard format of in storage objects 611, 625
Nested objects 26
Next method 220
No scribble state
  termination of 585
No scribble storage mode 139
No scribble storage state 515
Normal storage state 515
NoteChangeTime method 493
Notifications
  asynchronous 382, 400, 402, 405, 406, 415, 725, 780
  by in-place active objects 680, 681, 685
  compound document 123, 300
  data 123
  definition of 123
  deleting advisory connections for 402, 406
  enumerating advisory connections 402, 406
  for data changes 382, 780
  in-place active objects 686
  keeping track of 124
  paths of 126
  retrieving advisory connections for 416

Notifications *(continued)*
- setting advisory connections for 400, 405, 415
- setting up for 116
- synchronous and asynchronous 129
- types of 123
- updating advisory connections for 407
- view 123

O

OBJD
- description of 387

Object activation
- definition of 117

Object applications
- accessing its services 25
- accommodating OLE 1 versions 173
- closing of 147
- description of 13, 22
- implementing drag and drop 633
- installation issues 761
- installing newer version 267
- intercepting command keys 67
- interfaces implemented by 22
- locking in memory 212
- making visible 252
- revoking objects when closing 251
- specifying color palette to use 339
- typical structure of 22

Object class
- registering 29
- registration database 29

Object classes
- activating as different class 270
- automatic conversion of 267
- conversion of 266
- converting from one to another 268
- creating instances of 207, 210
- emulation of 266
- obtaining auto-convert data 274
- obtaining emulation data 272
- registering of 106
- retrieving conversion data 277
- setting conversion bit 276
- tagging for auto-conversion 275
- tagging for conversion 267

Object creation functions 756

Object creation functions common parameters 349

Object handler
- storing of monikers 321

Object handlers
- connected to object or not 256
- custom handlers 735
  - registered in 735
- default provided by OLE 14, 18
- defined 735
- DLL object applications written as 735
- general description of 14, 17
- handling object change notifications 126
- InprocHandler 735
- loading 756
- marshaling the CLSID of 232
- provide services for 736
- purpose of 14
- structure of 17
- types of 735
- unloading 756

Object pointers
- enumerations of 478
- finding 478
- registering 477

Object rendering 735

Object states
- active 53
- in a compound document 23
- inactive 50
- open 56
- selected 52
- transitions between 59

Object type
- conversion of 31, 32
- emulation of 31, 33
- listing of 32
- permanent conversion 32
- unregistered 32, 34

Object types
- user model 27

OBJECTDESCRIPTOR structure 387, 769

Objects
- access to the persistent storage of 451
- activating 117
  - IOleObject::DoVerb 117
- advise holders 124
- aggregating 99
- aggregation of 98
- and advisory connections 300
- and external connections 343
- and notifying of changes to view 295
- and persistent storage 296
- and requests for more or less room 308
- automatic conversion of 173, 717
- changes to 124
- checking for changes 582
- closing 319

Objects *(continued)*
closing from container 152
closing to the passive state 26
communication with container 317
compared to OLE 1 49
connecting to 322
controlling running the container 311
conversion/emulation of 266
converting OLE 1 to OLE 2 723
creating
Insert Object dialog 39
ole API functions used 116
creating embedded object from clipboard 364
creating embedded object from data transfer object 363
creating from link source format 361
creating linked object form data transfer object 365
creating pointer monikers for 499
creating static 362
creating static objects 362
creating with helper functions 115
creating with link to file 361
creating with link to file specification 361
creation of 114
data change notiifcations regarding 294
data source 636
data transfer 360, 363, 636
data transfer model 77
detecting OLE 1 classes 718
determine if object is up-to-date 461
determining if in running state 341
determining if registered as running 492
determining if running 344
determining if up-to-date 330
determining interfaces supported 204
determining supported interfaces 204
disconnecting
CoDisconnectObject 154
dragging and dropping 81, 633
drawing of 434
embedded
creating 351
embedded as containers 49
enumerating for current container 310
enumerating verbs available for 328
enumerating verbs of 328
external references 111
finding object pointers 478
functions for creating 348
get time of last change 494
getting current extent of 333
getting link update options 481
handling changes to 123
in the running state 26
indicating as contained as embedding 343

Objects *(continued)*
informing of space available to them 333
inidcating contained as embedding 347
initializing contents of 322
invisible 343
invisible window notifications 307
linked
automatic updates 45
creating from data transfer object 360
manual updates 45
linked versus embedded 44
locating and loading 449
lock in running state 342
locking and unlocking 347
locking in memory 251
locking in running state 346
maintaining links to 47
maintaining up-to-date cache 330
making visible to user 307
marshaling an instance to a stream 239
newly created 200
note time of last change 493
notification regarding monikers 321
obtaining access to the storage of 315
obtaining pointers to current client site 317
OnSave notifications 296
parse display name for 469
placing into running state 341, 345
proxy 10, 713
registering as needing to be released 471
registering for data change notifications
IDataObject::DAdvise 117
registering for OLE notifications
IOleObject::Advise 117
registering for view notifications
IViewObject::SetAdvise 117
registering in running object table 489
registering object pointers 477
release registered objects 472
releasing reference locks 148
removing previously registered objects 472
renaming 296
request to save 303
requesting objects to perform a verb 325
retrieving 486
retrieving display name of linked object's source 483
return running objects 492
returning 478
returning class identifier for 331
returning data transfer object 324
returning status information about 336
revoking from running object table 147
revoking registration of 479, 491
root storage 12

Objects *(continued)*
  saving changes incrementally 143
  saving in low memory 140
    methods guranteed to work 141
  saving in transacted mode 143
  saving to storage 134
  sending notification of name change 296
  setting link update options 480
  setting logical size 333
  setting rectangular limits of 333
  specifying window title information 318
  status information about stored in 337
  storage 11
  storage and stream 533
  stream 11
  stub 10, 713
  transferring data between 77
  transitioning embedded objects to loaded state 318
  transitioning strong lock to weak lock 343
  unbinding 487
  unlock from running state 342, 346
  unmarshaling an instance from a stream 241
  updating 461
  updating linked objects with latest data 487
  upgrading with new application 173, 717
  user readable identification string for 331
  visible 343
  visible window notifications 307
  visual appearance of 49
OLE
  architectural overview 1
  base interface 6
  compatibity issues 713
  Differences from Windows 807
  Differences in architecture 807
  explanation of 1
  function differences from Windows version 820, 821, 822, 823
  infrastructure described 2
  initialization functions 365
  initializing 368, 371
  interface differences from Windows version 817, 818, 819
  programming considerations 89
  registration database 158
  uninitializing 370
OLE 1
  communication with 713
  compatibility 164
  functions that support 719
  supporting data formats 715
  supporting storage media 715
OLE 1 applications
  coexisting with 175
  linking to OLE 2 objects 715
  loading OLE 2 objects 715
  registering 192
  running with on the same system 175, 717
  working with containers 714
OLE 1 compatibility
  database key 164
OLE 1 compatible formats
  left when flushing clipboard 433
OLE 1 format
  converting to 720
OLE 1 object applications 173
OLE 1 objects
  detecting 718
  prevent linking to 719
OLE 2 applications
  registering 158
  working with OLE 1 object applications 715
OLE 2 libraries
  registration of 172
OLE 2-to-OLE 1
  communication 713
  compatibility 713
OLE applications
  closing 148, 155
    sequence of events 150
  closing with File Quit 148
  compound documents
    useful constants 110
  general information on 103
  initializing the document structure 110
  opening compound documents 109
  started by user 106
  startup tasks 103
    determining the start-up method 106
    initializing the interface VTBLs 105
  types of 13
OLE Functions
  OleregOpenRegistration 193
OLE interface implementations
  relationship between 102
OLE libraries
  closing during shutdown 156
  verifying build version 104
OLE library
  initializing 367
  returning version number for 365
  unitializing 368
OLE object-creation functions 756
OLE objects
  aggregating 99
    controlling unknown 99

OLE Storage interfaces
summary of 511
OLE storage model
description of 511
OLE2.DLL 755
default entry in Registration Database file 755
OleaAdviseHolder
creation of 124
OleAddMBarMenu function 695
OleBuildVersion function 365, 367
OleClipWindow function 699
OleClipWindows function 698
OLECLOSE enumeration 319, 791
OLECONTF enumeration 310, 792
OleConvertIStorageToOLESTREAM function 719
OleConvertIStorageToOLESTREAMEx function 720
OleConvertOLESTREAMToIStorage function 722
OleConvertOLESTREAMToIStorageEx function 723
OleCreate function 116, 343, 351, 356
OleCreateDefaultHandler 753
and aggregation of default handler 753
how used 352
OleCreateDefaultHandler function 352
OleCreateEmbeddingHelper function 353
implementations of 354
OleCreateFromData function 355, 360, 363
OleCreateFromFile
used to 357
OleCreateFromFile function 357
OleCreateFromFSp function 358, 359
OleCreateLink function 359
OleCreateLinkFromData function 360
OleCreateLinkToFile function 361
OleCreateLinkToFSp function 361
OleCreateStaticFromData function 362, 363
OleDisposeMBar function 692
OleDoAutoConvert function 273
use during class conversion 268, 270
OleDragObjectWindow function 701
OleDragParentWindow function 701
OleDraw function 434
OleDuplicateData function 435
OleFlushClipboard function 433
leaving hGlobal-based formats behind 433
leaving OLE 1 compatible formats behind 433
OleFullPathFromFSSpec function 592
OleGetAutoConvert 274
OleGetClipboard function 363, 432
OleGetCursor function 707
OleGetIconFromIconSuite function 443
OleGetIconOfClass function 442
OleGetIconOfFile function 440, 441
OLEGETMONIKER enumeration 304, 793
OLEGROWHANDLES enumeration 793
OleGrowObjectWindow function 705
OleGrowParentWindow function 704
OleHashMenuID function 693
OleIconSource structure 438, 771
creating for an icon 442
OleInitDBCSCountry function 371
OleInitialize function 367
OLEINPLACEFRAMEINFO 813
OLEINPLACEFRAMEINFO structure 656, 773
OleInsertMenus function 692
OleIsCurrentClipboard function 433
OleIsRunning function 342, 344
OLELINKBIND enumeration 484, 486, 794
OleLoad function 247, 343, 629
use during class conversion 270
OleLoadFromStream function 630
OleLockRunning function 346
OleMakeFSSpec function 591
OLEMANAGER enumeration 794
OleMaskMouse function 711
OleMBarRec structure 658, 775
OLEMISC enumeration 337, 795
OleMoveWindow function 700
OleNewMBar function 691
OleNoteObjectVisible 343
locking/unlocking reference counts 252
OleNoteObjectVisible function 347
OlePatchGetMHandle function 694
OlePictFromIconAndLabel function 442
OleProcessClipboardAE function 373
OleProcessDdeAE function 372
OleProcessLrpcAE function 372
OleQueryCreateAll function 364
OleQueryCreateFromData function 363
OleQueryLinkFromData function 365
OLEREG_KEYWORD enumeration 797
OleregCloseRegistration function 194
OleRegEnumFormatEtc function 179
OleRegEnumVerbs function 178
OleRegGetMiscStatus function 177
OleRegGetUserType function 177
OleregGetValue function 194
OleregOpenRegistration function 193
OleregRemoveKey function 197
OleregSetValue function 196
OLERENDER enumeration 350, 797
OleRun 351
OleRun function 341, 345
OleSave function 521, 631
saving an object to storage 135
OleSaveToStream function 632
OleSendLLE function 691
OleSendLowLevelEvent function 689

OleSetAutoConvert
  use during class conversion 267
OleSetAutoConvert function 275
OleSetClipboard 324
OleSetClipboard function 323, 430, 431
OleSetContainedObject function 343, 347
OleSetCursor function 707
OleSetInFrontOf function 696
OleSetInPlaceRects function 709
OleSetInPlaceWindow function 697
OleSetParentRgns function 710
OleSizeObjectWindow function 703
OleSizeParentWindow function 702
OleUnclipWindow function 699
OleUnhashMenuID function 693
OleUninitialize
  and forced unloading of custom handlers 756
OleUninitialize function 156, 367, 368
OleUnpatchGetMHandle function 695
OleUnSetInPlaceWindow function 697
OLEUPDATE enumeration 481, 799
OleUpdate function
  value returned by OLE 1 714
OleUpdateCursor function 708
OLEVERB structure 298, 326, 328, 775
OleWhichGrowHandle function 706
OLEWHICHMK enumeration 304, 322, 799
OleZoomParentWindow function 704
OnClose change notification 123
OnClose method 129, 146, 296
OnDataChange method 129, 131, 147, 294
OnDataChange notification 123
OnDocWindowActivate method 668
OnFrameWindowActivate method 667
OnInPlaceActivate method 680
OnInPlaceDeactivate method 686
OnLinkSrcChange method 298
OnPosRectChange method 687
OnRename change notification 123
OnRename method 129, 131, 132, 296
OnRun method 428
OnSave change notification 123
OnSave method 129, 296
OnShowWindow method 147, 307
OnStop method 429
OnUIActivate method 681
OnUIDeactivate method 685
OnUIVisible method 682
OnViewChange method 131, 295
OnViewChange notification 123
Open object state 56
Open objects
  undo changes 60
Opening documents
  initializing the document structure 110
  registering for drag and drop 113
  setting the user interface 112
  showing the document 113
  tasks involved in 109
Opening storage objects 111
  File New command 111
  File Open command 112
OpenStorage method 539
OpenStream method 536
Options
  link update 480
Outside-in objects
  description of 59
  rules of 59

P

ParseDisplayName method 466, 469
Parsing
  display names 469, 502, 506
  names 308
Passive state
  objects entering 26
  of an object 23
Paste operations
  from the clipboard 391
Paste special dialog 78
  recommended text for 80
Path names
  monikers created from 497
Pathnames
  obtaining for files 578
PENDINGTYPE enumeration 732, 800
Persistent storage 296
PICT
  applications that support OLE 1 389
PICTs 737
Picture formats
  for icons 439
Pointer (cursor)
  appropriate feedback shapes 637
Pointer monikers
  creating for an object 499
Pointers See interface pointers
  registering object pointers 477
  releasing 297
  returning object pointers 478
  to the running object table 502
Popup menus 67
Prefix
  longest common 463, 508

Presentation data 738
description of 11
OLE 1 applications 717
Presentation transfer model
overview of 375
Private data
moving with storage objects 391
Process boundary
passing arguments across 223
Processes
assigning identifiers 263
ProgID 159
conversion to CLSID 160
obtaining readable string 159
Registration database keys 160
string 159
version-dependent 159
version-independent 159, 163
ProgIDFromCLSID 159
ProgIDFromCLSID function 289
PROGIDs
conversion functions 286
converting 159
creating from CLSID 289
string length 289
Programmatic identifiers 159
Programming considerations 89
PropagateResult function 284
Protocol\StdFileEditing
database key 160
Proxy function
definition of 234
Proxy objects 10, 713
Pseudo objects
closing 146
creation of 119
definition of 22
description of 13
moniker changes 137

Q

QueryContinueDrag method 637, 638
QueryGetData method 395
Querying objects
for interface pointers 204
QueryInterface method 204

R

ReactivateAndUndo method 664
Read method 554
ReadAt method 568
ReadClassStg function 610
ReadClassStm function 610
ReadFmtUserTypeStg function 611
use during class conversion 268, 270
Reading data
from ILockBytes byte arrays 568
from streams 554
ReadOle1FmtProgIDStgMac function 612
Realloc method 214
Reallocating memory 214
Receiving change notifications 130
Rect structure 671
Rectangle extents
in-place active objects 671
Reduce method 453
Reduction 453
Reference count
locking and unlocking 347
not incrementing 294
Reference counters
required size of 206
Reference counting 6
artificial for safeguarding 200
decrementing counts 206
definition of 199
incrementing counts 206
optimizing 202
releasing an object 26
rules of 200
See Also interface pointers
separate counts 200
Reference locks
releasing 148
Refernce counts
managing 251
RegCloseKey function 180
REGCLS enumeration 800
RegCreateKey function 180
RegDeleteKey function 181
RegDeleteValue function 181
RegEnumKey function 182
RegEnumProgID function 183
REGENUMPROGIDF enumeration 801
RegEnumValue function 185
RegFlush function 187
RegInitialize function 187
Register method 147, 489
RegisterDragDrop 641
RegisterDragDrop function 113, 640, 648
Registering as a drop target 641
Registering class objects 106, 248
Registering documents for drag and drop 113
Registering File Monikers 111
Registering object applications
for conversion of classes 268

RegisterObjectBound method 471
RegisterObjectParam method 477
Registration
  as a drop target 648
  revoking 491
Registration database 157, 158, 328, 755
  adding information to 166
  API functions 157
  associating text with keys 190
  associating values with data types 191
  AuxUserType entry 168
  CLSID entry 167
  CLSID subkey entry 167
  Conversion subkey entry 170
  DataFormats subkey entry 169
  decrementing lock count 194
  DefaultIcon subkey entry 170
  deleting keys 181
  Embedding Preferences file 192
  Entry point entry 167
  enumerating FORMATETC structure 179
  enumerating subkey entries 182, 183
  enumerating values for registry key 185
  File extension entry 171
  functions
    OLE 1 applications 192
    OLE 2 applications 176
  functions for OLE 2 applications 176
  getting status information 177
  Human-readable string entries 166
  identifying keys 180
  Information for OLE 1 applications entries 166
  initializing for OLE 187
  InprocHandler entry 168
  Insertable entry 166
  Insertable subkey entry 170
  keys for object conversion 267
  keys in 158
  Local Server entry 167
  localization issues 175
  MacFInfo key entry 171
  MiscStatus subkey entry 169
  Object Class entry 167
  object class registrations 29
  object status information stored in 337
  Oenumerating entries 178
  OLE 1 functions 192
  OLE 2 158
  OLE 2 libraries 172
  OleRegGetUserType function 177
  opening a key 188
  opening OLE 1 193
  OProgID subkey entry 170
  overview of 157
Registration database *(continued)*
  overwriting OLE 1 entries 173
  ProgID key 160
  ProgID key entry 166
  releasing keys 180
  removing data from 197
  removing name values 181
  retrieving data types 189
  retrieving text strings 188
  searching for information 194
  static versus DLL functions 176
  storing data values 196
  syntax 158
  Verb entry 168
  verifying entries 104
  Version-independent ProgID entry 171
  writing to disk 187
Registration Database file 158
  example of 165
Registration database functions
  calling at runtime 176
Registration database keys
  CLSID 160, 161
  CurVer 163
  file extension key 163
  file type 163
  InProcHandler 161
  InProcServer 161
  Insertable 160
  LocalServer 161
  OLE 1 compatibility 164
  Protocol\StdFileEditing key 160
  registering new interfaces 164
  Server 160
  UnknownUserType 175
  Verb 160, 161
Registration functions
  calling at runtime 821
  static and runtime support 822
RegOpenKey function 188
RegQueryValue function 188
RegQueryValueEx function 189
RegSetValue function 190
RegSetValueEx function 191
Relative moniker 446
Relative paths 464, 507
RelativePathTo method 464
Release method 206
ReleaseBoundObjects method 472
ReleaseConnection method 218
ReleaseMarshalData method 231
ReleaseStgMedium function 437
Releasing storage media 437

Remoting handlers
 definition of 18
RemoveMenus method 676
RenameElement method 549
Renaming storage objects 550
Rendering handler
 and implementing IAdviseSink 750
 and implementing IDataObject 750
 and implementing IOleCache2 750
 and implementing IPersistStorage 750
 and implementing IViewObject2 750
Rendering handlers 749
 coordination of storage with object application 750
 drawing functionality versus that of default handler 749
 interfaces implemented by 750
 to support embedded objects 750
 to support linked objects 750
Rendering objects 410
 freezing appearance of 414
 obtaining the size of 418
 retrieving the view extent 418
RequestBorderSpace method 671
RequestNewObjectLayout method 308
Reset method 222
ResizeBorder method 668
ResultFromScode function 285
Retrieving data
 from specific medium 393, 394
Retry calls
 with dialog boxes 729
RetryRejectedCall method 729
Return codes
 common to all interface methods 278
Revert method 547, 561
Revoke method 131, 147, 491
RevokeDragDrop function 641, 648
RevokeObjectBound method 472
RevokeObjectParam method 479
Rgn Handles
 of in-place active objects 663
Root compound files
 creation of 594
Run method 341, 345
Running object table 131, 138, 145
 access to 477
 enumerate monikers of objects registered as running 495
 implementing 457
 obtaining pointer to
  GetRunningObjectTable 111
 registering objects in 489
  IRunningObjectTable::Register 111
 returning a pointer to 502
 revoking registration 491
Running objects See binding objects
Running state 737
 objects entering 25
 of an object 23
 placing objects into 738
 transitioning into 339

S

Safeguarding objects
 artificial reference counts 200
Save
 IPersistStorage 358, 359
Save Copy As command 131
Save method 135, 139, 141, 356, 577, 584, 589
Save routines
 which are called 136
SaveCompleted method 136, 139, 142, 578, 585
SaveCompletedFSP method 581
SaveFSP method 579
SaveObject method 146, 303
Savign documents
 opening istorage 133
Saving compound documents
 procedure for 141
Saving documents 131
 incremental saves 143
 ole information 134
 setting the filename 132
 transacted mode 143
 using File Save 138
 using File Save As 132
Saving documents to storage 134
Saving files
 getting time of last save 145
Saving objects 516
 action to take with errors 516
 container responsibilities 521
 into storage 631
 into streams 632
 low memory situations 140, 141, 142
 OleSave 521
 overview of 511
 saving object's CLSID 521
 special data to save 522
 tasks required of container 521
 transacted mode 631
 using IPersistStorage::Save 135
 using OleSave function 135
Saving objects to storage 584
Saving static objects 632
SCODE
 obtaining HRESULT from 285
SCODE_CODE macro
 description of 285

SCODE_FACILITY macro
  description of 285
SCODE_SEVERITY macro
  description of 285
SCODEs
  obtaining from HRESULTs 284
Scroll method 685
Scrolling
  in-place active objects 685
Seek method 557
Seek pointers
  moving within a stream 557
Selected object menu 65
Selected object state 52
Semantics
  implementation 468
Sending change notifications 129
SendOnClose method 302
SendOnDataChange method 407
SendOnRename method 132, 137, 301
SendOnSave method 302
Server
  database key 160
SetActiveObject method 673
SetAdvise method 123, 295, 415
SetBindOptions method 473
SetBorderSpace method 672
SetClass method 551
SetClientSite method 116, 317
SetColorScheme method 339
SetContainedObject
  IRunnableObject 348
SetContainedObject method 343
SetConvertStg function 276
  use during class conversion 269
SetCursor 636
SetData method 397, 423
SetElementTimes method 550
SetExtent
  IOleObject 334
SetExtent method 333
SetHostNames method 318
SetMoniker method 132, 138, 321
SetObjectRects method 663
SetSize method 558, 570
SetSourceDisplayName method 483
SetSourceMoniker method 481
SetStateBits method 552
SetStatusText method 676
Setting the dirty flag 113
Setup programs
  converting object classes 267
SetUpdateOptions method 480
Shared memory 7
Shipping application disks 761
ShowObject method 307
Skip method 221
Starting OLE applications 103
Stat method 552, 564, 573
STATDATA 747
STATDATA structure 301, 336, 403, 776
  enumerating 336
States of objects
  visual 49
STATFLAG enumeration 553, 802
Static objects
  creating from data transfer object 362
  definition of 391
  saving 632
STATSTG structure 530, 776
  atime 531
  cbSize 531
  ctime 531
  mtime 531
  pspec 530, 777
  pwcsName 530
  type 531
Status code values
  macros that manage 285
Status reporting 9
Status text
  for in-place active objects 676
STG_SHARE_EXCLUSIVE 750
STGC enumeration 545, 802
StgCreateDocfile 111
StgCreateDocfile function 133, 594
StgCreateDocfileFSp function 597
StgCreateDocfileMac function 599
StgCreateDocfileOnILockBytes function 600
StgGetFRefFromIStorage function 627
StgGetFSpFromIStorage function 628
StgIsStorageFile function 603
StgIsStorageFileFSp function 604
StgIsStorageFileMac function 604
StgIsStorageILockBytes function 605
STGM_DELETEONRELEASE 111
STGMEDIUM structure 379, 778
STGMOVE enumeration 544, 803
StgOpenStorage function 132, 613
StgOpenStorageFSp function 616
StgOpenStorageMac function 618
StgOpenStorageOnILockBytes function 619
StgSetTimes function 621
StgSetTimesFSp function 623
StgSetTimesMac function 622
STGTY enumeration 531, 803
Storage
  obtaining access to 315

Storage access mode flags 522
STGM_CONVERT 522
STGM_CREATE 522
STGM_DELETEONRELEASE 522
STGM_DIRECT 522
STGM_FAILIFTHERE 522
STGM_PRIORITY 522
STGM_READ 522
STGM_READWRITE 522
STGM_SHARE_DENY_NONE 522
STGM_SHARE_DENY_READ 522
STGM_SHARE_DENY_WRITE 522
STGM_SHARE_EXCLUSIVE 522
STGM_TRANSACTED 522
STGM_WRITE 522
Storage access modes
opening IStorage objects with 514
STGM_DIRECT 514
STGM_READ 514
STGM_READWRITE 514
STGM_SHARE_DENY_WRITE 514
STGM_SHARE_EXCLUSIVE 514
STGM_TRANSACTED 514
Storage and stream objects
instantiating a collection of 533
Storage creation flags
STGM_CONVERT 524
STGM_CREATE 524
STGM_DELETEONRELEASE 524
STGM_FAILIFTHERE 524
Storage functions
calling at runtime 821
Storage media
release of 437
Storage mode flags 133
Storage model
description of 11
Storage modes
hands-off 139
no scribble 139
Storage object
child object
access modes 514
example of 513
Storage objects 11, 133
access modes 514
action to take with errors 516
changing byte array size 570
child objects 514
comitting changes to 544
converting OLE 2 to OLE 1 719, 720, 722
copying an instance of 541, 565
creating 514
creating an instance of 537
Storage objects *(continued)*
creating temporary root objects 111
creation functions 590
default state of 517
determining existence of in a file 603
determining ILockBytes existence 605
direct access mode
STG_SHARE_EXCLUSIVE 112
enumerating elements within 547
format of native data 611, 625
hands off after save 518
hands off from normal state 519
initializing 583
instantiating a collection of 533
IRootStorage interface 565
loading objects from 583
locking the byte array 571
moving 543
naming conventions 528
nesting of 514
no scribble state 517
normal state 517
transitions into and out of 517
obtaining CLSID 610
obtaining CLSID of 551
opening 514, 539
StgOpenStorage 112
opening of 613
opening of ILockBytes instance 619
protecting from data loss 570
query functions 602
release of 587
releasing pointers to 534
removing elements from 548
renaming 550
renaming elements within 549
root 514
opening 540
saving objects into 631
saving objects to 584
sending OnSave advise notifications 516
setting date and time stamps 550
state information on 552
states of 515
hands off 515
no scribble 515
normal 515
state transitions 515
statistical information on 552
storing the CLSID of 551
transitioning in and out of no scribble state 517
undoing changes to 547
unitialized 516
use on the Macintosh 520

Storage objects *(continued)*
- valid characters for names 528
- writing CLSIDs 624
- writing ole information to storage 134

Storage states
- hands off after save 518
- hands off from normal 519

Storage transaction flags 524
- STGM_DIRECT 525
- STGM_PRIORITY 525
- STGM_TRANSACTED 525

Stream objects 11
- comitting changes to 560
- CONTENTS stream 521
- copying 564
- copying data between 559
- creating 535
- determining size of 590
- instantiating a collection of 533
- loading into memory 588
- locking data within 562
- marshaling between processes 554
- obtaining CLSID 610
- obtaining memory handle 609
- opening existing streams 536
- opening with STGM_SHARE_EXCLUSIVE 537
- reading data from 554
- reading data using STGM_READ 555
- reverting changes to 561
- saving data to 589
- saving objects into 632
- seek pointer movement 557
- setting the size of 558
- statistical information on 564
- supported length of 554
- unlocking data within 563
- valid access mode 561
  - transacted 561
- valid access modes 514
- writing CLSIDs 625
- writing data to 555

STREAM_SEEK enumeration 558, 804

String Block Names (SNB) 530

StringFromCLSID function 290
- creating CLSIDs and IIDs 210

StringFromGUID2 function 292

StringFromIID function 292

Strong locks
- definition of 108
- when used 108

Structured data format
- definition of 378, 769

Structured storage
- information on arrays within 573
- overview of 513
- unlocking the byte array 572

Structures
- BIND_OPTS 473, 476, 763
- BORDERWIDTHS 656, 672, 673, 765
- DVTARGETDEVICE 380, 765
- FILETIME 258, 531, 767
- for marshaling functions 224
- FORMATETC 376, 384, 767
- initialization of 105
- INTERFACEINFO 769
- OBJECTDESCRIPTOR 387, 769
- OleIconSource 438, 442, 771
- OLEINPLACEFRAMEINFO 656, 773, 813
- OleMBarRec 658, 775
- OLEVERB 298, 326, 328, 775
- Rect 671
- STATDATA 301, 336, 403, 747, 776
- STATSTG 530, 776
- STGMEDIUM 379, 778

Stub function
- definition of 234

Stub objects 10, 713

SUCCEEDED macro
- description of 286

SwitchToFile method 142, 565

Synchronized calls 382, 725, 780

Synchronous calls 725
- waiting for 726

Synchronous communication 726

T

Target devices
- specifying data formats for 376, 768

Task memory 7

TDFLAGS enumeration 383, 804

Temporary files
- used during save operations 138

Tool space
- for in-place active objects 668, 671

Toolbars
- installing for in-place active objects 671

Transacted mode 133, 143

Transacted storage mode
- description of 514

Transferring data 394
- structures used for 375

TranslateAccelerator method 666, 678

Translating events
- in-place activation 666

Translating menu selections 678

Treat as
and class identifiers 331
TreatAs key 268
TYMED enumeration 378, 787, 805

U

UIDeactivate method 662
Unadvise
IOleObject 335
Unadvise method 300, 335, 406
UnbindSource method 487
Uncache method 421
Undo 60
Undo state
discarding 687
Undoing changes saved to storage 547
Unfreeze 131
Unfreeze method 415
UninitOleManager function 370
UnknownUserType
database key 175
Unloading DLLs 257, 258
Unloading DLLs from memory 257
Unlocking data
within a stream 563
UnLockRegion method 563, 572
Unmarshaling
description of 234
initialize newly created proxy 230
interface parameters 10
UnmarshalInterface method 230
Update method 330, 487
UpdateCache method 425
Updating links 145
Upgrading applications
from OLE 1 717
User interface
active editor menu 65
balloon help messages 87
control bars 71
floating pallettes 71
frame adornments 71
guidelines 27
menu summary 66
menus 63
model 27
removing during in-place activation 662
selected object menu 65
workspace menu 63
User messages
examples of 84
USERCLASSTYPE enumeration 332, 806

V

Verb
database key 160, 161
Verbs
definition of 122
determining set available 326
enumerating 328
relationship to linked objects 45
requests of objects to perform 325
user selectable 122
with predefined meanings 122
Verifying links 122
Version number
retruning major 365
returning minor 365
Version-independent
ProgID 163
View advisories
specifying information about 382, 779
View notifications 116
Virtual tables
description of 4
Visual appearance of objects 49
VTBL pointer 90
VTBLs 90
description of 4

W

Weak locks
definition of 254
Wildcard Advises 400
Window pointers
obtaining 659
to in-place window 659
Window title information
specifying when object is open for editing 318
Workspace menu 63
Write method 134, 555
WriteAt method 569
WriteClassStg function 132, 624
use during class conversion 268
WriteClassStm function 625
Writefmtusertypestg function 132, 134, 625
use during class conversion 269
WriteOle1FmtProgIDStgMac function 626
Writing data
to ILockbytes byte arrays 569
to streams 555
Writing data to storage 134